10TH AMENDMENT

SECURES A REPUBLIC

FORM OF GOVERNMENT

DANIEL H MARCHI

CONTENTS

THE WAY OF OUR DREAMS

This is amazing. I can barely hear the roaring of the engines—and after 17 missions, it still feels like riding on a magic carpet. I can see everything!

My Uncle Danny dreamed of flying from the age of ten. He would use a special stick to guide his imagination through the skies, envisioning a plane that could bring his dreams to life. Those dreams inspired a lifelong return to his imagination, as he worked out how to navigate life so that he could one day fly.

In school, when teachers asked students what they wanted to be, Uncle Danny would always say, "I'm going to be a pilot—like Charles Lindbergh!"

His time to fly came at the age of 19, though not as a pilot. World War II had other plans. He enlisted and trained as a nose gunner on a B-24 bomber, volunteering in the 15th Army Air Force.

In what way do your dreams go?

It's Valentine's Day, 1944—Uncle Danny's first mission.

As he recalls, the bomber is approaching its initial point to the target. Speed: 225 mph. Altitude: 24,000 feet. Anti-aircraft fire ahead.

Boom. Boom Boom. Boom!

Marchi jokingly says, "Hey, Lt. Ross, you might want to turn just a little to the right—we're about to enter the lower corner of that gunfire box."

Lt. Ross replies, "Thanks, Marchi. We're on the initial point. It's all about timing—we'll make it through."

Fifteen to twenty seconds later—**Boom. Boom!**

"We're hit!" yells the engineer.

Just five feet behind Marchi, through the flight deck, Lt. Ross is struck and killed—his legs blown out from beneath him. The plane enters a dive.

Marchi scrambles out of the gun turret and is just reaching for his parachute when he's slammed to the floor—the bomber suddenly levels out.

The co-pilot, comes over the radio: "We're dropping these bombs! Get to your stations!"

Marchi makes his way around the damage and sees blood running down the framework of the plane. Back in the gun mount, he swings around and sees the bomb bay doors opening.

Marchi: "Bomb bay doors open!"

Co-pilot: "Bombs away!"

Marchi: "First bomb drops—bombs away!"

Having lost their initial point, Marchi sees the bombs exploding on a town north of Vienna, Austria.

"The devastation was too hard to watch—but so was Lt. Ross's blood just behind me."

There was no way this bomber was making it back to Castelluccio, Italy.

"We're going down," Marchi thought silently.

Just then, the co-pilot announces, *"All right, men—we're landing this lady just over the southern border into Yugoslavia. There's a reserve airfield with our name on it."*

The co-pilot lands the bomber safely, and four days later, the crew is back at home base.

Uncle Danny flew 16 more missions during the final year of the war. Some came with close calls to death—but all were calls to serve. His path to the skies was nothing like Lindbergh's and changed his life forever.

After the war, he worked for Chance Vought, an aviation company, as a mechanic building and troubleshooting engines and hydraulic systems. One day, while getting a cup of coffee in the cafeteria, he recalls:

Marchi: "What do you say, Linny!"

Lindbergh: "Keep up the good work, Marchi!"

Marchi: "You got it, Mr. Lindbergh."

Lindbergh: "Thank you, my boy!"

It wasn't a historical conversation by any means—but for Uncle Danny, who idolized Lindbergh, it was a moment he never forgot.

In the years that followed, Uncle Danny completed his master's degree in mathematics and computer information science. He never left the aviation community, contributing to many projects. Perhaps the most notable was his work on the Apollo Lunar Module, where he helped develop the navigational system, before eventually retiring from IBM.

In his final years, Uncle Danny dedicated himself to writing books about the Constitution from a mathematical perspective—for the love of this country and its future. He shared his findings on the structural changes in government, their effects, and how we might restore our nation to the vision the Founders intended.

He did all of this while battling stage 4 cancer, grieving a heart-breaking lost love, and trying to heal a torn family. His dream came at the cost of war and the evolving shape of a nation. He put his own dreams aside to help rebuild this country—alongside the WWII men and women whose bravery and sacrifice saved us from fascist ideologies.

Or… were Uncle Danny's and others' bravery a distraction, while our freedoms diminished?

He is my hero and my compass. He is magnanimous.

In what way do your dreams go?

Thank you,
Donald D Marchi

EARLY AMERICAN HISTORY

Early Americans' mistrust of government power came from the colonial experience itself. Most historians believe that the pivotal event was the Stamp Act, which the English Parliament passed in 1765. Taxes were imposed on every legal and business document like newspapers, books, and pamphlets.

Even more than the taxes themselves, the Americans resented the fact that a distant government imposed the taxes without representation in the British government. The Early Americans were further enraged on how the Stamp Act was enforced through the efforts of British customs inspectors. Armed with Parliament-issued "writs of assistance," British customs inspectors entered people's homes regardless of having had no evidence of a Stamp Act violation. The British customs inspectors ransacked the people's possessions in search of contraband. The colonialists came to hate the enforcement procedures of the British customs inspectors. These experiences of the British customs inspector enforcing the Stamp Act taught the early American colonialist the exclusivity of power and liberty as natural enemies. The British customs inspector's "warrantless" searches became a rallying point toward the opposition of aristocratic government rule.

A federal government republic is a representative government that operates starting at local people organization and districts and ends at the executive branch.

SEPARATION OF POWERS

The separation of powers of the three branches of government—legislative, judiciary, and executive—is a checks and balances, but a second set of checks and balances are established via the representational government scheme of a federal government republic. Representational governing defines to be bottom-up. Representative lawmaking guaranties people sovereignty, state governments' sovereignties, and federal government republic sovereignty also in a bottom-up order. The federal government republic sovereignty is at the bottom of this pecking order.

The nation's founders believed the most important task was containing the government's power and protecting the people's liberties. The nation's founders declared a new purpose for government was the protection of people's individual rights. Not only the protection of people's rights was the government's only purpose, but to ensure economic growth. To conduct foreign affairs, the government was expected to protect the community against foreign and domestic threats. The government's job was not to tell how people should live their lives, what religion to practice, or what to write about in pamphlets and newspapers. Common sense made the idea of individual rights the oldest and most traditional of the American ideology.

In the United States, the people require the rule of law and social order. The United States government has need of cooperation among whose inhabitance are subject to the same general rule affecting others within the territory of the United States. As the organization size swells beyond a point, ideas and goals becomes extremely difficult to consolidate.

The planners of the Constitution formed a republic form of government, ensuring freedom, liberty, and equal protection under the law for all persons within the sovereign borders of the United States. As the planners of the Constitution foresaw, in order to perform properly, a federal government republic requires vigilance of the governed. People looked to a federal government republic for establishing and maintaining a social equitable order based upon the will of the people who wanted direct participation in the process. With the will of its people, a federal government republic has the unique ability of peacefully destroying itself. The planners of the Constitution, having realized this situation, among others, proposed what is now known as the Bill of Rights, the first ten amendments to the Constitution.

BILL OF RIGHTS

The Bill of Rights contains the first ten amendments to the United States Constitution. James Madison introduced the Bill of Rights in the first 1789 United States Congress as a series of constitutional amendments that came into effect on December 15, 1791. At that time, three-fourths of the state governments ratified the Bill of Rights, which limits the powers of the Federal Government Republic of the United States. The Bill of Rights protects the rights of all citizens on United States territory.

The Bill of Rights include a set of specific guarantees, among them the right to free speech, freedom of religion, due process of law, and freedom from governmental search and seizure along with the Tenth Amendment. The people ratified the Constitution only after the framers of the constitution pledged to add to the Constitution those protections.

The absence of a "bill of rights" turned out to be an obstacle to the Constitution's ratification. The state government legislatures demanded recognition of certain rights that the British government had violated during the occupation of the American colonies. Four more years of intense debate followed before the new federal government republic was formed to resolve the issue.

The Federalists argued that the Bill of Rights was not necessary. The Constitution was to be sufficient, and the Bill of Rights did not need to be included in the Constitution. Anti-Federalists, who feared a strong centralized federal government republic, refused to support the Constitution without a Bill of Rights.

Finally, popular sentiment was decisive. Recently freed from the despotic English monarchy, the American people within the colonies were granted strong guarantees. The newly formed federal government republic would not trample upon their newly won freedoms of speech, press and religion, nor upon their right to be free from warrantless searches and seizures.

The framers of the Constitution's paid attention to Thomas Jefferson, who argued, "A bill of rights is what the people are entitled to against every government on earth, general or particular, and what no just government should refuse, or rest on inference."

The planners of the Constitution demonstrated a clearness of vision formulating the Constitution based on knowledge of other countries' governmental structures of past history and existing ones at that time. The framers of the Constitution did not realize that they were creating a centralized federal government republic that had enormous powers. The centralized federal government republic might discover the power of the purse (Sixteenth Amendment). The centralized federal government may try to expand and control state governments using extortionary methods, which are a process that will cost the American taxpayer. The planners of the Constitution insisted on having the Tenth Amendment within the Bill of Rights that has the ability to rescind any tyrannical ideas of a federal government republic upon state government republics.

TENTH AMENDMENT OF THE CONSTITUTION

At the time that the Constitution was adopted, the Tenth Amendment was intended to confirm the understanding of the state government republics' people.

The Tenth Amendment expressly declares the constitutional policy of the federal government republic may not exercise power that prejudices the state governments' republics, which interfere with the state government republics' abilities to function. The state government republics and the state government republics' people are to retain all powers.

Without the Constitution, the federal government republic power diminishes. Since the Constitution created the federal government republic, eliminating the Constitution would obliterate the federal government republic. On the other hand, the state government republics and the state government republics' people, who created the Constitution, will endure. The state government republics and the state government republics' people are leading issues in the Tenth Amendment.

The Tenth Amendment states that the powers not delegated to the United States by the Constitution, nor prohibited by it to the states, are reserved to the states respectively or to the people.

In other words, the Tenth Amendment states, the powers not delegated to the United States by the Constitution, *or not* prohibited (not allowed) by it to the states, are reserved to the states respectively or to the people.

In other words, the Tenth Amendment states, the powers not given to the United States by the Constitution, or *not allowed* by it to the states, are reserved to the states respectively or to the people.

In other words, the Tenth Amendment states, the powers not given to the United States by the Constitution, or *allowed* by it to the states, are reserved to the states respectively or to the people.

Take two "or" logic steps through the Tenth Amendment.

The Tenth Amendment states the powers allowed by the Constitution to the states are reserved for the people.

CENSUS

The United States Constitution mandates that every ten years, a census be taken across the United States of a population count. The law requires participation in the census. Census data are used to distribute United States House of Congress seats to state governments and the assignment population statistics to each state government.

IDEAL DISTRICT POPULATION

Starting at the state government, the ideal district population for the state government assembly district is equal to the total state government's population divided by the total number of assigned districts. Likewise, the ideal district population for the state government Senate district is equal to the total state government's population divided by the total number of assigned districts.

United States House of Congress seat is assigned to a state government. The ideal district population for the state government United States House of Congress district is equal to the total state government's population divided by the total number of census-assigned districts.

At the state government's county level, the ideal district population for the state government county districts is equal to the total state government county's population divided by the total number of assigned county districts.

At the state government's city level, the ideal district population for the state government city districts is equal to the total state government city's population divided by the total number of assigned city districts. Designing ideal is practically impossible.

At the state government's town level, the ideal district population for the state government town districts is equal to the total state government town population divided by the total number of assigned town districts. Designing ideal is practically impossible.

QUASI-EQUAL POPULATION

The ideal districts cannot usually be constructed. In the real world, quasi-equal population districts can be estimated to felicitate district construction. Starting at the state government, the quasi-equal district population for the state government assembly district is equal to the total state government's population divided by the total number of assigned districts. Likewise, the quasi-equal district population for the state government Senate district is equal to the total state government population divided by the total number of assigned districts.

United States House of Representatives' seats are assigned to state governments. The quasi-equal district population for the state government's United States House of Representatives district is equal to the total state government population divided by the total number of census-assigned districts.

At the state government county level, the quasi-equal district population for the state government county districts is equal to the total state government county's population divided by the total number of assigned county districts.

At the state government city level, the quasi-equal district population for the state government city districts are equal to the total state government city population divided by the total number of assigned city districts.

At the state government town level, the quasi-equal district population for the state government town districts is equal to the total state government town population divided by the total number of assigned town districts.

Designing districts of equal or quasi-equal population for state governments, county governments, city governments, and town governments designate state government republic, county government republic, city government republic, and town government republic. Therefore, state governments, county governments, city governments, and town governments truly are republics forms of governments and are to be identified as state government republic, county republic, city republic, and town republic.

GOVERN BY BOTTOM-UP REPRESENTATIONAL MODE

State Governments

- The quasi-equal populated assembly districts of the state governments represent the area of a state's government.

- The elected representatives of the quasi-equal state government assembly districts of the state governments represent the quasi-equal populated assembly districts of the state governments.

- The quasi-equal populated senators' districts of the state governments represent an area of state governments.

- The elected representatives of the quasi-equal state government senators' districts of the state governments represent the quasi-equal populated senators' districts of the state governments.

- The state government legislatures represent the quasi-equal populated assembly districts and the quasi-equal senators' districts of the state governments.

- The state government governors represent the state government legislatures.

- The United States Senate represents the state government legislatures.

United States House of Representatives

- The quasi-equal populated United States House of Representatives' districts of the state governments represent the area of state governments.

- The elected representatives of the quasi-equal United States House of Representatives' districts of the state governments represent the quasi-equal populated United States House of Representatives' districts of the state governments.

President

- The president of the United States represents the elected representatives of the quasi-equal populated United States House of Representatives' districts and of the quasi-equal populated United States Senate districts, both in an area of state governments.

County Governments

- The quasi-equal populated districts of the county governments represent an area of state governments.

- The elected representatives of the quasi-equal populated county districts represent the quasi-equal populated county districts.

- The county legislatures represent the elected representatives of the quasi-equal populated county districts.

- The county executives represent the county legislatures.

City Governments

- The quasi-equal populated districts of the city governments represent an area of state governments.

- The elected representatives of the quasi-equal populated city districts represent the quasi-equal populated city districts.

- The city councils represent the elected representatives of the quasi-equal populated city districts.

- The city mayors represent the city councils.

Town Governments

- The quasi-equal populated districts of the town governments represent an area of state governments.

- The elected representatives of the quasi-equal populated town districts represent the quasi-equal populated town districts.

- The town councils represent the elected representatives of the quasi-equal populated town districts.

- The town mayors represent the town councils.

TENTH AMENDMENT CREATES A FEDERAL GOVERNMENT REPUBLIC

The Tenth Amendment states that the powers allowed by the Constitution to the state governments are reserved for the state governments' quasi-equal populated districts.

The powers allowed by the Constitution are the following:

- State governments assemblies are reserved for the state government assemblies' quasi-equal populated districts.

- State government Senates are reserved for the state government Senates' quasi-equal populated districts.

- State government legislatures are reserved for the state government Senate and assembly quasi-equal populated districts.

- United States Senate is reserved for the state government Senate and assembly quasi-equal populated districts.

- United States House of Representatives is reserved for the state governments' United States House of Representatives quasi-equal populated districts.

- Legislative branch of the Constitution is reserved for the state government Senate and assembly quasi-equal populated districts.

- Executive branch of the Constitution is reserved for the state government Senate and assembly quasi-equal populated districts.

- Judicial branch of the Constitution is reserved for the state government Senate and assembly quasi-equal populated districts.

- Federal government republic is reserved for the state government Senate and assembly quasi-equal populated districts.

If the state governments' quasi-equal populated districts are replaced with the entire state government area, then a referendum or winner-take-all prevails, which violates the Tenth Amendment.

STATE GOVERNMENTS' LOCAL REPUBLIC FORM OF GOVERNMENT

The Tenth Amendment states that the powers allowed by the Constitution to the state government counties are reserved to the state government counties' quasi-equal populated districts.

The powers allowed by the Constitution are the following:

- State government counties' governments are reserved for the state government counties' quasi-equal populated districts.

- The state government counties' executives are reserved for the state government counties' quasi-equal populated districts.

- The state government counties' legislatures are reserved for the state government counties' quasi-equal populated districts.

If the state government counties' quasi-equal populated districts are replaced with the entire state government county area, then a referendum or winner-take-all prevails, which violates the Tenth Amendment.

The powers allowed by the Constitution are the following:

- State government cities are reserved for the state government cities' quasi-equal populated districts.

- State government city mayors are reserved for the state government cities' quasi-equal populated districts.

- The state government city councils are reserved for the state government cities' quasi-equal populated districts.

If the state government cities' quasi-equal populated districts are replace with the entire state government city area, then a referendum or winner-take-all prevails, which violates the Tenth Amendment.

The powers allowed by the Constitution are the following:

- State government towns are reserved for the state government towns' quasi-equal populated districts.

- State government town mayors are reserved for the state government towns' quasi-equal populated districts.

- The state government town councils are reserved for the state government towns' quasi-equal populated districts.

If the state government towns' quasi-equal populated districts are replace with the entire state government town area, then a referendum or winner-take-all prevails, which violates the Tenth Amendment.

REFERENDUM TOP-DOWN MODE VIOLATES THE TENTH AMENDMENT

- When the state government assemblies use referendum voting, the state government areas replace the state government assemblies' quasi-equal populated districts.

- When the state government Senate uses referendum voting, the state government areas replace the state government assemblies' quasi-equal populated districts.

- When the state government legislatures use referendum voting, the state government areas replace the state government assemblies' and the state government Senate's quasi-equal populated districts.

- When the state government county legislatures use referendum voting, the state government county areas replace the state government counties' quasi-equal populated districts.

- When the state government city councils use referendum voting, the state government city areas replace the state government cities' quasi-equal populated districts.

- When the state government town councils use referendum voting, the state government town areas replace the state government towns' quasi-equal populated districts.

WINNER-TAKES-ALL TOP-DOWN MODE VIOLATES THE TENTH AMENDMENT

- When the state government assemblies use winner-takes-all voting, the state government areas replace the state government assemblies' quasi-equal populated districts.

- When the state government Senate uses winner-takes-all voting, the state government areas replace the state government Senate's quasi-equal populated districts.

- When the state government legislatures use winner-takes-all voting, the state government areas replace the state government assemblies' and the state government Senate's quasi-equal populated districts.

- When the state government county legislatures use winner-takes-all voting, the state government county areas replace the state government counties' quasi-equal populated districts.

- When the state government city councils use winner-takes-all voting, the state government city areas replace the state government cities' quasi-equal populated districts.

- When the state government town councils use winner-takes-all voting, the state government town areas replace the towns' quasi-equal populated districts.

The 60%–40% is derived from the statistical bell-shaped curve of the normal distribution where two standard deviations straddling the mean of the frequency's distribution encompasses two-thirds of its area $(^2/_3)$. Therefore, 40% divided by 60% (40% / 60%) equals two-thirds $(^2/_3)$.

The following mentioned groups must make decision using a 60%–40% voting to protect quasi-equal constituencies' populations to validate the Tenth Amendment:

- State government Senate member groups

- State government Assembly member groups

- County legislator member groups

- City council member groups

- Town council member groups

The Following Violate the Tenth Amendment:

- Referendums

- "Winner takes all"

- Getting rid of 60%–40% voting

FEDERAL GOVERNMENT REPUBLIC BOTTOM-UP REPRESENTATION MODE STARTING AT QUASI-EQUAL POPULATED CONSTITUENCY DISTRICTS:

- Elect president

- Presidential appointments

- Electoral College

- Elect state government republic governors

- Elect state government republic senators within each district

- Elect state government republic Assembly members within each district

- State government republic legislatures

- Elect United States House of Representatives members within each district

- United States House of Representatives

- Elect county republic legislators within each district

- County republic legislature

- County republic executive

- Elect city republic council members within each district

- City republic council

- City republic mayor

- Elect town republic council members within each district

- Town republic council

- Town republic mayor

PROPORTIONAL REPRESENTATION

The framers of the Constitution came to a great compromise at the Constitutional Convention of 1787. They provided for *proportional representation* and quasi-equal people districts for the House of Representatives and the United States Senate through the state governments within the United States territory. *Proportion representation* means that a sovereign state's area is subdivided into representative regions of equal or quasi-equal population, and the elected candidate representatives are *proportion representation*. The symbol for *proportion representation* in this paper is

Nonproportion representation means a person represents the entire population of the United States state governments, city governments, and town governments. The symbol for *nonproportion representation* in this paper is

The elected representatives of the quasi-equal populated state government assembly districts of the states governments are *proportional representation*.

The elected representatives of the quasi-equal populated state government senators' districts of the state government are *proportional representation*.

The elected representatives of the quasi-equal populated United States House of representatives' districts of the state governments are *proportional representation*.

The state government legislatures represent the *proportional representation* state government assemblies and the state government Senates; therefore, the state government legislatures are *proportional representation*.

The state government governors represent the state government legislatures; therefore, the state government governors are *proportional representation*.

The United States Senate represents the state government legislatures; therefore, the United States Senate is *proportional representation*.

The president of the United States represents the elected representatives of the United States House of Representative and the United States Senate; therefore, the president of the United States is *proportional representation*.

The elected representatives of the quasi-equal county districts are *proportional representation*.

The elected representatives of the quasi-equal city districts are *proportional representation*.

The elected representatives of the quasi-equal town districts are *proportional representation*.

The county legislatures represent the elected counties' *proportional representation* representatives; therefore, the county legislatures are *proportional representation*.

The city councils represent the elected cities' *proportional representation* representatives; therefore, the city councils are *proportional representation*.

The town councils represent the elected towns' *proportional representation* representatives; therefore, the town councils are *proportional representation*.

The county executives represent the counties' *proportional representation* legislatures; therefore, the county executives are *proportional representation*.

The city mayors represent the cities' *proportional representation* councils; therefore, the city mayors are *proportional representation*.

The town mayors represent the towns' *proportional representation* councils; therefore, the town mayors are *proportional representation*.

Referendum is a *mob rule* decision that takes away *bottom-up* representation mode starting at quasi-equal constituency districts.

A *referendum* decision used in any of the following violates the Tenth Amendment:

- State government republics' Senates

- State government republics' assemblies

- United States House of Representatives

- County legislatures

- City councils

- Town councils

The following are *referendum* types:

- Elect state government governors

- Elect state government senators within each district

- Elect state government assembly members within each district

- Elect United States House of Representatives members within each district

- Elect county members within each district

- Elect city council members within each district

- Elect town council members within each district

FEDERALISM VIOLATES THE TENTH AMENDMENT (A PRODUCT OF THE SEVENTEENTH AMENDMENT)

The Tenth Amendment is absent in the Bill of Rights. Referendum voting is allowed; therefore, mob rule prevails in elections. The following is true under federalism:

- A referendum elects United States senators with dictatorial powers.

- A referendum allows the state governments' people to impeach a rogue United States senator.

- A referendum could elect the president of the United States.

- A referendum allows the state governments' people to impeach a state's governor.

- A referendum allows the people to impeach local official like mayors and county executives.

Federal government republic notes the following:

- The framers of the Constitution created a federal government republic made up of elected representatives to govern.

- A federal government republic satisfies the desires of the country's people.

- A federal government republic governs by representation where people in a region are not allowed to pass laws (referendum or top-down voting).

- A federal government republic rules by representation where people have elected representatives to pass laws.

- A federal government republic exists to protect the rights of people.

- A federal government republic protects people's property.

- A federal government republic protects people's sovereignty.

- A federal government republic exclusively depends upon the advice of supporting representatives and their consultants.

- A federal government republic rules by law.

- A federal government republic's power is the consequent of people's election to choose the most excellent officials to represent them.

- A federal government republic's attitude toward the law is the administration of justice in accord with pre-set principles and well-known evidence regardless of the consequences.

- A federal government republic represents a great number of citizens in an extension of territory that may be brought within its compass.

- A federal government republic avoids the dangerous extreme of using referendums that might create either tyranny or mob rule (violates Tenth Amendment).

- A federal government republic encourages statesmanship, freedom, motivation, righteousness, contentment, and growth.

- A federal government republic respects the people's natural human rights.

- A federal government republic recognizes that a dissenting juror's decision prevents a person from being denied his rights in a jury trial.

- A federal government republic serves the people.

- A federal government republic denies the compulsion of people to govern.

- A federal government republic does not allow the people of the United States to elect the president (referendum, violates Tenth Amendment).

- A federal government republic allows state governments to pick the president through an electoral system of chosen state government legislatures' electors.

- A federal government republic allows representatives to pass laws that create a check against those elite persons who may not always do the common people's request.

- A federal government republic puts a check against the denial of a person's individual rights, which is the precursor of mob rule.

- A federal government republic gives a jury the final pronouncement over an individual right so as to also improve and defend such rights.

- A federal government republic allows a court assemblage to have the last word.

- A federal government republic assists in interpreting the Constitution.

- A federal government republic understands limits of Constitutional laws.

- A federal government republic's executive has the option of vetoing laws.

- A federal government republic accepts judicial review.

- A federal government republic allows the state government legislatures to participate.

- A federal government republic recognizes the stages where a particular piece of legislation must be scrutinize to safeguard against violating the Bill of Rights.

- A federal government republic has to condemn "judicial activism."

- A federal government republic thrives on the rule of law, which is hostile to both dictatorships and to anarchists.

- A federal government republic accepts Constitutional amendments that the people's elected representatives approve.

- A federal government republic includes the United States House of Representatives that has the power of the purse.

- A federal government republic includes United States Senate, which the state government legislatures elect to act as ambassadors.

- A federal government republic deals with Supreme Court encroachments.

- A federal government republic is a representative form of government that responds to people who discuss local affairs at political and social gatherings.

- A federal government republic respects the inalienable rights of individuals.

- A federal government republic's sovereignty is in line after a state government republic's sovereignty and a people's sovereignty.

- A federal government republic's lawmaking is slow but deliberate, requiring the approval of three branches of government: the judiciary, executive, and legislative.

- A federal government republic does not allow state government legislatures, county legislatures, city councils, and town councils to pass the responsibilities of decision-making to referendums (violates the Tenth Amendment).

- A federal government republic des not adhere to federalism (violates the Tenth Amendment).

- A federal government republic discourages mob rule, a possible outcome of referendums (violates the Tenth Amendment).

- A federal government republic begins a bottom-up representational mode at the people's end and ends at the executive branch through the state government legislatures.

- A federal government republic satisfies the Tenth Amendment, which prevents the destruction of the federal government republic itself.

- A federal government republic, according to the Tenth Amendment, recognizes that power belongs to the state government republics' people.

- A federal government republic, according to the Tenth Amendment, recognizes that power belongs to the county government republic's people.

- A federal government republic, according to the Tenth Amendment, recognizes that power belongs to the city government republics' people.

- A federal government republic, according to the Tenth Amendment, recognizes that power belongs to the town government republics' people.

- A federal government republic, according to the Tenth Amendment, recognizes that power starts at the state government, county government, city government, and town government quasi-equal districts, bringing into being a representation method of governing, which is bottom-up.

- A federal government republic creation forced the planners of the Constitution to inaugurate the Tenth Amendment into the Bill of Rights in order to decentralize federal government republic powers.

- A federal government republic regards as an unlawful act to transfer legislatives' responsibilities to referendums (violates the Tenth Amendment and the Bill of Rights).

DEFINITIONS

State government governor (elected)

Since the whole state votes for the state governor, the governor falls within realm of nonproportional representation.

Individual state government senator member (elected)

Since the district's population votes for a state senator, the state senator's district falls within the realm of nonproportional representation.

State government Senate (all members)

Since member districts have quasi-equal populations within the state's sovereign boundary, the state Senate falls within the realm of proportional representation.

Individual state government assembly member (elected)

Since the district's population votes for a state assembly member, the state assembly member's district falls within the realm of nonproportional representation.

State government assembly (all members)

Since all member districts have quasi-equal population, within the state's sovereign boundary, the state assembly falls within the realm of proportional representation.

State government legislature

The state legislature includes both the state government Senate and state government assembly and becomes classified as proportional representation.

State government electors (elected)

The state government electors includes states government legislature and is classified as proportional representation.

President of the United States (elected)

Since the electors of the state governments within the whole country picks the president of the United States, the president falls within the realm of proportional representation.

State government governor

The governor deals with the legislator and is classified as proportional representation.

A House of Representative member (elected)

Since the district's population votes for a House of Representative member, the House of Representative district falls within the realm of nonproportional representation.

House of Representatives (all members)

Since member districts have quasi-equal population within the United States, the House of Representatives falls within the realm of proportional representation.

President of the United States

The president deals with both the senators (ambassadors) and the House of Representatives and is classified as proportional representation.

HYPOTHETICAL STATE
GOVERNMENT DISTRICT MAPS

					1						

STATE GOVERNMENT REPUBLIC ASSEMBLY DISTRICTS!

HYPOTHETICAL STATE GOVERNMENT DISTRICT MAP TO ILLUSTRATE A STATE GOVERNMENT ASSEMBLY

					2	3	4				
					5	6	7				
					8	9	10				
					11	12	13				
				14	15	16	17	18			
19	20	21	22	23	24	25	26	27	28	29	30	31
32	33	34	35	36	37	38	39	40	41	42	43	44
45	46	47	48	49	50	51	52	53	54	55	56	57
58	59	60	61	62	63	64	65	66	67	68	69	70
71	72	73	74	75	76	77	78	79	80	81	82	
			83	84	85	86	87	88			

In this hypothetical example of a state government area, a state government republic assembly is simulated to demonstrate the construction of quasi-equal populated districts. In this situation, the population of the state government is divided into eighty-eight equally populated districts. Since it is not probability possible to construct equally populated districts, a quasi-equal population will have to suffice for each district in the real world. The displayed quasi-equal populated districts represent a hypothetical state government assembly area within the hypothetical state government area. These districts must be consecutively connected to one another, having at least one side in contact with one another, which, in reality, is very difficult to achieve. Finally, a district map depicting the state government assembly's district area within the state government boundary becomes a realization to behold.

Since the population of their districts are quasi-equal populated, there exists eighty-eight hypothetical state government assembly members who are said to be *proportional representative*. In electing these state government assembly members, this begins the first govern-by-representation election in a state government republic, putting the state government republic into a bottom-up representational mode starting at the quasi-equal districts and ending at the state governor. The power belongs to the people as described in the Tenth Amendment as follows: The powers allowed by the Constitution to the state government (assemblies) are reserved to the state government assemblies' people of quasi-equal populated districts.

| STATE GOVERNMENT REPUBLIC SENATE DISTRICT OVERLAYS ASSEMBLY DISTRICTS! | | HYPOTHETICAL STATE GOVERNMENT DISTRICT MAP TO ILLUSTRATE A STATE GOVERNMENT SENATE |

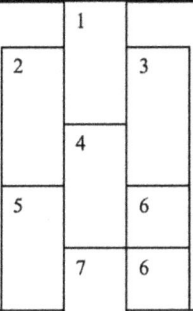

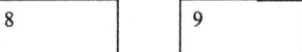

```
                    1
          2              3
               4
          5              6
               7    6
     8              9
10  11   12   13   14   15  16
22  21   20   19   18   17
23  24   25   26   27   28  29
35  34   33   32   31   30
36  37   38   39   40   41
        42   43   44
```

In this hypothetical example of a state government area, a state government republic Senate is simulated to demonstrate the construction of quasi-equal populated districts. In this situation, the population of the state government is divided into forty-four equally populated districts. Since it is not probability possible to construct equally populated districts, a quasi-equal population will have to suffice for each district in the real world. The displayed quasi-equal populated districts represent a hypothetical state government Senate area within the hypothetical state government area. These districts must be consecutively connected to one another, having at least one side in contact with one another, which, in reality, is very difficult to achieve. Finally, a district map depicting the state government Senate district area within the state government boundary becomes a realization to behold.

Since the population of their districts is quasi-equal populated, there exists forty-four hypothetical state government Senate members who are said to be *proportional representative*. In electing these state government Senate members, this begins the first govern-by-representation election in a state government republic, putting the state government republic into a bottom-up representational mode starting at the quasi-equal districts and ending at the state governor. The power belongs to the people as described in the Tenth Amendment as follows: The powers allowed by the Constitution to the state government (Senate) are reserved to the state government Senate's people of quasi-equal populated districts.

CITY GOVERNMENT MUTUAL EXCLUSIVE OF TOWN GOVERNMENTS!

HYPOTHETICAL STATE GOVERNMENT DISTRICT MAP TO ILLUSTRATE A CITY REPUBLIC

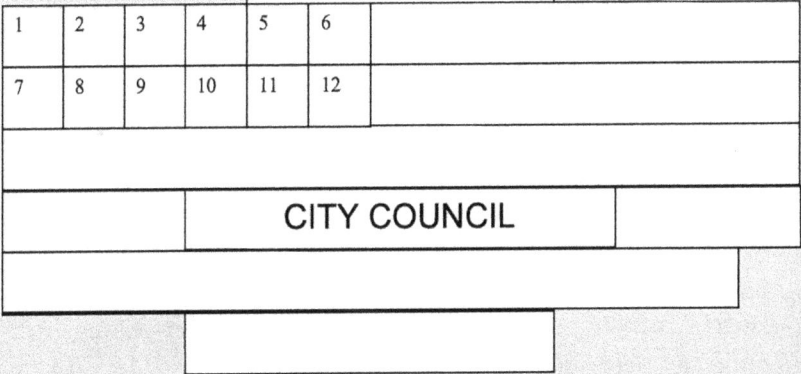

| 1 | 2 | 3 | 4 | 5 | 6 | |
| 7 | 8 | 9 | 10 | 11 | 12 | |

CITY COUNCIL

In this hypothetical example of a state government area, a city government republic is simulated to demonstrate the construction of quasi-equal populated districts. In this situation, the population of the city is divided into twelve equally populated districts. Since it is not probability possible to construct equally populated districts, a quasi-equal population will have to suffice for each district in the real world. The displayed quasi-equal populated districts represent a hypothetical city government legislature area within the hypothetical state government area. These districts must be consecutively connected to one another, having at least one side in contact with one another, which, in reality, is very difficult to achieve. Finally, a district map depicting the city legislature district area within the state government boundary becomes a realization to behold.

Since the population of their districts is quasi-equal populated, there exists twelve hypothetical city legislature members who are said to be *proportion representation*. In electing these city council members, this begins the first govern-by-representation election in a city government republic, putting the city government republic into a bottom-up representational mode starting at the quasi-equal districts and ending at the city mayor. The power belongs to the people as described in the Tenth Amendment as follows: The powers allowed by the Constitution to the state government (cities) are reserved to the state government cities' people of quasi-equal populated districts.

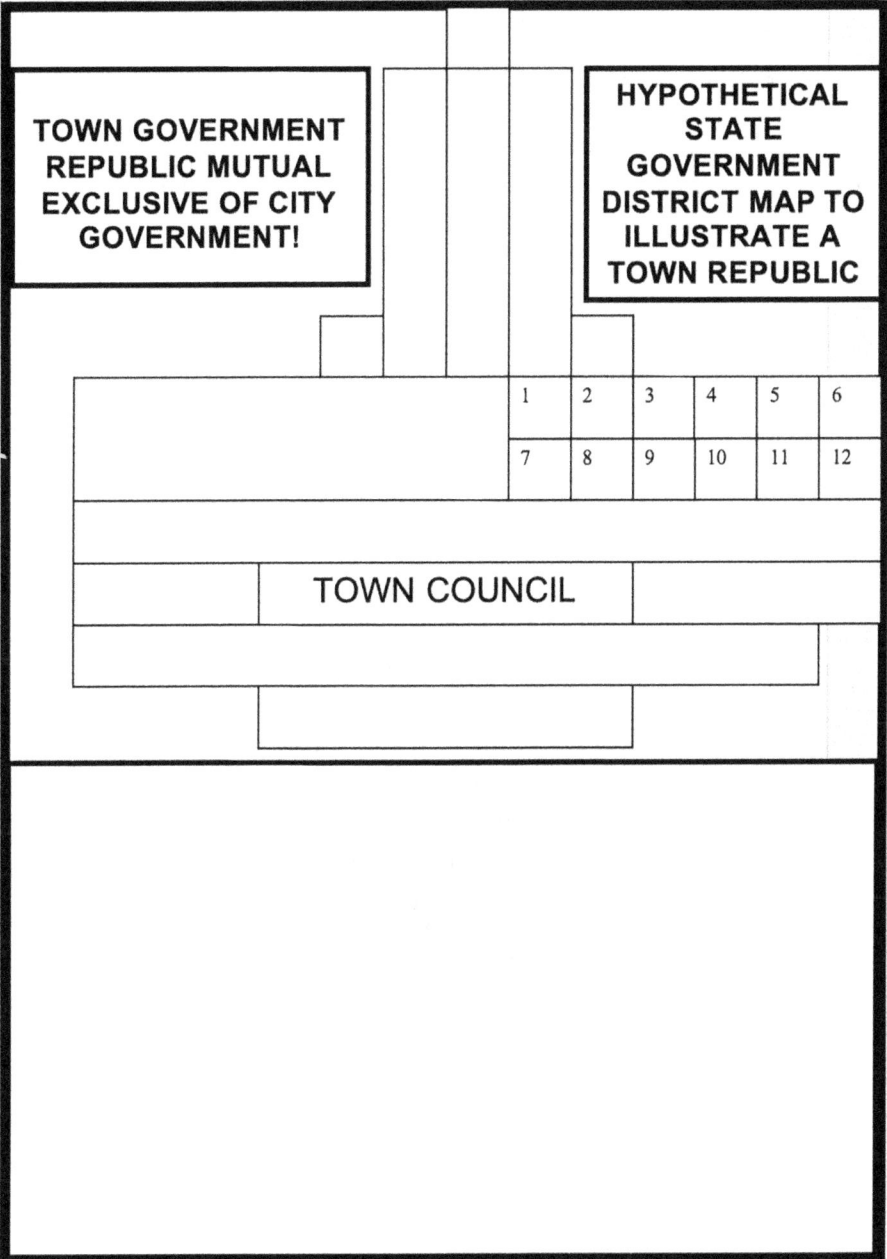

TOWN GOVERNMENT REPUBLIC MUTUAL EXCLUSIVE OF CITY GOVERNMENT!

HYPOTHETICAL STATE GOVERNMENT DISTRICT MAP TO ILLUSTRATE A TOWN REPUBLIC

| 1 | 2 | 3 | 4 | 5 | 6 |
| 7 | 8 | 9 | 10 | 11 | 12 |

TOWN COUNCIL

In this hypothetical example of a state government area, a town government republic is simulated to demonstrate the construction of quasi-equal populated districts. In this situation, the population of the town is divided into twelve equally populated districts. Since it is not probability possible to construct equally populated districts, a quasi-equal population will have to suffice for each district in the real world. The displayed quasi-equal populated districts represent a hypothetical town government legislature area within the hypothetical state government area. These districts must be consecutively connected to one another, having at least one side in contact with one another, which, in reality, is very difficult to achieve. Finally, a district map depicting the town legislature district area within the state government boundary becomes a realization to behold.

Since the population of their districts is quasi-equal populated, there exists twelve hypothetical town legislature members who are said to be *proportion representation*. In electing these town executive members, this begins the first govern-by-representation election in a town government republic, putting the town government republic into a bottom-up representational mode starting at the quasi-equal districts and ending at the town mayor. The power belongs to the people as described in the Tenth Amendment as follows: The powers allowed by the Constitution to the state government (towns) are reserved to the state government towns' people of quasi-equal populated districts.

TENTH AMENDMENT

The powers allowed by the Constitution to the states are reserved to the people.

STATE GOVERNMENT REPUBLIC

*Bottom-up representation mode
starting at quasi-equal proportion
representation state government
Senate districts going to the state
government's legislature.*

STATE GOVERNMENT LEGISLATURE

ELECTED STATE GOVERNMENT SENATE

PROPORTIONAL
REPRESENTATION

The Tenth Amendment definition in the Constitution ensures the maintaining of a state government republic. The state government Senate is compelled to follow through and complete any decision-making process, no matter the difficulty that might prevail, rather than to bail out and give up their responsibility to a referendum. The entire state government voting population votes in a referendum that settles the difficulty at hand, turning a bottom-up *representation mode* to a top-down mode, averting the concept away from starting government by representation at the quasi-equal state government Senate districts where the power of the state government or the state government's people exists as explained in the definition of the Tenth Amendment.

The powers allowed by the Constitution to the state government are reserved to the state governments' people of quasi-equal populated districts.

BOTTOM UP

TENTH AMENDMENT
The powers allowed by the Constitution to the states are reserved to the people.

STATE GOVERNMENT REPUBLIC

Bottom-up representation mode starting at quasi-equal proportional representation state government assembly districts going to the state government's legislature

STATE GOVERNMENT LEGISLATURE

ELECTED STATE GOVERNMENT ASSEMBLY

PROPORTIONAL REPRESENTATION

The Tenth Amendment definition in the Constitution ensures the maintaining of a state government republic. The state government assembly is compelled to follow through and complete any decision-making process, no matter the difficulty that might prevail, rather than to bail out and give up their responsibility to a referendum. The entire state government voting population votes in a referendum that settles the difficulty at hand, turning a bottom-up *representation mode* to a top-down mode, averting the concept away from starting government by representation at the quasi-equal state government assembly districts where the power of the state government or the state government's people exists as explained in the definition of the Tenth Amendment.

The powers allowed by the Constitution to the state government (assembly) are reserved to the state government assemblies' people of quasi-equal populated districts.

BOTTOM UP

TENTH AMENDMENT

The powers allowed by the Constitution to the states are reserved to the people.

STATE GOVERNMENT REPUBLIC

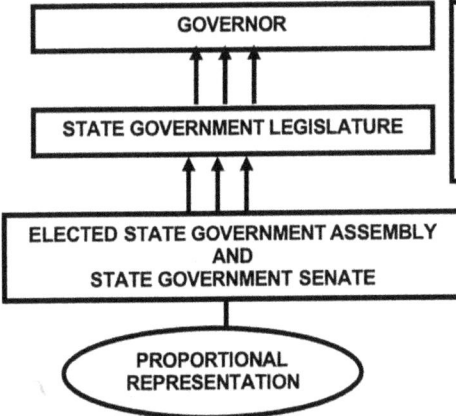

GOVERNOR

↑ ↑ ↑

STATE GOVERNMENT LEGISLATURE

↑ ↑ ↑

ELECTED STATE GOVERNMENT ASSEMBLY AND STATE GOVERNMENT SENATE

(PROPORTIONAL REPRESENTATION)

Bottom-up representation mode starting at quasi-equal proportion representation state government assembly districts and state government Senate districts going to the state government's legislature ending at the governor

   Government by representation starts at the quasi-equal state government Senate and assembly districts in bottom-up mode. The state government legislature members represent the quasi-equal *proportion representation* state government's assembly and Senate districts. The state government governors represent the *proportion representation* state government legislatures, which represent the state government or the state government's people.

   The Tenth Amendment definition in the Constitution ensures the maintaining of a state government republic. The state government legislature is compelled to follow through and complete any decision-making process, no matter the difficulty that might prevail, rather than to bail out and give up their responsibility to a referendum. The entire state government voting population votes in a referendum that settles the difficulty at hand, turning a bottom-up *representation mode* to a top-down mode, averting the concept away from starting government by representation at the quasi-equal state government Senate and assembly districts where the power of the state government or the state government's people exists as explained in the definition of the Tenth Amendment.

   The powers allowed by the Constitution to the state government (legislatures) are reserved to the state government Senate's and state government assemblies' people of quasi-equal populated districts.

BOTTOM UP

TENTH AMENDMENT

The powers allowed by the Constitution to the states are reserved to the people.

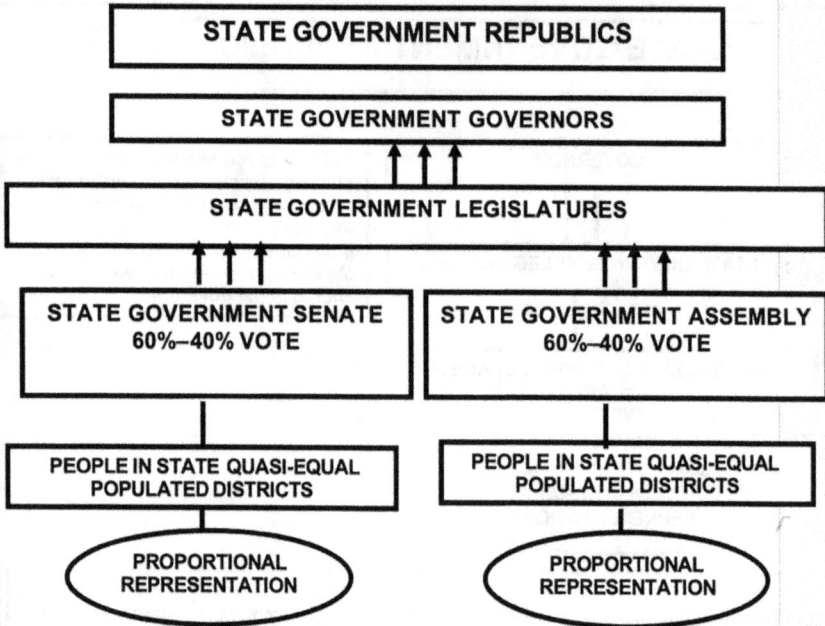

STATE GOVERNMENT REPUBLICS

STATE GOVERNMENT GOVERNORS

STATE GOVERNMENT LEGISLATURES

STATE GOVERNMENT SENATE 60%–40% VOTE	STATE GOVERNMENT ASSEMBLY 60%–40% VOTE
PEOPLE IN STATE QUASI-EQUAL POPULATED DISTRICTS	PEOPLE IN STATE QUASI-EQUAL POPULATED DISTRICTS
PROPORTIONAL REPRESENTATION	PROPORTIONAL REPRESENTATION

The 60%–40% voting interval protects minority members of states government Senate and assembly. Also, the 60%–40% voting interval protects quasi-equal population of the constructed districts where the govern by representation begins along with the *proportion representation* of both members of the state government Senate and state government assembly. It takes 60% or more of both state government Senate and assembly to win a decision or 40% or more to lose a decision.

The 60%–40% is derived from the statistical bell-shaped curve of the normal distribution, where two standard deviations straddling the mean of the frequency's distribution encompasses two-thirds of its area ($^2/_3$). Therefore, 40% divided by 60% (40% / 60%) equals two-thirds ($^2/_3$).

If the state government Senate or assembly decide on their own to vote "winner takes all" as with referendums, they will destroy the state government's constructed quasi-equal population districts and the *proportion representation* of the state government Senate and assembly members violating the Tenth Amendment.

The powers allowed by the Constitution to the state governments (legislatures) are reserved to the state government assemblies' and state governor Senate's people of quasi-equal populated districts.

BOTTOM UP

VIOLATES TENTH AMENDMENT

The powers allowed by the Constitution to the states are reserved to the people.

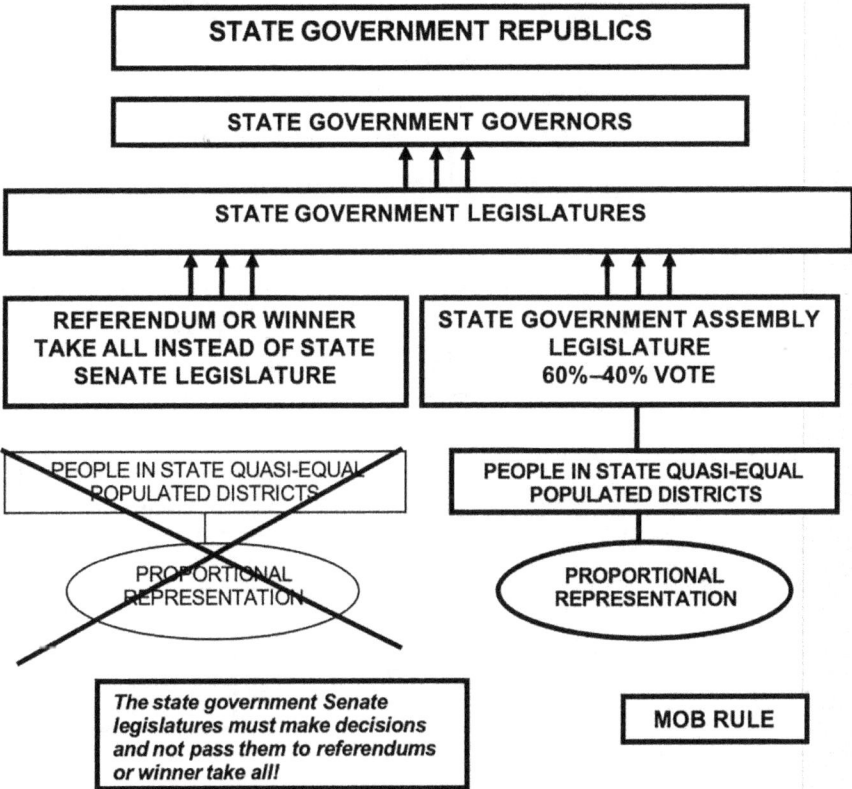

STATE GOVERNMENT REPUBLICS

STATE GOVERNMENT GOVERNORS

STATE GOVERNMENT LEGISLATURES

REFERENDUM OR WINNER TAKE ALL INSTEAD OF STATE SENATE LEGISLATURE	STATE GOVERNMENT ASSEMBLY LEGISLATURE 60%–40% VOTE
PEOPLE IN STATE QUASI-EQUAL POPULATED DISTRICTS	PEOPLE IN STATE QUASI-EQUAL POPULATED DISTRICTS
PROPORTIONAL REPRESENTATION	PROPORTIONAL REPRESENTATION

The state government Senate legislatures must make decisions and not pass them to referendums or winner take all!

MOB RULE

THE REPRESENTATION MODE HAS BEEN BROKEN!

VIOLATES TENTH AMENDMENT

The powers allowed by the Constitution to the states are reserved to the people.

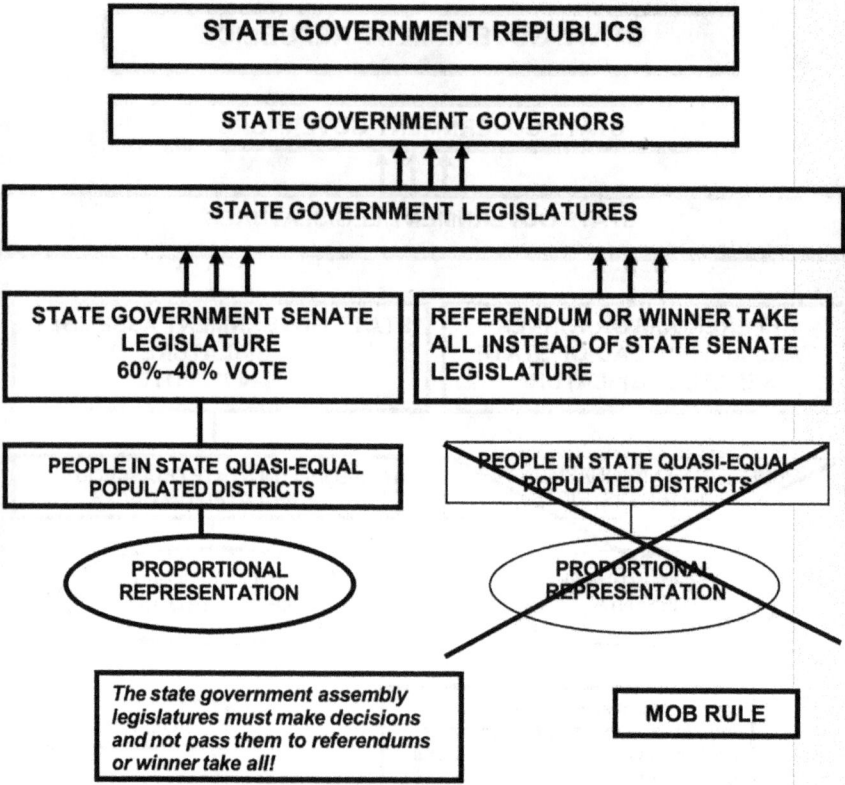

STATE GOVERNMENT REPUBLICS

STATE GOVERNMENT GOVERNORS

STATE GOVERNMENT LEGISLATURES

STATE GOVERNMENT SENATE LEGISLATURE 60%–40% VOTE	REFERENDUM OR WINNER TAKE ALL INSTEAD OF STATE SENATE LEGISLATURE

PEOPLE IN STATE QUASI-EQUAL POPULATED DISTRICTS	PEOPLE IN STATE QUASI-EQUAL POPULATED DISTRICTS

PROPORTIONAL REPRESENTATION

PROPORTIONAL REPRESENTATION

The state government assembly legislatures must make decisions and not pass them to referendums or winner take all!

MOB RULE

THE REPRESENTATION MODE HAS BEEN BROKEN!

VIOLATES TENTH AMENDMENT

The powers allowed by the Constitution to the states are reserved to the people.

STATE GOVERNMENT REPUBLICS

STATE GOVERNMENT GOVERNORS

STATE GOVERNMENT LEGISLATURES

| REFERENDUM OR WINNER TAKE ALL INSTEAD OF STATE SENATE LEGISLATURE | REFERENDUM OR WINNER TAKE ALL INSTEAD OF STATE ASSEMBLY LEGISLATURE |

PEOPLE IN STATE QUASI-EQUAL POPULATED DISTRICTS

PROPORTIONAL REPRESENTATION

PEOPLE IN STATE QUASI-EQUAL POPULATED DISTRICTS

PROPORTIONAL REPRESENTATION

The state Senate and assembly legislatures must make decisions and not pass them to referendums or winner take all!

MOB RULE

THE REPRESENTATION MODE HAS BEEN BROKEN!

TOP DOWN

TENTH AMENDMENT
The powers allowed by the Constitution to the states are reserved to the people.

COUNTY GOVERNMENT REPUBLIC

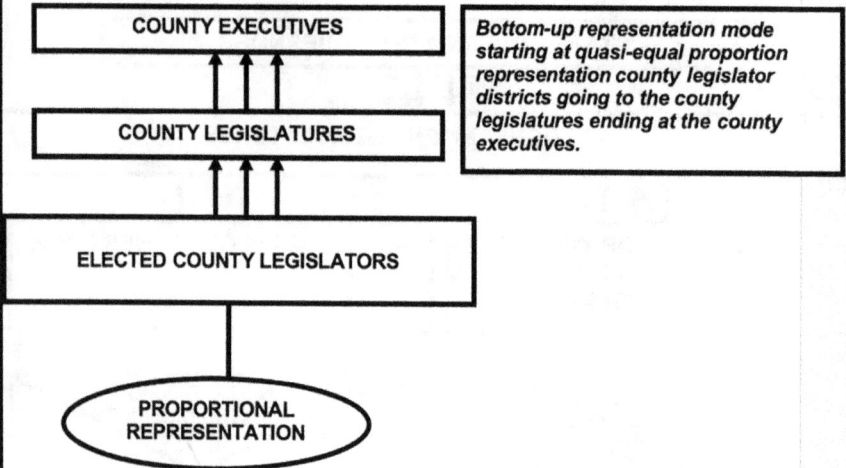

COUNTY EXECUTIVES

COUNTY LEGISLATURES

Bottom-up representation mode starting at quasi-equal proportion representation county legislator districts going to the county legislatures ending at the county executives.

ELECTED COUNTY LEGISLATORS

PROPORTIONAL REPRESENTATION

Government by representation starts at the quasi-equal county legislator districts in bottom-up mode. The county legislatures' reprehensive represent the quasi-equal *proportion representation* county legislator districts. The county executives represent the *proportion representation* county legislatures, which represent the county's people.

The Tenth Amendment definition in the Constitution ensures the maintaining of a county republic. The county legislatures are compelled to follow through and complete any decision-making process, no matter the difficulty that might prevail, rather than to bail out and give up their responsibility to a referendum. The entire county government's voting population votes in a referendum that settles the difficulty at hand, turning a bottom-up *representation mode* to a top-down mode, averting the concept away from starting government by representation at the quasi-equal population county government districts where the power of the county's people exists as explained in the definition of the Tenth Amendment.

The powers allowed by the Constitution to the state government (counties) are reserved to the state government county's people of quasi-equal populated districts.

BOTTOM UP

TENTH AMENDMENT

The powers allowed by the Constitution to the states are reserved to the people.

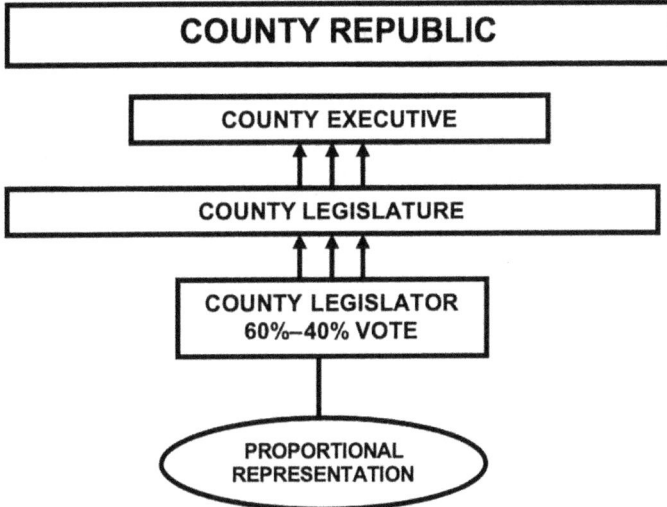

COUNTY REPUBLIC

COUNTY EXECUTIVE

COUNTY LEGISLATURE

COUNTY LEGISLATOR
60%–40% VOTE

PROPORTIONAL
REPRESENTATION

The 60%–40% voting interval protects minority members of the county legislatures. Also, the 60%–40% voting interval protects quasi-equal population of the constructed districts where the govern by representation begins along with the *proportion representation* of county legislature members. It takes 60% or more of county council members to win a decision or 40% or more to lose a decision.

The 60%–40% is derived from the statistical bell-shaped curve of the normal distribution, where two standard deviations straddling the mean of the frequency's distribution encompasses two-thirds ($^2/_3$) of its area. Therefore, 40% divided by 60% (40% / 60%) equals two-thirds ($^2/_3$).

If the county legislatures decide on their own to vote "winner takes all" as with referendums, they will destroy the county's constructed quasi-equal population districts and the *proportion representation* of the county legislature members, violating the Tenth Amendment.

The powers allowed by the Constitution to the state government (county legislatures) are reserved to the state government county legislatures' people of quasi-equal populated districts.

BOTTOM UP

VIOLATES TENTH AMENDMENT

The powers allowed by the Constitution to the states are reserved to the people.

NONCOUNTY GOVERNMENT REPUBLIC

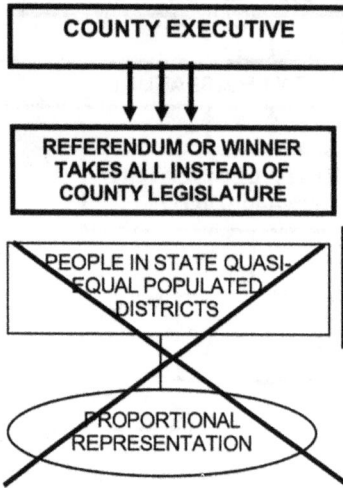

COUNTY EXECUTIVE

REFERENDUM OR WINNER TAKES ALL INSTEAD OF COUNTY LEGISLATURE

PEOPLE IN STATE QUASI-EQUAL POPULATED DISTRICTS

The county legislature must make decisions and not pass them to referendums or winner takes all!

PROPORTIONAL REPRESENTATION

MOB RULE

When a referendum replaces a county council procedure of passing bills or amendments, the county government republic becomes a noncounty government republic, destroying the quasi-equal populated districts, which violates the Tenth Amendment and, of course, the Bill of Rights.

THE REPRESENTATION MODE HAS BEEN BROKEN!

TOP DOWN

TENTH AMENDMENT
The powers allowed by the Constitution to the states are reserved to the people.

CITY GOVERNMENT REPUBLIC

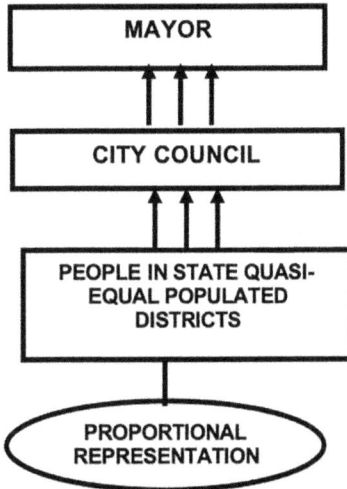

MAYOR

CITY COUNCIL

PEOPLE IN STATE QUASI-EQUAL POPULATED DISTRICTS

PROPORTIONAL REPRESENTATION

Bottom-up representation mode starting at quasi-equal proportion representation city districts going to the city legislature and ending at city mayor, giving power to the people.

The Tenth Amendment definition in the Constitution ensures the maintaining of a city government republic. The city council is compelled to follow through and complete any decision-making process, no matter the difficulty that might prevail, rather than to bail out and give up their responsibility to a referendum. The entire city government voting population votes in a referendum that settles the difficulty at hand, turning a bottom-up *representation mode* to a top-down mode, averting the concept away from starting government by representation at the quasi-equal populated city government districts where the power of the people exists as explained in the definition of the Tenth Amendment and transferring the power to the mayor, creating a dictatorial mode naturally leading to mob rule, destroying the efforts made in constructing consecutively city government districts relating to a *proportion representation* legislature. Winner takes all leads to mob rule, which favors majorities and discriminates against minorities. One vote might disclose a winner, whereas a city legislature decision requires more than a single vote. Anyway, a referendum violates the Tenth Amendment and, of course, the Bill of Rights.

The powers allowed by the Constitution to the state government (city councils) are reserved to the state government city councils' people of quasi-equal populated districts.

BOTTOM UP

TENTH AMENDMENT
The powers allowed by the Constitution to the states are reserved to the people.

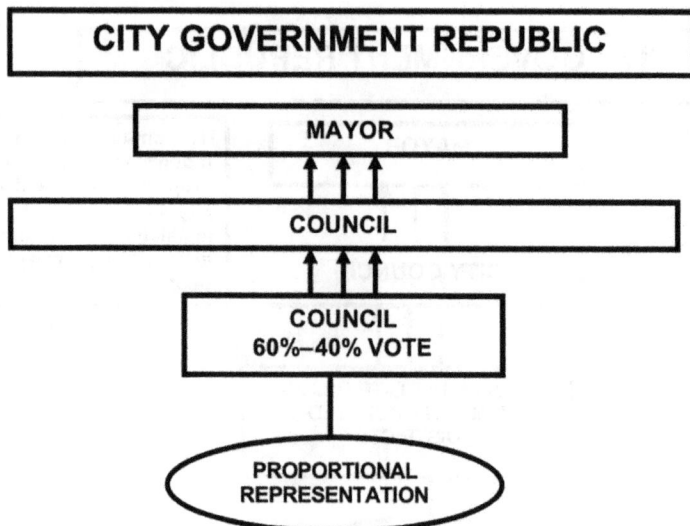

CITY GOVERNMENT REPUBLIC

MAYOR

COUNCIL

COUNCIL
60%–40% VOTE

PROPORTIONAL
REPRESENTATION

The 60%–40% voting interval protects minority members of the city councils. Also, the 60%–40% voting interval protects quasi-equal population of the constructed districts where the govern by representation begins along with the *proportion representation* of city members. It takes 60% or more of city council members to win a decision or 40% or more to lose a decision.

The 60%–40% is derived from the statistical bell-shaped curve of the normal distribution, where two standard deviations straddling the mean of the frequency's distribution encompasses two-thirds ($^2/_3$) of its area. Therefore, 40% divided by 60% (40% / 60%) equals two-thirds ($^2/_3$).

If the city councils decide on their own to vote "winner takes all" as with referendums, they will destroy the city's constructed quasi-equal population districts and the *proportion representation* of the city council members, violating the Tenth Amendment.

The powers allowed by the Constitution to the state government (city mayors) are reserved to the state government city mayors' people of quasi-equal populated districts.

BOTTOM UP

VIOLATES TENTH AMENDMENT
The powers allowed by the Constitution to the states are reserved to the people.

NONCITY GOVERNMENT REPUBLIC

MAYOR

REFERENDUM OR WINNER TAKES ALL INSTEAD OF CITY COUNCIL

PEOPLE IN STATE QUASI-EQUAL POPULATED DISTRICTS

The city council must make decisions and not pass them to referendums or winner takes all!

PROPORTIONAL REPRESENTATION

MOB RULE

When a referendum replaces a city council procedure of passing bills or amendments, the city government republic becomes a noncity government republic, destroying the quasi-equal populated districts, which violates the Tenth Amendment and, of course, the Bill of Rights.

THE REPRESENTATION MODE HAS BEEN BROKEN!

TOP DOWN

TENTH AMENDMENT
The powers allowed by the Constitution to the states are reserved to the people.

TOWN GOVERNMENT REPUBLIC

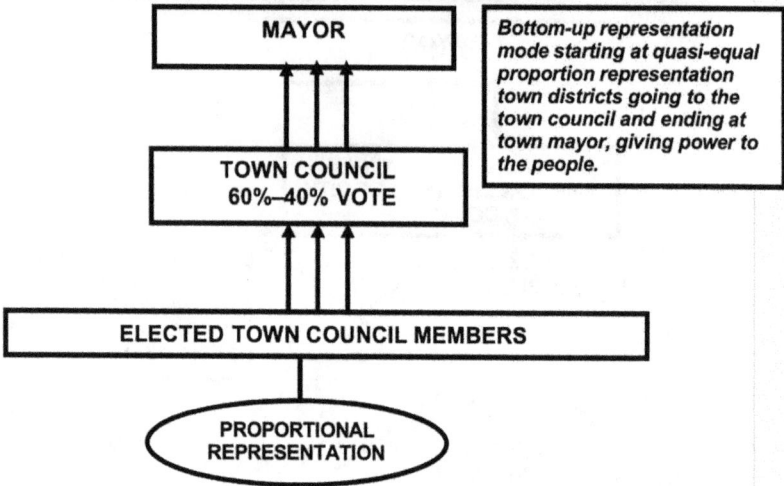

MAYOR

Bottom-up representation mode starting at quasi-equal proportion representation town districts going to the town council and ending at town mayor, giving power to the people.

TOWN COUNCIL
60%–40% VOTE

ELECTED TOWN COUNCIL MEMBERS

PROPORTIONAL
REPRESENTATION

The Tenth Amendment definition in the Constitution ensures the maintaining of a town government republic. The town legislature is compelled to follow through and complete any decision-making process, no matter the difficulty that might prevail, rather than to bail out and give up their responsibility to a referendum. The entire town government voting population votes in a referendum that settles the difficulty at hand, turning a bottom-up *representation mode* to a top-down mode, averting the concept away from starting government by representation at the quasi-equal populated town government districts where the power of the people exists as explained in definition of the Tenth Amendment and transferring the power to the mayor, creating a dictatorial mode naturally leading to mob rule, destroying the efforts made in constructing consecutive town government districts relating to a *proportion representation* legislature. Mob rule leads to winner takes all, which favors majorities and discriminates against minorities. One vote might disclose a winner, whereas a town legislature decision requires more than a single vote. Anyway, a referendum violates the Tenth Amendment and, of course, the Bill of Rights.

The powers allowed by the Constitution to the state government (town councils) are reserved to the state government town councils' people of quasi-equal populated districts.

BOTTOM UP

TENTH AMENDMENT

The powers allowed by the Constitution to the states are reserved to the people.

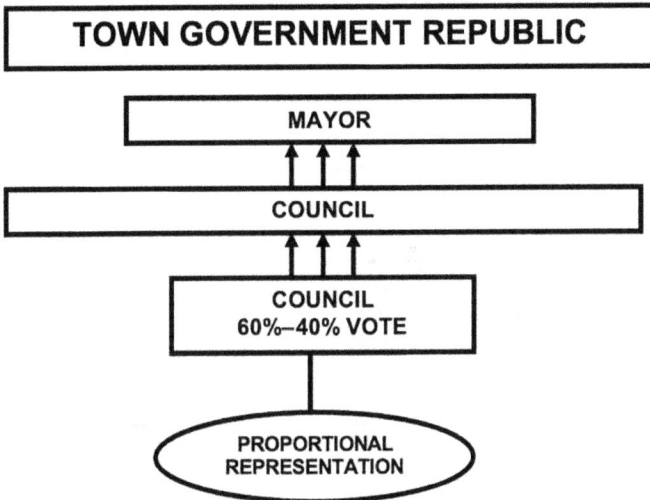

TOWN GOVERNMENT REPUBLIC

MAYOR

COUNCIL

COUNCIL
60%–40% VOTE

PROPORTIONAL
REPRESENTATION

Government by representation starts at the quasi-equal town council districts in bottom-up mode. The town councils represent the quasi-equal *proportion representation* town council districts. The town mayors represent the *proportion representation* town councils, which represent the townspeople.

The Tenth Amendment definition in the Constitution ensures the maintaining of a town government republic. The town's council is compelled to follow through and complete any decision-making process, no matter the difficulty that might prevail, rather than to bail out and give up their responsibility to a referendum. The entire town government republic's voting population votes in a referendum that settles the difficulty at hand, turning a bottom-up *representation mode* to a top-down mode, averting the concept away from starting government by representation at the quasi-equal town government districts where the power of the townspeople exists as explained in the definition of the Tenth Amendment.

The powers allowed by the Constitution to the state government (town mayors) are reserved to the state government town mayors' people of quasi-equal populated districts.

BOTTOM UP

VIOLATES TENTH AMENDMENT

The powers allowed by the Constitution to the states are reserved to the people.

NONTOWN GOVERNMENT REPUBLIC

MAYOR

REFERENDUM OR WINNER TAKES ALL INSTEAD OF TOWN COUNCIL

ELECTED COUNCILMEN

PROPORTIONAL REPRESENTATION

The town council must make decisions and not pass them to referendums or winner takes all!

MOB RULE

When a referendum replaces a town council legislature procedure of passing bills or amendments, the town government republic becomes a nontown government republic, which violates the Tenth Amendment and, of course, the Bill of Rights.

TOP DOWN

THE REPRESENTATION MODE HAS BEEN BROKEN!

TENTH AMENDMENT
The powers allowed by the Constitution to the states are reserved to the people.

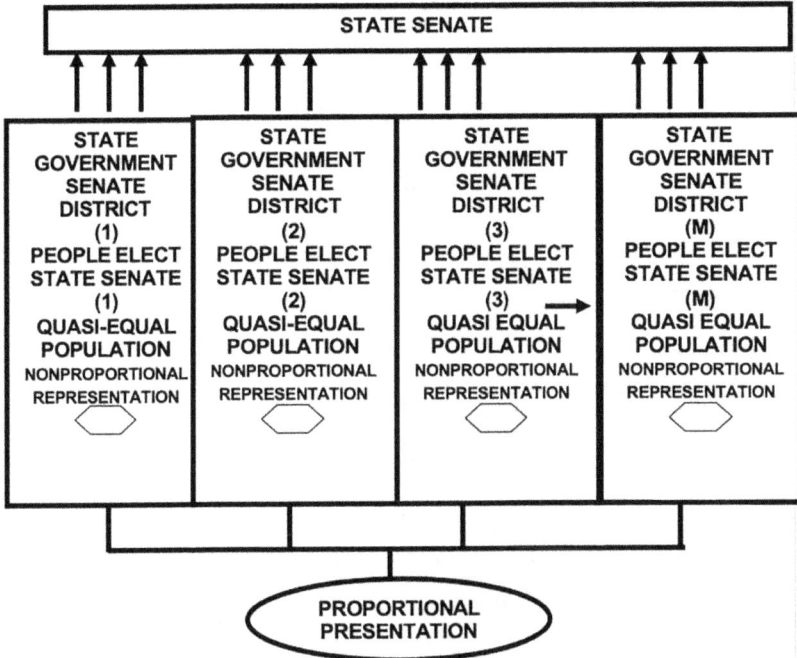

STATE SENATE

STATE GOVERNMENT SENATE DISTRICT (1) PEOPLE ELECT STATE SENATE (1) QUASI-EQUAL POPULATION NONPROPORTIONAL REPRESENTATION	STATE GOVERNMENT SENATE DISTRICT (2) PEOPLE ELECT STATE SENATE (2) QUASI-EQUAL POPULATION NONPROPORTIONAL REPRESENTATION	STATE GOVERNMENT SENATE DISTRICT (3) PEOPLE ELECT STATE SENATE (3) QUASI EQUAL POPULATION NONPROPORTIONAL REPRESENTATION	STATE GOVERNMENT SENATE DISTRICT (M) PEOPLE ELECT STATE SENATE (M) QUASI EQUAL POPULATION NONPROPORTIONAL REPRESENTATION

PROPORTIONAL PRESENTATION

Within each state government Senate district occurs a referendum-type voting procedure electing a state government senator who has dictatorial powers for two years. The flow of power is *top down* within each district. The state government senator's objective in *nonproportion representation* mode is the district's population goal.

The district's population is equal to the state government Senate population divided by the state government M chosen number of districts, which, in most cases, turns in constructing a quasi-equal district population of the M districts across the state government sovereign's territory. A republic form of government begins in this sequence of M quasi-equal populated districts, which are in the state government Senate's sovereign territory.

The sequence of *nonproportion representation* state government Senate members gathered together becomes *proportion representation*.

The state government Senate represents the *proportion representation* members.

BOTTOM UP

TENTH AMENDMENT

The powers allowed by the Constitution to the states are reserved to the people.

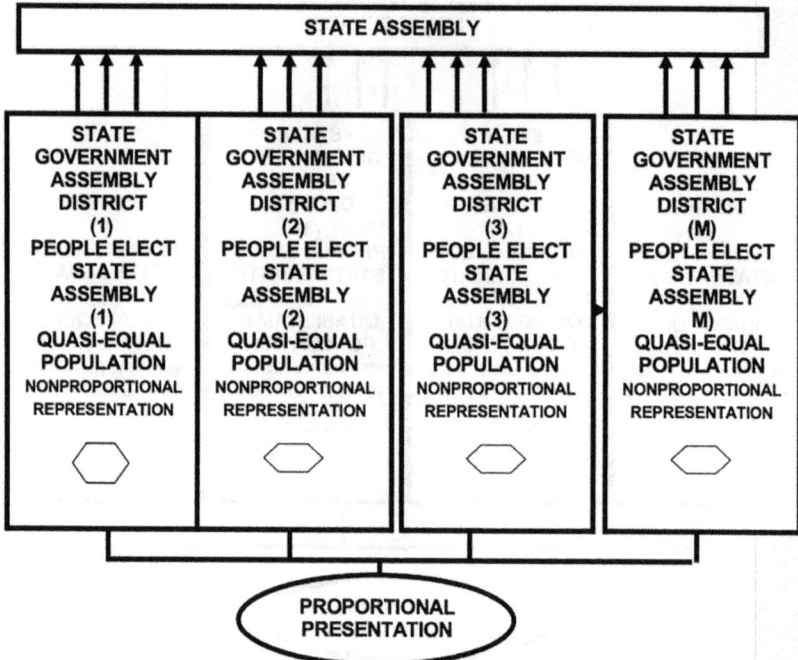

STATE ASSEMBLY

STATE GOVERNMENT ASSEMBLY DISTRICT (1) PEOPLE ELECT STATE ASSEMBLY (1) QUASI-EQUAL POPULATION NONPROPORTIONAL REPRESENTATION	STATE GOVERNMENT ASSEMBLY DISTRICT (2) PEOPLE ELECT STATE ASSEMBLY (2) QUASI-EQUAL POPULATION NONPROPORTIONAL REPRESENTATION	STATE GOVERNMENT ASSEMBLY DISTRICT (3) PEOPLE ELECT STATE ASSEMBLY (3) QUASI-EQUAL POPULATION NONPROPORTIONAL REPRESENTATION	STATE GOVERNMENT ASSEMBLY DISTRICT (M) PEOPLE ELECT STATE ASSEMBLY M) QUASI-EQUAL POPULATION NONPROPORTIONAL REPRESENTATION

PROPORTIONAL PRESENTATION

Within each state government assembly district occurs a referendum-type voting procedure electing a state government senator who has dictatorial powers for two years. The flow of power is *top down* within each district. The state government senator's objective in *nonproportion representation* mode is the district's population goal.

The district's population is equal to the state government assembly population divided by the states government's M chosen number of districts, which, in most cases, turns in constructing a quasi-equal district population of the M districts across the state government sovereign's territory. A republic form of government begins in this sequence of M quasi-equal populated districts, which are in the state government assembly's sovereign territory.

The sequence of *nonproportion representation* state government assembl members gathered together becomes *proportion representation*.

The state government assembly represents the *proportion representation members*.

BOTTOM UP

STATE GOVERNMENT LEGISLATURE

STATE GOVERNMENT SENATE

PROPORTIONAL REPRESENTATION

STATE GOVERNMENT ASSEMBLY

PROPORTIONAL REPRESENTATION

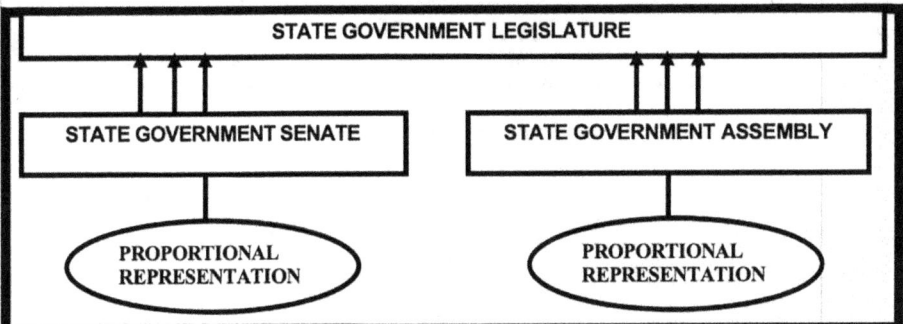

The state government legislature represents the state government's *proportion representation* Senate and assembly; the state government legislatures are *proportion representation.*

The most important group of members are in the state government legislatures. A state government legislature is made up of state government Senate and assembly members who the stats government's inhabitance elected into office; therefore, the state government people indirectly participate in the federal government republic's decision-making through the state government legislatures.

The framers of the Constitution authorized the state government legislatures to choose two senators (ambassadors). The tenure of these two United States senators (ambassadors) would be six (6) years. The state government legislatures are given the power to remove senators during the senator's tenure. Since elections are to be in sequence every two (2) years, one-third ($\frac{1}{3}$) of the United States' senators (ambassadors) would be up for election at anyone time. Two-thirds ($\frac{2}{3}$) of the United States' senators (ambassadors) would be in office, maintaining stability of the federal government republic during elections. At the end of a single senator's tenure, all senators of the federal government republic would have gone through elections.

In conclusion, the framers of the Constitution made the United States Senate the ambassadors of state government republics through the elected choice of the state government legislatures who would protect the rights of the state government republics' inhabitances, guaranteeing the sovereignty of the state government republics.

The state government Senate and assembly make up a bicameral system. Bicameralism merits a "checks and balances" system, which prevents the passage into law of not-thought-out legislation.

Bicameralism controls the potentially corrupt behavior of legislators. Since in the last two decades, rampant corruption scandals have cast dark shadows on the state government republic lawmakers' accountability, the effectiveness of state government republic bicameralism arrangements has gained momentum.

The security of the people requires the concurrence of two distinct bodies to avert schemes of usurpation or treachery of ambitious or corrupted individuals. The state government Senate becomes, in all cases, a salutary check on the state government assembly.

BOTTOM UP

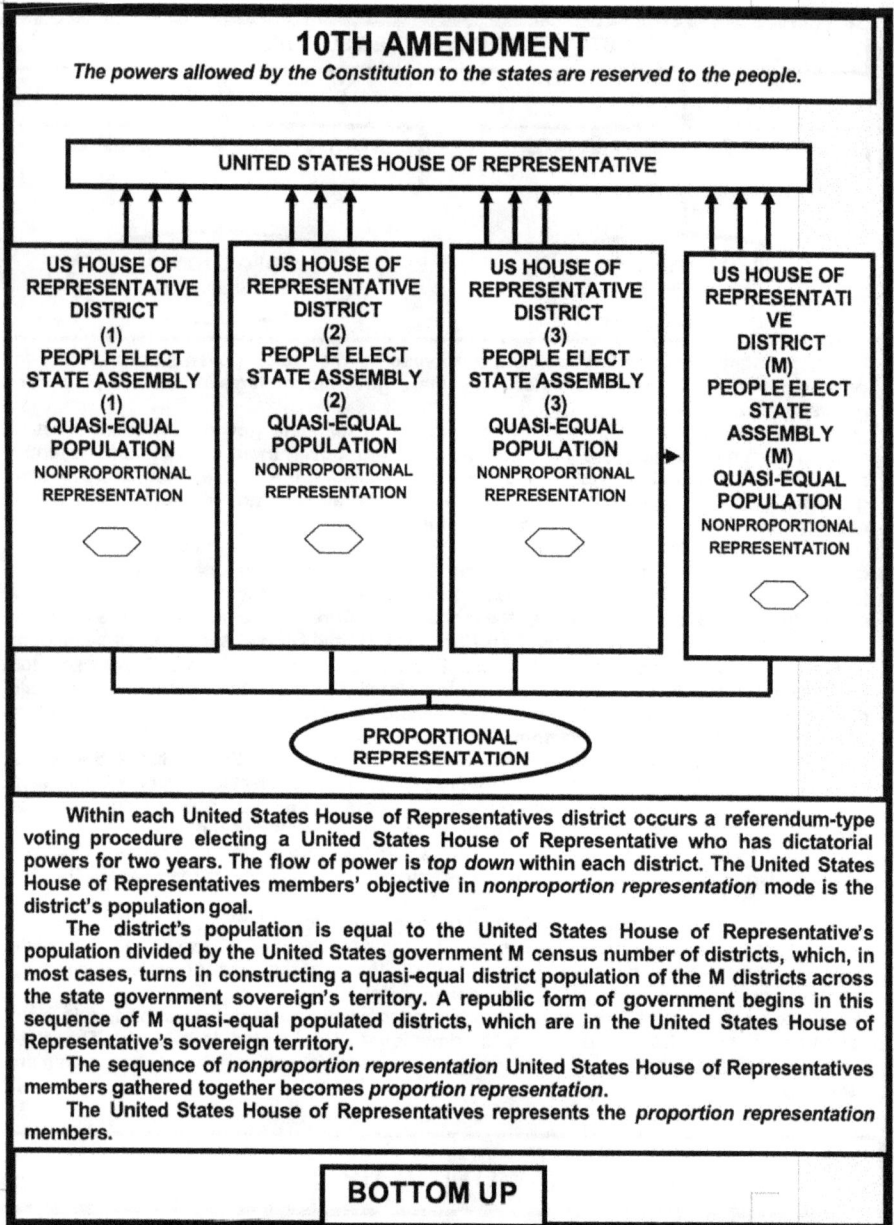

10TH AMENDMENT
The powers allowed by the Constitution to the states are reserved to the people.

UNITED STATES HOUSE OF REPRESENTATIVE

| US HOUSE OF REPRESENTATIVE DISTRICT (1) PEOPLE ELECT STATE ASSEMBLY (1) QUASI-EQUAL POPULATION NONPROPORTIONAL REPRESENTATION | US HOUSE OF REPRESENTATIVE DISTRICT (2) PEOPLE ELECT STATE ASSEMBLY (2) QUASI-EQUAL POPULATION NONPROPORTIONAL REPRESENTATION | US HOUSE OF REPRESENTATIVE DISTRICT (3) PEOPLE ELECT STATE ASSEMBLY (3) QUASI-EQUAL POPULATION NONPROPORTIONAL REPRESENTATION | US HOUSE OF REPRESENTATIVE DISTRICT (M) PEOPLE ELECT STATE ASSEMBLY (M) QUASI-EQUAL POPULATION NONPROPORTIONAL REPRESENTATION |

PROPORTIONAL REPRESENTATION

Within each United States House of Representatives district occurs a referendum-type voting procedure electing a United States House of Representative who has dictatorial powers for two years. The flow of power is *top down* within each district. The United States House of Representatives members' objective in *nonproportion representation* mode is the district's population goal.

The district's population is equal to the United States House of Representative's population divided by the United States government M census number of districts, which, in most cases, turns in constructing a quasi-equal district population of the M districts across the state government sovereign's territory. A republic form of government begins in this sequence of M quasi-equal populated districts, which are in the United States House of Representative's sovereign territory.

The sequence of *nonproportion representation* United States House of Representatives members gathered together becomes *proportion representation*.

The United States House of Representatives represents the *proportion representation* members.

BOTTOM UP

TENTH AMENDMENT

The powers allowed by the Constitution to the states are reserved to the people.

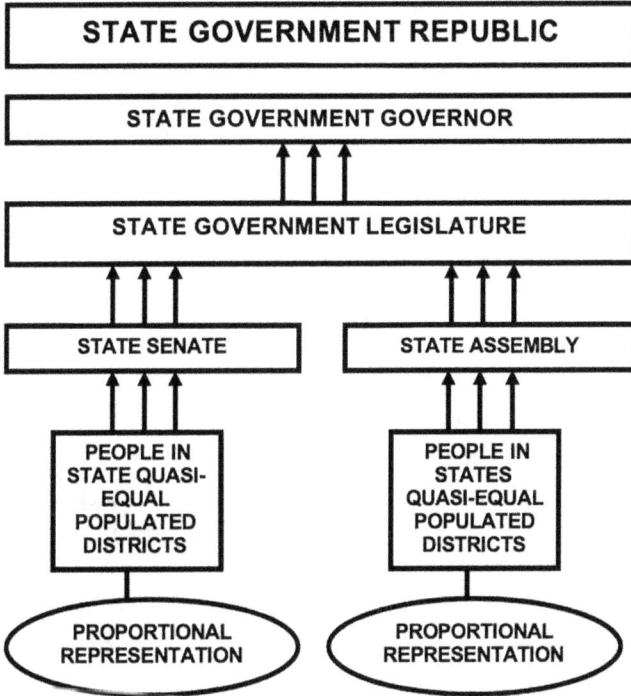

STATE GOVERNMENT REPUBLIC

STATE GOVERNMENT GOVERNOR

STATE GOVERNMENT LEGISLATURE

STATE SENATE	STATE ASSEMBLY

PEOPLE IN STATE QUASI-EQUAL POPULATED DISTRICTS	PEOPLE IN STATES QUASI-EQUAL POPULATED DISTRICTS

PROPORTIONAL REPRESENTATION	PROPORTIONAL REPRESENTATION

A state government republic operates in *representation mode*, which is a *bottom-up representation mode* starting at quasi-equal populated districts representing the state government's area. The *proportion representation* state government Senate and assembly members represent the quasi-equal populated districts. The *proportion representation* state government legislature represents the *proportion representation*, state government Senate, and the *proportion representation* state government assembly members. The state governors represent the state government legislatures.

The powers allowed by the Constitution to the state government (legislatures) are reserved to the state government Senate's and state government assemblies' people of quasi-equal populated districts.

BOTTOM UP

75

TENTTH AMENDMENT
The powers allowed by the Constitution to the states are reserved to the people.

PRESIDENTIAL APPOINTMENTS

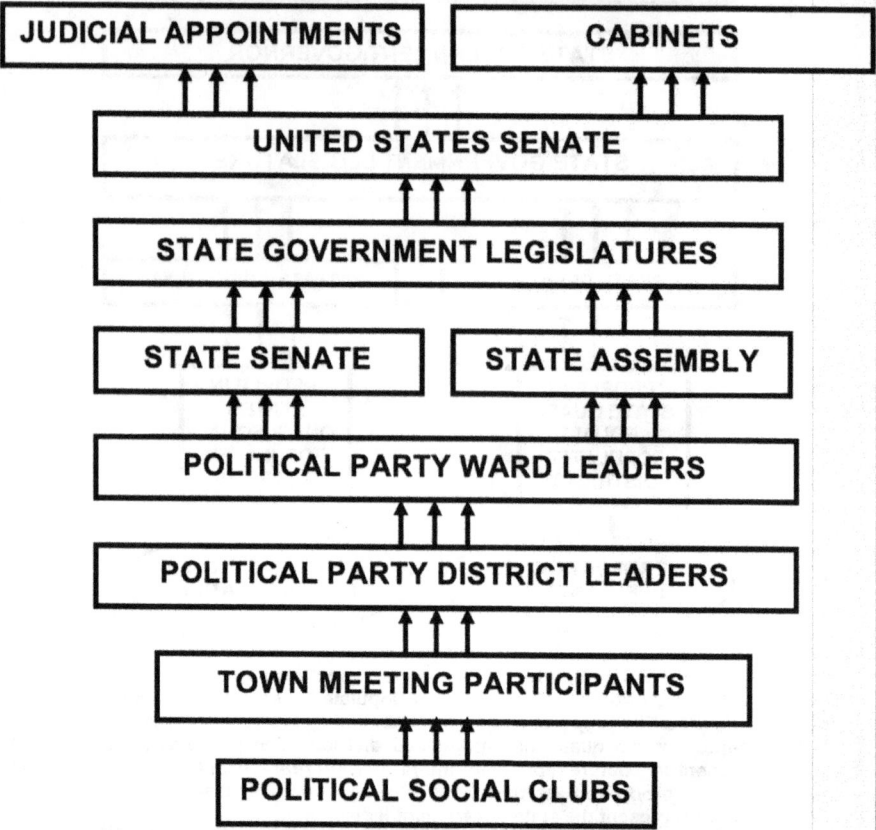

JUDICIAL APPOINTMENTS	CABINETS

UNITED STATES SENATE

STATE GOVERNMENT LEGISLATURES

STATE SENATE	STATE ASSEMBLY

POLITICAL PARTY WARD LEADERS

POLITICAL PARTY DISTRICT LEADERS

TOWN MEETING PARTICIPANTS

POLITICAL SOCIAL CLUBS

The United States Senate represents the state government legislatures. The state government legislatures represent the state government *proportion representation* senators and assembly members. The state government *proportional representation* senators and assemblymen represent political party ward leaders, political party district leaders, town meeting participants, and political social clubs.

BOTTOM UP

TENTH AMENDMENT

The powers allowed by the Constitution to the states are reserved to the people.

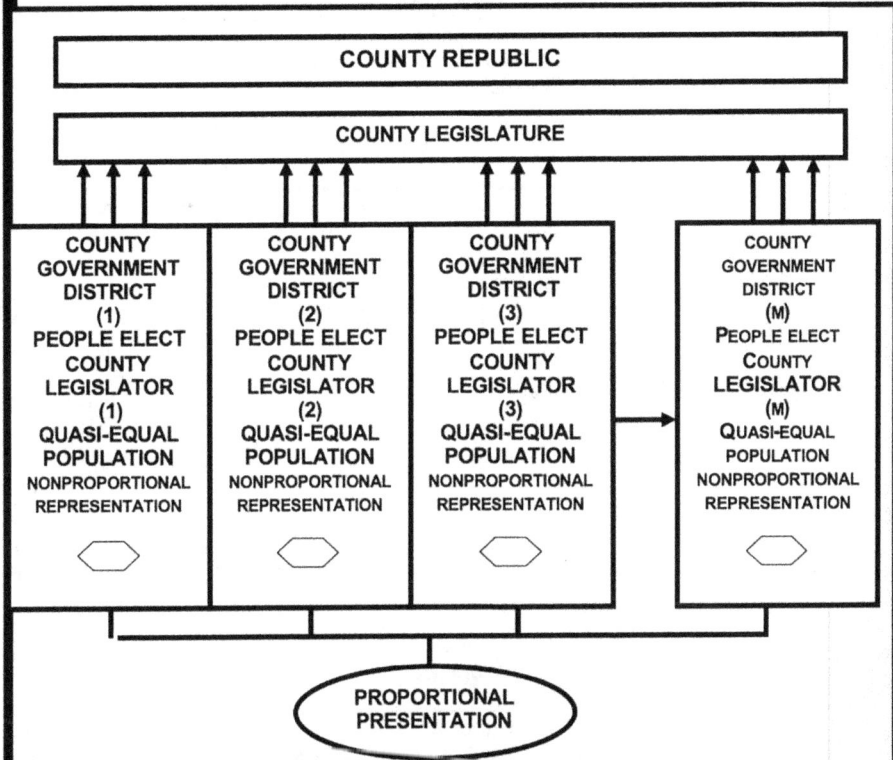

COUNTY REPUBLIC

COUNTY LEGISLATURE

COUNTY GOVERNMENT DISTRICT (1) PEOPLE ELECT COUNTY LEGISLATOR (1) QUASI-EQUAL POPULATION NONPROPORTIONAL REPRESENTATION	COUNTY GOVERNMENT DISTRICT (2) PEOPLE ELECT COUNTY LEGISLATOR (2) QUASI-EQUAL POPULATION NONPROPORTIONAL REPRESENTATION	COUNTY GOVERNMENT DISTRICT (3) PEOPLE ELECT COUNTY LEGISLATOR (3) QUASI-EQUAL POPULATION NONPROPORTIONAL REPRESENTATION	COUNTY GOVERNMENT DISTRICT (M) PEOPLE ELECT COUNTY LEGISLATOR (M) QUASI-EQUAL POPULATION NONPROPORTIONAL REPRESENTATION

PROPORTIONAL PRESENTATION

Within each county government district occurs a referendum-type voting procedure electing a county government legislator who has dictatorial powers for two years. The flow of power is *top down* within each district. The county government members' objective, in *nonproportion representation* mode, is the district's population goal.

The district's population is equal to the county government's population divided by the county government's M chosen number of districts, which, in most cases, turns in constructing a quasi-equal district population of the M districts across the state government sovereign's territory. A republic form of government begins in this sequence of M quasi-equal populated districts, which are in the county's sovereign territory.

The sequence of *nonproportion representation* county government members gathered together becomes *proportion representation*.

The county government represents the *proportion representation* members.

BOTTOM UP

TENTH AMENDMENT

The powers allowed by the Constitution to the states are reserved to the people.

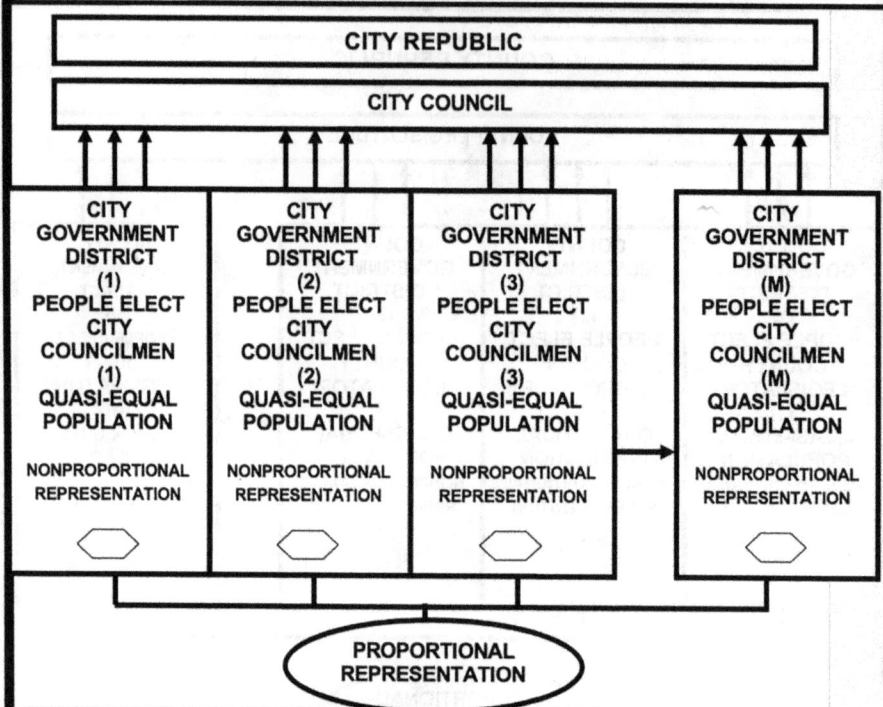

CITY REPUBLIC

CITY COUNCIL

CITY GOVERNMENT DISTRICT (1) PEOPLE ELECT CITY COUNCILMEN (1) QUASI-EQUAL POPULATION NONPROPORTIONAL REPRESENTATION	CITY GOVERNMENT DISTRICT (2) PEOPLE ELECT CITY COUNCILMEN (2) QUASI-EQUAL POPULATION NONPROPORTIONAL REPRESENTATION	CITY GOVERNMENT DISTRICT (3) PEOPLE ELECT CITY COUNCILMEN (3) QUASI-EQUAL POPULATION NONPROPORTIONAL REPRESENTATION	CITY GOVERNMENT DISTRICT (M) PEOPLE ELECT CITY COUNCILMEN (M) QUASI-EQUAL POPULATION NONPROPORTIONAL REPRESENTATION

PROPORTIONAL REPRESENTATION

Within each city government district occurs a referendum-type voting procedure electing a city government legislator who has dictatorial powers for two years. The flow of power is *top down* within each district. The city government member's objective in *nonproportion representation* mode is the district's population goal.

The district's population is equal to the city government's population divided by the city government's M chosen number of districts, which, in most cases, turns in constructing a quasi-equal district population of the M districts across the state government sovereign's territory. A republic form of government begins in this sequence of M quasi-equal populated districts, which are in the state government city's sovereign territory.

The sequence of *nonproportion representation* city government members gathered together becomes *proportion representation*.

The city government represents the *proportion representation* members.

BOTTOM UP

TENTH AMENDMENT

The powers allowed by the Constitution to the states are reserved to the people.

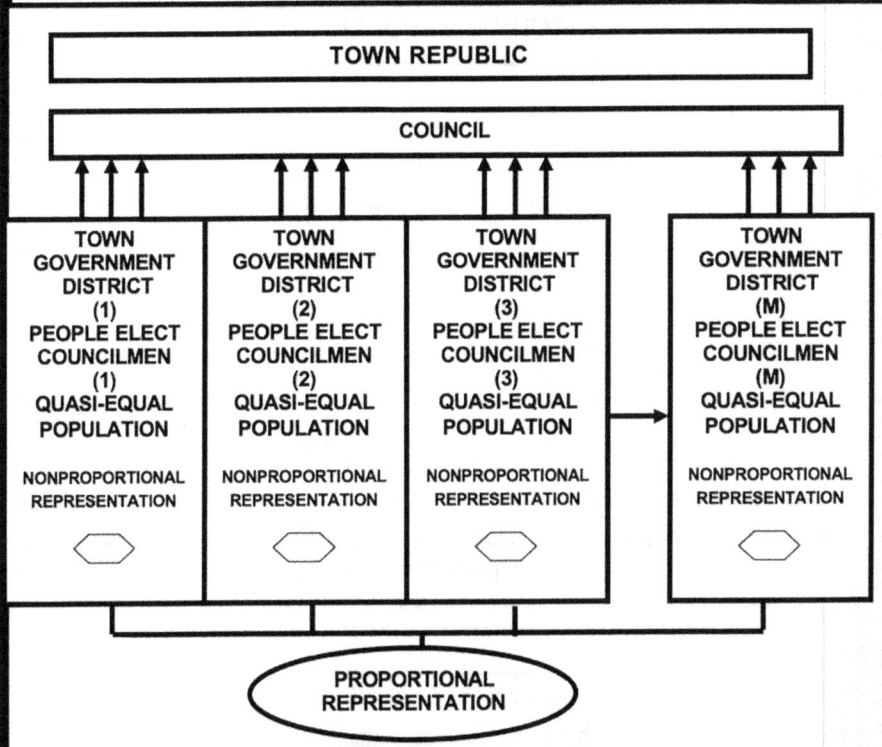

TOWN REPUBLIC

COUNCIL

TOWN GOVERNMENT DISTRICT (1) PEOPLE ELECT COUNCILMEN (1) QUASI-EQUAL POPULATION	TOWN GOVERNMENT DISTRICT (2) PEOPLE ELECT COUNCILMEN (2) QUASI-EQUAL POPULATION	TOWN GOVERNMENT DISTRICT (3) PEOPLE ELECT COUNCILMEN (3) QUASI-EQUAL POPULATION	TOWN GOVERNMENT DISTRICT (M) PEOPLE ELECT COUNCILMEN (M) QUASI-EQUAL POPULATION
NONPROPORTIONAL REPRESENTATION	NONPROPORTIONAL REPRESENTATION	NONPROPORTIONAL REPRESENTATION	NONPROPORTIONAL REPRESENTATION

PROPORTIONAL REPRESENTATION

Within each town government district occurs a referendum-type voting procedure electing a town government legislator who has dictatorial powers for two years. The flow of power is *top down* within each district. The town government member's objective in *nonproportion representation* mode is the district's population goal.

The district's population is equal to the town government's population divided by the town government's M chosen number of districts, which, in most cases, turns in constructing a quasi-equal populated district of the M districts across the state government sovereign's territory. A republic form of government begins in this sequence of M quasi-equal populated districts, which are in the town's sovereign territory town.

The sequence of *nonproportion representation* town government members gathered together becomes *proportion representation*.

The town government represents the *proportion representation* members.

BOTTOM UP

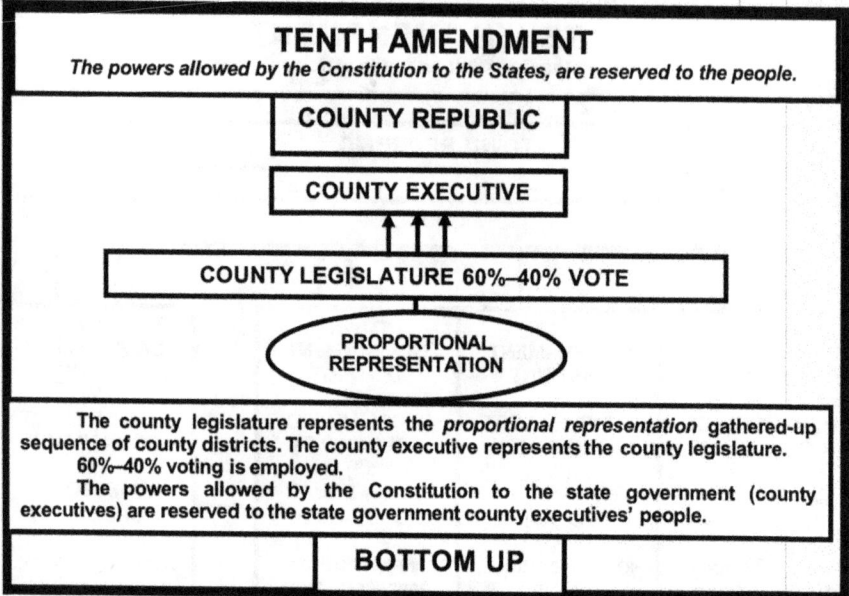

TENTH AMENDMENT

The powers allowed by the Constitution to the States, are reserved to the people.

COUNTY REPUBLIC

COUNTY EXECUTIVE

COUNTY LEGISLATURE 60%–40% VOTE

PROPORTIONAL REPRESENTATION

The county legislature represents the *proportional representation* gathered-up sequence of county districts. The county executive represents the county legislature. 60%–40% voting is employed.

The powers allowed by the Constitution to the state government (county executives) are reserved to the state government county executives' people.

BOTTOM UP

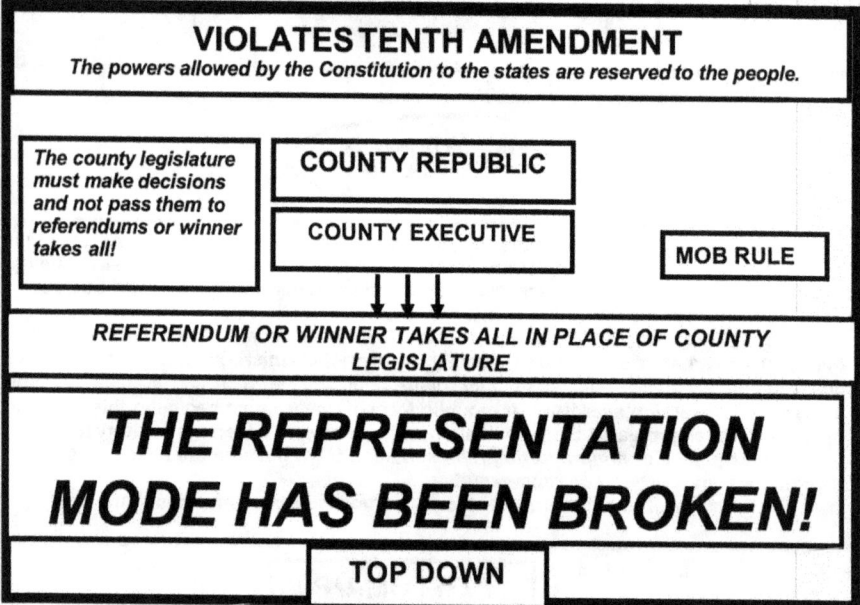

VIOLATES TENTH AMENDMENT

The powers allowed by the Constitution to the states are reserved to the people.

The county legislature must make decisions and not pass them to referendums or winner takes all!

COUNTY REPUBLIC

COUNTY EXECUTIVE

MOB RULE

REFERENDUM OR WINNER TAKES ALL IN PLACE OF COUNTY LEGISLATURE

THE REPRESENTATION MODE HAS BEEN BROKEN!

TOP DOWN

TENTH AMENDMENT
The powers allowed by the Constitution to the states are reserved to the people.

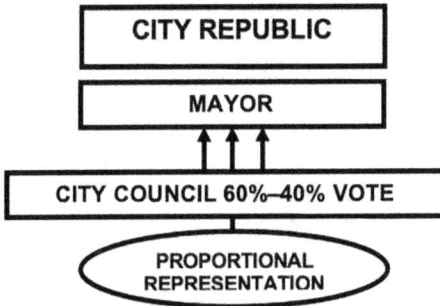

CITY REPUBLIC

MAYOR

CITY COUNCIL 60%–40% VOTE

PROPORTIONAL
REPRESENTATION

The city council represents the *proportional representation* gathered-up sequence of city districts. The mayor represents the city council.

60%–40% voting is employed. The powers allowed by the Constitution to the state government (county mayors) are reserved to the state government city mayor's people of quasi-equal populated districts.

BOTTOM UP

VIOLATES TENTH AMENDMENT
The powers allowed by the Constitution to the states are reserved to the people.

The city council must make decisions and not pass them to referendums or winner takes all!

CITY REPUBLIC

MAYOR

MOB RULE

REFERENDUM OR WINNER TAKES ALL IN PLACE OF CITY COUNCIL

THE REPRESENTATION MODE HAS BEEN BROKEN!

TOP DOWN

TENTH AMENDMENT
The powers allowed by the Constitution to the states are reserved to the people.

TOWN REPUBLIC

MAYOR

TOWN COUNCIL 60%–40% VOTE

PROPORTIONAL REPRESENTATION

The town legislature represents the *proportional representation* gathered-up sequence of town districts. The mayor represents the town's council.

60%–40% voting is employed. The powers allowed by the Constitution to the state government (town mayors) are reserved to the town mayors' people of quasi-equal populated districts.

BOTTOM UP

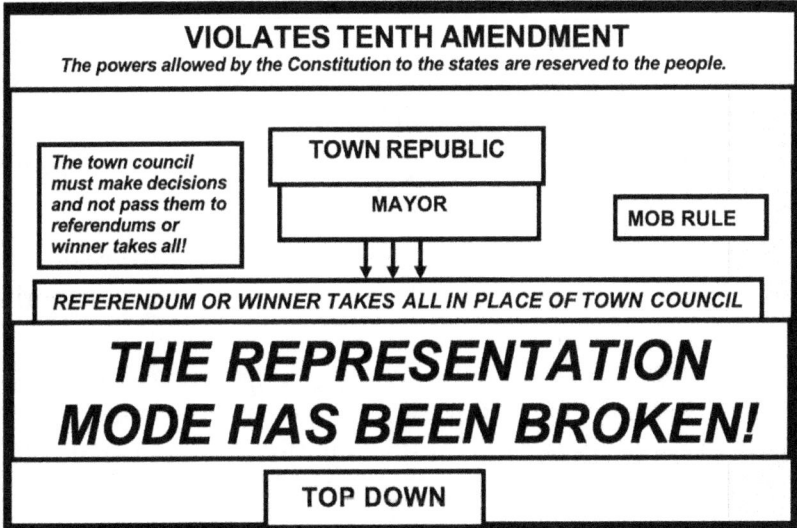

ELECTORAL COLLEGE (UNITED STATES)

Each state has a number of electors equal to the number of its senators and representatives in the United States Congress. Additionally, the District of Columbia is given a number of electors equal to the number held by the smallest states. US territories are not represented in the Electoral College.

Each elector casts one vote for president and one vote for vice president. In order to be elected, a candidate must have a majority (at least 270) of the electoral votes cast for that office. Should no candidate for president win a majority of the electoral votes, the choice is referred to the House of Representatives. Should no candidate for vice president possess a majority of the electoral votes, the choice is given to the Senate.

The Constitution allows each state legislature to designate a method of choosing electors. Fifty states and the District of Columbia have adopted a winner-take-all popular vote rule where voters choose between statewide slates of electors pledged to vote for a specific presidential and vice presidential candidate. The candidate that wins the most votes in the state wins the support of all of that state's electors (mob rule).

Maine and Nebraska use a tiered system. A single elector is chosen within each United States House of Representative district.

Statewide popular vote chose two electors (referendum violates the Tenth Amendment).

A statewide vote chooses the vast majority of electors. The United States presidential elections are effectively an amalgamation of fifty-one separate and simultaneous first past the post-elections rather than a single national election.

Candidates with less than a plurality of the nationwide popular vote can win a presidential election, which has happened on several occasions in American history. The Electoral College is a significant and unique feature of the federal government republic protecting the rights of smaller states. Numerous constitutional amendments have been submitted seeking a replacement of the Electoral College with a direct popular vote.

In the *Federalist Papers No. 39*, James Madison argued that the Constitution was designed to be a mixture of state-based and population-based government.

The legislative branch would have two houses, one state government legislatures elected Senate (state based) and the other United States House of Representatives (population based) in character. A mixture of the two models would elect the president, giving some electoral power to the states and some to the people in general.

Both the Congress and the president would be elected by mixed state-based and population-based means.

Article II, Section 1, Clause 2 of the Constitution states,

> Each State shall appoint, in such Manner as the Legislature thereof may direct, a Number of Electors, equal to the whole Number of Senators and Representatives to which the State may be entitled in the Congress: but no Senator or Representative, or Person holding

an Office of Trust or Profit under the United States, shall be appointed an Elector.

Article II, Section 1, Clause 4 of the Constitution states,

> The Congress may determine the Time of choosing the Electors, and the Day on which they shall give their Votes; which Day shall be the same throughout the United States.

Article II, Section 1, Clause 3 of the Constitution provided for the original fashion by which the president and vice president were to be chosen by the electors. The primary difference was that each elector voted for two persons for president rather than one vote for president and one vote for vice president. After the choosing of the president, whoever had the most electoral votes among the remaining candidates would become the vice president.

The constitutional theory behind the indirect election of both the president and vice president of the United States is that while the Congress is popularly elected by the people, the president and vice president are elected to be executives of a federal government republic made up of independent state government republics.

Presidential electors are selected on a state-by-state basis as determined by the laws of each state. Each state uses the popular vote on Election Day to appoint electors. Although ballots list the names of the presidential candidates, voters within the fifty states and Washington, DC, actually choose electors for their state when they vote for president and vice president. These presidential electors in turn cast electoral votes for those two offices. Even though the aggregate national popular vote and media organizations, the national popular vote is not the basis for electing a president or vice president.

A candidate must receive an absolute majority of electoral votes (currently 270) to win the presidency.

If no candidate receives a majority in the election for president or vice president, that election is determined via a contingency procedure in the Tenth Amendment, which is explained in detail below.

The size of the Electoral College is equal to the total membership of both Houses of Congress (435 representatives and 100 senators), plus the three electors allocated to Washington, DC, totaling 538 electors.

Each state is allocated as many electors as it has representatives and senators in the United States Congress. Since the most populous states have the most seats in the House of Representatives, they also have the most electors. The six states with the most electors are California (55), Texas (34), New York (31), Florida (27), Illinois (21), and Pennsylvania (21). The seven smallest states by population—Alaska, Delaware, Montana, North Dakota, South Dakota, Vermont, and Wyoming—each have three electors. The number of representatives for each state is determined decennially by the United States Census, thus determining the number of electoral votes for each state until the next census reallocation.

Candidates for elector are nominated by their state political parties in the months prior to Election Day. The US Constitution delegates to each state the authority for nominating and choosing its electors. In some states, the electors are nominated in primaries, the same way that other candidates are nominated. Other states such as Oklahoma, Virginia, and North Carolina nominate electors in party conventions. In Pennsylvania, the campaign committees of each candidate name their candidates for presidential elector (an attempt to discourage faithless electors). Under Article II, Section 1, Clause 2 of the US Constitution, no person holding a federal office, either elected or appointed, may become an elector. Under Section 3 of the Fourteenth Amendment, any person who has sworn an oath to support the United States Constitution in order to hold either a state or federal office and has then later rebelled against the United States is barred from serving in the Electoral College. However, the Congress may remove this disability by a two-thirds vote in both Houses.

The manner for choosing electors is determined within each state by its legislature. Currently, all states choose electors by popular election on the date specified by federal law. While many people may believe they are voting for their presidential candidate, they are in actuality casting their vote for that candidate's electors.

The number of electoral votes allocated to each state is equal to the number of representatives the state has in the Congress. The two votes that a candidate receives for winning the statewide popular vote come from the two electoral votes that each state receives from the members in the Senate to which each state is entitled. The other electoral votes that a state has come from the respective number of members of the House of Representatives to which each state is entitled.

The Congressional District Method allows for the chance for states to split their electoral vote between multiple candidates. However, even though Maine and Nebraska have been using the method for twenty-six and sixteen years respectively, neither has ever split their electoral, probably because of the small number of electoral districts. Therefore, if states with more congressional representatives used this method, more frequent split electoral votes would likely occur.

The Congressional District Method is closer to one man, one vote than the current winner-take-all system (mob rule) because an individual's vote has a larger weight to it. In addition, the Congressional District Method can be more easily implemented than other alternatives to the winner-take-all method (mob rule). Each state only has to pass legislation in order to use the new method instead of having to pass a constitutional amendment like some other Electoral College reform options.

The Congressional District Method has its benefits, but there are also criticisms of it. For instance, candidates might only spend time in certain battleground districts instead of the entire state, and cases of gerrymandering could arise with political parties trying to draw up as many safe districts as they can.

However, a result of the present functionality of the Electoral College is that the national popular vote bears no legal or factual significance on determining the outcome of the election. Since the national popular vote is irrelevant, both voters and candidates are assumed to base their campaign strategies around the existence of the Electoral College.

Altogether, the ultimate consequence of such functions in any close race has candidates campaigning to maximize electoral votes by capturing coveted swing states, not to maximize national popular vote totals.

Most states use a winner-take-all (violates Tenth Amendment) system, in which the candidate with the most votes in that state receives all of the state's electoral votes. This gives candidates an incentive to pay the most attention to states without a clear favorite, such as Pennsylvania, Ohio, and Florida. For example, California, Texas, and New York, in spite of having the largest populations, have, in recent elections, been considered safe for a particular party (Democratic for California and New York, Republican for Texas), and therefore, candidates typically devote relatively few resources, in both time and money, to such states.

Because it does not matter how many people turn out to vote in a given state, the Electoral College eliminates any advantage to a political party or campaign for encouraging voters to turn out (except in the few closely fought swing states). If the presidential election were decided by a national popular vote (*referendum*—violates Tenth Amendment), in contrast, campaigns and parties would have a strong incentive to work to increase turnout everywhere. Individuals would similarly have a strong incentive to persuade their friends and neighbors to turn out to vote. The differences in turnout between swing states and nonswing states under the current Electoral College system suggest that replacing the Electoral

College with direct election by popular vote (*referendum*—violates Tenth Amendment) would likely increase turnout and participation very significantly.

Because it does not matter how many people turn out to vote in a given state, the Electoral College eliminates any advantage to a political party or campaign for encouraging voters to turn out (except in the few closely fought swing states). If the presidential election were decided by a national popular vote (*referendum*—violates Tenth Amendment), in contrast, campaigns and parties would have a strong incentive to work to increase turnout everywhere. Individuals would similarly have a strong incentive to persuade their friends and neighbors to turn out to vote. The differences in turnout between swing states and nonswing states under the current Electoral College system suggest that replacing the Electoral College with direct election by popular vote (*referendum*—violates Tenth Amendment) would likely increase turnout and participation very significantly.

Proponents of the Electoral College claim the Electoral College prevents a candidate from winning the presidency by simply winning in heavily populated urban areas. This means that candidates must make a much wider appeal than they would if they simply had to win the national popular vote.

Maintains the Federal Character of the Nation

The United States of America is a federal coalition that consists of component states. Proponents of the current system argue that the collective opinion of even a small state merits attention at the federal level greater than that given to a small, though numerically equivalent, portion of a very populous state.

Enhances Status of Minority Groups

Far from decreasing the power of minority groups by depressing voter turnout, proponents argue that by making the votes of a given state an all-or-nothing (mob rule) affair, minority groups can provide the critical edge that allows a candidate to win. This encourages candidates to court a wide variety of such minorities and special interests. This argument does not apply to states that do not employ an all-or-nothing (mob rule) system for selecting their electors, Maine and Nebraska being the only such states at this time; the argument does apply to individual electors.

Encourages Stability Through the Two-Party System

Many proponents of the Electoral College see its negative effect on third parties as a good thing. They argue that the two-party system has provided stability through its ability to change during times of rapid political and cultural change. They believe it protects the most powerful office in the country from control by what these proponents view as regional minorities until they can moderate their views to win broad long-term support from across the entire nation.

Isolation of Election Problems

Some supporters of the Electoral College note that it isolates the impact of potential election fraud or other problems to the state where it occurs. The College prevents instances where a party dominant in one state may dishonestly inflate the votes for a candidate and thereby affect the election outcome. Recounts, for instance, occur only on a state-by-state basis, not nationwide. Similarly, the College acts to isolate less-malicious election problems to the state in which they occur.

Maintains Separation of Powers

The Constitution separated government into three branches that check each other to minimize threats to liberty and encourage deliberation of governmental acts. Under the original framework, only members of the House of Representatives were directly elected by the people, with members of the Senate chosen by state legislatures, the president by the Electoral College, and the judiciary by the president and the Senate. The president was not directly elected in part due to fears that he could assert a national popular mandate that would undermine the legitimacy of the other branches and potentially result in tyranny.

Electoral College Notes

- The Electoral College allows the individual states to elect the president.

- The Electoral College system is a system that makes an attempt to limit the federal government republic power.

- The Electoral College system is a system that makes an attempt to guarantee state Government rights.

- The Electoral College system is a system that is an essential part of the framers of the Constitution's balance power idea.

- The Electoral College system is a system that is compatible toward people's rights.

- The Electoral College system does not force candidates to focus on small states.

- The Electoral College system protects against mob rule.

- The Electoral College system was one way the framers of the Constitution reined in the mob rule impulse.

- The Electoral College system votes combine the number of 435 proportional Representative United States House of Representative seats with the 100 United States seats.

- The Electoral College system states that fifty states elect the president to guarantee so that states of low population took part in choosing the president.

- The Electoral College system declares if a state wants to adopt a process whereby electoral votes are parceled out according to the winner by congressional district, instead of a statewide winner-take-all (mob rule) approach, then it can do so. The Electoral College system accepts the few states have indeed adopted that approach, and it has much merit to it.

- The Electoral College system split decision between the popular and electoral votes occurred fifty-three times since George Washington was chosen in 1792.

- The Electoral College system, on the three previous occasions when a split decision between the popular and electoral votes occurred, was the mechanism for a decisive conclusion to an election and a certain transition to a final winner.

- The Electoral College system restricts to recounting of votes to a finite number of states instead of many.

- The Electoral College system does not allow the smaller less-populated states to be swallowed up or ignored by the larger more-populous states.

- The Electoral College system represented not only a compromise to accommodate the concerns of the small states, but also a singular act of genius on the part of the framers.

- The Electoral College system does not reject the notion of a truly democratic election (mob rule) that occurs in each state, which decides the state's vote for president in the Electoral College.

- The Electoral College system serves as a pillar of our federal system of government since the states created the central government in the first place, and therefore, the states should not be absorbed into a national popular (*referendum*—violates Tenth Amendment) mass vote.

- The Electoral College system compels a candidate to win a majority in the Electoral College and requires that he must focus all his resources and attention on campaigning in many states.

- The Electoral College system forces the candidate for president to fashion a truly national appeal.

- The Electoral College system helps assure that the winner will enjoy an added measure of support and legitimacy that is derives from a relatively broad base.

- The Electoral College system might have one reform that does make sense; it is one requiring that electors vote for the candidate who won their respective states. The framers assumed that they would, but left it to the states to settle the details. Twenty-six states have such a requirement, but fourteen do not.

- Advocates of the abolition of the Electoral College are those who favor a centralized federal government.

- Advocates of the abolition of the Electoral College are those who express contempt of state government rights.

TENTH AMENDMENT

The powers allowed by the Constitution to the states are reserved to the people.

UNITED STATES REPUBLIC

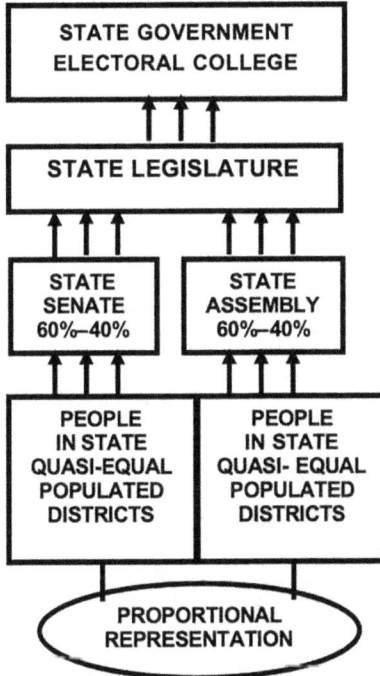

STATE GOVERNMENT
ELECTORAL COLLEGE

↑↑↑

STATE LEGISLATURE

↑↑↑   ↑↑↑

| STATE SENATE 60%–40% | STATE ASSEMBLY 60%–40% |

↑↑↑   ↑↑↑

| PEOPLE IN STATE QUASI-EQUAL POPULATED DISTRICTS | PEOPLE IN STATE QUASI- EQUAL POPULATED DISTRICTS |

PROPORTIONAL REPRESENTATION

Government by representation starts at the quasi-equal state government Senate and assembly districts in bottom-up mode. The state government legislature members represent the quasi-equal *proportion representation* state government assembly and Senate districts. The state government's Electoral College represents the *proportion representation* state government legislature, which represents the state government's people.

The powers allowed by the Constitution to the state government (legislature) are reserved to the state government Senate's and state government assemblies' people of quasi-equal populated districts.

BOTTOM UP

95

VIOLATES TENTH AMENDMENT
The powers allowed by the Constitution to the states are reserved to the people.

Government by representation starts at the quasi-equal state government Senate and assembly districts in bottom-up mode. The state government legislature members represent the quasi-equal *proportion representation* state government assembly and Senate districts. The state government Electoral College's members represent the *proportion representation* state government legislature, which represents the state government's people.

Decimal arithmetic must replace integral arithmetic. Use the following steps:

Calculate the percentage popular vote won in decimal times the electoral number.

Convert decimal to integral arithmetic.

Covert in such a way that the state government electoral number is satisfied.

See *percentage table!*

The calculations were done in decimal arithmetic and then converted to integral arithmetic. Using this method eliminates the possibility of having a national popular winner not getting the electoral vote. In other words, the electoral vote winner will always also be the national popular vote winner, reducing the possibility of mob rule!

According to the Tenth Amendment, the state government legislature has the power to pick the electors who represent the state government's people.

The power belongs to the people within the US House of Representatives quasi-equal populated districts, indicating that the US House of Representatives' districts should be electing the president. "Winner takes all" is eliminated, and integral arithmetic is acceptable. Adding the District of Columbia makes 436 districts across the USA. The winner of the election will win both the popular vote and the electoral vote. In other words, if a candidate wins a district in Alaska and another in New York, then those districts belong to him, abolishing mob rule!

STATE GOVERNMENT ELECTORAL COLLEGE WINNER TAKES ALL

STATE LEGISLATURES

STATE SENATE 60%–40%

STATE ASSEMBLY 60%–40%

PEOPLE IN STATE QUASI-EQUAL POPULATED DISTRICTS

PEOPLE IN STATES QUASI-EQUAL POPULATED DISTRICTS

PROPORTIONAL REPRESENTATION

THE REPRESENTATION MODE HAS BEEN BROKEN!

TENTH AMENDMENT

The powers allowed by the Constitution to the states are reserved to the people.

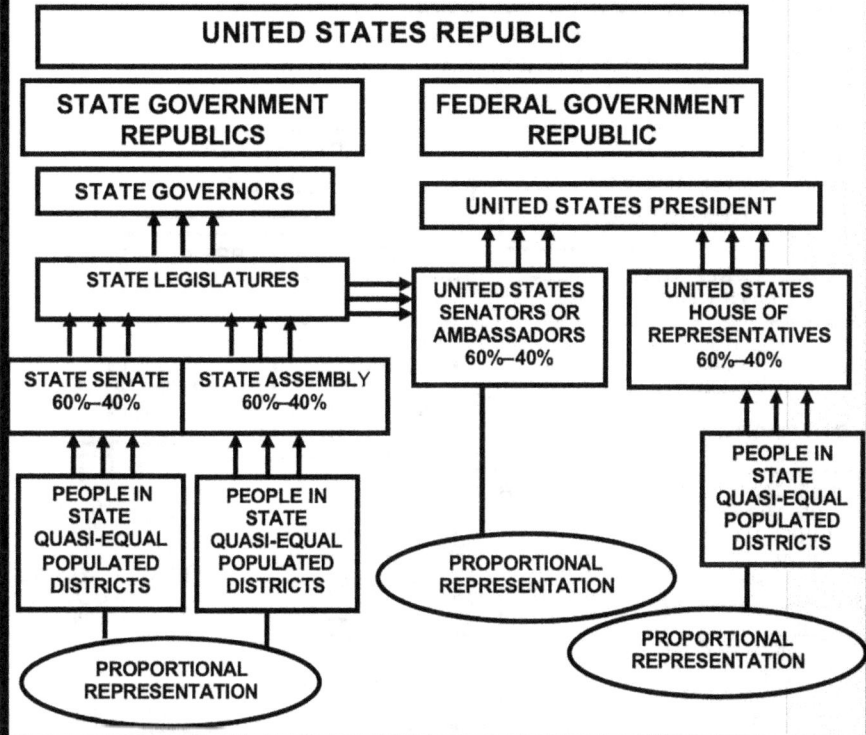

UNITED STATES REPUBLIC

STATE GOVERNMENT REPUBLICS

FEDERAL GOVERNMENT REPUBLIC

STATE GOVERNORS

UNITED STATES PRESIDENT

STATE LEGISLATURES

UNITED STATES SENATORS OR AMBASSADORS 60%–40%

UNITED STATES HOUSE OF REPRESENTATIVES 60%–40%

STATE SENATE 60%–40%

STATE ASSEMBLY 60%–40%

PEOPLE IN STATE QUASI-EQUAL POPULATED DISTRICTS

PEOPLE IN STATE QUASI-EQUAL POPULATED DISTRICTS

PEOPLE IN STATE QUASI-EQUAL POPULATED DISTRICTS

PROPORTIONAL REPRESENTATION

PROPORTIONAL REPRESENTATION

PROPORTIONAL REPRESENTATION

A federal government republic operates in a *bottom-up representation mode* starting at quasi-equal *proportion representation* state government Senate's and state government assemblies' districts. The *proportion representation* state government legislatures represent the *proportion representation* state government Senate and the *proportion representation* state government assembly. The *proportion representation* United States Senate represents the state government legislature. The president represents the *proportion representation* United States Senate and the *proportion representation* House of Representatives. The state government governor represents the state government legislature.

The powers allowed by the Constitution to the state government are reserved to the state government people of quasi-equal populated districts.

BOTTOM UP

VIOLATES TENTH AMENDMENT

The powers allowed by the Constitution to the states are reserved to the people.

NONUNITED STATES REPUBLIC

NONSTATE GOVERNMENT REPUBLICS

NONFEDERAL GOVERNMENT REPUBLIC

UNITED STATES PRESIDENT

STATE GOVERNORS

STATE LEGISLATURES

UNITED STATES SENATORS OR AMBASSADORS 60%–40%

UNITED STATES HOUSE OF REPRESENTATIVES 60%–40%

REFERENDUM OR WINNER TAKES ALL IN PLACE OF STATE SENATE

STATE ASSEMBLY 60%–40%

PEOPLE IN STATE QUASI-EQUAL POPULATED DISTRICTS

PROPORTIONAL REPRESENTATION

PEOPLE IN STATE QUASI-EQUAL POPULATED DISTRICTS

PEOPLE IN STATE QUASI-EQUAL POPULATED DISTRICTS

The state government Senate must make decisions and not pass them to referendums or winner takes all!

PROPORTIONAL REPRESENTATION

PROPORTIONAL REPRESENTATION

MOB RULE

THE REPRESENTATION MODE HAS BEEN BROKEN!

VIOLATES TENTH AMENDMENT

The powers allowed by the Constitution to the states are reserved to the people.

NONUNITED STATES REPUBLIC

NONSTATE GOVERNMENT REPUBLICS	NONFEDERAL GOVERNMENT REPUBLIC

STATE GOVERNORS

UNITED STATES PRESIDENT

STATE LEGISLATURES

UNITED STATES SENATORS OR AMBASSADORS 60%–40%

UNITED STATES HOUSE OF REPRESENTATIVES 60%–40%

STATE SENATE 60%–40%

REFERENDUM OR WINNER TAKES ALL IN PLACE OF STATE ASSEMBLY

PEOPLE IN STATES QUASI-EQUAL POPULATED DISTRICTS

PEOPLE IN STATE QUASI-EQUAL POPULATED DISTRICTS

PEOPLE IN STATE QUASI-EQUAL POPULATED DISTRICTS

PROPORTIONAL REPRESENTATION

The state government assembly must make decisions and not pass them to referendums or winner takes all!

PROPORTIONAL REPRESENTATION

PROPORTIONAL REPRESENTATION

MOB RULE

THE REPRESENTATION MODE HAS BEEN BROKEN!

VIOLATES TENTH AMENDMENT

The powers allowed by the Constitution to the states are reserved to the people.

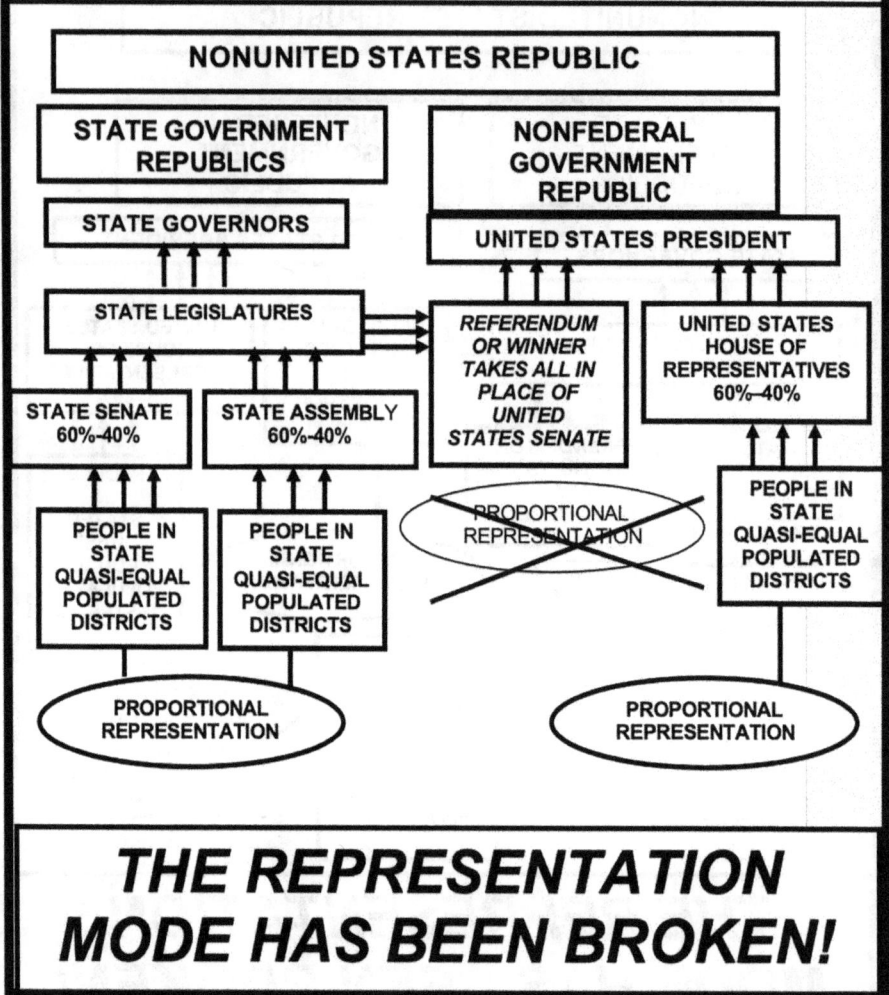

NONUNITED STATES REPUBLIC

STATE GOVERNMENT REPUBLICS

NONFEDERAL GOVERNMENT REPUBLIC

STATE GOVERNORS

UNITED STATES PRESIDENT

STATE LEGISLATURES

REFERENDUM OR WINNER TAKES ALL IN PLACE OF UNITED STATES SENATE

UNITED STATES HOUSE OF REPRESENTATIVES 60%–40%

STATE SENATE 60%–40%

STATE ASSEMBLY 60%-40%

PROPORTIONAL REPRESENTATION

PEOPLE IN STATE QUASI-EQUAL POPULATED DISTRICTS

PEOPLE IN STATE QUASI-EQUAL POPULATED DISTRICTS

PEOPLE IN STATE QUASI-EQUAL POPULATED DISTRICTS

PROPORTIONAL REPRESENTATION

PROPORTIONAL REPRESENTATION

THE REPRESENTATION MODE HAS BEEN BROKEN!

VIOLATES TENTH AMENDMENT

The powers allowed by the Constitution to the states are reserved to the people.

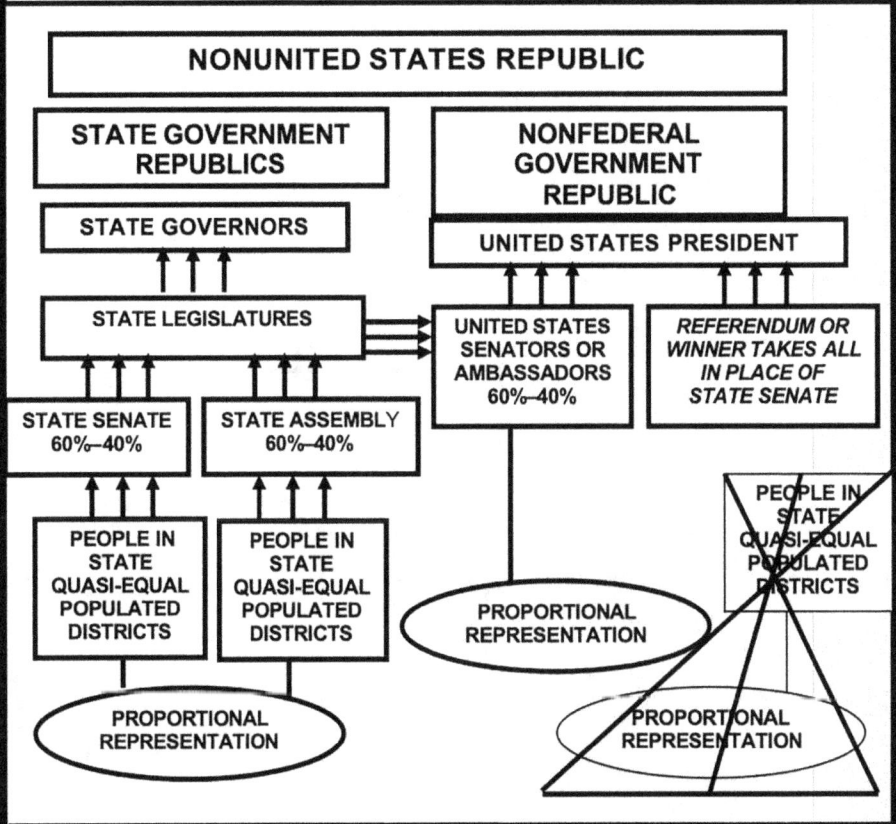

NONUNITED STATES REPUBLIC

STATE GOVERNMENT REPUBLICS

NONFEDERAL GOVERNMENT REPUBLIC

STATE GOVERNORS

UNITED STATES PRESIDENT

STATE LEGISLATURES

UNITED STATES SENATORS OR AMBASSADORS 60%–40%

REFERENDUM OR WINNER TAKES ALL IN PLACE OF STATE SENATE

STATE SENATE 60%–40%

STATE ASSEMBLY 60%–40%

PEOPLE IN STATE QUASI-EQUAL POPULATED DISTRICTS

PEOPLE IN STATE QUASI-EQUAL POPULATED DISTRICTS

PEOPLE IN STATE QUASI-EQUAL POPULATED DISTRICTS

PROPORTIONAL REPRESENTATION

PROPORTIONAL REPRESENTATION

PROPORTIONAL REPRESENTATION

THE REPRESENTATION MODE HAS BEEN BROKEN!

VIOLATES TENTH AMENDMENT
The powers allowed by the Constitution to the states are reserved to the people.

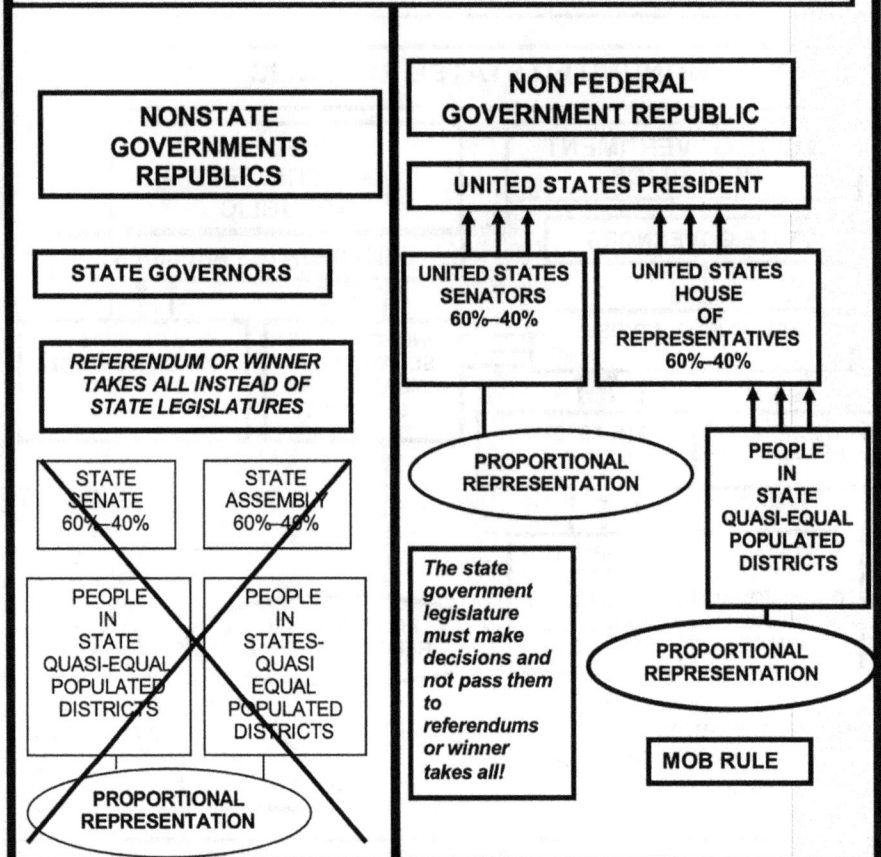

NONSTATE GOVERNMENTS REPUBLICS

STATE GOVERNORS

REFERENDUM OR WINNER TAKES ALL INSTEAD OF STATE LEGISLATURES

STATE SENATE 60%–40%

STATE ASSEMBLY 60%–40%

PEOPLE IN STATE QUASI-EQUAL POPULATED DISTRICTS

PEOPLE IN STATES-QUASI EQUAL POPULATED DISTRICTS

PROPORTIONAL REPRESENTATION

NON FEDERAL GOVERNMENT REPUBLIC

UNITED STATES PRESIDENT

UNITED STATES SENATORS 60%–40%

UNITED STATES HOUSE OF REPRESENTATIVES 60%–40%

PROPORTIONAL REPRESENTATION

The state government legislature must make decisions and not pass them to referendums or winner takes all!

PEOPLE IN STATE QUASI-EQUAL POPULATED DISTRICTS

PROPORTIONAL REPRESENTATION

MOB RULE

THE REPRESENTATION MODE HAS BEEN BROKEN!

VIOLATES TENTH AMENDMENT

The powers allowed by the Constitution to the states are reserved to the people.

NONUNITED STATES REPUBLIC

STATE GOVERNMENT REPUBLICS	NONFEDERAL GOVERNMENT REPUBLIC

STATE GOVERNORS

UNITED STATES PRESIDENT

REFERENDUM OR WINNER TAKES ALL IN STEAD OF STATE LEGISLATURES

REFERENDUM OR WINNER TAKES ALL INSTEAD OF UNITED STATES SENATORS

UNITED STATES HOUSE OF REPRESENTATIVES 60%–40%

STATE SENATE 60%–40%

STATE ASSEMBLY 60%–40%

PEOPLE IN STATE QUASI-EQUAL POPULATED DISTRICTS

PROPORTIONAL REPRESENTATION

PEOPLE IN STATE QUASI-EQUAL POPULATED DISTRICTS

PEOPLE IN STATE QUASI-EQUAL POPULATED DISTRICTS

The United States Senate and legislatures must make decisions and not pass them to referendums or winner takes all!

PROPORTIONAL REPRESENTATION

PROPORTIONAL REPRESENTATION

MOB RULE

THE REPRESENTATION MODE HAS BEEN BROKEN!

VIOLATES TENTH AMENDMENT
The powers allowed by the Constitution to the states are reserved to the people.

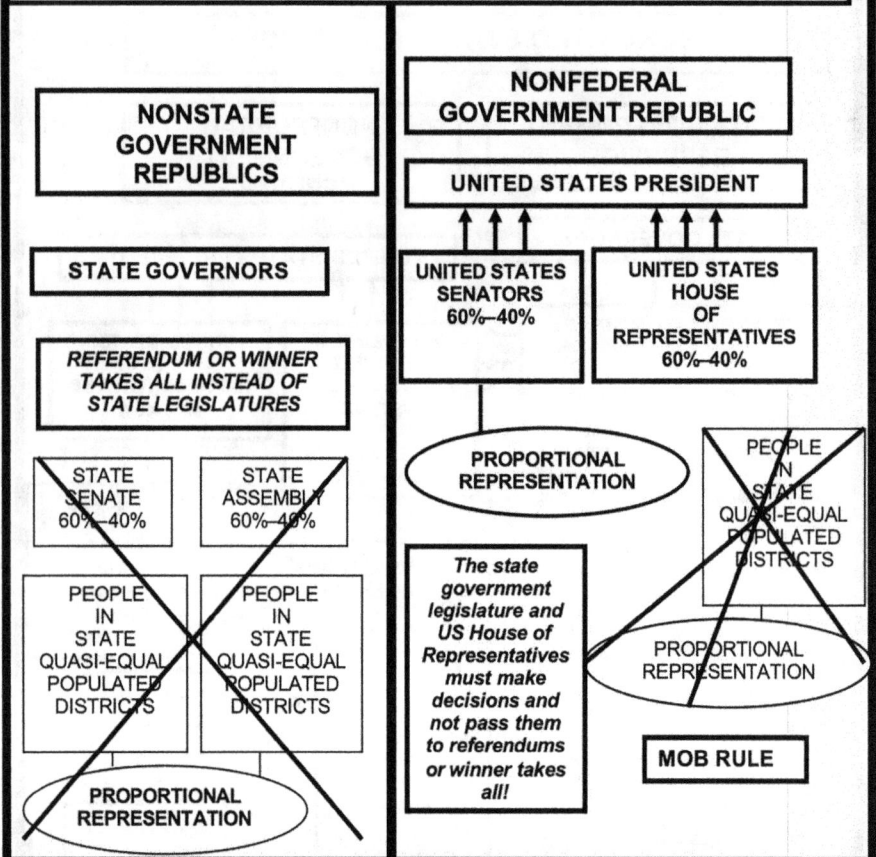

NONSTATE GOVERNMENT REPUBLICS

NONFEDERAL GOVERNMENT REPUBLIC

UNITED STATES PRESIDENT

STATE GOVERNORS

UNITED STATES SENATORS 60%–40%

UNITED STATES HOUSE OF REPRESENTATIVES 60%–40%

REFERENDUM OR WINNER TAKES ALL INSTEAD OF STATE LEGISLATURES

STATE SENATE 60%–40%

STATE ASSEMBLY 60%–40%

PROPORTIONAL REPRESENTATION

PEOPLE IN STATE QUASI-EQUAL POPULATED DISTRICTS

PEOPLE IN STATE QUASI-EQUAL POPULATED DISTRICTS

PEOPLE IN STATE QUASI-EQUAL POPULATED DISTRICTS

PROPORTIONAL REPRESENTATION

The state government legislature and US House of Representatives must make decisions and not pass them to referendums or winner takes all!

PROPORTIONAL REPRESENTATION

MOB RULE

THE REPRESENTATION MODE HAS BEEN BROKEN!

VIOLATES TENTH AMENDMENT

The powers allowed by the Constitution to the states are reserved to the people.

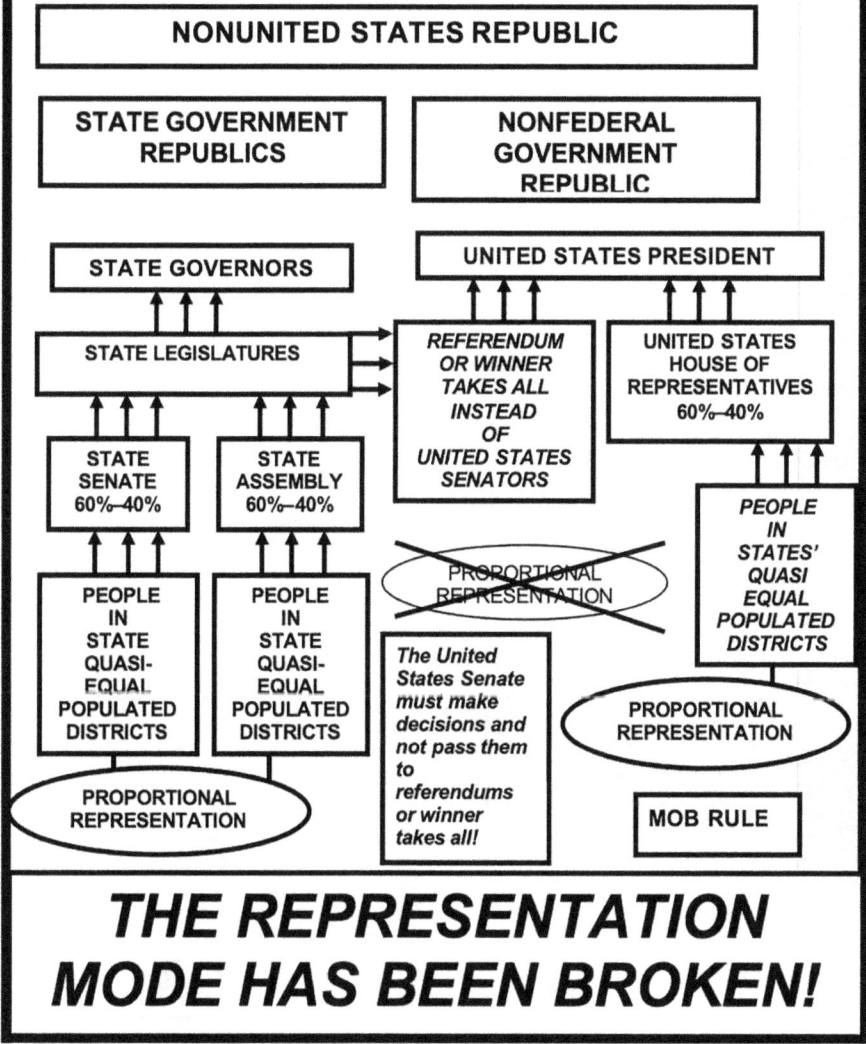

NONUNITED STATES REPUBLIC

STATE GOVERNMENT REPUBLICS

NONFEDERAL GOVERNMENT REPUBLIC

STATE GOVERNORS

UNITED STATES PRESIDENT

STATE LEGISLATURES

REFERENDUM OR WINNER TAKES ALL INSTEAD OF UNITED STATES SENATORS

UNITED STATES HOUSE OF REPRESENTATIVES 60%–40%

STATE SENATE 60%–40%

STATE ASSEMBLY 60%–40%

PEOPLE IN STATES' QUASI EQUAL POPULATED DISTRICTS

PEOPLE IN STATE QUASI-EQUAL POPULATED DISTRICTS

PEOPLE IN STATE QUASI-EQUAL POPULATED DISTRICTS

PROPORTIONAL REPRESENTATION

The United States Senate must make decisions and not pass them to referendums or winner takes all!

PROPORTIONAL REPRESENTATION

PROPORTIONAL REPRESENTATION

MOB RULE

THE REPRESENTATION MODE HAS BEEN BROKEN!

VIOLATES TENTH AMENDMENT

The powers allowed by the Constitution to the states are reserved to the people.

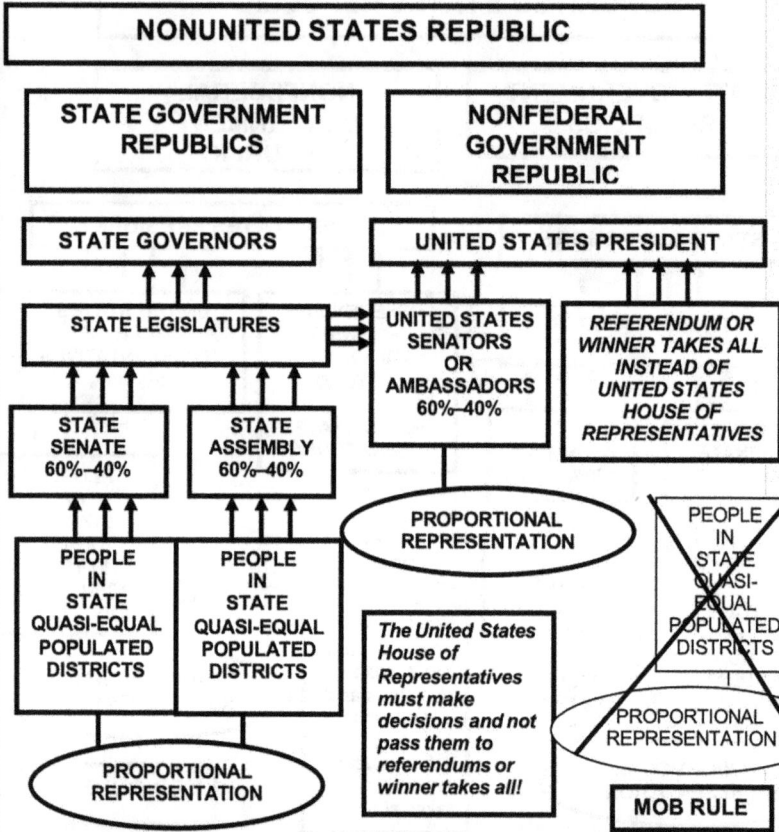

NONUNITED STATES REPUBLIC

STATE GOVERNMENT REPUBLICS	NONFEDERAL GOVERNMENT REPUBLIC

STATE GOVERNORS

UNITED STATES PRESIDENT

STATE LEGISLATURES

UNITED STATES SENATORS OR AMBASSADORS 60%–40%

REFERENDUM OR WINNER TAKES ALL INSTEAD OF UNITED STATES HOUSE OF REPRESENTATIVES

STATE SENATE 60%–40%

STATE ASSEMBLY 60%–40%

PROPORTIONAL REPRESENTATION

PEOPLE IN STATE QUASI-EQUAL POPULATED DISTRICTS

PEOPLE IN STATE QUASI-EQUAL POPULATED DISTRICTS

PEOPLE IN STATE QUASI-EQUAL POPULATED DISTRICTS

The United States House of Representatives must make decisions and not pass them to referendums or winner takes all!

PROPORTIONAL REPRESENTATION

PROPORTIONAL REPRESENTATION

MOB RULE

THE REPRESENTATION MODE HAS BEEN BROKEN!

VIOLATES TENTH AMENDMENT

The powers allowed by the Constitution to the states are reserved to the people.

NONUNITED STATES REPUBLIC

STATE GOVERNMENT REPUBLICS	NONFEDERAL GOVERNMENT REPUBLIC

STATE GOVERNORS

UNITED STATES PRESIDENT

STATE LEGISLATURES

REFERENDUM OR WINNER TAKES ALL INSTEAD OF UNITED STATES SENATORS

REFERENDUM OR WINNER TAKES ALL INSTEAD OF UNITED STATES HOUSE OF REPRESENTATIVES

STATE SENATE 60%–40%

STATE ASSEMBLY 60%–40%

PROPORTIONAL REPRESENTATION

PEOPLE IN STATE QUASI-EQUAL POPULATED DISTRICTS

PEOPLE IN STATE QUASI-EQUAL POPULATED DISTRICTS

PROPORTIONAL REPRESENTATION

The United States House of Representatives and Senate must make decisions and not pass them to referendums or winner takes all!

PROPORTIONAL REPRESENTATION

MOB RULE

THE REPRESENTATION MODE HAS BEEN BROKEN!

BICAMERALISM

Ideas of bicameralism can be traced back to the theories developed in ancient bicameral institutions that arose in medieval Europe where they were associated with separate representations of different estates of the realm. One house would represent the aristocracy, and the other would represent the commoners.

The Connecticut Compromise, also known as the Great Compromise, was an agreement between large and small states reached during the Philadelphia Convention of 1787 that, in part, defined the legislative structure and representation that each state government would have under the United States Constitution. Bicameral legislature was proposed, resulting in the current United States Senate and House of Representatives.

The framers of the Constitution also favored a bicameral legislature, though not based on class distinction. As part of the Great Compromise, the framers of the Constitution invented a new rationale for bicameralism. The upper house would have state government legislatures who elected the United States Senate represented equally with the United States House of Representatives of the lower house. Bicameralism brought together two independent power sources: the people's representatives in the United States House of Representatives and the state government legislature agents in the United States Senate. The idea was to have the United States Senate be more affluent and scholarly. Senators would be more knowledgeable and more deliberate, a sort of dignity reflecting the ideals of a federal government republic and a counter to any indecisiveness with passion that might suck up a United States House of Representatives. The United States Senate would be a stabilizing force, not a mob rule, people-elected end product like the United States House of Representatives.

The best known example is the British House of Lords, which includes a number of hereditary peers. The House of Lords represents a vestige of the aristocratic system that once predominated in British politics, while the other house, the House of Commons, is entirely elected. The framers of the Constitution borrowed bicameralism from the British system of government, dividing the legislative branch into two chambers: United States Senate (ambassadors) and House of Representatives. The upper bicameral chamber is the United States Senate (ambassadors), whose members represent quasi-equal contingency districts, and the lower bicameral chamber is the House of Representatives (people elected), whose members also represent quasi-equal contingency districts. Both United States Senate and United States House of Representatives members are *proportion representation.*

The need for two powers to concur would, in turn, thwart the influence of special interests groups. Bicameralism guarantees human rights of the individuals and suppresses corporate lobbyists and other special interest groups that might take those human rights away. Bicameralism (United States Senate [ambassadors] and House of Representatives) is preserved in the federal government republic. The bicameral mode is endowed with qualities of "checks and balances," which helps prevent the passage of not-thought-through legislation.

In the United States Senate, each state government is given the same number of seats in the United States Senate legislature's upper house no matter the dissimilarity of population among the state governments. The design ensures that more populous state governments do not overshadow the smaller state governments. In the United States House of Representatives, the lower houses, the seats are allocated based purely on population. The bicameral system combines the principle that all citizens are equal in the lower houses, while all states are equal in the upper houses.

Prior to the American Revolution, small minorities of ruling elites controlled all governments. Parts of the population were completely disfranchised. Even so, the widening of the franchise caused concern. The framers of the Constitution restated that the people were to have national sovereignty. Also, the framers of the Constitution labored to ensure that a simple majority of voters could not infringe upon the people's liberty. Bicameralism was one protection against the separation of powers. With the United States House of Representatives representing the common people and the United States Senate defending the interests of the state governments, bicameralism aims to serve as a constraint on popular movements that might threaten particular groups having a popular vote in quasi-equal populated districts elect the members who are *proportional representation* of the United States House of Representatives and letting the state government legislatures whose members were *proportion representation* from quasi-equal populated districts appoint United States senators.

Bicameralism eases of bearing the burden of transferring from the state government legislatures to the United States Senate idea of the bottom-up representation mode of a federal government republic.

The Constitution ascribes significant powers to the legislative branch as one of the three coequal branches of government. All legislative power in the government is vested in the legislative branch, which is the only part of the federal government republic that makes or changes laws. The executive branch issues regulations with the full force of law, which are laws under the authority of the legislative branch. The president may veto bills the legislative branch passes, and the legislative branch can override a veto with a two-thirds majority vote in both the Senate and the House of Representatives. Oversight of the executive branch is an important legislative branch check on the president's power. The legislative branch is a balance against the president's discretion in implementing laws and making regulations.

With most interest of state government delegates who are state governmentsambassadors to be called senators in mind, the United States Senate was made to be the representative body of state government legislatures.

The United States Senate (ambassadors) is the most important position in the federal government being given the authority of the most active component of the legislative federal governments republic's branch.

The Senate has the sole power to confirm those of the president's appointments that require consent and to ratify treaties. There are, however, two exceptions to this rule. The House must also approve appointments to the vice presidency and any treaty that involves foreign trade. The Senate also tries impeachment cases for federal officials referred to it by the House.

The United States Senate maintains several powers to itself. Using a two-thirds vote, the Senate ratifies treaties and confirms the president's appointments. The United States Senate and the consent of the House of Representatives is also needed for the ratification of trade agreements and the confirmation of the vice president.

The most important group of members is in the state government legislatures. A state government's legislature is made up of state Senate and state assembly members who the state's inhabitance elected into office; therefore, the state's people indirectly participate in the federal government's decision-making through the state government legislatures.

The framers of the Constitution authorized the state government legislatures to choose two senators (ambassadors). The tenure of these two United States senators (ambassadors) would be six (6) years. The state government legislatures are given the power to remove senators during the senator's tenure. Since elections are to be in sequence every two (2) years, one-third ($^1/_3$) of the United

States senators (ambassadors) would be up for election at any one time. Two-thirds ($^2/_3$) of the United States senators (ambassadors) would be in office maintaining stability of the federal government during elections. At the end of a single senator's tenure, all senators of the federal government would have gone through elections.

In conclusion, the framers of the Constitution made the United States Senate the ambassadors of state government republics through the elected choice of the state government legislatures who would protect the rights of the state government inhabitances, guaranteeing the sovereignty of state government republics.

STATE GOVERNMENT REPRESENTATION VIOLATION OF THE TOWNS

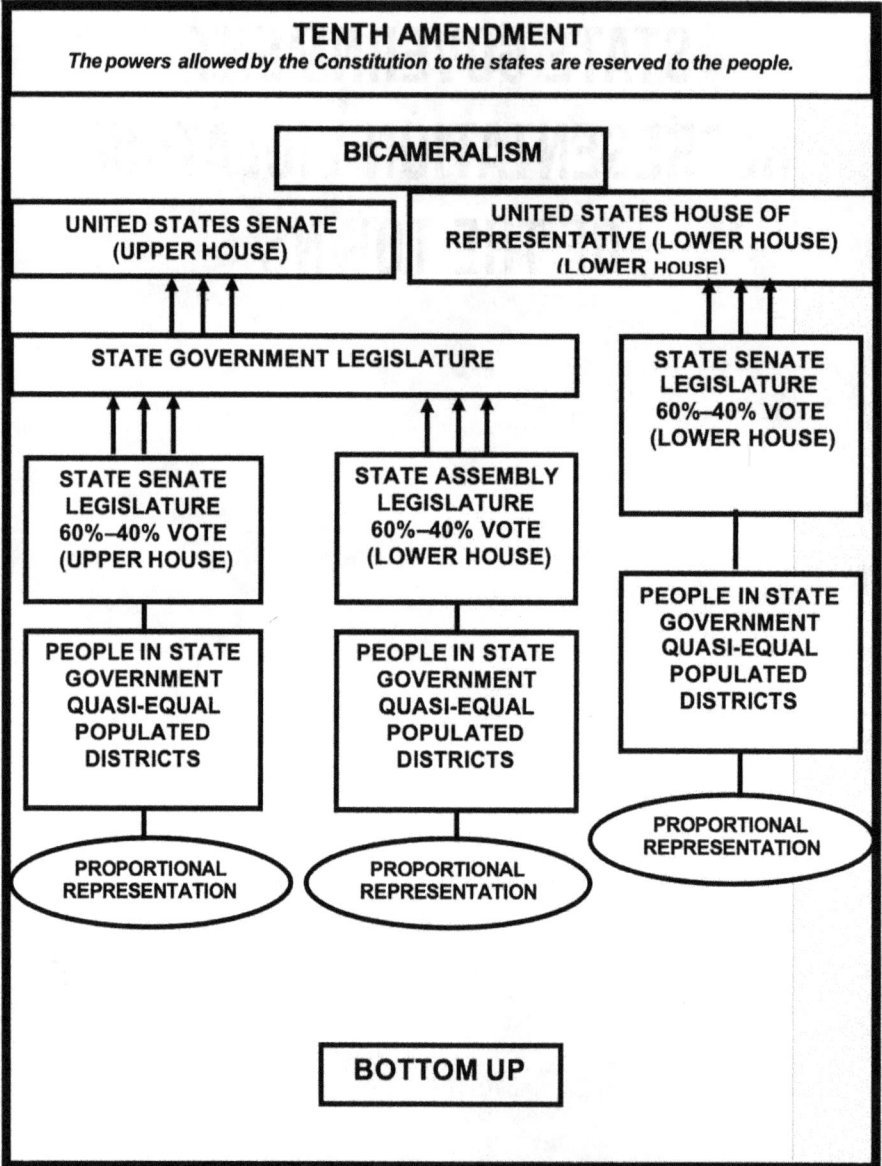

TENTH AMENDMENT
The powers allowed by the Constitution to the states are reserved to the people.

BICAMERALISM

UNITED STATES SENATE (UPPER HOUSE)

UNITED STATES HOUSE OF REPRESENTATIVE (LOWER HOUSE)
(LOWER HOUSE)

STATE GOVERNMENT LEGISLATURE

STATE SENATE LEGISLATURE 60%–40% VOTE (LOWER HOUSE)

STATE SENATE LEGISLATURE 60%–40% VOTE (UPPER HOUSE)

STATE ASSEMBLY LEGISLATURE 60%–40% VOTE (LOWER HOUSE)

PEOPLE IN STATE GOVERNMENT QUASI-EQUAL POPULATED DISTRICTS

PEOPLE IN STATE GOVERNMENT QUASI-EQUAL POPULATED DISTRICTS

PEOPLE IN STATE GOVERNMENT QUASI-EQUAL POPULATED DISTRICTS

PROPORTIONAL REPRESENTATION

PROPORTIONAL REPRESENTATION

PROPORTIONAL REPRESENTATION

BOTTOM UP

VIOLATES TENTH AMENDMENT

The powers allowed by the Constitution to the states are reserved to the people.

NONBICAMERALISM

UNITED STATES SENATE (UPPER HOUSE)	UNITED STATES HOUSE OF REPRESENTATIVE (LOWER HOUSE)

STATE GOVERNMENT LEGISLATURE

HOUSE OF REPRESENTATIVES LEGISLATURE 60%–40% VOTE (LOWER HOUSE)

REFERENDUM WINNER TAKES ALL INSTEAD OF STATE SENATE LEGISLATURE

STATE ASSEMBLY LEGISLATURE 60%–40% VOTE (LOWER HOUSE)

PEOPLE IN STATE GOVERNMENT QUASI-EQUAL POPULATED DISTRICTS

PEOPLE IN STATE GOVERNMENT QUASI-EQUAL POPULATED DISTRICTS

PEOPLE IN STATE GOVERNMENT QUASI-EQUAL POPULATED DISTRICTS

PROPORTIONAL REPRESENTATION

PROPORTIONAL REPRESENTATION

PROPORTIONAL REPRESENTATION

The state government Senate must make decisions and not pass them to referendums or winner takes all!

MOB RULE

THE REPRESENTATION MODE HAS BEEN BROKEN!

VIOLATES TENTH AMENDMENT
The powers allowed by the Constitution to the states are reserved to the people.

NONBICAMERALISM

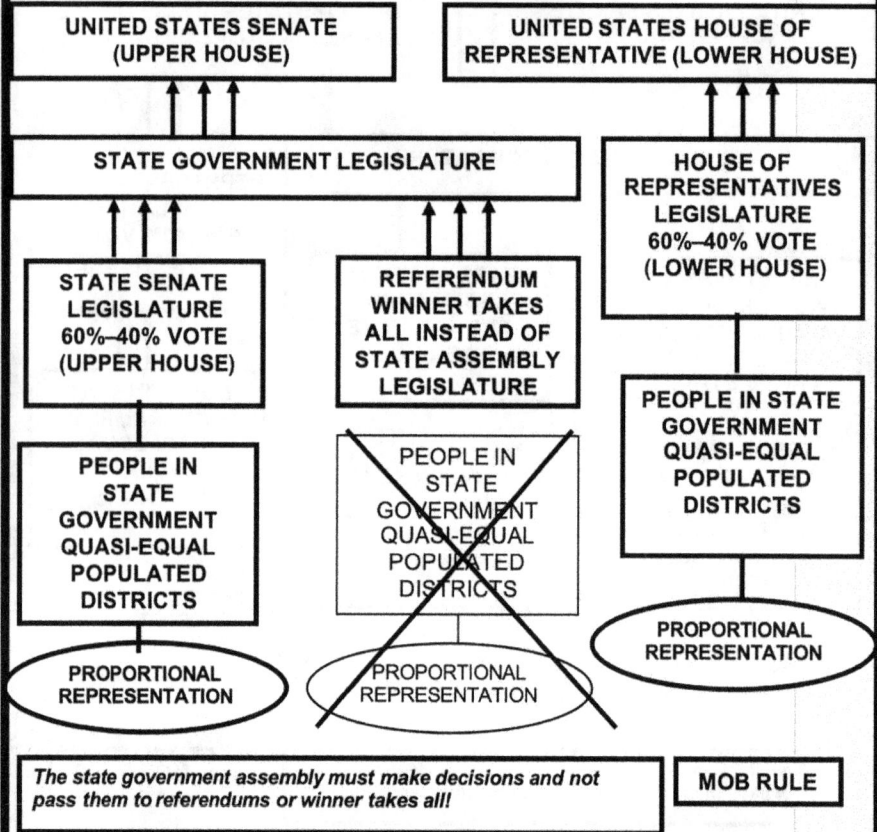

UNITED STATES SENATE (UPPER HOUSE)	UNITED STATES HOUSE OF REPRESENTATIVE (LOWER HOUSE)

STATE GOVERNMENT LEGISLATURE

HOUSE OF REPRESENTATIVES LEGISLATURE 60%–40% VOTE (LOWER HOUSE)

STATE SENATE LEGISLATURE 60%–40% VOTE (UPPER HOUSE)

REFERENDUM WINNER TAKES ALL INSTEAD OF STATE ASSEMBLY LEGISLATURE

PEOPLE IN STATE GOVERNMENT QUASI-EQUAL POPULATED DISTRICTS

PEOPLE IN STATE GOVERNMENT QUASI-EQUAL POPULATED DISTRICTS

PEOPLE IN STATE GOVERNMENT QUASI-EQUAL POPULATED DISTRICTS

PROPORTIONAL REPRESENTATION

PROPORTIONAL REPRESENTATION

PROPORTIONAL REPRESENTATION

The state government assembly must make decisions and not pass them to referendums or winner takes all!

MOB RULE

THE REPRESENTATION MODE HAS BEEN BROKEN!

VIOLATES TENTH AMENDMENT
The powers allowed by the Constitution to the states are reserved to the people.

NONBICAMERALISM

UNITED STATES SENATE (UPPER HOUSE)

UNITED STATES HOUSE OF REPRESENTATIVE (LOWER HOUSE)

STATE GOVERNMENT LEGISLATURE

STATE SENATE LEGISLATURE 60%–40% VOTE (LOWER HOUSE)

REFERENDUM WINNER TAKES ALL INSTEAD OF STATE SENATE LEGISLATURE

REFERENDUM WINNER TAKES ALL INSTEAD OF STATE ASSEMBLY LEGISLATURE

PEOPLE IN STATE GOVERNMENT QUASI-EQUAL POPULATED DISTRICTS

PEOPLE IN STATE GOVERNMENT QUASI-EQUAL POPULATED DISTRICTS

PEOPLE IN STATE GOVERNMENT QUASI-EQUAL POPULATED DISTRICTS

PROPORTIONAL REPRESENTATION

PROPORTIONAL REPRESENTATION

PROPORTIONAL REPRESENTATION

The state government Senate and assembly must make decisions and not pass them to referendums or winner takes all!

MOB RULE

THE REPRESENTATION MODE HAS BEEN BROKEN!

VIOLATES TENTH AMENDMENT
The powers allowed by the Constitution to the states are reserved to the people.

NONBICAMERALISM

UNITED STATES SENATE (UPPER HOUSE)	UNITED STATES HOUSE OF REPRESENTATIVE (LOWER HOUSE)

STATE GOVERNMENT LEGISLATURE

REFERENDUM WINNER TAKES ALL INSTEAD OF HOUSE OF REPRESENTATIVES LEGISLATURE

REFERENDUM WINNER TAKES ALL INSTEAD OF STATE SENATE LEGISLATURE

REFERENDUM WINNER TAKES ALL INSTEAD OF STATE ASSEMBLY LEGISLATURE

PEOPLE IN STATE GOVERNMENT QUASI-EQUAL POPULATED DISTRICTS

PEOPLE IN STATE GOVERNMENT QUASI-EQUAL POPULATED DISTRICTS

PEOPLE IN STATE GOVERNMENT QUASI-EQUAL POPULATED DISTRICTS

PROPORTIONAL REPRESENTATION

PROPORTIONAL REPRESENTATION

PROPORTIONAL REPRESENTATION

MOB RULE

The state government Senate and assembly and House of Representatives must make decisions and not pass them to referendums or winner takes all!

THE REPRESENTATION MODE HAS BEEN BROKEN!

TENTH AMENDMENT

The powers allowed by the Constitution to the states are reserved to the people.

UNITED STATES REPUBLIC

STATE GOVERNMENT REPUBLICS	FEDERAL GOVERNMENT REPUBLIC

STATE GOVERNORS	EXECUTIVE BRANCH (PRESIDENT)

STATE LEGISLATURES	LEGISLATIVE BRANCH (CONGRESS) UNITED STATES HOUSE OF REPRESENTATIVE UNITED STATES SENATE (AMBASSADORS)

STATE SENATE 60%–40%

STATE ASSEMBLY 60%–40%

PROPORTIONAL REPRESENTATION

FEDERAL STATE QUASI-EQUAL POPULATED DISTRICTS

PEOPLE IN STATE QUASI-EQUAL POPULATED DISTRICTS

PEOPLE IN STATES QUASI-EQUAL POPULATED DISTRICTS

PROPORTIONAL REPRESENTATION

PROPORTIONAL REPRESENTATION

A federal government republic operates in a *bottom-up representation mode* starting at quasi-equal *proportion representation* state government Senate's and state government assemblies' districts. The *proportion representation* state government legislatures represent the *proportion representation* state government Senate and the *proportion representation* state government assembly. The *proportion representation* United States Senate represents the state government legislature. The legislative branch (Congress) represents the *proportion representation* United States Senate and the *proportion representation* House of Representatives. The president represents the *proportion representation* legislative branch.

BOTTOM UP

TENTH AMENDMENT
The powers allowed by the Constitution to the states are reserved to the people.

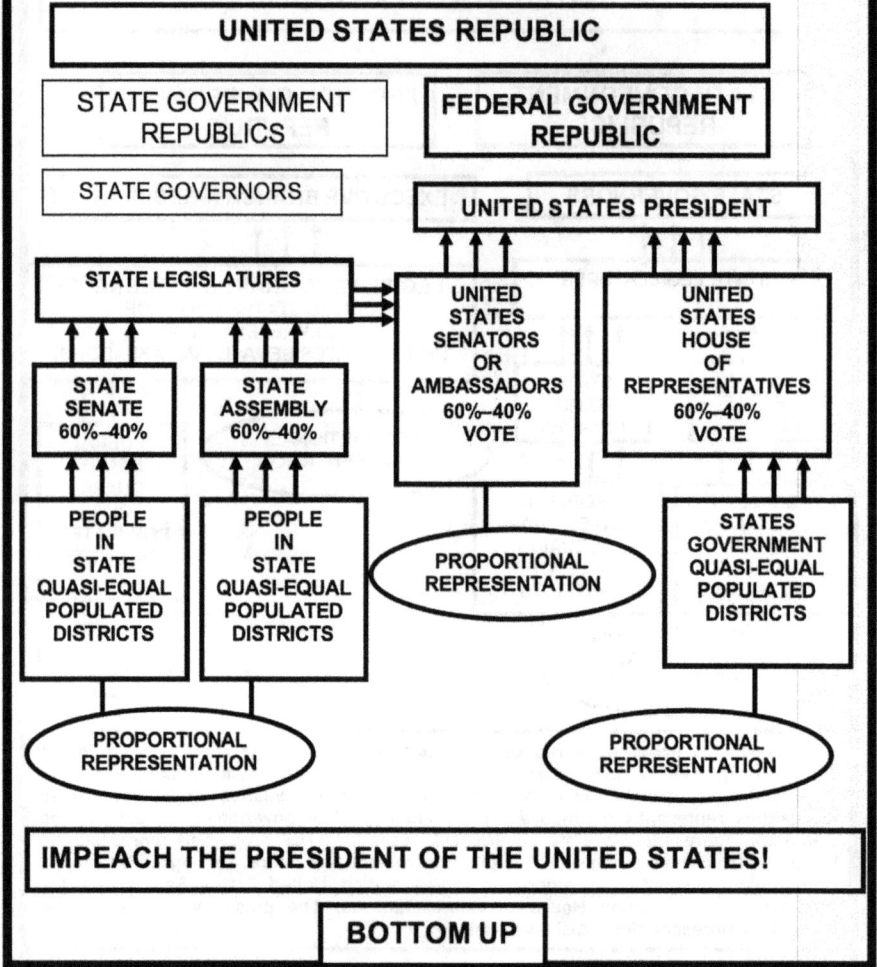

UNITED STATES REPUBLIC

STATE GOVERNMENT REPUBLICS

FEDERAL GOVERNMENT REPUBLIC

STATE GOVERNORS

UNITED STATES PRESIDENT

STATE LEGISLATURES

UNITED STATES SENATORS OR AMBASSADORS 60%–40% VOTE

UNITED STATES HOUSE OF REPRESENTATIVES 60%–40% VOTE

STATE SENATE 60%–40%

STATE ASSEMBLY 60%–40%

PEOPLE IN STATE QUASI-EQUAL POPULATED DISTRICTS

PEOPLE IN STATE QUASI-EQUAL POPULATED DISTRICTS

PROPORTIONAL REPRESENTATION

STATES GOVERNMENT QUASI-EQUAL POPULATED DISTRICTS

PROPORTIONAL REPRESENTATION

PROPORTIONAL REPRESENTATION

IMPEACH THE PRESIDENT OF THE UNITED STATES!

BOTTOM UP

VIOLATES TENTH AMENDMENT
The powers allowed by the Constitution to the states are reserved to the people.

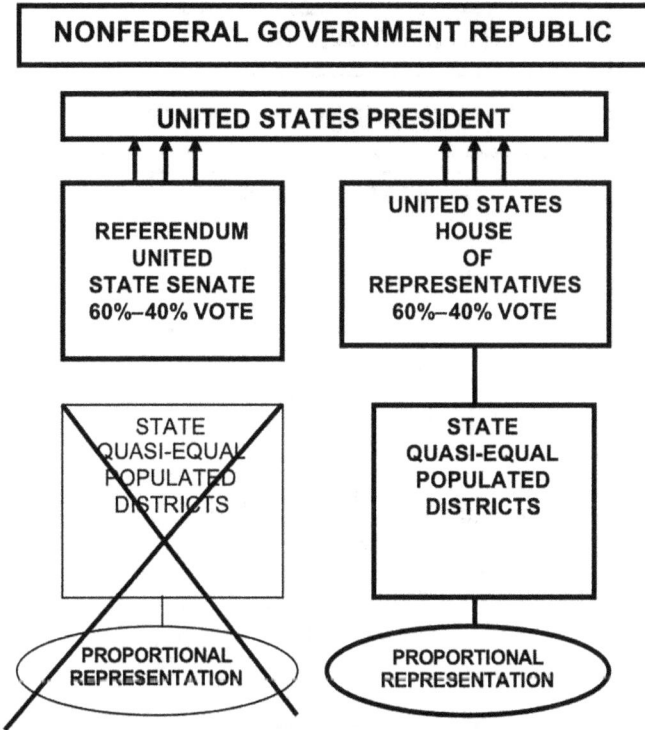

NONFEDERAL GOVERNMENT REPUBLIC

UNITED STATES PRESIDENT

REFERENDUM
UNITED
STATE SENATE
60%–40% VOTE

UNITED STATES
HOUSE
OF
REPRESENTATIVES
60%–40% VOTE

STATE
QUASI-EQUAL
POPULATED
DISTRICTS

STATE
QUASI-EQUAL
POPULATED
DISTRICTS

PROPORTIONAL
REPRESENTATION

PROPORTIONAL
REPRESENTATION

IMPEACH THE PRESIDENT OF THE UNITED STATES!

THE REPRESENTATION MODE HAS BEEN BROKEN!

TENTH AMENDMENT

The powers allowed by the Constitution to the states are reserved to the people.

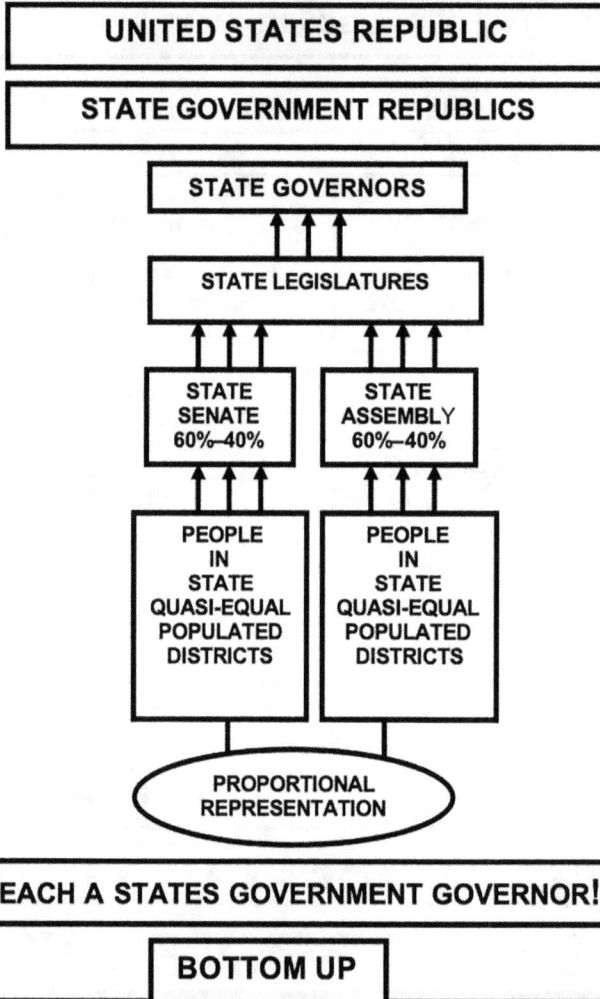

UNITED STATES REPUBLIC

STATE GOVERNMENT REPUBLICS

STATE GOVERNORS

STATE LEGISLATURES

STATE SENATE 60%–40%	STATE ASSEMBLY 60%–40%
PEOPLE IN STATE QUASI-EQUAL POPULATED DISTRICTS	PEOPLE IN STATE QUASI-EQUAL POPULATED DISTRICTS

PROPORTIONAL REPRESENTATION

IMPEACH A STATES GOVERNMENT GOVERNOR!

BOTTOM UP

VIOLATES TENTH AMENDMENT

The powers allowed by the Constitution to the states are reserved to the people.

UNITED STATES REPUBLIC

STATE GOVERNMENT REPUBLICS

STATE GOVERNORS

REFERENDUM OR WINNER TAKES ALL IN PLACE OF STATE LEGISLATURE

| STATE SENATE 60% 40% | STATE ASSEMBLY 60% 40% |

The state government legislatures must make decisions and not pass them to referendums or winner takes all!

| PEOPLE IN STATE QUASI-EQUAL POPULATED DISTRICTS | PEOPLE IN STATE QUASI-EQUAL POPULATED DISTRICTS |

MOB RULE

PROPORTIONAL REPRESENTATION

IMPEACH A STATE GOVERNMENT GOVERNOR!

THE REPRESENTATION MODE HAS BEEN BROKEN!

TOP DOWN

SUPREMACY CLAUSE

The Supremacy Clause is the common name given to Article VI, Clause 2 of the United States Constitution, which reads,

> This Constitution, and the Laws of the United States which shall be made in Pursuance thereof; and all Treaties made, or which shall be made, under the authority of the United States, shall be the supreme Law of the land; and the Judges in every State shall be bound thereby, any Thing in the Constitution or Laws of any State to the Contrary notwithstanding.

The Supremacy Clause establishes the Constitution, federal statutes, and US treaties as "the supreme law of the land." The Constitution is the highest form of law in the American legal system. State judges are required to uphold it, even if state laws or constitutions conflict with it.

Jefferson was a leader in developing republicanism in the United States. He insisted that the British aristocratic system was inherently corrupt and that Americans' devotion to civic virtue required independence. In the 1790s, he repeatedly warned that Hamilton and Adams were trying to impose a British-like monarchical system that threatened republicanism. He supported the War of 1812, hoping it would drive away the British military and ideological threat from Canada. Jefferson's vision for American virtue was that of an agricultural nation of yeoman farmers minding their own affairs. It stood in contrast to the vision of Alexander Hamilton, who envisioned a nation of commerce and manufacturing, which Jefferson said offered too many temptations to corruption. Jefferson's deep belief in the uniqueness and the potential of America made him the father of American exceptionalism. In particular, he was confident that an underpopulated America could avoid what he considered the horrors of class-divided industrialized Europe.

Jefferson believed that each individual has "certain inalienable rights." That is, these rights exist with or without government; man cannot create, take, or give them away. It is the right of "liberty" on which Jefferson is most notable for expounding. He defines it by saying, "Rightful liberty is unobstructed action according to our will within limits drawn around us by the equal rights of others. I do not add 'within the limits of the law,' because law is often but the tyrant's will, and always so when it violates the rights of the individual." Hence, for Jefferson, though government cannot create a right to liberty, it can indeed violate it. And the limit of an individual's rightful liberty is not what law says it is, but is simply a matter of stopping short of prohibiting other individuals from having the same liberty. A proper government, for Jefferson, is one that not only prohibits individuals in society from infringing on the liberty of other individuals, but also restrains itself from diminishing individual liberty.

Jefferson's very strong defense of state rights, especially in the Kentucky and Virginia Resolutions of 1798, set the tone for hostility to expansion of federal powers. However, some of his foreign policies did, in fact, strengthen the government. Most important was the Louisiana Purchase in 1803, when he used the implied powers to annex a huge foreign territory and all its French and Indian inhabitants. His enforcement of the Embargo Act of 1807, while it failed in terms of foreign policy, demonstrated that the federal government could intervene with great force at the local level in controlling trade that might lead to war.

Jefferson's commitment to liberty extended to many areas of individual freedom. In his *Commonplace Book*, he copied a passage from Cesare, Marquis of Beccaria, related to the issue of gun control. The quote reads, "Laws that forbid the carrying of arms...disarm only those who are neither inclined nor determined to commit crimes...Such laws make things worse for the assaulted and better for the assailants; they serve rather to encourage than to prevent homicides, for an unarmed man may be attacked with greater confidence than an armed man."

Jefferson's quote, "I hope we shall crush...in its birth the aristocracy of our moneyed corporations, which dare already to challenge our government to a trial of strength and bid defiance to the laws of our country," is often attributed to being a strong warning against corporations and their function in American government and society.

Numeric Scientific Mathematic Model

The framers of the Constitution deliberately or accidentally created a mathematic model baste on *proportion representation* and quasi-equal populated districts. The framers of the Constitution constructed a numerical scientific mathematical model that contains quasi-equal populated districts distributed within state government territories.

Representatives of these quasi-equal populated districts are classified as *proportion representation*. The state government senators are *proportion representation* as well as the state government assembly members along with the House of Representatives members whose quasi-equal populated districts are contained within the state government territory. This framers of the Constitution mathematical model is the foundation of a republic form of government, which is accurately designed to eliminate mob rule.

Progressive Era

The period from the 1890s to the 1920s became known as the Progressive Era in the United States, which was a period of reform. The United States Senate was the first target of the Progressives. Significant changes achieved at the national levels included the income tax with the Sixteenth Amendment, direct election of senators with the Seventeenth Amendment (violates Tenth Amendment). The state government legislatures elected the United States senators. On May 13, 1912, the Sixty-Second Congress proposed the Seventeenth Amendment (violates Tenth Amendment) to the Constitution to state government legislatures. The Seventeenth Amendment (violates Tenth Amendment) changed the procedure of electing United States senators from state government legislatures to people-direct election (*referendum* - violates Tenth Amendment).

On July 12, 1909, The Sixty-First Congress passed the income tax Sixteenth Amendment for ratification to United States Constitution, allowing the federal government to tax workers' incomes. Since the state governments were having problems of raising taxes, with the ratification of the Sixteenth Amendment, the federal government promised to return revenues to the state governments so as to entice the state government legislatures to ratify the Seventeenth Amendment (violates Tenth Amendment).

The state government legislatures sold out to the federal government republic for revenue relief, causing the loss of state government sovereignties as well as the people's sovereignties and freedom. The state government was separated from the federal government republic, resulting in two systems of governments—one a collection of state government republics and the other a nonfederal government republic. Both the Sixteenth Amendment and Seventeenth Amendment (violates the Tenth Amendment) were ratified within months of each other.

For the last ninety-plus years, the Seventeenth Amendment (violates Tenth Amendment) caused the nonfederal government republic to go out of control, which had become centralized where state government republics are treated as nonfederal government republic provinces carrying out commands of the nonfederal government republic as a state government republic does with counties.

The Seventeenth amendment (violates Tenth Amendment) allowed the nonfederal government republic to seize the power to govern the state government people away from the state government republics, which is more or less similar to the old federalism of Hamilton and Washington (Hamilton advocated getting rid of state government sovereignties, and Washington supported Hamilton). Hamilton's Constitutional plan leaned toward the British aristocracy, which was contrary to the ideals of antifederalists Jefferson and Madison, who favored the yeoman farmer and sovereignty of state government republics.

The Seventeenth Amendment (violates Tenth Amendment) tragedy eliminated the bicameral system and destroyed the framers of the Constitution's mathematical model, which changed the federal government republic to a nonfederal government republic. People electing of United States senators (violates Tenth Amendment) encouraged mob rule, which developed a perfect situation for lobbyists of elite corporations. Since senator (illegal) election expenses are in the range of between 6 million and 16 million, they spend their six-year term dealing with lobbyists who have an open door to senators' offices—not so with the United States senators' constituencies who the senators seldom confide in.

The senators' individual constituencies can range between California's 35,484,453 and Rhode Island's 1,076,164, resulting in dictatorial powers since their state territories are not quasi-equal, and constituencies are *nonproportion representation*. Not so with the state governors who the same constituencies elect every four years. The state governors have to deal with state government legislators who represent *proportion representation* of state government Senate and assembly quasi-equal districts. State governors deal with *proportion representation* state government legislatures, whereas *nonproportion representation* United States (illegal) senators dictate.

The Seventeenth Amendment (violates Tenth Amendment) has created an unchecked and out-of-balance nonfederal government republic. The passage of the Seventeenth Amendment (violates Tenth Amendment) lost the all-important vertical separation of powers, which divides the power to govern vertically between state government republics and the nonfederal government republic. Since 1913, the nonfederal government has exploded out of control, seizing the lawful power of state government republics to govern their people. Power was wrested from state government officials, transferring the power to groups of nonelected officials of a nonfederal government republic. These nonelected officials are not answerable for their mistakes to anyone. Since these government officials are political appointees, they remain in office and cannot be removed for passing awful bills to all state governments.

A fundamental issue of campaign financing in respect to United States senators became an issue that has been a hot topic in the United States Congress. United States senators need money to support an election within the next six years as they constantly fill their coffers, turning to the likes of Enron and other corporations for monetary assistance. The price for that support is in impending legislation decisions that will satisfy appetites of corporations instead of adhering to state government legislatures who happen to know the needs of the people as well as accomplishments to complete state government projects and satisfy state government objectives.

Under the Seventeenth Amendment (violates Tenth Amendment), voting for a United States senator denotes a *referendum*-type voting procedure that encourages mob rule, resulting in abolishing the mathematical model. The state government legislatures' right to appoint United States senators in favor of using a referendum-type election (violates Tenth Amendment) to elect those officials allow the nonfederal government republic to expand, through nonfederal government republic deficit spending, passing along inappropriate nonfederal government republic mandates to state government republics and taking control over some state government institutions.

The Seventeenth Amendment caused the state government republics' connection to the federal government republic to be broken, which decreased the present status of the state government legislatures. State government legislatures don't have the ability of decentralizing the nonfederal government republic's power and don't have direct influence over the selection of federal judges or their jurisdictions. The severing of flow of power between the state government republics and the nonfederal government republic also affects communicating the needs of the state government republic's people.

The same people also vote for state government senators and assemblymen as well as the United States senators. The conglomeration of state government senators and assemblymen make up the state government legislature, which reflects the views of the state government people. The people are represented in the state government and the United States Senate. This contradiction points to the fact there exists two separate entities of governmental systems, one a collection of state government republics and the other a nonfederal government republic.

The constituencies represented in the United States House of Representatives and Senate are the same that might facilitate the creation of logrolling agreements across the two houses of the federal government, making procurement of special-interest legislation easier and allowing special interests to directly lobby the Senate, especially critical in interstate commerce where development of group interests lies across state lines. In an era of increasing interstate commerce, there exists development groups across state lines whose procurement of special-interest legislation is made easy, especially through the United Sates Senate.

Huge concentrations of business, capital, and labor introduce the United States senators to the elite. Alliances are created with corporations and special interests during the United States senatorial elections, which might manipulate their decision-making. Tremendous power of the mass media on the United States senators may sway their individual deliberations. Popular opinion polls might determine the course of national policy.

United States Constitution Article I, Section 3
The Senate of the United States shall be composed of two Senators from each state, chosen by the legislature thereof, for six years; and each Senator shall have one vote.

TENTH AMENDMENT
The powers allowed by the Constitution to the states are reserved to the people.

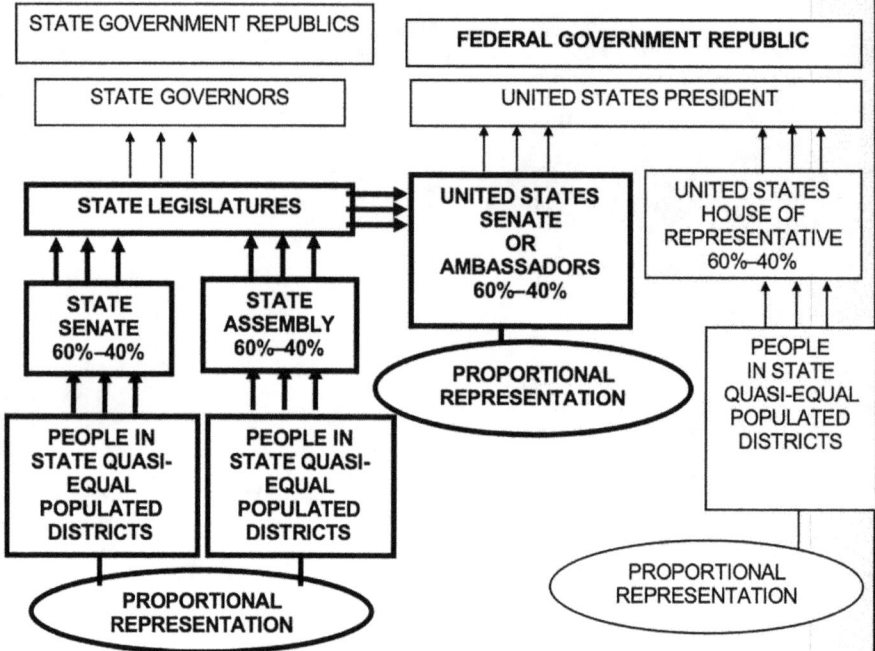

STATE GOVERNMENT REPUBLICS	FEDERAL GOVERNMENT REPUBLIC
STATE GOVERNORS	UNITED STATES PRESIDENT

STATE LEGISLATURES

| STATE SENATE 60%–40% | STATE ASSEMBLY 60%–40% | UNITED STATES SENATE OR AMBASSADORS 60%–40% | UNITED STATES HOUSE OF REPRESENTATIVE 60%–40% |

| PEOPLE IN STATE QUASI-EQUAL POPULATED DISTRICTS | PEOPLE IN STATE QUASI-EQUAL POPULATED DISTRICTS | PEOPLE IN STATE QUASI-EQUAL POPULATED DISTRICTS |

PROPORTIONAL REPRESENTATION

PROPORTIONAL REPRESENTATION

PROPORTIONAL REPRESENTATION

A state government republic operates in a *bottom-up representation mode* starting at quasi-equal *proportion representation* state government Senate and state government assemblies' districts. The *proportion representation* state government legislatures represent the PROPORTION REPRESENTATION state government Senate and the *proportion representation* state government assembly. The United States Senate represents the *proportion representation* state government legislatures. The *proportion representation* House of Representatives represents quasi-equal *proportion representation* districts. The president represents the *proportion representation* United States Senate and United States House of Representatives. Both United States Senate and United States House of Representatives influence the president!

BOTTOM UP

FEDERAL GOVERNMENT REPUBLIC

United States Constitution Seventeenth Amendment, Clause 1: The Senate of the United States shall be composed of two Senators from each state, elected by the people thereof, for six years; and each Senator shall have one vote.

TENTH AMENDMENT
The powers allowed by the Constitution to the states are reserved to the people.

TENTH AMENDMENT IS SATISFIED.

VIOLATES **TENTH AMENDMENT**
The powers allowed by the Constitution to the states are reserved to the people.

THE SEVENTEENTH AMENDMENT REPLACES THE TENTH AMENDMENT IN THE BILL OF RIGHTS!

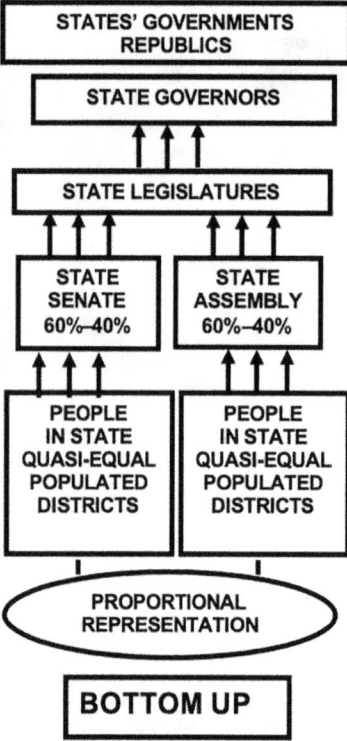

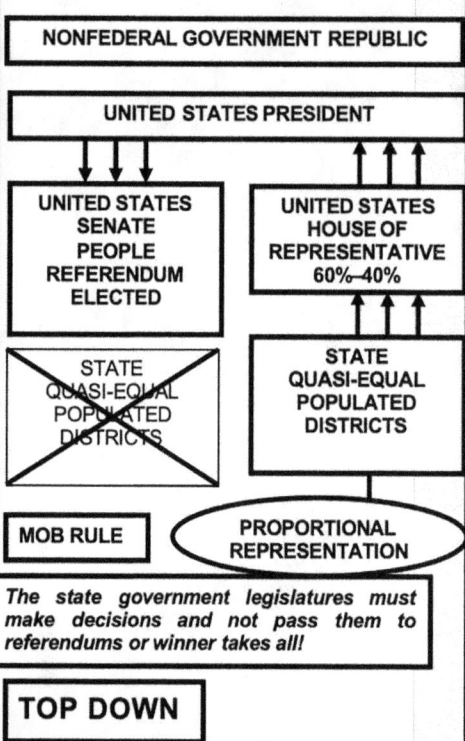

STATES' GOVERNMENTS REPUBLICS

NONFEDERAL GOVERNMENT REPUBLIC

STATE GOVERNORS

UNITED STATES PRESIDENT

STATE LEGISLATURES

| STATE SENATE 60%–40% | STATE ASSEMBLY 60%–40% |

UNITED STATES SENATE PEOPLE REFERENDUM ELECTED

UNITED STATES HOUSE OF REPRESENTATIVE 60%–40%

| PEOPLE IN STATE QUASI-EQUAL POPULATED DISTRICTS | PEOPLE IN STATE QUASI-EQUAL POPULATED DISTRICTS |

STATE QUASI-EQUAL POPULATED DISTRICTS

STATE QUASI-EQUAL POPULATED DISTRICTS

MOB RULE

PROPORTIONAL REPRESENTATION

PROPORTIONAL REPRESENTATION

The state government legislatures must make decisions and not pass them to referendums or winner takes all!

BOTTOM UP

TOP DOWN

THE REPRESENTATION MODE HAS BEEN BROKEN!

Federalism

VIOLATES TENTH AMENDMENT

The powers allowed by the Constitution to the states are reserved to the people.

NONUNITED STATES REPUBLIC

The mode is from a top-down in *nonrepresentation mode*, which is a dictatorial-type mode. The power goes to the president of the United States, not to the state government or the state government people, resulting in a centralized nonfederal government republic. The Seventeenth Amendment allows the state government people to elect the United States senator in place of the *proportion representation* state government's legislature, which eliminates the Tenth Amendment theorem as long as the Seventeenth Amendment exists, violating the Bill of Rights. The Seventeenth Amendment produced a centralized nonfederal government republic. The Seventeenth Amendment is illegal. In reality, the Seventeenth Amendment replaced the *proportion representation* state government legislatures with a referendum to elect a United States senator.

THE SEVENTEENTH AMENDMENT MUST BE REMOVED FROM THE EXISTING CONSTITUTION!

The state government legislatures must make decisions and not pass them to referendums or winner takes all!

NONFEDERAL GOVERNMENT REPUBLIC

UNITED STATES PRESIDENT

UNITED STATES PEOPLE-ELECTED SENATORS

UNITED STATES HOUSE OF REPRESENTATIVES 60%–40%

NONPROPORTIONAL REPRESENTATION

STATE QUASI-EQUAL POPULATED DISTRICTS

PROPORTIONAL REPRESENTATION

MOB RULE

TOP DOWN

FEDERALISM

Mob Rule

The Bill of Rights protects the natural rights of the minority from mob rule of the majority.

The framers of the Constitution created the Electoral College to guard against a mob rule dictatorship.

The framers of the Constitution tried to eliminated mob rule of dictators or demagogues.

- Mob rule could be the result of political propaganda and mass advertisement that manipulate the conscience of people, which can be called the manufacture of consent.

- Mob rule is where 51 percent of the people may take away the rights of the other 49 percent.

- Mob rule constitutes majority rule exists.

- Mob rule could be the result of the ignorant masses of people to address political leaders.

- Mob rule introduces tyranny.

- Mob rule allows a majority mob to pass whimsical laws.

- Mob rule allows a majority mob to pass existence laws based on the temperament of the mob at that moment.

- Mob rule allows modern scientific polling to convince people with the aid of modern communication media.

- Mob rule allows political pandering over modern communication media.

- Mob rule allows politicians to churns up political pressure over modern communication media.

- Mob rule allows the mostly socialist-minded liberal press to keep the general public ignorant of very important current events.

- Mob rule destroys limited government.

- Mob rule destroys liberty.

- Mob rule allows laws to be passed at breakneck speed.

- Mob rule allows laws to be passed that will have people injuring one another.

- Mob rule allows laws to be passed giving the government supreme power over the people.

- Mob rule allows laws to be made "legal" from a simple majority vote.

- Mob rule allows authority to be derived through mass meeting or any other form of expression.

- Mob rule indicates that the attitude toward laws is the will of the majority, whether the law is based upon deliberation, passion, prejudice, or impulse without regard to their consequences.

- Mob rule attitude toward property is communistic, which negates property rights.

- Mob rule places little virtue in the action of the masses.

- Mob rule results in authorization, agitation, discontent, and anarchy.

- Mob rule was not stopped; framers of the Constitution merely slowed it down somewhat.

- Mob rule comes under the constitutional protection of certain fundamental freedoms, like the freedom of speech used in describing varying impulses of popular opinion.

United States Constitution Article I, Section 3
The Senate of the United States shall be composed of two Senators from each state, chosen by the legislature thereof, for six years; and each Senator shall have one vote.

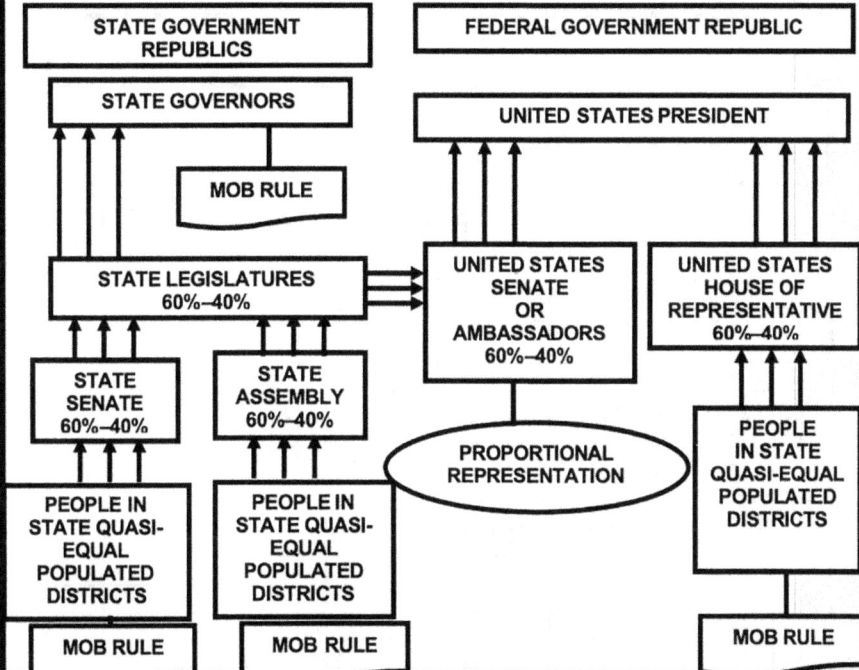

STATE GOVERNMENT REPUBLICS	FEDERAL GOVERNMENT REPUBLIC

STATE GOVERNORS

UNITED STATES PRESIDENT

MOB RULE

STATE LEGISLATURES
60%–40%

UNITED STATES SENATE OR AMBASSADORS 60%–40%

UNITED STATES HOUSE OF REPRESENTATIVE 60%–40%

STATE SENATE 60%–40%

STATE ASSEMBLY 60%–40%

PROPORTIONAL REPRESENTATION

PEOPLE IN STATE QUASI-EQUAL POPULATED DISTRICTS

PEOPLE IN STATE QUASI-EQUAL POPULATED DISTRICTS

PEOPLE IN STATE QUASI-EQUAL POPULATED DISTRICTS

MOB RULE   MOB RULE   MOB RULE

Referendum type of voting is done to elect a state government governor, state government assemblymen, state government senator, and House of Representatives member, which encourages mob rule. The state government governor's term is four years; therefore, the governor should be elected as is done for the president of the United States using an electoral-type process where the state government assembly district (quasi-equal populated to reduce mob rule) elects the governor. A spreadsheet method technique can be programmed in a computer. The computer automatically, with a spreadsheet operator, can process the data instantly as a vote is being cast at the poling station.

The same technique may be utilized for processing the presidential vote as well as processing the House of Representative members' vote. The state government assembly district is the lowest common denominator in the spreadsheet technique for electing the state government governor and House of Representative members, which, like the presidency, has a large constituency where mob rule becomes a probability. Hypothetically, mob rule is explained followed with programmed spreadsheet equation.

MOB RULE

MOB RULE STATE GOVERNOR

D = DEMOCRATIC VOTER.
R = REPUBLICAN VOTER.
LET'S ASSUME THAT THERE ARE VOTING MEMBERS IN THE ENTIRE STATE CONSTITUENCY REGARDLESS OF THE DISTRICTS.

D	D	D	D	D	D	D	D	D	D	D	D	D	D	D	D	D	D	D	D	D	D	D	D	D	D	D	D	D	D
D	D	D	D	D	D	D	D	D	D	D	D	D	D	D	D	D	D	D	D	D	D	D	D	D	D	D	D	D	D
D	D	D	D	D	D	D	D	D	D	D	D	D	D	D	D	D	D	D	D	D	D	D	D	D	D	D	D	D	D
D	D	D	D	D	D	D	D	D	D	D	D	D	D	D	D	D	D	D	D	D	D	D	D	D	D	D	D	D	D
D	D	D	D	D	R	R	R	R	R	R	R	R	R	R	R	R	R	R	R	R	R	R	R	R	D	D	D	D	D
D	D	D	D	D	R	R	R	R	R	R	R	R	R	R	R	R	R	R	R	R	R	R	R	R	D	D	D	D	D
D	D	D	D	D	R	R	R	R	R	R	R	R	R	R	R	R	R	R	R	R	R	R	R	R	D	D	D	D	D
D	D	D	D	D	R	R	R	R	R	R	R	R	R	R	R	R	R	R	R	R	R	R	R	R	D	D	D	D	D
D	D	D	D	D	R	R	R	R	R	R	R	R	R	R	R	R	R	R	R	R	R	R	R	R	D	D	D	D	D
D	D	D	D	D	R	R	R	R	R	R	R	R	R	R	R	R	R	R	R	R	R	R	R	R	D	D	D	D	D
D	D	D	D	D	R	R	R	R	R	R	R	R	R	R	R	R	R	R	R	R	R	R	R	R	D	D	D	D	D
D	D	D	D	D	R	R	R	R	R	R	R	R	R	R	R	R	R	R	R	R	R	R	R	R	D	D	D	D	D
D	D	D	D	D	R	R	R	R	R	R	R	R	R	R	R	R	R	R	R	R	R	R	R	R	D	D	D	D	D
D	D	D	D	D	R	R	R	R	R	R	R	R	R	R	R	R	R	R	R	R	R	R	R	R	D	D	D	D	D
D	D	D	D	D	R	R	R	R	R	R	R	R	R	R	R	R	R	R	R	R	R	R	R	R	D	D	D	D	D
D	D	D	D	D	R	R	R	R	R	R	R	R	R	R	R	R	R	R	R	R	R	R	R	R	D	D	D	D	D
D	D	D	D	D	R	R	R	R	R	R	R	R	R	R	R	R	R	R	R	R	R	R	R	R	D	D	D	D	D
D	D	D	D	D	R	R	R	R	R	R	R	R	R	R	R	R	R	R	R	R	R	R	R	R	D	D	D	D	D
D	D	D	D	D	R	R	R	R	R	R	R	R	R	R	R	R	R	R	R	R	R	R	R	R	D	D	D	D	D
D	D	D	D	D	D	D	D	D	D	D	D	D	D	D	D	D	D	D	D	D	D	D	D	D	D	D	D	D	D
D	D	D	D	D	D	D	D	D	D	D	D	D	D	D	D	D	D	D	D	D	D	D	D	D	D	D	D	D	D
D	D	D	D	D	D	D	D	D	D	D	D	D	D	D	D	D	D	D	D	D	D	D	D	D	D	D	D	D	D
D	D	D	D	D	D	D	D	D	D	D	D	D	D	D	D	D	D	D	D	D	D	D	D	D	D	D	D	D	D

MOB RULE WINNER TAKES ALL ASSEMBLY DISTRICTS' STATE GOVERNORS
NUMBER OF DEMOCRATIC VOTERS (D) 308** NUMBER OF REPUBLICAN VOTERS (R) 304
TOTAL NUMBER VOTED 612
** INDICATES TOTAL SUM OF VOTER WINNER

GOVERNOR 1

MOB RULE STATE GOVERNOR

D = VOTED FOR UNITED STATES DEMOCRATIC GOVERNOR.
R = VOTED FOR UNITED STATES REPUBLICAN GOVERNOR.
LET'S ASSUME THAT THERE ARE 36 QUASI EQUAL VOTING MEMBERS IN EACH DISTRICT OF 17 STATE DISTRICTS MAKING UP THE ENTIRE STATE CONSTITUENCY.

State Assembly District 1	State Assembly District 2	State Assembly District 3	State Assembly District 4	State Assembly District 5	State Assembly District 6	State Assembly District 7	State Assembly District 8	State Assembly District 9
D D D D D D D D D D D D D D D D D D D D D D D D D D D D D	D D D D D D D D D D D D D D D D D R R R R R R R R R R R R R	D D D D D D D D D D D D D D D D D R R R R R R R R R R R R R	D D D D D D D D D D D D D D D D D R R R R R R R R R R R R R	D D D D D D D D D D D D D D D D D R R R R R R R R R R R R R	D D D D D D D D D D D D D D D D D R R R R R R R R R R R R R	D D D D D D D D D D D D D D D D D R R R R R R R R R R R R R	D D D D D D D D D D D D D D D D D R R R R R R R R R R R R R	D D D D D D D D D D D D D D D D D R R R R R R R R R R R R R

State Assembly District 10	State Assembly District 11	State Assembly District 12	State Assembly District 13	State Assembly District 14	State Assembly District 15	State Assembly District 16	State Assembly District 17
D D D D D D D D D D D D D D D D D R R R R R R R R R R R R R	D D D D D D D D D D D D D D D D D R R R R R R R R R R R R R	D D D D D D D D D D D D D D D D D R R R R R R R R R R R R R	D D D D D D D D D D D D D D D D D R R R R R R R R R R R R R	D D D D D D D D D D D D D D D D D R R R R R R R R R R R R R	D D D D D D D D D D D D D D D D D R R R R R R R R R R R R R	D D D D D D D D D D D D D D D D D R R R R R R R R R R R R R	D D D D D D D D D D D D D D D D D R R R R R R R R R R R R R

MOB RULE WINNER TAKES ALL DISTRICT STATE GOVERNORS (DICTATORIAL)

NUMBER OF DEMOCRATIC VOTERS (D) 308** NUMBER OF REPUBLICAN VOTERS (R) 304
TOTAL NUMBER VOTED 512
** INDICATES TOTAL SUM OF VOTER WINNER

MOB RULE (FRAMERS OF THE CONSTITUTION) STATE GOVERNOR (STATE DISTRICTS DECIDE)
STATE ASSEMBLY DISTRICTS
ASSEMBLY DISTRICT 1 D* ASSEMBLY DISTRICT 2 R* ASSEMBLY DISTRICT 3 R*
ASSEMBLY DISTRICT 4 R* ASSEMBLY DISTRICT 5 R* ASSEMBLY DISTRICT 6 R*
ASSEMBLY DISTRICT 7 R* ASSEMBLY DISTRICT 8 R* ASSEMBLY DISTRICT 9 R*
ASSEMBLY DISTRICT 10 R* ASSEMBLY DISTRICT 11 R* ASSEMBLY DISTRICT 12 R*
ASSEMBLY DISTRICT 13 R* ASSEMBLY DISTRICT 14 R* ASSEMBLY DISTRICT 15 R*
ASSEMBLY DISTRICT 16 R* ASSEMBLY DISTRICT 17 R*
NUMBER OF DEMOCRATIC DISTRICTS WON 1; NUMBER OF REPUBLICAN DISTRICTS WON 16
THE 17 ASSEMBLY DISTRICTS WILL THE GOVERNOR!
*INDICATES WINNER OF DISTRICT

GOVERNOR 2

MOB RULE
UNITED STATES HOUSE OF REPRESENTATIVES

<u>D</u> = DEMOCRATIC VOTER.
<u>R</u>= REPUBLICAN VOTER.

LET'S ASSUME THAT THERE ARE VOTING MEMBERS IN A UNITED STATES HOUSE OF REPRESENTATIVES DISTRICT.

D	D	D	D	D	D	D	D	D	D	D	D	D	D	D	D	D	D	D	D	D	D	D	D	D	D	D	D
D	D	D	D	D	D	D	D	D	D	D	D	D	D	D	D	D	D	D	D	D	D	D	D	D	D	D	D
D	D	D	D	D	D	D	D	D	D	D	D	D	D	D	D	D	D	D	D	D	D	D	D	D	D	D	D
D	D	D	D	D	D	D	D	D	D	D	D	D	D	D	D	D	D	D	D	D	D	D	D	D	D	D	D
D	D	D	D	D	R	R	R	R	R	R	R	R	R	R	R	R	R	R	R	R	R	R	R	D	D	D	D
D	D	D	D	D	R	R	R	R	R	R	R	R	R	R	R	R	R	R	R	R	R	R	R	D	D	D	D
D	D	D	D	D	R	R	R	R	R	R	R	R	R	R	R	R	R	R	R	R	R	R	R	D	D	D	D
D	D	D	D	D	R	R	R	R	R	R	R	R	R	R	R	R	R	R	R	R	R	R	R	D	D	D	D
D	D	D	D	D	R	R	R	R	R	R	R	R	R	R	R	R	R	R	R	R	R	R	R	D	D	D	D
D	D	D	D	D	R	R	R	R	R	R	R	R	R	R	R	R	R	R	R	R	R	R	R	D	D	D	D
D	D	D	D	D	R	R	R	R	R	R	R	R	R	R	R	R	R	R	R	R	R	R	R	D	D	D	D
D	D	D	D	D	R	R	R	R	R	R	R	R	R	R	R	R	R	R	R	R	R	R	R	D	D	D	D
D	D	D	D	D	R	R	R	R	R	R	R	R	R	R	R	R	R	R	R	R	R	R	R	D	D	D	D
D	D	D	D	D	R	R	R	R	R	R	R	R	R	R	R	R	R	R	R	R	R	R	R	D	D	D	D
D	D	D	D	D	R	R	R	R	R	R	R	R	R	R	R	R	R	R	R	R	R	R	R	D	D	D	D
D	D	D	D	D	R	R	R	R	R	R	R	R	R	R	R	R	R	R	R	R	R	R	R	D	D	D	D
D	D	D	D	D	R	R	R	R	R	R	R	R	R	R	R	R	R	R	R	R	R	R	R	D	D	D	D
D	D	D	D	D	R	R	R	R	R	R	R	R	R	R	R	R	R	R	R	R	R	R	R	D	D	D	D
D	D	D	D	D	D	D	D	D	D	D	D	D	D	D	D	D	D	D	D	D	D	D	D	D	D	D	D
D	D	D	D	D	D	D	D	D	D	D	D	D	D	D	D	D	D	D	D	D	D	D	D	D	D	D	D
D	D	D	D	D	D	D	D	D	D	D	D	D	D	D	D	D	D	D	D	D	D	D	D	D	D	D	D
	D	D	D	D	D	D	D	D	D	D	D	D	D	D	D	D	D	D	D	D	D	D	D	D	D	D	

MOB RULE WINNER TAKES ALL STATE ASSEMBLY DISTRICTS
UNITED STATES HOUSE OF REPRESENTATIVES

NUMBER OF DEMOCRATIC VOTERS (D) **308**** NUMBER OF REPUBLICAN VOTERS (R) **304**
TOTAL NUMBER VOTED **612**
** INDICATES TOTAL SUM OF VOTER WINNER

US HOUSE 1

MOB RULE
UNITED STATE HOUSE OF REPRESENTATIVES

D = VOTED FOR UNITED STATES DEMOCRATIC SENATOR.
R̄ = VOTED FOR UNITED STATES REPUBLICAN SENATOR.
LET'S ASSUME THAT THERE ARE 36 QUASI-EQUAL 17 STATE ASSEMBLY DISTRICTS WITHIN A SINGLE UNITED STATES HOUSE OF REPRESENTATIVES DISTRICT.

State Assembly District 1	State Assembly District 2	State Assembly District 3	State Assembly District 4	State Assembly District 5	State Assembly District 6	State Assembly District 7	State Assembly District 8	State Assembly District 9
D D D D D	D D D D D	D D D D D	D D D D D	D D D D D	D D D D D	D D D D D	D D D D D	D D D D D
D D D D D	D D D D D	D D D D D	D D D D D	D D D D D	D D D D D	D D D D D	D D D D D	D D D D D
D D D D D	D D D D	D D D D D	D D D D D	D D D D D	D D D D D	D D D D D	D D D D	D D D D D
D D D D D								
D D D D D	R	R	R	R	R	R	R	R
D D D D D	R R R R R R	R R R R R R	R R R R R R	R R R R R R	R R R R R R	R R R R R R	R R R R R R	R R R R R R
	R R R R R R	R R R R R R	R R R R R R	R R R R R R	R R R R R R	R R R R R R	R R R R R R	R R R R R R
	R R R R R R	R R R R R R	R R R R R R	R R R R R R	R R R R R R	R R R R R R	R R R R R R	R R R R R R

State Assembly District 10	State Assembly District 11	State Assembly District 12	State Assembly District 13	State Assembly District 14	State Assembly District 15	State Assembly District 16	State Assembly District 17
D D D D D	D D D D D	D D D D D	D D D D D	D D D D D	D D D D D	D D D D D	D D D D D
D D D D D D	D D D D D D	D D D D D D	D D D D D D	D D D D D D	D D D D D D	D D D D D D	D D D D D D
D D D D	D D D D	D D D D	D D D D	D D D D	D D D D	D D D D	D D D D
R	R	R	R	R	R	R	R
R R R R R R	R R R R R R	R R R R R R	R R R R R R	R R R R R R	R R R R R R	R R R R R R	R R R R R R
R R R R R R	R R R R R R	R R R R R R	R R R R R R	R R R R R R	R R R R R R	R R R R R R	R R R R R R
R R R R R R	R R R R R R	R R R R R R	R R R R R R	R R R R R R	R R R R R R	R R R R R R	R R R R R R

MOB RULE WINNER TAKES ALL ASSEMBLY DISTRICTS
AND UNITED STATES HOUSE OF REPRESENTATIVES DISTRICT

NUMBER OF DEMOCRATIC VOTERS (D) 308** NUMBER OF REPUBLICAN VOTERS (R) 304
TOTAL NUMBER VOTED 512
** INDICATES TOTAL SUM OF VOTER WINNER

MOB RULE (FRAMERS OF THE CONSTITUTION)
A UNITED STATES HOUSE OF REPRESENTATIVES DISTRICT

ASSEMBLY DISTRICT 1 D* ASSEMBLY DISTRICT 2 R* ASSEMBLY DISTRICT 3 R*
ASSEMBLY DISTRICT 4 R̄* ASSEMBLY DISTRICT 5 R* ASSEMBLY DISTRICT 6 R*
ASSEMBLY DISTRICT 7 R* ASSEMBLY DISTRICT 8 R* ASSEMBLY DISTRICT 9 R*
ASSEMBLY DISTRICT 10 R* ASSEMBLY DISTRICT 11 R* ASSEMBLY DISTRICT 12 R*
ASSEMBLY DISTRICT 13 R* ASSEMBLY DISTRICT 14 R* ASSEMBLY DISTRICT 15 R*
ASSEMBLY DISTRICT 16 R*
ASSEMBLY DISTRICT 17 R*
NUMBER OF DEMOCRATIC DISTRICTS WON 1; NUMBER OF REPUBLICAN DISTRICTS WON 16
THE 17 STATE ASSEMBLY DISTRICT REPRESENTATIVES WILL PICK THE UNITED STATES HOUSE OF REPRESENTATIVES!
* INDICATES WINNER OF DISTRICT

US HOUSE 2

MOB RULE STATE SENATE

D = DEMOCRATIC VOTER.
R = REPUBLICAN VOTER.
LET'S ASSUME THAT THERE ARE VOTING MEMBERS IN A STATE SENATE DISTRICT.

```
D D D D D D D D D D D D D D D D D D D D D D D D D D D D D
D D D D D D D D D D D D D D D D D D D D D D D D D D D D D
D D D D D D D D D D D D D D D D D D D D D D D D D D D D D
D D D D D D D D D D D D D D D D D D D D D D D D D D D D D
D D D D D R R R R R R R R R R R R R R R R R R R D D D D D
D D D D D R R R R R R R R R R R R R R R R R R R D D D D D
D D D D D R R R R R R R R R R R R R R R R R R R D D D D D
D D D D D R R R R R R R R R R R R R R R R R R R D D D D D
D D D D D R R R R R R R R R R R R R R R R R R R D D D D D
D D D D D R R R R R R R R R R R R R R R R R R R D D D D D
D D D D D R R R R R R R R R R R R R R R R R R R D D D D D
D D D D D R R R R R R R R R R R R R R R R R R R D D D D D
D D D D D R R R R R R R R R R R R R R R R R R R D D D D D
D D D D D R R R R R R R R R R R R R R R R R R R D D D D D
D D D D D R R R R R R R R R R R R R R R R R R R D D D D D
D D D D D R R R R R R R R R R R R R R R R R R R D D D D D
D D D D D R R R R R R R R R R R R R R R R R R R D D D D D
D D D D D R R R R R R R R R R R R R R R R R R R D D D D D
D D D D D R R R R R R R R R R R R R R R R R R R D D D D D
D D D D D R R R R R R R R R R R R R R R R R R R D D D D D
D D D D D R R R R R R R R R R R R R R R R R R R D D D D D
D D D D D D D D D D D D D D D D D D D D D D D D D D D D D
D D D D D D D D D D D D D D D D D D D D D D D D D D D D D
D D D D D D D D D D D D D D D D D D D D D D D D D D D D D
  D D D D D D D D D D D D D D D D D D D D D D D D D D
```

MOB RULE WINNER TAKES ALL DISTRICTS STATE SENATE

NUMBER OF DEMOCRATIC VOTERS (D) 308** NUMBER OF REPUBLICAN VOTERS (R) 304
TOTAL NUMBER VOTED 612
** INDICATES TOTAL SUM OF VOTER WINNER

STATE SENATE 1

144

MOB RULE STATE ASSEMBLY

D = DEMOCRATIC VOTER.
R = REPUBLICAN VOTER.
LET'S ASSUME THAT THERE ARE VOTING MEMBERS IN A STATE ASSEMBLY DISTRICT.

D	D	D	D	D	D	D	D	D	D	D	D	D	D	D	D	D	D	D	D	D	D	D	D	D	D	D	D	D
D	D	D	D	D	D	D	D	D	D	D	D	D	D	D	D	D	D	D	D	D	D	D	D	D	D	D	D	D
D	D	D	D	D	D	D	D	D	D	D	D	D	D	D	D	D	D	D	D	D	D	D	D	D	D	D	D	D
D	D	D	D	D	D	D	D	D	D	D	D	D	D	D	D	D	D	D	D	D	D	D	D	D	D	D	D	D
D	D	D	D	D	R	R	R	R	R	R	R	R	R	R	R	R	R	R	R	R	R	R	R	D	D	D	D	D
D	D	D	D	D	R	R	R	R	R	R	R	R	R	R	R	R	R	R	R	R	R	R	R	D	D	D	D	D
D	D	D	D	D	R	R	R	R	R	R	R	R	R	R	R	R	R	R	R	R	R	R	R	D	D	D	D	D
D	D	D	D	D	R	R	R	R	R	R	R	R	R	R	R	R	R	R	R	R	R	R	R	D	D	D	D	D
D	D	D	D	D	R	R	R	R	R	R	R	R	R	R	R	R	R	R	R	R	R	R	R	D	D	D	D	D
D	D	D	D	D	R	R	R	R	R	R	R	R	R	R	R	R	R	R	R	R	R	R	R	D	D	D	D	D
D	D	D	D	D	R	R	R	R	R	R	R	R	R	R	R	R	R	R	R	R	R	R	R	D	D	D	D	D
D	D	D	D	D	R	R	R	R	R	R	R	R	R	R	R	R	R	R	R	R	R	R	R	D	D	D	D	D
D	D	D	D	D	R	R	R	R	R	R	R	R	R	R	R	R	R	R	R	R	R	R	R	D	D	D	D	D
D	D	D	D	D	R	R	R	R	R	R	R	R	R	R	R	R	R	R	R	R	R	R	R	D	D	D	D	D
D	D	D	D	D	R	R	R	R	R	R	R	R	R	R	R	R	R	R	R	R	R	R	R	D	D	D	D	D
D	D	D	D	D	R	R	R	R	R	R	R	R	R	R	R	R	R	R	R	R	R	R	R	D	D	D	D	D
D	D	D	D	D	R	R	R	R	R	R	R	R	R	R	R	R	R	R	R	R	R	R	R	D	D	D	D	D
D	D	D	D	D	R	R	R	R	R	R	R	R	R	R	R	R	R	R	R	R	R	R	R	D	D	D	D	D
D	D	D	D	D	R	R	R	R	R	R	R	R	R	R	R	R	R	R	R	R	R	R	R	D	D	D	D	D
D	D	D	D	D	R	R	R	R	R	R	R	R	R	R	R	R	R	R	R	R	R	R	R	D	D	D	D	D
D	D	D	D	D	D	D	D	D	D	D	D	D	D	D	D	D	D	D	D	D	D	D	D	D	D	D	D	D
D	D	D	D	D	D	D	D	D	D	D	D	D	D	D	D	D	D	D	D	D	D	D	D	D	D	D	D	D
D	D	D	D	D	D	D	D	D	D	D	D	D	D	D	D	D	D	D	D	D	D	D	D	D	D	D	D	D
	D	D	D	D	D	D	D	D	D	D	D	D	D	D	D	D	D	D	D	D	D	D	D	D	D	D	D	

MOB RULE WINNER TAKES ALL DISTRICTS STATE ASSEMBLY

NUMBER OF DEMOCRATIC VOTERS (D) 308** NUMBER OF REPUBLICAN VOTERS (R) 304
TOTAL NUMBER VOTED 612
** INDICATES TOTAL SUM OF VOTER WINNER

STATE ASSEMBLY 1

Electoral College

MOB RULE PRESIDENTIAL

D = DEMOCRATIC VOTER.
R = REPUBLICAN VOTER.
LET'S ASSUME THAT THERE ARE VOTING MEMBERS IN THE ENTIRE STATE CONSTITUENCY
REGARDLESS OF THE STATES WITHIN THE UNITED STATES TERRITORY.

D	D	D	D	D	D	D	D	D	D	D	D	D	D	D	D	D	D	D	D	D	D	D	D	D	D	D	D	D
D	D	D	D	D	D	D	D	D	D	D	D	D	D	D	D	D	D	D	D	D	D	D	D	D	D	D	D	D
D	D	D	D	D	D	D	D	D	D	D	D	D	D	D	D	D	D	D	D	D	D	D	D	D	D	D	D	D
D	D	D	D	D	D	D	D	D	D	D	D	D	D	D	D	D	D	D	D	D	D	D	D	D	D	D	D	D
D	D	D	D	D	R	R	R	R	R	R	R	R	R	R	R	R	R	R	R	R	R	R	R	R	D	D	D	D
D	D	D	D	D	R	R	R	R	R	R	R	R	R	R	R	R	R	R	R	R	R	R	R	R	D	D	D	D
D	D	D	D	D	R	R	R	R	R	R	R	R	R	R	R	R	R	R	R	R	R	R	R	R	D	D	D	D
D	D	D	D	D	R	R	R	R	R	R	R	R	R	R	R	R	R	R	R	R	R	R	R	R	D	D	D	D
D	D	D	D	D	R	R	R	R	R	R	R	R	R	R	R	R	R	R	R	R	R	R	R	R	D	D	D	D
D	D	D	D	D	R	R	R	R	R	R	R	R	R	R	R	R	R	R	R	R	R	R	R	R	D	D	D	D
D	D	D	D	D	R	R	R	R	R	R	R	R	R	R	R	R	R	R	R	R	R	R	R	R	D	D	D	D
D	D	D	D	D	R	R	R	R	R	R	R	R	R	R	R	R	R	R	R	R	R	R	R	R	D	D	D	D
D	D	D	D	D	R	R	R	R	R	R	R	R	R	R	R	R	R	R	R	R	R	R	R	R	D	D	D	D
D	D	D	D	D	R	R	R	R	R	R	R	R	R	R	R	R	R	R	R	R	R	R	R	R	D	D	D	D
D	D	D	D	D	R	R	R	R	R	R	R	R	R	R	R	R	R	R	R	R	R	R	R	R	D	D	D	D
D	D	D	D	D	R	R	R	R	R	R	R	R	R	R	R	R	R	R	R	R	R	R	R	R	D	D	D	D
D	D	D	D	D	R	R	R	R	R	R	R	R	R	R	R	R	R	R	R	R	R	R	R	R	D	D	D	D
D	D	D	D	D	R	R	R	R	R	R	R	R	R	R	R	R	R	R	R	R	R	R	R	R	D	D	D	D
D	D	D	D	D	R	R	R	R	R	R	R	R	R	R	R	R	R	R	R	R	R	R	R	R	D	D	D	D
D	D	D	D	D	R	R	R	R	R	R	R	R	R	R	R	R	R	R	R	R	R	R	R	R	D	D	D	D
D	D	D	D	D	D	D	D	D	D	D	D	D	D	D	D	D	D	D	D	D	D	D	D	D	D	D	D	D
D	D	D	D	D	D	D	D	D	D	D	D	D	D	D	D	D	D	D	D	D	D	D	D	D	D	D	D	D
D	D	D	D	D	D	D	D	D	D	D	D	D	D	D	D	D	D	D	D	D	D	D	D	D	D	D	D	D
D	D	D	D	D	D	D	D	D	D	D	D	D	D	D	D	D	D	D	D	D	D	D	D	D	D	D	D	

MOB RULE WINNER TAKES ALL UNITED STATES PRESIDENT

NUMBER OF **DEMOCRATIC** VOTERS (D) 308** NUMBER OF **REPUBLICAN** VOTERS (R) 304
TOTAL NUMBER VOTED 612
** INDICATES TOTAL SUM OF VOTER WINNER

PRESIDENTIAL 1

MOB RULE PRESIDENTIAL

D = VOTED FOR UNITED STATES DEMOCRATIC PRESIDENT.
R̄ = VOTED FOR UNITED STATES REPUBLICAN PRESIDENT.
LET'S ASSUME THAT THERE ARE 36 QUASI-EQUAL VOTING MEMBERS IN EACH DISTRICT OF 17 STATE DISTRICTS MAKING UP THE ENTIRE STATE CONSTITUENCY.

State 1	State t 2	State 3	State 4	State 5	State 6	State 7	State 8	State 9
D D D D D	D D D D D	D D D D D	D D D D D	D D D D D	D D D D D	D D D D D	D D D D D	D D D D D
D D D D D	D D D D D	D D D D D	D D D D D	D D D D D	D D D D D	D D D D D	D D D D D	D D D D D
D D D D D	D D D D	D D D D	D D D D	D D D D	D D D D	D D D D	D D D D	D D D D
D D D D D								
D D D D D								
D D D D D	R	R	R	R	R	R	R	R
	R R R R R R	R R R R R R	R R R R R R	R R R R R R	R R R R R R	R R R R R R	R R R R R R	R R R R R R
	R R R R R R	R R R R R R	R R R R R R	R R R R R R	R R R R R R	R R R R R R	R R R R R R	R R R R R R
	R R R R R R	R R R R R R	R R R R R R	R R R R R R	R R R R R R	R R R R R R	R R R R R R	R R R R R R

State 10	State 11	State 12	State 13	State 14	State 15	State 16	State 17
D D D D D	D D D D D	D D D D D	D D D D D	D D D D D	D D D D D	D D D D D	D D D D D
D D D D D	D D D D D	D D D D D	D D D D D	D D D D D	D D D D D	D D D D D	D D D D D
D D D D	D D D D	D D D D	D D D D	D D D D	D D D D	D D D D	D D D D
R	R	R	R	R	R	R	R
R R R R R R	R R R R R R	R R R R R R	R R R R R R	R R R R R R	R R R R R R	R R R R R R	R R R R R R
R R R R R R	R R R R R R	R R R R R R	R R R R R R	R R R R R R	R R R R R R	R R R R R R	R R R R R R
R R R R R R	R R R R R R	R R R R R R	R R R R R R	R R R R R R	R R R R R R	R R R R R R	R R R R R R

MOB RULE WINNER TAKES ALL UNITED STATES PRESIDENT

NUMBER OF DEMOCRATIC VOTERS (D) 308** NUMBER OF REPUBLICAN VOTERS (R) 304
TOTAL NUMBER VOTED 512
** INDICATES TOTAL SUM OF VOTER WINNER

MOB RULE (FRAMERS OF THE CONSTITUTION) PRESIDENT

STATE 1 D* STATE 2 R* STATE 3 R* STATE 4 R* STATE 5 R* STATE 6 R* STATE 7 R* STATE 8 R*
STATE 9 R̄* STATE 10 R* STATE 11 R* STATE 12 R*
STATE 13 R* STATE 14 R* STATE 15 R* STATE 16 R* STATE 17 R*

NUMBER OF DEMOCRATIC STATES WON 1; NUMBER OF REPUBLICAN STATES WON 16.
THE 17 STATE ELECTORAL COLLEGE REPRESENTATIVES WILL PICK THE PRESIDENT OF THE UNITED STATES!
* INDICATES WINNER OF STATE

PRESIDENTIAL 2

147

MCCAIN WINS STATE'S POPULAR VOTE AND COUNTIES' POPULAR VOTE

1. in alaska, mccain wins both counties and popular vote!

   mccain 136,348   obama 80,340
   mccain % 0.629237   obama % 0.370763

2. in alabama, mccain wins both counties and popular vote!

   mccain 797,145   obama 504,120
   mccain % 0.61259   obama % 0.38741

3. in arizona, mccain wins both counties and popular vote!

   mccain % 0.54418   obama % 0.45582

4. in arkansas, mccain wins both counties and popular vote!

   mccain % 0.602131   obama % 0.397869

5. in georgia, mccain wins both counties and popular vote!

   mccain % 0.527547   obama % 0.472453

6. in idaho, mccain wins both counties and popular vote!

    mccain % 0.63028   obama % 0.36972

7. in kansas, mccain wins both counties and popular vote!

    mccain 685,541   obama 499,979
    mccain % 0.578262   obama % 0.421738

8. in kentucky, mccain wins both counties and popular vote!

9. in louisiana, mccain wins both counties and popular vote!

    mccain 1,147,603   obama 787,152
    mccain % 0.59315   obama % 0.40685

10. in mississippi, mccain wins both counties and popular vote!

    mccain % 0.56927   obama % 0.43073

11. in missouri, mccain wins both counties and popular vote!

    mccain % 0.53177   obama % 0.46823

12. in montana, mccain wins both counties and popular vote!

    mccain 241,816   obama 229,725
    mccain % 0.51282   obama % 0.48718

13. in nebraska, mccain wins both counties and popular vote!

    mccain 439,421   obama 315,913
    mccain % 0.58176   obama % 0.41824

14. in north dakota, mccain wins both counties and popular vote!

mccain 168,523   obama 141,113
mccain % 0.544262   obama % 0.455738

15. in oklahoma, mccain wins both counties and popular vote!

mccain % 0.65642   obama % 0.34358

16. in south carolina, mccain wins both counties and popular vote!

mccain 1,018,418   obama 849,852
mccain % 0.54511   obama % 0.45489

17. in south dakota, mccain wins both counties and popular vote!

mccain 03,013   obama 170,880
mccain % 0.542971   obama % 0.457029

18. in tennessee, mccain wins both counties and popular vote!

mccain 1487564   obama 1093213
mccain % 0.5764016   obama % 0.4235984

19. in texas, mccain wins both counties and popular vote!

mccain % 0.55924   obama % 0.44076

20. in utah, mccain wins both counties and popular vote!

mccain % 0.64799   obama % 0.35201

21. in west virginia, mccain wins both counties and popular vote!

    mccain% 301,438   obama% 0.43328

22. in wyoming, mccain wins both counties and popular vote!

    mccain % 0.66618   obama % 0.33382

OBAMA WINS STATE POPULAR VOTE AND COUNTY POPULAR VOTE

1. in california, obama wins both counties and popular vote!

   obama 6,219,123   mccain 3,777,314
   obama % 0.62213   mccain % 0.37787

2. in connecticut, obama wins both counties and popular vote!

   obama 979,316   mccain 620,210
   difference 359,106
   obama % 0.612254   mccain % 0.387746

3. in delaware, obama wins both counties and popular vote!

   obama 255,394   mccain 152,356
   difference 103,038
   obama % 0.62635   mccain % 0.37365

4. in district of columbia, obama wins both counties and popular vote!

   obama 210,403   mccain 14,821
   difference 195,582

obama % 0.934194   mccain % 0.065806

5. in hawaii, obama wins both counties and popular vote!

    obama 298,621   mccain 110,848
    difference 187,773
    obama % 0.729288   mccain % 0.270712

6. in iowa, obama wins both counties and popular vote!

    obama 818,240   mccain 677,508
    difference 140,732
    obama % 0.54704   mccain % 0.45296

7. in maine, obama wins both counties and popular vote!

    obama 421,481   mccain 296,192
    difference 125,289
    mccain % 0.58729   obama % 0.41271

8. in massachusetts, obama wins both counties and popu-
    lar vote!

    obama 1,891,083   mccain 1,104,284
    difference 786,799
    obama % 0.631336   mccain % 0.368664

9. in michigan, obama wins both counties and popular vote!

    obama 2,867,680   mccain 2,044,405
    difference 823,275
    obama % 0.58380   mccain % 0.41620

10. in new hampshire, obama wins both counties and pop-
    ular vote!

    obama 384,591   mccain 384,591
    obama % 0.54822   mccain % 0.45178

11. in new jersey, mccain wins both counties and popular vote!

    obama 2,072,566   mccain 1,541,024
    obama % 0.57355   mccain % 0.42645

12. in new mexico, obama wins both counties and popular vote!

    obama 454,291   mccain 334,298
    difference 119,993
    obama % 0.576081   mccain % 0.423919

13. in new york, obama wins both counties and popular vote!

    obama 4,357,360   mccain 2,573,368
    difference 1,783,992
    obama % 0.62870   mccain % 0.37130

14. in rhode island, obama wins both counties and popular vote!

    obama 275,488   mccain 152,502
    difference 66,412
    obama % 0.64368   mccain % 0.35632

15. in vermont, obama wins both counties and popular vote!

    obama % 0.67890   mccain % 0.32110

16. in wisconsin, obama wins both counties and popular vote!

    obama 1,670,474   mccain 1,258,181
    obama % 0.57039

These two preceding tables cannot be used to show mob rule, but McCain had won more state government counties (22) than Obama (15). Obama and McCain won both state governments and state counties.

The following table shows differently where Obama wins state governments and McCain wins state counties. Nowhere does McCain win state governments and Obama wins counties. The following table indicates mob rule.

MOB RULE
OBAMA WINS STATE'S POPULAR VOTE MCCAIN WINS COUNTIES POPULAR VOTE

Colorado State #1

A	B	C	D	E	F	G	H	I
NUM-BER OF COUN-TIES	NAMES	COUNTY VOTE	PERCENT	OBAMA COUNT	MCCAIN COUNT	OBAMA VOTE	MCCAIN VOTE	OBAMA - MCCAIN VOTE
1	Obama	90,113	58%	1		90,113		
	McCain	62,321	40%		0		62,321	27,792
2	Obama	3,521	56%	1		3,521		
	McCain	2,635	42%		0		2,635	886
3	Obama	128,366	55%	1		128,366		
	McCain	100,409	43%		0		100,409	27,957
4	Obama	2,822	43%	0		2,822		
	McCain	3,618	55%		1		3,618	796
5	Obama	532	25%	0		532		
	McCain	1,568	72%		1		1,568	1,036
6	Obama	799	42%	0		799		
	McCain	1,077	56%		1		1,077	278
7	Obama	90,932	73%	1		90,932		
	McCain	32,167	26%		0		32,167	58,765
8	Obama	16,031	55%	1		16,031		
	McCain	12,675	43%		0		12,675	3,356
9	Obama	4,827	49%	0		4,827		
	McCain	4,832	49%		1		4,832	5
10	Obama	198	18%	0		198		

A	B	C	D	E	F	G	H	I
NUMBER OF COUNTIES	NAMES	COUNTY VOTE	PERCENT	OBAMA COUNT	MCCAIN COUNT	OBAMA VOTE	MCCAIN VOTE	OBAMA - MCCAIN VOTE
	McCain	890	80%		1		890	692
11	Obama	3,295	58%	1		3,295		
	McCain	2,278	40%		0		2,278	1,017
12	Obama	2,106	56%	1		2,106		
	McCain	1,616	43%		0		1,616	490
13	Obama	1,236	73%	1		1,236		
	McCain	411	25%		0		411	825
14	Obama	552	36%	0		552		
	McCain	976	63%		1		976	424
15	Obama	914	35%	0		914		
	McCain	1,668	63%		1		1,668	754
16	Obama	5,007	33%	0		5,007		
	McCain	9,905	65%		1		9,905	4,898
17	Obama	195,499	75%	1		195,499		
	McCain	60,226	23%		0		60,226	135,273
18	Obama	356	30%	0		356		
	McCain	803	67%		1		803	447
19	Obama	51,813	41%	0		51,813		
	McCain	73,225	58%		1		73,225	21,412
20	Obama	13,055	61%	1		13,055		
	McCain	8,112	38%		0		8,112	4,943
21	Obama	3,775	29%	0		3,775		
	McCain	9,030	69%		1		9,030	5,255
22	Obama	104,670	40%	0		104,670		
	McCain	155,914	59%		1		155,914	51,244
23	Obama	6,801	34%	0		6,801		
	McCain	12,595	64%		1		12,595	5,794
24	Obama	10,847	49%	0		10,847		
	McCain	10,932	50%		1		10,932	85
25	Obama	1,944	59%	1		1,944		
	McCain	1,249	38%		0		1,249	695
26	Obama	3,961	48%	0		3,961		
	McCain	4,088	50%		1		4,088	127
27	Obama	5,512	63%	1		5,512		
	McCain	3,112	35%		0		3,112	2,400
28	Obama	239	39%	0		239		
	McCain	343	56%		1		343	104
29	Obama	1,989	55%	1		1,989		
	McCain	1,582	44%		0		1,582	407
30	Obama	277	30%	0		277		
	McCain	624	68%		1		624	347
31	Obama	155,020	54%	1		155,020		
	McCain	129,291	45%		0		129,291	25,729
32	Obama	172	21%	0		172		
	McCain	630	76%		1		630	458
33	Obama	898	27%	0		898		
	McCain	2,420	71%		1		2,420	1,522
34	Obama	1,847	62%	1		1,847		
	McCain	1,076	36%		0		1,076	771
35	Obama	15,422	57%	1		15,422		
	McCain	11,170	41%		0		11,170	4,252
36	Obama	84,461	54%	1		84,461		
	McCain	68,932	44%		0		68,932	15,529
37	Obama	3,483	53%	1		3,483		
	McCain	3,033	46%		0		3,033	450
38	Obama	543	24%	0		543		
	McCain	1,683	74%		1		1,683	1,140
39	Obama	2,837	32%	1		2,837		

A	B	C	D	E	F	G	H	I
NUM- BER OF COUN- TIES	NAMES	COUNTY VOTE	PERCENT	OBAMA COUNT	MCCAIN COUNT	OBAMA VOTE	MCCAIN VOTE	OBAMA - MCCAIN VOTE
	McCain	5,986	67%		0		5,986	3,149
40	Obama	23,470	35%	0		23,470		
	McCain	43,669	64%		1		43,669	20,199
41	Obama	270	44%	0		270		
	McCain	334	54%		1		334	64
42	Obama	1,566	27%	0		1,566		
	McCain	4,101	71%		1		4,101	2,535
43	Obama	4,619	39%	0		4,619		
	McCain	6,913	59%		1		6,913	2,294
44	Obama	6,115	34%	0		6,115		
	McCain	11,525	64%		1		11,525	5,410
45	Obama	3,762	37%	0		3,762		
	McCain	6,222	62%		1		6,222	2,460
46	Obama	3,454	44%	0		3,454		
	McCain	4,324	55%		1		4,324	870
47	Obama	1,629	53%	1		1,629		
	McCain	1,360	45%		0		1,360	269
48	Obama	4,196	45%	0		4,196		
	McCain	4,835	52%		1		4,835	639
49	Obama	587	28%	0		587		
	McCain	1,513	71%		1		1,513	926
50	Obama	7,260	74%	1		7,260		
	McCain	2,448	25%		0		2,448	4,812
51	Obama	1,464	32%	0		1,464		
	McCain	3,026	66%		1		3,026	1,562
52	Obama	38,074	57%	1		38,074		
	McCain	28,523	42%		0		28,523	9,551
53	Obama	654	21%	0		654		
	McCain	2,425	77%		1		2,425	1,771
54	Obama	2,427	45%	0		2,427		
	McCain	2,916	54%		1		2,916	489
55	Obama	8,133	63%	1		8,133		
	McCain	4,634	36%		0		4,634	3,499
56	Obama	1,620	63%	1		1,620		
	McCain	913	35%		0		913	707
57	Obama	264	53%	1		264		
	McCain	218	44%		0		218	46
58	Obama	3,345	77%	1		3,345		
	McCain	930	21%		0		930	2,415
59	Obama	468	35%	0		468		
	McCain	857	64%		1		857	389
60	Obama	9,700	66%	1		9,700		
	McCain	4,845	33%		0		4,845	4,855
61	Obama	4,370	35%	0		4,370		
	McCain	7,939	63%		1		7,939	3,569
62	Obama	518	21%	0		518		
	McCain	1,935	78%		1		1,935	1,417
63	Obama	46,644	45%	0		46,644		
	McCain	55,913	54%		1		55,913	9,269
64	Obama	1,105	25%	0		1,105		
	McCain	3,238	73%	0	1	0	3,238	2,133
Total		2,203,044		27	37	1,192,386	1,010,658	181,728

In Colorado, mob rule Obama wins popular vote! McCain wins counties!

Mob Rule Difference 181,728

Obama % 0.54124475

McCain % 0.45875525

In column E total, Obama won *twenty-seven* counties whereas in column F total, McCain won *thirty-seven* counties.

In the *twenty-seven* counties, the differences between Obama and McCain is in column I. Since McCain could not over take the mob rule values, the difference in column I total is mob rule.

Especially notice the following counties in column G (county #1, #3, #7, #17, #31) and where the differences are more or equal five-digit numbers.

Florida State #2

A	B	C	D	E	F	G	H	I
COUNTY NUMBER	NAMES	COUNTY VOTE	PERCENT	OBAMA COUNT	MCCAIN COUNT	OBAMA VOTE	MCCAIN VOTE	OBAMA - MCCAIN VOTE
1	Obama	73,134	60%	1		73,134		
	McCain	47,025	39%		0		47,025	26,109
2	Obama	2,326	21%	0		2,326		
	McCain	8,672	79%		1		8,672	6,346
3	Obama	23,603	29%	0		23,603		
	McCain	56,597	70%		1		56,597	32,994
4	Obama	3,430	29%	0		3,430		
	McCain	8,135	70%		1		8,135	4,705
5	Obama	127,400	44%	0		127,400		
	McCain	157,402	55%		1		157,402	30,002
6	Obama	474,579	68%	1		474,579		
	McCain	225,453	32%		0		225,453	249,126
7	Obama	1,821	29%	0		1,821		
	McCain	4,344	70%		1		4,344	2,523
8	Obama	39,006	46%	0		39,006		
	McCain	45,180	53%		1		45,180	6,174
9	Obama	31,428	41%	0		31,428		
	McCain	43,666	58%		1		43,666	12,238
10	Obama	26,635	29%	0		26,635		
	McCain	66,847	71%		1		66,847	40,212
11	Obama	52,710	39%	0		52,710		
	McCain	83,238	61%		1		83,238	30,528
12	Obama	9,171	33%	0		9,171		
	McCain	18,668	66%		1		18,668	9,497
13	Obama	4,378	43%	0		4,378		
	McCain	5,625	56%		1		5,625	1,247
14	Obama	1,921	26%	0		1,921		
	McCain	5,188	72%		1		5,188	3,267

A	B	C	D	E	F	G	H	I
COUNTY NUMBER	NAMES	COUNTY VOTE	PERCENT	OBAMA COUNT	MCCAIN COUNT	OBAMA VOTE	MCCAIN VOTE	OBAMA - MCCAIN VOTE
15	Obama	192,173	49%	0		192,173		
	McCain	197,171	51%		1		197,171	4,998
16	Obama	61,152	40%	0		61,152		
	McCain	90,826	59%		1		90,826	29,674
17	Obama	24,682	51%	1		24,682		
	McCain	23,931	49%		0		23,931	751
18	Obama	2,122	36%	0		2,122		
	McCain	3,799	63%		1		3,799	1,677
19	Obama	15,566	69%	1		15,566		
	McCain	6,805	31%		0		6,805	8,761
20	Obama	1,993	26%	0		1,993		
	McCain	5,654	73%		1		5,654	3,661
21	Obama	1,674	40%	0		1,674		
	McCain	2,533	60%		1		2,533	859
22	Obama	2,144	30%	0		2,144		
	McCain	4,971	69%		1		4,971	2,827
23	Obama	2,360	42%	0		2,360		
	McCain	3,179	57%		1		3,179	819
24	Obama	2,561	35%	0		2,561		
	McCain	4,758	64%		1		4,758	2,197
25	Obama	4,998	46%	0		4,998		
	McCain	5,779	53%		1		5,779	781
26	Obama	18,980	43%	0		18,980		
	McCain	25,220	56%		1		25,220	6,240
27	Obama	17,913	40%	0		17,913		
	McCain	25,903	59%		1		25,903	7,990
28	Obama	192,320	50%	1		192,320		
	McCain	188,096	49%		0		188,096	4,224
29	Obama	1,443	17%	0		1,443		
	McCain	7,023	82%		1		7,023	5,580
30	Obama	29,565	42%	0		29,565		
	McCain	39,972	57%		1		39,972	10,407
31	Obama	7,632	36%	0		7,632		
	McCain	13,695	64%		1		13,695	6,063
32	Obama	4,082	52%	1		4,082		
	McCain	3,794	48%		0		3,794	288
33	Obama	640	19%	0		640		
	McCain	2,677	80%		1		2,677	2,037
34	Obama	62,710	43%	0		62,710		
	McCain	82,512	57%		1		82,512	19,802
35	Obama	117,878	45%	0		117,878		
	McCain	145,624	55%		1		145,624	27,746
36	Obama	91,356	62%	1		91,356		
	McCain	55,521	38%		0		55,521	35,835
37	Obama	6,707	36%	0		6,707		
	McCain	11,751	63%		1		11,751	5,044
38	Obama	892	27%	0		892		
	McCain	2,337	72%		1		2,337	1,445
39	Obama	4,270	48%	0		4,270		
	McCain	4,544	51%		1		4,544	274
40	Obama	67,785	46%	0		67,785		
	McCain	78,040	53%		1		78,040	10,255
41	Obama	70,771	44%	0		70,771		
	McCain	89,571	55%		1		89,571	18,800
42	Obama	33,474	43%	0		33,474		
	McCain	44,110	56%		1		44,110	10,636
43	Obama	491,195	58%	1		491,195		
	McCain	351,462	42%		0		351,462	139,733
44	Obama	20,868	52%	1		20,868		
	McCain	18,906	47%		0		18,906	1,962
45	Obama	10,577	28%	0		10,577		
	McCain	27,326	72%		1		27,326	16,749
46	Obama	25,623	27%	0		25,623		

A COUNTY NUMBER	B NAMES	C COUNTY VOTE	D PERCENT	E OBAMA COUNT	F MCCAIN COUNT	G OBAMA VOTE	H MCCAIN VOTE	I OBAMA - MCCAIN VOTE
	McCain	68,181	72%		1		68,181	42,558
47	Obama	5,102	40%	0		5,102		
	McCain	7,551	59%		1		7,551	2,449
48	Obama	271,866	59%	1		271,866		
	McCain	186,079	41%		0		186,079	85,787
49	Obama	59,081	60%	1		59,081		
	McCain	39,489	40%		0		39,489	19,592
50	Obama	342,527	62%	1		342,527		
	McCain	211,163	38%		0		211,163	131,364
51	Obama	102,217	48%	0		102,217		
	McCain	109,902	51%		1		109,902	7,685
52	Obama	243,994	54%	1		243,994		
	McCain	206,909	45%		0		206,909	37,085
53	Obama	113,552	47%	0		113,552		
	McCain	128,658	53%		1		128,658	15,106
54	Obama	13,201	40%	0		13,201		
	McCain	19,586	59%		1		19,586	6,385
55	Obama	19,394	26%	0		19,394		
	McCain	55,843	74%		1		55,843	36,449
56	Obama	102,413	50%	0		102,413		
	McCain	102,650	50%		1		102,650	237
57	Obama	99,140	48%	0		99,140		
	McCain	104,885	51%		1		104,885	5,745
58	Obama	35,578	34%	0		35,578		
	McCain	68,800	66%		1		68,800	33,222
59	Obama	66,830	56%	1		66,830		
	McCain	52,323	44%		0		52,323	14,507
60	Obama	17,644	36%	0		17,644		
	McCain	30,859	63%		1		30,859	13,215
61	Obama	4,572	28%	0		4,572		
	McCain	11,672	71%		1		11,672	7,100
62	Obama	2,787	30%	0		2,787		
	McCain	6,446	69%		1		6,446	3,659
63	Obama	1,299	25%	0		1,299		
	McCain	3,933	74%		1		3,933	2,634
64	Obama	127,474	53%	1		127,474		
	McCain	113,716	47%		0		113,716	13,758
65	Obama	5,303	37%	0		5,303		
	McCain	8,869	62%		1		8,869	3,566
66	Obama	7,158	27%	0		7,158		
	McCain	19,527	72%		1		19,527	12,369
67	Obama	2,858	26%	0		2,858		
	McCain	8,165	74%		1		8,165	5,307
Total		8,012,374		15	52	4,103,638	3,908,736	194,902

In Florida, mob rule Obama wins popular vote! McCain wins counties!

Mob rule difference 194,902

Obama % 0.512162563

McCain % 0.487837437

In column E total, Obama won fifteen counties whereas in column F total, McCain won fifty-two counties.

In the fifteen counties, the differences between Obama and McCain is in column I. Since McCain could not overtake the mob rule values, the difference in column I total is mob rule.

Especially notice the following counties in column G (counties #6, #43, and #50), where the differences are a six-digit number.

Illinois State #3

A	B	C	D	E	F	G	H	I
COUNTY NUMBER	NAMES	COUNTY VOTE	PERCENT	OBAMA COUNT	MCCAIN COUNT	OBAMA VOTE	MCCAIN VOTE	OBAMA - MCCAIN VOTE
1	Obama	11,700	38%	0		11,700		
	McCain	18,592	61%		1		18,592	6,892
2	Obama	2,189	56%	1		2,189		
	McCain	1,692	43%		0		1,692	497
3	Obama	3,832	49%	0		3,832		
	McCain	3,938	50%		1		3,938	106
4	Obama	11,324	51%	1		11,324		
	McCain	10,396	47%		0		10,396	928
5	Obama	985	39%	0		985		
	McCain	1,541	60%		1		1,541	556
6	Obama	8,872	52%	1		8,872		
	McCain	7,902	46%		0		7,902	970
7	Obama	1,421	53%	1		1,421		
	McCain	1,221	45%		0		1,221	200
8	Obama	3,956	52%	1		3,956		
	McCain	3,589	47%		0		3,589	367
9	Obama	2,690	50%	1		2,690		
	McCain	2,617	48%		0		2,617	73
10	Obama	48,351	58%	1		48,351		
	McCain	33,748	40%		0		33,748	14,603
11	Obama	898,655	85%	1		898,655		
	McCain	145,424	14%		0		145,424	753,231
12	Obama	6,912	46%	0		6,912		
	McCain	7,869	52%		1		7,869	957
13	Obama	3,737	45%	0		3,737		
	McCain	4,406	53%		1		4,406	669
14	Obama	2,423	38%	0		2,423		
	McCain	3,924	61%		1		3,924	1,501
15	Obama	7,653	44%	0		7,653		
	McCain	9,348	54%		1		9,348	1,695
16	Obama	11,704	51%	1		11,704		
	McCain	10,962	48%		0		10,962	742
17	Obama	684,318	67%	1		684,318		
	McCain	331,614	32%		0		331,614	352,704
18	Obama	3,877	43%	0		3,877		
	McCain	5,067	56%		1		5,067	1,190
19	Obama	2,052	39%	0		2,052		
	McCain	3,155	59%		1		3,155	1,103
20	Obama	25,765	57%	1		25,765		
	McCain	18,260	41%		0		18,260	7,505

A	B	C	D	E	F	G	H	I
COUNTY NUMBER	NAMES	COUNTY VOTE	PERCENT	OBAMA COUNT	MCCAIN COUNT	OBAMA VOTE	MCCAIN VOTE	OBAMA - MCCAIN VOTE
21	Obama	3,299	42%	0		3,299		
	McCain	4,345	56%		1		4,345	1,046
22	Obama	3,226	39%	0		3,226		
	McCain	5,001	60%		1		5,001	1,775
23	Obama	227,416	55%	1		227,416		
	McCain	182,860	44%		0		182,860	44,556
24	Obama	3,737	46%	0		3,737		
	McCain	4,393	53%		1		4,393	656
25	Obama	1,140	34%	0		1,140		
	McCain	2,136	64%		1		2,136	996
26	Obama	5,256	31%	0		5,256		
	McCain	11,313	67%		1		11,313	6,057
27	Obama	3,963	41%	0		3,963		
	McCain	5,493	57%		1		5,493	1,530
28	Obama	2,226	35%	0		2,226		
	McCain	4,075	64%		1		4,075	1,849
29	Obama	8,873	48%	0		8,873		
	McCain	9,390	51%		1		9,390	517
30	Obama	9,722	60%	1		9,722		
	McCain	6,244	38%		0		6,244	3,478
31	Obama	1,587	56%	1		1,587		
	McCain	1,211	42%		0		1,211	376
32	Obama	2,617	45%	0		2,617		
	McCain	3,048	53%		1		3,048	431
33	Obama	9,134	49%	0		9,134		
	McCain	9,144	49%		1		9,144	10
34	Obama	1,794	42%	0		1,794		
	McCain	2,353	55%		1		2,353	559
35	Obama	3,753	43%	0		3,753		
	McCain	4,778	55%		1		4,778	1,025
36	Obama	892	40%	0		892		
	McCain	1,330	59%		1		1,330	438
37	Obama	2,213	58%	1		2,213		
	McCain	1,540	41%		0		1,540	673
38	Obama	13,177	53%	1		13,177		
	McCain	11,247	46%		0		11,247	1,930
39	Obama	4,640	34%	0		4,640		
	McCain	8,686	64%		1		8,686	4,046
40	Obama	15,199	60%	1		15,199		
	McCain	9,665	38%		0		9,665	5,534
41	Obama	2,063	40%	0		2,063		
	McCain	2,963	58%		1		2,963	900
42	Obama	7,460	44%	0		7,460		
	McCain	9,293	54%		1		9,293	1,833
43	Obama	5,036	48%	0		5,036		
	McCain	5,320	50%		1		5,320	284
44	Obama	6,392	55%	1		6,392		
	McCain	5,163	44%		0		5,163	1,229
45	Obama	1,477	31%	0		1,477		
	McCain	3,138	67%		1		3,138	1,661
46	Obama	105,592	55%	1		105,592		
	McCain	84,223	44%		0		84,223	21,369
47	Obama	24,719	52%	1		24,719		
	McCain	22,508	47%		0		22,508	2,211
48	Obama	23,529	53%	1		23,529		
	McCain	20,675	46%		0		20,675	2,854
49	Obama	14,165	59%	1		14,165		
	McCain	9,396	39%		0		9,396	4,769
50	Obama	111,051	56%	1		111,051		
	McCain	85,284	43%		0		85,284	25,767

163

A	B	C	D	E	F	G	H	I
								OBAMA
COUNTY	NAMES	COUNTY	PERCENT	OBAMA	MCCAIN	OBAMA	MCCAIN	-
NUMBER		VOTE		COUNT	COUNT	VOTE	VOTE	MCCAIN VOTE
51	Obama	27,415	55%	1		27,415		
	McCain	21,855	44%		0		21,855	5,560
52	Obama	3,013	46%	0		3,013		
	McCain	3,401	52%		1		3,401	388
53	Obama	7,757	48%	0		7,757		
	McCain	8,243	51%		1		8,243	486
54	Obama	6,184	40%	0		6,184		
	McCain	9,180	59%		1		9,180	2,996
55	Obama	5,245	41%	0		5,245		
	McCain	7,424	58%		1		7,424	2,179
56	Obama	25,419	50%	1		25,419		
	McCain	24,901	49%		0		24,901	518
57	Obama	12,071	54%	1		12,071		
	McCain	9,879	44%		0		9,879	2,192
58	Obama	68,836	54%	1		68,836		
	McCain	57,059	45%		0		57,059	11,777
59	Obama	8,334	48%	0		8,334		
	McCain	8,687	50%		1		8,687	353
60	Obama	3,078	49%	0		3,078		
	McCain	3,142	50%		1		3,142	64
61	Obama	3,540	52%	1		3,540		
	McCain	3,139	46%		0		3,139	401
62	Obama	2,693	38%	0		2,693		
	McCain	4,371	61%		1		4,371	1,678
63	Obama	6,780	52%	1		6,780		
	McCain	6,047	47%		0		6,047	733
64	Obama	71,976	52%	1		71,976		
	McCain	64,595	47%		0		64,595	7,381
65	Obama	37,551	50%	1		37,551		
	McCain	36,657	49%		0		36,657	894
66	Obama	2,704	42%	0		2,704		
	McCain	3,672	57%		1		3,672	968
67	Obama	4,885	55%	1		4,885		
	McCain	3,830	44%		0		3,830	1,055
68	Obama	7,943	44%	0		7,943		
	McCain	9,870	55%		1		9,870	1,927
69	Obama	6,486	51%	1		6,486		
	McCain	6,141	48%		0		6,141	345
70	Obama	7,458	49%	0		7,458		
	McCain	7,585	49%		1		7,585	127
71	Obama	2,663	43%	0		2,663		
	McCain	3,466	55%		1		3,466	803
72	Obama	11,247	45%	0		11,247		
	McCain	13,131	53%		1		13,131	1,884
73	Obama	44,396	57%	1		44,396		
	McCain	33,018	42%		0		33,018	11,378
74	Obama	4,697	47%	0		4,697		
	McCain	5,077	51%		1		5,077	380
75	Obama	3,856	43%	0		3,856		
	McCain	4,988	55%		1		4,988	1,132
76	Obama	3,021	40%	0		3,021		
	McCain	4,451	58%		1		4,451	1,430
77	Obama	842	38%	0		842		
	McCain	1,339	60%		1		1,339	497
78	Obama	1,636	50%	1		1,636		
	McCain	1,592	49%		0		1,592	44
79	Obama	1,900	57%	1		1,900		
	McCain	1,376	41%		0		1,376	524
80	Obama	7,387	49%	0		7,387		
	McCain	7,536	50%		1		7,536	149

A COUNTY NUMBER	B NAMES	C COUNTY VOTE	D PERCENT	E OBAMA COUNT	F MCCAIN COUNT	G OBAMA VOTE	H MCCAIN VOTE	I OBAMA - MCCAIN VOTE
81	Obama	3,177	42%	0		3,177		
	McCain	4,320	57%		1		4,320	1,143
82	Obama	42,175	62%	1		42,175		
	McCain	25,338	37%		0		25,338	16,837
83	Obama	5,082	45%	0		5,082		
	McCain	6,096	53%		1		6,096	1,014
84	Obama	51,176	51%	1		51,176		
	McCain	46,857	47%		0		46,857	4,319
85	Obama	1,896	50%	1		1,896		
	McCain	1,830	48%		0		1,830	66
86	Obama	1,090	42%	0		1,090		
	McCain	1,453	56%		1		1,453	363
87	Obama	4,236	39%	0		4,236		
	McCain	6,390	59%		1		6,390	2,154
88	Obama	77,896	62%	1		77,896		
	McCain	47,005	37%		0		47,005	30,891
89	Obama	1,357	47%	0		1,357		
	McCain	1,513	52%		1		1,513	156
90	Obama	11,010	52%	1		11,010		
	McCain	9,686	46%		0		9,686	1,324
91	Obama	29,335	46%	0		29,335		
	McCain	33,203	52%		1		33,203	3,868
92	Obama	3,916	43%	0		3,916		
	McCain	4,999	55%		1		4,999	1,083
93	Obama	16,228	49%	0		16,228		
	McCain	16,046	49%		1		16,046	182
94	Obama	2,462	43%	0		2,462		
	McCain	3,252	56%		1		3,252	790
95	Obama	4,286	54%	1		4,286		
	McCain	3,637	45%		0		3,637	649
96	Obama	3,338	42%	0		3,338		
	McCain	4,468	57%		1		4,468	1,130
97	Obama	2,545	32%	0		2,545		
	McCain	5,381	67%		1		5,381	2,836
98	Obama	3,315	45%	0		3,315		
	McCain	3,985	54%		1		3,985	670
99	Obama	15,587	58%	1	1	15,587		
	McCain	10,867	41%		0		10,867	4,720
100	Obama	154,691	56%	1		154,691		
	McCain	119,049	43%		0		119,049	35,642
101	Obama	12,893	42%	0		12,893		
	McCain	17,351	56%		1		17,351	4,458
102	Obama	69,903	55%	1		69,903		
	McCain	53,806	43%		0		53,806	16,097
103	Obama	6,969	36%	0		6,969		
	McCain	12,137	63%		1		12,137	5,168
Total		5,269,141		45	58	3,293,340	1,975,801	1,317,539

In Illinois, mob rule Obama wins popular vote! McCain wins counties!

Mob rule difference 1,317,539

Obama % 0.625024079

McCain % 0.374975921

In column E total, Obama won forty-five counties whereas in column F total, McCain won fifty-eight counties.

In the forty-five counties, the differences between Obama and McCain is in column I. Since McCain could not overtake the mob rule values, the difference in column I total is mob rule.

Especially notice the following counties column G (counties #11 and #17), where the differences are a six-digit number.

Indiana State #4

A	b	c	d	e	f	g	h	I
COUNTY number	NAMES	COUNTY VOTE	PERCENT	OBAMA COUNT	MCCAIN COUNT	OBAMA VOTE	MCCAIN VOTE	OBAMA - MCCAIN VOTE
1	Obama	4,928	37%	0		4,928		
	McCain	8,402	62%		1		8,402	3,474
2	Obama	71,083	47%	0		71,083		
	McCain	77,668	52%		1		77,668	6,585
3	Obama	13,555	44%	0		13,555		
	McCain	17,061	55%		1		17,061	3,506
4	Obama	1,563	41%	0		1,563		
	McCain	2,180	57%		1		2,180	617
5	Obama	2,677	49%	0		2,677		
	McCain	2,690	50%		1		2,690	13
6	Obama	9,744	37%	0		9,744		
	McCain	16,616	62%		1		16,616	6,872
7	Obama	3,852	48%	0		3,852		
	McCain	4,060	50%		1		4,060	208
8	Obama	3,733	43%	0		3,733		
	McCain	4,845	56%		1		4,845	1,112
9	Obama	6,995	45%	0		6,995		
	McCain	8,339	53%		1		8,339	1,344
10	Obama	21,918	46%	0		21,918		
	McCain	25,299	53%		1		25,299	3,381
11	Obama	4,954	44%	0		4,954		
	McCain	6,264	55%		1		6,264	1,310
12	Obama	5,306	43%	0		5,306		
	McCain	6,915	56%		1		6,915	1,609
13	Obama	2,286	48%	0		2,286		
	McCain	2,393	51%		1		2,393	107
14	Obama	3,369	32%	0		3,369		

A COUNTY number	b NAMES	c COUNTY VOTE	d PERCENT	e OBAMA COUNT	f MCCAIN COUNT	g OBAMA VOTE	h MCCAIN VOTE	I OBAMA - MCCAIN VOTE
	McCain	7,096	67%		1		7,096	3,727
15	Obama	7,123	32%	0		7,123		
16	McCain	14,886	67%		1		14,886	7,763
	Obama	3,890	37%	0		3,890		
17	McCain	6,443	62%		1		6,443	2,553
	Obama	7,169	42%	0		7,169		
18	McCain	9,771	57%		1		9,771	2,602
	Obama	28,356	57%	1		28,356		
19	McCain	20,904	42%		0		20,904	7,452
	Obama	8,748	47%	0		8,748		
20	McCain	9,526	51%		1		9,526	778
	Obama	31,289	44%	0		31,289		
21	McCain	39,344	55%		1		39,344	8,055
	Obama	4,387	46%	0		4,387		
22	McCain	4,917	52%		1		4,917	530
	Obama	16,248	44%	0		16,248		
23	McCain	19,944	55%		1		19,944	3,696
	Obama	3,094	42%	0		3,094		
24	McCain	4,151	56%		1		4,151	1,057
	Obama	3,404	32%	0		3,404		
25	McCain	7,017	66%		1		7,017	3,613
	Obama	3,700	41%	0		3,700		
26	McCain	5,145	57%		1		5,145	1,445
	Obama	6,455	43%	0		6,455		
27	McCain	8,449	56%		1		8,449	1,994
	Obama	11,291	43%	0		11,291		
28	McCain	14,726	56%		1		14,726	3,435
	Obama	5,709	42%	0		5,709		
29	McCain	7,689	56%		1		7,689	1,980
	Obama	49,691	38%	0		49,691		
30	McCain	78,391	61%		1		78,391	28,700
	Obama	11,869	35%	0		11,869		
31	McCain	21,991	64%		1		21,991	10,122
	Obama	7,271	40%	0		7,271		
32	McCain	10,529	59%		1		10,529	3,258
	Obama	24,394	38%	0		24,394		
33	McCain	39,578	61%		1		39,578	15,184
	Obama	10,058	47%	0		10,058		
34	McCain	10,894	51%		1		10,894	836
	Obama	17,803	46%	0		17,803		
35	McCain	20,207	53%		1		20,207	2,404
	Obama	5,842	36%	0		5,842		
36	McCain	10,289	63%		1		10,289	4,447
	Obama	7,445	42%	0		7,445		
37	McCain	9,852	56%		1		9,852	2,407
	Obama	5,044	39%	0		5,044		
38	McCain	7,669	60%		1		7,669	2,625
	Obama	3,746	45%	0		3,746		
39	McCain	4,400	53%		1		4,400	654
	Obama	6,255	47%	0		6,255		
40	McCain	7,052	52%		1		7,052	797
	Obama	5,302	45%	0		5,302		
41	McCain	6,257	53%		1		6,257	955
	Obama	21,536	37%	0		21,536		
42	McCain	36,471	62%		1		36,471	14,935
	Obama	7,569	46%	0		7,569		
43	McCain	8,639	53%		1		8,639	1,070
	Obama	9,229	31%	0		9,229		
44	McCain	20,484	68%		1		20,484	11,255
	Obama	3,659	39%	0		3,659		
	McCain	5,697	60%		1		5,697	2,038

A	b	c	d	e	f	g	h	I
COUNTY number	NAMES	COUNTY VOTE	PERCENT	OBAMA COUNT	MCCAIN COUNT	OBAMA VOTE	MCCAIN VOTE	OBAMA - MCCAIN VOTE
45	Obama	138,603	67%	1		138,603		
	McCain	67,417	32%		0		67,417	71,186
46	Obama	28,247	60%	1		28,247		
	McCain	17,911	38%		0		17,911	10,336
47	Obama	7,208	39%	0		7,208		
	McCain	11,018	59%		1		11,018	3,810
48	Obama	30,152	53%	0		30,152		
	McCain	26,403	46%		1		26,403	3,749
49	Obama	237,275	64%	1		237,275		
	McCain	131,459	35%		0		131,459	105,816
50	Obama	7,880	43%	0		7,880		
	McCain	10,401	56%		1		10,401	2,521
51	Obama	1,706	35%	0		1,706		
	McCain	3,112	64%		1		3,112	1,406
52	Obama	5,559	39%	0		5,559		
	McCain	8,305	59%		1		8,305	2,746
53	Obama	41,332	66%	1		41,332		
	McCain	21,083	33%		0		21,083	20,249
54	Obama	6,005	40%	0		6,005		
	McCain	9,055	59%		1		9,055	3,050
55	Obama	10,314	36%	0		10,314		
	McCain	18,105	63%		1		18,105	7,791
56	Obama	2,623	43%	0		2,623		
	McCain	3,300	55%		1		3,300	677
57	Obama	7,063	42%	0		7,063		
	McCain	9,671	57%		1		9,671	2,608
58	Obama	1,158	40%	0		1,158		
	McCain	1,712	59%		1		1,712	554
59	Obama	3,390	42%	0		3,390		
	McCain	4,536	56%		1		4,536	1,146
60	Obama	3,570	44%	0		3,570		
	McCain	4,415	54%		1		4,415	845
61	Obama	2,913	42%	0		2,913		
	McCain	3,900	56%		1		3,900	987
62	Obama	5,140	60%	1		5,140		
	McCain	3,201	38%		0		3,201	1,939
63	Obama	2,700	45%	0		2,700		
	McCain	3,221	53%		1		3,221	521
64	Obama	39,046	53%	1		39,046		
	McCain	33,796	46%		0		33,796	5,250
65	Obama	5,820	46%	0		5,820		
	McCain	6,794	53%		1		6,794	974
66	Obama	2,466	41%	0		2,466		
	McCain	3,368	57%		1		3,368	902
67	Obama	6,331	43%	0		6,331		
	McCain	8,085	55%		1		8,085	1,754
68	Obama	4,839	45%	0		4,839		
	McCain	5,787	53%		1		5,787	948
69	Obama	4,187	34%	0		4,187		
	McCain	7,794	64%		1		7,794	3,607
70	Obama	3,228	42%	0		3,228		
	McCain	4,270	56%		1		4,270	1,042
71	Obama	4,268	48%	0		4,268		
	McCain	4,443	50%		1		4,443	175
72	Obama	6,983	40%	0		6,983		
	McCain	10,330	59%		1		10,330	3,347
73	Obama	5,037	50%	1		5,037		
	McCain	4,998	49%		0		4,998	39
74	Obama	68,708	58%	1		68,708		
	McCain	48,510	41%		0		48,510	20,198
75	Obama	4,778	51%	1		4,778		

A COUNTY number	b NAMES	c COUNTY VOTE	d PERCENT	e OBAMA COUNT	f MCCAIN COUNT	g OBAMA VOTE	h MCCAIN VOTE	I OBAMA - MCCAIN VOTE
	McCain	4,473	47%		0		4,473	305
76	Obama	6,283	45%	0		6,283		
	McCain	7,670	54%		1		7,670	1,387
77	Obama	4,282	49%	0		4,282		
	McCain	4,341	49%		1		4,341	59
78	Obama	1,638	45%	0		1,638		
	McCain	1,940	53%		1		1,940	302
79	Obama	37,709	55%	1		37,709		
	McCain	29,789	44%		0		29,789	7,920
80	Obama	3,250	41%	0		3,250		
	McCain	4,452	57%		1		4,452	1,202
81	Obama	1,220	36%	0		1,220		
	McCain	2,058	62%		1		2,058	838
82	Obama	39,368	51%	1		39,368		
	McCain	37,449	48%		0		37,449	1,919
83	Obama	4,002	56%	1		4,002		
	McCain	3,004	42%		0		3,004	998
84	Obama	25,023	57%	1		25,023		
	McCain	18,111	42%		0		18,111	6,912
85	Obama	5,455	39%	0		5,455		
	McCain	8,238	60%		1		8,238	2,783
86	Obama	1,753	44%	0		1,753		
	McCain	2,164	54%		1		2,164	411
87	Obama	12,329	43%	0		12,329	0	
	McCain	16,013	56%		1		16,013	3,684
88	Obama	4,561	40%	0		4,561	0	
	McCain	6,512	58%		1		6,512	1,951
89	Obama	13,459	47%	0		13,459	0	
	McCain	14,558	51%		1		14,558	1,099
90	Obama	4,403	34%	0		4,403	0	
	McCain	8,503	65%		1		8,503	4,100
91	Obama	4,839	45%	0		4,839	0	
	McCain	5,730	53%		1		5,730	891
92	Obama	5,861	39%	0		5,861	0	
	McCain	9,122	60%		1	0	9,122	3,261
Total		2,709,170		14	78	1,367,503	1,341,667	25,836

In Indiana, mob rule Obama wins popular vote!!! Mccain wins counties!!!

Mob rule difference 25,836

Obama % 0.50476825

McCain % 0.49523175

In column E total, Obama won fourteen counties whereas in column F total, McCain won seventy-eight counties.

In the fourteen counties, the differences between Obama and McCain is in column I. Since McCain could not overtake the mob rule values, the difference in column I total is mob rule. Especially notice the following county in column G, county #49, where the differences is a six-digit number.

Maryland State # 5

A	B	C	D	E	F	G	H	I
COUNTY NUMBER	NAMES	COUNTY VOTE	PERCENT	OBAMA COUNT	MCCAIN COUNT	OBAMA VOTE	MCCAIN VOTE	OBAMA - MCCAIN VOTE
1	Obama	9,824	36%	0		9,824		
	McCain	17,193	62%		1		17,193	7,369
2	Obama	113,963	48%	0		113,963		
	McCain	119,956	51%		1		119,956	5,993
3	Obama	190,991	56%	1		190,991		
	McCain	145,991	43%		0		145,991	45,000
4	Obama	197,262	88%	1		197,262		
	McCain	26,131	12%		0		26,131	171,131
5	Obama	18,382	46%	0		18,382		
	McCain	21,089	53%		1		21,089	2,707
6	Obama	4,538	37%	0		4,538		
	McCain	7,528	62%		1		7,528	2,990
7	Obama	25,798	33%	0		25,798		
	McCain	51,308	65%		1		51,308	25,510
8	Obama	16,331	41%	0		16,331		
	McCain	22,315	57%		1		22,315	5,984
9	Obama	40,127	63%	1		40,127		
	McCain	23,441	37%		0		23,441	16,686
10	Obama	6,272	45%	0		6,272		
	McCain	7,510	54%		1		7,510	1,238
11	Obama	48,842	48%	0		48,842		
	McCain	51,145	50%		1		51,145	2,303
12	Obama	3,285	28%	0		3,285		
	McCain	8,209	71%		1		8,209	4,924
13	Obama	44,479	39%	0		44,479		
	McCain	66,507	59%		1		66,507	22,028
14	Obama	77,800	60%	1		77,800		
	McCain	50,447	39%		0		50,447	27,353
15	Obama	4,397	49%	0		4,397		
	McCain	4,401	49%		1		4,401	4
16	Obama	271,132	71%	1		271,132		
	McCain	105,088	28%		0		105,088	166,044
17	Obama	247,464	89%	1		247,464		
	McCain	29,269	11%		0		29,269	218,195
18	Obama	7,704	36%	0		7,704		
	McCain	13,715	63%		1		13,715	6,011
19	Obama	4,356	48%	0		4,356		
	McCain	4,622	51%		1		4,622	266
20	Obama	17,056	43%	0		17,056		
	McCain	22,531	56%		1		22,531	5,475
21	Obama	7,702	44%	0		7,702		
	McCain	9,599	55%		1		9,599	1,897
22	Obama	23,953	42%	0		23,953		
	McCain	31,715	56%		1		31,715	7,762
23	Obama	17,455	46%	0		17,455		
	McCain	19,823	53%		1		19,823	2,368

A	B	C	D	E	F	G	H	I
COUNTY NUMBER	NAMES	COUNTY VOTE	PERCENT	OBAMA COUNT	MCCAIN COUNT	OBAMA VOTE	MCCAIN VOTE	OBAMA - MCCAIN VOTE
24	Obama	10,037	42%	0		10,037		
	McCain	13,787	57%		1		13,787	3,750
Total		2,282,470		6	18	1,409,150	873,320	535,830

In Maryland, mob rule Obama wins popular vote! McCain wins counties!

Mob rule difference 535,830

Obama % 0.617379

McCain % 0.382621

In column E total, Obama won six counties whereas in column F total, McCain won eighteen counties.

In the six counties, the differences between Obama and McCain is in column I. Since McCain could not over take the mob rule values, the difference in column I total is mob rule.

Especially notice the following counties in column G (counties #3, #4, #7, #16, and #17), where the differences are equal or greater than five numbers.

Minnesota State # 6

A	B	C	D	E	F	G	H	I
COUNTY NUMBER	NAMES	COUNTY VOTE	PERCENT	OBAMA COUNT	MCCAIN COUNT	OBAMA VOTE	MCCAIN VOTE	OBAMA - MCCAIN VOTE
1	Obama	4,601	49%	1		4,601		
	McCain	4,591	49%		0		4,591	10
2	Obama	86,977	48%	0		86,977		
	McCain	91,357	50%		1		91,357	4,380
3	Obama	7,687	46%	0		7,687		
	McCain	8,851	52%		1		8,851	1,164
4	Obama	12,019	54%	1		12,019		
	McCain	9,762	44%		0		9,762	2,257
5	Obama	8,452	44%	0		8,452		

171

A	B	C	D	E	F	G	H	I
COUNTY NUMBER	NAMES	COUNTY VOTE	PERCENT	OBAMA COUNT	MCCAIN COUNT	OBAMA VOTE	MCCAIN VOTE	OBAMA - MCCAIN VOTE
	McCain	10,338	54%		1		10,338	1,886
6	Obama	1,552	52%	1		1,552		
	McCain	1,362	46%		0		1,362	190
7	Obama	19,325	55%	1		19,325		
	McCain	14,782	42%		0		14,782	4,543
8	Obama	5,808	43%	0		5,808		
	McCain	7,454	55%		1		7,454	1,646
9	Obama	11,501	63%	1		11,501		
	McCain	6,549	36%		0		6,549	4,952
10	Obama	20,653	42%	0		20,653		
	McCain	28,158	57%		1		28,158	7,505
11	Obama	7,276	45%	0		7,276		
	McCain	8,660	53%		1		8,660	1,384
12	Obama	3,277	52%	1		3,277		
	McCain	2,906	46%		0		2,906	371
13	Obama	12,782	44%	0		12,782		
	McCain	15,788	54%		1		15,788	3,006
14	Obama	16,666	57%	1		16,666		
	McCain	11,978	41%		0		11,978	4,688
15	Obama	1,877	44%	0		1,877		
	McCain	2,291	54%		1		2,291	414
16	Obama	2,019	61%	1		2,019		
	McCain	1,240	37%		0		1,240	779
17	Obama	2,759	46%	0		2,759		
	McCain	3,157	53%		1		3,157	398
18	Obama	15,859	45%	0		15,859		
	McCain	18,566	53%		1		18,566	2,707
19	Obama	116,774	52%	1		116,774		
	McCain	104,363	47%		0		104,363	12,411
20	Obama	4,463	44%	0		4,463		
	McCain	5,468	54%		1		5,468	1,005
21	Obama	9,255	45%	0		9,255		
	McCain	11,241	54%		1		11,241	1,986
22	Obama	3,736	46%	0		3,736		
	McCain	4,197	52%		1		4,197	461
23	Obama	5,921	53%	1		5,921		
	McCain	4,993	45%		0		4,993	928
24	Obama	9,915	58%	1		9,915		
	McCain	6,955	40%		0		6,955	2,960
25	Obama	12,420	49%	0		12,420		
	McCain	12,775	50%		1		12,775	355
26	Obama	1,850	52%	1		1,850		
	McCain	1,646	46%		0		1,646	204
27	Obama	420,896	64%	1		420,896		
	McCain	231,024	35%		0		231,024	189,872
28	Obama	5,906	55%	1		5,906		
	McCain	4,743	44%		0		4,743	1,163
29	Obama	4,872	42%	0		4,872		
	McCain	6,559	57%		1		6,559	1,687
30	Obama	8,248	41%	0		8,248		
	McCain	11,325	57%		1		11,325	3,077
31	Obama	13,461	55%	1		13,461		
	McCain	10,309	43%		0		10,309	3,152
32	Obama	2,618	47%	0		2,618		
	McCain	2,858	51%		1		2,858	240
33	Obama	3,742	44%	0		3,742		
	McCain	4,479	53%		1		4,479	737
34	Obama	10,123	47%	0		10,123		
	McCain	11,318	52%		1		11,318	1,195
35	Obama	1,492	58%	1		1,492		

10TH AMENDMENT

A	B	C	D	E	F	G	H	I
COUNTY NUMBER	NAMES	COUNTY VOTE	PERCENT	OBAMA COUNT	MCCAIN COUNT	OBAMA VOTE	MCCAIN VOTE	OBAMA - MCCAIN VOTE
	McCain	1,016	40%		0		1,016	476
36	Obama	3,649	54%	1		3,649		
	McCain	2,962	44%		0		2,962	687
37	Obama	2,160	52%	1		2,160		
	McCain	1,913	46%		0		1,913	247
38	Obama	4,174	60%	1		4,174		
	McCain	2,636	38%		0		2,636	1,538
39	Obama	971	42%	0		971		
	McCain	1,278	56%		1		1,278	307
40	Obama	6,994	47%	0		6,994		
	McCain	7,636	51%		1		7,636	642
41	Obama	1,517	49%	1		1,517		
	McCain	1,491	48%		0		1,491	26
42	Obama	6,110	48%	0		6,110		
	McCain	6,315	50%		1		6,315	205
43	Obama	1,436	62%	1		1,436		
	McCain	843	36%		0		843	593
44	Obama	2,311	49%	0		2,311		
	McCain	2,285	49%		1		2,285	26
45	Obama	4,413	41%	0		4,413		
	McCain	6,053	57%		1		6,053	1,640
46	Obama	7,505	40%	0		7,505		
	McCain	10,993	58%		1		10,993	3,488
47	Obama	5,379	43%	0		5,379		
	McCain	6,737	54%		1		6,737	1,358
48	Obama	6,073	45%	0		6,073		
	McCain	7,049	52%		1		7,049	976
49	Obama	6,547	39%	0		6,547		
	McCain	9,734	58%		1		9,734	3,187
50	Obama	11,605	61%	1		11,605		
	McCain	7,075	37%		0		7,075	4,530
51	Obama	2,345	49%	0		2,345		
	McCain	2,320	48%		1		2,320	25
52	Obama	9,887	55%	1		9,887		
	McCain	7,968	44%		0		7,968	1,919
53	Obama	4,244	49%	0		4,244		
	McCain	4,368	50%		1		4,368	124
54	Obama	2,129	62%	1		2,129		
	McCain	1,204	35%		0		1,204	925
55	Obama	38,711	51%	1		38,711		
	McCain	36,202	48%		0		36,202	2,509
56	Obama	13,856	43%	0		13,856		
	McCain	18,077	56%		1		18,077	4,221
57	Obama	3,394	50%	1		3,394		
	McCain	3,248	48%		0		3,248	146
58	Obama	7,084	50%	1		7,084		
	McCain	6,862	48%		0		6,862	222
59	Obama	2,021	42%	0		2,021		
	McCain	2,652	56%		1		2,652	631
60	Obama	7,849	52%	1		7,849		
	McCain	7,148	47%		0		7,148	701
61	Obama	3,317	51%	1		3,317		
	McCain	3,068	47%		0		3,068	249
62	Obama	182,972	66%	1		182,972		
	McCain	88,942	32%		0		88,942	94,030
63	Obama	1,119	52%	1		1,119		
	McCain	983	45%		0		983	136
64	Obama	3,250	42%	0		3,250		
	McCain	4,308	55%		1		4,308	1,058
65	Obama	3,904	48%	0		3,904		

A	B	C	D	E	F	G	H	I
COUNTY NUMBER	NAMES	COUNTY VOTE	PERCENT	OBAMA COUNT	MCCAIN COUNT	OBAMA VOTE	MCCAIN VOTE	OBAMA - MCCAIN VOTE
	McCain	3,956	49%		1		3,956	52
66	Obama	17,381	55%	1		17,381		
	McCain	13,723	43%		0		13,723	3,658
67	Obama	2,078	42%	0		2,078		
	McCain	2,773	56%		1		2,773	695
68	Obama	3,096	41%	0		3,096		
	McCain	4,437	58%		1		4,437	1,341
69	Obama	29,209	44%	0		29,209		
	McCain	36,726	55%		1		36,726	7,517
70	Obama	17,960	40%	0		17,960		
	McCain	26,143	58%		1		26,143	8,183
71	Obama	2,998	39%	0		2,998		
	McCain	4,492	59%		1		4,492	1,494
72	Obama	77,330	66%	1		77,330		
	McCain	38,732	33%		0		38,732	38,598
73	Obama	35,690	46%	0		35,690		
	McCain	41,194	53%		1		41,194	5,504
74	Obama	9,016	46%	0		9,016		
	McCain	10,068	52%		1		10,068	1,052
75	Obama	2,780	50%	1		2,780		
	McCain	2,710	48%		0		2,710	70
76	Obama	2,907	56%	1		2,907		
	McCain	2,184	42%		0		2,184	723
77	Obama	5,277	43%	0		5,277		
	McCain	6,637	54%		1		6,637	1,360
78	Obama	1,041	51%	1		1,041		
	McCain	933	46%		0		933	108
79	Obama	5,646	48%	0		5,646		
	McCain	5,935	50%		1		5,935	289
80	Obama	2,882	40%	0		2,882		
	McCain	4,127	58%		1		4,127	1,245
81	Obama	4,401	45%	0		4,401		
	McCain	5,212	53%		1		5,212	811
82	Obama	70,281	52%	1		70,281		
	McCain	64,335	47%		0		64,335	5,946
83	Obama	2,562	49%	1		2,562		
	McCain	2,526	48%		0		2,526	36
84	Obama	1,550	46%	0		1,550		
	McCain	1,786	53%		1		1,786	236
85	Obama	16,308	59%	1		16,308		
	McCain	10,974	40%		0		10,974	5,334
86	Obama	26,343	40%	0		26,343		
	McCain	37,779	58%		1		37,779	11,436
87	Obama	2,816	51%	1		2,816		
	McCain	2,579	46%		0		2,579	237
Total		2,848,630		39	48	1,573,260	1,275,370	297,890

In Minnesota, mob rule Obama wins popular vote! McCain wins counties!

Mob rule difference 297,890

Obama % 0.5522865

McCain % 0.4477135

In column E total, Obama won thirty-nine counties whereas in column F total, McCain won forty-eight counties.

In the thirty-nine counties, the differences between Obama and McCain is in column I. Since McCain could not overtake the mob rule values, the difference in column I total is mob rule.

Especially notice the following county in column G, county #27, where the difference is a six-digit number.

Nevada State # 7

A	B	C	D	E	F	G	H	I
COUNTY NUMBEr	NAMES	COUNTY VOTE	PERCENT	OBAMA COUNT	MCCAIN COUNT	OBAMA VOTE	MCCAIN VOTE	OBAMA - MCCAIN VOTE
1	Obama	11,622	49%	1		11,622		
	McCain	11,419	48%		0		11,419	203
2	Obama	3,494	33%	0		3,494		
	McCain	6,831	65%		1		6,831	3,337
3	Obama	379,204	58%	1		379,204		
	McCain	256,401	40%		0		256,401	122,803
4	Obama	10,671	41%	0		10,671		
	McCain	14,645	57%		1		14,645	3,974
5	Obama	4,537	28%	0		4,537		
	McCain	10,958	68%		1		10,958	6,421
6	Obama	104	23%	0		104		
	McCain	303	68%		1		303	199
7	Obama	144	19%	0		144		
	McCain	564	76%		1		564	420
8	Obama	1,909	34%	0		1,909		
	McCain	3,584	63%		1		3,584	1,675
9	Obama	574	27%	0		574		
	McCain	1,462	70%		1		1,462	888
10	Obama	518	24%	0		518		
	McCain	1,498	71%		1		1,498	980
11	Obama	8,405	40%	0		8,405		
	McCain	12,154	58%		1		12,154	3,749
12	Obama	1,082	47%	0		1,082		
	McCain	1,131	49%		1		1,131	49
13	Obama	7,223	41%	0		7,223		
	McCain	9,535	55%		1		9,535	2,312
14	Obama	673	37%	0		673		
	McCain	1,075	59%		1		1,075	402
15	Obama	1,099	46%	0		1,099		
	McCain	1,245	52%		1		1,245	146
16	Obama	99,395	55%	1		99,395		
	McCain	76,743	43%		0		76,743	22,652
17	Obama	1,230	32%	0		1,230		
	McCain	2,440	63%		1		2,440	1,210
Total		943,872		3	14	531,884	411,988	119,896

In Nevada, mob rule Obama wins popular vote! McCain wins counties!

Mob rule difference 119,896

Obama % 0.563512849

McCain % 0.436487151

In column E total, Obama won three counties whereas in column F total, McCain won fourteen counties.

In the fifteen counties, the differences between Obama and McCain is in column I. Since McCain could not overtake the mob rule values, the difference in column I total is mob rule.

Especially notice the following county in column G, county #3, where the differences is a six-digit number.

North Carolina State #8

A	B	C	D	E	F	G	H	I
COUNTY NUMBER	NAMES	COUNTY VOTE	PERCENT	OBAMA COUNT	MCCAIN COUNT	OBAMA VOTE	MCCAIN VOTE	OBAMA - MCCAIN VOTE
1	McCain	34,501	54%		1		34,501	
	Obama	28,590	45%	0		28,590		5,911
2	McCain	11,747	69%		1		11,747	
	Obama	5,153	30%	0		5,153		6,594
3	McCain	3,117	60%		1		3,117	
	Obama	2,017	39%	0		2,017		1,100
4	McCain	4,067	39%		0		4,067	
	Obama	6,293	61%	1		6,293		2,226
5	McCain	7,885	61%		1		7,885	
	Obama	4,861	38%	0		4,861		3,024
6	McCain	5,619	72%		1		5,619	
	Obama	2,163	28%	0		2,163		3,456
7	McCain	13,437	59%		1		13,437	
	Obama	9,426	41%	0		9,426		4,011
8	McCain	3,338	35%		0		3,338	
	Obama	6,248	65%	1		6,248		2,910
9	McCain	7,530	49%		0		7,530	
	Obama	7,846	51%	1		7,846		316
10	McCain	30,662	59%		1		30,662	
	Obama	21,280	41%	0		21,280		9,382
11	McCain	52,236	42%		0		52,236	
	Obama	69,415	57%	1		69,415		17,179

A	B	C	D	E	F	G	H	I
COUNTY NUMBER	NAMES	COUNTY VOTE	PERCENT	OBAMA COUNT	MCCAIN COUNT	OBAMA VOTE	MCCAIN VOTE	OBAMA - MCCAIN VOTE
12	McCain	21,766	59%		1		21,766	
	Obama	14,623	40%	0		14,623		7,143
13	McCain	45,340	59%		1		45,340	
	Obama	31,191	40%	0		31,191		14,149
14	McCain	22,397	64%		1		22,397	
	Obama	12,007	35%	0		12,007		10,390
15	McCain	3,118	66%		1		3,118	
	Obama	1,587	33%	0		1,587		1,531
16	McCain	22,868	67%		1		22,868	
	Obama	11,079	32%	0		11,079		11,789
17	McCain	5,177	48%		0		5,177	
	Obama	5,466	51%	1		5,466		289
18	McCain	42,843	62%		1		42,843	
	Obama	25,535	37%	0		25,535		17,308
19	McCain	14,591	45%		0		14,591	
	Obama	17,783	54%	1		17,783		3,192
20	McCain	8,591	69%		1		8,591	
	Obama	3,748	30%	0		3,748		4,843
21	McCain	3,751	51%		1		3,751	
	Obama	3,652	49%	0		3,652		99
22	McCain	3,692	67%		1		3,692	
	Obama	1,731	32%	0		1,731		1,961
23	McCain	25,950	60%		1		25,950	
	Obama	17,274	40%	0		17,274		8,676
24	McCain	12,998	54%		1		12,998	
	Obama	11,088	46%	0		11,088		1,910
25	McCain	23,163	57%		1		23,163	
	Obama	17,335	43%	0		17,335		5,828
26	McCain	51,596	41%		0		51,596	
	Obama	73,926	59%	1		73,926		22,330
27	McCain	7,159	65%		1		7,159	
	Obama	3,685	34%	0		3,685		3,474
28	McCain	9,621	55%		1		9,621	
	Obama	7,760	44%	0		7,760		1,861
29	McCain	45,135	66%		1		45,135	
	Obama	22,192	33%	0		22,192		22,943
30	McCain	13,846	69%		1		13,846	
	Obama	6,102	30%	0		6,102		7,744
31	McCain	10,734	55%		1		10,734	
	Obama	8,866	45%	0		8,866		1,868
32	McCain	32,040	24%		0		32,040	
	Obama	102,237	76%	1		102,237		70,197
33	McCain	8,416	33%		0		8,416	
	Obama	17,365	67%	1		17,365		8,949
34	McCain	73,304	44%		0		73,304	
	Obama	90,712	55%	1		90,712		17,408
35	McCain	12,883	49%		0		12,883	
	Obama	13,026	50%	1		13,026		143
36	McCain	52,220	62%		1		52,220	
	Obama	31,247	37%	0		31,247		20,973
37	McCain	2,546	47%		0		2,546	
	Obama	2,827	53%	1		2,827		281
38	McCain	2,824	68%		1		2,824	
	Obama	1,265	31%	0		1,265		1,559
39	McCain	11,375	46%		0		11,375	
	Obama	13,011	53%	1		13,011		1,636
40	McCain	4,258	53%		1		4,258	
	Obama	3,774	47%	0		3,774		484
41	McCain	97,511	41%		0		97,511	
	Obama	141,680	59%	1		141,680		44,169

A	B	C	D	E	F	G	H	I
COUNTY NUMBER	NAMES	COUNTY VOTE	PERCENT	OBAMA COUNT	MCCAIN COUNT	OBAMA VOTE	MCCAIN VOTE	OBAMA - MCCAIN VOTE
42	McCain	8,867	36%		0		8,867	
	Obama	15,726	64%	1		15,726		6,859
43	McCain	23,311	58%		1		23,311	
	Obama	16,519	41%	0		16,519		6,792
44	McCain	14,902	53%		1		14,902	
	Obama	12,724	46%	0		12,724		2,178
45	McCain	30,903	60%		1		30,903	
	Obama	20,062	39%	0		20,062		10,841
46	McCain	3,083	29%		0		3,083	
	Obama	7,479	71%	1		7,479		4,396
47	McCain	6,197	40%		0		6,197	
	Obama	9,133	59%	1		9,133		2,936
48	McCain	1,203	49%		0		1,203	
	Obama	1,225	50%	1		1,225		22
49	McCain	44,979	62%		1		44,979	
	Obama	27,201	37%	0		27,201		17,778
50	McCain	7,793	47%		0		7,793	
	Obama	8,671	52%	1		8,671		878
51	McCain	43,164	62%		1		43,164	
	Obama	26,475	38%	0		26,475		16,689
52	McCain	2,807	54%		1		2,807	
	Obama	2,364	46%	0		2,364		443
53	McCain	12,652	54%		1		12,652	
	Obama	10,703	45%	0		10,703		1,949
54	McCain	13,281	50%		1		13,281	
	Obama	13,157	50%	0		13,157		124
55	McCain	23,561	66%		1		23,561	
	Obama	11,674	33%	0		11,674		11,887
56	McCain	10,262	60%		1		10,262	
	Obama	6,603	39%	0		6,603		3,659
57	McCain	5,175	50%		1		5,175	
	Obama	5,011	49%	0		5,011		164
58	McCain	5,914	48%		0		5,914	
	Obama	6,488	52%	1		6,488		574
59	McCain	11,382	63%		1		11,382	
	Obama	6,514	36%	0		6,514		4,868
60	McCain	152,957	38%		0		152,957	
	Obama	252,642	62%	1		252,642		99,685
61	McCain	5,472	70%		1		5,472	
	Obama	2,220	29%	0		2,220		3,252
62	McCain	6,125	55%		1		6,125	
	Obama	4,870	44%	0		4,870		1,255
63	McCain	27,165	60%		1		27,165	
	Obama	17,534	39%	0		17,534		9,631
64	McCain	23,660	51%		1		23,660	
	Obama	23,013	49%	0		23,013		647
65	McCain	50,004	50%		1		50,004	
	Obama	48,588	49%	0		48,588		1,416
66	McCain	3,662	35%		0		3,662	
	Obama	6,893	65%	1		6,893		3,231
67	McCain	29,942	60%		1		29,942	
	Obama	19,296	39%	0		19,296		10,646
68	McCain	20,226	27%		0		20,226	
	Obama	53,712	72%	1		53,712		33,486
69	McCain	3,809	57%		1		3,809	
	Obama	2,820	42%	0		2,820		989
70	McCain	7,720	43%		0		7,720	
	Obama	10,170	57%	1		10,170		2,450
71	McCain	13,517	57%		1		13,517	
	Obama	9,832	42%	0		9,832		3,685

A	B	C	D	E	F	G	H	I
COUNTY NUMBER	NAMES	COUNTY VOTE	PERCENT	OBAMA COUNT	MCCAIN COUNT	OBAMA VOTE	MCCAIN VOTE	OBAMA - MCCAIN VOTE
72	McCain	3,674	57%		1		3,674	
	Obama	2,761	43%	0		2,761		913
73	McCain	10,007	54%		1		10,007	
	Obama	8,410	45%	0		8,410		1,597
74	McCain	33,429	46%		0		33,429	
	Obama	39,763	54%	1		39,763		6,334
75	McCain	6,511	57%		1		6,511	
	Obama	4,723	42%	0		4,723		1,788
76	McCain	40,644	71%		1		40,644	
	Obama	16,280	28%	0		16,280		24,364
77	McCain	9,317	49%		0		9,317	
	Obama	9,586	50%	1		9,586		269
78	McCain	16,561	43%		0		16,561	
	Obama	22,146	57%	1		22,146		5,585
79	McCain	22,435	57%		1		22,435	
	Obama	16,730	42%	0		16,730		5,705
80	McCain	37,284	61%		1		37,284	
	Obama	23,272	38%	0		23,272		14,012
81	McCain	18,631	65%		1		18,631	
	Obama	9,595	34%	0		9,595		9,036
82	McCain	13,952	54%		1		13,952	
	Obama	11,753	46%	0		11,753		2,199
83	McCain	5,972	42%		0		5,972	
	Obama	8,105	58%	1		8,105		2,133
84	McCain	19,193	68%		1		19,193	
	Obama	8,815	31%	0		8,815		10,378
85	McCain	14,335	67%		1		14,335	
	Obama	6,816	32%	0		6,816		7,519
86	McCain	18,453	64%		1		18,453	
	Obama	10,279	35%	0		10,279		8,174
87	McCain	2,896	50%		1		2,896	
	Obama	2,803	49%	0		2,803		93
88	McCain	9,257	56%		1		9,257	
	Obama	7,180	43%	0		7,180		2,077
89	McCain	959	50%		1		959	
	Obama	932	49%	0		932		27
90	McCain	53,721	63%		1		53,721	
	Obama	30,945	36%	0		30,945		22,776
91	McCain	7,584	37%		0		7,584	
	Obama	13,110	63%	1		13,110		5,526
92	McCain	183,291	42%		0		183,291	
	Obama	247,914	57%	1		247,914		64,623
93	McCain	2,992	31%		0		2,992	
	Obama	6,663	69%	1		6,663		3,671
94	McCain	2,667	42%		0		2,667	
	Obama	3,734	58%	1		3,734		1,067
95	McCain	13,303	47%		0		13,303	
	Obama	14,513	52%	1		14,513		1,210
96	McCain	26,800	54%		1		26,800	
	Obama	22,507	46%	0		22,507		4,293
97	McCain	20,152	69%		1		20,152	
	Obama	8,889	30%	0		8,889		11,263
98	McCain	18,338	48%		0		18,338	
	Obama	19,754	52%	1		19,754		1,416
99	McCain	12,355	73%		1		12,355	
	Obama	4,501	26%	0		4,501		7,854
100	McCain	5,021	52%		1		5,021	
	Obama	4,470	47%	0		4,470		551
Total		4,232,615		34	66	2,123,334	2,109,281	14,053

In North Carolina, mob rule Obama wins popular vote! McCain wins counties!

Mob rule difference 14,053

Obama % 0.501660

McCain % 0.498340

In column E total, Obama won thirty-four counties whereas in column F total, McCain won sixty-six counties.

In the thirty-four counties, the differences between Obama and McCain is in column I. Since McCain could not overtake the mob rule values, the difference in column I total is mob rule.

Especially notice the following counties in column G (counties #11, #26, #32, #34, #60, #68, and #92), where the differences are five-digit numbers.

Ohio State # 9

A	B	C	D	E	F	G	H	I
COUNTY number	NAMES	COUNTY VOTE	PERCENT	OBAMA COUNT	MCCAIN COUNT	OBAMA VOTE	MCCAIN VOTE	OBAMA - MCCAIN VOTE
1	Obama	4,041	37%	0		4,041		
	McCain	6,725	61%		1		6,725	2,684
2	Obama	16,575	38%	0		16,575		
	McCain	26,167	60%		1		26,167	9,592
3	Obama	9,027	37%	0		9,027		
	McCain	14,788	60%		1		14,788	5,761
4	Obama	24,233	54%	1		24,233		
	McCain	18,464	41%		0		18,464	5,769
5	Obama	19,258	67%	1		19,258		
	McCain	9,107	31%		0		9,107	10,151
6	Obama	6,492	29%	0		6,492		
	McCain	15,938	70%		1		15,938	9,446
7	Obama	15,986	50%	1		15,986		
	McCain	15,127	48%		0		15,127	859
8	Obama	7,280	37%	0		7,280		
	McCain	11,873	61%		1		11,873	4,593
9	Obama	62,871	38%	0		62,871		
	McCain	101,537	61%		1		101,537	38,666
10	Obama	6,302	46%	0		6,302		
	McCain	6,952	51%		1		6,952	650

A	B	C	D	E	F	G	H	I
COUNTY number	NAMES	COUNTY VOTE	PERCENT	OBAMA COUNT	MCCAIN COUNT	OBAMA VOTE	MCCAIN VOTE	OBAMA - MCCAIN VOTE
11	Obama	7,161	39%	0		7,161		
	McCain	10,919	59%		1		10,919	3,758
12	Obama	29,122	47%	0		29,122		
	McCain	31,821	51%		1		31,821	2,699
13	Obama	30,124	33%	0		30,124		
	McCain	60,287	66%		1		60,287	30,163
14	Obama	6,267	34%	0		6,267		
	McCain	12,037	65%		1		12,037	5,770
15	Obama	21,222	45%	0		21,222		
	McCain	24,891	53%		1		24,891	3,669
16	Obama	7,580	46%	0		7,580		
	McCain	8,583	52%		1		8,583	1,003
17	Obama	8,045	39%	0		8,045		
	McCain	12,050	58%		1		12,050	4,005
18	Obama	441,836	69%	1		441,836		
	McCain	196,369	30%		0		196,369	245,467
19	Obama	7,456	30%	0		7,456		
	McCain	17,226	69%		1		17,226	9,770
20	Obama	7,394	43%	0		7,394		
	McCain	9,334	55%		1		9,334	1,940
21	Obama	35,848	40%	0		35,848		
	McCain	53,670	59%		1		53,670	17,822
22	Obama	22,277	56%	1		22,277		
	McCain	17,080	43%		0		17,080	5,197
23	Obama	28,487	41%	0		28,487		
	McCain	40,708	58%		1		40,708	12,221
24	Obama	4,199	37%	0		4,199		
	McCain	6,931	61%		1		6,931	2,732
25	Obama	305,447	59%	1		305,447		
	McCain	205,701	40%		0		205,701	99,746
26	Obama	9,627	45%	0		9,627		
	McCain	11,414	53%		1		11,414	1,787
27	Obama	4,616	36%	0		4,616		
	McCain	8,047	62%		1		8,047	3,431
28	Obama	20,692	42%	0		20,692		
	McCain	28,314	57%		1		28,314	7,622
29	Obama	27,162	41%	0		27,162		
	McCain	39,252	58%		1		39,252	12,090
30	Obama	7,369	44%	0		7,369		
	McCain	8,950	53%		1		8,950	1,581
31	Obama	208,802	52%	1		208,802		
	McCain	187,862	47%		0		187,862	20,940
32	Obama	13,357	37%	0		13,357		
	McCain	21,898	61%		1		21,898	8,541
33	Obama	4,847	38%	0		4,847		
	McCain	7,553	59%		1		7,553	2,706
34	Obama	3,495	47%	0		3,495		
	McCain	3,717	50%		1		3,717	222
35	Obama	6,163	42%	0		6,163		
	McCain	8,091	56%		1		8,091	1,928
36	Obama	6,437	35%	0		6,437		
	McCain	11,390	63%		1		11,390	4,953
37	Obama	6,083	48%	0		6,083		
	McCain	6,201	49%		1		6,201	118
38	Obama	3,074	28%	0		3,074		
	McCain	7,590	70%		1		7,590	4,516
39	Obama	9,461	48%	0		9,461		
	McCain	10,001	50%		1		10,001	540
40	Obama	5,108	39%	0		5,108		
	McCain	7,837	59%		1		7,837	2,729

A	B	C	D	E	F	G	H	I
COUNTY number	NAMES	COUNTY VOTE	PERCENT	OBAMA COUNT	MCCAIN COUNT	OBAMA VOTE	MCCAIN VOTE	OBAMA - MCCAIN VOTE
41	Obama	17,266	49%	1		17,266		
	McCain	17,216	49%		0		17,216	50
42	Obama	10,702	39%	0		10,702		
	McCain	16,207	59%		1		16,207	5,505
43	Obama	54,786	49%	0		54,786		
	McCain	54,441	49%		1		54,441	345
44	Obama	10,956	41%	0		10,956		
	McCain	15,055	57%		1		15,055	4,099
45	Obama	19,768	39%	0		19,768		
	McCain	30,545	60%		1		30,545	10,777
46	Obama	7,615	36%	0		7,615		
	McCain	13,440	63%		1		13,440	5,825
47	Obama	77,719	58%	1		77,719		
	McCain	55,031	41%		0		55,031	22,688
48	Obama	134,729	65%	1		134,729		
	McCain	70,865	34%		0		70,865	63,864
49	Obama	6,193	37%	0		6,193		
	McCain	10,178	61%		1		10,178	3,985
50	Obama	76,356	62%	1		76,356		
	McCain	44,339	36%		0		44,339	32,017
51	Obama	12,016	44%	0		12,016		
	McCain	14,840	54%		1		14,840	2,824
52	Obama	24,614	43%	0		24,614		
	McCain	31,785	56%		1		31,785	7,171
53	Obama	3,990	40%	0		3,990		
	McCain	5,891	58%		1		5,891	1,901
54	Obama	5,636	27%	0		5,636		
	McCain	14,730	71%		1		14,730	9,094
55	Obama	10,739	32%	0		10,739		
	McCain	22,217	66%		1		22,217	11,478
56	Obama	3,623	53%	1		3,623		
	McCain	2,973	44%		0		2,973	650
57	Obama	136,110	52%	1		136,110		
	McCain	123,040	47%		0		123,040	13,070
58	Obama	2,921	45%	0		2,921		
	McCain	3,387	52%		1		3,387	466
59	Obama	5,960	37%	0		5,960		
	McCain	9,787	61%		1		9,787	3,827
60	Obama	17,209	45%	0		17,209		
	McCain	20,174	53%		1		20,174	2,965
61	Obama	2,419	40%	0		2,419		
	McCain	3,387	56%		1		3,387	968
62	Obama	11,760	52%	1		11,760		
	McCain	10,417	46%		0		10,417	1,343
63	Obama	4,043	42%	0		4,043		
	McCain	5,204	55%		1		5,204	1,161
64	Obama	7,128	47%	0		7,128		
	McCain	7,585	50%		1		7,585	457
65	Obama	8,229	38%	0		8,229		
	McCain	13,087	60%		1		13,087	4,858
66	Obama	5,833	48%	0		5,833		
	McCain	6,005	50%		1		6,005	172
67	Obama	32,160	53%	1		32,160		
	McCain	26,959	45%		0		26,959	5,201
68	Obama	6,846	33%	0		6,846		
	McCain	13,340	65%		1		13,340	6,494
69	Obama	5,169	28%	0		5,169		
	McCain	12,855	70%		1		12,855	7,686
70	Obama	24,473	49%	0		24,473		
	McCain	32,590	56%		1		32,590	8,117

A	B	C	D	E	F	G	H	I
COUNTY number	NAMES	COUNTY VOTE	PERCENT	OBAMA COUNT	MCCAIN COUNT	OBAMA VOTE	MCCAIN VOTE	OBAMA - MCCAIN VOTE
71	Obama	13,636	45%	0		13,636		
	McCain	16,027	53%		1		16,027	2,391
72	Obama	15,101	51%	1		15,101		
	McCain	13,935	47%		0		13,935	1,166
73	Obama	14,470	46%	0		14,470		
	McCain	16,472	52%		1		16,472	2,002
74	Obama	12,751	48%	0		12,751		
	McCain	13,588	51%		1		13,588	837
75	Obama	6,777	31%	0		6,777		
	McCain	15,005	68%		1		15,005	8,228
76	Obama	66,712	50%	1		66,712		
	McCain	63,283	48%		0		63,283	3,429
78	Obama	151,932	58%	1		151,932		
	McCain	107,937	41%		0		107,937	43,995
79	Obama	62,254	60%	1		62,254		
	McCain	39,319	38%		0		39,319	22,935
80	Obama	20,957	50%	1		20,957		
	McCain	19,940	48%		0		19,940	1,017
81	Obama	8,348	35%	0		8,348		
	McCain	15,049	63%		1		15,049	6,701
82	Obama	5,046	35%	0		5,046		
	McCain	8,993	63%		1		8,993	3,947
83	Obama	2,405	44%	0		2,405		
	McCain	2,962	54%		1		2,962	557
84	Obama	32,372	31%	0		32,372		
	McCain	69,741	68%		1		69,741	37,369
85	Obama	12,082	41%	0		12,082		
	McCain	16,638	57%		1		16,638	4,556
86	Obama	21,144	42%	0		21,144		
	McCain	28,730	56%		1		28,730	7,586
87	Obama	7,892	44%	0		7,892		
	McCain	9,618	54%		1		9,618	1,726
88	Obama	32,956	52%	1		32,956		
	McCain	28,819	46%		0		28,819	4,137
89	Obama	4,362	41%	0		4,362		
	McCain	6,190	57%		1		6,190	1,828
Total		5,211,206		21	67	2,708,988	2,502,218	206,770

In Ohio, mob rule Obama wins popular vote! McCain wins counties!

Mob rule difference 206,770

Obama % 0.519838978

McCain % 0.480161022

In column E total, Obama won fifteen counties whereas in column F total, McCain won sixty-seven counties.

In the fifteen counties, the differences between Obama and McCain is in column I. Since McCain could not overtake the mob rule values, the difference in column I total is mob rule.

Especially notice the following county in column G, county #18, where the differences is a six-digit number.

Oregon State # 10

A	B	C	D	E	F	G	H	I
COUNTY NUMBER	NAMES	COUNTY VOTE	PERCENT	OBAMA COUNT	MCCAIN COUNT	OBAMA VOTE	MCCAIN VOTE	OBAMA - MCCAIN VOTE
1	Obama	2,795	32%	0		2,795		
	McCain	5,643	65%		1		5,643	2,848
2	Obama	20,345	69%	1		20,345		
	McCain	8,718	30%		0		8,718	11,627
3	Obama	81,910	56%	1		81,910		
	McCain	61,501	42%		0		61,501	20,409
4	Obama	7,311	59%	1		7,311		
	McCain	4,902	39%		0		4,902	2,409
5	Obama	13,253	55%	1		13,253		
	McCain	10,351	43%		0		10,351	2,902
6	Obama	12,413	48%	0		12,413		
	McCain	12,475	49%		1		12,475	62
7	Obama	3,623	35%	0		3,623		
	McCain	6,348	62%		1		6,348	2,725
8	Obama	5,216	43%	0		5,216		
	McCain	6,626	54%		1		6,626	1,410
9	Obama	38,612	49%	0		38,612		
	McCain	38,918	49%		1		38,918	306
10	Obama	19,153	39%	0		19,153		
	McCain	28,635	59%		1		28,635	9,482
11	Obama	429	39%	0		429		
	McCain	642	59%		1		642	213
12	Obama	980	26%	0		980		
	McCain	2,670	72%		1		2,670	1,690
13	Obama	946	26%	0		946		
	McCain	2,592	71%		1		2,592	1,646
14	Obama	6,229	64%	1		6,229		
	McCain	3,240	34%		0		3,240	2,989
15	Obama	34,091	52%	1		34,091		
	McCain	29,925	46%		0		29,925	4,166
16	Obama	3,648	45%	0		3,648		
	McCain	4,360	53%		1		4,360	712
17	Obama	16,697	42%	0		16,697		
	McCain	22,124	55%		1		22,124	5,427
18	Obama	9,015	32%	0		9,015		
	McCain	18,682	66%		1		18,682	9,667
19	Obama	954	26%	0		954		
	McCain	2,631	72%		1		2,631	1,677
20	Obama	43,987	63%	1		43,987		
	McCain	24,765	35%		0		24,765	19,222
21	Obama	13,991	60%	1		13,991		

A	B	C	D	E	F	G	H	I
COUNTY NUMBER	NAMES	COUNTY VOTE	PERCENT	OBAMA COUNT	MCCAIN COUNT	OBAMA VOTE	MCCAIN VOTE	OBAMA - MCCAIN VOTE
	McCain	8,649	37%		0		8,649	5,342
22	Obama	19,578	44%	0		19,578		
	McCain	24,191	54%		1		24,191	4,613
23	Obama	2,922	28%	0		2,922		
	McCain	7,099	69%		1		7,099	4,177
24	Obama	55,610	50%	1		55,610		
	McCain	53,174	48%		0		53,174	2,436
25	Obama	1,398	35%	0		1,398		
	McCain	2,501	62%		1		2,501	1,103
26	Obama	239,251	77%	1		239,251		
	McCain	65,251	21%		0		65,251	174,000
27	Obama	17,046	49%	0		17,046		
	McCain	17,272	49%		1		17,272	226
28	Obama	382	37%	0		382		
	McCain	632	61%		1		632	250
29	Obama	7,018	54%	1		7,018		
	McCain	5,732	44%		0		5,732	1,286
30	Obama	9,400	38%	0		9,400		
	McCain	15,126	60%		1		15,126	5,726
31	Obama	4,612	37%	0		4,612		
	McCain	7,563	61%		1		7,563	2,951
32	Obama	1,490	34%	0		1,490		
	McCain	2,832	64%		1		2,832	1,342
33	Obama	5,649	52%	1		5,649		
	McCain	4,900	45%		0		4,900	749
34	Obama	98,249	63%	1		98,249		
	McCain	55,956	36%		0		55,956	42,293
35	Obama	276	35%	0		276		
	McCain	497	62%		1		497	221
36	Obama	20,494	48%	0		20,494		
	McCain	21,068	50%		1		21,068	574
Total		1,407,164		13	23	818,973	588,191	230,782

In Oregon, mob rule Obama wins popular vote! McCain wins counties!

Mob rule difference 230,782

Obama % 0.582002524

McCain % 0. 0.417997476

In column E total, Obama won thirteen counties whereas in column F total, McCain won twenty-three counties.

In the thirteen counties, the differences between Obama and McCain is in column I. Since McCain could not overtake the mob rule values, the difference in column I total is mob rule.

185

Especially notice the following county in column G, county #26, where the differences is a six-digit number.

Pennsylvania State # 11

A	B	C	D	E	F	G	H	I
county number	names	COUNTY VOTE	PERCENT	OBAMA COUNT	MCCAIN COUNT	OBAMA VOTE	MCCAIN VOTE	OBAMA - MCCAIN VOTE
1	Obama	17,475	40%	0		17,475		
	McCain	26,134	59%		1		26,134	8,659
2	Obama	368,453	57%	1		368,453		
	McCain	269,819	42%		0		269,819	98,634
3	Obama	10,729	37%	0		10,729		
	McCain	17,715	61%		1		17,715	6,986
4	Obama	39,738	48%	0		39,738		
	McCain	42,358	51%		1		42,358	2,620
5	Obama	6,001	27%	0		6,001		
	McCain	15,928	72%		1		15,928	9,927
6	Obama	91,803	54%	1		91,803		
	McCain	75,868	45%		0		75,868	15,935
7	Obama	18,798	38%	0		18,798		
	McCain	30,812	61%		1		30,812	12,014
8	Obama	10,202	40%	0		10,202		
	McCain	14,911	58%		1		14,911	4,709
9	Obama	178,345	54%	1		178,345		
	McCain	149,860	45%		0		149,860	28,485
10	Obama	29,882	36%	0		29,882		
	McCain	52,294	63%		1		52,294	22,412
11	Obama	30,697	50%	1		30,697		
	McCain	29,981	48%		0		29,981	716
12	Obama	802	37%	0		802		
	McCain	1,239	58%		1		1,239	437
13	Obama	13,235	50%	1		13,235		
	McCain	12,646	48%		0		12,646	589
14	Obama	39,652	55%	1		39,652		
	McCain	31,971	44%		0		31,971	7,681
15	Obama	135,150	54%	1		135,150		
	McCain	112,266	45%		0		112,266	22,884
16	Obama	6,415	38%	0		6,415		
	McCain	10,126	60%		1		10,126	3,711
17	Obama	14,549	43%	0		14,549		
	McCain	18,656	55%		1		18,656	4,107
18	Obama	6,799	48%	0		6,799		
	McCain	7,126	51%		1		7,126	327
19	Obama	12,597	47%	0		12,597		
	McCain	13,704	52%		1		13,704	1,107
20	Obama	15,684	44%	0		15,684		
	McCain	19,265	54%		1		19,265	3,581
21	Obama	45,355	43%	0		45,355		
	McCain	59,693	56%		1		59,693	14,338
22	Obama	69,352	54%	1		69,352		
	McCain	57,964	45%		0		57,964	11,388
23	Obama	169,030	60%	1		169,030		
	McCain	109,322	39%		0		109,322	59,708

A county number	B names	C COUNTY VOTE	D PERCENT	E OBAMA COUNT	F MCCAIN COUNT	G OBAMA VOTE	H MCCAIN VOTE	I OBAMA - MCCAIN VOTE
24	Obama	6,910	51%	1		6,910		
	McCain	6,252	46%		0		6,252	658
25	Obama	74,206	59%	1		74,206		
	McCain	49,284	40%		0		49,284	24,922
26	Obama	25,509	49%	0		25,509		
	McCain	25,669	50%		1		25,669	160
27	Obama	1,014	42%	0		1,014		
	McCain	1,366	57%		1		1,366	352
28	Obama	21,052	33%	0		21,052		
	McCain	41,711	66%		1		41,711	20,659
29	Obama	1,562	25%	0		1,562		
	McCain	4,612	74%		1		4,612	3,050
30	Obama	7,365	49%	0		7,365		
	McCain	7,451	50%		1		7,451	86
31	Obama	6,989	36%	0		6,989		
	McCain	12,265	63%		1		12,265	5,276
32	Obama	16,964	46%	0		16,964		
	McCain	19,617	53%		1		19,617	2,653
33	Obama	6,132	35%	0		6,132		
	McCain	11,248	64%		1		11,248	5,116
34	Obama	3,055	32%	0		3,055		
	McCain	6,463	67%		1		6,463	3,408
35	Obama	67,112	63%	1		67,112		
	McCain	39,198	36%		0		39,198	27,914
36	Obama	97,290	43%	0		97,290		
	McCain	124,475	56%		1		124,475	27,185
37	Obama	19,371	47%	0		19,371		
	McCain	21,496	52%		1		21,496	2,125
38	Obama	22,004	40%	0		22,004		
	McCain	32,325	59%		1		32,325	10,321
39	Obama	86,226	57%	1		86,226		
	McCain	62,668	42%		0		62,668	23,558
40	Obama	71,903	54%	1		71,903		
	McCain	60,512	45%		0		60,512	11,391
41	Obama	18,335	37%	0		18,335		
	McCain	30,215	62%		1		30,215	11,880
42	Obama	6,186	41%	0		6,186		
	McCain	8,835	58%		1		8,835	2,649
43	Obama	24,319	49%	0		24,319		
	McCain	24,321	49%		1		24,321	2
44	Obama	5,364	33%	0		5,364		
	McCain	10,904	66%		1		10,904	5,540
45	Obama	36,655	58%	1		36,655		
	McCain	25,892	41%		0		25,892	10,763
46	Obama	249,493	60%	1		249,493		
	McCain	163,030	39%		0		163,030	86,463
47	Obama	3,347	42%	0		3,347		
	McCain	4,555	57%		1		4,555	1,208
48	Obama	74,956	56%	1		74,956		
	McCain	58,352	43%		0		58,352	16,604
49	Obama	13,555	42%	0		13,555		
	McCain	18,012	56%		1		18,012	4,457
50	Obama	6,384	32%	0		6,384		
	McCain	13,032	66%		1		13,032	6,648
51	Obama	571,635	83%	1		571,635		
	McCain	112,719	16%		0		112,719	458,916
52	Obama	11,448	47%	0		11,448		
	McCain	12,456	52%		1		12,456	1,008
53	Obama	2,277	31%	0		2,277		

A	B	C	D	E	F	G	H	I
county number	names	COUNTY VOTE	PERCENT	OBAMA COUNT	MCCAIN COUNT	OBAMA VOTE	MCCAIN VOTE	OBAMA - MCCAIN VOTE
	McCain	5,073	68%		1		5,073	2,796
54	Obama	28,187	45%	0		28,187		
	McCain	33,682	54%		1		33,682	5,495
55	Obama	5,375	35%	0		5,375		
	McCain	9,895	64%		1		9,895	4,520
56	Obama	12,437	37%	0		12,437		
	McCain	20,925	62%		1		20,925	8,488
57	Obama	1,228	39%	0		1,228		
	McCain	1,840	59%		1		1,840	612
58	Obama	8,314	44%	0		8,314		
	McCain	10,551	55%		1		10,551	2,237
59	Obama	6,012	36%	0		6,012		
	McCain	10,542	63%		1		10,542	4,530
60	Obama	7,207	42%	0		7,207		
	McCain	9,720	57%		1		9,720	2,513
61	Obama	8,708	40%	0		8,708		
	McCain	12,817	59%		1		12,817	4,109
62	Obama	8,669	46%	0		8,669		
	McCain	9,824	52%		1		9,824	1,155
63	Obama	44,286	47%	0		44,286		
	McCain	48,753	52%		1		48,753	4,467
64	Obama	9,824	43%	0		9,824		
	McCain	12,618	56%		1		12,618	2,794
65	Obama	69,004	41%	0		69,004		
	McCain	96,786	58%		1		96,786	27,782
66	Obama	5,631	46%	0		5,631		
	McCain	6,494	53%		1		6,494	863
67	Obama	81,748	43%	0		81,748		
	McCain	107,367	56%		1		107,367	25,619
Total		5,771,471		18	49	3,185,991	2,585,480	600,511

In Pennsylvania, mob rule Obama wins popular vote! McCain wins counties!

Mob rule difference 600,511

Obama % 0.552024085

McCain % 0.447975915

In column E total, Obama won eighteen counties whereas in column F total, McCain won forty-nine counties.

In the eighteen counties, the differences between Obama and McCain is in column I. Since McCain could not overtake the mob rule values, the difference in column I total is mob rule.

Especially notice the following county in column G, county #51, where the difference is a six-digit number.

Virginia State # 12

A	B	C	D	E	F	G	H	I
COUNTY NUMBER	NAMES	COUNTY VOTE	PERCENT	OBAMA COUNT	MCCAIN COUNT	OBAMA VOTE	MCCAIN VOTE	OBAMA - MCCAIN
1	Obama	7,696	49%	0		7,696		
	McCain	7,766	50%		1		7,766	70
2	Obama	29,766	59%	1		29,766		
	McCain	20,547	40%		0		20,547	9,219
3	Obama	50,415	72%	1		50,415		
	McCain	19,140	28%		0		19,140	31,275
4	Obama	3,549	48%	0		3,549		
	McCain	3,711	51%		1		3,711	162
5	Obama	2,479	38%	0		2,479		
	McCain	3,964	61%		1		3,964	1,485
6	Obama	6,094	42%	0		6,094		
	McCain	8,470	58%		1		8,470	2,376
7	Obama	2,641	35%	0		2,641		
	McCain	4,903	64%		1		4,903	2,262
8	Obama	78,953	72%	1		78,953		
	McCain	29,703	27%		0		29,703	49,250
9	Obama	9,825	30%	0		9,825		
	McCain	23,120	70%		1		23,120	13,295
10	Obama	1,043	43%	0		1,043		
	McCain	1,349	56%		1		1,349	306
11	Obama	11,007	31%	0		11,007		
	McCain	24,402	68%		1		24,402	13,395
12	Obama	1,208	44%	0		1,208		
	McCain	1,497	55%		1		1,497	289
13	Obama	864	29%	0		864		
	McCain	2,031	69%		1		2,031	1,167
14	Obama	5,693	33%	0		5,693		
	McCain	11,471	66%		1		11,471	5,778
15	Obama	2,662	36%	0		2,662		
	McCain	4,576	63%		1		4,576	1,914
16	Obama	4,772	64%	1		4,772		
	McCain	2,690	36%		0		2,690	2,082
17	Obama	4,063	47%	0		4,063		
	McCain	4,541	52%		1		4,541	478
18	Obama	3,493	50%	1		3,493		
	McCain	3,427	49%		0		3,427	66
19	Obama	1,108	46%	0		1,108		
	McCain	1,282	53%		1		1,282	174
20	Obama	8,089	32%	0		8,089		
	McCain	17,439	68%		1		17,439	9,350
21	Obama	6,908	55%	1		6,908		
	McCain	5,461	44%		0		5,461	1,447
22	Obama	4,109	33%	0		4,109		
	McCain	8,187	65%		1		8,187	4,078
23	Obama	2,811	68%	1		2,811		
	McCain	1,288	32%		0		1,288	1,523
24	Obama	2,702	44%	0		2,702		
	McCain	3,371	55%		1		3,371	669

A	B	C	D	E	F	G	H	I
COUNTY NUMBER	NAMES	COUNTY VOTE	PERCENT	OBAMA COUNT	MCCAIN COUNT	OBAMA VOTE	MCCAIN VOTE	OBAMA - MCCAIN
25	Obama	14,862	79%	1		14,862		
	McCain	3,908	21%		0		3,908	10,954
26	Obama	45,917	49%	0		45,917		
	McCain	47,539	51%		1		47,539	1,622
27	Obama	74,169	46%	0		74,169		
	McCain	86,318	54%		1		86,318	12,149
28	Obama	3,456	47%	0		3,456		
	McCain	3,839	52%		1		3,839	383
29	Obama	2,557	29%	0		2,557		
	McCain	6,160	70%		1		6,160	3,603
30	Obama	1,304	56%	1		1,304		
	McCain	1,020	43%		0		1,020	284
31	Obama	876	33%	0		876		
	McCain	1,695	65%		1		1,695	819
32	Obama	8,782	45%	0		8,782		
	McCain	10,701	55%		1		10,701	1,919
33	Obama	2,255	48%	0		2,255		
	McCain	2,418	51%		1		2,418	163
34	Obama	12,342	59%	1		12,342		
	McCain	8,359	40%		0		8,359	3,983
35	Obama	3,253	49%	0		3,253		
	McCain	3,293	49%		1		3,293	40
36	Obama	6,244	49%	0		6,244		
	McCain	6,521	51%		1		6,521	277
37	Obama	1,702	65%	1		1,702		
	McCain	897	35%		0		897	805
38	Obama	2,923	55%	1		2,923		
	McCain	2,377	45%		0		2,377	546
39	Obama	240,175	59%	1		240,175		
	McCain	167,057	41%		0		167,057	73,118
40	Obama	6,571	58%	1		6,571		
	McCain	4,686	41%		0		4,686	1,885
41	Obama	4,693	70%	1		4,693		
	McCain	1,967	29%		0		1,967	2,726
42	Obama	14,614	43%	0		14,614		
	McCain	19,224	57%		1		19,224	4,610
43	Obama	2,937	39%	0		2,937		
	McCain	4,441	59%		1		4,441	1,504
44	Obama	6,173	49%	0		6,173		
	McCain	6,414	51%		1		6,414	241
45	Obama	9,618	38%	0		9,618		
	McCain	15,414	61%		1		15,414	5,796
46	Obama	2,815	64%	1		2,815		
	McCain	1,574	36%		0		1,574	1,241
47	Obama	12,949	39%	0		12,949		
	McCain	20,148	60%		1		20,148	7,199
48	Obama	6,081	64%	1		6,081		
	McCain	3,381	36%		0		3,381	2,700
49	Obama	1,052	44%	0		1,052		
	McCain	1,316	55%		1		1,316	264
50	Obama	3,204	41%	0		3,204		
	McCain	4,462	57%		1		4,462	1,258
51	Obama	6,722	36%	0		6,722		
	McCain	11,737	63%		1		11,737	5,015
52	Obama	4,812	39%	0		4,812		
	McCain	7,640	61%		1		7,640	2,828
53	Obama	2,480	35%	0		2,480		
	McCain	4,540	63%		1		4,540	2,060
54	Obama	3,272	39%	0		3,272		
	McCain	4,978	60%		1		4,978	1,706
55	Obama	3,121	64%	1		3,121		

A	B	C	D	E	F	G	H	I
COUNTY NUMBER	NAMES	COUNTY VOTE	PERCENT	OBAMA COUNT	MCCAIN COUNT	OBAMA VOTE	MCCAIN VOTE	OBAMA - MCCAIN
	McCain	1,729	36%		0		1,729	1,392
56	Obama	8,107	49%	0		8,107		
	McCain	8,591	51%		1		8,591	484
57	Obama	38,846	67%	1		38,846		
	McCain	18,808	33%		0		18,808	20,038
58	Obama	18,443	33%	0		18,443		
	McCain	37,244	67%		1		37,244	18,801
59	Obama	7,687	57%	1		7,687		
	McCain	5,556	42%		0		5,556	2,131
60	Obama	86,063	56%	1		86,063		
	McCain	67,265	44%		0		67,265	18,798
61	Obama	11,116	44%	0		11,116		
	McCain	13,757	55%		1		13,757	2,641
62	Obama	590	38%	0		590		
	McCain	929	60%		1		929	339
63	Obama	5,285	56%	1		5,285		
	McCain	4,149	44%		0		4,149	1,136
64	Obama	8,569	43%	0		8,569		
	McCain	11,253	57%		1		11,253	2,684
65	Obama	17,218	45%	0		17,218		
	McCain	20,779	54%		1		20,779	3,561
66	Obama	1,917	52%	1		1,917		
	McCain	1,763	48%		0		1,763	154
67	Obama	4,471	43%	0		4,471		
	McCain	5,885	56%		1		5,885	1,414
68	Obama	3,344	40%	0		3,344		
	McCain	4,966	60%		1		4,966	1,622
69	Obama	3,232	47%	0		3,232		
	McCain	3,644	53%		1		3,644	412
70	Obama	3,212	35%	0		3,212		
	McCain	5,827	63%		1		5,827	2,615
71	Obama	1,540	62%	1		1,540		
	McCain	914	37%		0		914	626
72	Obama	62,560	53%	1		62,560		
	McCain	55,428	47%		0		55,428	7,132
73	Obama	6,938	46%	0		6,938		
	McCain	8,155	54%		1		8,155	1,217
74	Obama	2,702	48%	0		2,702		
	McCain	2,900	52%		1		2,900	198
75	Obama	16,256	48%	0		16,256		
	McCain	17,622	51%		1		17,622	1,366
76	Obama	2,862	43%	0		2,862		
	McCain	3,758	56%		1		3,758	896
77	Obama	6,114	54%	1		6,114		
	McCain	5,129	45%		0		5,129	985
78	Obama	2,460	60%	1		2,460		
	McCain	1,634	40%		0		1,634	826
79	Obama	4,134	64%	1		4,134		
	McCain	2,309	36%		0		2,309	1,825
80	Obama	1,943	36%	0		1,943		
	McCain	3,454	64%		1		3,454	1,511
81	Obama	7,124	48%	0		7,124		
	McCain	7,809	52%		1		7,809	685
82	Obama	2,390	40%	0		2,390		
	McCain	3,545	59%		1		3,545	1,155
83	Obama	19,139	51%	1		19,139		
	McCain	17,822	48%		0		17,822	1,317
84	Obama	4,383	54%	1		4,383		
	McCain	3,646	45%		0		3,646	737
85	Obama	3,490	35%	0		3,490		
	McCain	6,285	64%		1		6,285	2,795

A	B	C	D	E	F	G	H	I
COUNTY NUMBER	NAMES	COUNTY VOTE	PERCENT	OBAMA COUNT	MCCAIN COUNT	OBAMA VOTE	MCCAIN VOTE	OBAMA - MCCAIN
86	Obama	45,429	63%	1		45,429		
	McCain	26,355	37%		0		26,355	19,074
87	Obama	56,191	71%	1		56,191		
	McCain	22,726	29%		0		22,726	33,465
88	Obama	3,795	58%	1		3,795		
	McCain	2,711	41%		0		2,711	1,084
89	Obama	3,304	45%	0		3,304		
	McCain	4,036	55%		1		4,036	732
90	Obama	742	49%	0		742		
	McCain	744	49%		1		744	2
91	Obama	3,358	49%	0		3,358		
	McCain	3,437	50%		1		3,437	79
92	Obama	7,095	45%	0		7,095		
	McCain	8,492	54%		1		8,492	1,397
93	Obama	4,302	41%	0		4,302		
	McCain	5,992	58%		1		5,992	1,690
94	Obama	2,879	34%	0		2,879		
	McCain	5,489	64%		1		5,489	2,610
95	Obama	13,671	89%	1		13,671		
	McCain	1,582	10%		0		1,582	12,089
96	Obama	11,394	38%	0		11,394		
	McCain	18,718	62%		1		18,718	7,324
97	Obama	1,747	25%	0		1,747		
	McCain	5,229	74%		1		5,229	3,482
98	Obama	26,200	67%	1		26,200		
	McCain	12,760	33%		0		12,760	13,440
99	Obama	4,233	30%	0		4,233		
	McCain	10,084	70%		1		10,084	5,851
100	Obama	5,099	54%	1		5,099		
	McCain	4,174	45%		0		4,174	925
101	Obama	7,190	48%	0		7,190		
	McCain	7,750	52%		1		7,750	560
102	Obama	73,585	56%	1		73,585		
	McCain	57,177	44%		0		57,177	16,408
103	Obama	5,917	39%	0		5,917		
	McCain	8,855	59%		1		8,855	2,938
104	Obama	2,930	54%	1		2,930		
	McCain	2,418	45%		0		2,418	512
105	Obama	2,105	48%	0		2,105		
	McCain	2,227	51%		1		2,227	122
106	Obama	1,614	43%	0		1,614		
	McCain	2,092	56%		1		2,092	478
107	Obama	73,180	79%	1		73,180		
	McCain	18,472	20%		0		18,472	54,708
108	Obama	19,469	39%	0		19,469		
	McCain	30,171	60%		1		30,171	10,702
109	Obama	22,623	61%	1		22,623		
	McCain	14,131	38%		0		14,131	8,492
110	Obama	4,347	43%	0		4,347		
	McCain	5,732	57%		1		5,732	1,385
111	Obama	10,533	32%	0		10,533		
	McCain	22,459	68%		1		22,459	11,926
112	Obama	4,928	43%	0		4,928		
	McCain	6,387	56%		1		6,387	1,459
113	Obama	5,160	42%	0		5,160		
	McCain	7,083	57%		1		7,083	1,923
114	Obama	2,473	27%	0		2,473		
	McCain	6,372	71%		1		6,372	3,899
115	Obama	6,903	36%	0		6,903		
	McCain	12,005	63%		1		12,005	5,102
116	Obama	4,230	34%	0		4,230		

A	B	C	D	E	F	G	H	I
COUNTY NUMBER	NAMES	COUNTY VOTE	PERCENT	OBAMA COUNT	MCCAIN COUNT	OBAMA VOTE	MCCAIN VOTE	OBAMA - MCCAIN
	McCain	7,813	64%		1		7,813	3,583
117	Obama	4,402	49%	0		4,402		
	McCain	4,583	51%		1		4,583	181
118	Obama	24,893	46%	0		24,893		
	McCain	28,606	53%		1		28,606	3,713
119	Obama	25,704	47%	0		25,704		
	McCain	29,207	53%		1		29,207	3,503
120	Obama	5,570	51%	1		5,570		
	McCain	5,328	49%		0		5,328	242
121	Obama	19,193	55%	1		19,193		
	McCain	15,630	45%		0		15,630	3,563
122	Obama	2,623	61%	1		2,623		
	McCain	1,662	39%		0		1,662	961
123	Obama	3,195	61%	1		3,195		
	McCain	2,029	39%		0		2,029	1,166
124	Obama	5,592	33%	0		5,592		
	McCain	11,196	66%		1		11,196	5,604
125	Obama	83,856	48%	0		83,856		
	McCain	89,229	51%		1		89,229	5,373
126	Obama	6,994	44%	0		6,994		
	McCain	8,878	55%		1		8,878	1,884
127	Obama	8,052	33%	0		8,052		
	McCain	16,055	66%		1		16,055	8,003
128	Obama	3,905	44%	0		3,905		
	McCain	4,815	54%		1		4,815	910
129	Obama	4,576	55%	1		4,576		
	McCain	3,718	45%		0		3,718	858
130	Obama	4,322	64%	1		4,322		
	McCain	2,350	35%		0		2,350	1,972
Total		3,363,393		46	84	1,765,519	1,597,874	167,645

In Virginia, mob rule Obama wins popular vote! McCain wins counties!

Mob rule difference 167,645

Obama % 0.524922006

McCain % 0.475077994

In column E total, Obama won forty-six counties whereas in column F total, McCain won eighty-four counties.

In the forty-six counties, the differences between Obama and McCain is in column I. Since McCain could not overtake the mob rule values, the difference in column I total is mob rule.

Especially notice the following counties in column G (counties #3, #8, #25, #39, #57, #60, #86, #87, #95, #98, #102, and #107), where the differences are a five-digit number.

Washington State #13

A	B	C	D	E	F	G	H	I
COUNTY NUMBER	NAMES	COUNTY VOTE	PERCENT	OBAMA COUNT	MCCAIN COUNT	OBAMA VOTE	MCCAIN VOTE	OBAMA - MCCAIN VOTE
1	Obama	972	31%	0		972		
	McCain	2,085	67%		1		2,085	1,113
2	Obama	3,822	43%	0		3,822		
	McCain	4,873	55%		1		4,873	1,051
3	Obama	19,295	37%	0		19,295		
	McCain	32,242	62%		1		32,242	12,947
4	Obama	11,173	44%	0		11,173		
	McCain	13,946	55%		1		13,946	2,773
5	Obama	12,738	54%	1		12,738		
	McCain	10,679	45%		0		10,679	2,059
6	Obama	82,625	53%	1		82,625		
	McCain	69,989	45%		0		69,989	12,636
7	Obama	667	31%	0		667		
	McCain	1,447	67%		1		1,447	780
8	Obama	14,064	58%	1		14,064		
	McCain	9,568	40%		0		9,568	4,496
9	Obama	3,119	40%	0		3,119		
	McCain	4,617	59%		1		4,617	1,498
10	Obama	1,386	42%	0		1,386		
	McCain	1,817	55%		1		1,817	431
11	Obama	4,843	38%	0		4,843		
	McCain	7,789	61%		1		7,789	2,946
12	Obama	353	28%	0		353		
	McCain	876	70%		1		876	523
13	Obama	8,872	35%	0		8,872		
	McCain	15,861	63%		1		15,861	6,989
14	Obama	11,332	58%	1		11,332		
	McCain	7,737	40%		0		7,737	3,595
15	Obama	17,969	54%	1		17,969		
	McCain	15,199	45%		0		15,199	2,770
16	Obama	10,656	68%	1		10,656		
	McCain	4,844	31%		0		4,844	5,812
17	Obama	356,983	72%	1		356,983		
	McCain	136,062	27%		0		136,062	220,921
18	Obama	47,546	56%	1		47,546		
	McCain	35,793	42%		0		35,793	11,753
19	Obama	5,841	45%	0		5,841		
	McCain	6,829	53%		1		6,829	988
20	Obama	4,457	49%	0		4,457		
	McCain	4,482	49%		1		4,482	25
21	Obama	9,006	42%	0		9,006		
	McCain	12,164	56%		1		12,164	3,158
22	Obama	2,013	34%	0		2,013		
	McCain	3,779	64%		1		3,779	1,766
23	Obama	11,813	54%	0		11,813		
	McCain	9,456	44%		1		9,456	2,357
24	Obama	4,736	47%	0		4,736		
	McCain	5,100	51%		1		5,100	364
25	Obama	5,534	57%	0		5,534		
	McCain	3,989	41%		1		3,989	1,545
26	Obama	2,524	39%	0		2,524		
	McCain	3,671	57%		1		3,671	1,147
27	Obama	85,019	57%	0		85,019		
	McCain	62,018	42%		1		62,018	23,001

A	B	C	D	E	F	G	H	I
COUNTY NUMBER	NAMES	COUNTY VOTE	PERCENT	OBAMA COUNT	MCCAIN COUNT	OBAMA VOTE	MCCAIN VOTE	OBAMA - MCCAIN VOTE
28	Obama	6,334	71%	0		6,334		
	McCain	2,490	28%		1		2,490	3,844
29	Obama	20,604	55%	1		20,604		
	McCain	16,146	43%		0		16,146	4,458
30	Obama	2,773	51%	1		2,773		
	McCain	2,495	46%		0		2,495	278
31	Obama	116,472	61%	1		116,472		
	McCain	72,369	38%		0		72,369	44,103
32	Obama	87,290	49%	0		87,290		
	McCain	87,597	49%		1		87,597	307
33	Obama	4,842	41%	0		4,842		
	McCain	6,652	56%		1		6,652	1,810
34	Obama	66,139	60%	1		66,139		
	McCain	41,746	38%		0		41,746	24,393
35	Obama	1,112	49%	0		1,112		
	McCain	1,100	48%		1		1,100	12
36	Obama	6,209	41%	0		6,209		
	McCain	8,712	58%		1		8,712	2,503
37	Obama	39,054	60%	1		39,054		
	McCain	25,284	39%		0		25,284	13,770
38	Obama	5,208	51%	1		5,208		
	McCain	4,778	47%		0		4,778	430
39	Obama	22,565	44%	0		22,565		
	McCain	27,651	54%		1		27,651	5,086
Total		1,901,892		14	25	1,117,960	783,932	334,028

In Washington, mob rule Obama wins popular vote! McCain wins counties!

Mob rule difference 334,028

Obama % 0.58781466

McCain % 0.41218534

In column E total, Obama won fourteen counties whereas in column F total, McCain won twenty-five counties.

In the fourteen counties, the differences between Obama and McCain are in column I. Since McCain could not overtake the mob rule values, the difference in column I total is mob rule.

Especially notice the following county in column G, county #17, where the difference is a six-digit number.

WINNER TAKES ALL (MOB RULE) ELECTORAL VOTE VS. PERCENTAGE CALCULATION OF ELECTORAL VOTE

A	B	C	D	E	F	G	H
STATE	ELECTORAL VOTE (EV)	OBAMA EV WINNER TAKE ALL MOB RULE	MCCAIN EV WINNER TAKE ALL MOB RULE	OBAMA %	MCCAIN %	OBAMA EV %	MCCAIN EV %
Alabama	9	0	9	0.40	0.60	4	5
Alaska	3	0	3	0.39	0.61	1	2
Arizona	10	0	10	0.46	0.54	5	5
Arkansas	6	0	6	0.43	0.57	3	3
California	55	55	0	0.64	0.36	35	20
Colorado	9	9	0	0.55	0.45	5	4
Connecticut	7	7	0	0.61	0.39	4	3
Delaware	3	3	0	0.63	0.37	2	1
DC	3	3	0	0.93	0.07	3	0
Florida	27	27	0	0.52	0.48	14	13
Georgia	15	0	15	0.46	0.54	7	8
Hawaii	4	4	0	0.75	0.25	3	1
Idaho	4	0	4	0.38	0.62	2	2
Illinois	21	21	0	0.62	0.38	13	8
Indiana	11	11	0	0.51	0.49	6	5
Iowa	7	7	0	0.55	0.45	4	3
Kansas	6	0	6	0.44	0.56	3	3
Kentucky	8	0	8	0.43	0.57	3	5
Louisiana	9	0	9	0.41	0.59	4	5
Maine	4	4	0	0.61	0.39	2	2
Maryland	10	10	0	0.60	0.40	6	4
Massachusetts	12	12	0	0.64	0.36	8	4
Michigan	17	17	0	0.58	0.42	10	7
Minnesota	10	10	0	0.56	0.44	6	4
Mississippi	6	0	6	0.43	0.57	3	3
Missouri	11	11	0	0.50	0.50	6	5

A	B	C	D	E	F	G	H
STATE	ELECTORAL VOTE (EV)	OBAMA EV WINNER TAKE ALL MOB RULE	MCCAIN EV WINNER TAKE ALL MOB RULE	OBAMA %	MCCAIN %	OBAMA EV %	MCCAIN EV %
Montana	3	0	3	0.50	0.50	1	2
Nebraska	5	0	5	0.43	0.57	2	3
Nevada	5	5	0	0.61	0.39	3	2
New Hampshire	4	4	0	0.56	0.44	2	2
New Jersey	15	15	0	0.58	0.42	9	6
New Mexico	5	5	0	0.56	0.44	3	2
New York	31	31	0	0.63	0.37	20	11
North Carolina	15	15	0	0.51	0.49	8	7
North Dakota	3	0	3	0.47	0.53	1	2
Ohio	20	20	0	0.53	0.47	11	9
Oklahoma	7	0	7	0.34	0.66	2	5
Oregon	7	7	0	0.58	0.42	4	3
Pennsylvania	21	21	0	0.57	0.44	12	9
Rhode Island	4	4	0	0.66	0.34	3	1
South Carolina	8	0	8	0.47	0.53	4	4
South Dakota	3	0	3	0.46	0.54	1	2
Tennessee	11	0	11	0.39	0.61	4	7
Texas	34	0	34	0.45	0.55	15	19
Utah	5	0	5	0.37	0.63	2	3
Vermont	3	3	0	0.68	0.32	2	1
Virginia	13	13	0	0.51	0.49	7	6
Washington	11	11	0	0.59	0.41	7	4
West Virginia	5	0	5	0.45	0.55	2	3
Wisconsin	10	10	0	0.58	0.42	6	4
Wyoming	3	0	3	0.34	0.66	1	2
Total	538	349	162			290	248

PERCENTAGE TABLE

Columns C and F is winner takes all (mob rule) electoral vote. Columns G and H represent percentage calculation of electoral vote. The different in winner take all is 178, whereas the percentage different calculation winner is 42.

Total vote is 538. Obama percentage is 5.39%, and McCain percentage is 4.6%. The percentage calculation is more accurate in determining the winner of the presidential election, which does away with mob rule. In this era of computer technology, the Notepad++ integer technology must be done away with and replaced with decimal arithmetic. The decimal calculation can be done in double precision arithmetic, which is accurate within sixty-four places to reduce roundoff error.

The percentage technique would do away with the fact of having a popular vote winner who does not win the electoral vote like what occurred several times using winner takes all.

The computer era justifies using percentage calculation to determine the electoral winner instead of the winner-take-all electoral vote, which introduces the possibility of mob rule.

Since 2 divides into 538, two candidates could have even electoral votes in electoral vote winner take all (mob rule).

The most important thing is to get rid of mob rule. The planners of the Constitution tried to minimize the effects of the factor like mob rule in their historical Constitution design.

ELECTORAL COLLEGE SPREADSHEET CALCULATION USING PERCENTAGE

ALASKA, DELAWARE, MONTANA, NORTH DAKOTA,
SOUTH DAKOTA, VERMONT, WYOMING

PRESIDENTIAL SPREADSHEET #1

UNITED STATES HOUSE OF REPRESENTATIVES DISTRICT

	A	B	C	D	E
1			Alaska		
2					
3		Votes Cast		Elector Number	
4		0		0	
5					
6	US District	Votes	%	President A	President B
7	1				
8	President A	0	B8/B4	IF(B8>B9,1,0)	
9	President B	0	B9/B4		IF(C8<C9,1,0)
10	Total			SUM(D8:D9)	SUM(E8:E9)
	Total Electoral	Percentage	Calculation	D4/A7*D10	D4/A7*E10

199

HAWAII, MAINE, NEW HAMPSHIRE, AND RHODE ISLAND

PRESIDENTIAL SPREAD SHEET #2

UNITED STATES HOUSE OF REPRESENTATIVES DISTRICT

	A	B	C	D	E
1			Hawaii		
2					
3		Votes Cast		Elector Number	
4		0		0	
5					
6	US District	Votes	%	President A	President B
7	1				
8	President A	0	B8/B4	IF(B8>B9,1,0)	
9	President B	0	B9/B4		IF(C8<C9,1,0)
10	2				
11	President A	0	B11/B4	IF(B11>B12,1,0)	
12	President B	0	B12/B4		IF(C11<C12,1,0)
13	Total			SUM(D8:D12)	SUM(E8:E12)
	Total Electoral	Percentage	Calculation	D4/A10*D13	D4/A10*E13

NEBRASKA, NEVADA, NEW MEXICO, UTAH, AND WEST VIRGINIA

PRESIDENTIAL SPREADSHEET #3

UNITED STATES HOUSE OF REPRESENTATIVES DISTRICT

	A	B	C	D	E
1			Nebraska		
2					
3		Votes Cast		Elector Number	
4		0		0	
5					
6	US District	Votes	%	President A	President B
7	1				
8	President A	0	B8/B4	IF(B8>B9,1,0)	
9	President B	0	B9/B4		IF(C8<C9,1,0)
10	2				
11	President A	0	B11/B4	IF(B11>B12,1,0)	
12	President B	0	B12/B4		IF(C11<C12,1,0)
13	3				
14	President A	0	B14/B4	IF(B14>B15,1,0)	
15	President B	0	B15/B4		IF(C14<C15,1,0)
16	Total			SUM(D8:D15)	SUM(E8:E15)
	Total Electoral	Percentage	Calculation	D4/A13*D16	D4/A13*E16

ARKANSAS, KANSAS, AND MISSISSIPPI

PRESIDENTIAL SPREADSHEET #4

UNITED STATES HOUSE OF REPRESENTATIVES DISTRICT

	A	B	C	D	E
1					
2					
3		Votes Cast		Elector Number	
4		0		0	
5					
6	US District	Votes	%	President A	President B
7	1				
8	President A	0	B8/B4	IF(B8>B9,1,0)	
9	President B	0	B9/B4		IF(C8<C9,1,0)
10	2				
11	President A	0	B11/B4	IF(B11>B12,1,0)	
12	President B	0	B12/B4		IF(C11<C12,1,0)
13	3				
14	President A	0	B14/B4	IF(B14>B15,1,0)	
15	President B	0	B15/B4		IF(C14<C15,1,0)
14	4				
17	President A	0	B17/B4	IF(B17>B18,1,0)	
18	President B	0	B18/B4		IF(C17<C18,1,0)
19	Total			SUM(D8:D18)	SUM(E8:E18)
	Total Electoral	Percentage	Calculation	D4/A14*D19	D4/A14*E19

IOWA, OKLAHOMA, AND OREGON

PRESIDENTIAL SPREADSHEET #5

UNITED STATES HOUSE OF REPRESENTATIVES DISTRICT

	A	B	C	D	E
1			Iowa		
2					
3		Votes Cast		Elector Number	
4		0		0	
5					
6	US District	Votes		President A	President B
7	1				
8	President A	0	B8/B4	IF(B8>B9,1,0)	
9	President B	0	B9/B4		IF(C8<C9,1,0)
10	2				
11	President A	0	B11/B4	IF(B11>B12,1,0)	
12	President B	0	B12/B4		IF(C11<C12,1,0)
13	3				
14	President A	0	B14/B4	IF(B14>B15,1,0)	
15	President B	0	B15/B4		IF(C14<C15,1,0)
14	4				
17	President A	0	B17/B4	IF(B17>B18,1,0)	
18	President B	0	B18/B4		IF(C17<C18,1,0)
19	5				
20	President A	0	B20/B4	IF(B20>B21,1,0)	

	A	B	C	D	E
21	President B	0	B21/B4		IF(C20<C21,1,0)
22	Total			SUM(D8:D21)	SUM(E8:E21)
	Total Electoral	Percentage	Calculation	D4/A19*D22	D4/A19*E22

SOUTH CAROLINA

PRESIDENTIAL SPREADSHEET #6

UNITED STATES HOUSE OF REPRESENTATIVES DISTRICT

	A	B	C	D	E
1			South Carolina		
2					
3		Votes Cast	Records	Elector Number	
4		0	0	0	
5					
6	US District	Votes	%	President A	President B
7	1				
8	President A	0	B8/B4	IF(B8>B9,1,0)	
9	President B	0	B9/B4		IF(C8<C9,1,0)
10	2				
11	President A	0	B11/B4	IF(B11>B12,1,0)	
12	President B	0	B12/B4		IF(C11<C12,1,0)
13	3				
14	President A	0	B14/B4	IF(B14>B15,1,0)	
15	President B	0	B15/B4		IF(C14<C15,1,0)
14	4				
17	President A	0	B17/B4	IF(B17>B18,1,0)	
18	President B	0	B18/B4		IF(C17<C18,1,0)
19	5				
20	President A	0	B20/B4	IF(B20>B21,1,0)	
21	President B	0	B21/B4		IF(C20<C21,1,0)
22	6				
23	President A	0	B23/B4	IF(B23>B24,1,0)	
24	President B	0	B24/B4		IF(C23<C24,1,0)
25	Total			SUM(D8:D24)	SUM(E8:E24)
	Total Electoral	Percentage	Calculation	D4/A22*D25	D4/A22*E25

ALABAMA

PRESIDENTIAL SPREADSHEET #7

UNITED STATES HOUSE OF REPRESENTATIVES DISTRICT

	A	B	C	D	E
1			Alabama		
2					
3		Votes Cast		Elector Number	
4		0		0	
5					
6	District	Votes	%	Senator A	Senator B

202

	A	B	C	D	E
7	1				
8	Senator A	0	B8/B4	IF(B8>B9,1,0)	
9	Senator B	0	B9/B4		IF(C8<C9,1,0)
10	2				
11	Senator A	0	B11/B4	IF(B11>B12,1,0)	
12	Senator B	0	B12/B4		IF(C11<C12,1,0)
13	3				
14	Senator A	0	B14/B4	IF(B14>B15,1,0)	
15	Senator B	0	B15/B4		IF(C14<C15,1,0)
14	4				
17	Senator A	0	B17/B4	IF(B17>B18,1,0)	
18	Senator B	0	B18/B4		IF(C17<C18,1,0)
19	5				
20	Senator A	0	B20/B4	IF(B20>B21,1,0)	
21	Senator B	0	B21/B4		IF(C20<C21,1,0)
22	6				
23	Senator A	0	B23/B4	IF(B23>B24,1,0)	
24	Senator B	0	B24/B4		IF(C23<C24,1,0)
25	7				
26	Senator A	0	B26/B4	IF(B26>B27,1,0)	
27	Senator B	0	B27/B4		IF(C26<C27,1,0)
28	Total			SUM(D8:D27)	SUM(E8:E27)
	Total Electoral	Percentage	Calculation	D4/A25*D28	D4/A25*E28

MARYLAND, MINNESOTA, AND WISCONSIN

PRESIDENTIAL SPREADSHEET #8

UNITED STATES HOUSE OF REPRESENTATIVES DISTRICT

	A	B	C	D	E
1			Maryland		
2					
3		Votes Cast	Records	Elector Number	
4		0	0	0	
5					
6	US District	Votes	%	President A	President B
7	1				
8	President A	0	B8/B4	IF(B8>B9,1,0)	
9	President B	0	B9/B4		IF(C8<C9,1,0)
10	2				
11	President A	0	B11/B4	IF(B11>B12,1,0)	
12	President B	0	B12/B4		IF(C11<C12,1,0)
13	3				
14	President A	0	B14/B4	IF(B14>B15,1,0)	
15	President B	0	B15/B4		IF(C14<C15,1,0)
14	4				
17	President A	0	B17/B4	IF(B17>B18,1,0)	
18	President B	0	B18/B4		IF(C17<C18,1,0)
19	5				
20	President A	0	B20/B4	IF(B20>B21,1,0)	
21	President B	0	B21/B4		IF(C20<C21,1,0)
22	6				
23	President A	0	B23/B4	IF(B23>B24,1,0)	
24	President B	0	B24/B4		IF(C23<C24,1,0)
25	7				
26	President A	0	B26/B4	IF(B26>B27,1,0)	
27	President B	0	B27/B4		IF(C26<C27,1,0)
28	8				

	A	B	C	D	E
29	President A	0	B29/B4	IF(B29>B30,1,0)	
30	President B	0	B30/B4		IF(C29<C30,1,0)
31	Total			SUM(D8:D30)	SUM(E8:E30)
Total Electoral	Percentage	Calculation	D4/A28*D31	D4/A28*E31

MISSOURI, TENNESSEE, AND WASHINGTON

PRESIDENTIAL SPREAD SHEET #9

UNITED STATES HOUSE OF REPRESENTATIVES DISTRICT

	A	B	C	D	E
1			Tennessee		
2					
3		Votes Cast	Records	Elector Number	
4		0	0	0	
5					
6	US District	Votes	%	President A	President B
7	1				
8	President A	0	B8/B4	IF(B8>B9,1,0)	
9	President B	0	B9/B4		IF(C8<C9,1,0)
10	2				
11	President A	0	B11/B4	IF(B11>B12,1,0)	
12	President B	0	B12/B4		IF(C11<C12,1,0)
13	3				
14	President A	0	B14/B4	IF(B14>B15,1,0)	
15	President B	0	B15/B4		IF(C14<C15,1,0)
14	4				
17	President A	0	B17/B4	IF(B17>B18,1,0)	
18	President B	0	B18/B4		IF(C17<C18,1,0)
19	5				
20	President A	0	B20/B4	IF(B20>B21,1,0)	
21	President B	0	B21/B4		IF(C20<C21,1,0)
22	6				
23	President A	0	B23/B4	IF(B23>B24,1,0)	
24	President B	0	B24/B4		IF(C23<C24,1,0)
25	7				
26	President A	0	B26/B4	IF(B26>B27,1,0)	
27	President B	0	B27/B4		IF(C26<C27,1,0)
28	8				
29	President A	0	B29/B4	IF(B29>B30,1,0)	
30	President B	0	B30/B4		IF(C29<C30,1,0)
31	9				
32	President A	0	B32/B4	IF(B32>B33,1,0)	
33	President B	0	B33/B4		IF(C32<C33,1,0)
34	Total			SUM(D8:D33)	SUM(E8:E33)
	Total Electoral	Percentage	Calculation	D4/A31*D34	D4/A31*E34

MASSACHUSETTS

PRESIDENTIAL SPREADSHEET #10

UNITED STATES HOUSE OF REPRESENTATIVES DISTRICT

	A	B	C	D	E
1			Massachusetts		
2					
3		Votes Cast	Records	Elector Number	
4		0	0	0	
5					
6	US District	Votes	%	President A	President B
7	1				
8	President A	0	B8/B4	IF(B8>B9,1,0)	
9	President B	0	B9/B4		IF(C8<C9,1,0)
10	2				
11	President A	0	B11/B4	IF(B11>B12,1,0)	
12	President B	0	B12/B4		IF(C11<C12,1,0)
13	3				
14	President A	0	B14/B4	IF(B14>B15,1,0)	
15	President B	0	B15/B4		IF(C14<C15,1,0)
14	4				
17	President A	0	B17/B4	IF(B17>B18,1,0)	
18	President B	0	B18/B4		IF(C17<C18,1,0)
19	5				
20	President A	0	B20/B4	IF(B20>B21,1,0)	
21	President B	0	B21/B4		IF(C20<C21,1,0)
22	6				
23	President A	0	B23/B4	IF(B23>B24,1,0)	
24	President B	0	B24/B4		IF(C23<C24,1,0)
25	7				
26	President A	0	B26/B4	IF(B26>B27,1,0)	
27	President B	0	B27/B4		IF(C26<C27,1,0)
28	8				
29	President A	0	B29/B4	IF(B29>B30,1,0)	
30	President B	0	B30/B4		IF(C29<C30,1,0)
31	9				
32	President A	0	B32/B4	IF(B32>B33,1,0)	
33	President B	0	B33/B4		IF(C32<C33,1,0)
34	10				
35	President A	0	B35/B4	IF(B35>B36,1,0)	
36	President B	0	B36/B4		IF(C35<C36,1,0)
37	Total			SUM(D8:D36)	SUM(E8:E36)
	Total Electoral	Percentage	Calculation	D4/A34*D37	D4/A34*E37

VIRGINIA

PRESIDENTIAL SPREADSHEET #11

UNITED STATES HOUSE OF REPRESENTATIVES DISTRICT

	A	B	C	D	E
1			Virginia		
2					
3		Votes Cast	Records	Elector Number	

	A	B	C	D	E
4		0	0	0	
5					
6	US District	Votes	%	President A	President B
7	1				
8	President A	0	B8/B4	IF(B8>B9,1,0)	
9	President B	0	B9/B4		IF(C8<C9,1,0)
10	2				
11	President A	0	B11/B4	IF(B11>B12,1,0)	
12	President B	0	B12/B4		IF(C11<C12,1,0)
13	3				
14	President A	0	B14/B4	IF(B14>B15,1,0)	
15	President B	0	B15/B4		IF(C14<C15,1,0)
14	4				
17	President A	0	B17/B4	IF(B17>B18,1,0)	
18	President B	0	B18/B4		IF(C17<C18,1,0)
19	5				
20	President A	0	B20/B4	IF(B20>B21,1,0)	
21	President B	0	B21/B4		IF(C20<C21,1,0)
22	6				
23	President A	0	B23/B4	IF(B23>B24,1,0)	
24	President B	0	B24/B4		IF(C23<C24,1,0)
25	7				
26	President A	0	B26/B4	IF(B26>B27,1,0)	
27	President B	0	B27/B4		IF(C26<C27,1,0)
28	8				
29	President A	0	B29/B4	IF(B29>B30,1,0)	
30	President B	0	B30/B4		IF(C29<C30,1,0)
31	9				
32	President A	0	B32/B4	IF(B32>B33,1,0)	
33	President B	0	B33/B4		IF(C32<C33,1,0)
34	10				
35	President A	0	B35/B4	IF(B35>B36,1,0)	
36	President B	0	B36/B4		IF(C35<C36,1,0)
37	11				
38	President A	0	B38/B4	IF(B38>B39,1,0)	
39	President B	0	B39/B4		IF(C38<C39,1,0)
40	Total			SUM(D8:D39)	SUM(E8:E39)
	Total Electoral	Percentage	Calculation	D4/A37*D40	D4/A37*E40

GEORGIA, NEW JERSEY, AND NORTH CAROLINA

PRESIDENTIAL SPREADSHEET #12

UNITED STATES HOUSE OF REPRESENTATIVES DISTRICT

	A	B	C	D	E
1			Georgia		
2					
3					
4		Votes Cast		Electoral Number	
5		0		0	
6					
7	District	Votes	%	President A	President B
8	1				
9	President A	0	B8/B4	IF(C8>C9,1,0)	
10	President B	0	B9/B4		IF(C8<C9,1,0)
11	2				
12	President A	0	B11/B4	IF(C11>C12,1,0)	
13	President B	0	B12/B4		IF(C11<C12,1,0)

	A	B	C	D	E
14	3				
15	President A	0	B14/B4	IF(C14>C15,1,0)	
14	President B	0	B15/B4		IF(C14<C15,1,0)
17	4				
18	President A	0	B17/B4	IF(C17>C18,1,0)	
19	President B	0	B18/B4		IF(C17<C18,1,0)
20	5				
21	President A	0	B20/B4	IF(C20>C21,1,0)	
22	President B	0	B21/B4		IF(C20<C21,1,0)
23	6				
24	President A	0	B23/B4	IF(C23>C24,1,0)	
25	President B	0	B24/B4		IF(C23<C24,1,0)
26	7				
27	President A	0	B26/B4	IF(C26>C27,1,0)	
28	President B	0	B27/B4		IF(C26<C27,1,0)
29	8				
30	President A	0	B29/B4	IF(C29>C30,1,0)	
31	President B	0	B30/B4		IF(C29<C30,1,0)
32	9				
33	President A	0	B32/B4	IF(C32>C33,1,0)	
34	President B	0	B33/B4		IF(C32<C33,1,0)
35	10				
36	President A	0	B35/B4	IF(C35>C36,1,0)	
37	President B	0	B36/B4		IF(C35<C36,1,0)
38	11				
39	President A	0	B38/B4	IF(C38>C39,1,0)	
40	President B	0	B39/B4		IF(C38<C39,1,0)
41	12				
42	President A	0	B41/B4	IF(C41>C42,1,0)	
43	President B	0	B42/B4		IF(C41<C42,1,0)
44	13				
45	President A	0	B44/B4	IF(C44>C45,1,0)	
46	President B	0	B45/B4		IF(C44<C45,1,0)
47	Total			SUM(D8:D45)	SUM(E8:E45)
	Total Electoral	Percentage	Calculation	D5/A44*D47	D5/A44*E47

MICHIGAN

PRESIDENTIAL SPREADSHEET #13

UNITED STATES HOUSE OF REPRESENTATIVES DISTRICT

	A	B	C	D	E
1			Michigan		
2					
3		Votes Cast		Electoral Number	
4		0		0	
5					
6	District	Votes	%	President A	President B
7	1				
8	President A	0	B8/B4	IF(C8>C9,1,0)	
9	President B	0	B9/B4		IF(C8<C9,1,0)
10	2				
11	President A	0	B11/B4	IF(C11>C12,1,0)	
12	President B	0	B12/B4		IF(C11<C12,1,0)
13	3				
14	President A	0	B14/B4	IF(C14>C15,1,0)	

	A	B	C	D	E
15	President B	0	B15/B4		IF(C14<C15,1,0)
14	4				
17	President A	0	B17/B4	IF(C17>C18,1,0)	
18	President B	0	B18/B4		IF(C17<C18,1,0)
19	5				
20	President A	0	B20/B4	IF(C20>C21,1,0)	
21	President B	0	B21/B4		IF(C20<C21,1,0)
22	6				
23	President A	0	B23/B4	IF(C23>C24,1,0)	
24	President B	0	B24/B4		IF(C23<C24,1,0)
25	7				
26	President A	0	B26/B4	IF(C26>C27,1,0)	
27	President B	0	B27/B4		IF(C26<C27,1,0)
28	8				
29	President A	0	B29/B4	IF(C29>C30,1,0)	
30	President B	0	B30/B4		IF(C29<C30,1,0)
31	9				
32	President A	0	B32/B4	IF(C32>C33,1,0)	
33	President B	0	B33/B4		IF(C32<C33,1,0)
34	10				
35	President A	0	B35/B4	IF(C35>C36,1,0)	
36	President B	0	B36/B4		IF(C35<C36,1,0)
37	11				
38	President A	0	B38/B4	IF(C38>C39,1,0)	
39	President B	0	B39/B4		IF(C38<C39,1,0)
40	12				
41	President A	0	B41/B4	IF(C41>C42,1,0)	
42	President B	0	B42/B4		IF(C41<C42,1,0)
43	13				
44	President A	0	B44/B4	IF(C44>C45,1,0)	
45	President B	0	B45/B4		IF(C44<C45,1,0)
46	14				
47	President A	0	B47/B4	IF(C47>C48,1,0)	
48	President B	0	B48/B4		IF(C47<C48,1,0)
49	15				
50	President A	0	B50/B4	IF(C50>C51,1,0)	
51	President B	0	B51/B4		IF(C50<C51,1,0)
52	Total			SUM(D8:D51)	SUM(E8:E51)
53	Total Electoral	Percentage	Calculation	D4/A49*D52	D4/A49*E52

The demonstrated spreadsheets are designed for the presidential campaign using the state government United States House of Representatives districts as the base districts.

Input the state government district's presidential results in column B.

Using the spreadsheet's displayed instructions as a flowchart, a computer programmer can write a computer program that will tabulate votes as a voter goes through the act of voting. The technology already exists where a computer is used to process a vote being cast at polling stations.

At the end of the vote-casting day, the computer delivers the candidates' total popular and decimal electoral vote. The decimal electoral vote would be calculated in double precision, percentage addition.

Total electoral computes the total percentage electoral vote.

According to the Tenth Amendment, the state government legislatures have the power to pick the electors who represent the state governments and the people within the US House of Representatives quasi-equal populated districts. The power belongs to the people within the US House of Representatives quasi-equal populated districts, indicating that the US House of Representatives' districts should be electing the president.

Total computes the total number of US House of Representatives quasi-equal populated districts.

MOB RULE (AVOID)

Governor's Vote (State Government Assembly Districts)

Governor Spreadsheet State Government Assembly

400 Districts

	A	B	C	D	E	F
1						
2						
3						
4						
5	District	Total Votes	Votes	%	Candidate A	Candidate B
6	1	C7+C8				
7	Candidate A		0	B6/C7	IF(D7>D8,1,0)	
8	Candidate B		0	B6/C8		IF(D8>D7,1,0)
9	2	C10+C11				
10	Candidate A		0	B9/C10	IF(D10>D11,1,0)	
11	Candidate B		0	B9/C11		IF(D11>D10,1,0)
12	3	C13+C14				
13	Candidate A		0	B12/C13	IF(D13>D14,1,0)	
14	Candidate B		0	B12/C14		IF(D14>D13,1,0)
15	4	C16+C17				
16	Candidate A		0	B15/C16	IF(D16>D17,1,0)	
17	Candidate B		0	B15/C17		IF(D17>D16,1,0)
18	5	C19+C20				
19	Candidate A		0	B18/C19	IF(D19>D20,1,0)	
20	Candidate B		0	B18/C20		IF(D20>D19,1,0)
21	6	C22+C23				
22	Candidate A		0	B21/C22	IF(D22>D23,1,0)	
23	Candidate B		0	B21/C23		IF(D23>D22,1,0)
24	7	C25+C26				
25	Candidate A		0	B24/C25	IF(D25>D26,1,0)	

	A	B	C	D	E	F
26	Candidate B		0	B24/C26		IF(D26>D25,1,0)
27	8	C28+C29				
28	Candidate A		0	B27/C28	IF(D28>D29,1,0)	
29	Candidate B		0	B27/C29		IF(D29>D28,1,0)
30	9	C31+C32				
31	Candidate A		0	B30/C31	IF(D31>D32,1,0)	
32	Candidate B		0	B30/C32		IF(D32>D31,1,0)
33	10	C34+C35				
34	Candidate A		0	B33/C34	IF(D34>D35,1,0)	
35	Candidate B		0	B33/C35		IF(D35>D34,1,0)
36	11	C37+C38				
37	Candidate A		0	B36/C37	IF(D37>D38,1,0)	
38	Candidate B		0	B36/C38		IF(D38>D37,1,0)
39	12	C40+C41				
40	Candidate A		0	B39/C40	IF(D40>D41,1,0)	
41	Candidate B		0	B39/C41		IF(D41>D40,1,0)
42	13	C43+C44				
43	Candidate A		0	B42/C43	IF(D43>D44,1,0)	
44	Candidate B		0	B42/C44		IF(D44>D43,1,0)
45	14	C46+C47				
46	Candidate A		0	B45/C46	IF(D46>D47,1,0)	
47	Candidate B		0	B45/C47		IF(D47>D46,1,0)
48	15	C49+C50				
49	Candidate A		0	B48/C49	IF(D49>D50,1,0)	
50	Candidate B		0	B48/C50		IF(D50>D49,1,0)
51	16	C52+C53				
52	Candidate A		0	B51/C52	IF(D52>D53,1,0)	
53	Candidate B		0	B51/C53		IF(D53>D52,1,0)
54	17	C55+C56				
55	Candidate A		0	B54/C55	IF(D55>D56,1,0)	
56	Candidate B		0	B54/C56		IF(D56>D55,1,0)
57	18	C58+C59				
58	Candidate A		0	B57/C58	IF(D58>D59,1,0)	
59	Candidate B		0	B57/C59		IF(D59>D58,1,0)
60	19	C61+C62				

	A	B	C	D	E	F
61	Candidate A		0	B60/C61	IF(D61>D62,1,0)	
62	Candidate B		0	B60/C62		IF(D62>D61,1,0)
63	20	C64+C65				
64	Candidate A		0	B63/C64	IF(D64>D65,1,0)	
65	Candidate B		0	B63/C65		IF(D65>D64,1,0)
66	21	C67+C68				
67	Candidate A		0	B66/C67	IF(D67>D68,1,0)	
68	Candidate B		0	B66/C68		IF(D68>D67,1,0)
69	22	C70+C71				
70	Candidate A		0	B69/C70	IF(D70>D71,1,0)	
71	Candidate B		0	B69/C71		IF(D71>D70,1,0)
72	23	C73+C74				
73	Candidate A		0	B72/C73	IF(D73>D74,1,0)	
74	Candidate B		0	B72/C74		IF(D74>D73,1,0)
75	24	C76+C77				
76	Candidate A		0	B75/C76	IF(D76>D77,1,0)	
77	Candidate B		0	B75/C77		IF(D77>D76,1,0)
78	25	C79+C80				
79	Candidate A		0	B78/C79	IF(D79>D80,1,0)	
80	Candidate B		0	B78/C80		IF(D80>D79,1,0)
81	26	C82+C83				
82	Candidate A		0	B81/C82	IF(D82>D83,1,0)	
83	Candidate B		0	B81/C83		IF(D83>D82,1,0)
84	27	C85+C86				
85	Candidate A		0	B84/C85	IF(D85>D86,1,0)	
86	Candidate B		0	B84/C86		IF(D86>D85,1,0)
87	28	C88+C89				
88	Candidate A		0	B87/C88	IF(D88>D89,1,0)	
89	Candidate B		0	B87/C89		IF(D89>D88,1,0)
90	29	C91+C92				
91	Candidate A		0	B90/C91	IF(D91>D92,1,0)	
92	Candidate B		0	B90/C92		IF(D92>D91,1,0)
93	30	C94+C95				
94	Candidate A		0	B93/C94	IF(D94>D95,1,0)	
95	Candidate B		0	B93/C95		IF(D95>D94,1,0)

	A	B	C	D	E	F
96	31	C97+C98				
97	Candidate A		0	B96/C97	IF(D97>D98,1,0)	
98	Candidate B		0	B96/C98		IF(D98>D97,1,0)
99	32	C100+C101				
100	Candidate A		0	B99/C100	IF(D100>D101,1,0)	
101	Candidate B		0	B99/C101		IF(D101>D100,1,0)
102	33	C103+C104				
103	Candidate A		0	B102/C103	IF(D103>D104,1,0)	
104	Candidate B		0	B102/C104		IF(D104>D103,1,0)
105	34	C106+C107				
106	Candidate A		0	B105/C106	IF(D106>D107,1,0)	
107	Candidate B		0	B105/C107		IF(D107>D106,1,0)
108	35	C109+C110				
109	Candidate A		0	B108/C109	IF(D109>D110,1,0)	
110	Candidate B		0	B108/C110		IF(D110>D109,1,0)
111	36	C112+C113				
112	Candidate A		0	B111/C112	IF(D112>D113,1,0)	
113	Candidate B		0	B111/C113		IF(D113>D112,1,0)
114	37	C115+C116				
115	Candidate A		0	B114/C115	IF(D115>D116,1,0)	
116	Candidate B		0	B114/C116		IF(D116>D115,1,0)
117	38	C118+C119				
118	Candidate A		0	B117/C118	IF(D118>D119,1,0)	
119	Candidate B		0	B117/C119		IF(D119>D118,1,0)
120	39	C121+C122				
121	Candidate A		0	B120/C121	IF(D121>D122,1,0)	
122	Candidate B		0	B120/C122		IF(D122>D121,1,0)
123	40	C124+C125				
124	Candidate A		0	B123/C124	IF(D124>D125,1,0)	
125	Candidate B		0	B123/C125		IF(D125>D124,1,0)
126	41	C127+C128				
127	Candidate A		0	B126/C127	IF(D127>D128,1,0)	
128	Candidate B		0	B126/C128		IF(D128>D127,1,0)
129	42	C130+C131				
130	Candidate A		0	B129/C130	IF(D130>D131,1,0)	

	A	B	C	D	E	F
131	Candidate B		0	B129/C131		IF(D131>D130,1,0)
132	43	C133+C134				
133	Candidate A		0	B132/C133	IF(D133>D134,1,0)	
134	Candidate B		0	B132/C134		IF(D134>D133,1,0)
135	44	C136+C137				
136	Candidate A		0	B135/C136	IF(D136>D137,1,0)	
137	Candidate B		0	B135/C137		IF(D137>D136,1,0)
138	45	C139+C140				
139	Candidate A		0	B138/C139	IF(D139>D140,1,0)	
140	Candidate B		0	B138/C140		IF(D140>D139,1,0)
141	46	C142+C143				
142	Candidate A		0	B141/C142	IF(D142>D143,1,0)	
143	Candidate B		0	B141/C143		IF(D143>D142,1,0)
144	47	C145+C146				
145	Candidate A		0	B144/C145	IF(D145>D146,1,0)	
146	Candidate B		0	B144/C146		IF(D146>D145,1,0)
147	48	C148+C149				
148	Candidate A		0	B147/C148	IF(D148>D149,1,0)	
149	Candidate B		0	B147/C149		IF(D149>D148,1,0)
150	49	C151+C152				
151	Candidate A		0	B150/C151	IF(D151>D152,1,0)	
152	Candidate B		0	B150/C152		IF(D152>D151,1,0)
153	50	C154+C155				
154	Candidate A		0	B153/C154	IF(D154>D155,1,0)	
155	Candidate B		0	B153/C155		IF(D155>D154,1,0)
156	51	C157+C158				
157	Candidate A		0	B156/C157	IF(D157>D158,1,0)	
158	Candidate B		0	B156/C158		IF(D158>D157,1,0)
159	52	C160+C161				
160	Candidate A		0	B159/C160	IF(D160>D161,1,0)	
161	Candidate B		0	B159/C161		IF(D161>D160,1,0)
162	53	C163+C164				
163	Candidate A		0	B162/C163	IF(D163>D164,1,0)	
164	Candidate B		0	B162/C164		IF(D164>D163,1,0)
165	54	C166+C167				

	A	B	C	D	E	F
166	Candidate A		0	B165/C166	IF(D166>D167,1,0)	
167	Candidate B		0	B165/C167		IF(D167>D166,1,0)
168	55	C169+C170				
169	Candidate A		0	B168/C169	IF(D169>D170,1,0)	
170	Candidate B		0	B168/C170		IF(D170>D169,1,0)
171	56	C172+C173				
172	Candidate A		0	B171/C172	IF(D172>D173,1,0)	
173	Candidate B		0	B171/C173		IF(D173>D172,1,0)
174	57	C175+C176				
175	Candidate A		0	B174/C175	IF(D175>D176,1,0)	
176	Candidate B		0	B174/C176		IF(D176>D175,1,0)
177	58	C178+C179				
178	Candidate A		0	B177/C178	IF(D178>D179,1,0)	
179	Candidate B		0	B177/C179		IF(D179>D178,1,0)
180	59	C181+C182				
181	Candidate A		0	B180/C181	IF(D181>D182,1,0)	
182	Candidate B		0	B180/C182		IF(D182>D181,1,0)
183	60	C184+C185				
184	Candidate A		0	B183/C184	IF(D184>D185,1,0)	
185	Candidate B		0	B183/C185		IF(D185>D184,1,0)
186	61	C187+C188				
187	Candidate A		0	B186/C187	IF(D187>D188,1,0)	
188	Candidate B		0	B186/C188		IF(D188>D187,1,0)
189	62	C190+C191				
190	Candidate A		0	B189/C190	IF(D190>D191,1,0)	
191	Candidate B		0	B189/C191		IF(D191>D190,1,0)
192	63	C193+C194				
193	Candidate A		0	B192/C193	IF(D193>D194,1,0)	
194	Candidate B		0	B192/C194		IF(D194>D193,1,0)
195	64	C196+C197				
196	Candidate A		0	B195/C196	IF(D196>D197,1,0)	
197	Candidate B		0	B195/C197		IF(D197>D196,1,0)
198	65	C199+C200				
199	Candidate A		0	B198/C199	IF(D199>D200,1,0)	
200	Candidate B		0	B198/C200		IF(D200>D199,1,0)

	A	B	C	D	E	F
201	66	C202+C203				
202	Candidate A		0	B201/C202	IF(D202>D203,1,0)	
203	Candidate B		0	B201/C203		IF(D203>D202,1,0)
204	67	C205+C206				
205	Candidate A		0	B204/C205	IF(D205>D206,1,0)	
206	Candidate B		0	B204/C206		IF(D206>D205,1,0)
207	68	C208+C209				
208	Candidate A		0	B207/C208	IF(D208>D209,1,0)	
209	Candidate B		0	B207/C209		IF(D209>D208,1,0)
210	69	C211+C212				
211	Candidate A		0	B210/C211	IF(D211>D212,1,0)	
212	Candidate B		0	B210/C212		IF(D212>D211,1,0)
213	70	C214+C215				
214	Candidate A		0	B213/C214	IF(D214>D215,1,0)	
215	Candidate B		0	B213/C215		IF(D215>D214,1,0)
216	71	C217+C218				
217	Candidate A		0	B216/C217	IF(D217>D218,1,0)	
218	Candidate B		0	B216/C218		IF(D218>D217,1,0)
219	72	C220+C221				
220	Candidate A		0	B219/C220	IF(D220>D221,1,0)	
221	Candidate B		0	B219/C221		IF(D221>D220,1,0)
222	73	C223+C224				
223	Candidate A		0	B222/C223	IF(D223>D224,1,0)	
224	Candidate B		0	B222/C224		IF(D224>D223,1,0)
225	74	C226+C227				
226	Candidate A		0	B225/C226	IF(D226>D227,1,0)	
227	Candidate B		0	B225/C227		IF(D227>D226,1,0)
228	75	C229+C230				
229	Candidate A		0	B228/C229	IF(D229>D230,1,0)	
230	Candidate B		0	B228/C230		IF(D230>D229,1,0)
231	76	C232+C233				
232	Candidate A		0	B231/C232	IF(D232>D233,1,0)	
233	Candidate B		0	B231/C233		IF(D233>D232,1,0)
234	77	C235+C236				
235	Candidate A		0	B234/C235	IF(D235>D236,1,0)	

	A	B	C	D	E	F
236	Candidate B		0	B234/C236		IF(D236>D235,1,0)
237	78	C238+C239				
238	Candidate A		0	B237/C238	IF(D238>D239,1,0)	
239	Candidate B		0	B237/C239		IF(D239>D238,1,0)
240	79	C241+C242				
241	Candidate A		0	B240/C241	IF(D241>D242,1,0)	
242	Candidate B		0	B240/C242		IF(D242>D241,1,0)
243	80	C244+C245				
244	Candidate A		0	B243/C244	IF(D244>D245,1,0)	
245	Candidate B		0	B243/C245		IF(D245>D244,1,0)
246	81	C247+C248				
247	Candidate A		0	B246/C247	IF(D247>D248,1,0)	
248	Candidate B		0	B246/C248		IF(D248>D247,1,0)
249	82	C250+C251				
250	Candidate A		0	B249/C250	IF(D250>D251,1,0)	
251	Candidate B		0	B249/C251		IF(D251>D250,1,0)
252	83	C253+C254				
253	Candidate A		0	B252/C253	IF(D253>D254,1,0)	
254	Candidate B		0	B252/C254		IF(D254>D253,1,0)
255	84	C256+C257				
256	Candidate A		0	B255/C256	IF(D256>D257,1,0)	
257	Candidate B		0	B255/C257		IF(D257>D256,1,0)
258	85	C259+C260				
259	Candidate A		0	B258/C259	IF(D259>D260,1,0)	
260	Candidate B		0	B258/C260		IF(D260>D259,1,0)
261	86	C262+C263				
262	Candidate A		0	B261/C262	IF(D262>D263,1,0)	
263	Candidate B		0	B261/C263		IF(D263>D262,1,0)
264	87	C265+C266				
265	Candidate A		0	B264/C265	IF(D265>D266,1,0)	
266	Candidate B		0	B264/C266		IF(D266>D265,1,0)
267	88	C268+C269				
268	Candidate A		0	B267/C268	IF(D268>D269,1,0)	
269	Candidate B		0	B267/C269		IF(D269>D268,1,0)
270	89	C271+C272				

	A	B	C	D	E	F
271	Candidate A		0	B270/C271	IF(D271>D272,1,0)	
272	Candidate B		0	B270/C272		IF(D272>D271,1,0)
273	90	C274+C275				
274	Candidate A		0	B273/C274	IF(D274>D275,1,0)	
275	Candidate B		0	B273/C275		IF(D275>D274,1,0)
276	91	C277+C278				
277	Candidate A		0	B276/C277	IF(D277>D278,1,0)	
278	Candidate B		0	B276/C278		IF(D278>D277,1,0)
279	92	C280+C281				
280	Candidate A		0	B279/C280	IF(D280>D281,1,0)	
281	Candidate B		0	B279/C281		IF(D281>D280,1,0)
282	93	C283+C284				
283	Candidate A		0	B282/C283	IF(D283>D284,1,0)	
284	Candidate B		0	B282/C284		IF(D284>D283,1,0)
285	94	C286+C287				
286	Candidate A		0	B285/C286	IF(D286>D287,1,0)	
287	Candidate B		0	B285/C287		IF(D287>D286,1,0)
288	95	C289+C290				
289	Candidate A		0	B288/C289	IF(D289>D290,1,0)	
290	Candidate B		0	B288/C290		IF(D290>D289,1,0)
291	96	C292+C293				
292	Candidate A		0	B291/C292	IF(D292>D293,1,0)	
293	Candidate B		0	B291/C293		IF(D293>D292,1,0)
294	97	C295+C296				
295	Candidate A		0	B294/C295	IF(D295>D296,1,0)	
296	Candidate B		0	B294/C296		IF(D296>D295,1,0)
297	98	C298+C299				
298	Candidate A		0	B297/C298	IF(D298>D299,1,0)	
299	Candidate B		0	B297/C299		IF(D299>D298,1,0)
300	99	C301+C302				
301	Candidate A		0	B300/C301	IF(D301>D302,1,0)	
302	Candidate B		0	B300/C302		IF(D302>D301,1,0)
303	100	C304+C305				
304	Candidate A		0	B303/C304	IF(D304>D305,1,0)	
305	Candidate B		0	B303/C305		IF(D305>D304,1,0)

	A	B	C	D	E	F
306	101	C307+C308				
307	Candidate A		0	B306/C307	IF(D307>D308,1,0)	
308	Candidate B		0	B306/C308		IF(D308>D307,1,0)
309	102	C310+C311				
310	Candidate A		0	B309/C310	IF(D310>D311,1,0)	
311	Candidate B		0	B309/C311		IF(D311>D310,1,0)
312	103	C313+C314				
313	Candidate A		0	B312/C313	IF(D313>D314,1,0)	
314	Candidate B		0	B312/C314		IF(D314>D313,1,0)
315	104	C316+C317				
316	Candidate A		0	B315/C316	IF(D316>D317,1,0)	
317	Candidate B		0	B315/C317		IF(D317>D316,1,0)
318	105	C319+C320				
319	Candidate A		0	B318/C319	IF(D319>D320,1,0)	
320	Candidate B		0	B318/C320		IF(D320>D319,1,0)
321	106	C322+C323				
322	Candidate A		0	B321/C322	IF(D322>D323,1,0)	
323	Candidate B		0	B321/C323		IF(D323>D322,1,0)
324	107	C325+C326				
325	Candidate A		0	B324/C325	IF(D325>D326,1,0)	
326	Candidate B		0	B324/C326		IF(D326>D325,1,0)
327	108	C328+C329				
328	Candidate A		0	B327/C328	IF(D328>D329,1,0)	
329	Candidate B		0	B327/C929		IF(D329>D328,1,0)
330	109	C331+C332				
331	Candidate A		0	B330/C331	IF(D331>D332,1,0)	
332	Candidate B		0	B330/C332		IF(D332>D331,1,0)
333	110	C334+C335				
334	Candidate A		0	B333/C334	IF(D334>D335,1,0)	
335	Candidate B		0	B333/C335		IF(D335>D334,1,0)
336	111	C337+C338				
337	Candidate A		0	B336/C337	IF(D337>D338,1,0)	
338	Candidate B		0	B336/C338		IF(D338>D337,1,0)
339	112	C340+C341				
340	Candidate A		0	B339/C340	IF(D340>D341,1,0)	

	A	B	C	D	E	F
341	Candidate B		0	B339/C341		IF(D341>D340,1,0)
342	113	C343+C344				
343	Candidate A		0	B342/C343	IF(D343>D344,1,0)	
344	Candidate B		0	B342/C344		IF(D344>D343,1,0)
345	114	C346+C347				
346	Candidate A		0	B345/C346	IF(D346>D347,1,0)	
347	Candidate B		0	B345/C347		IF(D347>D346,1,0)
348	115	C349+C350				
349	Candidate A		0	B348/C349	IF(D349>D350,1,0)	
350	Candidate B		0	B348/C350		IF(D350>D349,1,0)
351	116	C352+C353				
352	Candidate A		0	B351/C352	IF(D352>D353,1,0)	
353	Candidate B		0	B351/C353		IF(D353>D352,1,0)
354	117	C355+C356				
355	Candidate A		0	B354/C355	IF(D355>D356,1,0)	
356	Candidate B		0	B354/C356		IF(D356>D355,1,0)
357	118	C358+C359				
358	Candidate A		0	B357/C358	IF(D358>D359,1,0)	
359	Candidate B		0	B357/C359		IF(D359>D358,1,0)
360	119	C361+C362				
361	Candidate A		0	B360/C361	IF(D361>D362,1,0)	
362	Candidate B		0	B360/C362		IF(D362>D361,1,0)
363	120	C364+C365				
364	Candidate A		0	B363/C364	IF(D364>D365,1,0)	
365	Candidate B		0	B363/C365		IF(D365>D364,1,0)
366	121	C367+C368				
367	Candidate A		0	B366/C367	IF(D367>D368,1,0)	
368	Candidate B		0	B366/C368		IF(D368>D367,1,0)
369	122	C370+C371				
370	Candidate A		0	B369/C370	IF(D370>D371,1,0)	
371	Candidate B		0	B369/C371		IF(D371>D370,1,0)
372	123	C373+C374				
373	Candidate A		0	B372/C373	IF(D373>D374,1,0)	
374	Candidate B		0	B372/C374		IF(D374>D373,1,0)
375	124	C376+C377				

	A	B	C	D	E	F
376	Candidate A		0	B375/C376	IF(D376>D377,1,0)	
377	Candidate B		0	B375/C377		IF(D377>D376,1,0)
378	125	C379+C380				
379	Candidate A		0	B378/C379	IF(D379>D380,1,0)	
380	Candidate B		0	B378/C380		IF(D380>D379,1,0)
381	126	C382+C383				
382	Candidate A		0	B381/C382	IF(D382>D383,1,0)	
383	Candidate B		0	B381/C383		IF(D383>D382,1,0)
384	127	C385+C386				
385	Candidate A		0	B384/C385	IF(D385>D386,1,0)	
386	Candidate B		0	B384/C386		IF(D386>D385,1,0)
387	128	C388+C389				
388	Candidate A		0	B387/C388	IF(D388>D389,1,0)	
389	Candidate B		0	B387/C389		IF(D389>D388,1,0)
390	129	C391+C392				
391	Candidate A		0	B390/C391	IF(D391>D392,1,0)	
392	Candidate B		0	B390/C392		IF(D392>D391,1,0)
393	130	C394+C395				
394	Candidate A		0	B393/C394	IF(D394>D395,1,0)	
395	Candidate B		0	B393/C395		IF(D395>D394,1,0)
396	131	C397+C398				
397	Candidate A		0	B396/C397	IF(D397>D398,1,0)	
398	Candidate B		0	B396/C398		IF(D398>D397,1,0)
399	132	C400+C401				
400	Candidate A		0	B399/C400	IF(D400>D401,1,0)	
401	Candidate B		0	B399/C401		IF(D401>D400,1,0)
402	133	C403+C404				
403	Candidate A		0	B402/C403	IF(D403>D404,1,0)	
404	Candidate B		0	B402/C404		IF(D404>D403,1,0)
405	134	C406+C407				
406	Candidate A		0	B405/C406	IF(D406>D407,1,0)	
407	Candidate B		0	B405/C407		IF(D407>D406,1,0)
408	135	C409+C410				
409	Candidate A		0	B408/C409	IF(D409>D410,1,0)	
410	Candidate B		0	B408/C410		IF(D410>D409,1,0)

	A	B	C	D	E	F
411	136	C412+C413				
412	Candidate A		0	B411/C412	IF(D412>D413,1,0)	
413	Candidate B		0	B411/C413		IF(D413>D412,1,0)
414	137	C415+C416				
415	Candidate A		0	B414/C415	IF(D415>D416,1,0)	
416	Candidate B		0	B414/C416		IF(D416>D415,1,0)
417	138	C418+C419				
418	Candidate A		0	B417/C418	IF(D418>D419,1,0)	
419	Candidate B		0	B417/C419		IF(D419>D418,1,0)
420	139	C421+C422				
421	Candidate A		0	B420/C421	IF(D421>D422,1,0)	
422	Candidate B		0	B420/C422		IF(D422>D421,1,0)
423	140	C424+C425				
424	Candidate A		0	B423/C424	IF(D424>D425,1,0)	
425	Candidate B		0	B423/C425		IF(D425>D424,1,0)
426	141	C427+C428				
427	Candidate A		0	B426/C427	IF(D427>D428,1,0)	
428	Candidate B		0	B426/C428		IF(D428>D427,1,0)
429	142	C430+C431				
430	Candidate A		0	B429/C430	IF(D430>D431,1,0)	
431	Candidate B		0	B429/C431		IF(D431>D430,1,0)
432	143	C433+C434				
433	Candidate A		0	B432/C433	IF(D433>D434,1,0)	
434	Candidate B		0	B432/C434		IF(D434>D433,1,0)
435	144	C436+C437				
436	Candidate A		0	B435/C436	IF(D436>D437,1,0)	
437	Candidate B		0	B435/C437		IF(D437>D436,1,0)
438	145	C439+C440				
439	Candidate A		0	B438/C439	IF(D439>D440,1,0)	
440	Candidate B		0	B438/C440		IF(D440>D439,1,0)
441	146	C442+C443				
442	Candidate A		0	B441/C442	IF(D442>D443,1,0)	
443	Candidate B		0	B441/C443		IF(D443>D442,1,0)
444	147	C445+C446				
445	Candidate A		0	B444/C445	IF(D445>D446,1,0)	

	A	B	C	D	E	F
446	Candidate B		0	B444/C446		IF(D446>D445,1,0)
447	148	C448+C449				
448	Candidate A		0	B447/C448	IF(D448>D449,1,0)	
449	Candidate B		0	B447/C449		IF(D449>D448,1,0)
450	149	C451+C452				
451	Candidate A		0	B450/C451	IF(D451>D452,1,0)	
452	Candidate B		0	B450/C452		IF(D452>D451,1,0)
453	150	C454+C455				
454	Candidate A		0	B453/C454	IF(D454>D455,1,0)	
455	Candidate B		0	B453/C455		IF(D455>D454,1,0)
456	151	C457+C458				
457	Candidate A		0	B456/C457	IF(D457>D458,1,0)	
458	Candidate B		0	B456/C458		IF(D458>D457,1,0)
459	152	C460+C461				
460	Candidate A		0	B459/C460	IF(D460>D461,1,0)	
461	Candidate B		0	B459/C461		IF(D461>D460,1,0)
462	153	C463+C464				
463	Candidate A		0	B462/C463	IF(D463>D464,1,0)	
464	Candidate B		0	B462/C464		IF(D464>D463,1,0)
465	154	C466+C467				
466	Candidate A		0	B465/C466	IF(D466>D467,1,0)	
467	Candidate B		0	B465/C467		IF(D467>D466,1,0)
468	155	C469+C470				
469	Candidate A		0	B468/C469	IF(D469>D470,1,0)	
470	Candidate B		0	B468/C470		IF(D470>D469,1,0)
471	156	C472+C473				
472	Candidate A		0	B471/C472	IF(D472>D473,1,0)	
473	Candidate B		0	B471/C473		IF(D473>D472,1,0)
474	157	C475+C476				
475	Candidate A		0	B474/C475	IF(D475>D476,1,0)	
476	Candidate B		0	B474/C476		IF(D476>D475,1,0)
477	158	C478+C479				
478	Candidate A		0	B477/C478	IF(D478>D479,1,0)	
479	Candidate B		0	B477/C479		IF(D479>D478,1,0)
480	159	C481+C482				

	A	B	C	D	E	F
481	Candidate A		0	B480/C481	IF(D481>D482,1,0)	
482	Candidate B		0	B480/C482		IF(D482>D481,1,0)
483	160	C484+C485				
484	Candidate A		0	B483/C484	IF(D484>D485,1,0)	
485	Candidate B		0	B483/C485		IF(D485>D484,1,0)
486	161	C487+C488				
487	Candidate A		0	B486/C487	IF(D487>D488,1,0)	
488	Candidate B		0	B486/C488		IF(D488>D487,1,0)
489	162	C490+C491				
490	Candidate A		0	B489/C490	IF(D490>D491,1,0)	
491	Candidate B		0	B489/C491		IF(D491>D490,1,0)
492	163	C493+C494				
493	Candidate A		0	B492/C493	IF(D493>D494,1,0)	
494	Candidate B		0	B492/C494		IF(D494>D493,1,0)
495	164	C496+C497				
496	Candidate A		0	B495/C496	IF(D496>D497,1,0)	
497	Candidate B		0	B495/C497		IF(D497>D496,1,0)
498	165	C499+C500				
499	Candidate A		0	B498/C499	IF(D499>D500,1,0)	
500	Candidate B		0	B498/C500		IF(D500>D499,1,0)
501	166	C502+C503				
502	Candidate A		0	B501/C502	IF(D502>D503,1,0)	
503	Candidate B		0	B501/C503		IF(D503>D502,1,0)
504	167	C505+C506				
505	Candidate A		0	B504/C505	IF(D505>D506,1,0)	
506	Candidate B		0	B504/C506		IF(D506>D505,1,0)
507	168	C508+C509				
508	Candidate A		0	B507/C508	IF(D508>D509,1,0)	
509	Candidate B		0	B507/C509		IF(D509>D508,1,0)
510	169	C511+C512				
511	Candidate A		0	B510/C511	IF(D511>D512,1,0)	
512	Candidate B		0	B510/C512		IF(D512>D511,1,0)
513	170	C514+C515				
514	Candidate A		0	B513/C514	IF(D514>D515,1,0)	
515	Candidate B		0	B513/C515		IF(D515>D514,1,0)

	A	B	C	D	E	F
516	171	C517+C518				
517	Candidate A		0	B516/C517	IF(D517>D518,1,0)	
518	Candidate B		0	B516/C518		IF(D518>D517,1,0)
519	172	C520+C521				
520	Candidate A		0	B519/C520	IF(D520>D521,1,0)	
521	Candidate B		0	B519/C521		IF(D521>D520,1,0)
522	173	C523+C524				
523	Candidate A		0	B522/C523	IF(D523>D524,1,0)	
524	Candidate B		0	B522/C524		IF(D524>D523,1,0)
525	174	C526+C527				
526	Candidate A		0	B525/C526	IF(D526>D527,1,0)	
527	Candidate B		0	B525/C527		IF(D527>D526,1,0)
528	175	C529+C530				
529	Candidate A		0	B528/C529	IF(D529>D530,1,0)	
530	Candidate B		0	B528/C530		IF(D530>D529,1,0)
531	176	C532+C533				
532	Candidate A		0	B531/C532	IF(D532>D533,1,0)	
533	Candidate B		0	B531/C533		IF(D533>D532,1,0)
534	177	C535+C536				
535	Candidate A		0	B534/C535	IF(D535>D536,1,0)	
536	Candidate B		0	B534/C536		IF(D536>D535,1,0)
537	178	C538+C539				
538	Candidate A		0	B537/C538	IF(D538>D539,1,0)	
539	Candidate B		0	B537/C539		IF(D539>D538,1,0)
540	179	C541+C542				
541	Candidate A		0	B540/C541	IF(D541>D542,1,0)	
542	Candidate B		0	B540/C542		IF(D542>D541,1,0)
543	180	C544+C545				
544	Candidate A		0	B543/C544	IF(D544>D545,1,0)	
545	Candidate B		0	B543/C545		IF(D545>D544,1,0)
546	181	C547+C548				
547	Candidate A		0	B546/C547	IF(D547>D548,1,0)	
548	Candidate B		0	B546/C548		IF(D548>D547,1,0)
549	182	C550+C551				
550	Candidate A		0	B549/C550	IF(D550>D551,1,0)	

	A	B	C	D	E	F
551	Candidate B		0	B549/C551		IF(D551>D550,1,0)
552	183	C553+C554				
553	Candidate A		0	B552/C553	IF(D553>D554,1,0)	
554	Candidate B		0	B552/C554		IF(D554>D553,1,0)
555	184	C556+C557				
556	Candidate A		0	B555/C556	IF(D556>D557,1,0)	
557	Candidate B		0	B555/C557		IF(D557>D556,1,0)
558	185	C559+C560				
559	Candidate A		0	B558/C559	IF(D559>D560,1,0)	
560	Candidate B		0	B558/C560		IF(D560>D559,1,0)
561	186	C562+C563				
562	Candidate A		0	B561/C562	IF(D562>D563,1,0)	
563	Candidate B		0	B561/C563		IF(D563>D562,1,0)
564	187	C565+C566				
565	Candidate A		0	B564/C565	IF(D565>D566,1,0)	
566	Candidate B		0	B564/C566		IF(D566>D565,1,0)
567	188	C568+C569				
568	Candidate A		0	B567/C568	IF(D568>D569,1,0)	
569	Candidate B		0	B567/C569		IF(D569>D568,1,0)
570	189	C571+C572				
571	Candidate A		0	B570/C571	IF(D571>D572,1,0)	
572	Candidate B		0	B570/C572		IF(D572>D571,1,0)
573	190	C574+C575				
574	Candidate A		0	B573/C574	IF(D574>D575,1,0)	
575	Candidate B		0	B573/C575		IF(D575>D574,1,0)
576	191	C577+C578				
577	Candidate A		0	B576/C577	IF(D577>D578,1,0)	
578	Candidate B		0	B576/C578		IF(D578>D577,1,0)
579	192	C580+C581				
580	Candidate A		0	B579/C580	IF(D580>D581,1,0)	
581	Candidate B		0	B579/C581		IF(D581>D580,1,0)
582	193	C583+C584				
583	Candidate A		0	B582/C583	IF(D583>D584,1,0)	
584	Candidate B		0	B582/C584		IF(D584>D583,1,0)
585	194	C586+C587				

	A	B	C	D	E	F
586	Candidate A		0	B585/C586	IF(D586>D587,1,0)	
587	Candidate B		0	B585/C587		IF(D587>D586,1,0)
588	195	C589+C590				
589	Candidate A		0	B588/C589	IF(D589>D590,1,0)	
590	Candidate B		0	B588/C590		IF(D590>D589,1,0)
591	196	C592+C593				
592	Candidate A		0	B591/C592	IF(D592>D593,1,0)	
593	Candidate B		0	B591/C593		IF(D593>D592,1,0)
594	197	C595+C596				
595	Candidate A		0	B594/C595	IF(D595>D596,1,0)	
596	Candidate B		0	B594/C596		IF(D596>D595,1,0)
597	198	C598+C599				
598	Candidate A		0	B597/C598	IF(D598>D599,1,0)	
599	Candidate B		0	B597/C599		IF(D599>D598,1,0)
600	199	C601+C602				
601	Candidate A		0	B600/C601	IF(D601>D602,1,0)	
602	Candidate B		0	B600/C602		IF(D602>D601,1,0)
603	200	C604+C605				
604	Candidate A		0	B603/C604	IF(D604>D605,1,0)	
605	Candidate B		0	B603/C605		IF(D605>D604,1,0)
606	201	C607+C608				
607	Candidate A		0	B606/C607	IF(D607>D608,1,0)	
608	Candidate B		0	B606/C608		IF(D608>D607,1,0)
609	202	C610+C611				
610	Candidate A		0	B609/C610	IF(D610>D611,1,0)	
611	Candidate B		0	B609/C611		IF(D611>D610,1,0)
612	203	C613+C614				
613	Candidate A		0	B612/C613	IF(D613>D614,1,0)	
614	Candidate B		0	B612/C614		IF(D614>D613,1,0)
615	204	C616+C617				
616	Candidate A		0	B615/C616	IF(D616>D617,1,0)	
617	Candidate B		0	B615/C617		IF(D617>D616,1,0)
618	205	C619+C620				
619	Candidate A		0	B618/C619	IF(D619>D620,1,0)	
620	Candidate B		0	B618/C620		IF(D620>D619,1,0)

	A	B	C	D	E	F
621	206	C622+C623				
622	Candidate A		0	B621/C622	IF(D622>D623,1,0)	
623	Candidate B		0	B621/C623		IF(D623>D622,1,0)
624	207	C625+C626				
625	Candidate A		0	B624/C625	IF(D625>D626,1,0)	
626	Candidate B		0	B624/C626		IF(D626>D625,1,0)
627	208	C628+C629				
628	Candidate A		0	B627/C628	IF(D628>D629,1,0)	
629	Candidate B		0	B627/C629		IF(D629>D628,1,0)
630	209	C631+C632				
631	Candidate A		0	B630/C631	IF(D631>D632,1,0)	
632	Candidate B		0	B630/C632		IF(D632>D631,1,0)
633	210	C634+C635				
634	Candidate A		0	B633/C634	IF(D634>D635,1,0)	
635	Candidate B		0	B633/C635		IF(D635>D634,1,0)
636	211	C637+C638				
637	Candidate A		0	B636/C637	IF(D637>D638,1,0)	
638	Candidate B		0	B636/C638		IF(D638>D637,1,0)
639	212	C640+C641				
640	Candidate A		0	B639/C640	IF(D640>D641,1,0)	
641	Candidate B		0	B639/C641		IF(D641>D640,1,0)
642	213	C643+C644				
643	Candidate A		0	B642/C643	IF(D643>D644,1,0)	
644	Candidate B		0	B642/C644		IF(D644>D643,1,0)
645	214	C646+C647				
646	Candidate A		0	B645/C646	IF(D646>D647,1,0)	
647	Candidate B		0	B645/C647		IF(D647>D646,1,0)
648	215	C649+C650				
649	Candidate A		0	B648/C649	IF(D649>D650,1,0)	
650	Candidate B		0	B648/C650		IF(D650>D649,1,0)
651	216	C652+C653				
652	Candidate A		0	B651/C652	IF(D652>D653,1,0)	
653	Candidate B		0	B651/C653		IF(D653>D652,1,0)
654	217	C655+C656				
655	Candidate A		0	B654/C655	IF(D655>D656,1,0)	

	A	B	C	D	E	F
656	Candidate B		0	B654/C656		IF(D656>D655,1,0)
657	218	C658+C659				
658	Candidate A		0	B657/C658	IF(D658>D659,1,0)	
659	Candidate B		0	B657/C659		IF(D659>D658,1,0)
660	219	C661+C662				
661	Candidate A		0	B660/C661	IF(D661>D662,1,0)	
662	Candidate B		0	B660/C662		IF(D662>D661,1,0)
663	220	C664+C665				
664	Candidate A		0	B663/C664	IF(D664>D665,1,0)	
665	Candidate B		0	B663/C665		IF(D665>D664,1,0)
666	221	C667+C668				
667	Candidate A		0	B666/C667	IF(D667>D668,1,0)	
668	Candidate B		0	B666/C668		IF(D668>D667,1,0)
669	222	C670+C671				
670	Candidate A		0	B669/C670	IF(D670>D671,1,0)	
671	Candidate B		0	B669/C671		IF(D671>D670,1,0)
672	223	C673+C674				
673	Candidate A		0	B672/C673	IF(D673>D674,1,0)	
674	Candidate B		0	B672/C674		IF(D674>D673,1,0)
675	224	C676+C677				
676	Candidate A		0	B675/C676	IF(D676>D677,1,0)	
677	Candidate B		0	B675/C677		IF(D677>D676,1,0)
678	225	C679+C680				
679	Candidate A		0	B678/C679	IF(D679>D680,1,0)	
680	Candidate B		0	B678/C680		IF(D680>D679,1,0)
681	226	C682+C683				
682	Candidate A		0	B681/C682	IF(D682>D683,1,0)	
683	Candidate B		0	B681/C683		IF(D683>D682,1,0)
684	227	C685+C686				
685	Candidate A		0	B684/C685	IF(D685>D686,1,0)	
686	Candidate B		0	B684/C686		IF(D686>D685,1,0)
687	228	C688+C689				
688	Candidate A		0	B687/C688	IF(D688>D689,1,0)	
689	Candidate B		0	B687/C689		IF(D689>D688,1,0)
690	229	C691+C692				

229

	A	B	C	D	E	F
691	Candidate A		0	B690/C691	IF(D691>D692,1,0)	
692	Candidate B		0	B690/C692		IF(D692>D691,1,0)
693	230	C694+C695				
694	Candidate A		0	B693/C694	IF(D694>D695,1,0)	
695	Candidate B		0	B693/C695		IF(D695>D694,1,0)
696	231	C697+C698				
697	Candidate A		0	B696/C697	IF(D697>D698,1,0)	
698	Candidate B		0	B696/C698		IF(D698>D697,1,0)
699	232	C700+C701				
700	Candidate A		0	B699/C700	IF(D700>D701,1,0)	
701	Candidate B		0	B699/C701		IF(D701>D700,1,0)
702	233	C703+C704				
703	Candidate A		0	B702/C703	IF(D703>D704,1,0)	
704	Candidate B		0	B702/C704		IF(D704>D703,1,0)
705	234	C706+C707				
706	Candidate A		0	B705/C706	IF(D706>D707,1,0)	
707	Candidate B		0	B705/C707		IF(D707>D706,1,0)
708	235	C709+C710				
709	Candidate A		0	B708/C709	IF(D709>D710,1,0)	
710	Candidate B		0	B708/C710		IF(D710>D709,1,0)
711	236	C712+C713				
712	Candidate A		0	B711/C712	IF(D712>D713,1,0)	
713	Candidate B		0	B711/C713		IF(D713>D712,1,0)
714	237	C715+C716				
715	Candidate A		0	B714/C715	IF(D715>D716,1,0)	
716	Candidate B		0	B714/C716		IF(D716>D715,1,0)
717	238	C718+C719				
718	Candidate A		0	B717/C718	IF(D718>D719,1,0)	
719	Candidate B		0	B717/C719		IF(D719>D718,1,0)
720	239	C721+C722				
721	Candidate A		0	B720/C721	IF(D721>D722,1,0)	
722	Candidate B		0	B720/C722		IF(D722>D721,1,0)
723	240	C724+C725				
724	Candidate A		0	B723/C724	IF(D724>D725,1,0)	
725	Candidate B		0	B723/C725		IF(D725>D724,1,0)

	A	B	C	D	E	F
726	241	C727+C728				
727	Candidate A		0	B726/ C727	IF(D727>D728,1,0)	
728	Candidate B		0	B726/ C728		IF(D728>D727,1,0)
729	242	C730+C731				
730	Candidate A		0	B729/ C730	IF(D730>D731,1,0)	
731	Candidate B		0	B729/ C731		IF(D731>D730,1,0)
732	243	C733+C734				
733	Candidate A		0	B732/ C733	IF(D733>D734,1,0)	
734	Candidate B		0	B732/ C734		IF(D734>D733,1,0)
735	244	C736+C737				
736	Candidate A		0	B735/ C736	IF(D736>D737,1,0)	
737	Candidate B		0	B735/ C737		IF(D737>D736,1,0)
738	245	C739+C740				
739	Candidate A		0	B738/ C739	IF(D739>D740,1,0)	
740	Candidate B		0	B738/ C740		IF(D740>D739,1,0)
741	246	C742+C743				
742	Candidate A		0	B741/ C742	IF(D742>D743,1,0)	
743	Candidate B		0	B741/ C743		IF(D743>D742,1,0)
744	247	C745+C746				
745	Candidate A		0	B744/ C745	IF(D745>D746,1,0)	
746	Candidate B		0	B744/ C746		IF(D746>D745,1,0)
747	248	C748+C749				
748	Candidate A		0	B747/ C748	IF(D748>D749,1,0)	
749	Candidate B		0	B747/ C749		IF(D749>D748,1,0)
750	249	C751+C752				
751	Candidate A		0	B750/ C751	IF(D751>D752,1,0)	
752	Candidate B		0	B750/ C752		IF(D752>D751,1,0)
753	250	C754+C755				
754	Candidate A		0	B753/ C754	IF(D754>D755,1,0)	
755	Candidate B		0	B753/ C755		IF(D755>D754,1,0)
756	251	C757+C758				
757	Candidate A		0	B756/ C757	IF(D757>D758,1,0)	
758	Candidate B		0	B756/ C758		IF(D758>D757,1,0)
759	252	C760+C761				
760	Candidate A		0	B759/ C760	IF(D760>D761,1,0)	

	A	B	C	D	E	F
761	Candidate B		0	B759/C761		IF(D761>D760,1,0)
762	253	C763+C764				
763	Candidate A		0	B762/C763	IF(D763>D764,1,0)	
764	Candidate B		0	B762/C764		IF(D764>D763,1,0)
765	254	C766+C767				
766	Candidate A		0	B765/C766	IF(D766>D767,1,0)	
767	Candidate B		0	B765/C767		IF(D767>D766,1,0)
768	255	C769+C770				
769	Candidate A		0	B768/C769	IF(D769>D770,1,0)	
770	Candidate B		0	B768/C770		IF(D770>D769,1,0)
771	256	C772+C773				
772	Candidate A		0	B771/C772	IF(D772>D773,1,0)	
773	Candidate B		0	B771/C773		IF(D773>D772,1,0)
774	257	C775+C776				
775	Candidate A		0	B774/C775	IF(D775>D776,1,0)	
776	Candidate B		0	B774/C776		IF(D776>D775,1,0)
777	258	C778+C779				
778	Candidate A		0	B777/C778	IF(D778>D779,1,0)	
779	Candidate B		0	B777/C779		IF(D779>D778,1,0)
780	259	C781+C782				
781	Candidate A		0	B780/C781	IF(D781>D782,1,0)	
782	Candidate B		0	B780/C782		IF(D782>D781,1,0)
783	260	C784+C785				
784	Candidate A		0	B783/C784	IF(D784>D785,1,0)	
785	Candidate B		0	B783/C785		IF(D785>D784,1,0)
786	261	C787+C788				
787	Candidate A		0	B786/C787	IF(D787>D788,1,0)	
788	Candidate B		0	B786/C788		IF(D788>D787,1,0)
789	262	C790+C791				
790	Candidate A		0	B789/C790	IF(D790>D791,1,0)	
791	Candidate B		0	B789/C791		IF(D791>D790,1,0)
792	263	C793+C794				
793	Candidate A		0	B792/C793	IF(D793>D794,1,0)	
794	Candidate B		0	B792/C794		IF(D794>D793,1,0)
795	264	C796+C797				

	A	B	C	D	E	F
796	Candidate A		0	B795/ C796	IF(D796>D797,1,0)	
797	Candidate B		0	B795/ C797		IF(D797>D796,1,0)
798	265	C799+C800				
799	Candidate A		0	B798/ C799	IF(D799>D800,1,0)	
800	Candidate B		0	B798/ C800		IF(D800>D799,1,0)
801	266	C802+C803				
802	Candidate A		0	B801/ C802	IF(D802>D803,1,0)	
803	Candidate B		0	B801/ C803		IF(D803>D802,1,0)
804	267	C805+C806				
805	Candidate A		0	B804/ C805	IF(D805>D806,1,0)	
806	Candidate B		0	B804/ C806		IF(D806>D805,1,0)
807	268	C808+C809				
808	Candidate A		0	B807/ C808	IF(D808>D809,1,0)	
809	Candidate B		0	B807/ C809		IF(D809>D808,1,0)
810	269	C811+C812				
811	Candidate A		0	B810/ C811	IF(D811>D812,1,0)	
812	Candidate B		0	B810/ C812		IF(D812>D811,1,0)
813	270	C814+C815				
814	Candidate A		0	B813/ C814	IF(D814>D815,1,0)	
815	Candidate B		0	B813/ C815		IF(D815>D814,1,0)
816	271	C817+C818				
817	Candidate A		0	B816/ C817	IF(D817>D818,1,0)	
818	Candidate B		0	B816/ C818		IF(D818>D817,1,0)
819	272	C820+C821				
820	Candidate A		0	B819/ C820	IF(D820>D821,1,0)	
821	Candidate B		0	B819/ C821		IF(D821>D820,1,0)
822	273	C823+C824				
823	Candidate A		0	B822/ C823	IF(D823>D824,1,0)	
824	Candidate B		0	B822/ C824		IF(D824>D823,1,0)
825	274	C826+C827				
826	Candidate A		0	B825/ C826	IF(D826>D827,1,0)	
827	Candidate B		0	B825/ C827		IF(D827>D826,1,0)
828	275	C829+C830				
829	Candidate A		0	B828/ C829	IF(D829>D830,1,0)	
830	Candidate B		0	B828/ C830		IF(D830>D829,1,0)

	A	B	C	D	E	F
831	276	C832+C833				
832	Candidate A		0	B831/C832	IF(D832>D833,1,0)	
833	Candidate B		0	B831/C833		IF(D833>D832,1,0)
834	277	C835+C836				
835	Candidate A		0	B834/C835	IF(D835>D836,1,0)	
836	Candidate B		0	B834/C836		IF(D836>D835,1,0)
837	278	C838+C839				
838	Candidate A		0	B837/C838	IF(D838>D839,1,0)	
839	Candidate B		0	B837/C839		IF(D839>D838,1,0)
840	279	C841+C842				
841	Candidate A		0	B840/C841	IF(D841>D842,1,0)	
842	Candidate B		0	B840/C842		IF(D842>D841,1,0)
843	280	C844+C845				
844	Candidate A		0	B843/C844	IF(D844>D845,1,0)	
845	Candidate B		0	B843/C845		IF(D845>D844,1,0)
846	281	C847+C848				
847	Candidate A		0	B846/C847	IF(D847>D848,1,0)	
848	Candidate B		0	B846/C848		IF(D848>D847,1,0)
849	282	C850+C851				
850	Candidate A		0	B849/C850	IF(D850>D851,1,0)	
851	Candidate B		0	B849/C851		IF(D851>D850,1,0)
852	283	C853+C854				
853	Candidate A		0	B852/C853	IF(D853>D854,1,0)	
854	Candidate B		0	B852/C854		IF(D854>D853,1,0)
855	284	C856+C857				
856	Candidate A		0	B855/C856	IF(D856>D857,1,0)	
857	Candidate B		0	B855/C857		IF(D857>D856,1,0)
858	285	C859+C860				
859	Candidate A		0	B858/C859	IF(D859>D860,1,0)	
860	Candidate B		0	B858/C860		IF(D860>D859,1,0)
861	286	C862+C863				
862	Candidate A		0	B861/C862	IF(D862>D863,1,0)	
863	Candidate B		0	B861/C863		IF(D863>D862,1,0)
864	287	C865+C866				
865	Candidate A		0	B864/C865	IF(D865>D866,1,0)	

	A	B	C	D	E	F
866	Candidate B		0	B864/ C866		IF(D866>D865,1,0)
867	288	C868+C869				
868	Candidate A		0	B867/ C868	IF(D868>D869,1,0)	
869	Candidate B		0	B867/ C869		IF(D869>D868,1,0)
870	289	C871+C872				
871	Candidate A		0	B870/ C871	IF(D871>D872,1,0)	
872	Candidate B		0	B870/ C872		IF(D872>D871,1,0)
873	290	C874+C875				
874	Candidate A		0	B873/ C874	IF(D874>D875,1,0)	
875	Candidate B		0	B873/ C875		IF(D875>D874,1,0)
876	291	C877+C878				
877	Candidate A		0	B876/ C877	IF(D877>D878,1,0)	
878	Candidate B		0	B876/ C878		IF(D878>D877,1,0)
879	292	C880+C881				
880	Candidate A		0	B879/ C880	IF(D880>D881,1,0)	
881	Candidate B		0	B879/ C881		IF(D881>D880,1,0)
882	293	C883+C884				
883	Candidate A		0	B882/ C883	IF(D883>D884,1,0)	
884	Candidate B		0	B882/ C884		IF(D884>D883,1,0)
885	294	C886+C887				
886	Candidate A		0	B885/ C886	IF(D886>D887,1,0)	
887	Candidate B		0	B885/ C887		IF(D887>D886,1,0)
888	295	C889+C890				
889	Candidate A		0	B888/ C889	IF(D889>D890,1,0)	
890	Candidate B		0	B888/ C890		IF(D890>D889,1,0)
891	296	C892+C893				
892	Candidate A		0	B891/ C892	IF(D892>D893,1,0)	
893	Candidate B		0	B891/ C893		IF(D893>D892,1,0)
894	297	C895+C896				
895	Candidate A		0	B894/ C895	IF(D895>D896,1,0)	
896	Candidate B		0	B894/ C896		IF(D896>D895,1,0)
897	298	C898+C899				
898	Candidate A		0	B897/ C898	IF(D898>D899,1,0)	
899	Candidate B		0	B897/ C899		IF(D899>D898,1,0)
900	299	C901+C902				

	A	B	C	D	E	F
901	Candidate A		0	B900/C901	IF(D901>D902,1,0)	
902	Candidate B		0	B900/C902		IF(D902>D901,1,0)
903	300	C904+C905				
904	Candidate A		0	B903/C904	IF(D904>D905,1,0)	
905	Candidate B		0	B903/C905		IF(D905>D904,1,0)
906	301	C907+C908				
907	Candidate A		0	B906/C907	IF(D907>D908,1,0)	
908	Candidate B		0	B906/C908		IF(D908>D907,1,0)
909	302	C910+C911				
910	Candidate A		0	B909/C910	IF(D910>D911,1,0)	
911	Candidate B		0	B909/C911		IF(D911>D910,1,0)
912	303	C913+C914				
913	Candidate A		0	B912/C913	IF(D913>D914,1,0)	
914	Candidate B		0	B912/C914		IF(D914>D913,1,0)
915	304	C916+C917				
916	Candidate A		0	B915/C916	IF(D916>D917,1,0)	
917	Candidate B		0	B915/C917		IF(D917>D916,1,0)
918	305	C919+C920				
919	Candidate A		0	B918/C919	IF(D919>D920,1,0)	
920	Candidate B		0	B918/C920		IF(D920>D919,1,0)
921	306	C922+C923				
922	Candidate A		0	B921/C922	IF(D922>D923,1,0)	
923	Candidate B		0	B921/C923		IF(D923>D922,1,0)
924	307	C925+C926				
925	Candidate A		0	B924/C925	IF(D925>D926,1,0)	
926	Candidate B		0	B924/C926		IF(D926>D925,1,0)
927	308	C928+C929				
928	Candidate A		0	B927/C928	IF(D928>D929,1,0)	
929	Candidate B		0	B927/C929		IF(D929>D928,1,0)
930	309	C931+C932				
931	Candidate A		0	B930/C931	IF(D931>D932,1,0)	
932	Candidate B		0	B930/C932		IF(D932>D931,1,0)
933	310	C934+C935				
934	Candidate A		0	B933/C934	IF(D934>D935,1,0)	
935	Candidate B		0	B933/C935		IF(D935>D934,1,0)

	A	B	C	D	E	F
936	311	C937+C938				
937	Candidate A		0	B936/C937	IF(D937>D938,1,0)	
938	Candidate B		0	B936/C938		IF(D938>D937,1,0)
939	312	C940+C941				
940	Candidate A		0	B939/C940	IF(D940>D941,1,0)	
941	Candidate B		0	B939/C941		IF(D941>D940,1,0)
942	313	C943+C944				
943	Candidate A		0	B942/C943	IF(D943>D944,1,0)	
944	Candidate B		0	B942/C944		IF(D944>D943,1,0)
945	314	C946+C947				
946	Candidate A		0	B945/C946	IF(D946>D947,1,0)	
947	Candidate B		0	B945/C947		IF(D947>D946,1,0)
948	315	C949+C950				
949	Candidate A		0	B948/C949	IF(D949>D950,1,0)	
950	Candidate B		0	B948/C950		IF(D950>D949,1,0)
951	316	C952+C953				
952	Candidate A		0	B951/C952	IF(D952>D953,1,0)	
953	Candidate B		0	B951/C953		IF(D953>D952,1,0)
954	317	C955+C956				
955	Candidate A		0	B954/C955	IF(D955>D956,1,0)	
956	Candidate B		0	B954/C956		IF(D956>D955,1,0)
957	318	C958+C959				
958	Candidate A		0	B957/C958	IF(D958>D959,1,0)	
959	Candidate B		0	B957/C959		IF(D959>D958,1,0)
960	319	C961+C962				
961	Candidate A		0	B960/C961	IF(D961>D962,1,0)	
962	Candidate B		0	B960/C962		IF(D962>D961,1,0)
963	320	C964+C965				
964	Candidate A		0	B963/C964	IF(D964>D965,1,0)	
965	Candidate B		0	B963/C965		IF(D965>D964,1,0)
966	321	C967+C968				
967	Candidate A		0	B966/C967	IF(D967>D968,1,0)	
968	Candidate B		0	B966/C968		IF(D968>D967,1,0)
969	322	C970+C971				
970	Candidate A		0	B969/C970	IF(D970>D971,1,0)	

	A	B	C	D	E	F
971	Candidate B		0	B969/C971		IF(D971>D970,1,0)
972	323	C973+C974				
973	Candidate A		0	B972/C973	IF(D973>D974,1,0)	
974	Candidate B		0	B972/C974		IF(D974>D973,1,0)
975	324	C976+C977				
976	Candidate A		0	B975/C976	IF(D976>D977,1,0)	
977	Candidate B		0	B975/C977		IF(D977>D976,1,0)
978	325	C979+C980				
979	Candidate A		0	B978/C979	IF(D979>D980,1,0)	
980	Candidate B		0	B978/C980		IF(D980>D979,1,0)
981	326	C982+C983				
982	Candidate A		0	B981/C982	IF(D982>D983,1,0)	
983	Candidate B		0	B981/C983		IF(D983>D982,1,0)
984	327	C985+C986				
985	Candidate A		0	B984/C985	IF(D985>D986,1,0)	
986	Candidate B		0	B984/C986		IF(D986>D985,1,0)
987	328	C988+C989				
988	Candidate A		0	B987/C988	IF(D988>D989,1,0)	
989	Candidate B		0	B987/C989		IF(D989>D988,1,0)
990	329	C991+C992				
991	Candidate A		0	B990/C991	IF(D991>D992,1,0)	
992	Candidate B		0	B990/C992		IF(D992>D991,1,0)
993	330	C994+C995				
994	Candidate A		0	B993/C994	IF(D994>D995,1,0)	
995	Candidate B		0	B993/C995		IF(D995>D994,1,0)
996	331	C997+C998				
997	Candidate A		0	B996/C997	IF(D997>D998,1,0)	
998	Candidate B		0	B996/C998		IF(D998>D997,1,0)
999	332	C1000+C1001				
1000	Candidate A		0	B999/C1000	IF(D1000>D1001,1,0)	
1001	Candidate B		0	B999/C1001		IF(D1001>D1000,1,0)
1002	333	C1003+C1004				
1003	Candidate A		0	B1002/C1003	IF(D1003>D1004,1,0)	
1004	Candidate B		0	B1002/C1004		IF(D1004>D1003,1,0)
1005	334	C1006+C1007				

	A	B	C	D	E	F
1006	Candidate A		0	B1005/C1006	IF(D1006>D1007,1,0)	
1007	Candidate B		0	B1005/C1007		IF(D1007>D1006,1,0)
1008	335	C1009+C1010				
1009	Candidate A		0	B1008/C1009	IF(D1009>D1010,1,0)	
1010	Candidate B		0	B1008/C1010		IF(D1010>D1009,1,0)
1011	336	C1012+C1013				
1012	Candidate A		0	B1011/C1012	IF(D1012>D1013,1,0)	
1013	Candidate B		0	B1011/C1013		IF(D1013>D1012,1,0)
1014	337	C1015+C1016				
1015	Candidate A		0	B1014/C1015	IF(D1015>D1016,1,0)	
1016	Candidate B		0	B1014/C1016		IF(D1016>D1015,1,0)
1017	338	C1018+C1019				
1018	Candidate A		0	B1017/C1018	IF(D1018>D1019,1,0)	
1019	Candidate B		0	B1017/C1019		IF(D1019>D1018,1,0)
1020	339	C1021+C1022				
1021	Candidate A		0	B1020/C1021	IF(D1021>D1022,1,0)	
1022	Candidate B		0	B1020/C1022		IF(D1022>D1021,1,0)
1023	340	C1024+C1025				
1024	Candidate A		0	B1023/C1024	IF(D1024>D1025,1,0)	
1025	Candidate B		0	B1023/C1025		IF(D1025>D1024,1,0)
1026	341	C1027+C1028				
1027	Candidate A		0	B1026/C1027	IF(D1027>D1028,1,0)	
1028	Candidate B		0	B1026/C1028		IF(D1028>D1027,1,0)
1029	342	C1030+C1031				
1030	Candidate A		0	B1029/C1030	IF(D1030>D1031,1,0)	
1031	Candidate B		0	B1029/C1031		IF(D1031>D1030,1,0)
1032	343	C1033+C1034				
1033	Candidate A		0	B1032/C1033	IF(D1033>D1034,1,0)	
1034	Candidate B		0	B1032/C1034		IF(D1034>D1033,1,0)
1035	344	C1036+C1037				
1036	Candidate A		0	B1035/C1036	IF(D1036>D1037,1,0)	
1037	Candidate B		0	B1035/C1037		IF(D1037>D1036,1,0)
1038	345	C1039+C1040				
1039	Candidate A		0	B1038/C1039	IF(D1039>D1040,1,0)	
1040	Candidate B		0	B1038/C1040		IF(D1040>D1039,1,0)

	A	B	C	D	E	F
1041	346	C1042+C1043				
1042	Candidate A		0	B1041/C1042	IF(D1042>D1043,1,0)	
1043	Candidate B		0	B1041/C1043		IF(D1043>D1042,1,0)
1044	347	C1045+C1046				
1045	Candidate A		0	B1044/C1045	IF(D1045>D1046,1,0)	
1046	Candidate B		0	B1044/C1046		IF(D1046>D1045,1,0)
1047	348	C1048+C1049				
1048	Candidate A		0	B1047/C1048	IF(D1048>D1049,1,0)	
1049	Candidate B		0	B1047/C1049		IF(D1049>D1048,1,0)
1050	349	C1051+C1052				
1051	Candidate A		0	B1050/C1051	IF(D1051>D1052,1,0)	
1052	Candidate B		0	B1050/C1052		IF(D1052>D1051,1,0)
1053	350	C1054+C1055				
1054	Candidate A		0	B1053/C1054	IF(D1054>D1055,1,0)	
1055	Candidate B		0	B1053/C1055		IF(D1055>D1054,1,0)
1056	351	C1057+C1058				
1057	Candidate A		0	B1056/C1057	IF(D1057>D1058,1,0)	
1058	Candidate B		0	B1056/C1058		IF(D1058>D1057,1,0)
1059	352	C1060+C1061				
1060	Candidate A		0	B1059/C1060	IF(D1060>D1061,1,0)	
1061	Candidate B		0	B1059/C1061		IF(D1061>D1060,1,0)
1062	353	C1063+C1064				
1063	Candidate A		0	B1062/C1063	IF(D1063>D1064,1,0)	
1064	Candidate B		0	B1062/C1064		IF(D1064>D1063,1,0)
1065	354	C1066+C1067				
1066	Candidate A		0	B1065/C1066	IF(D1066>D1067,1,0)	
1067	Candidate B		0	B1065/C1067		IF(D1067>D1066,1,0)
1068	355	C1069+C1070				
1069	Candidate A		0	B1068/C1069	IF(D1069>D1070,1,0)	
1070	Candidate B		0	B1068/C1070		IF(D1070>D1069,1,0)
1071	356	C1072+C1073				
1072	Candidate A		0	B1071/C1072	IF(D1072>D1073,1,0)	
1073	Candidate B		0	B1071/C1073		IF(D1073>D1072,1,0)
1074	357	C1075+C1076				
1075	Candidate A		0	B1074/C1075	IF(D1075>D1076,1,0)	

	A	B	C	D	E	F
1076	Candidate B		0	B1074/ C1076		IF(D1076>D1075,1,0)
1077	358	C1078+C1079				
1078	Candidate A		0	B1077/ C1078	IF(D1078>D1079,1,0)	
1079	Candidate B		0	B1077/ C1079		IF(D1079>D1078,1,0)
1080	359	C1081+C1082				
1081	Candidate A		0	B1080/ C1081	IF(D1081>D1082,1,0)	
1082	Candidate B		0	B1080/ C1082		IF(D1082>D1081,1,0)
1083	360	C1084+C1085				
1084	Candidate A		0	B1083/ C1084	IF(D1084>D1085,1,0)	
1085	Candidate B		0	B1083/ C1085		IF(D1085>D1084,1,0)
1086	361	C1087+C1088				
1087	Candidate A		0	B1086/ C1087	IF(D1087>D1088,1,0)	
1088	Candidate B		0	B1086/ C1088		IF(D1088>D1087,1,0)
1089	362	C1090+C1091				
1090	Candidate A		0	B1089/ C1090	IF(D1090>D1091,1,0)	
1091	Candidate B		0	B1089/ C1091		IF(D1091>D1090,1,0)
1092	363	C1093+C1094				
1093	Candidate A		0	B1092/ C1093	IF(D1093>D1094,1,0)	
1094	Candidate B		0	B1092/ C1094		IF(D1094>D1093,1,0)
1095	364	C1096+C1097				
1096	Candidate A		0	B1095/ C1096	IF(D1096>D1097,1,0)	
1097	Candidate B		0	B1095/ C1097		IF(D1097>D1096,1,0)
1098	365	C1099+C1100				
1099	Candidate A		0	B1098/ C1099	IF(D1099>D1100,1,0)	
1100	Candidate B		0	B1098/ C1100		IF(D1100>D1099,1,0)
1101	366	C1102+C1103				
1102	Candidate A		0	B1101/ C1102	IF(D1102>D1103,1,0)	
1103	Candidate B		0	B1101/ C1103		IF(D1103>D1102,1,0)
1104	367	C1105+C1106				
1105	Candidate A		0	B1104/ C1105	IF(D1105>D1106,1,0)	
1106	Candidate B		0	B1104/ C1106		IF(D1106>D1105,1,0)
1107	368	C1108+C1109				
1108	Candidate A		0	B1107/ C1108	IF(D1108>D1109,1,0)	
1109	Candidate B		0	B1107/ C1109		IF(D1109>D1108,1,0)
1110	369	C1111+C1112				

	A	B	C	D	E	F
1111	Candidate A		0	B1110/C1111	IF(D1111>D1112,1,0)	
1112	Candidate B		0	B1110/C1112		IF(D1112>D1111,1,0)
1113	370	C1114+C1115				
1114	Candidate A		0	B1113/C1114	IF(D1114>D1115,1,0)	
1115	Candidate B		0	B1113/C1115		IF(D1115>D1114,1,0)
1116	371	C1117+C1118				
1117	Candidate A		0	B1116/C1117	IF(D1117>D1118,1,0)	
1118	Candidate B		0	B1116/C1118		IF(D1118>D1117,1,0)
1119	372	C1120+C1121				
1120	Candidate A		0	B1119/C1120	IF(D1120>D1121,1,0)	
1121	Candidate B		0	B1119/C1121		IF(D1121>D1120,1,0)
1122	373	C1123+C1124				
1123	Candidate A		0	B1122/C1123	IF(D1123>D1124,1,0)	
1124	Candidate B		0	B1122/C1124		IF(D1124>D1123,1,0)
1125	374	C1126+C1127				
1126	Candidate A		0	B1125/C1126	IF(D1126>D1127,1,0)	
1127	Candidate B		0	B1125/C1127		IF(D1127>D1126,1,0)
1128	375	C1129+C1130				
1129	Candidate A		0	B1128/C1129	IF(D1129>D1130,1,0)	
1130	Candidate B		0	B1128/C1130		IF(D1130>D1129,1,0)
1131	376	C1132+C1133				
1132	Candidate A		0	B1131/C1132	IF(D1132>D1133,1,0)	
1133	Candidate B		0	B1131/C1133		IF(D1133>D1132,1,0)
1134	377	C1135+C1136				
1135	Candidate A		0	B1134/C1135	IF(D1135>D1136,1,0)	
1136	Candidate B		0	B1134/C1136		IF(D1136>D1135,1,0)
1137	378	C1138+C1139				
1138	Candidate A		0	B1137/C1138	IF(D1138>D1139,1,0)	
1139	Candidate B		0	B1137/C1139		IF(D1139>D1138,1,0)
1140	379	C1141+C1142				
1141	Candidate A		0	B1140/C1141	IF(D1141>D1142,1,0)	
1142	Candidate B		0	B1140/C1142		IF(D1142>D1141,1,0)
1143	380	C1144+C1145				
1144	Candidate A		0	B1143/C1144	IF(D1144>D1145,1,0)	
1145	Candidate B		0	B1143/C1145		IF(D1145>D1144,1,0)

	A	B	C	D	E	F
1146	381	C1147+C1148				
1147	Candidate A		0	B1146/C1147	IF(D1147>D1148,1,0)	
1148	Candidate B		0	B1146/C1148		IF(D1148>D1147,1,0)
1149	382	C1150+C1151				
1150	Candidate A		0	B1149/C1150	IF(D1150>D1151,1,0)	
1151	Candidate B		0	B1149/C1151		IF(D1151>D1150,1,0)
1152	383	C1153+C1154				
1153	Candidate A		0	B1152/C1153	IF(D1153>D1154,1,0)	
1154	Candidate B		0	B1152/C1154		IF(D1154>D1153,1,0)
1155	384	C1156+C1157				
1156	Candidate A		0	B1155/C1156	IF(D1156>D1157,1,0)	
1157	Candidate B		0	B1155/C1157		IF(D1157>D1156,1,0)
1158	385	C1159+C1160				
1159	Candidate A		0	B1158/C1159	IF(D1159>D1160,1,0)	
1160	Candidate B		0	B1158/C1160		IF(D1160>D1159,1,0)
1161	386	C1162+C1163				
1162	Candidate A		0	B1161/C1162	IF(D1162>D1163,1,0)	
1163	Candidate B		0	B1161/C1163		IF(D1163>D1162,1,0)
1164	387	C1165+C1166				
1165	Candidate A		0	B1164/C1165	IF(D1165>D1166,1,0)	
1166	Candidate B		0	B1164/C1166		IF(D1166>D1165,1,0)
1167	388	C1168+C1169				
1168	Candidate A		0	B1167/C1168	IF(D1168>D1169,1,0)	
1169	Candidate B		0	B1167/C1169		IF(D1169>D1160,1,0)
1170	389	C1171+C1172				
1171	Candidate A		0	B1170/C1171	IF(D1171>D1172,1,0)	
1172	Candidate B		0	B1170/C1172		IF(D1172>D1171,1,0)
1173	390	C1174+C1175				
1174	Candidate A		0	B1173/C1174	IF(D1174>D1175,1,0)	
1175	Candidate B		0	B1173/C1175		IF(D1175>D1174,1,0)
1176	391	C1177+C1178				
1177	Candidate A		0	B1176/C1177	IF(D1177>D1178,1,0)	
1178	Candidate B		0	B1176/C1178		IF(D1178>D1177,1,0)
1179	392	C1180+C1181				
1180	Candidate A		0	B1179/C1180	IF(D1180>D1181,1,0)	

	A	B	C	D	E	F
1181	Candidate B		0	B1179/ C1181		IF(D1181>D1180,1,0)
1182	393	C1183+C1184				
1183	Candidate A		0	B1182/ C1183	IF(D1183>D1184,1,0)	
1184	Candidate B		0	B1182/ C1184		IF(D1184>D1183,1,0)
1185	394	C1186+C1187				
1186	Candidate A		0	B1185/ C1186	IF(D1186>D1187,1,0)	
1187	Candidate B		0	B1185/ C1187		IF(D1187>D1186,1,0)
1188	395	C1189+C1190				
1189	Candidate A		0	B1188/ C1189	IF(D1189>D1190,1,0)	
1190	Candidate B		0	B1188/ C1190		IF(D1190>D1189,1,0)
1191	396	C1192+C1193				
1192	Candidate A		0	B1191/ C1192	IF(D1192>D1193,1,0)	
1193	Candidate B		0	B1191/ C1193		IF(D1193>D1192,1,0)
1194	397	C1195+C1196				
1195	Candidate A		0	B1194/ C1195	IF(D1195>D1196,1,0)	
1196	Candidate B		0	B1194/ C1196		IF(D1196>D1195,1,0)
1197	398	C1198+C1199				
1198	Candidate A		0	B1197/ C1198	IF(D1198>D1199,1,0)	
1199	Candidate B		0	B1197/ C1199		IF(D1199>D1198,1,0)
1200	399	C1201+C1202				
1201	Candidate A		0	B1200/ C1201	IF(D1201>D1202,1,0)	
1202	Candidate B		0	B1200/ C1202		IF(D1202>D1201,1,0)
1203	400	C1204+C1205				
1204	Candidate A		0	B1203/ C1204	IF(D1204>D1205,1,0)	
1205	Candidate B		0	B1203/ C1205		IF(D1205>D1204,1,0)
1206	Total		SUM (C7:C1205)		F1207/A1203*E1204	E3/A1203*F1205

In the table above, the state government governor mob rule is shown.

The demonstration spreadsheets are designed for the state government governors' campaign. The state government assembly is the base district that will discourage mob rule.

Input candidates' election results in column C. There can be several candidates. For example, here, two are used to demonstrate. The spreadsheet calculates the candidates' sums of votes.

Using the spreadsheet's displayed instructions as a flowchart, a computer programmer can write a computer program that will tabulate and count the votes as a voter goes through the act of voting. The computer technology already exists where a computer is used to process a vote being cast at polling stations.

At the end of the vote-casting day, the computer automatically delivers the candidates' sums of districts won and the sum popular vote.

Instead of using a *referendum* type of voting method to elect a state's governor, the state government assemblies' districts will choose the governor. The state governor who receives the greater acceptances of districts wins the election.

Since the districts are quasi-equal populated, the group of people within the districts form a district's representative election. Mob rule diminishes and practically disappears. In case of a tie vote where the candidates receive the same acceptances of districts, the election goes to the candidate who wins the popular vote. Even though the election goes to a popular vote, the probability of mob rule diminishes. The action of receiving the same number of districts where one district nullifies another practically determines that mob rule will not be prevalent.

Since the population of state governments is high, using a state government's districts to elect a governor is justified to eliminate mob rule.

A programmer can tailor this presentation to any particular state government district.

A UNITED HOUSE OF REPRESENTATIVES DISTRICT

(STATE GOVERNMENT ASSEMBLY DISTRICTS)

GOVERNOR SPREADSHEET STATES GOVERNMENT ASSEMBLY

400 DISTRICTS

	a	B	C	D	E	F
1						
2						
3						
4						
5	District	Total Votes	Votes	%	Candidate A	Candidate B
6	1	C7+C8				
7	Candidate A		0	B6/C7	IF(D7>D8,1,0)	
8	Candidate B		0	B6/C8		IF(D8>D7,1,0)
9	2	C10+C11				
10	Candidate A		0	B9/C10	IF(D10>D11,1,0)	
11	Candidate B		0	B9/C11		IF(D11>D10,1,0)
12	3	C13+C14				
13	Candidate A		0	B12/C13	IF(D13>D14,1,0)	
14	Candidate B		0	B12/C14		IF(D14>D13,1,0)
15	4	C16+C17				
16	Candidate A		0	B15/C16	IF(D16>D17,1,0)	
17	Candidate B		0	B15/C17		IF(D17>D16,1,0)
18	5	C19+C20				
19	Candidate A		0	B18/C19	IF(D19>D20,1,0)	
20	Candidate B		0	B18/C20		IF(D20>D19,1,0)
21	6	C22+C23				
22	Candidate A		0	B21/C22	IF(D22>D23,1,0)	
23	Candidate B		0	B21/C23		IF(D23>D22,1,0)
24	7	C25+C26				
25	Candidate A		0	B24/C25	IF(D25>D26,1,0)	
26	Candidate B		0	B24/C26		IF(D26>D25,1,0)
27	8	C28+C29				
28	Candidate A		0	B27/C28	IF(D28>D29,1,0)	
29	Candidate B		0	B27/C29		IF(D29>D28,1,0)
30	9	C31+C32				
31	Candidate A		0	B30/C31	IF(D31>D32,1,0)	
32	Candidate B		0	B30/C32		IF(D32>D31,1,0)

	a	B	C	D	E	F
33	10	C34+C35				
34	Candidate A		0	B33/C34	IF(D34>D35,1,0)	
35	Candidate B		0	B33/C35		IF(D35>D34,1,0)
36	11	C37+C38				
37	Candidate A		0	B36/C37	IF(D37>D38,1,0)	
38	Candidate B		0	B36/C38		IF(D38>D37,1,0)
39	12	C40+C41				
40	Candidate A		0	B39/C40	IF(D40>D41,1,0)	
41	Candidate B		0	B39/C41		IF(D41>D40,1,0)
42	13	C43+C44				
43	Candidate A		0	B42/C43	IF(D43>D44,1,0)	
44	Candidate B		0	B42/C44		IF(D44>D43,1,0)
45	14	C46+C47				
46	Candidate A		0	B45/C46	IF(D46>D47,1,0)	
47	Candidate B		0	B45/C47		IF(D47>D46,1,0)
48	15	C49+C50				
49	Candidate A		0	B48/C49	IF(D49>D50,1,0)	
50	Candidate B		0	B48/C50		IF(D50>D49,1,0)
51	16	C52+C53				
52	Candidate A		0	B51/C52	IF(D52>D53,1,0)	
53	Candidate B		0	B51/C53		IF(D53>D52,1,0)
54	17	C55+C56				
55	Candidate A		0	B54/C55	IF(D55>D56,1,0)	
56	Candidate B		0	B54/C56		IF(D56>D55,1,0)
57	18	C58+C59				
58	Candidate A		0	B57/C58	IF(D58>D59,1,0)	
59	Candidate B		0	B57/C59		IF(D59>D58,1,0)
60	19	C61+C62				
61	Candidate A		0	B60/C61	IF(D61>D62,1,0)	
62	Candidate B		0	B60/C62		IF(D62>D61,1,0)
63	20	C64+C65				
64	Candidate A		0	B63/C64	IF(D64>D65,1,0)	
65	Candidate B		0	B63/C65		IF(D65>D64,1,0)
66	21	C67+C68				
67	Candidate A		0	B66/C67	IF(D67>D68,1,0)	
68	Candidate B		0	B66/C68		IF(D68>D67,1,0)
69	22	C70+C71				
70	Candidate A		0	B69/C70	IF(D70>D71,1,0)	
71	Candidate B		0	B69/C71		IF(D71>D70,1,0)
72	23	C73+C74				
73	Candidate A		0	B72/C73	IF(D73>D74,1,0)	
74	Candidate B		0	B72/C74		IF(D74>D73,1,0)
75	24	C76+C77				
76	Candidate A		0	B75/C76	IF(D76>D77,1,0)	
77	Candidate B		0	B75/C77		IF(D77>D76,1,0)
78	25	C79+C80				
79	Candidate A		0	B78/C79	IF(D79>D80,1,0)	
80	Candidate B		0	B78/C80		IF(D80>D79,1,0)
81	26	C82+C83				
82	Candidate A		0	B81/C82	IF(D82>D83,1,0)	
83	Candidate B		0	B81/C83		IF(D83>D82,1,0)
84	27	C85+C86				
85	Candidate A		0	B84/C85	IF(D85>D86,1,0)	
86	Candidate B		0	B84/C86		IF(D86>D85,1,0)
87	28	C88+C89				
88	Candidate A		0	B87/C88	IF(D88>D89,1,0)	
89	Candidate B		0	B87/C89		IF(D89>D88,1,0)
90	29	C91+C92				
91	Candidate A		0	B90/C91	IF(D91>D92,1,0)	
92	Candidate B		0	B90/C92		IF(D92>D91,1,0)
93	30	C94+C95				
94	Candidate A		0	B93/C94	IF(D94>D95,1,0)	
95	Candidate B		0	B93/C95		IF(D95>D94,1,0)
96	31	C97+C98				

	a	B	C	D	E	F
97	Candidate A		0	B96/C97	IF(D97>D98,1,0)	
98	Candidate B		0	B96/C98		IF(D98>D97,1,0)
99	32	C100+C101				
100	Candidate A		0	B99/C100	IF(D100>D101,1,0)	
101	Candidate B		0	B99/C101		IF(D101>D100,1,0)
102	33	C103+C104				
103	Candidate A		0	B102/C103	IF(D103>D104,1,0)	
104	Candidate B		0	B102/C104		IF(D104>D103,1,0)
105	34	C106+C107				
106	Candidate A		0	B105/C106	IF(D106>D107,1,0)	
107	Candidate B		0	B105/C107		IF(D107>D106,1,0)
108	35	C109+C110				
109	Candidate A		0	B108/C109	IF(D109>D110,1,0)	
110	Candidate B		0	B108/C110		IF(D110>D109,1,0)
111	36	C112+C113				
112	Candidate A		0	B111/C112	IF(D112>D113,1,0)	
113	Candidate B		0	B111/C113		IF(D113>D112,1,0)
114	37	C115+C116				
115	Candidate A		0	B114/C115	IF(D115>D116,1,0)	
116	Candidate B		0	B114/C116		IF(D116>D115,1,0)
117	38	C118+C119				
118	Candidate A		0	B117/C118	IF(D118>D119,1,0)	
119	Candidate B		0	B117/C119		IF(D119>D118,1,0)
120	39	C121+C122				
121	Candidate A		0	B120/C121	IF(D121>D122,1,0)	
122	Candidate B		0	B120/C122		IF(D122>D121,1,0)
123	40	C124+C125				
124	Candidate A		0	B123/C124	IF(D124>D125,1,0)	
125	Candidate B		0	B123/C125		IF(D125>D124,1,0)
126	41	C127+C128				
127	Candidate A		0	B126/C127	IF(D127>D128,1,0)	
128	Candidate B		0	B126/C128		IF(D128>D127,1,0)
129	42	C130+C131				
130	Candidate A		0	B129/C130	IF(D130>D131,1,0)	
131	Candidate B		0	B129/C131		IF(D131>D130,1,0)
132	43	C133+C134				

	a	B	C	D	E	F
133	Candidate A		0	B132/C133	IF(D133>D134,1,0)	
134	Candidate B		0	B132/C134		IF(D134>D133,1,0)
135	44	C136+C137				
136	Candidate A		0	B135/C136	IF(D136>D137,1,0)	
137	Candidate B		0	B135/C137		IF(D137>D136,1,0)
138	45	C139+C140				
139	Candidate A		0	B138/C139	IF(D139>D140,1,0)	
140	Candidate B		0	B138/C140		IF(D140>D139,1,0)
141	46	C142+C143				
142	Candidate A		0	B141/C142	IF(D142>D143,1,0)	
143	Candidate B		0	B141/C143		IF(D143>D142,1,0)
144	47	C145+C146				
145	Candidate A		0	B144/C145	IF(D145>D146,1,0)	
146	Candidate B		0	B144/C146		IF(D146>D145,1,0)
147	48	C148+C149				
148	Candidate A		0	B147/C148	IF(D148>D149,1,0)	
149	Candidate B		0	B147/C149		IF(D149>D148,1,0)
150	49	C151+C152				
151	Candidate A		0	B150/C151	IF(D151>D152,1,0)	
152	Candidate B		0	B150/C152		IF(D152>D151,1,0)
153	50	C154+C155				
154	Candidate A		0	B153/C154	IF(D154>D155,1,0)	
155	Candidate B		0	B153/C155		IF(D155>D154,1,0)
156	51	C157+C158				
157	Candidate A		0	B156/C157	IF(D157>D158,1,0)	
158	Candidate B		0	B156/C158		IF(D158>D157,1,0)
159	52	C160+C161				
160	Candidate A		0	B159/C160	IF(D160>D161,1,0)	
161	Candidate B		0	B159/C161		IF(D161>D160,1,0)
162	53	C163+C164				
163	Candidate A		0	B162/C163	IF(D163>D164,1,0)	
164	Candidate B		0	B162/C164		IF(D164>D163,1,0)
165	54	C166+C167				
166	Candidate A		0	B165/C166	IF(D166>D167,1,0)	
167	Candidate B		0	B165/C167		IF(D167>D166,1,0)

	a	B	C	D	E	F
168	55	C169+C170				
169	Candidate A		0	B168/C169	IF(D169>D170,1,0)	
170	Candidate B		0	B168/C170		IF(D170>D169,1,0)
171	56	C172+C173				
172	Candidate A		0	B171/C172	IF(D172>D173,1,0)	
173	Candidate B		0	B171/C173		IF(D173>D172,1,0)
174	57	C175+C176				
175	Candidate A		0	B174/C175	IF(D175>D176,1,0)	
176	Candidate B		0	B174/C176		IF(D176>D175,1,0)
177	58	C178+C179				
178	Candidate A		0	B177/C178	IF(D178>D179,1,0)	
179	Candidate B		0	B177/C179		IF(D179>D178,1,0)
180	59	C181+C182				
181	Candidate A		0	B180/C181	IF(D181>D182,1,0)	
182	Candidate B		0	B180/C182		IF(D182>D181,1,0)
183	60	C184+C185				
184	Candidate A		0	B183/C184	IF(D184>D185,1,0)	
185	Candidate B		0	B183/C185		IF(D185>D184,1,0)
186	61	C187+C188				
187	Candidate A		0	B186/C187	IF(D187>D188,1,0)	
188	Candidate B		0	B186/C188		IF(D188>D187,1,0)
189	62	C190+C191				
190	Candidate A		0	B189/C190	IF(D190>D191,1,0)	
191	Candidate B		0	B189/C191		IF(D191>D190,1,0)
192	63	C193+C194				
193	Candidate A		0	B192/C193	IF(D193>D194,1,0)	
194	Candidate B		0	B192/C194		IF(D194>D193,1,0)
195	64	C196+C197				
196	Candidate A		0	B195/C196	IF(D196>D197,1,0)	
197	Candidate B		0	B195/C197		IF(D197>D196,1,0)
198	65	C199+C200				
199	Candidate A		0	B198/C199	IF(D199>D200,1,0)	
200	Candidate B		0	B198/C200		IF(D200>D199,1,0)
201	66	C202+C203				
202	Candidate A		0	B201/C202	IF(D202>D203,1,0)	

	a	B	C	D	E	F
203	Candidate B		0	B201/C203		IF(D203>D202,1,0)
204	67	C205+C206				
205	Candidate A		0	B204/C205	IF(D205>D206,1,0)	
206	Candidate B		0	B204/C206		IF(D206>D205,1,0)
207	68	C208+C209				
208	Candidate A		0	B207/C208	IF(D208>D209,1,0)	
209	Candidate B		0	B207/C209		IF(D209>D208,1,0)
210	69	C211+C212				
211	Candidate A		0	B210/C211	IF(D211>D212,1,0)	
212	Candidate B		0	B210/C212		IF(D212>D211,1,0)
213	70	C214+C215				
214	Candidate A		0	B213/C214	IF(D214>D215,1,0)	
215	Candidate B		0	B213/C215		IF(D215>D214,1,0)
216	71	C217+C218				
217	Candidate A		0	B216/C217	IF(D217>D218,1,0)	
218	Candidate B		0	B216/C218		IF(D218>D217,1,0)
219	72	C220+C221				
220	Candidate A		0	B219/C220	IF(D220>D221,1,0)	
221	Candidate B		0	B219/C221		IF(D221>D220,1,0)
222	73	C223+C224				
223	Candidate A		0	B222/C223	IF(D223>D224,1,0)	
224	Candidate B		0	B222/C224		IF(D224>D223,1,0)
225	74	C226+C227				
226	Candidate A		0	B225/C226	IF(D226>D227,1,0)	
227	Candidate B		0	B225/C227		IF(D227>D226,1,0)
228	75	C229+C230				
229	Candidate A		0	B228/C229	IF(D229>D230,1,0)	
230	Candidate B		0	B228/C230		IF(D230>D229,1,0)
231	76	C232+C233				
232	Candidate A		0	B231/C232	IF(D232>D233,1,0)	
233	Candidate B		0	B231/C233		IF(D233>D232,1,0)
234	77	C235+C236				
235	Candidate A		0	B234/C235	IF(D235>D236,1,0)	
236	Candidate B		0	B234/C236		IF(D236>D235,1,0)
237	78	C238+C239				

	a	B	C	D	E	F
238	Candidate A		0	B237/C238	IF(D238>D239,1,0)	
239	Candidate B		0	B237/C239		IF(D239>D238,1,0)
240	79	C241+C242				
241	Candidate A		0	B240/C241	IF(D241>D242,1,0)	
242	Candidate B		0	B240/C242		IF(D242>D241,1,0)
243	80	C244+C245				
244	Candidate A		0	B243/C244	IF(D244>D245,1,0)	
245	Candidate B		0	B243/C245		IF(D245>D244,1,0)
246	81	C247+C248				
247	Candidate A		0	B246/C247	IF(D247>D248,1,0)	
248	Candidate B		0	B246/C248		IF(D248>D247,1,0)
249	82	C250+C251				
250	Candidate A		0	B249/C250	IF(D250>D251,1,0)	
251	Candidate B		0	B249/C251		IF(D251>D250,1,0)
252	83	C253+C254				
253	Candidate A		0	B252/C253	IF(D253>D254,1,0)	
254	Candidate B		0	B252/C254		IF(D254>D253,1,0)
255	84	C256+C257				
256	Candidate A		0	B255/C256	IF(D256>D257,1,0)	
257	Candidate B		0	B255/C257		IF(D257>D256,1,0)
258	85	C259+C260				
259	Candidate A		0	B258/C259	IF(D259>D260,1,0)	
260	Candidate B		0	B258/C260		IF(D260>D259,1,0)
261	86	C262+C263				
262	Candidate A		0	B261/C262	IF(D262>D263,1,0)	
263	Candidate B		0	B261/C263		IF(D263>D262,1,0)
264	87	C265+C266				
265	Candidate A		0	B264/C265	IF(D265>D266,1,0)	
266	Candidate B		0	B264/C266		IF(D266>D265,1,0)
267	88	C268+C269				
268	Candidate A		0	B267/C268	IF(D268>D269,1,0)	
269	Candidate B		0	B267/C269		IF(D269>D268,1,0)
270	89	C271+C272				
271	Candidate A		0	B270/C271	IF(D271>D272,1,0)	
272	Candidate B		0	B270/C272		IF(D272>D271,1,0)

	a	B	C	D	E	F
273	90	C274+C275				
274	Candidate A		0	B273/C274	IF(D274>D275,1,0)	
275	Candidate B		0	B273/C275		IF(D275>D274,1,0)
276	91	C277+C278				
277	Candidate A		0	B276/C277	IF(D277>D278,1,0)	
278	Candidate B		0	B276/C278		IF(D278>D277,1,0)
279	92	C280+C281				
280	Candidate A		0	B279/C280	IF(D280>D281,1,0)	
281	Candidate B		0	B279/C281		IF(D281>D280,1,0)
282	93	C283+C284				
283	Candidate A		0	B282/C283	IF(D283>D284,1,0)	
284	Candidate B		0	B282/C284		IF(D284>D283,1,0)
285	94	C286+C287				
286	Candidate A		0	B285/C286	IF(D286>D287,1,0)	
287	Candidate B		0	B285/C287		IF(D287>D286,1,0)
288	95	C289+C290				
289	Candidate A		0	B288/C289	IF(D289>D290,1,0)	
290	Candidate B		0	B288/C290		IF(D290>D289,1,0)
291	96	C292+C293				
292	Candidate A		0	B291/C292	IF(D292>D293,1,0)	
293	Candidate B		0	B291/C293		IF(D293>D292,1,0)
294	97	C295+C296				
295	Candidate A		0	B294/C295	IF(D295>D296,1,0)	
296	Candidate B		0	B294/C296		IF(D296>D295,1,0)
297	98	C298+C299				
298	Candidate A		0	B297/C298	IF(D298>D299,1,0)	
299	Candidate B		0	B297/C299		IF(D299>D298,1,0)
300	99	C301+C302				
301	Candidate A		0	B300/C301	IF(D301>D302,1,0)	
302	Candidate B		0	B300/C302		IF(D302>D301,1,0)
303	100	C304+C305				
304	Candidate A		0	B303/C304	IF(D304>D305,1,0)	
305	Candidate B		0	B303/C305		IF(D305>D304,1,0)
306	101	C307+C308				
307	Candidate A		0	B306/C307	IF(D307>D308,1,0)	

	a	B	C	D	E	F
308	Candidate B		0	B306/C308		IF(D308>D307,1,0)
309	102	C310+C311				
310	Candidate A		0	B309/C310	IF(D310>D311,1,0)	
311	Candidate B		0	B309/C311		IF(D311>D310,1,0)
312	103	C313+C314				
313	Candidate A		0	B312/C313	IF(D313>D314,1,0)	
314	Candidate B		0	B312/C314		IF(D314>D313,1,0)
315	104	C316+C317				
316	Candidate A		0	B315/C316	IF(D316>D317,1,0)	
317	Candidate B		0	B315/C317		IF(D317>D316,1,0)
318	105	C319+C320				
319	Candidate A		0	B318/C319	IF(D319>D320,1,0)	
320	Candidate B		0	B318/C320		IF(D320>D319,1,0)
321	106	C322+C323				
322	Candidate A		0	B321/C322	IF(D322>D323,1,0)	
323	Candidate B		0	B321/C323		IF(D323>D322,1,0)
324	107	C325+C326				
325	Candidate A		0	B324/C325	IF(D325>D326,1,0)	
326	Candidate B		0	B324/C326		IF(D326>D325,1,0)
327	108	C328+C329				
328	Candidate A		0	B327/C328	IF(D328>D329,1,0)	
329	Candidate B		0	B327/C329		IF(D329>D328,1,0)
330	109	C331+C332				
331	Candidate A		0	B330/C331	IF(D331>D332,1,0)	
332	Candidate B		0	B330/C332		IF(D332>D331,1,0)
333	110	C334+C335				
334	Candidate A		0	B333/C334	IF(D334>D335,1,0)	
335	Candidate B		0	B333/C335		IF(D335>D334,1,0)
336	111	C337+C338				
337	Candidate A		0	B336/C337	IF(D337>D338,1,0)	
338	Candidate B		0	B336/C338		IF(D338>D337,1,0)
339	112	C340+C341				
340	Candidate A		0	B339/C340	IF(D340>D341,1,0)	
341	Candidate B		0	B339/C341		IF(D341>D340,1,0)
342	113	C343+C344				

	a	B	C	D	E	F
343	Candidate A		0	B342/C343	IF(D343>D344,1,0)	
344	Candidate B		0	B342/C344		IF(D344>D343,1,0)
345	114	C346+C347				
346	Candidate A		0	B345/C346	IF(D346>D347,1,0)	
347	Candidate B		0	B345/C347		IF(D347>D346,1,0)
348	115	C349+C350				
349	Candidate A		0	B348/C349	IF(D349>D350,1,0)	
350	Candidate B		0	B348/C350		IF(D350>D349,1,0)
351	116	C352+C353				
352	Candidate A		0	B351/C352	IF(D352>D353,1,0)	
353	Candidate B		0	B351/C353		IF(D353>D352,1,0)
354	117	C355+C356				
355	Candidate A		0	B354/C355	IF(D355>D356,1,0)	
356	Candidate B		0	B354/C356		IF(D356>D355,1,0)
357	118	C358+C359				
358	Candidate A		0	B357/C358	IF(D358>D359,1,0)	
359	Candidate B		0	B357/C359		IF(D359>D358,1,0)
360	119	C361+C362				
361	Candidate A		0	B360/C361	IF(D361>D362,1,0)	
362	Candidate B		0	B360/C362		IF(D362>D361,1,0)
363	120	C364+C365				
364	Candidate A		0	B363/C364	IF(D364>D365,1,0)	
365	Candidate B		0	B363/C365		IF(D365>D364,1,0)
366	121	C367+C368				
367	Candidate A		0	B366/C367	IF(D367>D368,1,0)	
368	Candidate B		0	B366/C368		IF(D368>D367,1,0)
369	122	C370+C371				
370	Candidate A		0	B369/C370	IF(D370>D371,1,0)	
371	Candidate B		0	B369/C371		IF(D371>D370,1,0)
372	123	C373+C374				
373	Candidate A		0	B372/C373	IF(D373>D374,1,0)	
374	Candidate B		0	B372/C374		IF(D374>D373,1,0)
375	124	C376+C377				
376	Candidate A		0	B375/C376	IF(D376>D377,1,0)	
377	Candidate B		0	B375/C377		IF(D377>D376,1,0)

	a	B	C	D	E	F
378	125	C379+C380				
379	Candidate A		0	B378/C379	IF(D379>D380,1,0)	
380	Candidate B		0	B378/C380		IF(D380>D379,1,0)
381	126	C382+C383				
382	Candidate A		0	B381/C382	IF(D382>D383,1,0)	
383	Candidate B		0	B381/C383		IF(D383>D382,1,0)
384	127	C385+C386				
385	Candidate A		0	B384/C385	IF(D385>D386,1,0)	
386	Candidate B		0	B384/C386		IF(D386>D385,1,0)
387	128	C388+C389				
388	Candidate A		0	B387/C388	IF(D388>D389,1,0)	
389	Candidate B		0	B387/C389		IF(D389>D388,1,0)
390	129	C391+C392				
391	Candidate A		0	B390/C391	IF(D391>D392,1,0)	
392	Candidate B		0	B390/C392		IF(D392>D391,1,0)
393	130	C394+C395				
394	Candidate A		0	B393/C394	IF(D394>D395,1,0)	
395	Candidate B		0	B393/C395		IF(D395>D394,1,0)
396	131	C397+C398				
397	Candidate A		0	B396/C397	IF(D397>D398,1,0)	
398	Candidate B		0	B396/C398		IF(D398>D397,1,0)
399	132	C400+C401				
400	Candidate A		0	B399/C400	IF(D400>D401,1,0)	
401	Candidate B		0	B399/C401		IF(D401>D400,1,0)
402	133	C403+C404				
403	Candidate A		0	B402/C403	IF(D403>D404,1,0)	
404	Candidate B		0	B402/C404		IF(D404>D403,1,0)
405	134	C406+C407				
406	Candidate A		0	B405/C406	IF(D406>D407,1,0)	
407	Candidate B		0	B405/C407		IF(D407>D406,1,0)
408	135	C409+C410				
409	Candidate A		0	B408/C409	IF(D409>D410,1,0)	
410	Candidate B		0	B408/C410		IF(D410>D409,1,0)
411	136	C412+C413				
412	Candidate A		0	B411/C412	IF(D412>D413,1,0)	

	a	B	C	D	E	F
413	Candidate B		0	B411/ C413		IF(D413>D412,1,0)
414	137	C415+C416				
415	Candidate A		0	B414/ C415	IF(D415>D416,1,0)	
416	Candidate B		0	B414/ C416		IF(D416>D415,1,0)
417	138	C418+C419				
418	Candidate A		0	B417/ C418	IF(D418>D419,1,0)	
419	Candidate B		0	B417/ C419		IF(D419>D418,1,0)
420	139	C421+C422				
421	Candidate A		0	B420/ C421	IF(D421>D422,1,0)	
422	Candidate B		0	B420/ C422		IF(D422>D421,1,0)
423	140	C424+C425				
424	Candidate A		0	B423/ C424	IF(D424>D425,1,0)	
425	Candidate B		0	B423/ C425		IF(D425>D424,1,0)
426	141	C427+C428				
427	Candidate A		0	B426/ C427	IF(D427>D428,1,0)	
428	Candidate B		0	B426/ C428		IF(D428>D427,1,0)
429	142	C430+C431				
430	Candidate A		0	B429/ C430	IF(D430>D431,1,0)	
431	Candidate B		0	B429/ C431		IF(D431>D430,1,0)
432	143	C433+C434				
433	Candidate A		0	B432/ C433	IF(D433>D434,1,0)	
434	Candidate B		0	B432/ C434		IF(D434>D433,1,0)
435	144	C436+C437				
436	Candidate A		0	B435/ C436	IF(D436>D437,1,0)	
437	Candidate B		0	B435/ C437		IF(D437>D436,1,0)
438	145	C439+C440				
439	Candidate A		0	B438/ C439	IF(D439>D440,1,0)	
440	Candidate B		0	B438/ C440		IF(D440>D439,1,0)
441	146	C442+C443				
442	Candidate A		0	B441/ C442	IF(D442>D443,1,0)	
443	Candidate B		0	B441/ C443		IF(D443>D442,1,0)
444	147	C445+C446				
445	Candidate A		0	B444/ C445	IF(D445>D446,1,0)	
446	Candidate B		0	B444/ C446		IF(D446>D445,1,0)
447	148	C448+C449				

	a	B	C	D	E	F
448	Candidate A		0	B447/C448	IF(D448>D449,1,0)	
449	Candidate B		0	B447/C449		IF(D449>D448,1,0)
450	149	C451+C452				
451	Candidate A		0	B450/C451	IF(D451>D452,1,0)	
452	Candidate B		0	B450/C452		IF(D452>D451,1,0)
453	150	C454+C455				
454	Candidate A		0	B453/C454	IF(D454>D455,1,0)	
455	Candidate B		0	B453/C455		IF(D455>D454,1,0)
456	151	C457+C458				
457	Candidate A		0	B456/C457	IF(D457>D458,1,0)	
458	Candidate B		0	B456/C458		IF(D458>D457,1,0)
459	152	C460+C461				
460	Candidate A		0	B459/C460	IF(D460>D461,1,0)	
461	Candidate B		0	B459/C461		IF(D461>D460,1,0)
462	153	C463+C464				
463	Candidate A		0	B462/C463	IF(D463>D464,1,0)	
464	Candidate B		0	B462/C464		IF(D464>D463,1,0)
465	154	C466+C467				
466	Candidate A		0	B465/C466	IF(D466>D467,1,0)	
467	Candidate B		0	B465/C467		IF(D467>D466,1,0)
468	155	C469+C470				
469	Candidate A		0	B468/C469	IF(D469>D470,1,0)	
470	Candidate B		0	B468/C470		IF(D470>D469,1,0)
471	156	C472+C473				
472	Candidate A		0	B471/C472	IF(D472>D473,1,0)	
473	Candidate B		0	B471/C473		IF(D473>D472,1,0)
474	157	C475+C476				
475	Candidate A		0	B474/C475	IF(D475>D476,1,0)	
476	Candidate B		0	B474/C476		IF(D476>D475,1,0)
477	158	C478+C479				
478	Candidate A		0	B477/C478	IF(D478>D479,1,0)	
479	Candidate B		0	B477/C479		IF(D479>D478,1,0)
480	159	C481+C482				
481	Candidate A		0	B480/C481	IF(D481>D482,1,0)	
482	Candidate B		0	B480/C482		IF(D482>D481,1,0)

	a	B	C	D	E	F
483	160	C484+C485				
484	Candidate A		0	B483/C484	IF(D484>D485,1,0)	
485	Candidate B		0	B483/C485		IF(D485>D484,1,0)
486	161	C487+C488				
487	Candidate A		0	B486/C487	IF(D487>D488,1,0)	
488	Candidate B		0	B486/C488		IF(D488>D487,1,0)
489	162	C490+C491				
490	Candidate A		0	B489/C490	IF(D490>D491,1,0)	
491	Candidate B		0	B489/C491		IF(D491>D490,1,0)
492	163	C493+C494				
493	Candidate A		0	B492/C493	IF(D493>D494,1,0)	
494	Candidate B		0	B492/C494		IF(D494>D493,1,0)
495	164	C496+C497				
496	Candidate A		0	B495/C496	IF(D496>D497,1,0)	
497	Candidate B		0	B495/C497		IF(D497>D496,1,0)
498	165	C499+C500				
499	Candidate A		0	B498/C499	IF(D499>D500,1,0)	
500	Candidate B		0	B498/C500		IF(D500>D499,1,0)
501	166	C502+C503				
502	Candidate A		0	B501/C502	IF(D502>D503,1,0)	
503	Candidate B		0	B501/C503		IF(D503>D502,1,0)
504	167	C505+C506				
505	Candidate A		0	B504/C505	IF(D505>D506,1,0)	
506	Candidate B		0	B504/C506		IF(D506>D505,1,0)
507	168	C508+C509				
508	Candidate A		0	B507/C508	IF(D508>D509,1,0)	
509	Candidate B		0	B507/C509		IF(D509>D508,1,0)
510	169	C511+C512				
511	Candidate A		0	B510/C511	IF(D511>D512,1,0)	
512	Candidate B		0	B510/C512		IF(D512>D511,1,0)
513	170	C514+C515				
514	Candidate A		0	B513/C514	IF(D514>D515,1,0)	
515	Candidate B		0	B513/C515		IF(D515>D514,1,0)
516	171	C517+C518				
517	Candidate A		0	B516/C517	IF(D517>D518,1,0)	

	a	B	C	D	E	F
518	Candidate B		0	B516/ C518		IF(D518>D517,1,0)
519	172	C520+C521				
520	Candidate A		0	B519/ C520	IF(D520>D521,1,0)	
521	Candidate B		0	B519/ C521		IF(D521>D520,1,0)
522	173	C523+C524				
523	Candidate A		0	B522/ C523	IF(D523>D524,1,0)	
524	Candidate B		0	B522/ C524		IF(D524>D523,1,0)
525	174	C526+C527				
526	Candidate A		0	B525/ C526	IF(D526>D527,1,0)	
527	Candidate B		0	B525/ C527		IF(D527>D526,1,0)
528	175	C529+C530				
529	Candidate A		0	B528/ C529	IF(D529>D530,1,0)	
530	Candidate B		0	B528/ C530		IF(D530>D529,1,0)
531	176	C532+C533				
532	Candidate A		0	B531/ C532	IF(D532>D533,1,0)	
533	Candidate B		0	B531/ C533		IF(D533>D532,1,0)
534	177	C535+C536				
535	Candidate A		0	B534/ C535	IF(D535>D536,1,0)	
536	Candidate B		0	B534/ C536		IF(D536>D535,1,0)
537	178	C538+C539				
538	Candidate A		0	B537/ C538	IF(D538>D539,1,0)	
539	Candidate B		0	B537/ C539		IF(D539>D538,1,0)
540	179	C541+C542				
541	Candidate A		0	B540/ C541	IF(D541>D542,1,0)	
542	Candidate B		0	B540/ C542		IF(D542>D541,1,0)
543	180	C544+C545				
544	Candidate A		0	B543/ C544	IF(D544>D545,1,0)	
545	Candidate B		0	B543/ C545		IF(D545>D544,1,0)
546	181	C547+C548				
547	Candidate A		0	B546/ C547	IF(D547>D548,1,0)	
548	Candidate B		0	B546/ C548		IF(D548>D547,1,0)
549	182	C550+C551				
550	Candidate A		0	B549/ C550	IF(D550>D551,1,0)	
551	Candidate B		0	B549/ C551		IF(D551>D550,1,0)
552	183	C553+C554				

	a	B	C	D	E	F
553	Candidate A		0	B552/C553	IF(D553>D554,1,0)	
554	Candidate B		0	B552/C554		IF(D554>D553,1,0)
555	184	C556+C557				
556	Candidate A		0	B555/C556	IF(D556>D557,1,0)	
557	Candidate B		0	B555/C557		IF(D557>D556,1,0)
558	185	C559+C560				
559	Candidate A		0	B558/C559	IF(D559>D560,1,0)	
560	Candidate B		0	B558/C560		IF(D560>D559,1,0)
561	186	C562+C563				
562	Candidate A		0	B561/C562	IF(D562>D563,1,0)	
563	Candidate B		0	B561/C563		IF(D563>D562,1,0)
564	187	C565+C566				
565	Candidate A		0	B564/C565	IF(D565>D566,1,0)	
566	Candidate B		0	B564/C566		IF(D566>D565,1,0)
567	188	C568+C569				
568	Candidate A		0	B567/C568	IF(D568>D569,1,0)	
569	Candidate B		0	B567/C569		IF(D569>D568,1,0)
570	189	C571+C572				
571	Candidate A		0	B570/C571	IF(D571>D572,1,0)	
572	Candidate B		0	B570/C572		IF(D572>D571,1,0)
573	190	C574+C575				
574	Candidate A		0	B573/C574	IF(D574>D575,1,0)	
575	Candidate B		0	B573/C575		IF(D575>D574,1,0)
576	191	C577+C578				
577	Candidate A		0	B576/C577	IF(D577>D578,1,0)	
578	Candidate B		0	B576/C578		IF(D578>D577,1,0)
579	192	C580+C581				
580	Candidate A		0	B579/C580	IF(D580>D581,1,0)	
581	Candidate B		0	B579/C581		IF(D581>D580,1,0)
582	193	C583+C584				
583	Candidate A		0	B582/C583	IF(D583>D584,1,0)	
584	Candidate B		0	B582/C584		IF(D584>D583,1,0)
585	194	C586+C587				
586	Candidate A		0	B585/C586	IF(D586>D587,1,0)	
587	Candidate B		0	B585/C587		IF(D587>D586,1,0)

	a	B	C	D	E	F
588	195	C589+C590				
589	Candidate A		0	B588/C589	IF(D589>D590,1,0)	
590	Candidate B		0	B588/C590		IF(D590>D589,1,0)
591	196	C592+C593				
592	Candidate A		0	B591/C592	IF(D592>D593,1,0)	
593	Candidate B		0	B591/C593		IF(D593>D592,1,0)
594	197	C595+C596				
595	Candidate A		0	B594/C595	IF(D595>D596,1,0)	
596	Candidate B		0	B594/C596		IF(D596>D595,1,0)
597	198	C598+C599				
598	Candidate A		0	B597/C598	IF(D598>D599,1,0)	
599	Candidate B		0	B597/C599		IF(D599>D598,1,0)
600	199	C601+C602				
601	Candidate A		0	B600/C601	IF(D601>D602,1,0)	
602	Candidate B		0	B600/C602		IF(D602>D601,1,0)
603	200	C604+C605				
604	Candidate A		0	B603/C604	IF(D604>D605,1,0)	
605	Candidate B		0	B603/C605		IF(D605>D604,1,0)
606	201	C607+C608				
607	Candidate A		0	B606/C607	IF(D607>D608,1,0)	
608	Candidate B		0	B606/C608		IF(D608>D607,1,0)
609	202	C610+C611				
610	Candidate A		0	B609/C610	IF(D610>D611,1,0)	
611	Candidate B		0	B609/C611		IF(D611>D610,1,0)
612	203	C613+C614				
613	Candidate A		0	B612/C613	IF(D613>D614,1,0)	
614	Candidate B		0	B612/C614		IF(D614>D613,1,0)
615	204	C616+C617				
616	Candidate A		0	B615/C616	IF(D616>D617,1,0)	
617	Candidate B		0	B615/C617		IF(D617>D616,1,0)
618	205	C619+C620				
619	Candidate A		0	B618/C619	IF(D619>D620,1,0)	
620	Candidate B		0	B618/C620		IF(D620>D619,1,0)
621	206	C622+C623				
622	Candidate A		0	B621/C622	IF(D622>D623,1,0)	

	a	B	C	D	E	F
623	Candidate B		0	B621/C623		IF(D623>D622,1,0)
624	207	C625+C626				
625	Candidate A		0	B624/C625	IF(D625>D626,1,0)	
626	Candidate B		0	B624/C626		IF(D626>D625,1,0)
627	208	C628+C629				
628	Candidate A		0	B627/C628	IF(D628>D629,1,0)	
629	Candidate B		0	B627/C629		IF(D629>D628,1,0)
630	209	C631+C632				
631	Candidate A		0	B630/C631	IF(D631>D632,1,0)	
632	Candidate B		0	B630/C632		IF(D632>D631,1,0)
633	210	C634+C635				
634	Candidate A		0	B633/C634	IF(D634>D635,1,0)	
635	Candidate B		0	B633/C635		IF(D635>D634,1,0)
636	211	C637+C638				
637	Candidate A		0	B636/C637	IF(D637>D638,1,0)	
638	Candidate B		0	B636/C638		IF(D638>D637,1,0)
639	212	C640+C641				
640	Candidate A		0	B639/C640	IF(D640>D641,1,0)	
641	Candidate B		0	B639/C641		IF(D641>D640,1,0)
642	213	C643+C644				
643	Candidate A		0	B642/C643	IF(D643>D644,1,0)	
644	Candidate B		0	B642/C644		IF(D644>D643,1,0)
645	214	C646+C647				
646	Candidate A		0	B645/C646	IF(D646>D647,1,0)	
647	Candidate B		0	B645/C647		IF(D647>D646,1,0)
648	215	C649+C650				
649	Candidate A		0	B648/C649	IF(D649>D650,1,0)	
650	Candidate B		0	B648/C650		IF(D650>D649,1,0)
651	216	C652+C653				
652	Candidate A		0	B651/C652	IF(D652>D653,1,0)	
653	Candidate B		0	B651/C653		IF(D653>D652,1,0)
654	217	C655+C656				
655	Candidate A		0	B654/C655	IF(D655>D656,1,0)	
656	Candidate B		0	B654/C656		IF(D656>D655,1,0)
657	218	C658+C659				

	a	B	C	D	E	F
658	Candidate A		0	B657/C658	IF(D658>D659,1,0)	
659	Candidate B		0	B657/C659		IF(D659>D658,1,0)
660	219	C661+C662				
661	Candidate A		0	B660/C661	IF(D661>D662,1,0)	
662	Candidate B		0	B660/C662		IF(D662>D661,1,0)
663	220	C664+C665				
664	Candidate A		0	B663/C664	IF(D664>D665,1,0)	
665	Candidate B		0	B663/C665		IF(D665>D664,1,0)
666	221	C667+C668				
667	Candidate A		0	B666/C667	IF(D667>D668,1,0)	
668	Candidate B		0	B666/C668		IF(D668>D667,1,0)
669	222	C670+C671				
670	Candidate A		0	B669/C670	IF(D670>D671,1,0)	
671	Candidate B		0	B669/C671		IF(D671>D670,1,0)
672	223	C673+C674				
673	Candidate A		0	B672/C673	IF(D673>D674,1,0)	
674	Candidate B		0	B672/C674		IF(D674>D673,1,0)
675	224	C676+C677				
676	Candidate A		0	B675/C676	IF(D676>D677,1,0)	
677	Candidate B		0	B675/C677		IF(D677>D676,1,0)
678	225	C679+C680				
679	Candidate A		0	B678/C679	IF(D679>D680,1,0)	
680	Candidate B		0	B678/C680		IF(D680>D679,1,0)
681	226	C682+C683				
682	Candidate A		0	B681/C682	IF(D682>D683,1,0)	
683	Candidate B		0	B681/C683		IF(D683>D682,1,0)
684	227	C685+C686				
685	Candidate A		0	B684/C685	IF(D685>D686,1,0)	
686	Candidate B		0	B684/C686		IF(D686>D685,1,0)
687	228	C688+C689				
688	Candidate A		0	B687/C688	IF(D688>D689,1,0)	
689	Candidate B		0	B687/C689		IF(D689>D688,1,0)
690	229	C691+C692				
691	Candidate A		0	B690/C691	IF(D691>D692,1,0)	
692	Candidate B		0	B690/C692		IF(D692>D691,1,0)

	a	B	C	D	E	F
693	230	C694+C695				
694	Candidate A		0	B693/C694	IF(D694>D695,1,0)	
695	Candidate B		0	B693/C695		IF(D695>D694,1,0)
696	231	C697+C698				
697	Candidate A		0	B696/C697	IF(D697>D698,1,0)	
698	Candidate B		0	B696/C698		IF(D698>D697,1,0)
699	232	C700+C701				
700	Candidate A		0	B699/C700	IF(D700>D701,1,0)	
701	Candidate B		0	B699/C701		IF(D701>D700,1,0)
702	233	C703+C704				
703	Candidate A		0	B702/C703	IF(D703>D704,1,0)	
704	Candidate B		0	B702/C704		IF(D704>D703,1,0)
705	234	C706+C707				
706	Candidate A		0	B705/C706	IF(D706>D707,1,0)	
707	Candidate B		0	B705/C707		IF(D707>D706,1,0)
708	235	C709+C710				
709	Candidate A		0	B708/C709	IF(D709>D710,1,0)	
710	Candidate B		0	B708/C710		IF(D710>D709,1,0)
711	236	C712+C713				
712	Candidate A		0	B711/C712	IF(D712>D713,1,0)	
713	Candidate B		0	B711/C713		IF(D713>D712,1,0)
714	237	C715+C716				
715	Candidate A		0	B714/C715	IF(D715>D716,1,0)	
716	Candidate B		0	B714/C716		IF(D716>D715,1,0)
717	238	C718+C719				
718	Candidate A		0	B717/C718	IF(D718>D719,1,0)	
719	Candidate B		0	B717/C719		IF(D719>D718,1,0)
720	239	C721+C722				
721	Candidate A		0	B720/C721	IF(D721>D722,1,0)	
722	Candidate B		0	B720/C722		IF(D722>D721,1,0)
723	240	C724+C725				
724	Candidate A		0	B723/C724	IF(D724>D725,1,0)	
725	Candidate B		0	B723/C725		IF(D725>D724,1,0)
726	241	C727+C728				
727	Candidate A		0	B726/C727	IF(D727>D728,1,0)	

	a	B	C	D	E	F
728	Candidate B		0	B726/C728		IF(D728>D727,1,0)
729	242	C730+C731				
730	Candidate A		0	B729/C730	IF(D730>D731,1,0)	
731	Candidate B		0	B729/C731		IF(D731>D730,1,0)
732	243	C733+C734				
733	Candidate A		0	B732/C733	IF(D733>D734,1,0)	
734	Candidate B		0	B732/C734		IF(D734>D733,1,0)
735	244	C736+C737				
736	Candidate A		0	B735/C736	IF(D736>D737,1,0)	
737	Candidate B		0	B735/C737		IF(D737>D736,1,0)
738	245	C739+C740				
739	Candidate A		0	B738/C739	IF(D739>D740,1,0)	
740	Candidate B		0	B738/C740		IF(D740>D739,1,0)
741	246	C742+C743				
742	Candidate A		0	B741/C742	IF(D742>D743,1,0)	
743	Candidate B		0	B741/C743		IF(D743>D742,1,0)
744	247	C745+C746				
745	Candidate A		0	B744/C745	IF(D745>D746,1,0)	
746	Candidate B		0	B744/C746		IF(D746>D745,1,0)
747	248	C748+C749				
748	Candidate A		0	B747/C748	IF(D748>D749,1,0)	
749	Candidate B		0	B747/C749		IF(D749>D748,1,0)
750	249	C751+C752				
751	Candidate A		0	B750/C751	IF(D751>D752,1,0)	
752	Candidate B		0	B750/C752		IF(D752>D751,1,0)
753	250	C754+C755				
754	Candidate A		0	B753/C754	IF(D754>D755,1,0)	
755	Candidate B		0	B753/C755		IF(D755>D754,1,0)
756	251	C757+C758				
757	Candidate A		0	B756/C757	IF(D757>D758,1,0)	
758	Candidate B		0	B756/C758		IF(D758>D757,1,0)
759	252	C760+C761				
760	Candidate A		0	B759/C760	IF(D760>D761,1,0)	
761	Candidate B		0	B759/C761		IF(D761>D760,1,0)
762	253	C763+C764				

	a	B	C	D	E	F
763	Candidate A		0	B762/C763	IF(D763>D764,1,0)	
764	Candidate B		0	B762/C764		IF(D764>D763,1,0)
765	254	C766+C767				
766	Candidate A		0	B765/C766	IF(D766>D767,1,0)	
767	Candidate B		0	B765/C767		IF(D767>D766,1,0)
768	255	C769+C770				
769	Candidate A		0	B768/C769	IF(D769>D770,1,0)	
770	Candidate B		0	B768/C770		IF(D770>D769,1,0)
771	256	C772+C773				
772	Candidate A		0	B771/C772	IF(D772>D773,1,0)	
773	Candidate B		0	B771/C773		IF(D773>D772,1,0)
774	257	C775+C776				
775	Candidate A		0	B774/C775	IF(D775>D776,1,0)	
776	Candidate B		0	B774/C776		IF(D776>D775,1,0)
777	258	C778+C779				
778	Candidate A		0	B777/C778	IF(D778>D779,1,0)	
779	Candidate B		0	B777/C779		IF(D779>D778,1,0)
780	259	C781+C782				
781	Candidate A		0	B780/C781	IF(D781>D782,1,0)	
782	Candidate B		0	B780/C782		IF(D782>D781,1,0)
783	260	C784+C785				
784	Candidate A		0	B783/C784	IF(D784>D785,1,0)	
785	Candidate B		0	B783/C785		IF(D785>D784,1,0)
786	261	C787+C788				
787	Candidate A		0	B786/C787	IF(D787>D788,1,0)	
788	Candidate B		0	B786/C788		IF(D788>D787,1,0)
789	262	C790+C791				
790	Candidate A		0	B789/C790	IF(D790>D791,1,0)	
791	Candidate B		0	B789/C791		IF(D791>D790,1,0)
792	263	C793+C794				
793	Candidate A		0	B792/C793	IF(D793>D794,1,0)	
794	Candidate B		0	B792/C794		IF(D794>D793,1,0)
795	264	C796+C797				
796	Candidate A		0	B795/C796	IF(D796>D797,1,0)	
797	Candidate B		0	B795/C797		IF(D797>D796,1,0)

	a	B	C	D	E	F
798	265	C799+C800				
799	Candidate A		0	B798/C799	IF(D799>D800,1,0)	
800	Candidate B		0	B798/C800		IF(D800>D799,1,0)
801	266	C802+C803				
802	Candidate A		0	B801/C802	IF(D802>D803,1,0)	
803	Candidate B		0	B801/C803		IF(D803>D802,1,0)
804	267	C805+C806				
805	Candidate A		0	B804/C805	IF(D805>D806,1,0)	
806	Candidate B		0	B804/C806		IF(D806>D805,1,0)
807	268	C808+C809				
808	Candidate A		0	B807/C808	IF(D808>D809,1,0)	
809	Candidate B		0	B807/C809		IF(D809>D808,1,0)
810	269	C811+C812				
811	Candidate A		0	B810/C811	IF(D811>D812,1,0)	
812	Candidate B		0	B810/C812		IF(D812>D811,1,0)
813	270	C814+C815				
814	Candidate A		0	B813/C814	IF(D814>D815,1,0)	
815	Candidate B		0	B813/C815		IF(D815>D814,1,0)
816	271	C817+C818				
817	Candidate A		0	B816/C817	IF(D817>D818,1,0)	
818	Candidate B		0	B816/C818		IF(D818>D817,1,0)
819	272	C820+C821				
820	Candidate A		0	B819/C820	IF(D820>D821,1,0)	
821	Candidate B		0	B819/C821		IF(D821>D820,1,0)
822	273	C823+C824				
823	Candidate A		0	B822/C823	IF(D823>D824,1,0)	
824	Candidate B		0	B822/C824		IF(D824>D823,1,0)
825	274	C826+C827				
826	Candidate A		0	B825/C826	IF(D826>D827,1,0)	
827	Candidate B		0	B825/C827		IF(D827>D826,1,0)
828	275	C829+C830				
829	Candidate A		0	B828/C829	IF(D829>D830,1,0)	
830	Candidate B		0	B828/C830		IF(D830>D829,1,0)
831	276	C832+C833				
832	Candidate A		0	B831/C832	IF(D832>D833,1,0)	

	a	B	C	D	E	F
833	Candidate B		0	B831/ C833		IF(D833>D832,1,0)
834	277	C835+C836				
835	Candidate A		0	B834/ C835	IF(D835>D836,1,0)	
836	Candidate B		0	B834/ C836		IF(D836>D835,1,0)
837	278	C838+C839				
838	Candidate A		0	B837/ C838	IF(D838>D839,1,0)	
839	Candidate B		0	B837/ C839		IF(D839>D838,1,0)
840	279	C841+C842				
841	Candidate A		0	B840/ C841	IF(D841>D842,1,0)	
842	Candidate B		0	B840/ C842		IF(D842>D841,1,0)
843	280	C844+C845				
844	Candidate A		0	B843/ C844	IF(D844>D845,1,0)	
845	Candidate B		0	B843/ C845		IF(D845>D844,1,0)
846	281	C847+C848				
847	Candidate A		0	B846/ C847	IF(D847>D848,1,0)	
848	Candidate B		0	B846/ C848		IF(D848>D847,1,0)
849	282	C850+C851				
850	Candidate A		0	B849/ C850	IF(D850>D851,1,0)	
851	Candidate B		0	B849/ C851		IF(D851>D850,1,0)
852	283	C853+C854				
853	Candidate A		0	B852/ C853	IF(D853>D854,1,0)	
854	Candidate B		0	B852/ C854		IF(D854>D853,1,0)
855	284	C856+C857				
856	Candidate A		0	B855/ C856	IF(D856>D857,1,0)	
857	Candidate B		0	B855/ C857		IF(D857>D856,1,0)
858	285	C859+C860				
859	Candidate A		0	B858/ C859	IF(D859>D860,1,0)	
860	Candidate B		0	B858/ C860		IF(D860>D859,1,0)
861	286	C862+C863				
862	Candidate A		0	B861/ C862	IF(D862>D863,1,0)	
863	Candidate B		0	B861/ C863		IF(D863>D862,1,0)
864	287	C865+C866				
865	Candidate A		0	B864/ C865	IF(D865>D866,1,0)	
866	Candidate B		0	B864/ C866		IF(D866>D865,1,0)
867	288	C868+C869				

	a	B	C	D	E	F
868	Candidate A		0	B867/C868	IF(D868>D869,1,0)	
869	Candidate B		0	B867/C869		IF(D869>D868,1,0)
870	289	C871+C872				
871	Candidate A		0	B870/C871	IF(D871>D872,1,0)	
872	Candidate B		0	B870/C872		IF(D872>D871,1,0)
873	290	C874+C875				
874	Candidate A		0	B873/C874	IF(D874>D875,1,0)	
875	Candidate B		0	B873/C875		IF(D875>D874,1,0)
876	291	C877+C878				
877	Candidate A		0	B876/C877	IF(D877>D878,1,0)	
878	Candidate B		0	B876/C878		IF(D878>D877,1,0)
879	292	C880+C881				
880	Candidate A		0	B879/C880	IF(D880>D881,1,0)	
881	Candidate B		0	B879/C881		IF(D881>D880,1,0)
882	293	C883+C884				
883	Candidate A		0	B882/C883	IF(D883>D884,1,0)	
884	Candidate B		0	B882/C884		IF(D884>D883,1,0)
885	294	C886+C887				
886	Candidate A		0	B885/C886	IF(D886>D887,1,0)	
887	Candidate B		0	B885/C887		IF(D887>D886,1,0)
888	295	C889+C890				
889	Candidate A		0	B888/C889	IF(D889>D890,1,0)	
890	Candidate B		0	B888/C890		IF(D890>D889,1,0)
891	296	C892+C893				
892	Candidate A		0	B891/C892	IF(D892>D893,1,0)	
893	Candidate B		0	B891/C893		IF(D893>D892,1,0)
894	297	C895+C896				
895	Candidate A		0	B894/C895	IF(D895>D896,1,0)	
896	Candidate B		0	B894/C896		IF(D896>D895,1,0)
897	298	C898+C899				
898	Candidate A		0	B897/C898	IF(D898>D899,1,0)	
899	Candidate B		0	B897/C899		IF(D899>D898,1,0)
900	299	C901+C902				
901	Candidate A		0	B900/C901	IF(D901>D902,1,0)	
902	Candidate B		0	B900/C902		IF(D902>D901,1,0)

	a	B	C	D	E	F
903	300	C904+C905				
904	Candidate A		0	B903/C904	IF(D904>D905,1,0)	
905	Candidate B		0	B903/C905		IF(D905>D904,1,0)
906	301	C907+C908				
907	Candidate A		0	B906/C907	IF(D907>D908,1,0)	
908	Candidate B		0	B906/C908		IF(D908>D907,1,0)
909	302	C910+C911				
910	Candidate A		0	B909/C910	IF(D910>D911,1,0)	
911	Candidate B		0	B909/C911		IF(D911>D910,1,0)
912	303	C913+C914				
913	Candidate A		0	B912/C913	IF(D913>D914,1,0)	
914	Candidate B		0	B912/C914		IF(D914>D913,1,0)
915	304	C916+C917				
916	Candidate A		0	B915/C916	IF(D916>D917,1,0)	
917	Candidate B		0	B915/C917		IF(D917>D916,1,0)
918	305	C919+C920				
919	Candidate A		0	B918/C919	IF(D919>D920,1,0)	
920	Candidate B		0	B918/C920		IF(D920>D919,1,0)
921	306	C922+C923				
922	Candidate A		0	B921/C922	IF(D922>D923,1,0)	
923	Candidate B		0	B921/C923		IF(D923>D922,1,0)
924	307	C925+C926				
925	Candidate A		0	B924/C925	IF(D925>D926,1,0)	
926	Candidate B		0	B924/C926		IF(D926>D925,1,0)
927	308	C928+C929				
928	Candidate A		0	B927/C928	IF(D928>D929,1,0)	
929	Candidate B		0	B927/C929		IF(D929>D928,1,0)
930	309	C931+C932				
931	Candidate A		0	B930/C931	IF(D931>D932,1,0)	
932	Candidate B		0	B930/C932		IF(D932>D931,1,0)
933	310	C934+C935				
934	Candidate A		0	B933/C934	IF(D934>D935,1,0)	
935	Candidate B		0	B933/C935		IF(D935>D934,1,0)
936	311	C937+C938				
937	Candidate A		0	B936/C937	IF(D937>D938,1,0)	

	a	B	C	D	E	F
938	Candidate B		0	B936/C938		IF(D938>D937,1,0)
939	312	C940+C941				
940	Candidate A		0	B939/C940	IF(D940>D941,1,0)	
941	Candidate B		0	B939/C941		IF(D941>D940,1,0)
942	313	C943+C944				
943	Candidate A		0	B942/C943	IF(D943>D944,1,0)	
944	Candidate B		0	B942/C944		IF(D944>D943,1,0)
945	314	C946+C947				
946	Candidate A		0	B945/C946	IF(D946>D947,1,0)	
947	Candidate B		0	B945/C947		IF(D947>D946,1,0)
948	315	C949+C950				
949	Candidate A		0	B948/C949	IF(D949>D950,1,0)	
950	Candidate B		0	B948/C950		IF(D950>D949,1,0)
951	316	C952+C953				
952	Candidate A		0	B951/C952	IF(D952>D953,1,0)	
953	Candidate B		0	B951/C953		IF(D953>D952,1,0)
954	317	C955+C956				
955	Candidate A		0	B954/C955	IF(D955>D956,1,0)	
956	Candidate B		0	B954/C956		IF(D956>D955,1,0)
957	318	C958+C959				
958	Candidate A		0	B957/C958	IF(D958>D959,1,0)	
959	Candidate B		0	B957/C959		IF(D959>D958,1,0)
960	319	C961+C962				
961	Candidate A		0	B960/C961	IF(D961>D962,1,0)	
962	Candidate B		0	B960/C962		IF(D962>D961,1,0)
963	320	C964+C965				
964	Candidate A		0	B963/C964	IF(D964>D965,1,0)	
965	Candidate B		0	B963/C965		IF(D965>D964,1,0)
966	321	C967+C968				
967	Candidate A		0	B966/C967	IF(D967>D968,1,0)	
968	Candidate B		0	B966/C968		IF(D968>D967,1,0)
969	322	C970+C971				
970	Candidate A		0	B969/C970	IF(D970>D971,1,0)	
971	Candidate B		0	B969/C971		IF(D971>D970,1,0)
972	323	C973+C974				

	a	B	C	D	E	F
973	Candidate A		0	B972/C973	IF(D973>D974,1,0)	
974	Candidate B		0	B972/C974		IF(D974>D973,1,0)
975	324	C976+C977				
976	Candidate A		0	B975/C976	IF(D976>D977,1,0)	
977	Candidate B		0	B975/C977		IF(D977>D976,1,0)
978	325	C979+C980				
979	Candidate A		0	B978/C979	IF(D979>D980,1,0)	
980	Candidate B		0	B978/C980		IF(D980>D979,1,0)
981	326	C982+C983				
982	Candidate A		0	B981/C982	IF(D982>D983,1,0)	
983	Candidate B		0	B981/C983		IF(D983>D982,1,0)
984	327	C985+C986				
985	Candidate A		0	B984/C985	IF(D985>D986,1,0)	
986	Candidate B		0	B984/C986		IF(D986>D985,1,0)
987	328	C988+C989				
988	Candidate A		0	B987/C988	IF(D988>D989,1,0)	
989	Candidate B		0	B987/C989		IF(D989>D988,1,0)
990	329	C991+C992				
991	Candidate A		0	B990/C991	IF(D991>D992,1,0)	
992	Candidate B		0	B990/C992		IF(D992>D991,1,0)
993	330	C994+C995				
994	Candidate A		0	B993/C994	IF(D994>D995,1,0)	
995	Candidate B		0	B993/C995		IF(D995>D994,1,0)
996	331	C997+C998				
997	Candidate A		0	B996/C997	IF(D997>D998,1,0)	
998	Candidate B		0	B996/C998		IF(D998>D997,1,0)
999	332	C1000+C1001				
1000	Candidate A		0	B999/C1000	IF(D1000>D1001,1,0)	
1001	Candidate B		0	B999/C1001		IF(D1001>D1000,1,0)
1002	333	C1003+C1004				
1003	Candidate A		0	B1002/C1003	IF(D1003>D1004,1,0)	
1004	Candidate B		0	B1002/C1004		IF(D1004>D1003,1,0)
1005	334	C1006+C1007				
1006	Candidate A		0	B1005/C1006	IF(D1006>D1007,1,0)	
1007	Candidate B		0	B1005/C1007		IF(D1007>D1006,1,0)

	a	B	C	D	E	F
1008	335	C1009+C1010				
1009	Candidate A		0	B1008/C1009	IF(D1009>D1010,1,0)	
1010	Candidate B		0	B1008/C1010		IF(D1010>D1009,1,0)
1011	336	C1012+C1013				
1012	Candidate A		0	B1011/C1012	IF(D1012>D1013,1,0)	
1013	Candidate B		0	B1011/C1013		IF(D1013>D1012,1,0)
1014	337	C1015+C1016				
1015	Candidate A		0	B1014/C1015	IF(D1015>D1016,1,0)	
1016	Candidate B		0	B1014/C1016		IF(D1016>D1015,1,0)
1017	338	C1018+C1019				
1018	Candidate A		0	B1017/C1018	IF(D1018>D1019,1,0)	
1019	Candidate B		0	B1017/C1019		IF(D1019>D1018,1,0)
1020	339	C1021+C1022				
1021	Candidate A		0	B1020/C1021	IF(D1021>D1022,1,0)	
1022	Candidate B		0	B1020/C1022		IF(D1022>D1021,1,0)
1023	340	C1024+C1025				
1024	Candidate A		0	B1023/C1024	IF(D1024>D1025,1,0)	
1025	Candidate B		0	B1023/C1025		IF(D1025>D1024,1,0)
1026	341	C1027+C1028				
1027	Candidate A		0	B1026/C1027	IF(D1027>D1028,1,0)	
1028	Candidate B		0	B1026/C1028		IF(D1028>D1027,1,0)
1029	342	C1030+C1031				
1030	Candidate A		0	B1029/C1030	IF(D1030>D1031,1,0)	
1031	Candidate B		0	B1029/C1031		IF(D1031>D1030,1,0)
1032	343	C1033+C1034				
1033	Candidate A		0	B1032/C1033	IF(D1033>D1034,1,0)	
1034	Candidate B		0	B1032/C1034		IF(D1034>D1033,1,0)
1035	344	C1036+C1037				
1036	Candidate A		0	B1035/C1036	IF(D1036>D1037,1,0)	
1037	Candidate B		0	B1035/C1037		IF(D1037>D1036,1,0)
1038	345	C1039+C1040				
1039	Candidate A		0	B1038/C1039	IF(D1039>D1040,1,0)	
1040	Candidate B		0	B1038/C1040		IF(D1040>D1039,1,0)
1041	346	C1042+C1043				
1042	Candidate A		0	B1041/C1042	IF(D1042>D1043,1,0)	

	a	B	C	D	E	F
1043	Candidate B		0	B1041/C1043		IF(D1043>D1042,1,0)
1044	347	C1045+C1046				
1045	Candidate A		0	B1044/C1045	IF(D1045>D1046,1,0)	
1046	Candidate B		0	B1044/C1046		IF(D1046>D1045,1,0)
1047	348	C1048+C1049				
1048	Candidate A		0	B1047/C1048	IF(D1048>D1049,1,0)	
1049	Candidate B		0	B1047/C1049		IF(D1049>D1048,1,0)
1050	349	C1051+C1052				
1051	Candidate A		0	B1050/C1051	IF(D1051>D1052,1,0)	
1052	Candidate B		0	B1050/C1052		IF(D1052>D1051,1,0)
1053	350	C1054+C1055				
1054	Candidate A		0	B1053/C1054	IF(D1054>D1055,1,0)	
1055	Candidate B		0	B1053/C1055		IF(D1055>D1054,1,0)
1056	351	C1057+C1058				
1057	Candidate A		0	B1056/C1057	IF(D1057>D1058,1,0)	
1058	Candidate B		0	B1056/C1058		IF(D1058>D1057,1,0)
1059	352	C1060+C1061				
1060	Candidate A		0	B1059/C1060	IF(D1060>D1061,1,0)	
1061	Candidate B		0	B1059/C1061		IF(D1061>D1060,1,0)
1062	353	C1063+C1064				
1063	Candidate A		0	B1062/C1063	IF(D1063>D1064,1,0)	
1064	Candidate B		0	B1062/C1064		IF(D1064>D1063,1,0)
1065	354	C1066+C1067				
1066	Candidate A		0	B1065/C1066	IF(D1066>D1067,1,0)	
1067	Candidate B		0	B1065/C1067		IF(D1067>D1066,1,0)
1068	355	C1069+C1070				
1069	Candidate A		0	B1068/C1069	IF(D1069>D1070,1,0)	
1070	Candidate B		0	B1068/C1070		IF(D1070>D1069,1,0)
1071	356	C1072+C1073				
1072	Candidate A		0	B1071/C1072	IF(D1072>D1073,1,0)	
1073	Candidate B		0	B1071/C1073		IF(D1073>D1072,1,0)
1074	357	C1075+C1076				
1075	Candidate A		0	B1074/C1075	IF(D1075>D1076,1,0)	
1076	Candidate B		0	B1074/C1076		IF(D1076>D1075,1,0)
1077	358	C1078+C1079				

	a	B	C	D	E	F
1078	Candidate A		0	B1077/C1078	IF(D1078>D1079,1,0)	
1079	Candidate B		0	B1077/C1079		IF(D1079>D1078,1,0)
1080	359	C1081+C1082				
1081	Candidate A		0	B1080/C1081	IF(D1081>D1082,1,0)	
1082	Candidate B		0	B1080/C1082		IF(D1082>D1081,1,0)
1083	360	C1084+C1085				
1084	Candidate A		0	B1083/C1084	IF(D1084>D1085,1,0)	
1085	Candidate B		0	B1083/C1085		IF(D1085>D1084,1,0)
1086	361	C1087+C1088				
1087	Candidate A		0	B1086/C1087	IF(D1087>D1088,1,0)	
1088	Candidate B		0	B1086/C1088		IF(D1088>D1087,1,0)
1089	362	C1090+C1091				
1090	Candidate A		0	B1089/C1090	IF(D1090>D1091,1,0)	
1091	Candidate B		0	B1089/C1091		IF(D1091>D1090,1,0)
1092	363	C1093+C1094				
1093	Candidate A		0	B1092/C1093	IF(D1093>D1094,1,0)	
1094	Candidate B		0	B1092/C1094		IF(D1094>D1093,1,0)
1095	364	C1096+C1097				
1096	Candidate A		0	B1095/C1096	IF(D1096>D1097,1,0)	
1097	Candidate B		0	B1095/C1097		IF(D1097>D1096,1,0)
1098	365	C1099+C1100				
1099	Candidate A		0	B1098/C1099	IF(D1099>D1100,1,0)	
1100	Candidate B		0	B1098/C1100		IF(D1100>D1099,1,0)
1101	366	C1102+C1103				
1102	Candidate A		0	B1101/C1102	IF(D1102>D1103,1,0)	
1103	Candidate B		0	B1101/C1103		IF(D1103>D1102,1,0)
1104	367	C1105+C1106				
1105	Candidate A		0	B1104/C1105	IF(D1105>D1106,1,0)	
1106	Candidate B		0	B1104/C1106		IF(D1106>D1105,1,0)
1107	368	C1108+C1109				
1108	Candidate A		0	B1107/C1108	IF(D1108>D1109,1,0)	
1109	Candidate B		0	B1107/C1109		IF(D1109>D1108,1,0)
1110	369	C1111+C1112				
1111	Candidate A		0	B1110/C1111	IF(D1111>D1112,1,0)	
1112	Candidate B		0	B1110/C1112		IF(D1112>D1111,1,0)

	a	B	C	D	E	F
1113	370	C1114+C1115				
1114	Candidate A		0	B1113/C1114	IF(D1114>D1115,1,0)	
1115	Candidate B		0	B1113/C1115		IF(D1115>D1114,1,0)
1116	371	C1117+C1118				
1117	Candidate A		0	B1116/C1117	IF(D1117>D1118,1,0)	
1118	Candidate B		0	B1116/C1118		IF(D1118>D1117,1,0)
1119	372	C1120+C1121				
1120	Candidate A		0	B1119/C1120	IF(D1120>D1121,1,0)	
1121	Candidate B		0	B1119/C1121		IF(D1121>D1120,1,0)
1122	373	C1123+C1124				
1123	Candidate A		0	B1122/C1123	IF(D1123>D1124,1,0)	
1124	Candidate B		0	B1122/C1124		IF(D1124>D1123,1,0)
1125	374	C1126+C1127				
1126	Candidate A		0	B1125/C1126	IF(D1126>D1127,1,0)	
1127	Candidate B		0	B1125/C1127		IF(D1127>D1126,1,0)
1128	375	C1129+C1130				
1129	Candidate A		0	B1128/C1129	IF(D1129>D1130,1,0)	
1130	Candidate B		0	B1128/C1130		IF(D1130>D1129,1,0)
1131	376	C1132+C1133				
1132	Candidate A		0	B1131/C1132	IF(D1132>D1133,1,0)	
1133	Candidate B		0	B1131/C1133		IF(D1133>D1132,1,0)
1134	377	C1135+C1136				
1135	Candidate A		0	B1134/C1135	IF(D1135>D1136,1,0)	
1136	Candidate B		0	B1134/C1136		IF(D1136>D1135,1,0)
1137	378	C1138+C1139				
1138	Candidate A		0	B1137/C1138	IF(D1138>D1139,1,0)	
1139	Candidate B		0	B1137/C1139		IF(D1139>D1138,1,0)
1140	379	C1141+C1142				
1141	Candidate A		0	B1140/C1141	IF(D1141>D1142,1,0)	
1142	Candidate B		0	B1140/C1142		IF(D1142>D1141,1,0)
1143	380	C1144+C1145				
1144	Candidate A		0	B1143/C1144	IF(D1144>D1145,1,0)	
1145	Candidate B		0	B1143/C1145		IF(D1145>D1144,1,0)
1146	381	C1147+C1148				
1147	Candidate A		0	B1146/C1147	IF(D1147>D1148,1,0)	

	a	B	C	D	E	F
1148	Candidate B		0	B1146/C1148		IF(D1148>D1147,1,0)
1149	382	C1150+C1151				
1150	Candidate A		0	B1149/C1150	IF(D1150>D1151,1,0)	
1151	Candidate B		0	B1149/C1151		IF(D1151>D1150,1,0)
1152	383	C1153+C1154				
1153	Candidate A		0	B1152/C1153	IF(D1153>D1154,1,0)	
1154	Candidate B		0	B1152/C1154		IF(D1154>D1153,1,0)
1155	384	C1156+C1157				
1156	Candidate A		0	B1155/C1156	IF(D1156>D1157,1,0)	
1157	Candidate B		0	B1155/C1157		IF(D1157>D1156,1,0)
1158	385	C1159+C1160				
1159	Candidate A		0	B1158/C1159	IF(D1159>D1160,1,0)	
1160	Candidate B		0	B1158/C1160		IF(D1160>D1159,1,0)
1161	386	C1162+C1163				
1162	Candidate A		0	B1161/C1162	IF(D1162>D1163,1,0)	
1163	Candidate B		0	B1161/C1163		IF(D1163>D1162,1,0)
1164	387	C1165+C1166				
1165	Candidate A		0	B1164/C1165	IF(D1165>D1166,1,0)	
1166	Candidate B		0	B1164/C1166		IF(D1166>D1165,1,0)
1167	388	C1168+C1169				
1168	Candidate A		0	B1167/C1168	IF(D1168>D1169,1,0)	
1169	Candidate B		0	B1167/C1169		IF(D1169>D1168,1,0)
1170	389	C1171+C1172				
1171	Candidate A		0	B1170/C1171	IF(D1171>D1172,1,0)	
1172	Candidate B		0	B1170/C1172		IF(D1172>D1171,1,0)
1173	390	C1174+C1175				
1174	Candidate A		0	B1173/C1174	IF(D1174>D1175,1,0)	
1175	Candidate B		0	B1173/C1175		IF(D1175>D1174,1,0)
1176	391	C1177+C1178				
1177	Candidate A		0	B1176/C1177	IF(D1177>D1178,1,0)	
1178	Candidate B		0	B1176/C1178		IF(D1178>D1177,1,0)
1179	392	C1180+C1181				
1180	Candidate A		0	B1179/C1180	IF(D1180>D1181,1,0)	
1181	Candidate B		0	B1179/C1181		IF(D1181>D1180,1,0)
1182	393	C1183+C1184				

	a	B	C	D	E	F
1183	Candidate A		0	B1182/C1183	IF(D1183>D1184,1,0)	
1184	Candidate B		0	B1182/C1184		IF(D1184>D1183,1,0)
1185	394	C1186+C1187				
1186	Candidate A		0	B1185/C1186	IF(D1186>D1187,1,0)	
1187	Candidate B		0	B1185/C1187		IF(D1187>D1186,1,0)
1188	395	C1189+C1190				
1189	Candidate A		0	B1188/C1189	IF(D1189>D1190,1,0)	
1190	Candidate B		0	B1188/C1190		IF(D1190>D1189,1,0)
1191	396	C1192+C1193				
1192	Candidate A		0	B1191/C1192	IF(D1192>D1193,1,0)	
1193	Candidate B		0	B1191/C1193		IF(D1193>D1192,1,0)
1194	397	C1195+C1196				
1195	Candidate A		0	B1194/C1195	IF(D1195>D1196,1,0)	
1196	Candidate B		0	B1194/C1196		IF(D1196>D1195,1,0)
1197	398	C1198+C1199				
1198	Candidate A		0	B1197/C1198	IF(D1198>D1199,1,0)	
1199	Candidate B		0	B1197/C1199		IF(D1199>D1198,1,0)
1200	399	C1201+C1202				
1201	Candidate A		0	B1200/C1201	IF(D1201>D1202,1,0)	
1202	Candidate B		0	B1200/C1202		IF(D1202>D1201,1,0)
1203	400	C1204+C1205				
1204	Candidate A		0	B1203/C1204	IF(D1204>D1205,1,0)	
1205	Candidate B		0	B1203/C1205		IF(D1205>D1204,1,0)
1206	Total		SUM (C7:C1205)		F1207/A1203*E1204	E3/A1203*F1205

In flowchart *mob rule*, the United States House of Representatives mob rule is shown.

Since the population of the United States House of Representatives is in the range of six hundred thousand, mob rule should be eliminated.

The demonstration spreadsheets are designed for the United States House of Representatives' campaign. The state government assembly is the base district that will discourage mob rule. There will be one or more United States House of Representatives district per state government. This spreadsheet has to be executed for each United States House of Representatives district.

Input candidates' election results in column C. There can be several candidates. For example, here, two are used to demonstrate. The spreadsheet calculates the candidates' sums of votes.

Using the spreadsheet's displayed instructions as a flowchart, a computer programmer can write a computer program that will tabulate and count the votes as a voter goes through the act of voting. The computer technology already exists where a computer is used to process a vote being cast at polling stations.

At the end of the vote-casting day, the computer automatically delivers the candidates' sums of districts won and the sum popular vote.

Instead of using a *referendum* type of voting method to elect a United States House of Representatives, the state government assemblies' districts will choose the United States House of Representatives delegate.

Since the districts are quasi-equal populated, the group of people within the districts form a district's representative election. Mob rule diminishes and practically disappears. In case of a tie vote where the candidates receive the same acceptances of districts, the election goes to the candidate who wins the popular vote. Even though the election goes to a popular vote, the probability of mob rule diminishes. The action of receiving the same number of districts where one district nullifies another practically determines that mob rule will not be prevalent.

Since the population of United States House of Representatives is high, using a state government district to elect a United States House of Representatives member is justified to eliminate mob rule.

A programmer can tailor this presentation to any particular state government district.

UNITED STATES PRESIDENTIAL SPREADSHEET (ALL STATES)

UNITED STATES HOUSE OF REPRESENTATIVES DISTRICTS

USING PERCENTAGES TO DETERMINE
ELECTORAL PRESIDENTIAL WINNER!

	A	B		C	D
1					
2				Alabama	
3				Elector Number	
4				0	
5	District	Votes		President A	President B
6	1				
7	President A	0		IF(B7>B8,1,0)	
8	President B	0			IF(B7<B8,1,0)
9	2				
10	President A	0		IF(B10>B11,1,0)	
11	President B	0			IF(B10<B11,1,0)
12	3				
13	President A	0		IF(B13>B14,1,0)	
14	President B	0			IF(B13<B14,1,0)
15	4				
16	President A	0		IF(B16>B17,1,0)	
17	President B	0			IF(B16<B17,1,0)
18	5				
19	President A	0		IF(B19>B20,1,0)	
20	President B	0			IF(B19<B20,1,0)
21	6				
22	President A	0		IF(B22>B23,1,0)	
23	President B	0			IF(B22<B23,1,0)
24	7				
25	President A	0		IF(B25>B26,1,0)	
26	President B	0			IF(B25<B26,1,0)
27	Total	Alabama		SUM(C7:C25)	SUM(D6:D26)
28					
29				Alaska	
30				Elector Number	
31				IF(B32>B33,1,0)	
32					
33	District	Votes		President A	President B
34	1				
35	President A	0		IF(B36>B37,1,0)	
36	President B	0			IF(B36<B37,1,0)
37	Total	Alaska		SUM(C36)	SUM(D37)
38					
39				Arizona	
40				Elector Number	
41				0	
42					
43	District	Votes		President A	President B
44	1				
45	President A	0		IF(B47>B48,1,0)	
46	President B	0			IF(B47<B48,1,0)
47	2				
48	President A	0		IF(B50>B51,1,0)	
49	President B	0			IF(B50<B51,1,0)
50	3				
51	President A	0		IF(B53>B54,1,0)	
52	President B	0			IF(B53<B54,1,0)
53	4				
54	President A	0		IF(B56>B57,1,0)	
55	President B	0			IF(B56<B57,1,0)
56	5				
57	President A	0		IF(B59>B60,1,0)	

	A	B		C	D
58	President B	0			IF(B59<B60,1,0)
59	6				
60	President A	0		IF(B62>B63,1,0)	
61	President B	0			IF(B62<B63,1,0)
62	7				
63	President A	0		IF(B65>B66,1,0)	
64	President B	0			IF(B65<B66,1,0)
65	8				
66	President A	0		IF(B68>B69,1,0)	
67	President B	0			IF(B68<B69,1,0)
68	Total	Arizona		SUM(C47:C68)	SUM(D48:D69)
69					
70				Arkansas	
71				Elector Number	
72				0	
73					
74	District	Votes		President A	President B
75	1				
76	President A	0		IF(B79>B80,1,0)	
77	President B	0			IF(B79<B80,1,0)
78	2				
79	President A	0		IF(B82>B83,1,0)	
80	President B	0			IF(B82<B83,1,0)
81	3				
82	President A	0		IF(B85>B86,1,0)	
83	President B	0			IF(B85<B86,1,0)
84	4				
85	President A	0		IF(B88>B89,1,0)	
86	President B	0			IF(B88<B89,1,0)
87	Total	Arkansas		SUM(C79:C88)	SUM(D80:D89)
88					
89				California	
90				Elector Number	
91				0	
92					
93	District	Votes		President A	President B
94	1				
95	President A	0		IF(B99>B100,1,0)	
96	President B	0			IF(B99<B100,1,0)
97	2	0			
98	President A	0		IF(B102>B103,1,0)	
99	President B	0			IF(B102<B103,1,0)
100	3	0			
101	President A	0		IF(B105>B106,1,0)	
102	President B	0			IF(B105<B106,1,0)
103	4	0			
104	President A	0		IF(B108>B109,1,0)	
105	President B	0			IF(B108<B109,1,0)
106	5				
107	President A	0		IF(B111>B112,1,0)	
108	President B	0			IF(B111<B112,1,0)
109	6				
110	President A	0		IF(B114>B115,1,0)	
111	President B	0			IF(B114<B115,1,0)
112	7				
113	President A	0		IF(B117>B118,1,0)	
114	President B	0			IF(B117<B118,1,0)
115	8				
116	President A	0		IF(B120>B121,1,0)	
117	President B	0			IF(B120<B121,1,0)
118	9				
119	President A	0		IF(B123>B124,1,0)	
120	President B	0			IF(B123<B124,1,0)
121	10				
122	President A	0		IF(B126>B127,1,0)	
123	President B	0			IF(B126<B127,1,0)
124	11				
125	President A	0		IF(B129>B130,1,0)	
126	President B	0			IF(B129<B130,1,0)
127	12				
128	President A	0		IF(B132>B133,1,0)	

	A	B		C	D
129	President B	0			IF(B132<B133,1,0)
130	13				
131	President A	0		IF(B135>B136,1,0)	
132	President B	0			IF(B135<B136,1,0)
133	14				
134	President A	0		IF(B138>B139,1,0)	
135	President B	0			IF(B138<B139,1,0)
136	15				
137	President A	0		IF(B141>B142,1,0)	
138	President B	0			IF(B141<B142,1,0)
139	16				
140	President A	0		IF(B144>B145,1,0)	
141	President B	0			IF(B144<B145,1,0)
142	17				
143	President A	0		IF(B147>B148,1,0)	
144	President B	0			IF(B147<B148,1,0)
145	18				
146	President A	0		IF(B150>B151,1,0)	
147	President B	0			IF(B150<B151,1,0)
148	19				
149	President A	0		IF(B153>B154,1,0)	
150	President B	0			IF(B153<B154,1,0)
151	20				
152	President A	0		IF(B156>B157,1,0)	
153	President B	0			IF(B156<B157,1,0)
154	21				
155	President A	0		IF(B159>B160,1,0)	
156	President B	0			IF(B159<B160,1,0)
157	22				
158	President A	0		IF(B162>B163,1,0)	
159	President B	0			IF(B162<B163,1,0)
160	23				
161	President A	0		IF(B165>B166,1,0)	
162	President B	0			IF(B165<B166,1,0)
163	24				
164	President A	0		IF(B168>B169,1,0)	
165	President B	0			IF(B168<B169,1,0)
166	25				
167	President A	0		IF(B171>B172,1,0)	
168	President B	0			IF(B171<B172,1,0)
169	26				
170	President A	0		IF(B174>B175,1,0)	
171	President B	0			IF(B174<B175,1,0)
172	27				
173	President A	0		IF(B177>B178,1,0)	
174	President B	0			IF(B177<B178,1,0)
175	28				
176	President A	0		IF(B180>B181,1,0)	
177	President B	0			IF(B180<B181,1,0)
178	29				
179	President A	0		IF(B183>B184,1,0)	
180	President B	0			IF(B183<B184,1,0)
181	30				
182	President A	0		IF(B186>B187,1,0)	
183	President B	0			IF(B186<B187,1,0)
184	31				
185	President A	0		IF(B189>B190,1,0)	
186	President B	0			IF(B189<B190,1,0)
187	32				
188	President A	0		IF(B192>B193,1,0)	
189	President B	0			IF(B192<B193,1,0)
190	33				
191	President A	0		IF(B195>B196,1,0)	
192	President B	0			IF(B195<B196,1,0)
193	34				
194	President A	0		IF(B198>B199,1,0)	
195	President B	0			IF(B198<B199,1,0)
196	35				
197	President A	0		IF(B201>B202,1,0)	
198	President B	0			IF(B201<B202,1,0)
199	36				

	A	B		C	D
200	President A	0		IF(B204>B205,1,0)	
201	President B	0			IF(B204<B205,1,0)
202	37				
203	President A	0		IF(B207>B208,1,0)	
204	President B	0			IF(B207<B208,1,0)
205	38				
206	President A	0		IF(B210>B211,1,0)	
207	President B	0			IF(B210<B211,1,0)
208	39				
209	President A	0		IF(B213>B214,1,0)	
210	President B	0			IF(B213<B214,1,0)
211	40				
212	President A	0		IF(B216>B217,1,0)	
213	President B	0			IF(B216<B217,1,0)
214	41				
215	President A	0		IF(B219>B220,1,0)	
216	President B	0			IF(B219<B220,1,0)
217	42				
218	President A	0		IF(B222>B223,1,0)	
219	President B	0			IF(B222<B223,1,0)
220	43				
221	President A	0		IF(B225>B226,1,0)	
222	President B	0			IF(B225<B226,1,0)
223	44				
224	President A	0		IF(B228>B229,1,0)	
225	President B	0			IF(B228<B229,1,0)
226	45				
227	President A	0		IF(B231>B232,1,0)	
228	President B	0			IF(B231<B232,1,0)
229	46				
230	President A	0		IF(B234>B235,1,0)	
231	President B	0			IF(B234<B235,1,0)
232	47				
233	President A	0		IF(B237>B238,1,0)	
234	President B	0			IF(B237<B238,1,0)
235	48				
236	President A	0		IF(B240>B241,1,0)	
237	President B	0			IF(B240<B241,1,0)
238	49				
239	President A	0		IF(B243>B244,1,0)	
240	President B	0			IF(B243<B244,1,0)
241	50				
242	President A	0		IF(B246>B247,1,0)	
243	President B	0			IF(B246<B247,1,0)
244	51				
245	President A	0		IF(B249>B250,1,0)	
246	President B	0			IF(B249<B250,1,0)
247	52				
248	President A	0		IF(B252>B253,1,0)	
249	President B	0			IF(B252<B253,1,0)
250	53				
251	President A	0		IF(B255>B256,1,0)	
252	President B	0			IF(B255<B256,1,0)
253	Total	California		SUM(C99:C255)	SUM(D100:D256)
254					
255				Colorado	
256				Elector Number	
257				0	
258					
259	District	Votes		President A	President B
260	1				
261	President A	0		IF(B266>B267,1,0)	
262	President B	0			IF(B266<B267,1,0)
263	2				
264	President A	0		IF(B269>B270,1,0)	
265	President B	0			IF(B269<B270,1,0)
266	3				
267	President A	0		IF(B272>B273,1,0)	
268	President B	0			IF(B272<B273,1,0)
269	4				
270	President A	0		IF(B275>B276,1,0)	

	A	B		C	D
271	President B	0			IF(B275<B276,1,0)
272	5				
273	President A	0		IF(B278>B279,1,0)	
274	President B	0			IF(B278<B279,1,0)
275	6				
276	President A	0		IF(B281>B282,1,0)	
277	President B	0			IF(B281<B282,1,0)
278	7				
279	President A	0		IF(B284>B285,1,0)	
280	President B	0			IF(B284<B285,1,0)
281	Total	Colorado		SUM(C266:C284)	SUM(D267:D285)
282					
283				Connecticut	
284				Elector Number	
285				0	
286					
287	District	Votes		President A	President B
288	1				
289	President A	0		IF(B295>B296,1,0)	
290	President B	0			IF(B295<B296,1,0)
291	2				
292	President A	0		IF(B298>B299,1,0)	
293	President B	0			IF(B298<B299,1,0)
294	3				
295	President A	0		IF(B301>B302,1,0)	
296	President B	0			IF(B301<B302,1,0)
297	4				
298	President A	0		IF(B304>B305,1,0)	
299	President B	0			IF(B304<B305,1,0)
300	5				
301	President A	0		IF(B307>B308,1,0)	
302	President B	0			IF(B307<B308,1,0)
303	Total	Connecticut		SUM(C295:C307)	SUM(D296:D308)
304					
305				Delaware	
306				Elector Number	
307				0	
308					
309	District	Votes		President A	President B
310	1				
311	President A	0		IF(B318>B319,1,0)	
312	President B	0			IF(B318<B319,1,0)
313	Total	Delaware		SUM(C318)	SUM(D318:D319)
314					
315				Florida	
316				Elector Number	
317				0	
318					
319	District	Votes		President A	President B
320	1				
321	President A	0		IF(B329>B330,1,0)	
322	President B	0			IF(B329<B330,1,0)
323	2				
324	President A	0		IF(B332>B333,1,0)	
325	President B	0			IF(B332<B333,1,0)
326	3				
327	President A	0		IF(B335>B336,1,0)	
328	President B	0			IF(B335<B336,1,0)
329	4				
330	President A	0		IF(B338>B339,1,0)	
331	President B	0			IF(B338<B339,1,0)
332	5				
333	President A	0		IF(B341>B342,1,0)	
334	President B	0			IF(B341<B342,1,0)
335	6				
336	President A	0		IF(B344>B345,1,0)	
337	President B	0			IF(B344<B345,1,0)
338	7				
339	President A	0		IF(B347>B348,1,0)	
340	President B	0			IF(B347<B348,1,0)
341	8				

	A	B		C	D
342	President A	0		IF(B350>B351,1,0)	
343	President B	0			IF(B350<B351,1,0)
344	9				
345	President A	0		IF(B353>B354,1,0)	
346	President B	0			IF(B353<B354,1,0)
347	10				
348	President A	0		IF(B356>B357,1,0)	
349	President B	0			IF(B356<B357,1,0)
350	11				
351	President A	0		IF(B359>B360,1,0)	
352	President B	0			IF(B359<B360,1,0)
353	12				
354	President A	0		IF(B362>B363,1,0)	
355	President B	0			IF(B362<B363,1,0)
356	13				
357	President A	0		IF(B365>B366,1,0)	
358	President B	0			IF(B365<B366,1,0)
359	14				
360	President A	0		IF(B368>B369,1,0)	
361	President B	0			IF(B368<B369,1,0)
362	15				
363	President A	0		IF(B371>B372,1,0)	
364	President B	0			IF(B371<B372,1,0)
365	16				
366	President A	0		IF(B374>B375,1,0)	
367	President B	0			IF(B374<B375,1,0)
368	17				
369	President A	0		IF(B377>B378,1,0)	
370	President B	0			IF(B377<B378,1,0)
371	18				
372	President A	0		IF(B380>B381,1,0)	
373	President B	0			IF(B380<B381,1,0)
374	19				
375	President A	0		IF(B383>B384,1,0)	
376	President B	0			IF(B383<B384,1,0)
377	20				
378	President A	0		IF(B386>B387,1,0)	
379	President B	0			IF(B386<B387,1,0)
380	21				
381	President A	0		IF(B389>B390,1,0)	
382	President B	0			IF(B389<B390,1,0)
383	22				
384	President A	0		IF(B392>B393,1,0)	
385	President B	0			IF(B392<B393,1,0)
386	23				
387	President A	0		IF(B395>B396,1,0)	
388	President B	0			IF(B395<B396,1,0)
389	24				
390	President A	0		IF(B398>B399,1,0)	
391	President B	0			IF(B398<B399,1,0)
392	25				
393	President A	0		IF(B401>B402,1,0)	
394	President B	0			IF(B401<B402,1,0)
395	Total	Florida		SUM(C329:C401)	SUM(D330:D402)
396					
397				Georgia	
398				Elector Number	
399				0	
400					
401	District	Votes		President A	President B
402	1				
403	President A	0		IF(B412>B413,1,0)	
404	President B	0			IF(B412<B413,1,0)
405	2				
406	President A	0		IF(B415>B416,1,0)	
407	President B	0			IF(B415<B416,1,0)
408	3				
409	President A	0		IF(B418>B419,1,0)	
410	President B	0			IF(B418<B419,1,0)
411	4				
412	President A	0		IF(B421>B422,1,0)	

	A	B		C	D
413	President B	0			IF(B421<B422,1,0)
414	5				
415	President A	0		IF(B424>B425,1,0)	
416	President B	0			IF(B424<B425,1,0)
417	6				
418	President A	0		IF(B427>B428,1,0)	
419	President B	0			IF(B427<B428,1,0)
420	7				
421	President A	0		IF(B430>B431,1,0)	
422	President B	0			IF(B430<B431,1,0)
423	8				
424	President A	0		IF(B433>B434,1,0)	
425	President B	0			IF(B433<B434,1,0)
426	9				
427	President A	0		IF(B436>B437,1,0)	
428	President B	0			IF(B436<B437,1,0)
429	10				
430	President A	0		IF(B439>B440,1,0)	
431	President B	0			IF(B439<B440,1,0)
432	11				
433	President A	0		IF(B442>B443,1,0)	
434	President B	0			IF(B442<B443,1,0)
435	12				
436	President A	0		IF(B445>B446,1,0)	
437	President B	0			IF(B445<B446,1,0)
438	13				
439	President A	0		IF(B448>B449,1,0)	
440	President B	0			IF(B448<B449,1,0)
441	Total			SUM(C412:C448)	SUM(D413:D449)
442					
443				Hawaii	
444				Elector Number	
445				0	
446					
447	District	Votes		President A	President B
448	1				
449	President A	0		IF(B459>B460,1,0)	
450	President B	0			IF(B459<B460,1,0)
451	2				
452	President A	0		IF(B462>B463,1,0)	
453	President B	0			IF(B462<B463,1,0)
454	Total	Hawaii		SUM(C459:C462)	SUM(D460:D463)
455					
456				Idaho	
457				Elector Number	
458				0	
459					
460	District	Votes		President A	President B
461	1				
462	President A	0		IF(B473>B474,1,0)	
463	President B	0			IF(B473<B474,1,0)
464	2				
465	President A	0		IF(B476>B477,1,0)	
466	President B	0			IF(B476<B477,1,0)
467	Total	Idaho		SUM(C473:C476)	SUM(D474:D477)
468					
469				Illinois	
470				Elector Number	
471				0	
472					
473	District	Votes		President A	President B
474	1				
475	President A	0		IF(B487>B488,1,0)	
476	President B	0			IF(B487<B488,1,0)
477	2				
478	President A	0		IF(B490>B491,1,0)	
479	President B	0			IF(B490<B491,1,0)
480	3				
481	President A	0		IF(B493>B494,1,0)	
482	President B	0			IF(B493<B494,1,0)
483	4				

	A	B		C	D
484	President A	0		IF(B496>B497,1,0)	
485	President B	0			IF(B496<B497,1,0)
486	5				
487	President A	0		IF(B499>B500,1,0)	
488	President B	0			IF(B499<B500,1,0)
489	6				
490	President A	0		IF(B502>B503,1,0)	
491	President B	0			IF(B502<B503,1,0)
492	7				
493	President A	0		IF(B505>B506,1,0)	
494	President B	0			IF(B505<B506,1,0)
495	8				
496	President A	0		IF(B508>B509,1,0)	
497	President B	0			IF(B508<B509,1,0)
498	9				
499	President A	0		IF(B511>B512,1,0)	
500	President B	0			IF(B511<B512,1,0)
501	10				
502	President A	0		IF(B514>B515,1,0)	
503	President B	0			IF(B514<B515,1,0)
504	11				
505	President A	0		IF(B517>B518,1,0)	
506	President B	0			IF(B517<B518,1,0)
507	12				
508	President A	0		IF(B520>B521,1,0)	
509	President B	0			IF(B520<B521,1,0)
510	13				
511	President A	0		IF(B523>B524,1,0)	
512	President B	0			IF(B523<B524,1,0)
513	14				
514	President A	0		IF(B526>B527,1,0)	
515	President B	0			IF(B526<B527,1,0)
516	15				
517	President A	0		IF(B529>B530,1,0)	
518	President B	0			IF(B529<B530,1,0)
519	16				
520	President A	0		IF(B532>B533,1,0)	
521	President B	0			IF(B532<B533,1,0)
522	17				
523	President A	0		IF(B535>B536,1,0)	
524	President B	0			IF(B535<B536,1,0)
525	18				
526	President A	0		IF(B538>B539,1,0)	
527	President B	0			IF(B538<B539,1,0)
528	19				
529	President A	0		IF(B541>B542,1,0)	
530	President B	0			IF(B541<B542,1,0)
531	Total	Illinois		SUM(C487:C541)	SUM(D488:D542)
532					
533				Indiana	
534				Elector Number	
535				0	
536					
537	District	Votes		President A	President B
538	1				
539	President A	0		IF(B552>B553,1,0)	
540	President B	0			IF(B552<B553,1,0)
541	2				
542	President A	0		IF(B555>B556,1,0)	
543	President B	0			IF(B555<B556,1,0)
544	3				
545	President A	0		IF(B558>B559,1,0)	
546	President B	0			IF(B558<B559,1,0)
547	4				
548	President A	0		IF(B561>B562,1,0)	
549	President B	0			IF(B561<B562,1,0)
550	5				
551	President A	0		IF(B564>B565,1,0)	
552	President B	0			IF(B564<B565,1,0)
553	6				
554	President A	0		IF(B567>B568,1,0)	

	A	B		C	D
555	President B	0			IF(B567<B568,1,0)
556	7				
557	President A	0		IF(B570>B571,1,0)	
558	President B	0			IF(B570<B571,1,0)
559	8				
560	President A	0		IF(B573>B574,1,0)	
561	President B	0			IF(B573<B574,1,0)
562	9				SUM(D553:D574)
563	President A	0		IF(B576>B577,1,0)	
564	President B	0			IF(B576<B577,1,0)
565	Total	Indiana		SUM(C552:C576)	SUM(D577,D575)
566					
567				Iowa	
568				Elector Number	
569				0	
570					
571	District	Votes		President A	President B
572	1				
573	President A	0		IF(B587>B588,1,0)	
574	President B	0			IF(B587<B588,1,0)
575	2				
576	President A	0		IF(B590>B591,1,0)	
577	President B	0			IF(B590<B591,1,0)
578	3				
579	President A	0		IF(B593>B594,1,0)	
580	President B	0			IF(B593<B594,1,0)
581	4				
582	President A	0		IF(B596>B597,1,0)	
583	President B	0			IF(B596<B597,1,0)
584	5				
585	President A	0		IF(B599>B600,1,0)	
586	President B	0			IF(B599<B600,1,0)
587	Total	Iowa		SUM(C587:C599)	SUM(D588:D600)
588					
589				Kansas	
590				Elector Number	
591				0	
592					
593					
594	District	Votes		President A	President B
595	1				
596	President A	0		IF(B611>B612,1,0)	
597	President B	0			IF(B611<B612,1,0)
598	2				
599	President A	0		IF(B614>B615,1,0)	
600	President B	0			IF(B614<B615,1,0)
601	3				
602	President A	0		IF(B617>B618,1,0)	
603	President B	0			IF(B617<B618,1,0)
604	4				
605	President A	0		IF(B620>B621,1,0)	
606	President B	0			IF(B620<B621,1,0)
607	Total	Kansas		SUM(C611:C620)	SUM(D612:D621)
608					
609				Kentucky	
610				Elector Number	
611				0	
612					
613	District	Votes		President A	President B
614	1				
615	President A	0		IF(B631>B632,1,0)	
616	President B	0			IF(B631<B632,1,0)
617	2				
618	President A	0		IF(B634>B635,1,0)	
619	President B	0			IF(B634<B635,1,0)
620	3				
621	President A	0		IF(B637>B638,1,0)	
622	President B	0			IF(B637<B638,1,0)
623	4				
624	President A	0		IF(B640>B641,1,0)	
625	President B	0			IF(B640<B641,1,0)

	A	B		C	D
626	5				
627	President A	0		IF(B643>B644,1,0)	
628	President B	0			IF(B643<B644,1,0)
629	6				
630	President A	0		IF(B646>B647,1,0)	
631	President B	0			IF(B646<B647,1,0)
632	Total	Kentucky		SUM(C631:C646)	SUM(D632:D647)
633					
634				Louisiana	
635				Elector Number	
636				0	
637					
638	District	Votes		President A	President B
639	1				
640	President A	0		IF(B657>B658,1,0)	
641	President B	0			IF(B657<B658,1,0)
642	2				
643	President A	0		IF(B660>B661,1,0)	
644	President B	0			IF(B660<B661,1,0)
645	3				
646	President A	0		IF(B663>B664,1,0)	
647	President B	0			IF(B663<B664,1,0)
648	4				
649	President A	0		IF(B666>B667,1,0)	
650	President B	0			IF(B666<B667,1,0)
651	5				
652	President A	0		IF(B669>B670,1,0)	
653	President B	0			IF(B669<B670,1,0)
654	6				
655	President A	0		IF(B672>B673,1,0)	
656	President B	0			IF(B672<B673,1,0)
657	7				
658	President A	0		IF(B675>B676,1,0)	
659	President B	0			IF(B675<B676,1,0)
660	Total	Louisiana		SUM(C657:C675)	SUM(D658:D676)
661					
662				Maine	
663				Elector Number	
664				0	
665					
666	District	Votes		President A	President B
667	1				
668	President A	0		IF(B686>B687,1,0)	
669	President B	0			IF(B686<B687,1,0)
670	2				
671	President A	0		IF(B689>B690,1,0)	
672	President B	0			IF(B689<B690,1,0)
673	Total			SUM(C686:C689)	SUM(D687:D690)
674					
675				Maryland	
676				Elector Number	
677				0	
678					
679	District	Votes		President A	President B
680	1				
681	President A	0		IF(B700>B701,1,0)	
682	President B	0			IF(B700<B701,1,0)
683	2				
684	President A	0		IF(B703>B704,1,0)	
685	President B	0			IF(B703<B704,1,0)
686	3				
687	President A	0		IF(B706>B707,1,0)	
688	President B	0			IF(B706<B707,1,0)
689	4				
690	President A	0		IF(B709>B710,1,0)	
691	President B	0			IF(B709<B710,1,0)
692	5				
693	President A	0		IF(B712>B713,1,0)	
694	President B	0			IF(B712<B713,1,0)
695	6				
696	President A	0		IF(B715>B716,1,0)	

	A	B		C	D
697	President B	0			IF(B715<B716,1,0)
698	7				
699	President A	0		IF(B718>B719,1,0)	
700	President B	0			IF(B718<B719,1,0)
701	8				
702	President A	0		IF(B721>B722,1,0)	
703	President B	0			IF(B721<B722,1,0)
704	Total	Maine		SUM(C700:C721)	SUM(D701:D722)
705					
706				Massachusetts	
707				Elector Number	
708				0	
709					
710	District	Votes		President A	President B
711	President A	0		IF(B731>B732,1,0)	
712	President B	0			IF(B731<B732,1,0)
713	2				
714	President A	0		IF(B734>B735,1,0)	
715	President B	0			IF(B734<B735,1,0)
716	3				
717	President A	0		IF(B737>B738,1,0)	
718	President B	0			IF(B737<B738,1,0)
719	4				
720	President A	0		IF(B740>B741,1,0)	
721	President B	0			IF(B740<B741,1,0)
722	5				
723	President A	0		IF(B743>B744,1,0)	
724	President B	0			IF(B743<B744,1,0)
725	6				
726	President A	0		IF(B746>B747,1,0)	
727	President B	0			IF(B746<B747,1,0)
728	7				
729	President A	0		IF(B749>B750,1,0)	
730	President B	0			IF(B749<B750,1,0)
731	8				
732	President A	0		IF(B752>B753,1,0)	
733	President B	0			IF(B752<B753,1,0)
734	9				
735	President A	0		IF(B755>B756,1,0)	
736	President B	0			IF(B755<B756,1,0)
737	10				
738	President A	0		IF(B758>B759,1,0)	
739	President B	0			IF(B758<B759,1,0)
740	Total	Massachusetts		SUM(C731:C758)	SUM(D732:D759)
741					
742				Michigan	
743				Elector Number	
744				0	
745					
746	District	Votes		President A	President B
747	1				
748	President A	0		IF(B769>B770,1,0)	
749	President B	0			IF(B769<B770,1,0)
750	2				
751	President A	0		IF(B772>B773,1,0)	
752	President B	0			IF(B772<B773,1,0)
753	3				
754	President A	0		IF(B775>B776,1,0)	
755	President B	0			IF(B775<B776,1,0)
756	4				
757	President A	0		IF(B778>B779,1,0)	
758	President B	0			IF(B778<B779,1,0)
759	5				
760	President A	0		IF(B781>B782,1,0)	
761	President B	0			IF(B781<B782,1,0)
762	6				
763	President A	0		IF(B784>B785,1,0)	
764	President B	0			IF(B784<B785,1,0)
765	7				
766	President A	0		IF(B787>B788,1,0)	
767	President B	0			IF(B787<B788,1,0)

	A	B		C	D
768	8				
769	President A	0		IF(B790>B791,1,0)	
770	President B	0			IF(B790<B791,1,0)
771	9				
772	President A	0		IF(B793>B794,1,0)	
773	President B	0			IF(B793<B794,1,0)
774	10				
775	President A	0		IF(B796>B797,1,0)	
776	President B	0			IF(B796<B797,1,0)
777	11				
778	President A	0		IF(B799>B800,1,0)	
779	President B	0			IF(B799<B800,1,0)
780	12				
781	President A	0		IF(B802>B803,1,0)	
782	President B	0			IF(B802<B803,1,0)
783	13				
784	President A	0		IF(B805>B806,1,0)	
785	President B	0			IF(B805<B806,1,0)
786	14				
787	President A	0		IF(B808>B809,1,0)	
788	President B	0			IF(B808<B809,1,0)
789	15				
790	President A	0		IF(B811>B812,1,0)	
791	President B	0			IF(B811<B812,1,0)
792	Total	Michigan		SUM(C769:C811)	SUM(D770:D812)
793					
794				Minnesota	
795				Elector Number	
796				0	
797					
798	District	Votes		President A	President B
799	1				
800	President A	0		IF(B822>B823,1,0)	
801	President B	0			IF(B822<B823,1,0)
802	2				
803	President A	0		IF(B825>B826,1,0)	
804	President B	0			IF(B825<B826,1,0)
805	3				
806	President A	0		IF(B828>B829,1,0)	
807	President B	0			IF(B828<B829,1,0)
808	4				
809	President A	0		IF(B831>B832,1,0)	
810	President B	0			IF(B831<B832,1,0)
811	5				
812	President A	0		IF(B834>B835,1,0)	
813	President B	0			IF(B834<B835,1,0)
814	6				
815	President A	0		IF(B837>B838,1,0)	
816	President B	0			IF(B837<B838,1,0)
817	7				
818	President A	0		IF(B840>B841,1,0)	
819	President B	0			IF(B840<B841,1,0)
820	8				
821	President A	0		IF(B843>B844,1,0)	
822	President B	0			IF(B843<B844,1,0)
823	Total	Minnesota		SUM(C822:C843)	SUM(D823:D844)
824					
825				Mississippi	
826				Elector Number	
827				0	
828					
829	District	Votes		President A	President B
830	1				
831	President A	0		IF(B854>B855,1,0)	
832	President B	0			IF(B854<B855,1,0)
833	2				
834	President A	0		IF(B857>B858,1,0)	
835	President B	0			IF(B857<B858,1,0)
836	3				
837	President A	0		IF(B860>B861,1,0)	
838	President B	0			IF(B860<B861,1,0)

	A	B		C	D
839	4				
840	President A	0		IF(B863>B864,1,0)	
841	President B	0			IF(B863<B864,1,0)
842	Total	Mississippi		SUM(C854:C863)	SUM(D855:D864)
843					
844				Missouri	
845				Elector Number	
846				0	
847					
848	District	Votes		President A	President B
849	1				
850	President A	0		IF(B874>B875,1,0)	
851	President B	0			IF(B874<B875,1,0)
852	2				
853	President A	0		IF(B877>B878,1,0)	
854	President B	0			IF(B877<B878,1,0)
855	3				
856	President A	0		IF(B880>B881,1,0)	
857	President B	0			IF(B880<B881,1,0)
858	4				
859	President A	0		IF(B883>B884,1,0)	
860	President B	0			IF(B883<B884,1,0)
861	5				
862	President A	0		IF(B886>B887,1,0)	
863	President B	0			IF(B886<B887,1,0)
864	6				
865	President A	0		IF(B889>B890,1,0)	
866	President B	0			IF(B889<B890,1,0)
867	7				
868	President A	0		IF(B892>B893,1,0)	
869	President B	0			IF(B892<B893,1,0)
870	8				
871	President A	0		IF(B895>B896,1,0)	
872	President B	0			IF(B895<B896,1,0)
873	9				
874	President A	0		IF(B898>B899,1,0)	
875	President B	0			IF(B898<B899,1,0)
876	Total	Missouri		SUM(C874:C898)	SUM(D875:D899)
877					
878				Montana	
879				Elector Number	
880				0	
881					
882	District	Votes		President A	President B
883	1				
884	President A	0		IF(B909>B910,1,0)	
885	President B	0			IF(B909<B910,1,0)
886	Total	Montana		SUM(C909)	SUM(D909:D910)
887					
888				Nebraska	
889				Elector Number	
890				0	
891					
892	District	Votes		President A	President B
893	1				
894	President A	0		IF(B920>B921,1,0)	
895	President B	0			IF(B920<B921,1,0)
896	2				
897	President A	0		IF(B923>B924,1,0)	
898	President B	0			IF(B923<B924,1,0)
899	3				
900	President A	0		IF(B926>B927,1,0)	
901	President B	0			IF(B926<B927,1,0)
902	Total	Nebraska		SUM(C920:C926)	SUM(D921:D927)
903					
904				Nevada	
905				Elector Number	
906				0	
907					
908	District	Votes		President A	President B
909	1				

	A	B		C	D
910	President A	0		IF(B937>B938,1,0)	
911	President B	0			IF(B937<B938,1,0)
912	2				
913	President A	0		IF(B940>B941,1,0)	
914	President B	0			IF(B940<B941,1,0)
915	3				
916	President A	0		IF(B943>B944,1,0)	
917	President B	0			IF(B943<B944,1,0)
918	Total	Nevada		SUM(C937:C943)	SUM(D938:D944)
919					
920				New Hampshire	
921				Elector Number	
922				0	
923					
924	District	Votes		President A	President B
925	1				
926	President A	0		IF(B954>B955,1,0)	
927	President B	0			IF(B954<B955,1,0)
928	2				
929	President A	0		IF(B957>B958,1,0)	
930	President B	0			IF(B957<B958,1,0)
931	Total	New Hampshire		SUM(C954:C957)	SUM(D955:D958)
932					
933				New Jersey	
934				Elector Number	
935				0	
936					
937	District	Votes		President A	President B
938	1				
939	President A	0		IF(B968>B969,1,0)	
940	President B	0			IF(B968<B969,1,0)
941	2				
942	President A	0		IF(B971>B972,1,0)	
943	President B	0			IF(B971<B972,1,0)
944	3				
945	President A	0		IF(B974>B975,1,0)	
946	President B	0			IF(B974<B975,1,0)
947	4				
948	President A	0		IF(B977>B978,1,0)	
949	President B	0			IF(B977<B978,1,0)
950	5				
951	President A	0		IF(B980>B981,1,0)	
952	President B	0			IF(B980<B981,1,0)
953	6				
954	President A	0		IF(B983>B984,1,0)	
955	President B	0			IF(B983<B984,1,0)
956	7				
957	President A	0		IF(B986>B987,1,0)	
958	President B	0			IF(B986<B987,1,0)
959	8				
960	President A	0		IF(B989>B990,1,0)	
961	President B	0			IF(B989<B990,1,0)
962	9				
963	President A	0		IF(B992>B993,1,0)	
964	President B	0			IF(B992<B993,1,0)
965	10				
966	President A	0		IF(B995>B996,1,0)	
967	President B	0			IF(B995<B996,1,0)
968	11				
969	President A	0		IF(B998>B999,1,0)	
970	President B	0			IF(B998<B999,1,0)
971	12				
972	President A	0		IF(B1001>B1002,1,0)	
973	President B	0			IF(B1001<B1002,1,0)
974	13				
975	President A	0		IF(B1004>B1005,1,0)	
976	President B	0			IF(B1004<B1005,1,0)
977	Total	New Jersey		SUM(C968:C1004)	SUM(D969:D1005)
978					
979				New Mexico	

	A	B		C	D
980				Elector Number	
981				0	
982					
983	District	Votes		President A	President B
984	1				
985	President A	0		IF(B1015>B1016,1,0)	
986	President B	0			IF(B1015<B1016,1,0)
987	2				
988	President A	0		IF(B1018>B1019,1,0)	
989	President B	0			IF(B1018<B1019,1,0)
990	3				
991	President A	0		IF(B1021>B1022,1,0)	
992	President B	0			IF(B1021<B1022,1,0)
993	Total	New Mexico		SUM(C1015:C1021)	SUM(D1016:D1022)
994					
995				New York	
996				Elector Number	
997				0	
998					
999	District	Votes		President A	President B
1000	1				
1001	President A	0		IF(B1032>B1033,1,0)	
1002	President B	0			IF(B1032<B1033,1,0)
1003	2				
1004	President A	0		IF(B1035>B1036,1,0)	
1005	President B	0			IF(B1035<B1036,1,0)
1006	3				
1007	President A	0		IF(B1038>B1039,1,0)	
1008	President B	0			IF(B1038<B1039,1,0)
1009	4				
1010	President A	0		IF(B1041>B1042,1,0)	
1011	President B	0			IF(B1041<B1042,1,0)
1012	5				
1013	President A	0		IF(B1044>B1045,1,0)	
1014	President B	0			IF(B1044<B1045,1,0)
1015	6				
1016	President A	0		IF(B1047>B1048,1,0)	
1017	President B	0			IF(B1047<B1048,1,0)
1018	7				
1019	President A	0		IF(B1050>B1051,1,0)	
1020	President B	0			IF(B1050<B1051,1,0)
1021	8				
1022	President A	0		IF(B1053>B1054,1,0)	
1023	President B	0			IF(B1053<B1054,1,0)
1024	9				
1025	President A	0		IF(B1056>B1057,1,0)	
1026	President B	0			IF(B1056<B1057,1,0)
1027	10				
1028	President A	0		IF(B1059>B1060,1,0)	
1029	President B	0			IF(B1059<B1060,1,0)
1030	11				
1031	President A	0		IF(B1062>B1063,1,0)	
1032	President B	0			IF(B1062<B1063,1,0)
1033	12				
1034	President A	0		IF(B1065>B1066,1,0)	
1035	President B	0			IF(B1065<B1066,1,0)
1036	13				
1037	President A	0		IF(B1068>B1069,1,0)	
1038	President B	0			IF(B1068<B1069,1,0)
1039	14				
1040	President A	0		IF(B1071>B1072,1,0)	
1041	President B	0			IF(B1071<B1072,1,0)
1042	15				
1043	President A	0		IF(B1074>B1075,1,0)	
1044	President B	0			IF(B1074<B1075,1,0)
1045	16				
1046	President A	0		IF(B1077>B1078,1,0)	
1047	President B	0			IF(B1077<B1078,1,0)
1048	17				
1049	President A	0		IF(B1080>B1081,1,0)	
1050	President B	0			IF(B1080<B1081,1,0)

	A	B		C	D
1051	18				
1052	President A	0		IF(B1083>B1084,1,0)	
1053	President B	0			IF(B1083<B1084,1,0)
1054	19				
1055	President A	0		IF(B1086>B1087,1,0)	
1056	President B	0			IF(B1086<B1087,1,0)
1057	20				
1058	President A	0		IF(B1089>B1090,1,0)	
1059	President B	0			IF(B1089<B1090,1,0)
1060	21				
1061	President A	0		IF(B1092>B1093,1,0)	
1062	President B	0			IF(B1092<B1093,1,0)
1063	22				
1064	President A	0		IF(B1095>B1096,1,0)	
1065	President B	0			IF(B1095<B1096,1,0)
1066	23				
1067	President A	0		IF(B1098>B1099,1,0)	
1068	President B	0			IF(B1098<B1099,1,0)
1069	24				
1070	President A	0		IF(B1101>B1102,1,0)	
1071	President B	0			IF(B1101<B1102,1,0)
1072	25				
1073	President A	0		IF(B1104>B1105,1,0)	
1074	President B	0			IF(B1104<B1105,1,0)
1075	26				
1076	President A	0		IF(B1107>B1108,1,0)	
1077	President B	0			IF(B1107<B1108,1,0)
1078	27				
1079	President A	0		IF(B1110>B1111,1,0)	
1080	President B	0			IF(B1110<B1111,1,0)
1081	28				
1082	President A	0		IF(B1113>B1114,1,0)	
1083	President B	0			IF(B1113<B1114,1,0)
1084	29				
1085	President A	0		IF(B1116>B1117,1,0)	
1086	President B	0			IF(B1116<B1117,1,0)
1087	Total	New York		SUM(C1032:C1116)	SUM(D1033:D1117)
1088					
1089				North Carolina	
1090				Elector Number	
1091				0	
1092					
1093	District	Votes		President A	President B
1094	1				
1095	President A	0		IF(B1127>B1128,1,0)	
1096	President B	0			IF(B1127<B1128,1,0)
1097	2				
1098	President A	0		IF(B1130>B1131,1,0)	
1099	President B	0			IF(B1130<B1131,1,0)
1100	3				
1101	President A	0		IF(B1133>B1134,1,0)	
1102	President B	0			IF(B1133<B1134,1,0)
1103	4				
1104	President A	0		IF(B1136>B1137,1,0)	
1105	President B	0			IF(B1136<B1137,1,0)
1106	5				
1107	President A	0		IF(B1139>B1140,1,0)	
1108	President B	0			IF(B1139<B1140,1,0)
1109	6				
1110	President A	0		IF(B1142>B1143,1,0)	
1111	President B	0			IF(B1142<B1143,1,0)
1112	7				
1113	President A	0		IF(B1145>B1146,1,0)	
1114	President B	0			IF(B1145<B1146,1,0)
1115	8				
1116	President A	0		IF(B1148>B1149,1,0)	
1117	President B	0			IF(B1148<B1149,1,0)
1118	9				
1119	President A	0		IF(B1151>B1152,1,0)	
1120	President B	0			IF(B1151<B1152,1,0)
1121	10				

	A	B		C	D
1122	President A	0		IF(B1154>B1155,1,0)	
1123	President B	0			IF(B1154<B1155,1,0)
1124	11				
1125	President A	0		IF(B1157>B1158,1,0)	
1126	President B	0			IF(B1157<B1158,1,0)
1127	12				
1128	President A	0		IF(B1160>B1161,1,0)	
1129	President B	0			IF(B1160<B1161,1,0)
1130	13				
1131	President A	0		IF(B1163>B1164,1,0)	
1132	President B	0			IF(B1163<B1164,1,0)
1133	Total	North Carolina		SUM(C1127:C1163)	SUM(D1128:D1164)
1134					
1135				North Dakota	
1136				Elector Number	
1137				0	
1138					
1139	District	Votes		President A	President B
1140	1				
1141	President A	0		IF(B1174>B1175,1,0)	
1142	President B	0			IF(B1174<B1175,1,0)
1143	Total	North Dakota		SUM(C1174)	SUM(D1174:D1175)
1144					
1145				Ohio	
1146				Electro Number	
1147				0	
1148					
1149					
1150	District	Votes		President A	President B
1151	1				
1152	President A	0		IF(B1186>B1187,1,0)	
1153	President B	0			IF(B1186<B1187,1,0)
1154	2				
1155	President A	0		IF(B1189>B1190,1,0)	
1156	President B	0			IF(B1189<B1190,1,0)
1157	3				
1158	President A	0		IF(B1192>B1193,1,0)	
1159	President B	0			IF(B1192<B1193,1,0)
1160	4				
1161	President A	0		IF(B1195>B1196,1,0)	
1162	President B	0			IF(B1195<B1196,1,0)
1163	5				
1164	President A	0		IF(B1198>B1199,1,0)	
1165	President B	0			IF(B1198<B1199,1,0)
1166	6				
1167	President A	0		IF(B1201>B1202,1,0)	
1168	President B	0			IF(B1201<B1202,1,0)
1169	7				
1170	President A	0		IF(B1204>B1205,1,0)	
1171	President B	0			IF(B1204<B1205,1,0)
1172	8				
1173	President A	0		IF(B1207>B1208,1,0)	
1174	President B	0			IF(B1207<B1208,1,0)
1175	9				
1176	President A	0		IF(B1210>B1211,1,0)	
1177	President B	0			IF(B1210<B1211,1,0)
1178	10				
1179	President A	0		IF(B1213>B1214,1,0)	
1180	President B	0			IF(B1213<B1214,1,0)
1181	11				
1182	President A	0		IF(B1216>B1217,1,0)	
1183	President B	0			IF(B1216<B1217,1,0)
1184	12				
1185	President A	0		IF(B1219>B1220,1,0)	
1186	President B	0			IF(B1219<B1220,1,0)
1187	13				
1188	President A	0		IF(B1222>B1223,1,0)	
1189	President B	0			IF(B1222<B1223,1,0)
1190	14				
1191	President A	0		IF(B1225>B1226,1,0)	
1192	President B	0			IF(B1225<B1226,1,0)

	A	B		C	D
1193	15				
1194	President A	0		IF(B1228>B1229,1,0)	
1195	President B	0			IF(B1228<B1229,1,0)
1196	16				
1197	President A	0		IF(B1231>B1232,1,0)	
1198	President B	0			IF(B1231<B1232,1,0)
1199	17				
1200	President A	0		IF(B1234>B1235,1,0)	
1201	President B	0			IF(B1234<B1235,1,0)
1202	18				
1203	President A	0		IF(B1237>B1238,1,0)	
1204	President B	0			IF(B1237<B1238,1,0)
1205	Total	Ohio		SUM(C1186:C1237)	SUM(D1187:D1238)
1206					
1207				Oklahoma	
1208				Elector Number	
1109				0	
1110					
1211	District	Votes		President A	President B
1212	1				
1213	President A	0		IF(B1248>B1249,1,0)	
1214	President B	0			IF(B1248<B1249,1,0)
1215	2				
1216	President A	0		IF(B1251>B1252,1,0)	
1217	President B	0			IF(B1251<B1252,1,0)
1218	3				
1219	President A	0		IF(B1254>B1255,1,0)	
1220	President B	0			IF(B1254<B1255,1,0)
1221	4				
1222	President A	0		IF(B1257>B1258,1,0)	
1223	President B	0			IF(B1257<B1258,1,0)
1224	5				
1225	President A	0		IF(B1260>B1261,1,0)	
1226	President B	0			IF(B1260<B1261,1,0)
1227	Total	Oklahoma		SUM(C1248:C1260)	SUM(D1249:D1261)
1228					
1229				Oregon	
1230				Electro Number	
1231				0	
1232					
1233	District	Votes		President A	President B
1234	1				
1235	President A	0		IF(B1271>B1272,1,0)	
1236	President B	0			IF(B1271<B1272,1,0)
1237	2				
1238	President A	0		IF(B1274>B1275,1,0)	
1239	President B	0			IF(B1274<B1275,1,0)
1240	3				
1241	President A	0		IF(B1277>B1278,1,0)	
1242	President B	0			IF(B1277<B1278,1,0)
1243	4				
1244	President A	0		IF(B1280>B1281,1,0)	
1245	President B	0			IF(B1280<B1281,1,0)
1246	5				
1247	President A	0		IF(B1283>B1284,1,0)	
1248	President B	0			IF(B1283<B1284,1,0)
1249	Total	Oregon		SUM(C1271:C1283)	SUM(D1272:D1284)
1250					
1251				Pennsylvania	
1252				Elector Number	
1253				0	
1254					
1255	District	Votes		President A	President B
1256	1				
1257	President A	0		IF(B1294>B1295,1,0)	
1258	President B	0			IF(B1294<B1295,1,0)
1259	2				
1260	President A	0		IF(B1297>B1298,1,0)	
1261	President B	0			IF(B1297<B1298,1,0)
1262	3				
1263	President A	0		IF(B1300>B1301,1,0)	

	A	B		C	D
1264	President B	0			IF(B1300<B1301,1,0)
1265	4				
1266	President A	0		IF(B1303>B1304,1,0)	
1267	President B	0			IF(B1303<B1304,1,0)
1268	5				
1269	President A	0		IF(B1306>B1307,1,0)	
1270	President B	0			IF(B1306<B1307,1,0)
1271	6				
1272	President A	0		IF(B1309>B1310,1,0)	
1273	President B	0			IF(B1309<B1310,1,0)
1274	7				
1275	President A	0		IF(B1312>B1313,1,0)	
1276	President B	0			IF(B1312<B1313,1,0)
1277	8				
1278	President A	0		IF(B1315>B1316,1,0)	
1279	President B	0			IF(B1315<B1316,1,0)
1280	9				
1281	President A	0		IF(B1318>B1319,1,0)	
1282	President B	0			IF(B1318<B1319,1,0)
1283	10				
1284	President A	0		IF(B1321>B1322,1,0)	
1285	President B	0			IF(B1321<B1322,1,0)
1286	11				
1287	President A	0		IF(B1324>B1325,1,0)	
1288	President B	0			IF(B1324<B1325,1,0)
1289	12				
1290	President A	0		IF(B1327>B1328,1,0)	
1291	President B	0			IF(B1327<B1328,1,0)
1292	13				
1293	President A	0		IF(B1330>B1331,1,0)	
1294	President B	0			IF(B1330<B1331,1,0)
1295	14				
1296	President A	0		IF(B1333>B1334,1,0)	
1297	President B	0			IF(B1333<B1334,1,0)
1298	15				
1299	President A	0		IF(B1336>B1337,1,0)	
1300	President B	0			IF(B1336<B1337,1,0)
1301	16				
1302	President A	0		IF(B1339>B1340,1,0)	
1303	President B	0			IF(B1339<B1340,1,0)
1304	17				
1305	President A	0		IF(B1342>B1343,1,0)	
1306	President B	0			IF(B1342<B1343,1,0)
1307	18				
1308	President A	0		IF(B1345>B1346,1,0)	
1309	President B	0			IF(B1345<B1346,1,0)
1310	19				
1311	President A	0		IF(B1348>B1349,1,0)	
1312	President B	0			IF(B1348<B1349,1,0)
1313	Total	Pennsylvania		SUM(C1294:C1348)	SUM(D1295:D1349)
1314					
1315				Rhode Island	
1316				Elector Number	
1317				0	
1318					
1319	District	Votes		President A	President B
1320	1				
1321	President A	0		IF(B1359>B1360,1,0)	
1322	President B	0			IF(B1359<B1360,1,0)
1323	2				
1324	President A	0		IF(B1362>B1363,1,0)	
1325	President B	0			IF(B1362<B1363,1,0)
1326	Total	Rhode Island		SUM(C1359:C1362)	SUM(D1360:D1363)
1327					
1328				South Carolina	
1329				Elector Number	
1330				0	
1331					
1332	District	Votes		President A	President B
1333	1				
1334	President A	0		IF(B1373>B1374,1,0)	

	A	B		C	D
1335	President B	0			IF(B1373<B1374,1,0)
1336	2				
1337	President A	0		IF(B1376>B1377,1,0)	
1338	President B	0			IF(B1376<B1377,1,0)
1339	3				
1340	President A	0		IF(B1379>B1380,1,0)	
1341	President B	0			IF(B1379<B1380,1,0)
1342	4				
1343	President A	0		IF(B1382>B1383,1,0)	
1344	President B	0			IF(B1382<B1383,1,0)
1345	5				
1346	President A	0		IF(B1385>B1386,1,0)	
1347	President B	0			IF(B1385<B1386,1,0)
1348	6				
1349	President A	0		IF(B1388>B1389,1,0)	
1350	President B	0			IF(B1388<B1389,1,0)
1351	Total	South Carolina		SUM(C1373:C1388)	SUM(D1374:D1389)
1352					
1353				South Dakota	
1354				Elector Number	
1355				0	
1356					
1357	District	Votes		President A	President B
1358	1				
1359	President A	0		IF(B1399>B1400,1,0)	
1360	President B	0			IF(B1399<B1400,1,0)
1361	Total	South Dakota		SUM(C1399)	SUM(D1399:D1400)
1362					
1363				Tennessee	
1364				Elector Number	
1365				0	
1366					
1367	District	Votes		President A	President B
1368	1				
1369	President A	0		IF(B1410>B1411,1,0)	
1370	President B	0			IF(B1410<B1411,1,0)
1371	2				
1372	President A	0		IF(B1413>B1414,1,0)	
1373	President B	0			IF(B1413<B1414,1,0)
1374	3				
1375	President A	0		IF(B1416>B1417,1,0)	
1376	President B	0			IF(B1416<B1417,1,0)
1377	4				
1378	President A	0		IF(B1419>B1420,1,0)	
1379	President B	0			IF(B1419<B1420,1,0)
1380	5				
1381	President A	0		IF(B1422>B1423,1,0)	
1382	President B	0			IF(B1422<B1423,1,0)
1383	6				
1384	President A	0		IF(B1425>B1426,1,0)	
1385	President B	0			IF(B1425<B1426,1,0)
1386	7				
1387	President A	0		IF(B1428>B1429,1,0)	
1388	President B	0			IF(B1428<B1429,1,0)
1389	8				
1390	President A	0		IF(B1431>B1432,1,0)	
1391	President B	0			IF(B1431<B1432,1,0)
1392	9				
1393	President A	0		IF(B1434>B1435,1,0)	
1394	President B	0			IF(B1434<B1435,1,0)
1395	Total	Tennessee		SUM(C1410:C1434)	SUM(D1411:D1435)
1396					
1397				Texas	
1398				Elector Number	
1399				0	
1400					
1401	District	Votes		President A	President B
1402	1				
1403	President A	0		IF(B1445>B1446,1,0)	
1404	President B	0			IF(B1445<B1446,1,0)
1405	2				

	A	B		C	D
1406	President A	0		IF(B1448>B1449,1,0)	
1407	President B	0			IF(B1448<B1449,1,0)
1408	3				
1409	President A	0		IF(B1451>B1452,1,0)	
1410	President B	0			IF(B1451<B1452,1,0)
1411	4				
1412	President A	0		IF(B1454>B1455,1,0)	
1413	President B	0			IF(B1454<B1455,1,0)
1414	5				
1415	President A	0		IF(B1457>B1458,1,0)	
1416	President B	0			IF(B1457<B1458,1,0)
1417	6				
1418	President A	0		IF(B1460>B1461,1,0)	
1419	President B	0			IF(B1460<B1461,1,0)
1420	7				
1421	President A	0		IF(B1463>B1464,1,0)	
1422	President B	0			IF(B1463<B1464,1,0)
1423	8				
1424	President A	0		IF(B1466>B1467,1,0)	
1425	President B	0			IF(B1466<B1467,1,0)
1426	9				
1427	President A	0		IF(B1469>B1470,1,0)	
1428	President B	0			IF(B1469<B1470,1,0)
1429	10				
1430	President A	0		IF(B1472>B1473,1,0)	
1431	President B	0			IF(B1472<B1473,1,0)
1432	11				
1433	President A	0		IF(B1475>B1476,1,0)	
1434	President B	0			IF(B1475<B1476,1,0)
1435	12				
1436	President A	0		IF(B1478>B1479,1,0)	
1437	President B	0			IF(B1478<B1479,1,0)
1438	13				
1439	President A	0		IF(B1481>B1482,1,0)	
1440	President B	0			IF(B1481<B1482,1,0)
1441	14				
1442	President A	0		IF(B1484>B1485,1,0)	
1443	President B	0			IF(B1484<B1485,1,0)
1444	15				
1445	President A	0		IF(B1487>B1488,1,0)	
1446	President B	0			IF(B1487<B1488,1,0)
1447	16				
1448	President A	0		IF(B1490>B1491,1,0)	
1449	President B	0			IF(B1490<B1491,1,0)
1450	17				
1451	President A	0		IF(B1493>B1494,1,0)	
1452	President B	0			IF(B1493<B1494,1,0)
1453	18				
1454	President A	0		IF(B1496>B1497,1,0)	
1455	President B	0			IF(B1496<B1497,1,0)
1456	19				
1457	President A	0		IF(B1499>B1500,1,0)	
1458	President B	0			IF(B1499<B1500,1,0)
1459	20				
1460	President A	0		IF(B1502>B1503,1,0)	
1461	President B	0			IF(B1502<B1503,1,0)
1462	21				
1463	President A	0		IF(B1505>B1506,1,0)	
1464	President B	0			IF(B1505<B1506,1,0)
1465	22				
1466	President A	0		IF(B1508>B1509,1,0)	
1467	President B	0			IF(B1508<B1509,1,0)
1468	23				
1469	President A	0		IF(B1511>B1512,1,0)	
1470	President B	0			IF(B1511<B1512,1,0)
1471	24				
1472	President A	0		IF(B1514>B1515,1,0)	
1473	President B	0			IF(B1514<B1515,1,0)
1474	25				
1475	President A	0		IF(B1517>B1518,1,0)	
1476	President B	0			IF(B1517<B1518,1,0)

	A	B		C	D
1477	26				
1478	President A	0		IF(B1520>B1521,1,0)	
1479	President B	0			IF(B1520<B1521,1,0)
1480	27				
1481	President A	0		IF(B1523>B1524,1,0)	
1482	President B	0			IF(B1523<B1524,1,0)
1483	28				
1484	President A	0		IF(B1526>B1527,1,0)	
1485	President B	0			IF(B1526<B1527,1,0)
1486	29				
1487	President A	0		IF(B1529>B1530,1,0)	
1488	President B	0			IF(B1529<B1530,1,0)
1489	30				
1490	President A	0		IF(B1532>B1533,1,0)	
1491	President B	0			IF(B1532<B1533,1,0)
1492	31				
1493	President A	0		IF(B1535>B1536,1,0)	
1494	President B	0			IF(B1535<B1536,1,0)
1495	32				
1496	President A	0		IF(B1538>B1539,1,0)	
1497	President B	0			IF(B1538<B1539,1,0)
1498	Total	Texas		SUM(C1445:C1538)	SUM(D1446:D1539)
1499					
1500				Utah	
1501				Elector Number	
1502				0	
1503					
District	Votes		President A	President B	
1					
President A	0		IF(B1549>B1550,1,0)		
President B	0			IF(B1549<B1550,1,0)	
2					
President A	0		IF(B1552>B1553,1,0)		
President B	0			IF(B1552<B1553,1,0)	
3					
President A	0		IF(B1555>B1556,1,0)		
President B	0			IF(B1555<B1556,1,0)	
Total	Utah		SUM(C1549:C1555)	SUM(D1550:D1556)	
			Vermont		
			Elector Number		
			0		
District	Votes		President A	President B	
1					
President A	0		IF(B1566>B1567,1,0)		
President B	0			IF(B1566<B1567,1,0)	
Total	Vermont		SUM(C1566)	SUM(D1566:D1567)	
			Virginia		
			Elector Number		
			0		
District	Votes		President A	President B	
1					
President A	0		IF(B1577>B1578,1,0)		
President B	0			IF(B1577<B1578,1,0)	
2					
President A	0		IF(B1580>B1581,1,0)		
President B	0			IF(B1580<B1581,1,0)	
3					
President A	0		IF(B1583>B1584,1,0)		
President B	0			IF(B1583<B1584,1,0)	
4					
President A	0		IF(B1586>B1587,1,0)		
President B	0			IF(B1586<B1587,1,0)	
5					
President A	0		IF(B1589>B1590,1,0)		
President B	0			IF(B1589<B1590,1,0)	
6					
President A	0		IF(B1592>B1593,1,0)		

	A	B		C	D
President B	0			IF(B1592<B1593,1,0)	
7					
President A	0		IF(B1595>B1596,1,0)		
President B	0			IF(B1595<B1596,1,0)	
8					
President A	0		IF(B1598>B1599,1,0)		
President B	0			IF(B1598<B1599,1,0)	
9					
President A	0		IF(B1601>B1602,1,0)		
President B	0			IF(B1601<B1602,1,0)	
10					
President A	0		IF(B1604>B1605,1,0)		
President B	0			IF(B1604<B1605,1,0)	
11					
President A	0		IF(B1607>B1608,1,0)		
President B	0			IF(B1607<B1608,1,0)	
Total	Virginia		SUM(C1577:C1607)	SUM(D1578:D1608)	
			Washington		
			Elector Number		
			0		
District	Votes		President A	President B	
1					
President A	0		IF(B1618>B1619,1,0)		
President B	0			IF(B1618<B1619,1,0)	
2					
President A	0		IF(B1621>B1622,1,0)		
President B	0			IF(B1621<B1622,1,0)	
3					
President A	0		IF(B1624>B1625,1,0)		
President B	0			IF(B1624<B1625,1,0)	
4					
President A	0		IF(B1627>B1628,1,0)		
President B	0			IF(B1627<B1628,1,0)	
5					
President A	0		IF(B1630>B1631,1,0)		
President B	0			IF(B1630<B1631,1,0)	
6					
President A	0		IF(B1633>B1634,1,0)		
President B	0			IF(B1633<B1634,1,0)	
7					
President A	0		IF(B1636>B1637,1,0)		
President B	0			IF(B1636<B1637,1,0)	
8					
President A	0		IF(B1639>B1640,1,0)		
President B	0			IF(B1639<B1640,1,0)	
9					
President A	0		IF(B1642>B1643,1,0)		
President B	0			IF(B1642<B1643,1,0)	
Total	Washington		SUM(C1618:C1642)	SUM(D1619:D1643)	
			West Virginia		
			Elector Number		
			0		
District	Votes		President A	President B	
1					
President A	0		IF(B1653>B1654,1,0)		
President B	0			IF(B1653<B1654,1,0)	
2					
President A	0		IF(B1656>B1657,1,0)		
President B	0			IF(B1656<B1657,1,0)	
3					
President A	0		IF(B1659>B1660,1,0)		
President B	0			IF(B1659<B1660,1,0)	
Total	West Virginia		SUM(C1653:C1659)	SUM(D1654:D1660)	
			Wisconsin		
			Elector Number		
			0		

	A	B		C	D
District	Votes		President A	President B	
1					
President A	0		IF(B1670>B1671,1,0)		
President B	0			IF(B1670<B1671,1,0)	
2					
President A	0		IF(B1673>B1674,1,0)		
President B	0			IF(B1673<B1674,1,0)	
3					
President A	0		IF(B1676>B1677,1,0)		
President B	0			IF(B1676<B1677,1,0)	
4					
President A	0		IF(B1679>B1680,1,0)		
President B	0			IF(B1679<B1680,1,0)	
5					
President A	0		IF(B1682>B1683,1,0)		
President B	0			IF(B1682<B1683,1,0)	
6					
President A	0		IF(B1685>B1686,1,0)		
President B	0			IF(B1685<B1686,1,0)	
7					
President A	0		IF(B1688>B1689,1,0)		
President B	0			IF(B1688<B1689,1,0)	
8					
President A	0		IF(B1691>B1692,1,0)		
President B	0			IF(B1691<B1692,1,0)	
Total	Wisconsin		SUM(C1670:C1691)	SUM(D1671:D1692)	
			Wyoming		
			Elector Number		
			0		
District	Votes		President A	President B	
1					
President A	0		IF(B1702>B1703,1,0)		
President B	0			IF(B1702<B1703,1,0)	
Total	Wyoming		SUM(C1702)	SUM(D1702:D1703)	
Alabama	Electoral Total		C4/A24*C27	C4/A24*D27	
Alaska	Electoral Total		C32/A35*C38	C32/A35*D38	
Arizona	Electoral Total		C43/A67*C70	C43/A67*D70	
Arkansas	Electoral Total		C75/A87*C90	C75/A87*D90	
California	Electoral Total		C95/A254*C257	C95/A254*D257	
Colorado	Electoral Total		C262/A283*C286	C262/A283*D286	
Connecticut	Electoral Total		C291/A306*C309	C291/A306*D309	
Delaware	Electoral Total		C314/A317*C320	C314/A317*D320	
Florida	Electoral Total		C329/A400*C403	C325/A400*D403	
Georgia	Electoral Total		C408/A447*C450	C408/A447*D450	
Hawaii	Electoral Total		C455/A461*C464	C455/A461*D464	
Idaho	Electoral Total		C469/A475*C478	C469/A475*D478	
Illinois	Electoral Total		C483/A540*C543	C483/A540*D543	
Indiana	Electoral Total		C548/A575*C578	C548/A575*D577	
Iowa	Electoral Total		C583/A598*C601	C583/A598*D601	
Kansas	Electoral Total		C606/A619*C622	C606/A619*D622	
Kentucky	Electoral Total		C627/A645*C648	C627/A645*D648	
Louisiana	Electoral Total		C653/A674*C677	C653/A674*D677	
Maine	Electoral Total		C682/A688*C691	C682/A688*D691	
Maryland	Electoral Total		C696/A720*C723	C696/A720*D723	
Massachusetts	Electoral Total		C728/A757*C760	C728/A757*D760	
Michigan	Electoral Total		C765/A810*C813	C765/A810*D813	
Minnesota	Electoral Total		C818/A842*C845	C818/A842*D845	
Mississippi	Electoral Total		C850/A862*C865	C850/A862*D865	
Missouri	Electoral Total		C870/A897*C900	C870/A897*D900	
Montana	Electoral Total		C905/A908*C911	C905/A908*D911	
Nebraska	Electoral Total		C916/A925*C928	C916/A925*D928	
Nevada	Electoral Total		C933/A942*C945	C933/A942*D945	
New Hampshire	Electoral Total		C950/A956*C959	C950/A956*D959	
New Jersey	Electoral Total		C964/A1003*C1006	C964/A1003*D1006	
New Mexico	Electoral Total		C1011/A1020*C1023	C1011/A1020*D1023	
New York	Electoral Total		C1028/A1115*C1118	C1028/A1115*D1118	

	A	B		C	D
North Carolina	Electoral Total		C1123/A1162*C1165	C1123/A1162*D1165	
North Dakota	Electoral Total		C1170/A1173*C1176	C1170/A1173*D1176	
Ohio	Electoral Total		C1181/A1236*C1239	C1181/A1236*D1239	
Oklahoma	Electoral Total		C1244/A1259*C1262	C1244/A1259*D1262	
Oregon	Electoral Total		C1267/A1282*C1285	C1267/A1282*D1285	
Pennsylvania	Electoral Total		C1290/A1347*C1350	C1290/A1347*D1350	
Rhode Island	Electoral Total		C1355/A1361*C1364	C1355/A1361*D1364	
South Carolina	Electoral Total		C1369/A1387*C1390	C1369/A1387*D1390	
South Dakota	Electoral Total		C1395/A1398*C1401	C1395/A1398*D1401	
Tennessee	Electoral Total		C1406/A1433*C1436	C1406/A1433*D1436	
Texas	Electoral Total		C1441/A1537*C1540	C1441/A1537*D1540	
Utah	Electoral Total		C1545/A1554*C1557	C1545/A1554*D1557	
Vermont	Electoral Total		C1562/A1565*C1568	C1562/A1565*D1568	
Virginia	Electoral Total		C1573/A1606*C1609	C1573/A1606*D1609	
Washington	Electoral Total		C1614/A1641*C1644	C1614/A1641*D1644	
West Virginia	Electoral Total		C1649/A1658*C1661	C1649/A1658*D1661	
Wisconsin	Electoral Total		C1666/A1690*C1693	C1666/A1690*D1693	
Wyoming	Electoral Total		C1698/A1701*C1704	C1698/A1701*D1704	

If the electoral vote is 436, one electoral for each United States House of Representatives and DC of Columbia, then the total vote for each state government is read.

The demonstrated spreadsheet is designed for the United States presidential election campaign. The state governments, United States House of Representatives' districts, are the base districts that will eliminate mob rule.

The percentage calculations are to be done using double precision floating point arithmetic to eliminate roundoff error in the computer's operation of performing addition, multiplication, and especially division. A double precision floating number is accurate within sixty-four digits replacing the existing eight-digit integer arithmetic, which uses winner takes all that encourages mob rule. Using percentages to calculate the electoral vote eliminates the situation where the winner does not win the popular vote.

Input state government's electoral number. Fill in the number of votes cast for each candidate in each district. There can be several candidates. For example, a person is needed to input the election results and work the spreadsheet.

Using the spreadsheet's displayed instructions as a flowchart, a programmer can write a computer program for a computer that will tabulate and count the votes as the voter goes through the act of voting. The computer technology already exists where a computer is used to process a vote being cast at polling stations.

At the end of the vote-casting day, the computer automatically delivers the candidates' sums of electoral votes. Utilizing a spreadsheet or computer-programmed instruction, no living human being can be as accurate as a computer. The old days of using integer arithmetic to calculate is out of sync with moon landings and cell phones.

PRESIDENTIAL ELECTION

STATE GOVERNMENT ASSEMBLY

400 DISTRICTS

	A	B	C	D	E	F
1						
2					Electoral Number	
3					0	
4						
5	District	Total Votes	Votes	%	President A	President B
6	1	C7+C8				
7	President A		0	B6/C7	IF(D7>D8,1,0)	
8	President B		0	B6/C8		IF(D8>D7,1,0)
9	2	C10+C11				
10	President A		0	B9/C10	IF(D10>D11,1,0)	
11	President B		0	B9/C11		IF(D11>D10,1,0)
12	3	C13+C14				
13	President A		0	B12/C13	IF(D13>D14,1,0)	
14	President B		0	B12/C14		IF(D14>D13,1,0)
15	4	C16+C17				
16	President A		0	B15/C16	IF(D16>D17,1,0)	
17	President B		0	B15/C17		IF(D17>D16,1,0)
18	5	C19+C20				
19	President A		0	B18/C19	IF(D19>D20,1,0)	
20	President B		0	B18/C20		IF(D20>D19,1,0)
21	6	C22+C23				
22	President A		0	B21/C22	IF(D22>D23,1,0)	
23	President B		0	B21/C23		IF(D23>D22,1,0)
24	7	C25+C26				
25	President A		0	B24/C25	IF(D25>D26,1,0)	
26	President B		0	B24/C26		IF(D26>D25,1,0)
27	8	C28+C29				
28	President A		0	B27/C28	IF(D28>D29,1,0)	
29	President B		0	B27/C29		IF(D29>D28,1,0)
30	9	C31+C32				
31	President A		0	B30/C31	IF(D31>D32,1,0)	
32	President B		0	B30/C32		IF(D32>D31,1,0)
33	10	C34+C35				
34	President A		0	B33/C34	IF(D34>D35,1,0)	
35	President B		0	B33/C35		IF(D35>D34,1,0)
36	11	C37+C38				
37	President A		0	B36/C37	IF(D37>D38,1,0)	
38	President B		0	B36/C38		IF(D38>D37,1,0)
39	12	C40+C41				
40	President A		0	B39/C40	IF(D40>D41,1,0)	
41	President B		0	B39/C41		IF(D41>D40,1,0)
42	13	C43+C44				
43	President A		0	B42/C43	IF(D43>D44,1,0)	

	A	B	C	D	E	F
44	President B		0	B42/C44		IF(D44>D43,1,0)
45	14	C46+C47				
46	President A		0	B45/C46	IF(D46>D47,1,0)	
47	President B		0	B45/C47		IF(D47>D46,1,0)
48	15	C49+C50				
49	President A		0	B48/C49	IF(D49>D50,1,0)	
50	President B		0	B48/C50		IF(D50>D49,1,0)
51	16	C52+C53				
52	President A		0	B51/C52	IF(D52>D53,1,0)	
53	President B		0	B51/C53		IF(D53>D52,1,0)
54	17	C55+C56				
55	President A		0	B54/C55	IF(D55>D56,1,0)	
56	President B		0	B54/C56		IF(D56>D55,1,0)
57	18	C58+C59				
58	President A		0	B57/C58	IF(D58>D59,1,0)	
59	President B		0	B57/C59		IF(D59>D58,1,0)
60	19	C61+C62				
61	President A		0	B60/C61	IF(D61>D62,1,0)	
62	President B		0	B60/C62		IF(D62>D61,1,0)
63	20	C64+C65				
64	President A		0	B63/C64	IF(D64>D65,1,0)	
65	President B		0	B63/C65		IF(D65>D64,1,0)
66	21	C67+C68				
67	President A		0	B66/C67	IF(D67>D68,1,0)	
68	President B		0	B66/C68		IF(D68>D67,1,0)
69	22	C70+C71				
70	President A		0	B69/C70	IF(D70>D71,1,0)	
71	President B		0	B69/C71		IF(D71>D70,1,0)
72	23	C73+C74				
73	President A		0	B72/C73	IF(D73>D74,1,0)	
74	President B		0	B72/C74		IF(D74>D73,1,0)
75	24	C76+C77				
76	President A		0	B75/C76	IF(D76>D77,1,0)	
77	President B		0	B75/C77		IF(D77>D76,1,0)
78	25	C79+C80				
79	President A		0	B78/C79	IF(D79>D80,1,0)	
80	President B		0	B78/C80		IF(D80>D79,1,0)
81	26	C82+C83				
82	President A		0	B81/C82	IF(D82>D83,1,0)	
83	President B		0	B81/C83		IF(D83>D82,1,0)
84	27	C85+C86				
85	President A		0	B84/C85	IF(D85>D86,1,0)	
86	President B		0	B84/C86		IF(D86>D85,1,0)
87	28	C88+C89				
88	President A		0	B87/C88	IF(D88>D89,1,0)	
89	President B		0	B87/C89		IF(D89>D88,1,0)
90	29	C91+C92				
91	President A		0	B90/C91	IF(D91>D92,1,0)	
92	President B		0	B90/C92		IF(D92>D91,1,0)
93	30	C94+C95				
94	President A		0	B93/C94	IF(D94>D95,1,0)	
95	President B		0	B93/C95		IF(D95>D94,1,0)
96	31	C97+C98				
97	President A		0	B96/C97	IF(D97>D98,1,0)	
98	President B		0	B96/C98		IF(D98>D97,1,0)
99	32	C100+C101				
100	President A		0	B99/C100	IF(D100>D101,1,0)	
101	President B		0	B99/C101		IF(D101>D100,1,0)
102	33	C103+C104				
103	President A		0	B102/C103	IF(D103>D104,1,0)	
104	President B		0	B102/C104		IF(D104>D103,1,0)
105	34	C106+C107				
106	President A		0	B105/C106	IF(D106>D107,1,0)	
107	President B		0	B105/C107		IF(D107>D106,1,0)
108	35	C109+C110				
109	President A		0	B108/C109	IF(D109>D110,1,0)	
110	President B		0	B108/C110		IF(D110>D109,1,0)
111	36	C112+C113				
112	President A		0	B111/C112	IF(D112>D113,1,0)	
113	President B		0	B111/C113		IF(D113>D112,1,0)
114	37	C115+C116				

	A	B	C	D	E	F
115	President A		0	B114/C115	IF(D115>D116,1,0)	
116	President B		0	B114/C116		IF(D116>D115,1,0)
117	38	C118+C119				
118	President A		0	B117/C118	IF(D118>D119,1,0)	
119	President B		0	B117/C119		IF(D119>D118,1,0)
120	39	C121+C122				
121	President A		0	B120/C121	IF(D121>D122,1,0)	
122	President B		0	B120/C122		IF(D122>D121,1,0)
123	40	C124+C125				
124	President A		0	B123/C124	IF(D124>D125,1,0)	
125	President B		0	B123/C125		IF(D125>D124,1,0)
126	41	C127+C128				
127	President A		0	B126/C127	IF(D127>D128,1,0)	
128	President B		0	B126/C128		IF(D128>D127,1,0)
129	42	C130+C131				
130	President A		0	B129/C130	IF(D130>D131,1,0)	
131	President B		0	B129/C131		IF(D131>D130,1,0)
132	43	C133+C134				
133	President A		0	B132/C133	IF(D133>D134,1,0)	
134	President B		0	B132/C134		IF(D134>D133,1,0)
135	44	C136+C137				
136	President A		0	B135/C136	IF(D136>D137,1,0)	
137	President B		0	B135/C137		IF(D137>D136,1,0)
138	45	C139+C140				
139	President A		0	B138/C139	IF(D139>D140,1,0)	
140	President B		0	B138/C140		IF(D140>D139,1,0)
141	46	C142+C143				
142	President A		0	B141/C142	IF(D142>D143,1,0)	
143	President B		0	B141/C143		IF(D143>D142,1,0)
144	47	C145+C146				
145	President A		0	B144/C145	IF(D145>D146,1,0)	
146	President B		0	B144/C146		IF(D146>D145,1,0)
147	48	C148+C149				
148	President A		0	B147/C148	IF(D148>D149,1,0)	
149	President B		0	B147/C149		IF(D149>D148,1,0)
150	49	C151+C152				
151	President A		0	B150/C151	IF(D151>D152,1,0)	
152	President B		0	B150/C152		IF(D152>D151,1,0)
153	50	C154+C155				
154	President A		0	B153/C154	IF(D154>D155,1,0)	
155	President B		0	B153/C155		IF(D155>D154,1,0)
156	51	C157+C158				
157	President A		0	B156/C157	IF(D157>D158,1,0)	
158	President B		0	B156/C158		IF(D158>D157,1,0)
159	52	C160+C161				
160	President A		0	B159/C160	IF(D160>D161,1,0)	
161	President B		0	B159/C161		IF(D161>D160,1,0)
162	53	C163+C164				
163	President A		0	B162/C163	IF(D163>D164,1,0)	
164	President B		0	B162/C164		IF(D164>D163,1,0)
165	54	C166+C167				
166	President A		0	B165/C166	IF(D166>D167,1,0)	
167	President B		0	B165/C167		IF(D167>D166,1,0)
168	55	C169+C170				
169	President A		0	B168/C169	IF(D169>D170,1,0)	
170	President B		0	B168/C170		IF(D170>D169,1,0)
171	56	C172+C173				
172	President A		0	B171/C172	IF(D172>D173,1,0)	
173	President B		0	B171/C173		IF(D173>D172,1,0)
174	57	C175+C176				
175	President A		0	B174/C175	IF(D175>D176,1,0)	
176	President B		0	B174/C176		IF(D176>D175,1,0)
177	58	C178+C179				
178	President A		0	B177/C178	IF(D178>D179,1,0)	
179	President B		0	B177/C179		IF(D179>D178,1,0)
180	59	C181+C182				
181	President A		0	B180/C181	IF(D181>D182,1,0)	
182	President B		0	B180/C182		IF(D182>D181,1,0)
183	60	C184+C185				
184	President A		0	B183/C184	IF(D184>D185,1,0)	
185	President B		0	B183/C185		IF(D185>D184,1,0)

	A	B	C	D	E	F
186	61	C187+C188				
187	President A		0	B186/C187	IF(D187>D188,1,0)	
188	President B		0	B186/C188		IF(D188>D187,1,0)
189	62	C190+C191				
190	President A		0	B189/C190	IF(D190>D191,1,0)	
191	President B		0	B189/C191		IF(D191>D190,1,0)
192	63	C193+C194				
193	President A		0	B192/C193	IF(D193>D194,1,0)	
194	President B		0	B192/C194		IF(D194>D193,1,0)
195	64	C196+C197				
196	President A		0	B195/C196	IF(D196>D197,1,0)	
197	President B		0	B195/C197		IF(D197>D196,1,0)
198	65	C199+C200				
199	President A		0	B198/C199	IF(D199>D200,1,0)	
200	President B		0	B198/C200		IF(D200>D199,1,0)
201	66	C202+C203				
202	President A		0	B201/C202	IF(D202>D203,1,0)	
203	President B		0	B201/C203		IF(D203>D202,1,0)
204	67	C205+C206				
205	President A		0	B204/C205	IF(D205>D206,1,0)	
206	President B		0	B204/C206		IF(D206>D205,1,0)
207	68	C208+C209				
208	President A		0	B207/C208	IF(D208>D209,1,0)	
209	President B		0	B207/C209		IF(D209>D208,1,0)
210	69	C211+C212				
211	President A		0	B210/C211	IF(D211>D212,1,0)	
212	President B		0	B210/C212		IF(D212>D211,1,0)
213	70	C214+C215				
214	President A		0	B213/C214	IF(D214>D215,1,0)	
215	President B		0	B213/C215		IF(D215>D214,1,0)
216	71	C217+C218				
217	President A		0	B216/C217	IF(D217>D218,1,0)	
218	President B		0	B216/C218		IF(D218>D217,1,0)
219	72	C220+C221				
220	President A		0	B219/C220	IF(D220>D221,1,0)	
221	President B		0	B219/C221		IF(D221>D220,1,0)
222	73	C223+C224				
223	President A		0	B222/C223	IF(D223>D224,1,0)	
224	President B		0	B222/C224		IF(D224>D223,1,0)
225	74	C226+C227				
226	President A		0	B225/C226	IF(D226>D227,1,0)	
227	President B		0	B225/C227		IF(D227>D226,1,0)
228	75	C229+C230				
229	President A		0	B228/C229	IF(D229>D230,1,0)	
230	President B		0	B228/C230		IF(D230>D229,1,0)
231	76	C232+C233				
232	President A		0	B231/C232	IF(D232>D233,1,0)	
233	President B		0	B231/C233		IF(D233>D232,1,0)
234	77	C235+C236				
235	President A		0	B234/C235	IF(D235>D236,1,0)	
236	President B		0	B234/C236		IF(D236>D235,1,0)
237	78	C238+C239				
238	President A		0	B237/C238	IF(D238>D239,1,0)	
239	President B		0	B237/C239		IF(D239>D238,1,0)
240	79	C241+C242				
241	President A		0	B240/C241	IF(D241>D242,1,0)	
242	President B		0	B240/C242		IF(D242>D241,1,0)
243	80	C244+C245				
244	President A		0	B243/C244	IF(D244>D245,1,0)	
245	President B		0	B243/C245		IF(D245>D244,1,0)
246	81	C247+C248				
247	President A		0	B246/C247	IF(D247>D248,1,0)	
248	President B		0	B246/C248		IF(D248>D247,1,0)
249	82	C250+C251				
250	President A		0	B249/C250	IF(D250>D251,1,0)	
251	President B		0	B249/C251		IF(D251>D250,1,0)
252	83	C253+C254				
253	President A		0	B252/C253	IF(D253>D254,1,0)	
254	President B		0	B252/C254		IF(D254>D253,1,0)
255	84	C256+C257				
256	President A		0	B255/C256	IF(D256>D257,1,0)	

	A	B	C	D	E	F
257	President B		0	B255/C257		IF(D257>D256,1,0)
258	85	C259+C260				
259	President A		0	B258/C259	IF(D259>D260,1,0)	
260	President B		0	B258/C260		IF(D260>D259,1,0)
261	86	C262+C263				
262	President A		0	B261/C262	IF(D262>D263,1,0)	
263	President B		0	B261/C263		IF(D263>D262,1,0)
264	87	C265+C266				
265	President A		0	B264/C265	IF(D265>D266,1,0)	
266	President B		0	B264/C266		IF(D266>D265,1,0)
267	88	C268+C269				
268	President A		0	B267/C268	IF(D268>D269,1,0)	
269	President B		0	B267/C269		IF(D269>D268,1,0)
270	89	C271+C272				
271	President A		0	B270/C271	IF(D271>D272,1,0)	
272	President B		0	B270/C272		IF(D272>D271,1,0)
273	90	C274+C275				
274	President A		0	B273/C274	IF(D274>D275,1,0)	
275	President B		0	B273/C275		IF(D275>D274,1,0)
276	91	C277+C278				
277	President A		0	B276/C277	IF(D277>D278,1,0)	
278	President B		0	B276/C278		IF(D278>D277,1,0)
279	92	C280+C281				
280	President A		0	B279/C280	IF(D280>D281,1,0)	
281	President B		0	B279/C281		IF(D281>D280,1,0)
282	93	C283+C284				
283	President A		0	B282/C283	IF(D283>D284,1,0)	
284	President B		0	B282/C284		IF(D284>D283,1,0)
285	94	C286+C287				
286	President A		0	B285/C286	IF(D286>D287,1,0)	
287	President B		0	B285/C287		IF(D287>D286,1,0)
288	95	C289+C290				
289	President A		0	B288/C289	IF(D289>D290,1,0)	
290	President B		0	B288/C290		IF(D290>D289,1,0)
291	96	C292+C293				
292	President A		0	B291/C292	IF(D292>D293,1,0)	
293	President B		0	B291/C293		IF(D293>D292,1,0)
294	97	C295+C296				
295	President A		0	B294/C295	IF(D295>D296,1,0)	
296	President B		0	B294/C296		IF(D296>D295,1,0)
297	98	C298+C299				
298	President A		0	B297/C298	IF(D298>D299,1,0)	
299	President B		0	B297/C299		IF(D299>D298,1,0)
300	99	C301+C302				
301	President A		0	B300/C301	IF(D301>D302,1,0)	
302	President B		0	B300/C302		IF(D302>D301,1,0)
303	100	C304+C305				
304	President A		0	B303/C304	IF(D304>D305,1,0)	
305	President B		0	B303/C305		IF(D305>D304,1,0)
306	101	C307+C308				
307	President A		0	B306/C307	IF(D307>D308,1,0)	
308	President B		0	B306/C308		IF(D308>D307,1,0)
309	102	C310+C311				
310	President A		0	B309/C310	IF(D310>D311,1,0)	
311	President B		0	B309/C311		IF(D311>D310,1,0)
312	103	C313+C314				
313	President A		0	B312/C313	IF(D313>D314,1,0)	
314	President B		0	B312/C314		IF(D314>D313,1,0)
315	104	C316+C317				
316	President A		0	B315/C316	IF(D316>D317,1,0)	
317	President B		0	B315/C317		IF(D317>D316,1,0)
318	105	C319+C320				
319	President A		0	B318/C319	IF(D319>D320,1,0)	
320	President B		0	B318/C320		IF(D320>D319,1,0)
321	106	C322+C323				
322	President A		0	B321/C322	IF(D322>D323,1,0)	
323	President B		0	B321/C323		IF(D323>D322,1,0)
324	107	C325+C326				
325	President A		0	B324/C325	IF(D325>D326,1,0)	
326	President B		0	B324/C326		IF(D326>D325,1,0)
327	108	C328+C329				

	A	B	C	D	E	F
328	President A		0	B327/C328	IF(D328>D329,1,0)	
329	President B		0	B327/C329		IF(D329>D328,1,0)
330	109	C331+C332				
331	President A		0	B330/C331	IF(D331>D332,1,0)	
332	President B		0	B330/C332		IF(D332>D331,1,0)
333	110	C334+C335				
334	President A		0	B333/C334	IF(D334>D335,1,0)	
335	President B		0	B333/C335		IF(D335>D334,1,0)
336	111	C337+C338				
337	President A		0	B336/C337	IF(D337>D338,1,0)	
338	President B		0	B336/C338		IF(D338>D337,1,0)
339	112	C340+C341				
340	President A		0	B339/C340	IF(D340>D341,1,0)	
341	President B		0	B339/C341		IF(D341>D340,1,0)
342	113	C343+C344				
343	President A		0	B342/C343	IF(D343>D344,1,0)	
344	President B		0	B342/C344		IF(D344>D343,1,0)
345	114	C346+C347				
346	President A		0	B345/C346	IF(D346>D347,1,0)	
347	President B		0	B345/C347		IF(D347>D346,1,0)
348	115	C349+C350				
349	President A		0	B348/C349	IF(D349>D350,1,0)	
350	President B		0	B348/C350		IF(D350>D349,1,0)
351	116	C352+C353				
352	President A		0	B351/C352	IF(D352>D353,1,0)	
353	President B		0	B351/C353		IF(D353>D352,1,0)
354	117	C355+C356				
355	President A		0	B354/C355	IF(D355>D356,1,0)	
356	President B		0	B354/C356		IF(D356>D355,1,0)
357	118	C358+C359				
358	President A		0	B357/C358	IF(D358>D359,1,0)	
359	President B		0	B357/C359		IF(D359>D358,1,0)
360	119	C361+C362				
361	President A		0	B360/C361	IF(D361>D362,1,0)	
362	President B		0	B360/C362		IF(D362>D361,1,0)
363	120	C364+C365				
364	President A		0	B363/C364	IF(D364>D365,1,0)	
365	President B		0	B363/C365		IF(D365>D364,1,0)
366	121	C367+C368				
367	President A		0	B366/C367	IF(D367>D368,1,0)	
368	President B		0	B366/C368		IF(D368>D367,1,0)
369	122	C370+C371				
370	President A		0	B369/C370	IF(D370>D371,1,0)	
371	President B		0	B369/C371		IF(D371>D370,1,0)
372	123	C373+C374				
373	President A		0	B372/C373	IF(D373>D374,1,0)	
374	President B		0	B372/C374		IF(D374>D373,1,0)
375	124	C376+C377				
376	President A		0	B375/C376	IF(D376>D377,1,0)	
377	President B		0	B375/C377		IF(D377>D376,1,0)
378	125	C379+C380				
379	President A		0	B378/C379	IF(D379>D380,1,0)	
380	President B		0	B378/C380		IF(D380>D379,1,0)
381	126	C382+C383				
382	President A		0	B381/C382	IF(D382>D383,1,0)	
383	President B		0	B381/C383		IF(D383>D382,1,0)
384	127	C385+C386				
385	President A		0	B384/C385	IF(D385>D386,1,0)	
386	President B		0	B384/C386		IF(D386>D385,1,0)
387	128	C388+C389				
388	President A		0	B387/C388	IF(D388>D389,1,0)	
389	President B		0	B387/C389		IF(D389>D388,1,0)
390	129	C391+C392				
391	President A		0	B390/C391	IF(D391>D392,1,0)	
392	President B		0	B390/C392		IF(D392>D391,1,0)
393	130	C394+C395				
394	President A		0	B393/C394	IF(D394>D395,1,0)	
395	President B		0	B393/C395		IF(D395>D394,1,0)
396	131	C397+C398				
397	President A		0	B396/C397	IF(D397>D398,1,0)	
398	President B		0	B396/C398		IF(D398>D397,1,0)

	A	B	C	D	E	F
399	132	C400+C401				
400	President A		0	B399/C400	IF(D400>D401,1,0)	
401	President B		0	B399/C401		IF(D401>D400,1,0)
402	133	C403+C404				
403	President A		0	B402/C403	IF(D403>D404,1,0)	
404	President B		0	B402/C404		IF(D404>D403,1,0)
405	134	C406+C407				
406	President A		0	B405/C406	IF(D406>D407,1,0)	
407	President B		0	B405/C407		IF(D407>D406,1,0)
408	135	C409+C410				
409	President A		0	B408/C409	IF(D409>D410,1,0)	
410	President B		0	B408/C410		IF(D410>D409,1,0)
411	136	C412+C413				
412	President A		0	B411/C412	IF(D412>D413,1,0)	
413	President B		0	B411/C413		IF(D413>D412,1,0)
414	137	C415+C416				
415	President A		0	B414/C415	IF(D415>D416,1,0)	
416	President B		0	B414/C416		IF(D416>D415,1,0)
417	138	C418+C419				
418	President A		0	B417/C418	IF(D418>D419,1,0)	
419	President B		0	B417/C419		IF(D419>D418,1,0)
420	139	C421+C422				
421	President A		0	B420/C421	IF(D421>D422,1,0)	
422	President B		0	B420/C422		IF(D422>D421,1,0)
423	140	C424+C425				
424	President A		0	B423/C424	IF(D424>D425,1,0)	
425	President B		0	B423/C425		IF(D425>D424,1,0)
426	141	C427+C428				
427	President A		0	B426/C427	IF(D427>D428,1,0)	
428	President B		0	B426/C428		IF(D428>D427,1,0)
429	142	C430+C431				
430	President A		0	B429/C430	IF(D430>D431,1,0)	
431	President B		0	B429/C431		IF(D431>D430,1,0)
432	143	C433+C434				
433	President A		0	B432/C433	IF(D433>D434,1,0)	
434	President B		0	B432/C434		IF(D434>D433,1,0)
435	144	C436+C437				
436	President A		0	B435/C436	IF(D436>D437,1,0)	
437	President B		0	B435/C437		IF(D437>D436,1,0)
438	145	C439+C440				
439	President A		0	B438/C439	IF(D439>D440,1,0)	
440	President B		0	B438/C440		IF(D440>D439,1,0)
441	146	C442+C443				
442	President A		0	B441/C442	IF(D442>D443,1,0)	
443	President B		0	B441/C443		IF(D443>D442,1,0)
444	147	C445+C446				
445	President A		0	B444/C445	IF(D445>D446,1,0)	
446	President B		0	B444/C446		IF(D446>D445,1,0)
447	148	C448+C449				
448	President A		0	B447/C448	IF(D448>D449,1,0)	
449	President B		0	B447/C449		IF(D449>D448,1,0)
450	149	C451+C452				
451	President A		0	B450/C451	IF(D451>D452,1,0)	
452	President B		0	B450/C452		IF(D452>D451,1,0)
453	150	C454+C455				
454	President A		0	B453/C454	IF(D454>D455,1,0)	
455	President B		0	B453/C455		IF(D455>D454,1,0)
456	151	C457+C458				
457	President A		0	B456/C457	IF(D457>D458,1,0)	
458	President B		0	B456/C458		IF(D458>D457,1,0)
459	152	C460+C461				
460	President A		0	B459/C460	IF(D460>D461,1,0)	
461	President B		0	B459/C461		IF(D461>D460,1,0)
462	153	C463+C464				
463	President A		0	B462/C463	IF(D463>D464,1,0)	
464	President B		0	B462/C464		IF(D464>D463,1,0)
465	154	C466+C467				
466	President A		0	B465/C466	IF(D466>D467,1,0)	
467	President B		0	B465/C467		IF(D467>D466,1,0)
468	155	C469+C470				
469	President A		0	B468/C469	IF(D469>D470,1,0)	

	A	B	C	D	E	F
470	President B		0	B468/C470		IF(D470>D469,1,0)
471	156	C472+C473				
472	President A		0	B471/C472	IF(D472>D473,1,0)	
473	President B		0	B471/C473		IF(D473>D472,1,0)
474	157	C475+C476				
475	President A		0	B474/C475	IF(D475>D476,1,0)	
476	President B		0	B474/C476		IF(D476>D475,1,0)
477	158	C478+C479				
478	President A		0	B477/C478	IF(D478>D479,1,0)	
479	President B		0	B477/C479		IF(D479>D478,1,0)
480	159	C481+C482				
481	President A		0	B480/C481	IF(D481>D482,1,0)	
482	President B		0	B480/C482		IF(D482>D481,1,0)
483	160	C484+C485				
484	President A		0	B483/C484	IF(D484>D485,1,0)	
485	President B		0	B483/C485		IF(D485>D484,1,0)
486	161	C487+C488				
487	President A		0	B486/C487	IF(D487>D488,1,0)	
488	President B		0	B486/C488		IF(D488>D487,1,0)
489	162	C490+C491				
490	President A		0	B489/C490	IF(D490>D491,1,0)	
491	President B		0	B489/C491		IF(D491>D490,1,0)
492	163	C493+C494				
493	President A		0	B492/C493	IF(D493>D494,1,0)	
494	President B		0	B492/C494		IF(D494>D493,1,0)
495	164	C496+C497				
496	President A		0	B495/C496	IF(D496>D497,1,0)	
497	President B		0	B495/C497		IF(D497>D496,1,0)
498	165	C499+C500				
499	President A		0	B498/C499	IF(D499>D500,1,0)	
500	President B		0	B498/C500		IF(D500>D499,1,0)
501	166	C502+C503				
502	President A		0	B501/C502	IF(D502>D503,1,0)	
503	President B		0	B501/C503		IF(D503>D502,1,0)
504	167	C505+C506				
505	President A		0	B504/C505	IF(D505>D506,1,0)	
506	President B		0	B504/C506		IF(D506>D505,1,0)
507	168	C508+C509				
508	President A		0	B507/C508	IF(D508>D509,1,0)	
509	President B		0	B507/C509		IF(D509>D508,1,0)
510	169	C511+C512				
511	President A		0	B510/C511	IF(D511>D512,1,0)	
512	President B		0	B510/C512		IF(D512>D511,1,0)
513	170	C514+C515				
514	President A		0	B513/C514	IF(D514>D515,1,0)	
515	President B		0	B513/C515		IF(D515>D514,1,0)
516	171	C517+C518				
517	President A		0	B516/C517	IF(D517>D518,1,0)	
518	President B		0	B516/C518		IF(D518>D517,1,0)
519	172	C520+C521				
520	President A		0	B519/C520	IF(D520>D521,1,0)	
521	President B		0	B519/C521		IF(D521>D520,1,0)
522	173	C523+C524				
523	President A		0	B522/C523	IF(D523>D524,1,0)	
524	President B		0	B522/C524		IF(D524>D523,1,0)
525	174	C526+C527				
526	President A		0	B525/C526	IF(D526>D527,1,0)	
527	President B		0	B525/C527		IF(D527>D526,1,0)
528	175	C529+C530				
529	President A		0	B528/C529	IF(D529>D530,1,0)	
530	President B		0	B528/C530		IF(D530>D529,1,0)
531	176	C532+C533				
532	President A		0	B531/C532	IF(D532>D533,1,0)	
533	President B		0	B531/C533		IF(D533>D532,1,0)
534	177	C535+C536				
535	President A		0	B534/C535	IF(D535>D536,1,0)	
536	President B		0	B534/C536		IF(D536>D535,1,0)
537	178	C538+C539				
538	President A		0	B537/C538	IF(D538>D539,1,0)	
539	President B		0	B537/C539		IF(D539>D538,1,0)
540	179	C541+C542				

	A	B	C	D	E	F
541	President A		0	B540/C541	IF(D541>D542,1,0)	
542	President B		0	B540/C542		IF(D542>D541,1,0)
543	180	C544+C545				
544	President A		0	B543/C544	IF(D544>D545,1,0)	
545	President B		0	B543/C545		IF(D545>D544,1,0)
546	181	C547+C548				
547	President A		0	B546/C547	IF(D547>D548,1,0)	
548	President B		0	B546/C548		IF(D548>D547,1,0)
549	182	C550+C551				
550	President A		0	B549/C550	IF(D550>D551,1,0)	
551	President B		0	B549/C551		IF(D551>D550,1,0)
552	183	C553+C554				
553	President A		0	B552/C553	IF(D553>D554,1,0)	
554	President B		0	B552/C554		IF(D554>D553,1,0)
555	184	C556+C557				
556	President A		0	B555/C556	IF(D556>D557,1,0)	
557	President B		0	B555/C557		IF(D557>D556,1,0)
558	185	C559+C560				
559	President A		0	B558/C559	IF(D559>D560,1,0)	
560	President B		0	B558/C560		IF(D560>D559,1,0)
561	186	C562+C563				
562	President A		0	B561/C562	IF(D562>D563,1,0)	
563	President B		0	B561/C563		IF(D563>D562,1,0)
564	187	C565+C566				
565	President A		0	B564/C565	IF(D565>D566,1,0)	
566	President B		0	B564/C566		IF(D566>D565,1,0)
567	188	C568+C569				
568	President A		0	B567/C568	IF(D568>D569,1,0)	
569	President B		0	B567/C569		IF(D569>D568,1,0)
570	189	C571+C572				
571	President A		0	B570/C571	IF(D571>D572,1,0)	
572	President B		0	B570/C572		IF(D572>D571,1,0)
573	190	C574+C575				
574	President A		0	B573/C574	IF(D574>D575,1,0)	
575	President B		0	B573/C575		IF(D575>D574,1,0)
576	191	C577+C578				
577	President A		0	B576/C577	IF(D577>D578,1,0)	
578	President B		0	B576/C578		IF(D578>D577,1,0)
579	192	C580+C581				
580	President A		0	B579/C580	IF(D580>D581,1,0)	
581	President B		0	B579/C581		IF(D581>D580,1,0)
582	193	C583+C584				
583	President A		0	B582/C583	IF(D583>D584,1,0)	
584	President B		0	B582/C584		IF(D584>D583,1,0)
585	194	C586+C587				
586	President A		0	B585/C586	IF(D586>D587,1,0)	
587	President B		0	B585/C587		IF(D587>D586,1,0)
500	195	C589+C590				
589	President A		0	B588/C589	IF(D589>D590,1,0)	
590	President B		0	B588/C590		IF(D590>D589,1,0)
591	196	C592+C593				
592	President A		0	B591/C592	IF(D592>D593,1,0)	
593	President B		0	B591/C593		IF(D593>D592,1,0)
594	197	C595+C596				
595	President A		0	B594/C595	IF(D595>D596,1,0)	
596	President B		0	B594/C596		IF(D596>D595,1,0)
597	198	C598+C599				
598	President A		0	B597/C598	IF(D598>D599,1,0)	
599	President B		0	B597/C599		IF(D599>D598,1,0)
600	199	C601+C602				
601	President A		0	B600/C601	IF(D601>D602,1,0)	
602	President B		0	B600/C602		IF(D602>D601,1,0)
603	200	C604+C605				
604	President A		0	B603/C604	IF(D604>D605,1,0)	
605	President B		0	B603/C605		IF(D605>D604,1,0)
606	201	C607+C608				
607	President A		0	B606/C607	IF(D607>D608,1,0)	
608	President B		0	B606/C608		IF(D608>D607,1,0)
609	202	C610+C611				
610	President A		0	B609/C610	IF(D610>D611,1,0)	
611	President B		0	B609/C611		IF(D611>D610,1,0)

	A	B	C	D	E	F
612	203	C613+C614				
613	President A		0	B612/C613	IF(D613>D614,1,0)	
614	President B		0	B612/C614		IF(D614>D613,1,0)
615	204	C616+C617				
616	President A		0	B615/C616	IF(D616>D617,1,0)	
617	President B		0	B615/C617		IF(D617>D616,1,0)
618	205	C619+C620				
619	President A		0	B618/C619	IF(D619>D620,1,0)	
620	President B		0	B618/C620		IF(D620>D619,1,0)
621	206	C622+C623				
622	President A		0	B621/C622	IF(D622>D623,1,0)	
623	President B		0	B621/C623		IF(D623>D622,1,0)
624	207	C625+C626				
625	President A		0	B624/C625	IF(D625>D626,1,0)	
626	President B		0	B624/C626		IF(D626>D625,1,0)
627	208	C628+C629				
628	President A		0	B627/C628	IF(D628>D629,1,0)	
629	President B		0	B627/C629		IF(D629>D628,1,0)
630	209	C631+C632				
631	President A		0	B630/C631	IF(D631>D632,1,0)	
632	President B		0	B630/C632		IF(D632>D631,1,0)
633	210	C634+C635				
634	President A		0	B633/C634	IF(D634>D635,1,0)	
635	President B		0	B633/C635		IF(D635>D634,1,0)
636	211	C637+C638				
637	President A		0	B636/C637	IF(D637>D638,1,0)	
638	President B		0	B636/C638		IF(D638>D637,1,0)
639	212	C640+C641				
640	President A		0	B639/C640	IF(D640>D641,1,0)	
641	President B		0	B639/C641		IF(D641>D640,1,0)
642	213	C643+C644				
643	President A		0	B642/C643	IF(D643>D644,1,0)	
644	President B		0	B642/C644		IF(D644>D643,1,0)
645	214	C646+C647				
646	President A		0	B645/C646	IF(D646>D647,1,0)	
647	President B		0	B645/C647		IF(D647>D646,1,0)
648	215	C649+C650				
649	President A		0	B648/C649	IF(D649>D650,1,0)	
650	President B		0	B648/C650		IF(D650>D649,1,0)
651	216	C652+C653				
652	President A		0	B651/C652	IF(D652>D653,1,0)	
653	President B		0	B651/C653		IF(D653>D652,1,0)
654	217	C655+C656				
655	President A		0	B654/C655	IF(D655>D656,1,0)	
656	President B		0	B654/C656		IF(D656>D655,1,0)
657	218	C658+C659				
658	President A		0	B657/C658	IF(D658>D659,1,0)	
659	President B		0	B657/C659		IF(D659>D658,1,0)
660	219	C661+C662				
661	President A		0	B660/C661	IF(D661>D662,1,0)	
662	President B		0	B660/C662		IF(D662>D661,1,0)
663	220	C664+C665				
664	President A		0	B663/C664	IF(D664>D665,1,0)	
665	President B		0	B663/C665		IF(D665>D664,1,0)
666	221	C667+C668				
667	President A		0	B666/C667	IF(D667>D668,1,0)	
668	President B		0	B666/C668		IF(D668>D667,1,0)
669	222	C670+C671				
670	President A		0	B669/C670	IF(D670>D671,1,0)	
671	President B		0	B669/C671		IF(D671>D670,1,0)
672	223	C673+C674				
673	President A		0	B672/C673	IF(D673>D674,1,0)	
674	President B		0	B672/C674		IF(D674>D673,1,0)
675	224	C676+C677				
676	President A		0	B675/C676	IF(D676>D677,1,0)	
677	President B		0	B675/C677		IF(D677>D676,1,0)
678	225	C679+C680				
679	President A		0	B678/C679	IF(D679>D680,1,0)	
680	President B		0	B678/C680		IF(D680>D679,1,0)
681	226	C682+C683				
682	President A		0	B681/C682	IF(D682>D683,1,0)	

	A	B	C	D	E	F
683	President B		0	B681/C683		IF(D683>D682,1,0)
684	227	C685+C686				
685	President A		0	B684/C685	IF(D685>D686,1,0)	
686	President B		0	B684/C686		IF(D686>D685,1,0)
687	228	C688+C689				
688	President A		0	B687/C688	IF(D688>D689,1,0)	
689	President B		0	B687/C689		IF(D689>D688,1,0)
690	229	C691+C692				
691	President A		0	B690/C691	IF(D691>D692,1,0)	
692	President B		0	B690/C692		IF(D692>D691,1,0)
693	230	C694+C695				
694	President A		0	B693/C694	IF(D694>D695,1,0)	
695	President B		0	B693/C695		IF(D695>D694,1,0)
696	231	C697+C698				
697	President A		0	B696/C697	IF(D697>D698,1,0)	
698	President B		0	B696/C698		IF(D698>D697,1,0)
699	232	C700+C701				
700	President A		0	B699/C700	IF(D700>D701,1,0)	
701	President B		0	B699/C701		IF(D701>D700,1,0)
702	233	C703+C704				
703	President A		0	B702/C703	IF(D703>D704,1,0)	
704	President B		0	B702/C704		IF(D704>D703,1,0)
705	234	C706+C707				
706	President A		0	B705/C706	IF(D706>D707,1,0)	
707	President B		0	B705/C707		IF(D707>D706,1,0)
708	235	C709+C710				
709	President A		0	B708/C709	IF(D709>D710,1,0)	
710	President B		0	B708/C710		IF(D710>D709,1,0)
711	236	C712+C713				
712	President A		0	B711/C712	IF(D712>D713,1,0)	
713	President B		0	B711/C713		IF(D713>D712,1,0)
714	237	C715+C716				
715	President A		0	B714/C715	IF(D715>D716,1,0)	
716	President B		0	B714/C716		IF(D716>D715,1,0)
717	238	C718+C719				
718	President A		0	B717/C718	IF(D718>D719,1,0)	
719	President B		0	B717/C719		IF(D719>D718,1,0)
720	239	C721+C722				
721	President A		0	B720/C721	IF(D721>D722,1,0)	
722	President B		0	B720/C722		IF(D722>D721,1,0)
723	240	C724+C725				
724	President A		0	B723/C724	IF(D724>D725,1,0)	
725	President B		0	B723/C725		IF(D725>D724,1,0)
726	241	C727+C728				
727	President A		0	B726/C727	IF(D727>D728,1,0)	
728	President B		0	B726/C728		IF(D728>D727,1,0)
729	242	C730+C731				
730	President A		0	B729/C730	IF(D730>D731,1,0)	
731	President D		0	B729/C731		IF(D731>D730,1,0)
732	243	C733+C734				
733	President A		0	B732/C733	IF(D733>D734,1,0)	
734	President B		0	B732/C734		IF(D734>D733,1,0)
735	244	C736+C737				
736	President A		0	B735/C736	IF(D736>D737,1,0)	
737	President B		0	B735/C737		IF(D737>D736,1,0)
738	245	C739+C740				
739	President A		0	B738/C739	IF(D739>D740,1,0)	
740	President B		0	B738/C740		IF(D740>D739,1,0)
741	246	C742+C743				
742	President A		0	B741/C742	IF(D742>D743,1,0)	
743	President B		0	B741/C743		IF(D743>D742,1,0)
744	247	C745+C746				
745	President A		0	B744/C745	IF(D745>D746,1,0)	
746	President B		0	B744/C746		IF(D746>D745,1,0)
747	248	C748+C749				
748	President A		0	B747/C748	IF(D748>D749,1,0)	
749	President B		0	B747/C749		IF(D749>D748,1,0)
750	249	C751+C752				
751	President A		0	B750/C751	IF(D751>D752,1,0)	
752	President B		0	B750/C752		IF(D752>D751,1,0)
753	250	C754+C755				

	A	B	C	D	E	F
754	President A		0	B753/C754	IF(D754>D755,1,0)	
755	President B		0	B753/C755		IF(D755>D754,1,0)
756	251	C757+C758				
757	President A		0	B756/C757	IF(D757>D758,1,0)	
758	President B		0	B756/C758		IF(D758>D757,1,0)
759	252	C760+C761				
760	President A		0	B759/C760	IF(D760>D761,1,0)	
761	President B		0	B759/C761		IF(D761>D760,1,0)
762	253	C763+C764				
763	President A		0	B762/C763	IF(D763>D764,1,0)	
764	President B		0	B762/C764		IF(D764>D763,1,0)
765	254	C766+C767				
766	President A		0	B765/C766	IF(D766>D767,1,0)	
767	President B		0	B765/C767		IF(D767>D766,1,0)
768	255	C769+C770				
769	President A		0	B768/C769	IF(D769>D770,1,0)	
770	President B		0	B768/C770		IF(D770>D769,1,0)
771	256	C772+C773				
772	President A		0	B771/C772	IF(D772>D773,1,0)	
773	President B		0	B771/C773		IF(D773>D772,1,0)
774	257	C775+C776				
775	President A		0	B774/C775	IF(D775>D776,1,0)	
776	President B		0	B774/C776		IF(D776>D775,1,0)
777	258	C778+C779				
778	President A		0	B777/C778	IF(D778>D779,1,0)	
779	President B		0	B777/C779		IF(D779>D778,1,0)
780	259	C781+C782				
781	President A		0	B780/C781	IF(D781>D782,1,0)	
782	President B		0	B780/C782		IF(D782>D781,1,0)
783	260	C784+C785				
784	President A		0	B783/C784	IF(D784>D785,1,0)	
785	President B		0	B783/C785		IF(D785>D784,1,0)
786	261	C787+C788				
787	President A		0	B786/C787	IF(D787>D788,1,0)	
788	President B		0	B786/C788		IF(D788>D787,1,0)
789	262	C790+C791				
790	President A		0	B789/C790	IF(D790>D791,1,0)	
791	President B		0	B789/C791		IF(D791>D790,1,0)
792	263	C793+C794				
793	President A		0	B792/C793	IF(D793>D794,1,0)	
794	President B		0	B792/C794		IF(D794>D793,1,0)
795	264	C796+C797				
796	President A		0	B795/C796	IF(D796>D797,1,0)	
797	President B		0	B795/C797		IF(D797>D796,1,0)
798	265	C799+C800				
799	President A		0	B798/C799	IF(D799>D800,1,0)	
800	President B		0	B798/C800		IF(D800>D799,1,0)
801	266	C802+C803				
802	President A		0	B801/C802	IF(D802>D803,1,0)	
803	President B		0	B801/C803		IF(D803>D802,1,0)
804	267	C805+C806				
805	President A		0	B804/C805	IF(D805>D806,1,0)	
806	President B		0	B804/C806		IF(D806>D805,1,0)
807	268	C808+C809				
808	President A		0	B807/C808	IF(D808>D809,1,0)	
809	President B		0	B807/C809		IF(D809>D808,1,0)
810	269	C811+C812				
811	President A		0	B810/C811	IF(D811>D812,1,0)	
812	President B		0	B810/C812		IF(D812>D811,1,0)
813	270	C814+C815				
814	President A		0	B813/C814	IF(D814>D815,1,0)	
815	President B		0	B813/C815		IF(D815>D814,1,0)
816	271	C817+C818				
817	President A		0	B816/C817	IF(D817>D818,1,0)	
818	President B		0	B816/C818		IF(D818>D817,1,0)
819	272	C820+C821				
820	President A		0	B819/C820	IF(D820>D821,1,0)	
821	President B		0	B819/C821		IF(D021>D820,1,0)
822	273	C823+C824				
823	President A		0	B822/C823	IF(D823>D824,1,0)	
824	President B		0	B822/C824		IF(D824>D823,1,0)

	A	B	C	D	E	F
825	274	C826+C827				
826	President A		0	B825/C826	IF(D826>D827,1,0)	
827	President B		0	B825/C827		IF(D827>D826,1,0)
828	275	C829+C830				
829	President A		0	B828/C829	IF(D829>D830,1,0)	
830	President B		0	B828/C830		IF(D830>D829,1,0)
831	276	C832+C833				
832	President A		0	B831/C832	IF(D832>D833,1,0)	
833	President B		0	B831/C833		IF(D833>D832,1,0)
834	277	C835+C836				
835	President A		0	B834/C835	IF(D835>D836,1,0)	
836	President B		0	B834/C836		IF(D836>D835,1,0)
837	278	C838+C839				
838	President A		0	B837/C838	IF(D838>D839,1,0)	
839	President B		0	B837/C839		IF(D839>D838,1,0)
840	279	C841+C842				
841	President A		0	B840/C841	IF(D841>D842,1,0)	
842	President B		0	B840/C842		IF(D842>D841,1,0)
843	280	C844+C845				
844	President A		0	B843/C844	IF(D844>D845,1,0)	
845	President B		0	B843/C845		IF(D845>D844,1,0)
846	281	C847+C848				
847	President A		0	B846/C847	IF(D847>D848,1,0)	
848	President B		0	B846/C848		IF(D848>D847,1,0)
849	282	C850+C851				
850	President A		0	B849/C850	IF(D850>D851,1,0)	
851	President B		0	B849/C851		IF(D851>D850,1,0)
852	283	C853+C854				
853	President A		0	B852/C853	IF(D853>D854,1,0)	
854	President B		0	B852/C854		IF(D854>D853,1,0)
855	284	C856+C857				
856	President A		0	B855/C856	IF(D856>D857,1,0)	
857	President B		0	B855/C857		IF(D857>D856,1,0)
858	285	C859+C860				
859	President A		0	B858/C859	IF(D859>D860,1,0)	
860	President B		0	B858/C860		IF(D860>D859,1,0)
861	286	C862+C863				
862	President A		0	B861/C862	IF(D862>D863,1,0)	
863	President B		0	B861/C863		IF(D863>D862,1,0)
864	287	C865+C866				
865	President A		0	B864/C865	IF(D865>D866,1,0)	
866	President B		0	B864/C866		IF(D866>D865,1,0)
867	288	C868+C869				
868	President A		0	B867/C868	IF(D868>D869,1,0)	
869	President B		0	B867/C869		IF(D869>D868,1,0)
870	289	C871+C872				
871	President A		0	B870/C871	IF(D871>D872,1,0)	
872	President B		0	B870/C072		IF(D872>D871,1,0)
873	290	C874+C875				
874	President A		0	B873/C874	IF(D874>D875,1,0)	
875	President B		0	B873/C875		IF(D875>D874,1,0)
876	291	C877+C878				
877	President A		0	B876/C877	IF(D877>D878,1,0)	
878	President B		0	B876/C878		IF(D878>D877,1,0)
879	292	C880+C881				
880	President A		0	B879/C880	IF(D880>D881,1,0)	
881	President B		0	B879/C881		IF(D881>D880,1,0)
882	293	C883+C884				
883	President A		0	B882/C883	IF(D883>D884,1,0)	
884	President B		0	B882/C884		IF(D884>D883,1,0)
885	294	C886+C887				
886	President A		0	B885/C886	IF(D886>D887,1,0)	
887	President B		0	B885/C887		IF(D887>D886,1,0)
888	295	C889+C890				
889	President A		0	B888/C889	IF(D889>D890,1,0)	
890	President B		0	B888/C890		IF(D890>D889,1,0)
891	296	C892+C893				
892	President A		0	B891/C892	IF(D892>D893,1,0)	
893	President B		0	B891/C893		IF(D893>D892,1,0)
894	297	C895+C896				
895	President A		0	B894/C895	IF(D895>D896,1,0)	

	A	B	C	D	E	F
896	President B		0	B894/C896		IF(D896>D895,1,0)
897	298	C898+C899				
898	President A		0	B897/C898	IF(D898>D899,1,0)	
899	President B		0	B897/C899		IF(D899>D898,1,0)
900	299	C901+C902				
901	President A		0	B900/C901	IF(D901>D902,1,0)	
902	President B		0	B900/C902		IF(D902>D901,1,0)
903	300	C904+C905				
904	President A		0	B903/C904	IF(D904>D905,1,0)	
905	President B		0	B903/C905		IF(D905>D904,1,0)
906	301	C907+C908				
907	President A		0	B906/C907	IF(D907>D908,1,0)	
908	President B		0	B906/C908		IF(D908>D907,1,0)
909	302	C910+C911				
910	President A		0	B909/C910	IF(D910>D911,1,0)	
911	President B		0	B909/C911		IF(D911>D910,1,0)
912	303	C913+C914				
913	President A		0	B912/C913	IF(D913>D914,1,0)	
914	President B		0	B912/C914		IF(D914>D913,1,0)
915	304	C916+C917				
916	President A		0	B915/C916	IF(D916>D917,1,0)	
917	President B		0	B915/C917		IF(D917>D916,1,0)
918	305	C919+C920				
919	President A		0	B918/C919	IF(D919>D920,1,0)	
920	President B		0	B918/C920		IF(D920>D919,1,0)
921	306	C922+C923				
922	President A		0	B921/C922	IF(D922>D923,1,0)	
923	President B		0	B921/C923		IF(D923>D922,1,0)
924	307	C925+C926				
925	President A		0	B924/C925	IF(D925>D926,1,0)	
926	President B		0	B924/C926		IF(D926>D925,1,0)
927	308	C928+C929				
928	President A		0	B927/C928	IF(D928>D929,1,0)	
929	President B		0	B927/C929		IF(D929>D928,1,0)
930	309	C931+C932				
931	President A		0	B930/C931	IF(D931>D932,1,0)	
932	President B		0	B930/C932		IF(D932>D931,1,0)
933	310	C934+C935				
934	President A		0	B933/C934	IF(D934>D935,1,0)	
935	President B		0	B933/C935		IF(D935>D934,1,0)
936	311	C937+C938				
937	President A		0	B936/C937	IF(D937>D938,1,0)	
938	President B		0	B936/C938		IF(D938>D937,1,0)
939	312	C940+C941				
940	President A		0	B939/C940	IF(D940>D941,1,0)	
941	President B		0	B939/C941		IF(D941>D940,1,0)
942	313	C943+C944				
943	President A		0	B942/C943	IF(D943>D944,1,0)	
944	President B		0	B942/C944		IF(D944>D943,1,0)
945	314	C946+C947				
946	President A		0	B945/C946	IF(D946>D947,1,0)	
947	President B		0	B945/C947		IF(D947>D946,1,0)
948	315	C949+C950				
949	President A		0	B948/C949	IF(D949>D950,1,0)	
950	President B		0	B948/C950		IF(D950>D949,1,0)
951	316	C952+C953				
952	President A		0	B951/C952	IF(D952>D953,1,0)	
953	President B		0	B951/C953		IF(D953>D952,1,0)
954	317	C955+C956				
955	President A		0	B954/C955	IF(D955>D956,1,0)	
956	President B		0	B954/C956		IF(D956>D955,1,0)
957	318	C958+C959				
958	President A		0	B957/C958	IF(D958>D959,1,0)	
959	President B		0	B957/C959		IF(D959>D958,1,0)
960	319	C961+C962				
961	President A		0	B960/C961	IF(D961>D962,1,0)	
962	President B		0	B960/C962		IF(D962>D961,1,0)
963	320	C964+C965				
964	President A		0	B963/C964	IF(D964>D965,1,0)	
965	President B		0	B963/C965		IF(D965>D964,1,0)
966	321	C967+C968				

	A	B	C	D	E	F
967	President A		0	B966/C967	IF(D967>D968,1,0)	
968	President B		0	B966/C968		IF(D968>D967,1,0)
969	322	C970+C971				
970	President A		0	B969/C970	IF(D970>D971,1,0)	
971	President B		0	B969/C971		IF(D971>D970,1,0)
972	323	C973+C974				
973	President A		0	B972/C973	IF(D973>D974,1,0)	
974	President B		0	B972/C974		IF(D974>D973,1,0)
975	324	C976+C977				
976	President A		0	B975/C976	IF(D976>D977,1,0)	
977	President B		0	B975/C977		IF(D977>D976,1,0)
978	325	C979+C980				
979	President A		0	B978/C979	IF(D979>D980,1,0)	
980	President B		0	B978/C980		IF(D980>D979,1,0)
981	326	C982+C983				
982	President A		0	B981/C982	IF(D982>D983,1,0)	
983	President B		0	B981/C983		IF(D983>D982,1,0)
984	327	C985+C986				
985	President A		0	B984/C985	IF(D985>D986,1,0)	
986	President B		0	B984/C986		IF(D986>D985,1,0)
987	328	C988+C989				
988	President A		0	B987/C988	IF(D988>D989,1,0)	
989	President B		0	B987/C989		IF(D989>D988,1,0)
990	329	C991+C992				
991	President A		0	B990/C991	IF(D991>D992,1,0)	
992	President B		0	B990/C992		IF(D992>D991,1,0)
993	330	C994+C995				
994	President A		0	B993/C994	IF(D994>D995,1,0)	
995	President B		0	B993/C995		IF(D995>D994,1,0)
996	331	C997+C998				
997	President A		0	B996/C997	IF(D997>D998,1,0)	
998	President B		0	B996/C998		IF(D998>D997,1,0)
999	332	C1000+C1001				
1000	President A		0	B999/C1000	IF(D1000>D1001,1,0)	
1001	President B		0	B999/C1001		IF(D1001>D1000,1,0)
1002	333	C1003+C1004				
1003	President A		0	B1002/C1003	IF(D1003>D1004,1,0)	
1004	President B		0	B1002/C1004		IF(D1004>D1003,1,0)
1005	334	C1006+C1007				
1006	President A		0	B1005/C1006	IF(D1006>D1007,1,0)	
1007	President B		0	B1005/C1007		IF(D1007>D1006,1,0)
1008	335	C1009+C1010				
1009	President A		0	B1008/C1009	IF(D1009>D1010,1,0)	
1010	President B		0	B1008/C1010		IF(D1010>D1009,1,0)
1011	336	C1012+C1013				
1012	President A		0	B1011/C1012	IF(D1012>D1013,1,0)	
1013	President B		0	B1011/C1013		IF(D1013>D1012,1,0)
1014	337	C1015+C1016				
1015	President A		0	B1014/C1015	IF(D1015>D1016,1,0)	
1016	President B		0	B1014/C1016		IF(D1016>D1015,1,0)
1017	338	C1018+C1019				
1018	President A		0	B1017/C1018	IF(D1018>D1019,1,0)	
1019	President B		0	B1017/C1019		IF(D1019>D1018,1,0)
1020	339	C1021+C1022				
1021	President A		0	B1020/C1021	IF(D1021>D1022,1,0)	
1022	President B		0	B1020/C1022		IF(D1022>D1021,1,0)
1023	340	C1024+C1025				
1024	President A		0	B1023/C1024	IF(D1024>D1025,1,0)	
1025	President B		0	B1023/C1025		IF(D1025>D1024,1,0)
1026	341	C1027+C1028				
1027	President A		0	B1026/C1027	IF(D1027>D1028,1,0)	
1028	President B		0	B1026/C1028		IF(D1028>D1027,1,0)
1029	342	C1030+C1031				
1030	President A		0	B1029/C1030	IF(D1030>D1031,1,0)	
1031	President B		0	B1029/C1031		IF(D1031>D1030,1,0)
1032	343	C1033+C1034				
1033	President A		0	B1032/C1033	IF(D1033>D1034,1,0)	
1034	President B		0	B1032/C1034		IF(D1034>D1033,1,0)
1035	344	C1036+C1037				
1036	President A		0	B1035/C1036	IF(D1036>D1037,1,0)	
1037	President B		0	B1035/C1037		IF(D1037>D1036,1,0)

	A	B	C	D	E	F
1038	345	C1039+C1040				
1039	President A		0	B1038/C1039	IF(D1039>D1040,1,0)	
1040	President B		0	B1038/C1040		IF(D1040>D1039,1,0)
1041	346	C1042+C1043				
1042	President A		0	B1041/C1042	IF(D1042>D1043,1,0)	
1043	President B		0	B1041/C1043		IF(D1043>D1042,1,0)
1044	347	C1045+C1046				
1045	President A		0	B1044/C1045	IF(D1045>D1046,1,0)	
1046	President B		0	B1044/C1046		IF(D1046>D1045,1,0)
1047	348	C1048+C1049				
1048	President A		0	B1047/C1048	IF(D1048>D1049,1,0)	
1049	President B		0	B1047/C1049		IF(D1049>D1048,1,0)
1050	349	C1051+C1052				
1051	President A		0	B1050/C1051	IF(D1051>D1052,1,0)	
1052	President B		0	B1050/C1052		IF(D1052>D1051,1,0)
1053	350	C1054+C1055				
1054	President A		0	B1053/C1054	IF(D1054>D1055,1,0)	
1055	President B		0	B1053/C1055		IF(D1055>D1054,1,0)
1056	351	C1057+C1058				
1057	President A		0	B1056/C1057	IF(D1057>D1058,1,0)	
1058	President B		0	B1056/C1058		IF(D1058>D1057,1,0)
1059	352	C1060+C1061				
1060	President A		0	B1059/C1060	IF(D1060>D1061,1,0)	
1061	President B		0	B1059/C1061		IF(D1061>D1060,1,0)
1062	353	C1063+C1064				
1063	President A		0	B1062/C1063	IF(D1063>D1064,1,0)	
1064	President B		0	B1062/C1064		IF(D1064>D1063,1,0)
1065	354	C1066+C1067				
1066	President A		0	B1065/C1066	IF(D1066>D1067,1,0)	
1067	President B		0	B1065/C1067		IF(D1067>D1066,1,0)
1068	355	C1069+C1070				
1069	President A		0	B1068/C1069	IF(D1069>D1070,1,0)	
1070	President B		0	B1068/C1070		IF(D1070>D1069,1,0)
1071	356	C1072+C1073				
1072	President A		0	B1071/C1072	IF(D1072>D1073,1,0)	
1073	President B		0	B1071/C1073		IF(D1073>D1072,1,0)
1074	357	C1075+C1076				
1075	President A		0	B1074/C1075	IF(D1075>D1076,1,0)	
1076	President B		0	B1074/C1076		IF(D1076>D1075,1,0)
1077	358	C1078+C1079				
1078	President A		0	B1077/C1078	IF(D1078>D1079,1,0)	
1079	President B		0	B1077/C1079		IF(D1079>D1078,1,0)
1080	359	C1081+C1082				
1081	President A		0	B1080/C1081	IF(D1081>D1082,1,0)	
1082	President B		0	B1080/C1082		IF(D1082>D1081,1,0)
1083	360	C1084+C1085				
1084	President A		0	B1083/C1084	IF(D1084>D1085,1,0)	
1085	President B		0	B1083/C1085		IF(D1085>D1084,1,0)
1086	361	C1087+C1088				
1087	President A		0	B1086/C1087	IF(D1087>D1088,1,0)	
1088	President B		0	B1086/C1088		IF(D1088>D1087,1,0)
1089	362	C1090+C1091				
1090	President A		0	B1089/C1090	IF(D1090>D1091,1,0)	
1091	President B		0	B1089/C1091		IF(D1091>D1090,1,0)
1092	363	C1093+C1094				
1093	President A		0	B1092/C1093	IF(D1093>D1094,1,0)	
1094	President B		0	B1092/C1094		IF(D1094>D1093,1,0)
1095	364	C1096+C1097				
1096	President A		0	B1095/C1096	IF(D1096>D1097,1,0)	
1097	President B		0	B1095/C1097		IF(D1097>D1096,1,0)
1098	365	C1099+C1100				
1099	President A		0	B1098/C1099	IF(D1099>D1100,1,0)	
1100	President B		0	B1098/C1100		IF(D1100>D1099,1,0)
1101	366	C1102+C1103				
1102	President A		0	B1101/C1102	IF(D1102>D1103,1,0)	
1103	President B		0	B1101/C1103		IF(D1103>D1102,1,0)
1104	367	C1105+C1106				
1105	President A		0	B1104/C1105	IF(D1105>D1106,1,0)	
1106	President B		0	B1104/C1106		IF(D1106>D1105,1,0)
1107	368	C1108+C1109				
1108	President A		0	B1107/C1108	IF(D1108>D1109,1,0)	

	A	B	C	D	E	F
1109	President B		0	B1107/C1109		IF(D1109>D1108,1,0)
1110	369	C1111+C1112				
1111	President A		0	B1110/C1111	IF(D1111>D1112,1,0)	
1112	President B		0	B1110/C1112		IF(D1112>D1111,1,0)
1113	370	C1114+C1115				
1114	President A		0	B1113/C1114	IF(D1114>D1115,1,0)	
1115	President B		0	B1113/C1115		IF(D1115>D1114,1,0)
1116	371	C1117+C1118				
1117	President A		0	B1116/C1117	IF(D1117>D1118,1,0)	
1118	President B		0	B1116/C1118		IF(D1118>D1117,1,0)
1119	372	C1120+C1121				
1120	President A		0	B1119/C1120	IF(D1120>D1121,1,0)	
1121	President B		0	B1119/C1121		IF(D1121>D1120,1,0)
1122	373	C1123+C1124				
1123	President A		0	B1122/C1123	IF(D1123>D1124,1,0)	
1124	President B		0	B1122/C1124		IF(D1124>D1123,1,0)
1125	374	C1126+C1127				
1126	President A		0	B1125/C1126	IF(D1126>D1127,1,0)	
1127	President B		0	B1125/C1127		IF(D1127>D1126,1,0)
1128	375	C1129+C1130				
1129	President A		0	B1128/C1129	IF(D1129>D1130,1,0)	
1130	President B		0	B1128/C1130		IF(D1130>D1129,1,0)
1131	376	C1132+C1133				
1132	President A		0	B1131/C1132	IF(D1132>D1133,1,0)	
1133	President B		0	B1131/C1133		IF(D1133>D1132,1,0)
1134	377	C1135+C1136				
1135	President A		0	B1134/C1135	IF(D1135>D1136,1,0)	
1136	President B		0	B1134/C1136		IF(D1136>D1135,1,0)
1137	378	C1138+C1139				
1138	President A		0	B1137/C1138	IF(D1138>D1139,1,0)	
1139	President B		0	B1137/C1139		IF(D1139>D1138,1,0)
1140	379	C1141+C1142				
1141	President A		0	B1140/C1141	IF(D1141>D1142,1,0)	
1142	President B		0	B1140/C1142		IF(D1142>D1141,1,0)
1143	380	C1144+C1145				
1144	President A		0	B1143/C1144	IF(D1144>D1145,1,0)	
1145	President B		0	B1143/C1145		IF(D1145>D1144,1,0)
1146	381	C1147+C1148				
1147	President A		0	B1146/C1147	IF(D1147>D1148,1,0)	
1148	President B		0	B1146/C1148		IF(D1148>D1147,1,0)
1149	382	C1150+C1151				
1150	President A		0	B1149/C1150	IF(D1150>D1151,1,0)	
1151	President B		0	B1149/C1151		IF(D1151>D1150,1,0)
1152	383	C1153+C1154				
1153	President A		0	B1152/C1153	IF(D1153>D1154,1,0)	
1154	President B		0	B1152/C1154		IF(D1154>D1153,1,0)
1155	384	C1156+C1157				
1156	President A		0	B1155/C1156	IF(D1156>D1157,1,0)	
1157	President B		0	B1155/C1157		IF(D1157>D1156,1,0)
1158	385	C1159+C1160				
1159	President A		0	B1158/C1159	IF(D1159>D1160,1,0)	
1160	President B		0	B1158/C1160		IF(D1160>D1159,1,0)
1161	386	C1162+C1163				
1162	President A		0	B1161/C1162	IF(D1162>D1163,1,0)	
1163	President B		0	B1161/C1163		IF(D1163>D1162,1,0)
1164	387	C1165+C1166				
1165	President A		0	B1164/C1165	IF(D1165>D1166,1,0)	
1166	President B		0	B1164/C1166		IF(D1166>D1165,1,0)
1167	388	C1168+C1169				
1168	President A		0	B1167/C1168	IF(D1168>D1169,1,0)	
1169	President B		0	B1167/C1169		IF(D1169>D1168,1,0)
1170	389	C1171+C1172				
1171	President A		0	B1170/C1171	IF(D1171>D1172,1,0)	
1172	President B		0	B1170/C1172		IF(D1172>D1171,1,0)
1173	390	C1174+C1175				
1174	President A		0	B1173/C1174	IF(D1174>D1175,1,0)	
1175	President B		0	B1173/C1175		IF(D1175>D1174,1,0)
1176	391	C1177+C1178				
1177	President A		0	B1176/C1177	IF(D1177>D1178,1,0)	
1178	President B		0	B1176/C1178		IF(D1178>D1177,1,0)
1179	392	C1180+C1181				

323

	A	B	C	D	E	F
1180	President A		0	B1179/C1180	IF(D1180>D1181,1,0)	
1181	President B		0	B1179/C1181		IF(D1181>D1180,1,0)
1182	393	C1183+C1184				
1183	President A		0	B1182/C1183	IF(D1183>D1184,1,0)	
1184	President B		0	B1182/C1184		IF(D1184>D1183,1,0)
1185	394	C1186+C1187				
1186	President A		0	B1185/C1186	IF(D1186>D1187,1,0)	
1187	President B		0	B1185/C1187		IF(D1187>D1186,1,0)
1188	395	C1189+C1190				
1189	President A		0	B1188/C1189	IF(D1189>D1190,1,0)	
1190	President B		0	B1188/C1190		IF(D1190>D1189,1,0)
1191	396	C1192+C1193				
1192	President A		0	B1191/C1192	IF(D1192>D1193,1,0)	
1193	President B		0	B1191/C1193		IF(D1193>D1192,1,0)
1194	397	C1195+C1196				
1195	President A		0	B1194/C1195	IF(D1195>D1196,1,0)	
1196	President B		0	B1194/C1196		IF(D1196>D1195,1,0)
1197	398	C1198+C1199				
1198	President A		0	B1197/C1198	IF(D1198>D1199,1,0)	
1199	President B		0	B1197/C1199		IF(D1199>D1198,1,0)
1200	399	C1201+C1202				
1201	President A		0	B1200/C1201	IF(D1201>D1202,1,0)	
1202	President B		0	B1200/C1202		IF(D1202>D1201,1,0)
1203	400	C1204+C1205				
1204	President A		0	B1203/C1204	IF(D1204>D1205,1,0)	
1205	President B		0	B1203/C1205		IF(D1205>D1204,1,0)
1206	Total		SUM(C7:C1205)		F1207/A1203*E1204	E3/A1203*F1205
1207	Total					

The demonstrated spreadsheet is designed for the United States presidential election campaign. The state government assemblies' districts are the base districts that will eliminate mob rule. Going from state government United States House of Representatives to the state government assemblies' districts, the state government districts become the representative vote in the election.

Since the number of state government assemblies' districts is greater than the state government United States House Representatives' districts, the population of a state government's quasi-equal population district is less than the population of a state government United States House of Representatives' quasi-equal population district. Since there are less people in the assemblies' districts, the accuracy of district representative voting increases to extent that mob rule practically disappears.

The percentage calculations are to be done using double-precision floating point arithmetic to eliminate roundoff error in the computer's operation of performing addition, multiplication, and especially division. A double-precision floating number contains sixty-four digits, replacing the existing eight-digit integer arithmetic, which uses winner takes all that encourages mob rule. Using percentages to calculate the electoral vote eliminates the situation where the winner doesn't win the popular vote.

Input state government's electoral number. Fill in the number of votes cast for each candidate in each district. There can be several candidates. For example, a person is needed to input the election results and work the spreadsheet.

Using the spreadsheet's displayed instructions as a flowchart, a programmer can write a computer program for a computer that will tabulate and count the votes as the voter goes through the act of voting. The computer technology already exists where a computer is used to process a vote being cast at polling stations.

At the end of the vote-casting day, the computer automatically delivers the candidates' sums of electoral votes or the winner of the presidential races. Utilizing a spreadsheet or computer-programmed instruction, no living human been can be as accurate as a computer. The old days of using integer arithmetic to calculate is out of sync with moon landings and cell phones.

TENTH AMENDMENT

The Tenth Amendment states that the powers allowed by the Constitution to the states are reserved for the people.

The following violates the Tenth Amendment:

- Referendums

- "Winner takes all"

- Rid of 60%–40% voting

Construct Quasi-Equal Populated Districts

- State government assemblies' districts

- State government Senates' districts

- United States House of Representatives' districts

- States government counties' districts

- State government cities' districts

- States government towns' districts

Republic Form of Governments

- State government republic

- County republic

- City republic

- Town republic

Initial People's Constitutional Powers

- State government assemblies' quasi-equal populated districts

- State government Senate's quasi-equal populated districts

- United States House of Representatives' quasi-equal populated districts

- State government counties' quasi-equal populated districts

- State government cities' quasi-equal populated districts

- State government towns' quasi-equal populated districts

- Bottom-Up Representation Mode Starts At

- State government assemblies' quasi-equal populated districts

- State government Senate's quasi-equal populated districts

- United States House of Representatives' quasi-equal populated districts

- States government counties' quasi-equal populated districts

- State government cities' quasi-equal populated districts

- States government towns' quasi-equal populated districts

Election of the President

United States House of Representatives' quasi-equal populated districts (*initial people's Constitutional powers*) plus District of Columbia elects the president to avoid winner takes all, which violates the Tenth Amendment. A mesh of 436 districts across the United

States elects the president, not 50 states. In case of a tie vote, the United States House of Representatives gets to pick the president.

Otherwise, double-precision decimal arithmetic must be used instead of winner takes all to be acceptable to the Tenth Amendment, which brings the election of the president back to the United States House of Representatives instead of the states where it doesn't belong for 537 electoral votes.

Choosing Electors

State government legislatures represent state government assemblies' and state government Senate's quasi-equal populated districts that have *initial people's Constitutional powers*. The state government legislatures must choose the electors, not a statewide governmental referendum, which violates the Tenth Amendment.

A Republic Way of Electing States Governors

Use state government assemblies' quasi-equal populated districts instead of a statewide referendum to avoid mob rule. In case of a tie, vote goes to the popular vote.

A Republic Way of Electing County Executives

Use counties' quasi-equal populated districts instead of a county-wide referendum to avoid mob rule. In case of a tie, vote goes to the popular vote.

A Republic Way of Electing City Mayors

Use cities' quasi-equal populated districts instead of a citywide referendum to avoid mob rule. In case of a tie, vote goes to the popular vote.

A Republic Way of Electing Town Mayors

Use towns' quasi-equal populated districts instead of a townwide referendum to avoid mob rule. In case of a tie, vote goes to the popular vote.

Secret society groups influence United States president (mob rule).

THE COUNCIL ON FOREIGN RELATIONS (CFR)

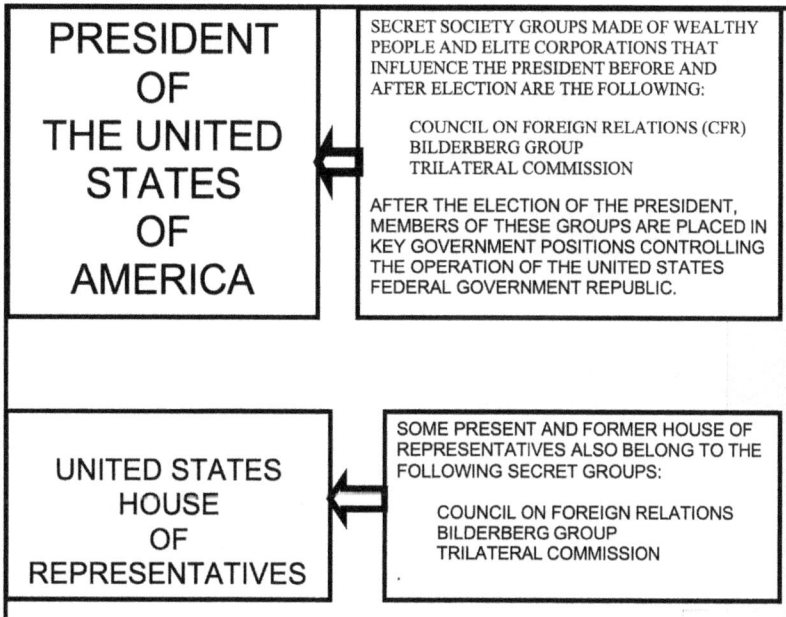

PRESIDENT OF THE UNITED STATES OF AMERICA	SECRET SOCIETY GROUPS MADE OF WEALTHY PEOPLE AND ELITE CORPORATIONS THAT INFLUENCE THE PRESIDENT BEFORE AND AFTER ELECTION ARE THE FOLLOWING: COUNCIL ON FOREIGN RELATIONS (CFR) BILDERBERG GROUP TRILATERAL COMMISSION AFTER THE ELECTION OF THE PRESIDENT, MEMBERS OF THESE GROUPS ARE PLACED IN KEY GOVERNMENT POSITIONS CONTROLLING THE OPERATION OF THE UNITED STATES FEDERAL GOVERNMENT REPUBLIC.
UNITED STATES HOUSE OF REPRESENTATIVES	SOME PRESENT AND FORMER HOUSE OF REPRESENTATIVES ALSO BELONG TO THE FOLLOWING SECRET GROUPS: COUNCIL ON FOREIGN RELATIONS BILDERBERG GROUP TRILATERAL COMMISSION

Council on Foreign Relations Members in Special Group

Agencies Controlled by 100+ Council on Foreign Relations Members who are part of the SPECIAL GROUP. The SECRET TEAM are the rest of the 3000+ CFR members and the members of their branch organizations in other nations.

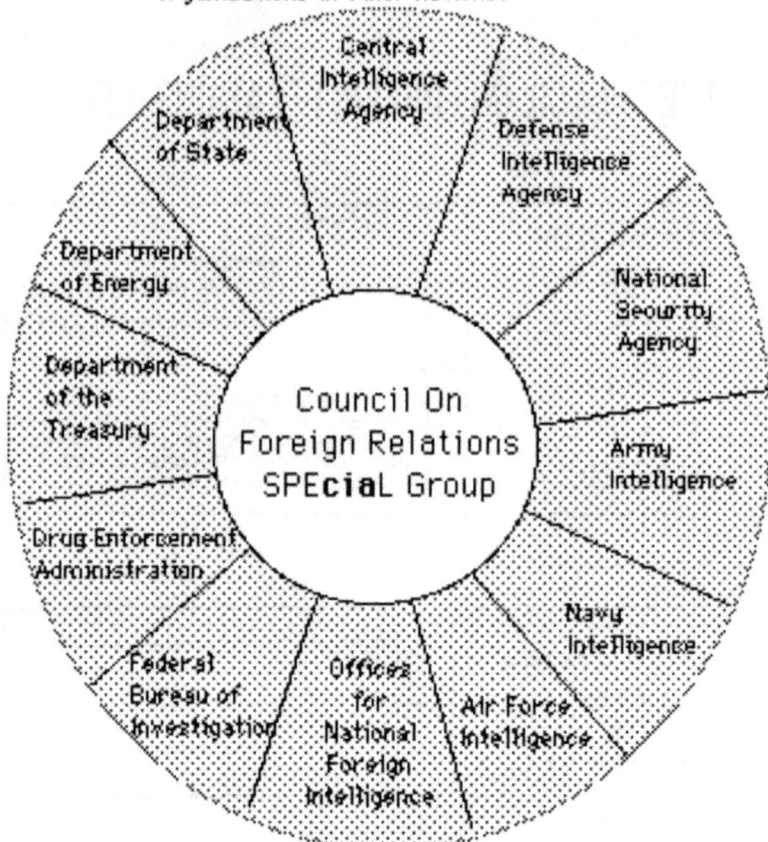

The Council on Foreign Relations is a branch of an international group of coconspirators called the Round Table Group.

Council on Foreign Relations members control both government agency and "private industry" news sources. Round Table Group members in different nations control the news sources in their countries. The Council on Foreign Relations propaganda machine manipulates American citizens to accept the particular climate of opinion the Round Table Groups are seeking to achieve in the world. Council on Foreign Relations members working in an ad hoc committee called the Special Group, through a vast intragovernmental undercover infrastructure called the Secret Team, formulate this opinion in the United States.

Other branches include Britain's Royal Institute of International Affairs, the Canadian Institute of International Affairs, the New Zealand Institute of International Affairs, the Australian Institute of International Affairs, the South African Institute of International Affairs, the Indian Institute of International Affairs, the Netherlands Institute of International Affairs, the Japanese Institute of Pacific Relations, the Chinese Institute of Pacific Relations, and the Russian Institute of Pacific Relations.

The Joint Chiefs of Staff have defined psychological operations (PSYOPS) as those that "include psychological warfare and, in addition, encompass those political, military, economic and ideological actions planned and conducted to create in neutral or friendly foreign groups the emotions, attitudes, or behavior to support achievement of national objectives. Another proposal develops the concept of 'strategic psychological operations' as aimed at influencing and shaping decision-makers' power to govern or control their followers."

Wake up, America. We, the American people, are among the groups being targeted and controlled.

Council on Foreign Relations members in the State Department, the National Security Council, the Central Intelligence Agency, and in the Department of Defense continue to control the lives of the American people through well-planned psychopolitical operations. These psychological operations rob American citizens of the present by creating false-reality worlds. These false-reality worlds are created to trick the American public into acting not in their own best interest but in the best interest of a group of subtle fascists intent on creating one world order under their control.

COUNCIL ON FOREIGN RELATIONS

Special Group and Secret Team Members in Government

Presidential Candidates

- Bill Clinton ('96, '92)

- Reubin Askew ('84)

- Alan Cranston('84)

- John Glenn ('84)

- Walter Mondale ('84)

- John Anderson ('80)

- Howard Baker ('80)

- George Bush ('80)

- Jimmy Carter ('80)

- Dwight Eisenhower ('80)

- Adlai Stevenson III ('80)

Department of State Members (1995)

- Secretary of State Warren Christopher

- Deputy Secretary Cliff R. Wharton Jr.

- Undersecretary of State for Political Affairs Peter Tarnoff

- Undersecretary of State for Management Richard M. Moose

- Undersecretary of State for Democracy and Global Affairs Tim Wirth

- Assistant Secretary, East Asian Pacific Affairs Winston Lord (Pres. and Rep.)

- Assistant Secretary, Europe Canadian Affairs Stephen Oxman

- Assistant Secretary of State for Intelligence and Research Toby Trister Gati

- Assistant Secretary Inter-American Affairs Alexander F. Watson

CIA Directors Members

- Richard Helms ('66–'73, Johnson)

- James R. Schlesinger ('73, Nixon)

- William E. Colby ('73–'76, Nixon)

- George Bush ('76–'77, Ford)

- Adm. Stansfield Turner ('77–'81, Carter)

- William J. Casey ('81–'87, Reagan)

- William H. Webster ('87–'91, Reagan)

- Robert M. Gates ('91–'93, Bush)

- Robert James Woolsey ('93, Clinton)

- John Deutch, chosen to replace Woolsey as CIA Director

Department of the Treasury
(Past and Present Partial Listing)

- Donald Regan

- John Helmann

- Lord William Simon

- Michael Blumenthal

- C. Fred Bergsten

- Anthony M. Solomon

- Arnold Nachmanoff

- Helen B. Junz

- Richard Fisher

- Roger Altman

- George Pratt Shultz

Union Presidents

- I. W. Abel (United Steelworkers)

- Sol Chick Chaikin (Pres., Ladies Garment Workers)

- Tom R. Donahue (Sec./Treas., AFL/CIO)

- Murray H. Finley (Pres., Amal Clothing Textile Workers)

- Victor Gautbaum (Amer. Fed. of State County Muni Employees)

- Lane Kirkland (Pres., AFL/CIO)

- H. D. Samuel (Pres, Ind. Union Dept. AFL/CIO)

- M. J. Ward (Pres., U. Ass. Plumbing Pipe)

- Glenn E. Watts (Pres., Comm. Workers of Amer.)

- Len Woodcock (Pres., UAW)

- Jerry Wurf (Pres., Amer. F. County. and Muni. Emp.)

Presidents Commission Executive Exchange

- David Rockefeller

- Willard Butcher (Pres., Chase Manhattan Bank)

- Thorton Bradshaw (Pres., Atlantic Richfield)

- John McKinley (Pres., Texico)

- Ruben Mettler (Pres., TRW)

- John Whitehead (Goldman Sachs)

- Marina N. Whitman (GM Corp)

CFR Secret Team Members in the Military (Partial List)
Allied Supreme Command

- '49–'52, Eisenhower

- '52–'53, Ridgeway

- '53–'56, Gruenther

- '56–'63, Norstad

- '63–'69, Lemnitzer

- '69–'74, Good Paster

- '80, Rogers

Secretaries of Defense

- '57–'59, McElroy

- '59–'61, Gates

- '61–'68, McNamara

- '69–'73, Laird

- '73, Richardson

- '77, Rumsfield

- '77, Brown

- '80, Weinberger

- '87–'89, Frank Carlucci

- '93–'95, Les Aspin

Deputy Secretary of Defense

- Frank Carlucci

- John Deutch

Undersecretary of Defense

- Fred Ikel

- Gen. Stillwell

- Frank Wisner

Assistant Secretary of Defense

- Lawrence Korb

Military Fellows

- Air Force Col. K. Baker

- Air Force Col. E. Foote

- Air Force Maj. Gen. R. Ginsburgh

- Air Force Col. R. Head

- Air Force Brig. Gen. T. Julian

- Air Force Col. I. Klette

- Air Force Lt. Col. J. Levy

- Air Force Lt. Gen. G. Loving

- Air Force Col. M. McPeak

- Air Force Lt. Gen. J. Pfautz

- Air Force Col. L. Pfeiffer

- Air Force Col. M. Sanders

- Air Force Col. F. Thayer

- Air Force Maj. Gen. W. Usher

- Air Force Col. J. Wolcott

- Air Force Col. T. Eggers

- Army Maj. Gen. J. Thompson

- Army Maj. Gen. T. Ayers

- Army Lt. Gen. S. Berry Jr.

- Army Capt. Dewienter

- Army Col. A. Dewey

- Army Lt. Gen. R. Gard

- Army Brig. Gen. M. Green

- Army Col. G. Loeftke

- Army Col. J. Sewall

- Army Gen. S. Walker

- Navy Rad. R. Welander
- Navy Rear Adm. C. Tesh
- Navy Capt. H Fiske
- Navy Capt. W. Kerr
- Navy Capt. R. Kurth
- Navy Capt. R. Miale
- Navy Capt. S. Ring
- Navy Capt. Gentry

Superintendents, United States Military West Point

- '60–'63, Westmoreland
- '63–'66, Lampert
- '66–'68, Bennett
- '70–'74, Knowlton
- '74–'77, Berry Jr.
- '77, Goodpaster

President, National Defense University

- Lt. Gen. Robert Gard, Jr.

Secretary of Navy

- John Lehman Jr.

Chief of Staff, Army

- Gen. J. Wickham

Joint Chief of Staff

- Gen. David Jones
- Vice Adm. Thor Hanson
- Lt. Gen. Paul Gorman
- Maj. Gen. R. C. Bowman
- Brig. Gen. F. Brown
- Lt. Col. W. Clark
- Capt. Ralph Crosby
- Adm. Wm. Crowe
- Col. P. Dawkins
- Vice Adm. Thor Hanson
- Col. W. Hauser
- Col. B. Hosmer
- Maj. R. Kimmitt
- Capt. F. Klotz
- Gen. W. Knowlton
- Vice Adm. J. Lee
- Capt. T. Lupter
- Col. D. Mead
- Maj. Gen. Jack Merritt
- Gen. E. Meyer
- Col. Wm. E. Odom
- Col. L. Olvey

- Col. Geo. K. Osborn

- Maj. Gen. J. Pustuay

- Capt. P. A. Putignano

- Lt. Gen. E. L. Rowny

- Capt. Gary Sick

- Maj. Gen. J. Siegal

- Maj. Gen. Dewitt Smith

- Brig. Gen. Perry Smith

- Col. W. Taylor

- Maj. Gen. J. N. Thompson

- Rear Adm. C. A. H. Trost

- Adm. S. Turner

- Maj. Gen. J. Welch

THE PSYCHOLOGICAL STRATEGY BOARD, AKA THE OPERATIONS COORDINATION BOARD, AKA THE SPECIAL GROUP

On June 20, 1951, Harry S. Truman signed a directive establishing the Psychological Strategy Board. The directive read,

> Directive to: the Secretary of State, The Secretary of Defense, The Director of Central Intelligence: It is the purpose of this directive to authorize and provide for the more effective planning, coordination and conduct, within the framework of approved national policies, of psychological operations. There is hereby established a Psychological Strategy Board responsible, within the purposes and terms of this directive, for the formulation and promulgation, as guidance to the departments and agencies responsible for psychological operations, of over-all national psychological

objectives, policies and programs, and for the coordination and evaluation of the national psychological effort.

The Board will report to the National Security Council on the Board's activities and on its evaluation of the national psychological operations, including implementation of approved objectives, policies, and programs by the departments and agencies concerned. The Board shall be composed of:

a. The Undersecretary of State, the Deputy Secretary of Defense, and the Director of Central Intelligence, or, in their absence, their appropriate designees;

b. An appropriate representative of the head of each such other department or agency of the Government as may, from time to time, be determined by the Board. The Board shall designate one of its members as Chairman. A representative of the Joint Chiefs of Staff shall sit with the Board as its principal military adviser in order that the Board may ensure that its objectives, policies and programs shall be related to approved plans for military operations.

The director and architect of the Psychological Strategy Board was Gordon Gray. Henry Kissinger was Gray's consultant. Kissinger was also the paid political consultant to the Rockefeller family. Gray, Kissinger, and Rockefeller were members of the Council on Foreign Relations. Gray served in the administrations of Truman, Eisenhower, Kennedy, Johnson, Nixon, and Ford. Gordon Gray was heir to the R. J. Reynolds tobacco fortune and president of the University of North Carolina. Gray was a broadcast and publication media specialist. Gray was instrumental in keeping the uniformed electorate uninformed by.

Eisenhower signed Presidential Executive Order 10483, replacing the Psychological Strategy board with the Operations Coordinating Board. The Operations Coordinating Board was composed of the following:

- The Undersecretary of State, who shall represent the Secretary of State and shall be the chairman of the board

- The Deputy Secretary of Defense, who shall represent the Secretary of Defense

- The Director of the Foreign Operations Administration

- The Director of Central Intelligence

- A representative of the president to be designated by the president

- The undersecretary or corresponding official of any presidential agency that has been assigned responsibilities for implementation of national security policy

- The special assistant to the president for National Security Affairs

- The director of the United States Information Agency

On 19 February 1961, President John F. Kennedy issued a Statement abolishing the Operations Coordinating Board.

No president ever wrote or signed an executive order establishing the Special Group. No president had a way of abolishing the Special Group. The Special Group was not established by executive order; it established itself. This was no accident. This was illegal. When Kennedy killed the Operations Coordinating Board, the Special Group operated as normal without the designated presidential representative.

The Special Group is alive and well today.

It consists of the Secretary of State, the Secretary of Defense, and the Director of the CIA—none of which are elected officials.

The only way to abolish this ad hoc committee is to abolish the Department of Defense, the Central Intelligence Agency, and the Department of State.

President Clinton, Secretary of State Warren Christopher, and Director of the CIA John Deutch and his predecessor James Woolsey belong to the Council on Foreign Relations. Les Aspin, Secretary of Defense William Perry's predecessor, also belonged to the Council on Foreign Relations.

The Joint Chiefs of Staff have defined psychological operations as those that include psychological warfare and, in addition, encompass those political, military, economic, and ideological actions planned and conducted to create in neutral or friendly foreign groups the emotions, attitudes, or behavior to support achievement of national objectives. Another proposal develops the concept of strategic psychological operations as aimed at influencing and shaping decision-makers the power to govern or control their followers.

CFR SECRET TEAM MEMBERS IN THE MEDIA

(Partial List, Past and Present)

CBS

- William Paley

- William Burden

- Roswell Gilpatric

- Henry Schact

- Manetta Tree
- C. C. Collingwood
- Lawrence LeSuer
- Dan Rather
- Harry Reasoner
- Richard Hottelet
- Frank Stanton
- Bill Moyers

NBC/RCA

- Jane Pfeiffer
- Lester Crystal
- R. W. Sonnenfeldt
- T. F. Bradshaw
- John Petty
- David Brinkley
- John Chancellor
- Marvin Kalb
- Irvine Levine
- P. G. Peterson
- John Sawhill

abc

- Ray Adam

- Frank Cary
- T. M. Macioce
- Ted Koppel
- John Scali
- Barbara Walters

Cable News Network

- Daniel Schorr

Public Broadcast Service

- Hartford Gunn
- Robert McNeil
- Jim Lehrer
- C. Hunter-Gault
- Hodding Carter III

Associated Press

- Keith Fuller
- Stanley Swinton
- Louis Boccardi
- Harold Anderson
- UPI
- H. L. Stevenson

Reuters

- Michael Posner

Boston Globe

- David Rogers

A. Times Syndicate

- Tom Johnson

- Joseph Kraft

Los Angeles Times Mirror

- Richard W. Murphy

- Charles A. Kupchan

- Michael Clough

- Zygmunt Nagorski

- Nancy Bodurtha

- Richard T. Childress

- Carl W. Ford Jr.

- Nomsa Daniels

- Alton Frye

- Gregory F. Treverton

Newsday

- Jessica Mathew

- Michael Mandelbaum

- Richard N. Haass

- Richard W. Murphy

- John L. Hirsch

- Alexander J. Motyl

- Nicholas X. Rizopoulos

- Alan D. Romberg

- C. V. Starr

- Gidion Gottlieb

- Charles A. Kupchan

Baltimore Sun

- Henry Trewhitt

Chicago Sun Times

- James Hoge

Minneapolis Starr/Tribune

- John Cowles Jr.

Houston Post

- William P. Hobby

New York Times Co.

- Richard Gelb

- James Reston

- William Scranton

- A. M. Rosenthal

- Seymour Topping

- James Greenfield

- Max Frankel

- Jack Rosenthal
- Harding Bancroft
- Amory Bradford
- Orvil Dryfoos
- David Halberstram
- Walter Lippmann
- L. E. Markel
- H. L. Matthews
- John Oakes
- Harrison Salisbury
- A. Hays Sulzberger
- A. Ochs Sulzberger
- C. L. Sulzberger
- H. L. Smith
- Steven Rattner
- Richard Burt

Time Inc.

- Ralph Davidson
- Donald M. Wilson
- Louis Banks
- Henry Grunwald
- Alexander Herard

- Sol Lionwitz

- Rawleigh Warner Jr.

- Thomas Watson Jr.

Newsweek/Washington Post

- Katherine Graham

- Philip Graham

- Arjay Miller

- TCN. deB. Katzenbach

- Frederick Beebe

- Robert Christopher

- A. De Borchgrave

- Osborne Elliot

- Phillipo Geyelin

- Kermit Lausner

- Murry Marder

- Eugene Meyer

- Malcolm Muir

- Maynard Parker

- George Will

- Robert Kaiser

- Meg Greenfield

- Walter Pincus

- Murray Gart

- Peter Osnos

- Don Oberdorfer

Dow Jones Co. (Wall Street Journal)

- William Agee

- J. Paul Austin

- T. C. Charles Meyer

- Robert Potter

- Richard Wood

- Robert Bartley

- Karen House

National Review

- Wm. F. Buckley Jr.

- Richard Brookhiser

The late Carroll Quigley, professor of history at Georgetown University, member of the CFR, stated in his book *Tragedy and Hope: A History of the World in Our Time*, "The CFR is the American Branch of a society which originated in England, and which believes that national boundaries should be obliterated, and a one-world rule established."

In 1921, Edward Mandell House, who had been the chief advisor of President Woodrow Wilson, founded the CFR. House was a Marxist, and his goal was to socialize the United States.

In 1912, House wrote the book *Philip Dru: Administrator* and mentioned that "socialism as dreamed of by Karl Marx. Using his book, House planned for the conquest of America. Both Democratic and

Republican parties would be controlled and utilized as instruments in the creation of a socialistic government.

House asked for the establishment of a United States–controlled central bank. The Federal Reserve Act was passed. A private central bank was brought into power to create United States money taking away power from the federal government.

As Karl Marx proposed, the Sixteenth Amendment (the graduated income tax) to the United States Constitution was also ratified.

In 1921, House formed the CFR, whose result would destroy the freedom and independence of the United States and lead the country toward one world government.

The CFR began to attract men of power and influence. In the late 1920s, the Rockefeller Foundation (taxpayer money) and the Carnegie Foundation (taxpayer money) financed the CFR.

In 1940, CFR members gained domination over the state department at the invitation of President Roosevelt. CFR members have maintained this domination to date.

Dan Smoot's *The Invisible Government* notes that the "crowning moment of achievement for the CFR came at San Francisco in 1945, when over forty members of the United States Delegation to the organizational meeting of the United Nations…were members of the CFR."

In his book *With No Apologies* (1979), Senator Barry Goldwater writes, "The CFR is the American branch of a society which originated in England. Internationalist in viewpoint, the CFR., along with the Atlantic Union Movement, and the Atlantic Council of the U.S., believes national boundaries should be obliterated."

Changing Presidents Does Not Mean Changing Administrations

Changing presidents means changing administrations, but, however, CFR members who had been held in office during the election of both Republican and Democratic presidents whom the people of the United States elected to office have controlled the operation of the executive branch of the United States government from 1945 to the present day. The United States government's strategies have been under the control of CFR members whom both Republican and Democratic presidents have placed in key presidential advisory positions under the pressure of the CFR, who supported their elections. As an example, Nixon placed Henry Kissinger, a CFR member and Nelson Rockefeller protégé, in charge of foreign policy. After his election, Jimmy Carter replaced Kissinger with Zbigniew Brzezinski, who was a CFR member and also a David Rockefeller protégé. Irregardless of different administration changes, CFR member were at times carried over to the next administration while new CFR members were added to guide the latest elected president who the people elected to carry on a supposedly new administration's policy.

CFR Intentions

Rear Admiral Chester Ward, a former member of the CFR for sixteen years, warned the American people of the organization's intentions: "The most powerful clique in these elitist groups have one objective in common—they want to bring about the surrender of the sovereignty of the national independence of the United States. A second clique of international members in the CFR comprises the Wall Street international bankers and their key agents. Primarily, they want the world banking monopoly from whatever power ends up in the control of global government."

Dan Smoot, a former member of the FBI headquarters staff in Washington, DC, summarized the organization's purpose: "The ultimate aim of the CFR is to create a one-world socialist system, and to make the US an official part of it."

In other words, the CFR's treasonous activities to the United States Constitution puts an end to the United States of America making the country a part of their global government scheme.

CFR Members

In 1944 and in 1948, Thomas Dewey, the Republican candidate for president, was a CFR member.

In later years, CFR membership included Republicans Eisenhower and Nixon, as were Democrats Stevenson, Kennedy, Humphrey, and McGovern.

Published in 1978, CFR's annual reports listed a membership of 1,878 members. Eleven of CFR's members' names were United States senators' names, and moreover, the CFR members' names list contained more United States House of Congressmen's names than United States senators' names. The CFR members' names list contained 284 United States government officials. The Chairman of the Board at the time of this impressive CFR members' names list was none other than David Rockefeller himself.

Jack Newell states that "its members have run, or are running, NBC and CBS, *The New York Times*, *The Washington Post*, *The Des Moines Register*, and many other important newspapers. The leaders of *Time*, *Newsweek*, *Fortune*, *Business Week*, and numerous other publications are CFR members. The organization's members also dominate the academic world, top corporations, the huge tax-exempt foundations, labor unions, the military, and just about every segment of American life."

Jack Newell continues to write, "Not every member of the CFR is fully committed to carrying out Edward Mandell House's conspiratorial plan. Many have been flattered by an invitation to join a study group, which is what the CFR calls itself. Others go along because of personal benefits, such as a nice job and a new importance. But all are used to promote the destruction of US sovereignty."

The CFR membership dominates almost every aspect of American life. Most Americans have never even heard of the CFR. A reason is that over 170 journalists, correspondents and communications executives are members of the CFR, and they do not mention the CFR organization in their written words. Also, an express condition of membership is not to disclose CFR meetings' minutes.

CFR Influence

The American people are led to believe that they pick the presidential candidates of the United States; however, CFR members make the choice, with exceptions of the few. For decades, CFR members have been choosing presidential candidates.

Jack Newell and Devvy Kidd wrote *Why a Bankrupt America?* (Project Liberty, PO Box 741075, Arvada, CO 80006-9075).

Barry Goldwater states in his book *With No Apologies* on page 231, "Does it not seem strange to you that these men just happened to be CFR and just happened to be on the Board of Governors of the Federal Reserve, that absolutely controls the money and interest rates of this great country without benefit of Congress? A privately owned organization, the Federal Reserve, which has absolutely nothing to do with the United States of America!"

Aspects of American Life Is Dominated

Congressmen John R. Rarick had warned, "The CFR, dedicated to one-world government, financed by a number of the largest tax-exempt foundations, and wielding such power and influence over our lives in the areas of finance, business, labor, military, education, and mass communication-media, should be familiar to every American concerned with good government, and with preserving and defending the U.S. Constitution and our free-enterprise system. Yet, the nation's right-to-know machinery, the news media, usually so aggressive in exposures to inform our people, remain conspicuously silent when it comes to the CFR, its members and their activities.

"The CFR is the establishment. Not only does it have influence and power in key decision-making positions at the highest levels of government to apply pressure from above, but it also finances and uses individuals and groups to bring pressure from below, to justify the high level decisions for converting the U.S. from a sovereign Constitution Republic into a servile member of a one-world dictatorship."

To create a one-world government is the main goal of the CFR's function resulting in destroying the freedom and independence of all nations, especially including the United States complements of David Rockefeller, who continues to be the chairman of the board.

CFR Effects

The common everyday American citizen does not need to be told that there is a controlled government running the United States. But when we understand exactly what the CFR is and how its members hold key positions in the government, it becomes all the more clear.

Jack Newell writes, "The real goal of our own Government's leaders is to make the United States into a carbon copy of a Communist state, and then to merge all nations into a one-world system run by a powerful few."

The key to obtain our freedom, to have true independence, is to free ourselves from the yoke of international finance. How true it is to state that those who control the money of a country control everything in that country.

Every citizen of the United States should become informed about the CFR organization and make it a point not to vote nor to promote those who are members. Every citizen of the United States should demand a reform of the financial laws of the country, especially to repeal the Federal Reserve Act of 1913.

Since 1952, almost every person elected to the office of president of the United States and nearly every opponent also has belonged to this secretive global-oriented organization known as CFR.

http://www.thenewamerican.com/node/3193

"Link unavailable. Please use your discretion and explore current sources to learn more."

Behind the bias

By: william norman grigg
february 10, 2003

David Rockefeller

"We are grateful to the Washington Post, the New York Times, Time magazine, and other great publications whose directors have attended our meetings and respected their promises of discretion for almost forty years."

The speaker was David Rockefeller, the "Chairman of the Establishment." The scene was the June 5, 1991, Bilderberg meeting in Sand, Germany—an ultra-elite conclave of banking, political, media, and industrial elites committed to world government. The subject of this particular address was the media's role in promoting the power elite's objectives.

"It would have been impossible for us to develop our plan for the world if we had been subject to the bright lights of publicity during these years," continued Rockefeller. "But the world is now more sophisticated and prepared to march towards a world government which will never again know war but only peace and prosperity for the whole of humanity."

The way in which Rockefeller's remarks were made public ironically illustrates the power of the elite's chokehold on the mass media. Excerpts from Rockefeller's opening address were leaked to two independent French publications. They then came to the attention of Hilaire du Berrier, an international correspondent living in Monaco, who published them in his newsletter, *HduB Reports*. As he relayed Rockefeller's breathtakingly brazen admissions to his readers, du Berrier knowingly commented that he would "lay odds that not a word of Mr. Rockefeller's speech will be reported in America." As far as the major media are concerned, du Berrier's prediction came true.

Nonsense, you say? "The power elite would never conspire to consolidate economic and political power on a global scale." Many Europeans reacted in a similar way when they heard certain "alarmists" outside their mainstream media claim that elitists among them had created the Common Market for the purpose of gradually building it into a government of Europe. Now that the Common Market has become the EU through a series of steps and the EU has begun sapping political and economic powers from once-sovereign European nations, a power grab once dismissed as preposterous is widely recognized as fact. But that power grab could not have succeeded without the complicity of the media moguls on both sides of the Atlantic, who portrayed earlier manifestations of the EU as a "free trade" agreement, thereby providing protective coloration for their counterparts in the political elite.

Thomas Jefferson once famously remarked that it is better to have a newspaper without a government than a government without a newspaper. The free press in whatever manifestation—from Revolutionary-era broadsides to "streaming video" and "blogs" on the Internet—plays an indispensable role in holding government accountable to the public. But the media cannot perform this duty if it is itself part of the ruling establishment—the self-appointed elitists like Rockefeller who busy themselves planning the future, supposedly on behalf of "the whole of humanity."

The Globalist Elite Control the Media

The Morgan interests figured prominently in the "international Anglophile network" identified by the late Georgetown University historian Carroll Quigley as the spine of the global power elite.

Quigley was more than just another tweedy academic. From his position at Georgetown, he played a key role in mentoring many individuals who went on to occupy critical positions.

Among his students was Bill Clinton, who paid homage to Quigley in his acceptance speech at the 1992 Democratic Convention.

In his 1966 work *Tragedy and Hope*, Quigley—after writing disdainfully of "conspiracy theorists"—admitted the existence of a partially submerged elite that "operates, to some extent, in the way the radical Right believes the Communists act.

In fact, this network, which we may identify as the Round Table Groups, has no aversion to cooperating with the Communists, or any other groups, and frequently does so.

I know of the operations of this network because I have studied it for twenty years and was permitted for two years, in the early 1960s, to examine its papers and secret records.

I have no aversion to it or to most of its aims and have, for much of my life, been close to it and many of its instruments."

The network's "aim," Quigley continued, is "nothing less than to create a world system of financial control in private hands able to dominate the political system of each country and the economy of the world as a whole."

The Round Table Groups stemmed from a secret society (Quigley's phrase) created by British magnate Cecil Rhodes to unite the world—beginning with the English-speaking dominions—under "enlightened" elitists like himself.

World War I and the post-war proposal for a League of Nations resulted from the Round Table cabal's machinations.

During the post-war Versailles Peace Conference, noted Quigley, this covert network decided to establish "in England and in each dominion, a front organization to the existing Round Table Group.

This front organization, called the Royal Institute of International Affairs, had as its nucleus in each area the existing submerged Round Table Group.

In New York it was known as the Council on Foreign Relations."

The Council on Foreign Relations (CFR) boasts a membership of only about four thousand. But its roster includes literally hundreds of powerful figures occupying key positions in the media—not merely writers, reporters, and news anchors who deliver the news, but also editors, publishers, and executives who define what news is and how it is covered.

(See "CFR Elitists Pulling the Strings" for a partial list of CFR members in the media.)

Just as significantly, the tiny CFR clique has, for decades, had a virtual stranglehold on the executive branch of the US government as well as much of academe.

Voice of the Ruling Class

Carroll Quigley—like David Rockefeller—specifically identified the *New York Times* and the *Washington Post* as key media organs of the power elite.

The *Times*, with utterly unwarranted self-assurance, designates itself the arbiter of "All the News That's Fit to Print" while the *Post* is the voice of official Washington.

Even in the cyber age, these two hoary papers (both of which are longtime CFR redoubts) set the tone for most news coverage, defining issues and setting the limits of "respectable" opinion.

But the CFR's chokehold on media influence extends well beyond the Manhattan-Washington corridor.

In his October 30, 1993, "Ruling Class Journalists" essay, *Washington Post* ombudsman Richard Harwood candidly remarked about how the CFR dominates our news media.

Harwood described the council as "the closest thing we have to a ruling establishment in the United States....[Its members are] the people who, for more than half a century, have managed our international affairs and our military-industrial complex."

After listing the executive branch positions then occupied by CFR members, Harwood continued: "What is distinctively modern about the council these days is the considerable involvement of journalists and other media figures, who account for more than 10 percent of the membership.

"The editorial page editor, deputy editorial page editor, executive editor, managing editor, foreign editor, national affairs editor, business and financial editor and various writers as well as Katharine Graham, the paper's principal owner, represent the Washington Post in the council's membership," observed Harwood.

He went on to describe CFR representation among the owners, management, and editorial personnel for the other media giants—the *New York Times*, *Wall Street Journal*, *Los Angeles Times*, NBC, CBS, ABC, and so on.

These media heavyweights "do not merely analyze and interpret foreign policy for the United States; they help make it," he concluded.

Harwood's stunning exposé confirms that the news media, rather than providing a check against the abuse of power by our ruling elite, are instead a key part of a political cartel.

Rather than offering an independent perspective on our rulers' actions, the establishment media act as the ruling elite's voice, conditioning the public to accept, and even embrace, insider designs that otherwise might not be politically attainable.

Cheerleaders for Globalism

Of course, media cheerleading for insider objectives is not confined to foreign policy. For example, the media elitists focus on crimes committed with guns while ignoring crimes prevented by law-abiding gun owners to condition the public for stricter gun-control laws leading to confiscation. They point to "hard case" examples of Americans without health insurance to create support for socialized medicine. They fan the flames of fear regarding supposed environmental crises to "justify" regulating all human activity that supposedly harms the environment.

In a sense, the "news" media generally tell one story: the saga of government as savior. On nearly every conceivable issue, domestic or foreign, news stories are designed to encourage readers and viewers to look to government intervention as a solution.

In brief, the mass media are guilty of something more serious than mere sloppiness in reporting facts or chronic liberal bias. The Establishment media are conscious, willing accomplices in the power elite's drive for global control.

To control the world, the power elite must conquer the public mind. Americans can avoid that fate if they learn to recognize the strategy and tactics used by the media to advance the drive for global control—and then unite with like-minded people in an organized effort to educate and mobilize the public.

THE COUNCIL ON FOREIGN RELATIONS MEMBERSHIP

MEDIA

ABC News	Google	Nike
Alcoa	Goldman Sachs	PepsiCo
American Express	Halliburton	Pfizer
AIG	Heinz	Shell Oil
Bank of America	Hess	Sony Corporation of America
Bloomberg L.P.	IBM	Tata Group
Boeing	JPMorgan Chase	Time Warner
BP	Kohlberg Kravis Roberts	Total S.A.
Chevron	Lehman Brothers	Toyota Motor North America
Citigroup	Lockheed Martin	UBS
Coca-Cola	MasterCard	United Technologies
De Beers	McGraw-Hill	United States Chamber of Commerce
Deutsche Bank	McKinsey	U.S. Trust Corporation
ExxonMobil	Merck	Verizon
FedEx	Merrill Lynch	Visa [31]
Ford Motor	Motorola	Nike
General Electric	NASDAQ	Google
GlaxoSmithKline	News Corp	ABC News

the council on foreign relations membership

NOTABLE CURRENT COUNCIL MEMBERS

John Abizaid	Christopher Heinz (Heir to the Heinz fortune)	Diane Sawyer
Robert F. Agostinelli (Founder and Chairman of Rhone group.)	Teresa Heinz	Karenna Gore Schiff (daughter of Al Gore)
Fouad Ajami	Warren Hoge (American journalist)	Brent Scowcroft (United States National Security Advisor under Gerald Ford and George H. W. Bush)
Graham Allison	Richard Holbrooke	George P. Shultz (former United States Secretary of State, former United States Secretary of the Treasury, former Secretary of Labor)
Roger Altman	Jesse Jackson	Ron Silver (actor, director, producer, confounded the organization One Jerusalem)
James A. Baker	Angelina Jolie (UN Goodwill Ambassador)[32]	Walter B. Slocombe (former Under Secretary of Defense for Policy)
Evan Bayh	Vernon Jordan, Jr. (close advisor to President William J. Clinton)	Olympia Snowe
	Robert Kagan (confounded Project for the New American Century)	George Soros
Warren Beatty		
Sandy Berger (United States National Security Advisor under President Bill Clinton)	Thomas Kean	Jonathan Soros
Michael Bloomberg (current Mayor of New York City)	Caroline Bouvier Kennedy	Lesley Stahl
Cory Booker	John Kerry	Diana Taylor

363

THE COUNCIL ON FOREIGN RELATIONS MEMBERSHIP

MEDIA

David Boren

L. Paul Bremer

Bill Brock (former Republican United States Senator from Tennessee)

Edgar Bronfman, Sr. (a member of the Bronfman dynasty, president of the World Jewish Congress)

Ethan Bronner (deputy foreign editor of The New York Times)

Zbigniew Brzezinski (United States National Security Advisor to President Jimmy Carter)

Jonathan S. Bush (healthcare CEO, son of Jonathan Bush, brother of NBC entertainment reporter Billy Bush)

Jimmy Carter (Past President of the United States, Nobel Peace Prize Winner)

Dick Cheney (Vice President of the United States under George W. Bush, Past CEO of Halliburton)

Warren Christopher (former United States Secretary of State)

Henry Cisneros

Wesley Clark (Retired US General, Past Contender for the Democratic Presidencial Nomination)

Bill Clinton (Past President of the United States)

Hillary Clinton

Zalmay Khalilzad

Henry Kissinger

Irving Kristol (founder of American neo-conservatism, Senior Fellow at the American Enterprise Institute)

Paul R. Krugman

Richard D. Land

Jim Lehrer

Lewis Libby

Joseph Lieberman

Consuelo Mack (Anchor and Managing Editor of Wealthtrack and former CNBC television personality)

John McCain

George Mitchell

Walter Mondale (Former US Vice President under Jimmy Carter and 1984 Democratic Presidential Candidate)

Paula Zahn (news media, formerly an anchor on CNN)

Janet Napolitano

Fred Thompson (Actor, former Senator from Tennessee, former Presidential candidate)

Kathleen Kennedy Townsend

Laura Tyson

Paul Volcker (former Chairman of the Federal Reserve)

Barbara Walters

John Warner

Margaret Warner

Mark Warner

Rick Warren

Steven Weinberg (American physicist)

William Weld

John C. Whitehead (chairman of the World Trade Center Memorial Foundation, former United States Deputy Secretary of State under Ronald Reagan, former Goldman Sachs chairman)

Christine Todd Whitman

Brian Williams

364

THE COUNCIL ON FOREIGN
RELATIONS MEMBERSHIP

MEDIA

William Cohen

Jon Corzine

Katie Couric

Michael Crow
(president of Arizona
State University)

Al D'Amato

Thomas Daschle

John Deutch

David Dinkins

Christopher Dodd

Michael Douglas

Richard Dreyfuss

Peggy Dulany
(fourth child of
David Rockefeller)

Lawrence Eagleburger
(former United
States Secretary of
State under George
H. W. Bush)

Dianne Feinstein

Roger W. Ferguson, Jr.

Noah Feldman (academic and author)

John Negroponte (Deputy
Secretary of State, former
Director of National
Intelligence, former U.S.
ambassador to Honduras)

Sam Nunn

Joseph Nye

William Odom

Stanley O'Neal (Former
Chief Executive Officer
and Chairman of the
Board of Merrill Lynch)

Henry Paulson
(Treasury Secretary)

David Petraeus

Kitty Pilgrim

Richard Pipes (founder
of Middle East Forum)

Norman Podhoretz
(former editor-in-chief
of "Commentary",
senior fellow at the
Hudson Institute, Project
for the New American
Century signatory)

Steve Poizner (California
businessman and
Republican politician)

Colin Powell (Retired
US General, Former
US Secretary of State
under George W Bush)

Charles Prince (former
chief executive offi-
cer of Citigroup)

Charles Rangel

Dan Rather

William R. Rhodes

Shirley Williams, Baroness
Williams of Crosby (International
Advisory Board member)

Adam Wolfensohn

James Wolfensohn (former president of the World Bank Group)

Paul Wolfowitz (former president
of the World Bank Group, former
U.S. Deputy Secretary of Defense)

R. James Woolsey, Jr. (former
Director of Central Intelligence
and former head of the CIA)

Robert Zoellick (President of
the World Bank Group)

Mortimer Zuckerman

Newt Gingrich (Former Speaker of
the US House of Representatives)

Alan Greenspan (former Chairman
of the Federal Reserve)

Donald Gregg

Chuck Hagel

Lee Hamilton

Jane Harman

Gary Hart (former Democratic U.S.
Senator representing Colorado,
Council for a Livable World chairman,
advisory board member for the
Partnership for a Secure America)

Leslie Gelb

Richard Gephardt

THE COUNCIL ON FOREIGN RELATIONS MEMBERSHIP

MEDIA

Mikhail Fridman (Russian oligarch, International Advisory Board member)

Thomas Friedman (journalist, The New York Times)

Evan Galbraith

Robert Gates (Secretary of Defense, former Director of Central Intelligence)

Jay Rockefeller

John Abizaid

Robert F. Agostinelli (Founder and Chairman of Rhone group.)

Fouad Ajami

Graham Allison

Roger Altman

James A. Baker

Evan Bayh

Warren Beatty

Sandy Berger (United States National Security Advisor under President Bill Clinton)

Michael Bloomberg (current Mayor of New York City)

Cory Booker

Condoleezza Rice (US Secretary of State under George W Bush, Former National Security Advisor under George W Bush)

Bill Richardson

Alice Rivlin (economist, former U.S. cabinet member)

David Rockefeller, Jr.

Charles Robb

Christopher Heinz (Heir to the Heinz fortune)

Teresa Heinz

Warren Hoge (American journalist)

Richard Holbrooke

Jesse Jackson

Angelina Jolie (UN Goodwill Ambassador)[32]

Vernon Jordan, Jr. (close advisor to President William J. Clinton)

Robert Kagan (confounded Project for the New American Century)

Thomas Kean

Caroline Bouvier Kennedy

John Kerry

James S. Gilmore

Charlie Rose

Diane Sawyer

Karenna Gore Schiff (daughter of Al Gore)

Brent Scowcroft (United States National Security Advisor under Gerald Ford and George H. W. Bush)

George P. Shultz (former United States Secretary of State, former United States Secretary of the Treasury, former Secretary of Labor)

Ron Silver (actor, director, producer, confounded the organization One Jerusalem)

Walter B. Slocombe (former Under Secretary of Defense for Policy)

Olympia Snowe

George Soros

Jonathan Soros

Lesley Stahl

Diana Taylor

THE COUNCIL ON FOREIGN
RELATIONS MEMBERSHIP

NOTABLE HISTORICAL MEMBERS

John B. Anderson
Robert O. Anderson
Birch Bayh
Lloyd Bentsen
Conrad Black (International
Advisory Board member)
Shirley Temple Black
Bill Bradley
William F. Buckley, Jr.
McGeorge Bundy
William Bundy
Arthur Burns
George H. W. Bush
Joseph Califano, Jr.
Hugh Carey
E. Gerald Corrigan
Monica Crowley
Mario Cuomo

Thomas Dewey

C. Douglas Dillon
Michael Dukakis
John Foster Dulles
Dwight D. Eisenhower
Geraldine Ferraro
Tom Foley
Gerald Ford
John B. Anderson

George C. Marshall
Charles Peter McColough
George S. McGovern
Robert McNamara

Susan Molinari

Paul Nitze
Richard Nixon
Charles Percy
Ann Richards
Nelson Rockefeller
John D. Rockefeller III
Felix Rohatyn
Eugene V. Rostow
Walt Whitman Rostow
Dean Rusk
Arthur M. Schlesinger, Jr.
James Schlesinger

Charles Schumer

R. Sargent Shriver, Jr.
Jean Kennedy Smith
Robert Schwarz Strauss
Strobe Talbott
Maurice Tempelsman
Stansfield Turner
Cyrus Vance
George C. Marshall

George F. Will
Albert Wohlstetter
Roberta Wohlstetter
Paul Warburg

Caspar Weinberger

Wendell Willkie
Andrew Young
J. William Fulbright
Katherine Graham
Alexander Haig
Averell Harriman
Pamela Harriman
Christian Herter
Herbert Hoover
Hubert H. Humphrey
Bobby Ray Inman
Jacob Javits
Sergei Karaganov
(International Advisory
Board member)
George Kennan
Robert F. Kennedy
Jeane Kirkpatrick
Melvin Laird
John Lindsay
Robert A. Lovett
George F. Will

THE COUNCIL ON FOREIGN RELATIONS MEMBERSHIP
List of chairmen and chairwomen

Russell Cornell Leffingwell 1946–1953

John J. McCloy 1953–1970

David Rockefeller 1970–1985

Peter George Peterson 1985–2007

Carla A. Hills (co-chairman) 2007
Robert E. Rubin (co-chairman) 2007

THE COUNCIL ON FOREIGN RELATIONS MEMBERSHIP
List of presidents

John W. Davis 1921–1933

George W. Wickersham 1933–1936

Norman Davis 1936–1944

Russell Cornell Leffingwell 1944–1946

Allen Welsh Dulles 1946–1950

Henry Merritt Wriston 1951–1964

Grayson L. Kirk 1964–1971

Bayless Manning 1971–1977

Winston Lord 1977–1985

John Temple Swing 1985–1986 (Pro tempore)

Peter Tarnoff 1986–1993

Alton Frye 1993

Leslie Gelb 1993–2003

Richard N. Haass 2003

Bilderberg Group

Joseph Retinger (an American Freemason) and Prince Bernhard of the Netherlands founded in 1954 the Bilderberg Group. The founder, Joseph Retinger, was concerned about the growth of anti-Americanism in Western Europe. The Bilderberg Group name was the name of the hotel in Oosterbeck Holland where the group met for the first time.

After the Second World War, the Bilderberg Group was formed during the Cold War period. The Bilderberg, like the NATO organization, aimed at strengthening the bond of the western nations against the threat of communism. The declared purpose of the Bilderberg Group was to bind politically the United States of America with Europe against the United Socialistic Soviet Republic, diminishing the global communist threat to the monetary interests of the United States and Europe.

Bilderberg members meet regularly, presumably once a year at various locations around the world. The invited members are made up of some of the most influential people within the global arena, and they are all informed persons of authority and influence in their respective countries.

Bilderberg's membership is heavily laden with the Council on Foreign Relations, the Pilgrims Society, the Trilateral Commission, and the famous "Round Table" members, which was founded in 1910 and who denies its existence. The Round Table group prescribes for a more efficient form of global empire such that Anglo-American domination could be extended throughout the twentieth century.

The Bilderberg's membership includes dominant leaders in the business, media, and political world. Attendees of Bilderberg include central bankers, defense experts, mass media press barons, government ministers, prime ministers, royalty, international financiers, and political leaders from Europe and North America. This powerful group of politicians and businesspeople want to create a One World Government where international and national sovereignties disappear. The invited members are a sinister ministered group of elitists who operate entirely through self-interest.

The Bilderberg meetings are held under strict secrecy as the invited members plan for the future global world or One World

Government. The Bilderberg organization maintains an extremely low profile. Written reports or studies rarely are published for the public under the official sponsorship of the Bilderberg organization. Participants have denied for many years the very existence of the Bilderberg's dynasty until the now-extinct *Spotlight* newspaper forcibly exposed the Bilderberg group through media's publicity.

The members of the Bilderberg press (*The New York Times*, *The Washington Post*, *Newsweek Magazine*, *The Financial Times*, and *Time Magazine*) are usually in attendance; therefore, under the code of silence, publicity is avoided to the outside world. Only when events happen will corporate media report them, even though selected media people would have been aware of what has been decided weeks or even months in advance.

Literally speaking, the Bilderbergers want to produce a dictatorial One World Empire with the following ideals:

- Intermediaries are eliminated, placing political power into the hands of a few chosen people.

- Suppress unwarranted competition to maximize concentration of industries.

- Bilderbergers make it possible through their iron-grip control of the World Bank, the International Monetary Fund, and the World Trade Organization to establish absolute control over prices, goods, and raw materials.

- Analyze the present into primitive components and their interrelations.

- Architecting a strategy of selective manipulation, reconstruction, introduction, and abolition of components and interrelations.

The Rockefeller family of the United States and Rothschild family of Europe are the forces within the Bilderberg Group sharing the Bilderberg's power.

Scarcely few people in the world know of the existence of the Bilderberg organization.

Conspiracy Theories

Conspiracy theorists maintain the Bilderberg Group had orchestrated the move to a common European currency and had Bill Clinton elected president of the United States after he agreed to sign onto NAFTA.

The Serbs of Yugoslavia placed the blame on the Bilderbergers for instigating the war within Yugoslavia, disposing the dictator Slobodan Milosevic.

Criticism

The term *nationalism* is an obscenity to Bilderberg, being equated with patriotism.

The group's secrecy and its connections to power elites has provided fodder for many who believe that the group is part of a conspiracy that the Bilderberg Society are the puppet masters of a New World Order and have been pulling the strings of humankind since at least 1954.

Radio host Alex Jones promotes the theory that the group intends to dissolve the sovereignty of the United States and other countries into a supranational structure similar to the European Union.

Madrid-based author Daniel Estulin claims that the long-term purpose of Bilderberg is to "build a One-World Empire." He states the group "is not the end but the means to a future One World Government."

Another opponent of the group, Tony Gosling, has registered the domain name bilderberg.org, largely hosting material critical of Bilderberg.

Reporter Jonathan Duffy, writing in *BBC News Online Magazine* states, "In the void created by such aloofness, an extraordinary conspiracy theory has grown up around the group that alleges the fate of the world is largely decided by Bilderberg."

Central Banks' Names

Bank of England, Bank of Canada, Bank of Russia, National Bank of Ukraine, European Central Bank, Central Bank of Ireland, USSR's Gosbank

Bilderberg Attendees

- Al Gore (2007)

- Bill Clinton (1991), former US President, 1993 - 2001

- Hillary Clinton (1997), current US Senator, Democratic presidential candidate 2008

- Gerald R. Ford (1964, 1966), former US President

- Dan Quayle (1990, 1991), former US Vice President

- Walter F. Mondale, former US Vice President

- Nelson A. Rockefeller, former US Vice President, former Governor of New York

- Dean Acheson, former United States Secretary of State

- Christian Herter (1961, 1963, 1964), former Secretary of State

- Dean Rusk, former United States Secretary of State

- Cyrus Vance, former United States Secretary of State

- Henry Kissinger (1957, 1964, 1966, 1971, 1973, 1977–2003, 2004, 2005, 2006, 2007), former Secretary of State (1973–1977)

- Richard Perle (1985, 2003), assistant Secretary of Defense (1981–1987)

- Donald Rumsfeld (1975, 2002), Secretary of Defense (2001–2006)

- David L. Aaron, Deputy National Security Advisor

- Colin L. Powell (1997), former United States Secretary of State

- William J. Perry (1996), former United States Secretary of Defense

- Lloyd Bentsen (1989, 1995, 1996, 1997), former United States Secretary of the Treasury

- Robert S. McNamara, former US Secretary of Defense, former President of the World Bank

- McGeorge Bundy, former National Security Advisor (United States)

- Walt Whitman Rostow, former National Security Advisor (United States)

- James Steinberg, former Deputy National Security Advisor

- Brent Scowcroft (1985, 1994), former National Security Advisor (United States)

- Sandy Berger, former National Security Advisor (United States)

- Nicholas F. Brady (1991), former United States Secretary of the Treasury

- Robert Zoellick (1991, 2003, 2006), former Deputy Secretary of State and current President of the World Bank

- Richard Holbrooke (1995, 1996, 1997, 1998, 1999, 2004, 2005, 2006), former US Ambassador to the United Nations

- Lawrence Summers (1998, 2002), former United States Secretary of the Treasury

- C. Douglas Dillon, former United States Secretary of the Treasury

- Kenneth W. Dam, former United States Deputy Secretary of the Treasury

- Stuart Eizenstat, former United States Deputy Secretary of the Treasury

- Robert M. Kimmitt, current United States Deputy Secretary of the Treasury

- Richard N. Haass (2004), President, Council on Foreign Relations

- John Edwards (2004), former US Senator

- Bill Bradley (1985), former US Senator

- Jay Rockefeller (1971), current US Senator

- L. Douglas Wilder (1991), former Governor of Virginia, current Mayor of Richmond, Virginia

- Bill Richardson (1999, 2000), current Governor of New Mexico

- Christopher Dodd (1999, 2000, 2001), current US Senator

- Chuck Hagel (1999, 2000, 2001), current US Senator

- Evan Bayh (1999), current US Senator

- Kay Bailey Hutchison (2000, 2002), current US Senator

- Dianne Feinstein (1991), current US Senator

- Jon Corzine (1995, 1996, 1997, 1999, 2003, 2004), current Governor of New Jersey

- James Florio (1994), former Governor of New Jersey

- Christine Todd Whitman (1998), former Governor of New Jersey

- Sam Nunn (1996, 1997), former US Senator

- Tom Foley (1995, 2002), former Speaker of the US House of Representatives

- Lee H. Hamilton (1997), former US Congressman

- Ross Wilson (ambassador) (2007), current United States Ambassador to Turkey

- Alexander Haig, former United States Secretary of State

- Winston Lord, former United States Ambassador to China

- George J. Mitchell, former US Senator

- Claiborne Pell, former US Senator

- Nancy Kassebaum Baker, former US Senator

- Daniel J. Evans, former US Senator, former Governor of Washington

- Larry Pressler, former US Senator

- Donald W. Riegle Jr., former US Senator

- Charles Mathias, Jr., former US Senator

- Adlai Stevenson III, former US Senator

- Edward Brooke, former US Senator

- Fred R. Harris, former US Senator

- Bennett Johnston Jr., former US Senator

- Donald M. Fraser, former US Congressman

- Cornelius Edward Gallagher, former US Congressman

- Peter Hood Ballantine Frelinghuysen Jr., former US Congressman

- James Robert Jones, former US Congressman

- John B. Anderson, former US Congressman

- Dan Glickman, former US Congressman

- John LaFalce, former US Congressman

- John H. Sununu (1990), former Governor of New Hampshire

- Terry McAuliffe, former Chairman of the Democratic National Committee

- Ken Mehlman, former Chairman of the Republican National Committee

- Robert Schwarz Strauss, former Chairman of the Democratic National Committee

- Shirley Temple (1982), former United States Ambassador, former child actress

- Donald Gregg (1985), former United States Ambassador

- Ralph E. Reed Jr., former first executive director of the Christian Coalition

- Rick Perry (2007), current Governor of Texas

- Philip D. Zelikow (2007), executive director of the 9/11 Commission and Counselor of the United States Department of State

- Kathleen Sebelius (2007), current Governor of Kansas

- Vin Weber (2007), former US Congressman

- Kristen Silverberg (2007), Bureau of International Organization Affairs, part of the State Department

- Marc Grossman (2007), former Undersecretary of State for Political Affairs

- William J. Luti, Senior Director for Defense Policy and Strategy for the National Security Council

- David Gergen (1995), political consultant and presidential adviser during the Republican administrations of Nixon, Ford, and Reagan, campaign staffer for George H. W. Bush, and adviser to Democratic President Bill Clinton

- George W. Ball (1954–1992), US diplomat

- Joseph E. Johnson (1954), President, Carnegie Endowment for International Peace

- David Rockefeller, original US founding member, life member, and member of the Steering Committee (1954–)

- Zbigniew Brzezinski (Guest, 1966, 1968, 1972, 1973, 1975, 1978, 1985), President Carter's National Security Advisor

- Daniel B. Baker (Guest, 2005, 2006, 2007), Emergency Management Advisor

- http://www.truefacts.co.uk/articles/a0002.html

"Link unavailable. Please use your discretion and explore current sources to learn more."

THE BILDERBERG GROUP BY PAUL VIGAY (25TH MAR 2000)

Paul Vgay Looks Into The Shady World Of
Global Conspiracies And Manipulations.

Have you ever wondered if there really is a 'global elite'? Some secret group of people who control world events and hide their agenda from public knowledge?

Could there be a group of people; politicians, heads of multinational companies, directors of world banking organizations and even royalty, who decide what policies will determine the way ordinary people live - and die?

As David Icke says, it is relatively easy for a small group of people to control the masses when everyday we give our power and freedom away, fearing to step out from the comfort of our 'hassle free zone'.

Who perpetrate the 'Problem, Reaction, Solution' events which shape and manipulate our perceived 'democracy and freedom'?

If you control governments and the media you control the world, or do you? What if a problem so terrible, so grotesque, so 'unbelievable' begins to occur with startling regularity? Do you demand answers? Do you demand what 'the government' is going to do about it? Do you pass the problem to someone else do deal with? What happens if that person you hand the solution to, is the person who created the problem in the first place? So forms the basis for the problem, reaction, solution method of controlling the people with the minimum of effort.

No wonder The Sun newspaper decided to back Tony Blair of New Labour (what a joke) in the May 1997 UK general election. The chief executive of News International (the parent of The Sun) is Mr. Andrew Knight, a member of the Bilderberg Group.

Mr. Tony Blair was a guest of the annual Bilderberg meeting in 1993, together with his colleague Kenneth Clarke. Hang on a minute though….. Aren't those two on opposite sides? What about Bilderberg attendees Margaret Thatcher and Denis Healey - and you thought we lived in a democracy where your vote actually counted.

Incidentally, this could account for why Margaret Thatcher was one of Tony Blair's first guests at Number Ten, something the independent media were quick to pick up on after New Labour won power.

The same goes for US presidents. Every one since Jimmy Carter has been a Bilderberg representative. Democrat, Republican - it doesn't matter. They all have the same policies, decided upon at top secret meetings held annually in hidden locations.

The CFR And Royal Institute For International Affairs (RIIA)

It was at the Majestic Hotel in Paris in 1919 that the Round Table Groups of the United States and Britain emerged out from under a cloak of secrecy and officially became the (American) Council on Foreign Relations and the (British) Royal Institute for International Affairs.

To Mr. Rittenhouse and his breed of religious isolationists at Liberty Lobby, Bilderberg evolved directly from the 'satanic-communist' Illuminati, and the Council on Foreign Relations - Royal Institute of International Affairs relationship.

The World's Most Powerful Secret Society

http://www.newsconfidential.com/FS/
FS_Story.php?RequestID=60001

> *"Link unavailable. Please use your discretion
> and explore current sources to learn more."*

Richard Creasy and Pete Sawyer investigate.

Tony Blair first attended when he was a junior opposition spokes-man and Bill Clinton attended the 1991 meeting in Baden-Baden, Germany before he announced that he was running for president.

In 1974 a Financial Times columnist, Gordon Tether; took a keen interest in the group's activities. He wrote: "if the Bilderberg group is not a conspiracy of some sort, it is conducted in such away as to give a remarkably good impression of one." Tether found himself sidelined and eventually lost his FT column.

The Bilderbergers "own" the central banks, such as the Federal Reserve in the US, and are therefore in a position to determine discount rates, money-supply levels, the price of gold and which countries should receive loans. They decide who should be allowed to run for the offices of president, prime minister, chancellor and other leading positions in governments around the world.

New Book In German : 'Bilderberger, The Timetable Of The New World Order' By Andreas's

VON RETIE

http://www.bilderberg.org/2006.htm

*"Link unavailable. Please use your discretion
and explore current sources to learn more."*

Our world history is not the result of coincidences, but rather precise planning. More than half a century ago a powerful group was formed to take the fate of this planet into hand and steer the world in the direction of a secret brand of internationalism. Numerous crucial events in politics and economics can be traced back to subtle manipulation by Bilderberg. Their goal: total global control.

The book explains:- A Bilderberg meeting in Germany selected Bill Clinton to become United States president.

Bilderberg has a proven history of acting in a kingmaker capacity, yet they are unelected and unaccountable to anyone. Their directives are driven towards undermining national sovereignty and establishing a world order that benefits their elite interests. Both Bill Clinton and Tony Blair were "groomed" by Bilderberg before becoming President and Prime Minister and the mainstream media reported that Bilderberg selected John Edwards as John Kerry's running mate in 2004.

Jocelan Caldwell

What would you think if all of the North-American sports team owners, for instance, met secretly every year where no media were allowed in or to interview any of the participants, where there were armed guards at all the doors and when they exited that meeting, the individuals hid their faces so as not to get photographed and refused to talk to reporters? What would the reaction be? Sports fans - and most everyone else - would be furious! We would wonder what kind of deals were they hatching, what were they plotting and planning that they didn't want the rest of us to know?

Sounds pretty weird, eh? But did you know that recently at a 5-star hotel in Ottawa, Ontario, Canada, more than 100 of the world's most wealthy and powerful individuals - called the Bilderbergers or the Illuminati or Synarchists - (and confirmed as including Hillary Clinton, George H.W. Bush, David Rockefeller, Gov. George Pataki of New York, the President of the Federal Reserve Bank, Henry Kissinger and Queen Beatrix of the Netherlands, whose family owns Royal Dutch Shell Oil) got together under just such circumstances to discuss the future of not baseball but the world as the rich and powerful want it to look like. At the end of their meeting they covered their faces, ashamed, as they sneaked out to their limousines to the airport.

"The Democratic and Republican parties are well-represented at Bilderberg, but Greens are never invited. Alas, we wouldn't fit it in. The Bilderberg conferences stand for everything the Green Party opposes -- concentration of the world's wealth and power among a small group of elite corporate and governmental leaders, whose agenda have become largely realized," said Julia Willebrand, Green candidate for Comptroller of New York, who noted reports that Bill Clinton was persuaded to support NAFTA as a result of his attendance at least one Bilderberg meeting in the early 1990s.

According to Koru's 'theory' Bilderberg participants are chosen very carefully to be assisted by secret world power centers through their careers. And when they reach the key positions in a country's political scene, all begin to implant the Bilderberg decisions, plans and programs.

The United States is no longer a democratic representative republic, but rather it is controlled by foreign interests, stemming from the Enlightenment, Washout's and Mazzini's Illuminati and Free Masonry where man is considered his own God and whose future lies in the Godless, U.N. run world government without borders, without sovereignty; the U.N.'s Charter replacing the Constitution and where there will be a world based on Hilliary's International Socialism with an unelected elite class dictating the rules and the judgments over mankind. It is Luciferian and it is visibly happening in the silent invasion from Mexico and the undeclared non-war wars that are bringing down our economy and our once proud society.

Megan Gillis, Ottawa Sun

Bilderbergers say they're building transatlantic understanding, frankly talking about the issues but prefer to do it in private where invited participants can speak freely.

Even mainstream critics say they are elitist, undemocratic and unaccountable. Others finger Bilderbergers as building a self-serving world government, pulling strings behind the scenes and planting their candidates in politics and other positions of power to serve their needs.

Ottawa Citizen

John F. Kennedy and Margaret Thatcher, the latter after criticizing the Bilderberg Group, were ousted from power by the group. Bill Clinton, on the other hand, was "selected" U.S. president in 1992.

James P. Tucker Jr.

President Bush will have a top White House aide representing him at Bilderberg, and high officials of the state, defense and treasury departments will attend. Heads of state and other high officials in government and banking will attend from Europe and Canada.

Daniel Estulin

THE BILDERBERGERS MUST BE STOPPED.

The Bilderberg Club has grown beyond its idealistic beginnings to become a shadow world government, which decides in total secrecy at annual meetings how their plans are to be carried out. They threaten to take away our right to direct our own destinies. And it is becoming easier because the development of telecommunication technology, together with profound present-day knowledge and new methods of behavior engineering to manipulate individual conduct convert what, at other epochs of history, were only evil intentions into a disturbing reality. Each new measure, viewed on its own, may seem an aberration, but a whole host of changes, as part of an ongoing continuum, constitutes a shift towards total enslavement.

This is why it is time to look behind the scenes. We are at a crossroads. And the roads we take from here will determine the very future of humanity. We have to wake up to the true objectives and actions of the Bilderberg Club and its parallel kin if we hope to retain the freedoms fought for by our grandfathers in the Second World War. It is not up to God to bring us back from the "New Dark Age" planned for us. IT IS UP TO US. Whether we go into the next century as an electronic global police state or as free human beings depends on the action we take now.

If you can help us in any way to spread the word through your contacts, friends and acquaintances, all of us would very much appreciate it.

THE LOGAN ACT

Although participants emphatically attest that they attend the Club's annual meeting as private citizens and not in their official government capacity, that affirmation is dubious-particularly when you compare the Chatham House Rule with the Logan Act in the United States, where it is absolutely illegal for elected officials to meet in private with influential business executives to debate and design public policy.

Bilderberg meetings follow a traditional protocol founded in 1919, in the wake of the Paris Peace Conference held at Versailles, by the Royal Institute of International Affairs (RIIA) based at Chatham House in London. While the name Chatham House is commonly used to refer to the Institute itself, the Royal Institute of International Affairs is the foreign policy executive arm of the British monarchy.

According to RIIA procedures: "When a meeting, or part thereof, is held under the Chatham House Rule, participants are free to use the information received, but neither the identity nor the affiliation of the speaker(s), nor that of any other participant, may be revealed; nor may it be mentioned that the information was received at a meeting of the Institute."

The Logan Act was intended to prohibit United States citizens without authority from interfering in relations between the United States and foreign governments. However, there have been a number of judicial references to the Act, and it is not uncommon for it to be used as a political weapon.

Those who have attended Bilderberg Group meetings over the years and flouted the Logan Act include:

- Allen Dulles (CIA);

- Senator William J. Fulbright (from Arkansas, a Rhodes Scholar);

- Dean Acheson (Secretary of State under President Truman);

- Nelson Rockefeller and Laurance Rockefeller;

- former President Gerald Ford;

- Henry J. Heinz II (former CEO, H. J. Heinz Co.);

- Thomas L. Hughes (former President of the Carnegie Endowment for International Peace);

- Robert S. McNamara (President Kennedy's Secretary of Defense and former President of the World Bank);

- William P. Bundy (former President of the Ford Foundation, and former editor of the Council on Foreign Relations' Foreign Affairs journal);

- John J. McCloy (former President of Chase Manhattan Bank);

- George F. Kennan (former US Ambassador to the Soviet Union);

- Paul H. Nitze (former representative of Schroeder Bank;

- Robert O. Anderson (former Chairman, Atlantic Richfield Co., and Chairman, Aspen Institute for Humanistic Studies);

- John D. Rockefeller IV (former Governor of West Virginia, now US Senator);

- Cyrus Vance (Secretary of State under President Carter);

- Eugene Black (former President of the World Bank);

- Joseph Johnson (former President, Carnegie Endowment for International Peace);

- Gen. Andrew J. Goodpaster (former Supreme Allied Commander in Europe, and later Superintendent of West Point Academy);

- Zbigniew Brzezinski (National Security Adviser to President Carter, co-founder of the Trilateral Commission);

- General Alexander Haig (once European NATO Commander, former assistant to Henry Kissinger, and later Secretary of State under President Reagan);

- James S. Rockefeller (former President and Chairman, First National City Bank, now Citibank).

A MEANS TO AN END

The Bilderberg Group is not the end but the means to a future One World Government. This organization has grown beyond its secretive beginnings to become a virtual shadow government which decides in total secrecy at annual meetings how its plans are to be carried out. The ultimate goal of this nightmare future is to transform Earth into a prison planet by bringing about a single globalize marketplace, controlled by a One World Government, policed by a United World Army, financially regulated by a World Bank, and populated by a micro chipped population whose life's needs have been stripped down to materialism and survival-work, buy, procreate, sleep-all connected to a global computer that monitors our every move.

Istanbul - Turkish Daily News

PEOPLE THAT RUN THE WORLD:

If one aspect of Bilderberg that irks many is its secrecy, another one is the identity of its participants. Looking at the list of regular "Bilderbergers," one cannot but think that these are really "the people that run the world". Veterans like Henry Kissinger, David Rockefeller and Zbigniew Brzezinski are joined every year by newcomers such as former U.S. President Bill Clinton, soon-to-be-former-PM Tony Blair, NATO Secretary-General Jaap de Hoop Scheffer, former Pentagon adviser Richard Perle and countless others. Every year, the list also includes important "media people" from influential outlets such as The Financial Times, Washington Post, The Economist, The Times, Le Figaro and Die Zeit. The picture becomes complete with CEOs from the world's biggest companies such as Coca-Cola, Fiat, Suez-Tractebel, Royal Dutch Shell and British Petroleum.

ZBIGNIEW BRZEZINSKI

In Zbigniew Brzezinski's 1997 book The Grand Chessboard "Russia" and "vital energy reserves", as it turns out, are mentioned more frequently than any other country and subject in the book. Brzezinski is President Carter's former National Security Advisor, a co-founder of the Trilateral Commission, a member of the Council on Foreign Relations and the Bilderberg Club and a close associate of David Rockefeller and Henry Kissinger. He is the proverbial insider's insider. According to Brzezinski, global US and thus Bilderberg hegemony depended on having complete control of Russia's vital energy reserves in Central Asia. As long as Russia remained strong, it remained a threat-a potential block to the complete imposition of Bilderberg-led economic and military will.

Brzezinski spelled out in The Grand Chessboard the compelling energy issue driving American policy: "A power that dominates Eurasia would control two of the world's three most advanced and economically productive regions. A mere glance at the map also suggests that control over Eurasia would almost automatically entail Africa's subordination, rendering the Western Hemisphere and Oceania geopolitically peripheral to the world's central continent. About 75 percent of the world's people live in Eurasia, and most of the world's physical wealth is there as well, both in its enterprise and underneath its soil. Eurasia accounts for 60 percent of the world's GNP and about three-fourths of the world's known energy resources."

The energy theme appears again later in Brzezinski's book, written four years before 9/11: "The world's energy consumption is bound to vastly increase over the next two or three decades. Estimates by the US Department of Energy anticipate that world demand will rise by more than 50 percent between 1993 and 2015, with the most significant increase in consumption occurring in the Far East. The momentum of Asia's economic development is already generating massive pressures for the exploration and exploitation of new sources of energy."

INSIDE THE SECRETIVE BILDERBERG GROUP

Jim Tucker, editor of a right-wing newspaper, the American Free Press for example, alleges they organize wars and elect and depose political leaders. He describes the group as simply 'evil'. So where does the truth lie?

Will Hutton, an economic analyst and former newspaper editor who attended a Bilderberg meeting in 1997, says people take part in these networks in order to influence the way the world works, to create what he calls "the international common sense" about policy.

"On every issue that might influence your business you will hear at first-hand the people who are actually making those decisions and you will play a part in helping them to make those decisions and formulating the common sense," he says.

And that "common sense" is one which supports the interests of Bilderberg's main participants - in particular free trade. Viscount Davignon says that at the annual meetings, "automatically around the table you have internationalists" - people who support the work of the World Trade Organization, trans-Atlantic co-operation and European integration

Bilderberg meetings often feature future political leaders shortly before they become household names. Bill Clinton went in 1991 while still governor of Arkansas, Tony Blair was there two years later while still an opposition

MP. All the recent presidents of the European Commission attended Bilderberg meetings before they were appointed.

'SECRET GOVERNMENT'

This has led to accusations that the group pushes its favored politicians into high office. But Viscount Davignon says his steering committee are simply excellent talent spotters. The steering committee "does its best assessment of who are the bright new boys or girls in the beginning phase of their career who would like to get known."

"It's not a total accident, but it's not a forecast and if they go places it's not because of Bilderberg, it's because of themselves," Viscount Davignon says.

But its critics say Bilderberg's selection process gives an extra boost to aspiring politicians whose views are friendly to big business. None of this, however, is easy to prove - or disprove.

Observers like Will Hutton argue that such private networks have both good and bad sides. They are unaccountable to voters but, at the same time, they do keep the international system functioning. And there are limits to their power - a point which Bilderberg chairman was keen to stress, "When people say this is a secret government of the world I say that if we were a secret government of the world we should be bloody ashamed of ourselves."

Informal and private networks like Bilderberg have helped to oil the wheels of global politics and globalization for the past half a century. In the eyes of critics they have undermined democracy, but their supporters believe they are crucial to modern democracy's success. And so long as business and politics remain mutually dependent, they will continue to thrive

Bilderberg Group (Organization)

http://www.nndb.com/org/514/000042388/

The Bilderberg Group holds "by invitation only" annual meetings of the rich and powerful. About two-thirds of the attendees are European, the rest American.

Name	Occupation	Birth	Known For
Fouad Ajami	Author	9-Sep-1945	Director of Middle East Studies, SAIS
Paul Allaire	Business	21-Jul-1938	Twice CEO of Xerox
Graham T. Allison	Scholar	23-Mar-1940	Kennedy School of Government
Ed Balls	Politician	25-Feb-1967	British MP, Normanton
Evan Bayh	Politician	26-Dec-1955	US Senator from Indiana
Queen Beatrix I	Royalty	31-Jan-1938	Queen of the Netherlands
Carl Bildt	Head of State	15-Jul-1949	Foreign Minister of Sweden
Conrad Black	Business	25-Aug-1944	Rapacious newspaper mogul
John Browne	Business	20-Feb-1948	CEO of British Petroleum, 1995-2007
John H. Bryan	Business	5-Oct-1936	CEO of Sara Lee, 1975-2000
William F. Buckley	Columnist	24-Nov-1925	National Review
Peter Carington	Government	6-Jun-1919	UK Foreign Secretary, 1979-82
Ahmed Chalabi	Government	30-Oct-1944	Prominent on the Iraqi Provisional Council
Bill Clinton	Head of State	19-Aug-1946	42nd US President, 1993-2001
Marshall A. Cohen	Business	c. 1935	CEO of Molson, 1988-96
Timothy C. Collins	Business	c. 1956	Private equity, Ripplewood Holdings
Jon Corzine	Politician	1-Jan-1947	Governor of New Jersey
Claes Dahlbäck	Business	c. 1948	CEO of Investor AB, 1978-99
Paul G. Desmarais, Jr.	Business	3-Jul-1954	Co-CEO of Power Corporation of Canada
John Deutch	Government	27-Jul-1938	CIA Director, 1995-96
Chris Dodd	Politician	27-May-1944	US Senator from Connecticut
Thomas E. Donilon	Attorney	c. 1955	O'Melvany and Myers
Esther Dyson	Business	14-Jul-1951	EDventure Holdings, former ICANN director
Dianne Feinstein	Politician	22-Jun-1933	US Senator from California
Martin Feldstein	Economist	25-Nov-1939	Reagan economist
Anthony S. Fell	Business	c. 1941	Chairman, RBC Capital Markets

Name	Occupation	Birth	Known For
Stephen Friedman	Business	21-Dec-1937	Former Partner, Goldman Sachs
Thomas Friedman	Journalist	20-Jul-1953	New York Times
Melinda Gates	Philanthropist	15-Aug-1964	Married to Bill Gates
Timothy F. Geithner	Government	18-Aug-1961	President of the New York Fed
David Gergen	Columnist	9-May-1942	Advisor to Nixon, Reagan, Bush, Clinton
Paul Gigot	Columnist	c. 1955	Wall Street Journal columnist
Donald E. Graham	Journalist	22-Apr-1945	Washington Post CEO
Richard Haass	Government	1951	President, Council on Foreign Relations
Chuck Hagel	Politician	4-Oct-1946	US Senator from Nebraska
Richard C. Holbrooke	Diplomat	24-Apr-1941	US Ambassador to UN, 1998-2001
Allan Hubbard	Economist	8-Sep-1947	George W. Bush economist
Merit E. Janow	Educator	13-May-1958	Professor of Int'l Affairs, Columbia University
James A. Johnson	Business	24-Dec-1943	CEO of Fannie Mae, 1991-98
J. Bennett Johnston	Politician	10-Jun-1932	US Senator from Louisiana, 1972-97
Vernon Jordan	Business	15-Aug-1935	Advisor to Bill Clinton
Henry Kissinger	Government	27-May-1923	Secretly bombed Cambodia
Andrew S. B. Knight	Journalist	1-Nov-1939	Editor of The Economist, 1974-86
Henry Kravis	Business	6-Jan-1944	Kohlberg Kravis Roberts
Marie-Josée Kravis	Economist	11-Sep-1949	President of MoMA
Bill Kristol	Columnist	23-Dec-1952	Editor of The Weekly Standard
Jan Leschly	Business	?	CEO of SmithKline Beecham, 1994-2000
William J. Luti	Military	c. 1952	NSC Defense Policy Adviser
Jessica Tuchman Mathews	Administrator	1946	Carnegie Endowment for International Peace
Charles Mathias	Politician	24-Jul-1922	US Senator from Maryland, 1969-87
William J. McDonough	Business	c. 1934	President of New York Fed, 1993-2003
George J. Mitchell	Politician	20-Aug-1933	US Senator from Maine, 1980-95
Bill Moyers	Journalist	6-Jun-1934	NOW with Bill Moyers
Craig Mundie	Business	c. 1949	Microsoft CTO
George Pataki	Politician	24-Jun-1945	Governor of New York, 1995-2006
Richard Perle	Government	16-Sep-1941	Prince of Darkness
Fredrik Reinfeldt	Head of State	4-Aug-1965	Prime Minister of Sweden
Bill Richardson	Politician	15-Nov-1947	Governor of New Mexico
Rozanne L. Ridgway	Diplomat	22-Aug-1935	Asst. Secy. of State for Europe, 1985-89
Don Riegle	Politician	4-Feb-1938	US Senator from Michigan, 1976-95
David Rockefeller	Business	12-Jun-1915	Founder of the Trilateral Commission
Robert B. Shapiro	Business	4-Aug-1938	CEO of Monsanto, 1995-2000
George Soros	Business	12-Aug-1930	Hungarian financial speculator
Lesley Stahl	Journalist	16-Dec-1941	60 Minutes
James B. Steinberg	Government	c. 1951	Deputy National Security Advisor, 1997-2001
Dennis Stevenson	Business	19-Jul-1945	Chairman of HBOS

Name	Occupation	Birth	Known For
Peter Sutherland	Government	25-Apr-1946	First Director General of the WTO
Jean-Claude Trichet	Business	20-Dec-1942	President, European Central Bank
John Vinocur	Journalist	?	International Herald Tribune correspondent
John C. Whitehead	Business	1922	US Deputy Secretary of State, 1985-89
Daniel Yergin	Author	6-Feb-1947	The Prize
Robert Zoellick	Government	25-Jul-1953	World Bank president

Central Intelligence Agency (CIA)

John J. McCloy (former chairman of the CFR and chairman of Chase Manhattan Bank) used his position as coordinator of information for the US government to build the framework of what was to become the Office of Strategic Services (OSS), created in the 1941–1942 era, headed by Bill Donovan. During 1947, the OSS was rolled into a new group called the Central Intelligence Agency (CIA) by the 1947 National Security Act, which made the activities of the CIA immune from all civil and criminal laws. In 1950, General Walter Bedel Smith became director of the CIA. The CIA helped organize and sponsored the formation and operation of the Bilderberg Conferences. There is little doubt that the CIA sponsored the formation of the Bilderbergs and continue to do so to this day.

Kai Bird

Kai Bird's excellent account in *The Chairman: John J. McCloy and the Making of the American Establishment* states, "In late 1952, Retinger went to America to try the idea out on his American contacts. Among others, he saw such old friends as Averell Harriman, David Rockefeller, and Bedel Smith, then director of the CIA. After Retinger explained his proposal, Smith said, 'Why the hell didn't you come to me in the first place?' He quickly referred Retinger to C. D. Jackson, who was about to become Eisenhower's special assistant for psychological warfare. It took a while for Jackson to organize the American wing of the group, but finally, in May 1954, the first conference was held in the Hotel de Bilderberg, a secluded hotel in Holland, near the German border. Prince Bernhard, and Retinger drew up the list of invitees from the European countries, while Jackson controlled the American list.''

US Senator Jacob Javits

The Congressional Record, US Senate, April 11, 1964, states, "Mr. [Jacob] Javits, Mr. President, the 13th in a series of Bilderberg meetings on international affairs, in which I participated, was held in Williamsburg, VA, on March 20, 21, and 22. I ask unanimous consent to have printed in the Record a background paper entitled 'The Bilderberg Meetings.'''

The Bilderberg Meetings

The idea of the Bilderberg meetings originated in the early fifties. Changes had taken place on the international political and economic scene after World War II. The countries of the Western World felt the need for closer collaboration to protect their moral and ethical values, their democratic institutions, and their independence against the growing Communist threat. The Marshall plan and NATO were examples of collective efforts of Western countries to join hands in economic and military matters after World War II.

In the early 1950s, a number of people on both sides of the Atlantic sought a means of bringing together leading citizens, not necessarily connected with government, for informal discussions of problems facing the Atlantic community. Such meetings, they felt, would create a better understanding of the forces and trends affecting Western nations in particular. They believed that direct exchanges could help to clear up differences and misunderstandings that might weaken the West.

One of the men who saw the need for such discussions was the late Dr. Joseph H. (Heironymus) Retinger (as a matter of interest, the name *Heironymus* is literally translated to be "member of the occult"). In 1952, he approached His Royal Highness, Prince Bernhard of the Netherlands, with the suggestion of informal and unofficial meetings to discuss the problems facing the Atlantic community. Others in Europe wholeheartedly supported the idea, and proposals were submitted to American friends to join in the undertaking. A number of Americans—including C. D. Jackson, the late General Walter Bedel Smith, and the late John Coleman—agreed to cooperate. (Very reliable information from a former CIA member now reveals that the CIA financed Dr. Retinger's efforts to convince Prince Bernhard to form this group that was later to be called the Bilderbergs. This is confirmed by the fact that General Walter Bedel Smith was the CIA director from 1950 to 1953, so, is it surprising that he would agree to join this group?)

Carroll Quigley

In his 1966 work *Tragedy and Hope*, Quigley—after writing disdainfully of "conspiracy theorists"—admitted the existence of a partially submerged elite that "operates, to some extent, in the way the radical Right believes the Communists act. In fact, this network, which we may identify as the Round Table Groups, has no aversion to cooperating with the Communists, or any other groups, and frequently does so. I know of the operations of this network because I have studied it for twenty years and was permitted for two years, in the early 1960s, to examine its papers and secret records. I have no aversion to it or to most of its aims and have, for much of my life, been close to it and many of its instruments." The network's "aim," Quigley continued, is "nothing less than to create a world system of financial control in private hands able to dominate the political system of each country and the economy of the world as a whole."

The "Round Table Groups" stemmed from a secret society (Quigley's phrase) created by British magnate Cecil Rhodes to unite the world — beginning with the English-speaking dominions — under "enlightened" elitists like himself. World War I and the post-war proposal for a League of Nations resulted from the Round Table cabal's machinations. During the post-war Versailles "Peace Conference," noted Quigley, this covert network decided to establish "in England and in each dominion, a front organization to the existing Round Table Group. This front organization, called the Royal Institute of International Affairs, had as its nucleus in each area the existing submerged Round Table Group. In New York it was known as the Council on Foreign Relations...."

The Council on Foreign Relations (CFR) boasts a membership of only about 4,000. But its roster includes literally hundreds of powerful figures occupying key positions in the media — not merely writers, reporters, and news anchors who deliver the news, but also editors, publishers, and executives who define what news is and how it is covered. (See "CFR Elitists Pulling the Strings" for a partial list of CFR members in the media.) Just as significantly, the tiny CFR clique has for decades had a virtual stranglehold on the executive branch of the U.S. government, as well as much of academe.

Voice of the "Ruling Class"

Carroll Quigley — like David Rockefeller — specifically identified the New York Times and the Washington Post as key media organs of the power elite. The Times, with utterly unwarranted self-assurance, designates itself the arbiter of "All the News that's Fit to Print," while the Post is the voice of official Washington. Even in the cyber age, these two hoary papers (both of which are longtime CFR redoubts) set the tone for most news coverage, defining issues and setting the limits of "respectable" opinion. But the CFR's chokehold on media influence extends well beyond the Manhattan-Washington corridor.

In his October 30, 1993 "Ruling Class Journalists" essay, Washington Post ombudsman Richard Harwood candidly remarked about how the CFR dominates our news media. Harwood described the council as "the closest thing we have to a ruling Establishment in the United States.... [Its members are] the people who, for more than half a century, have managed our international affairs and our military-industrial complex." After listing the executive branch positions then occupied by CFR members, Harwood continued: "What is distinctively modern about the council these days is the considerable involvement of journalists and other media figures, who account for more than 10 percent of the membership."

"The editorial page editor, deputy editorial page editor, executive editor, managing editor, foreign editor, national affairs editor, business and financial editor and various writers as well as Katharine Graham, the paper's principal owner, represent the Washington Post in the council's membership," observed Harwood. He went on to describe CFR representation among the owners, management, and editorial personnel for the other media giants — the New York Times, Wall Street Journal, Los Angeles Times, NBC, CBS, ABC, and so on. These media heavyweights "do not merely analyze and interpret foreign policy for the United States; they help make it," he concluded.

Harwood's stunning exposé confirms that the news media, rather than providing a check against the abuse of power by our ruling elite, are instead a key part of a political cartel. Rather than offering an independent perspective on our rulers' actions, the Establishment media act as the ruling elite's voice — conditioning the public to accept, and even embrace, Insider designs that otherwise might not be politically attainable.

Cold War Ends

Japan and European Communities progressed within the world economy.

The Socialist Republic of the Soviet Union breaks up and Communism ends within Russia. Adhesiveness of three world regions (Europe, North America, and Asia-Pacific) does not exist.

North America, Japan, and Western Europe

The European Union, North America (United States and Canada), and Japan, who are the three main democratic industrialized areas of the world, correspond to the three sides of the Trilateral Commission.

Most important is the European Union, North America, and Japan wealth deriving primarily from industrial production.

Since the three regions represent 70 percent of the world's trade, the theory was that America's role should be diminished and made equal to the Common markets of European Union and Japan.

Kenichi Ohmae, in his book *Triad Power*, states "The vast majority of new patents registered and exchanged among Free World countries are concentrated within five nations: Japan, the United States, West Germany, France and the United Kingdom. During 1982, these five nations represented 85 percent of the 10,000 patents registered in the world."

Trilateral Commission (TC)

The TC was formed to redirect attention away from the CFR. The TC represents a union of the three noncommunist industrial regions of the world—North America, Europe, and Japan. The opportunity existed to legalize the creation of the TC. With the blessing of the Bilderbergers group and the CFR, the TC began organizing on July 23–24, 1972, at the 3,500-acre Rockefeller estate at Pocantico Hills, New York.

In 1970, David Rockefeller was chairman of the CFR for fifteen years, and he also is a member of the Bilderberg Group advisory council. David Rockefeller was the longtime chairman of the Rockefeller family–controlled Chase Manhattan Bank and became the undisputed overlord of his family's global corporate empire.

Later, David Rockefeller became the founding chairman of the TC that was made of leaders in business, banking, government, and mass media in North America, Europe, and Japan.

Rockefeller's idea for establishing the TC emerged after Rockefeller read Zbigniew Brzezinski's book entitled *Between Two Ages*. In 1970, Zbigniew Brzezinski, who idealized the theories of Karl Marx in his book, describes that the initial world order was to be a trilateral economic linkage between Japan, Europe, and the United States. According to Brzezinski, changes in the modern world required it. Brzezinski wrote elsewhere, "The American system is compelled gradually to accommodate itself to this emerging international context, with the U.S. government called upon to negotiate, to guarantee, and, to some extent, to protect the various arrangements that have been contrived even by private business." (The international upper class must band together in order to protect their interests. Political leaders of developed nations were brought to power to ensure that the global financial interests of the Rockefellers and other ruling elites are protected from the masses.)

As Jack Newell writes, "The original literature of The TC also states, exactly as Brzezinski's book had proposed, that the more advanced Communist States could become partners in the alliance leading to world government. In short, David Rockefeller implemented Brzezinski's proposal.

"The effects of the Council on Foreign Relation and The TC on the affairs of our nation is easy to see. Our own Government no longer acts in its own interest, we no longer win any wars we fight, and we constantly tie ourselves to international agreements, pacts, and conventions. And, our leaders have developed blatant preferences for Communist U.S.S.R., Communist Cuba, and

Communist China, while they continue to work for world government, which has always been the goal of Communism."

David Rockefeller oversees the TC activities, providing guidance in policy-making, resulting in the control of the TC.

Trilateral Commission Expansion

In 2001, the TC expanded its dominant membership base to incorporate economically smaller but emerging countries within its regional structure.

In a Holy Globalism tinfoil festival, Mexico was accorded a handful of members, as were Asia-Pacific countries such as Australia, Indonesia, Malaysia, New Zealand, the Philippines, Singapore, South Korea, and Thailand.

As Newell writes: "The original literature of The TC also states, exactly as Brzezinski's book had proposed, that the more advanced Communist States could become partners in the alliance leading to world government. In short, David Rockefeller implemented Brzezinski's proposal."

"This is probably one of the very best illustrations of the great power of the Elite. They can make or break any president or candidate for president. They made Jimmy Carter in his efforts to become president, and broke Senator Barry Goldwater in his failed attempt."

An Archery Target Representation of the Elite

Center or Bull's-Eye. This is made up of the czar and the members of the Inner Circle. They are the decision-makers and are therefore 100 percent informed and involved in the Global Union movement. David Rockefeller is the only "obvious" member of this group. We can speculate about the members of the Inner Circle, but we will probably never have these speculations confirmed.

Inner Ring. This group is made up of the officers and directors and triple members of all three Elite groups. They are probably 90 percent informed by the czar and the members of the Inner Circle and are heavily involved in the Global Union movement (see the preceding listing and following charts for these members).

Center Ring. This group is made up of the leaders, implementers, and double members of the three Elite groups and who are probably 80 percent informed by the czar and the members of the Inner Circle and are moderately involved in the Global Union movement.

Outer Ring. These members are included for camouflage purposes only and are made up of many of those who belong to only the CFR. These members are aware of only about 50 percent or less of the goals and objectives of the Global Union movement. A large number of these people are members for ego and social reasons only and would very likely resign immediately when they find out what the Global Union is "really" up to. An example is Douglas Fairbanks Jr., the Hollywood actor, who probably falls completely off the above target. He would be classified as true camouflage. Another example of another possible member of the Outer Ring is Ben J. Wattenberg. He would be in the Outer Ring if he told the absolute truth on C-SPAN with Bryan Lamb on August 29, 1995, when he stated, "I plead guilty to being a member of the CFR, and I only pay my dues, but never, or rarely attends their meetings." If he was truthful, I would place him in the Outer Ring.

On the other hand, the CFR's bylaws absolutely prohibit their members from discussing this Elite organization. For this reason, he could have just been complying with their bylaws, and in all reality, he may be a very active member and really belongs in one of the inner rings.

Odds Favor Membership (Elite Secret Groups)

- In 1960, John F. Kennedy and Richard M. Nixon were members.

- In 1964, President Lyndon B. Johnson was not a member (but Johnson had already staffed his administration with plenty of insiders of these elite secret groups).

- In 1968, it was Nixon versus club member Hubert H. Humphrey.

- In 1972, it was Nixon again against Democratic Party CFR member George McGovern.

- In 1976, it was CFR Republican Gerald Ford losing to CFR Democrat Jimmy Carter.

- In 1980, Ronald Reagan was not a member, but his running mate, George H. W. Bush, was. So were both of his opponents, Carter and independent John Anderson. But on assuming office, Reagan quickly named 313 CFR members to his team.

- In 1984, the Democratic Party nominated CFR member Walter Mondale to challenge Reagan.

- In 1988, both Bush and Michael Dukakis were CFR members. In 1992, an obscure CFR member governor from Arkansas, Bill Clinton, who won the "trifecta" award of being a member of the CFR, TC, and Bilderberg Group, challenged Bush.

- In 1996, CFR member Bob Dole challenged Clinton.

- In 2000, CFR member Al Gore ran against George W. Bush, who was a nonmember, but George W. Bush's running mate, Dick Cheney, was.

- In 2004, CFR member John Kerry challenged Bush.

TRILATERAL COMMISSION MEMBERSHIP LIST (PARTIAL)

PRESS RELATED

David G. Bradley	Chairman, Atlantic Media Company, Washington, DC
David Gergen	Professor of Public Service, John F. Kennedy School of Government, Harvard University, Cambridge, MA; Editor-at-Large, US News and World Report
Donald E. Graham	Chairman and Chief Executive Officer, The Washington Post Company, Washington, DC
Karen Elliott House	Senior Vice President, Dow Jones & Company, and Publisher, The Wall Street Journal, New York, NY
Gerald M. Levin	Chief Executive Officer Emeritus, AOL Time Warner, Inc., New York, NY
Fareed Zakaria	Editor, Newsweek International, New York, NY
Mortimer B. Zuckerman	Chairman and Editor-in-Chief, US News & World Report, New York, NY

Labor Related

Sandra Feldman	President Emeritus, American Federation of Teachers, Washington, DC
John J. Sweeney	President, AFL-CIO, Washington, DC

Senate/Congress

Richard A. Gephardt	former Member (D-MO), US House of Representatives
Jim Leach	Member (R-IA), US House of Representatives
Charles B. Rangel	Member (D-NY), US House of Representatives
John D. Rockefeller IV	Member (D-WV), U.S. Senate
Dianne Feinstein	Member (D-CA), U.S. Senate

Thomas S. Foley	US Ambassador to Japan; former Speaker of the U.S. House of Representatives (D-WA); North American Chairman, TC
Other Political	

George H. W. Bush	President of the United States
Bill Clinton	President of the United States
Richard B. Cheney	Vice President of the United States
Paula J. Dobriansky	US Undersecretary of State for Global Affairs
Robert B. Zoellick	Former US Deputy Secretary of State
Madeleine K. Albright	US Secretary of State
C. Fred Bergsten	Assistant Secretary of the Treasury for International Affairs
William T. Coleman Jr.	US Secretary of Transportation
Lynn Davis	US Undersecretary of State for Arms Control and International Security
Richard N. Haass	US Department of State
Carla A. Hills	US Secretary of Housing and Urban Development
Richard Holbrooke	US Ambassador to the United Nations, former US Assistant Secretary of State for European and Canadian Affairs, former US Assistant Secretary of State for East Asian and Pacific Affairs, and former US Ambassador to Germany
Winston Lord	US Assistant Secretary of State for East Asian and Pacific Affairs, former US Ambassador to China
Joseph S. Nye Jr.	US Assistant Secretary of Defense for International Security Affairs
Richard N. Perle	US Department of Defense; former US Assistant Secretary of Defense for International Security Policy
Thomas R. Pickering	Undersecretary of State for Political Affairs, former US Ambassador to the Russian Federation, India, Israel, El Salvador, Nigeria, the Hashemite Kingdom of Jordan, and the United Nations
Strobe Talbott	US Deputy Secretary of State

A Global New World Order of Economics and Politics

The TC reproduced a powerful commercial and political interest that was committed to private enterprises, economic freedoms, and stronger collective management of global problems. The TC's members are influential politicians; banking and business executives; media, civic, and intellectual leaders; and a few trade union chiefs. The TC became known to be the Shadow Government of the West.

The leaders of the CFR created the TC as a tool to develop a Global Government throughout the world. The fact is that the TC reveals that David Rockefeller and other elites want a Global Government dictatorship. These world elites utilize secretive organizations (CFR, the Bilderberg Society, and the TC) to further its ultimate goal of global domination.

Although all these groups (CFR, the Bilderberg Society, and the TC) play a part in the movement toward a One World Government, the facts on the TC all lead us more specifically to the CFR.

Governor Jimmy Carter Joins the Trilateral Commission

Rockefeller appointed Zbigniew Brzezinski to be the director of the TC.

One of the TC's primary goals was to place a Trilateral-influenced president in the White House in 1976, and to achieve that goal, it was necessary to groom an appropriate candidate who would be willing to cooperate with TC's aims.

Rockefeller and Brzezinski selected a handful of well-known liberal Democrats and a scattering of Republicans (liberal-internationalist) to serve on the TC.

In an effort to give regional balance to the commission, Rockefeller invited the then-obscure one-term Democratic governor Jimmy Carter to join the commission. Rockefeller had longtime ties to the local Atlanta political and economic establishment. In fact, much of Rockefeller's personal investment portfolio is in Atlanta real estate (according to David Horowitz, coauthor of *The Rockefellers*, "Atlanta is Rockefeller Center South").

During the 1976 political campaign, Carter repeatedly told the nation that he was going to get rid of the establishment insiders if he became president. But when he took office, he promptly filled his administration with members of the CFR and TC (284), the two most prominent insider organizations in America. Included in this list of members of the TC were Walter Mondale and Dr. Henry Kissinger.

On March 21, 1978, *The New York Times* featured an article about Zbigniew Brzezinski's close relationship with the president. In part, it reads, "The two men met for the first time four years ago when Mr. Brzezinski was executive director of The TC...and had the foresight to ask the then obscure former Governor of Georgia to join its distinguished ranks. Their initial teacher-student relationship blossomed during the campaign, and appears to have grown closer still."

Senator Barry Goldwater wrote, "David Rockefeller and Zbigniew Brzezinski found Jimmy Carter to be their ideal candidate. They helped him win the nomination, and the presidency. To accomplish this purpose, they mobilized the money power of the Wall Street bankers, the intellectual influence of the academic community—which is subservient to the wealth of the great tax-free foundations—and the media controllers represented in the membership of the CFR and the TC.

"Seven months before the Democratic nominating convention, the Gallup Poll found less than four percent of Democrats favoring Jimmy Carter for President. But, almost overnight—like Willkie, and Eisenhower before him—he became the candidate."

With the power of the TC and the Rockefeller empire and its media influence behind him, Carter made his way to the presidency, establishing the first full-fledged Trilateral administration, appointing numerous Trilateralists to key policymaking positions and carrying out the Trilateral agenda to the hilt."

The Federal Reserve

The same founders who formed the CFR that started the TC also formed the Federal Reserve.

The privileged who created the CFR and TC acquire funds for their plans through illegal taxation and fraudulent debt creation. Using federal taxes and maintaining debt, the people of the United States are forced to fund these privileged of the CFR and TC in their totalitarian plans of creating a New World Order.

Barry Goldwater once stated on this subject: "The TC is international, and it is intended to be the vehicle for multinational consolidation of the commercial and banking interests by seizing control of the political government of the United States. The TC represents a skillful, coordinated effort to seize control and consolidate the four centers of power—political, monetary, intellectual, and ecclesiastical.

"The Trilateral organization created by David Rockefeller was a surrogate—the members selected by Rockefeller, its purposes defined by Rockefeller, its funding supplied by Rockefeller. David Rockefeller screened and selected every individual who was invited to participate."

Coolie Countries

The people of these United States didn't perceive that the United States was to be lowered to the position of using coolie countries who have nothing but raw material and supply the manpower.

International bankers and international industrialists acting together control the United States, a super state, to enslave the world for their own pleasure. The wealth of these United States and the working capital have been taken away from them and has either been locked in the vaults of certain banks and the great corporations or exported to foreign countries for the benefit of the foreign customers of these banks and corporations. The warehouses and coal yards and grain elevators are full, but these are padlocked, and the great banks and corporations hold the keys.

Many of the original TC members are still in positions of power. These individuals are capable to put into practice the TC's recommendations under the TC's supervision.

Bush Administration (Trilateral Commission Members)

Bush Administration

- Brent Scowcroft (National Security Advisor)

408

- Nicholas F. Brady (Secretary of Treasury)

Bill Clinton Administration (Members of the Trilateral Commission Members)

Bill Clinton (who is a member) Administration

- Al Gore (Vice President)

- Donna E. Shalala (Secretary of Health and Human Services)

- Alice M. Rivlin (Deputy Budget Director)

- Madeleine Albright (UN Ambassador)

- Peter Tarnoff (Undersecretary of State for International Security of Affairs)

- Warren M. Christopher (Secretary of State)

- Ronald H. Brown (Secretary of Commerce)

- Henry G. Cisneros (Secretary of Housing and Urban Development)

- Bruce Babbitt (Secretary of Interior)

- Walter Mondale (US Ambassador to Japan)

- William J. Crowe (Chairman of the Foreign Intelligence Advisory Board)

- Lloyd N. Cutler (Counsel to the President)

Trilateral Commission Criticism and Quotes

In *Kissinger on the Couch* (1975), authors Phyllis Schlafly and former CFR member Chester Ward state, "Once the ruling members of the CFR have decided that the US Government should adopt a particular policy, the very substantial research facilities of the CFR are put to work to develop arguments, intellectual and emotional, to support the new policy, and to confound and discredit, intellectually and politically, any opposition."

According to Chester Ward, the CFR's goal is the "submergence of US sovereignty and national independence into an all-powerful one-world government…This lust to surrender the sovereignty and independence of the United States is pervasive throughout most of the membership…In the entire CFR lexicon, there is no term of revulsion carrying a meaning so deep as 'America First.'"

The US News and World Report assessed the impact of Trilateralists' power under Carter: "The 'Trilateralists' have taken charge of foreign policy making in the Carter Administration, and already the immense power they wield is sparking some controversy. Active or former members of the TC now head every key agency involved in mapping U.S. strategy for dealing with the rest of the world…some see this concentration of power as a conspiracy at work."

David Rockefeller stated in 1973 after his visit to China, "The social experiment of China under Chairman Mao's leadership is one of the most important and successful in human history" (quoted by The New York Times, "From a China Traveler," August 10, 1973). "The family unit is broken up…The children are taken away from the parents and placed in government-run nurseries… The parents may see their children once a week and when they see them they cannot show affection toward the children. The idea is to have the children and the family sever their affection and direct it toward the state. Names are taken away from the children and they are given numbers. There is no individual identity…The commune system is destroying morality in Red China: There is no morality because the love of the family is taken away. There is no honesty and respect among men or between men. There is no human dignity: they are all like animals. There is no guilt associated with murder of individuals for the improvement of the state."

In the 1981 book *Democratic Dictatorship: The Emergent Constitution of Control*, Arthur S. Miller describes a "new feudal order" controlled by elitists and asserts that "dictatorship will come—is coming—but with the acquiescence of the people. The goal is 'predictable' man."

Carter administration's Global 2000 Report states, "With the persistence of human poverty and misery, the staggering growth of human population, and ever increasing human demands, the possibilities of further stress and permanent damage to the planet's resource base are very real."

Jim Marrs quotes from his book, *Rule by Secrecy*, "The concept of the TC was originally brought to (David) Rockefeller by Zbigniew Brzezinski, then head of the Russian Studies Department at Columbia University. While at the Brookings Institution, Brzezinski had been researching the need for closer cooperation between the trilateral nations of Europe, North America, and Asia.

"With the blessing of the Bilderbergers and the CFR, the TC began organizing on July 23-24, 1972, at the 3,500-acre Rockefeller estate at Pocantico Hills, New York.

"The TC officially was founded on July 1, 1973, with David Rockefeller as chairman. Brzezinski was named founding North American director."

Journalist and TC researcher Robert Eringer states, "Many of the original members of the TC are now in positions of power where they are able to implement policy recommendations of the Commission; recommendations that they, themselves, prepared on behalf of the Commission. It is for this reason that the Commission has acquired a reputation for being the Shadow Government of the West."

Journalist Bill Moyers (a CFR member), wrote about the power of David Rockefeller in 1980: "David Rockefeller is the most conspicuous representative today of the ruling class, a multinational fraternity of men who shape the global economy and manage the flow of its capital…Private citizen David Rockefeller is accorded privileges of a head of state…He is untouched by customs or passport offices and hardly pauses for traffic lights."

In his 1979 book *Who's Running America?*, Thomas Dye said that Rockefeller was the most powerful man in America.

A TC Task Force Report presented at the 1975 meeting in Kyoto, Japan, called "An Outline for Remaking World Trade and Finance," said: "Close Trilateral cooperation in keeping the peace, in managing the world economy, and in fostering economic development and in alleviating world poverty, will improve the chances of a smooth and peaceful evolution of the global system."

Another Commission document read: "The overriding goal is to make the world safe for interdependence by protecting the benefits which it provides for each country against external and internal threats which will constantly emerge from those willing to pay a price for more national autonomy. This may sometimes require slowing the pace at which interdependence proceeds, and checking some aspects of it. More frequently however, it will call for checking the intrusion of national government into the international exchange of both economic and non-economic goods."

In the late 1800s, at an annual dinner of the American Press Association, John Swinton, an editor at *The New York Times*, said, "There is no such thing, at this date, of the world's history, in America, as an independent press. You know it and I know it. There is not one of you who dares to write your honest opinions, and if you did, you know beforehand that it would never appear in print. I am paid weekly for keeping my honest opinions out of the paper I am connected with. Others of you are paid similar salaries for similar things, and any of you who would be so foolish as to write honest opinions would be out on the streets looking for another job. If I allowed my honest opinions to appear in one issue of my paper, before twenty-four hours my occupation would be gone. The business of the journalist is to destroy truth; to lie outright; to pervert; to vilify; to fawn at the feet of mammon, and to sell his country and his race for his daily bread. You know it and I know it and what folly is this toasting an independent press? We are the tools and vassals for rich men behind the scenes. We are the jumping jacks, they pull the strings and we dance. Our talents, our possibilities, and our lives are all the property of other men. We are intellectual prostitutes."

Holly Sklar, in her book *Trilateralism*, says, "These men make the most important foreign, economic, and domestic policy decisions of the U. S. government today; they set the goals and direction for the administration."

The Reform of International Institutions, "A Report of the Trilateral Tank Force on International Institutions to the TC" (New York: The TC, 1976), states, "The economic officials of... the largest countries must begin to think in terms of managing a single world economy, in addition to managing international economic relations among countries."

On January 7, 1977, *Time Magazine*, whose editor-in-chief, Hedley Donovan, was a powerful Trilateral, named President Carter "Man of the Year." The sixteen-page article in that issue not only failed to mention Carter's connection with the Commission but also stated the following: "As he searched for Cabinet appointees, Carter seemed at times hesitant and frustrated disconcertingly out of character. His lack of ties to Washington—and the Party Establishment—qualities that helped raise him to the White House—carry potential dangers. He does not know the Federal Government or the pressures it creates. He does not really know the politicians whom he will need to help him run the country."

Carter had already chosen his cabinet. Three of his cabinet members—Cyrus Vance, Michael Blumenthal, and Harold Brown—were TCers, and the other non-Commission members were not unsympathetic to Commission objectives and operations. In addition, Carter had appointed another fourteen TCers to top government posts, including the following:

- C. Fred Bergsten (Undersecretary of Treasury)

- James Schlesinger (Secretary of Energy)

- Elliot Richardson (Delegate to Law of the Sea)

- Leonard Woodcock (Chief Envoy to China)

- Andrew Young (Ambassador to the United Nations)

As of December 25, 1976, therefore, there were nineteen Trilaterals, including Carter and Mondale, holding tremendous political power. These presidential appointees represented almost one-third of the TC members from the United States

The TC held their annual plenary meeting in Tokyo, Japan, in January 1977. Carter and Brzezinski obviously could not attend as they were still in the process of reorganizing the White House. They did, however, address personal letters to the meeting, which were reprinted in *Trialogue*, the official magazine of the Commission: "It gives me special pleasure to send greetings to all of you gathering for the TC meeting in Tokyo. I have warm memories of our meeting in Tokyo some eighteen months ago, and am sorry I cannot be with you now.

"My active service on the Commission since its inception in 1973 has been a splendid experience for me, and it provided me with excellent opportunities to come to know leaders in our three regions.

"As I emphasized in my campaign, a strong partnership among us is of the greatest importance. We share economic, political and security concerns that make it logical we should seek ever-increasing cooperation and understanding. And this cooperation is essential not only for our three regions, but in the global search for a more just and equitable world order [emphasis added]. I hope to see you on the occasion of your next meeting in Washington, and I look forward to receiving reports on your work in Tokyo" (Jimmy Carter).

The Christian Science Monitor indicates the fantastic power the CFR has had during the last six administrations (before Mr. Reagan's second term): "Almost half of the Council members have been invited to assume official government positions or to act as consultants at one time or another."

Richard Barnet, with the Institute for Policy Studies, observed that "the TC was barely mentioned in the 1976 campaign. When the Carter cabinet was announced, a few columnists noted the coincidence that so many of them belonged to Mr. Rockefeller's new organization. By the time Jimmy Carter ran for a second term, however, the TC was a major campaign issue."

Jeremiah Novak made this observation in the July 1977 edition of *The Atlantic*: "The Trilaterists' emphasis on international economics is not entirely disinterested, for the oil crisis forced many developing nations, with doubtful repayment abilities, to borrow excessively. All told, private multinational banks, particularly Rockefeller's Chase Manhattan, have loaned nearly $52 billion to developing countries. An overhauled IMF would provide another source of credit for these nations, and would take the big private banks off the hook. This proposal is the cornerstone of the Trilateral plan."

Christopher Lydon also stated in the July 1977 edition of *The Atlantic*, "The TC was David Rockefeller's brainchild."

Sen. Barry Goldwater wrote that the Commission was "intended to be the vehicle for multinational consolidation of the commercial and banking interests by seizing control of the political government of the United States." Goldwater wrote in his book *With No Apologies*, "What the Trilaterals truly intend is the creation of a worldwide economic power superior to the political government of the nation-states involved. As managers and creators of the system they will rule the world....In my view, the TC represents a skillful, coordinated effort to seize control and consolidate the four centers of power: political, monetary, intellectual, and ecclesiastical."

David Rockefeller said in a *Saturday Evening Post* article he wrote to defend his group, "My point is that far from being a coterie of international conspirators with designs on covertly ruling the world, the TC is, in reality, a group of concerned citizens interested in fostering greater understanding and cooperation among international allies."

However, persons who have penetrated the inner actions of the TC's organization have revealed the real purpose of the TC, and these people found out that the real purpose of the TC is to take over all key policymaking positions in the United States government.

Critics of the conservative political class make claims that the TC constitutes a conspiracy to seek and gain control of the United States government in order to create a New World Order government.

Mike Thompson, chairman of the Florida Conservative Union, said, "It puts emphasis on interdependence, which is a nice euphemism for one-world government."

Sen. Barry Goldwater, in his book *With No Apologies*, wrote the following: "In my view, the TC represents a skillful, coordinated effort to seize control and consolidate the four centers of power: political, monetary, intellectual, and ecclesiastical. All this is to be done in the interest of creating a more, peaceful, more productive world community. What the Trilateralists truly intend is the creation of a worldwide economic power superior to the political governments of the nation-states involved. They believe the abundant materialism they propose to create will overwhelm existing differences. As managers and creators of the system they will rule the future.

"The Trilateralists have taken charge of foreign policy-making in the Carter Administration, and already the immense power they wield is sparking some controversy. Active or former members of the TC now head every key agency involved in mapping U.S. strategy for dealing with the rest of the world.

"I think there is an elite in this country and they are the very ones who run an elitist government. They want a government by a handful of people because they don't believe the people themselves can run their lives...Are we going to have an elitist government that makes decisions for people's lives, or are we going to believe as we have for so many decades, that the people can make these decisions for themselves?"

As an example, before being elected president in 1980, Ronald Reagan vocally spoke against anyone who had become involved with the TC. During Reagan's campaign for the president of the United States, he criticized Jimmy Carter for being a Trilateral member and for having nineteen TC members in Jimmy Carter's administration. Reagan pledged that he would investigate the TC, and George Bush Sr., who was a TC and a CFR member, would not have a place in his administration.

The CFR controllers like David Rockefeller used the media to convince Reagan to make their puppet, George Bush, Reagan's vice presidential running mate.

Reagan never again uttered a word against the TC or the CFR.

After Ronald Reagan's election, Reagan's fifty-nine–member transition team contained twenty-eight CFR members, ten members of the elite Bilderberg group, and at least ten TC members. Reagan also appointed prominent CFR members very sensitive offices to the Secretary of State (Alexander Haig, a TC founding member), to the Secretary of Defense (Casper Weinberger), and to the Secretary of the Treasury (Donald Regan).

The obvious fact is that the TC, CFR bankers, and industrialists like David Rockefeller controlled the decision-making of the United States government in the 1980s.

TC and its originator, the CFR, are still in charge. The elite class of individual members keep moving the United States toward accepting a totalitarian New World Order.

Conservative critics claim, "The Commission constitutes a conspiracy seeking to gain control of the US government to create a New World Order."

Sen. Barry Goldwater wrote that the Commission was "intended to be the vehicle for multinational consolidation of the commercial and banking interests by seizing control of the political government of the United States." Goldwater wrote in his book With No Apologies: "What the Trilateralist truly intend is the creation of a worldwide economic power superior to the political government of the nation-states involved. As managers and creators of the system they will rule the world….In my view, the TC represents a skillful, coordinated effort to seize control and consolidate the four centers of power: political, monetary, intellectual, and ecclesiastical."

On the left, the US Labor Party alleges that the Commission was created by multinational companies in order to dominate American foreign policy. Upon analysis, their economic plans leaned toward the controlling of energy sources, food production, and the international monetary system, so was there any reason to doubt that there were ulterior motives to their agenda?

Late in 1972, W. Averell Harriman (known at that time as the "grand old man of the Democrats"), establishment strategist and CFR member, told Milton Katz (also a CFR member), director of International Studies at Harvard, "We've got to get off our high horses and look at some of those southern governors."

Brzezinski said in an October 1973 speech, "The Democratic candidate will have to emphasize work, family, religion, and increasingly, patriotism, if he has any desire to be elected."

This led former Georgia governor Lester Maddox to say, "Based on false, misleading and deceiving statements and actions…Jimmy Carter in my opinion, neither deserves or should expect one vote from the American people."

After Carter beat Ford, Hamilton Jordan, his chief aide, said, "If, after the inauguration, you find Cy Vance [former president of the Rockefeller Foundation] as Secretary of State and Zbigniew Brzezinski as head of National Security, then I would say we have failed."

Henry Kissinger had called Brzezinski his "distinguished presumptive successor." It was Brzezinski who said, "The approaching two-hundredth anniversary of the Declaration of Independence could justify the call for a national constitutional convention to re-examine the nation's formal institutional framework. Either 1976 or 1989—the two-hundredth anniversary of the Constitution—could serve as a suitable target date culminating a national dialogue on the relevance of existing arrangements."

When James Earl Carter took the oath of office, he said that the "United States will help erect...a World Order." This self-proclaimed "outsider" filled many of his administrative posts with establishment insiders from the Rockefeller Foundation, the Brookings Institution, and Coca-Cola. Extracted from Coke were George Ball, Clark Clifford, Samuel P. Huntingdon, Marshall Shulman, Richard Gardner, Henry Owen, Robert Roosa, and J. Paul Austin. Because of the extent to which he used the company when he was governor, he called the Coca-Cola company his "own state department."

In the book *With No Apologies* by Sen. Barry M. Goldwater, he said, "This may cost me everything that I have, but I've got to get out an alert to the American people. The TC represents a skillfully coordinated effort to seize control and consolidate the four centers of power, political, monetary, intellectual, and ecclesiastical. What the Trilateralists intend is the creation of a world-wide economic power superior to the government of the nation states. In other words, what they are driving, orchestrating, meshing and gearing to accomplish is the New World Order, the one-world government."

Antony Sutton wrote in *The Trilateral Observer* that the Trilateralists have rejected the US Constitution and the democratic political process, and their objective is to obtain the wealth of the world for their own use, under the guise of "public service," and to have, ultimately, a one-world socialist government, with them in control.

The Atlantic Monthly reported, "Although the Commission's primary concern is economic, the Trilateralists pinpointed a vital political objective: to gain control of the American Presidency."

Jeremiah Novak said that their purpose was to "fashion a New World Order" and that they had achieved one of their objectives, which was to "gain control of the American presidency."

Craig S. Karpel wrote in his book *Cartergate: The Death of Democracy*, "The presidency of the United States and the key cabinet departments of the federal government have been taken over by a private organization dedicated to the subordination of the domestic interests of the United States to the international interests of the multi-national banks and corporations. It would be unfair to say that the TC dominates the Carter Administration. The TC is the Carter Administration."

Perhaps no one has described the Trilateral operation as succinctly as veteran reporter Jeremiah Novak in *The Christian Science Monitor* (February 7, 1977): "Today a new crop of economists, working in an organization known as the TC, is on the verge of creating a new international economic system, one designed by men as brilliant as Keynes and White. Their names are not well known, but these modern thinkers are as important to our age as Keynes and White were to theirs.

"Moreover, these economists, like their World War II counterparts, are working closely with high government officials, in this case President Jimmy Carter and Vice President Walter Mondale. And what is now being discussed at the highest levels of government, in both the United States and abroad, is the creation of a new world economic system—a system that will affect jobs in America and elsewhere, the prices consumers pay, and the freedom of individuals, corporations, and nations to enter into a truly planetary economic system. Indeed, many observers see the advent of the Carter administration and what is now being called the 'Trilateral' cabinet as the harbinger of this new era."

Trilateral Commission Members

The TC membership is made up of present and past presidents, ambassadors, Secretaries of State, Wall Street investors, international bankers, foundation executives, Think Tank executives, lobbyist lawyers, NATO and Pentagon military leaders, wealthy industrialist, media owners and executives, university presidents and key professors, select senators and congressmen, and wealthy entrepreneurs.

The TC contains influential members who probably are on the CFR membership list. Members of the TC are placed in extremely important government positions that form the United States government's course of action. Today, many of the original members of the TC are in positions of power throughout the world and in the United States. TC's members hold key positions in the United States government and other member government countries.

These TC members implement strategies under the direction of the TC; therefore, the dictatorial commands of the TC acquired a reputation of it being a shadow government.

The TC membership is made up of over three hundred members who only are interested in promoting close international cooperation, especially among noncommunist industrial nations. Many United States Cabinet-level officers and advisors have served on the TC in every United States past and recent administration. The North America region has 107 members. The European region has 150 members. The Pacific-Asian region has 117 members. The TC members are top bankers, industrialists, businessmen, labor leaders, scholars, politicians, senators, and governors. Each region contains a chairman, deputy chairman, and director as well as a forty-four member Executive Committee. The regions also have a small full-time staff in Washington, Paris, and Tokyo.

The following is outlined by Holly Sklar, who has conducted extensive research into the history and background of the TC in her book, *Trilateralism: the TC and Elite Planning for World Management*.

Ruling Class Unite

"The Commission's purpose is to engineer an enduring partnership among the ruling classes of North America, Western Europe and Japan—hence the term 'Trilateral'—in order to safeguard the interests of Western capitalism in an explosive world. The private commission is attempting to mold public policy and construct a framework for international stability in the coming decades.

"To put it simply, Trilateralists are saying: The people, governments and economies of all nations must serve the needs of multinational banks and corporations.

"In short, Trilateralism is the current attempt by ruling elites to manage both dependence and democracy—at home and abroad."

Another Trilateral critic, now-retired Sen. Barry Goldwater (R-Ariz.), views the commission as a Rockefeller family operation through and through. According to Goldwater, "The Trilateral organization created by David Rockefeller was a surrogate—the members selected by Rockefeller, its purposes defined by Rockefeller, its funding supplied by Rockefeller. David Rockefeller screened and selected every individual who was invited to participate."

Picking Policymakers

David Rockefeller and Brzezinski then began the process of selecting from among the "Trilateral" nations the several hundred elite power brokers who would be permitted to join in Trilateral policymaking in the coming years.

One of the commission's primary goals was to place a Trilateral-influenced president in the White House in 1976, and to achieve that goal, it was necessary to groom an appropriate candidate who would be willing to cooperate with Trilateral aims.

Rockefeller and Brzezinski selected a handful of well-known liberal Democrats and a scattering of Republicans (primarily of the liberal-internationalist bent) to serve on the commission.

And in an effort to give regional balance to the commission, Rockefeller invited the then-obscure one-term Democratic governor of Georgia, Jimmy Carter, to join the commission.

Rockefeller Center South

Rockefeller had longtime ties to the local Atlanta political and economic establishment. In fact, much of Rockefeller's personal investment portfolio is in Atlanta real estate (according to David Horowitz, coauthor of *The Rockefellers*, "Atlanta is Rockefeller Center South").

And Rockefeller himself had once even invited Carter to dine with him at the Chase Manhattan Bank several years before, as early as 1971, the year Carter began serving as governor.

Carter very definitely impressed Rockefeller and Brzezinski, more so than another Southern Democrat, Florida Gov. Reuben Askew, who was also selected to serve on the commission and viewed, like Carter, as a possible Trilateral candidate.

In fact, according to Brzezinski, "It was a close thing between Carter and Askew, but we were impressed that Carter had opened up trade offices for the state of Georgia in Brussels and Tokyo. That seemed to fit perfectly into the concept of the Trilateral."

Carter, in fact, like Askew, did announce for the 1976 Democratic presidential nomination, but because of Rockefeller's interest, Carter had the inside shot.

So much so that in a speech at the commission's first annual meeting in Kyoto, Japan, in May 1975, Rockefeller's man Brzezinski promoted the then-still obscure Carter to his fellow Trilateralists as an ideal presidential candidate.

Cut and Dry

From that point on, it was all cut and dried. According to Goldwater, "Rockefeller and Brzezinski found Carter to be their ideal candidate. They helped him win the Democratic nomination and the presidency.

"To accomplish this purpose they mobilized the money-power of the Wall Street bankers, the intellectual influence of the academic community—which is subservient to the wealth of the great tax-free foundations—and the media controllers represented in the membership of the CFR and the Trilateralists."

The aforementioned CFR is another Rockefeller-financed foreign policy pressure group similar to the Trilateralists and the Bilderberg group, although the CFR is composed solely of American citizens.

In other words, it was necessary for the international upper class to band together to protect its interests and to ensure, in the developed nations, that political leaders were brought to power who would ensure that the global financial interests (of the Rockefellers and the other ruling elites) would be protected over those of the hoi polloi.

Pocantico Hills Confabs

Although the initial arrangements for the commission were laid out in a series of meetings held at the Rockefeller's famous Pocantico

Hills estate outside New York City, Rockefeller first introduced the idea of the commission at an annual meeting of the Bilderberg group, this one held in Knokke, Belgium, in the spring of 1972.

The Bilderberg group is similar to the TC in that it is funded and heavily influenced by the Rockefeller empire and composed of international financiers, industrialists, media magnates, union bosses, and academics and political figures.

However, the much older Bilderberg group's membership is strictly limited to participants from the United States, Canada, and Western Europe (i.e., the NATO alliance). For more on the Bilderberg group, keep an eye out for future stories in this paper.

The TC was unique, though, in that it brought the Japanese ruling elite into the inner councils of the global power brokers, a recognition of Japan's growing influence in the world economic and political arena.

Zbigniew Brzezinski

From Brzezinski's *Between Two Ages*:

Though Stalinism may have been a needless tragedy for both the Russian people and communism as an ideal, there is the intellectually tantalizing possibility that for the world at large it was, as we shall see, a blessing in disguise.

Marxism represents a further vital and creative stage in the maturing of man's universal vision. Marxism is simultaneously a victory of the external man over the inner, passive man and a victory of reason over belief.

In the absence of social consensus society's emotional and rational needs may be fused—

mass media makes this easier to achieve—in the person of an individual who is seen as... making the necessary innovations in the social order.

Such a society would be dominated by an elite whose claim to political power would rest on allegedly superior scientific know-how. Unhindered by the restraints of traditional liberal values, this elite would not hesitate to achieve its political ends by the latest modern techniques for influencing public behavior and keeping society under close surveillance and control.

Movement toward such a community [of developed nations]...would involve the forging of community links among the United States, Western Europe, and Japan [a TC-stated objective].

Though the objective of shaping a community of the developed nations is less ambitious than the goal of world government, it is more attainable.

The Soviet Union could have emerged as the standard-bearer of this century's most influential system of thought and as the social model for resolving the key dilemmas facing modern man.

Marxism "supplied the best available insight into contemporary reality. Marxist theory [is] this century's most influential system of thought."

The approaching 200th anniversary of the Declaration of Independence could justify the call for a national Constitutional convention to reexamine the nation's formal institutional framework."

Zbigniew Brzezinski, a professor at Columbia University and a Rockefeller advisor who was a specialist on international affairs, left his post to organize the group with Henry Owen (a Foreign Policy Studies director with the Brookings Institution), George S. Franklin, Robert Bowie (of the Foreign Policy Association and director of the Harvard Center for International Affairs), Gerard Smith (Salt I negotiator , Rockefeller in-law , and First North American Chairman) , Marshall Hornblower, William Scranton (former governor of Pennsylvania), Edwin Reischauer (a professor at Harvard), and Max Kohnstamn.

Brzezinski was the author of the book *Between Two Ages*, which was published in 1970, in which he called for a new international monetary system and is considered to be the "bible" of the Trilateralists. On page 72, he said, "Marxism is simultaneously a victory of the external, active man over the inner, passive man and a victory of reason over belief." He calls for "deliberate management of the American future" (pg. 260), a "community of nations" (pg. 296), and a "world government" (pg. 308). He became the first director (1973–1976), drafted its Charter, and became its driving force.

In this book *Between Two Ages*, Brzezinski praised Marxism, thought of the United States as obsolete, and praised the formation of a one-world government. His thinking closely parallels that of CFR founder Edward Mandell House. On page 83, he states, "Marxism disseminated on the popular level in the form of Communism, represented a major advance in man's ability to conceptualize his relationship to his world."

On page 123, we find the following: "Marxism supplied the best available insight into contemporary reality."

In his White House memoirs, Brzezinski acknowledged, "Moreover, all the key foreign policy decision-makers of the Carter Administration had previously served in the TC."

Zbigniew Brzezinski's *Between Two Ages* was published in 1970 while he was a professor in New York City. David Rockefeller read the book and, in 1973, launched the new TC, whose purposes include linking North America, Western Europe, and Japan "in their economic relations, their political and defense relations, their relations with developing countries, and their relations with Communist countries."

Brzezinski's letter, in a similar vein, follows:

The TC has meant a great deal to me over the last few years. It has been the stimulus for intellectual creativity and a source of personal satisfaction. I have formed close ties with new friends and colleagues in all three regions, ties which I value highly and which I am sure will continue.

I remain convinced that, on the larger architectural issues of today, collaboration among our regions is of the utmost necessity. This collaboration must be dedicated to the fashioning of a more just and equitable world order [emphasis added]. This will require a prolonged process, but I think we can look forward with confidence and take some pride in the contribution which the Commission is making.

Zbigniew Brzezinski

In September 1974, Brzezinski was asked in an interview by the Brazilian newspaper *Vega*, "How would you define this New World Order?"

Brzezinski answered, "When I speak of the present international system I am referring to relations in specific fields, most of all among the Atlantic countries; commercial, military, mutual security relations, involving the international monetary fund, NATO etc. We need to change the international system for a global system in which new, active and creative forces recently developed—should be integrated. This system needs to include Japan. Brazil, the oil producing countries, and even the USSR, to the extent which the Soviet Union is willing to participate in a global system."

When asked if Congress would have an expanded or diminished role in the new system, Brzezinski declared, "The reality of our times is that a modern society such as the U.S. needs a central coordinating and renovating organ which cannot be made up of six hundred people."

In considering our structure of governance, Brzezinski stated, "Tension is unavoidable as man strives to assimilate the new into the framework of the old. For a time the established framework resiliently integrates the new by adapting it in a more familiar shape. But at some point the old framework becomes overloaded. The newer input can no longer be redefined into traditional forms, and eventually it asserts itself with compelling force. Today, though, the old framework of international politics—with their spheres of influence, military alliances between nation-states, the fiction of Sovereignty, doctrinal conflicts arising from nineteenth century crises—is clearly no longer compatible with reality."

One of the most important "frameworks" in the world, and especially to Americans, was the United States Constitution. It was this document that outlined the most prosperous nation in the history of the world. Was our sovereignty really fiction? Was the US vision no longer compatible with reality?

Brzezinski further stated, "The approaching two-hundredth anniversary of the Declaration of Independence could justify the call for a national constitutional convention to reexamine the nation's formal institutional framework. Either 1976 or 1989—the two-hundredth anniversary of the Constitution—could serve as a suitable target date culminating a national dialogue on the relevance of existing arrangements...Realism, however, forces us to recognize that the necessary political innovation will not come from direct constitutional reform, desirable as that would be. The needed change is more likely to develop incrementally and less overtly...in keeping with the American tradition of blurring distinctions between public and private institution."

In Brzezinski's Technetronic Era then, the "nation-state as a fundamental unit of man's organized life has ceased to be the principal creative force: International banks and multinational corporations are acting and planning in terms that are far in advance of the political concepts of the nation-state."

Brzezinski's philosophy clearly pointed forward to Richard Gardner's *The Hard Road to World Order* that appeared in *Foreign Affairs* in 1974, where Gardner stated, "In short, the 'house of world order' would have to be built from the bottom up rather than from the top down. It will look like a great 'booming, buzzing confusion,' to use William James' famous description of reality, but an end run around national sovereignty, eroding it piece by piece, will accomplish much more than the old-fashioned frontal assault."

Senator Goldwater

Senator Goldwater revealed (*With No Apologies*, p. 286.), "David Rockefeller and Zbigniew Brzezinski found Jimmy Carter their ideal candidate. They helped him win the nomination and the presidency. To accomplish this purpose, they mobilized the money power of the Wall Street bankers, the intellectual influence of the academic community-which is subservient to the wealth of the great tax-free foundations—and the media controllers represented in the membership of the CFR and the Trilateral."

Senator Goldwater continued (*With No Apologies*, p. 299.), "Brzezinski and Rockefeller invited Carter to be a member of the TC in 1973. They immediately began grooming him for the Presidency...We have arrived at our present position of peril in the world and at home because our leaders have refused to tell us the truth...unless we, who profess to believe in freedom, wake up, the world is headed for a period of slavery."

Senator Barry Goldwater warns in his 1979 book *With No Apologies*, "The TC is international and is intended to be the vehicle for multinational consolidation of the commercial and banking interests by seizing control of the political government of the United States. The TC represents a skillful, coordinated effort to seize control and consolidate the four centers of power—political, monetary, intellectual and ecclesiastical."

President Bush

On September 11, President Bush added a fifth objective. He said, and I quote, "Out of these troubled times, our fifth objective—a New World Order can emerge...We are now in sight of a United Nations that performs as envisioned by its founders."

On October 1, 1990, President Bush told the General Assembly of the United Nations (again I quote), "The United Nations can help bring about a new day...a New World Order, and a long era of peace."

Appointments

Anthony Lukas of *The New York Times* reported, "Of the first 82 names on a list prepared to help President Kennedy staff his State

Department, 63 were Council members. Kennedy once complained, 'I'd like to have some new faces here, but all I get is the same old names.'"

(James W. Wardner, *The Planned Destruction of America*, PO Box 163141, Altamonte Springs, Florida 32716-3141; 407-865-9722 , p. 60.)

President Nixon appointed 110 CFR members to the highest unelected offices in the land (Wardner, op. cit., p. 59).

President Carter appointed more than seventy men from the CFR and over twenty members of the TC to the highest unelected offices of government (Wardner, op. cit., p. 58).

President Reagan appointed over eighty individuals to his administration who were members of the CFR, the TC, or both. Note especially his running mate, Trilateralist George Bush. Reagan appointed to the highest offices in government 64 CFR members, 6 Trilateral members, 6 both CFR and Trilateral members, and 5 former members of the TC (Wardner, op. cit., p. 56).

Most of President Clinton's first-term cabinet officers were CFR members, including Secretary of State, Deputy Secretary of State, Secretary of Defense, National Security Advisor, Deputy National Security Advisor, CIA Director, Chairman of the Foreign Intelligence Advisory Board, Secretary of Treasury, Deputy Secretary of the Treasury, Secretary of Health and Human Services, Secretary of Housing and Urban Development, Secretary of the Interior, Undersecretary for Political Affairs, Assistant Secretary of State for East Asian and Pacific Affairs, Aid Coordinator to the Commonwealth of Independent States, Deputy Director, Office of Management and Budget, Chairman, Council of Economic Advisors, US Ambassador to the United Nations (Madeleine Albright, who was responsible for foreign policy legislation during the Carter years and was director of the world government–promoting Atlantic Council, now Secretary of State under Clinton) (Wardner, op. cit., pp. 51–52).

Dr. James W. Wardner, in his well-documented book, lists the following:

> Of the eighteen secretaries of the treasury since 1921, twelve have been members of the CFR.
>
> Of the sixteen secretaries of state, twelve have been CFR members (four have been presidents of Rockefeller Foundation).
>
> The Defense Department, created in 1947, has had fifteen secretaries; nine have been CFR.
>
> The CIA, also created in 1947, has had eleven directors seven have been CFR.
>
> Six of seven superintendents at West Point have been CFR.
>
> Every supreme Allied commander in Europe has been CFR
>
> Every U.S. ambassador to NATO has been CFR.

The Four key positions in every administration, Republican or Democratic, are routinely filled by CFR members:

National Security Advisor, Secretary of State, Secretary of Defense, Secretary of Treasury

There are increasing numbers of CFR members in the legislative branch of government. Pat Schroeder (D-CO), Christopher Dodd (D-CT), Newt Gingrich (R-GA), Warren Rudman (R-NH), Bob Graham (D-FL), Thomas Foley (D- WA), Charles Robb (D-VA), John D. Rockefeller, IV (D-WV) are all members.

George Bush had 387 members of the CFR in his administration. Ronald Reagan had 313. The team of Clinton and Gore is financed and supported by the CFR as well. Clinton is a member of the CFR and the TC.

Perot, the outsider in the 1992 elections, picked CFR people to run his campaign.

Total CFR membership as of December 1992 was 2905.

The objective of the CFR and CFR-controlled State Department is to completely disarm the whole world including America and let the United Nations has monopoly on armed forces which they called the U.N. Peace Force.

(Wardner, op. cit., pp. 67–68)

Pat Robertson

In *The New World Order* by Pat Robertson, it states, "In 1970 a young Polish intellectual named Zbigniew Brzezinski foresaw the rising economic power of Japan, and postwar Europe. Brzezinski idealized the theories of Karl Marx. In his book, Between Two Ages, as in subsequent writings, he argued that balance-of-power politics was out, and world-order politics was in. The initial world order was to be a trilateral economic linkage between Japan, Europe, and the United States. David Rockefeller funded Brzezinski, and called together an organization, named the TC, with Brzezinski as its first executive secretary, and director."

Trilateral Commission's Stated Goals

GOLDWATER SEES ELITIST SENTIMENTS
THREATENING LIBERTIES

By U.S. Senator Barry M. Goldwater (1979)

In September 1939, two members of the CFR visited the State Department to offer the council's services.

They proposed to do research and make recommendations for the department without formal assignment or responsibility, particularly in four areas—security armaments, economic and financial problems, political problems, and territorial problems. The Rockefeller Foundation agreed to finance the operation of this plan.

From that day forward, the CFR has placed its members in policy-making positions with the State Department and other federal agencies. Every Secretary of State since 1944, with the exception of James F. Byrnes, has been a member fo the council.

Almost without exception, its members are united by a congeniality of birth, economic status and educational background. The organization itself began in 1919 in Paris when scholars turned their attention to foreign affairs after the end of World War I. It remains a non-governmental private grouping of specialists in foreign affairs.

A number of writers, disturbed by the influential role that this organization has played in determining foreign policy, have concluded that the council and its members are an active part of the communist conspiracy for world domination.

Their syllogistic argument goes like this: The council has dominated American foreign policy since 1945. All American policy decisions have resulted in losses to the Communists. Therefore, all members of the council are communist sympathizers.

Many of the policies advocated by the council have been damaging to the cause of freedom and particularly to the United States. But this is not because the members are communists or communist sympathizers. This explanation of our foreign policy reversals is too pat, too simplistic.

I believe that the CFR and its ancillary elitist groups are indifferent to communism. They have no ideological anchors. In their pursuit of a New World Order they are prepared to deal without prejudice with a communist state a socialist state, a democratic state, a monarchy, an oligarchy—its all the same to them.

Their goal is to impose a benign stability on the quarreling family of nations through merger and consolidation. They see the elimination of national boundaries, the suppression of racial and ethnic loyalties, as the most expeditious avenue to world peace. They believe economic competition is the root cause of international tension.

Perhaps if the council's vision of the future were realized, it would reduce wars, lessen poverty and bring about a more efficient utilization of the world's resources. To my mind, this would inevitably be accompanied by a loss in personal freedom of choice and reestablishment of the restraints that provoked the American Revolution.

When we change presidents, it is understood to mean that the voters are ordering a change in national policy. Since 1945, three different Republicans have occupied the White House for 16 years, and four Democrats have held this most powerful post for 17 years. With the exception of the first seven years of the Eisenhower administration, there has been no appreciable change in foreign or domestic policy direction.

There has been a great turnover in personnel but no change in policy. Example: during the Nixon years, Henry Kissinger, a council member and Nelson Rockefeller protégé was in charge of foreign policy. When Jimmy Carter was elected, Kissinger was replaced by Zbigniew Brzezinski, a council member and David Rockefeller protégé.

Starting in the '30s and continuing through World War II, our official attitude toward the Far East reflected the thinking of the Institute of Pacific Relations. Members of the institute were placed in important teaching positions. They dominated the Asian affairs section of the State Department. Their publications were standard reading material for the armed forces, in most American colleges, and were used in 1,300 public school systems.

The Institute of Pacific Relations was behind the decision to cut off aid to Chiang Kai-Shek unless he embraced the communists, and the CFR is the parent reorganization of the Institute of Pacific Relations.

Everything he said was true. We are dependent on other nations for raw materials and for markets. It is necessary to have defense alliances with other nations in order to balance the military power of those who would destroy us.

Where I differ from Rockefeller is in the suggestion that to achieve this new federalism, the United States must submerge its national identity and surrender substantial matters of sovereignty to a new political order.

The implications in Nelson Rockefeller's presentation have become concrete proposals advanced by David Rockefeller's newest international cabal, the TC.

Whereas the CFR is distinctly national, representation is allocated equally to Western Europe, Japan and the United States. It is intended to act as the vehicle for multinational consolidation of the commercial and banking interests by seizing control of the political government of the United States.

Zbigniew Brzezinski and David Rockefeller screened and selected every individual who was invited to participate in shaping and administering The proposed New World Order.

In the late 1950s, Brzezinski, an accepted member of the inner circle of academics, asserting the need for global strategies, was openly anti-communist. By 1964, he had modified his criticism of communism.

In his prospectus describing the TC, David Rockefeller said that he intended to bring the best brains of the world together to bear on the problems of the future.

I find nothing inherently sinister in this original proposal, although the name he gave his new creation strikes me as both grandiose and presumptuous. The accepted definition of a commission is a group nominated by some higher authority to perform a specific function.

The Trilateral organization created by David Rockefeller was a surrogate - its members selected by Rockefeller, its purposes defined by Rockefeller, Its funding supplied by Rockefeller.

Whether or not the approximately 200 individuals selected for membership on the commission represent the "best brains" in the world is an arguable proposition.

Examination of the membership roster establishes beyond question that all those invited to join were members of the power elite, enlisted with great skill and singleness of purpose from the banking, commercial, political and communications sectors.

Nor was the governmental community over-looked, Invitations to join were extended to Sen. Walter Mondale, Gov. Jimmy Carter of Georgia, George Ball, Cyrus Vance, Paul Warnke and Reps. Donald Fraser and John Brademas, among others.

In my view, the TC represents a skillful, coordinated effort to seize control and consolidate the four centers of power—political, monetary, intellectual and ecclesiastical.

All this is to be done in the interest of creating a more peaceful, more productive world community. I have no hesitancy about judging its wisdom and the results of its actions.

A report presented at the plenary meeting of the TC in May 1975, at Kyoto, Japan, called for an enlargement of central authority and expressed a lack of confidence in democratically arrived at public decisions.

It also suggested that it would be helpful to impose prior restrictions on the press and to restructure the laws of libel to check the power of the press.

I've suffered as greatly from an abusive press as any man in public life, but I get an itchy, uncomfortable feeling at the base of my spine when someone suggest that government should control the news.

The entire TC approach is strictly economic. No recognition is given to the political condition. Total reliance is placed on materialism. The commission emphasizes the necessity of eliminating artificial barriers to world commerce, tariff, export duties, quota— an objective that I strongly support. What it proposes to substitute is an international economy managed and controlled by international monetary groups.

No attempt has been made to explain why the people of the western world enjoy economic abundance. Freedom - spiritual, political, economic—is denied any importance in the Trilateral construction of the next century.

The TC even selects and elevates its candidates to positions of political power.

David Rockefeller and Zbigniew Brzezinski found Jimmy Carter to be an ideal candidate, for example. They helped him win the democratic nomination and the presidency.

To accomplish their purpose, they mobilized the money power of the wall street bankers, The intellectual influence of the academic community—which is subservient to the wealthy of the great tax-free foundations—and the media controllers represented in the membership of the CFR and the TC.

It was no accident that Brzezinski and Rockefeller invited Carter to join the commission in 1973. But they weren't ready to bet all their chips on Carter.

They made him a founding member of the commission but to keep their options open, they also brought in Walter Mondale and Elliot Richardson, a highly visible Republican member of the Nixon administration, and they looked at other potential nominees.

After his nomination, Carter chose Mondale as his vice president. He chose Brzezinski as his foreign affairs adviser and Cyrus Vance as his secretary of state.

Accepting the democratic presidential nomination in New York, carter denounced those "unholy, self-perpetuating alliances that have formed between money and politics."

In 1962, Nelson Rockefeller, in a lecture at Harvard University on the interdependence of nations in the modern world, said: "And so the nation-state, standing alone, threatens in many ways to seem as anachronistic as the Greek city-state eventually became in ancient times.

Jeremiah Novak, in *The Christian Science Monitor* (February 7, 1977), stated, "Today a new crop of economists, working in an organization known as the TC, is on the verge of creating a new international economic system, one designed by men as brilliant as Keynes and White. Their names are not well known, but these modern thinkers are as important to our age as Keynes and White were to theirs.

"Moreover, these economists, like their World War II counterparts, are working closely with high government officials, in this case President Jimmy Carter and Vice President Walter Mondale. And what is now being discussed at the highest levels of government, in both the United States and abroad, is the creation of a new world economic system - a system that will affect jobs in America and elsewhere, the prices consumers pay, and the freedom of individuals, corporations, and nations to enter into a truly planetary economic system. Indeed, many observers see the advent of the Carter administration and what is now being called the 'Trilateral' cabinet as the harbinger of this new era.

"The CFR is the establishment. Not only does it have influence and power in key decision-making positions at the highest levels of government to apply pressure from above, but it also finances and uses individuals and groups to bring pressure from below, to justify the high level decisions for converting the U.S. from a sovereign Constitution Republic into a servile member of a one-world dictatorship."

In 1973, Jimmy Carter became a student of Brzezinski and a founding member of the TC.

Barry Goldwater once stated on this subject: "The TC is international, and it is intended to be the vehicle for multinational consolidation of the commercial and banking interests by seizing control of the political government of the United States. The TC represents a skillful, coordinated effort to seize control and consolidate the four centers of power—political, monetary, intellectual, and ecclesiastical."

The Trilateral Commission Force
Economic Nature

What was the economic nature of the driving force within the TC? It was the giant multinational corporations—those with Trilateral representation—which consistently benefited from Trilateral policy and actions.

Polished academics such as Brzezinski, Gardner, Allison, McCracken, Henry Owen, etc., served only to give "philosophical" justification to the exploitation of the world.

Don't underestimate their power or the distance they had already come by 1976. Their economic base was already established. Giants like Coca-Cola, IBM, CBS, Caterpillar Tractor, Bank of America, Chase Manhattan Bank, Deere & Company, Exxon, and others virtually dwarf whatever remains of American businesses. The market value of IBM's stock alone, for instance, was greater than the value of all the stocks on the American Stock Exchange. Chase Manhattan Bank had some fifty thousand branches or correspondent banks throughout the world. What reached our eyes and ears was highly regulated by CBS, *The New York Times*, *Time Magazine*, etc.

The most important thing of all is to remember that the political coup de grâce preceded the economic coup de grâce. The domination of the Executive Branch of the US government provided all the necessary political leverage needed to skew US and global economic policies to their own benefit.

By 1977, the TC had notably become expert at using crises (and creating them in some instances) to manage countries toward the New World Order, yet they found menacing backlashes from those very crises.

In the end, the biggest crisis of all was that of the American way of life. Americans never counted on such powerful and influential groups working against the Constitution and freedom, either inadvertently or purposefully, and even now, the principles that helped to build this great country are all but reduced to the sound of meaningless babblings.

Trilateral Entrenchment: 1980–2007

It would have been damaging enough if the Trilateral domination of the Carter administration was merely a one-time anomaly; but it was not!

Subsequent presidential elections brought George H.W. Bush (under Reagan), William Jefferson Clinton, Albert Gore and Richard Cheney (under G. W. Bush) to power.

Thus, every Administration since Carter has had top-level TC representation through the President or Vice-president, or both!

It is important to note that Trilateral domination has transcended political parties: they dominated both the Republican and Democrat parties with equal aplomb.

In addition, the Administration before Carter was very friendly and useful to Trilateral doctrine as well: President Gerald Ford took the reins after President Richard Nixon resigned, and then appointed Nelson Rockefeller as his Vice President. Neither Ford nor Rockefeller were members of the TC, but Nelson was David Rockefeller's brother and that says enough. According to Nelson Rockefeller's memoirs, he originally introduced then-governor Jimmy Carter to David and Brzezinski.

How has the TC effected their goal of creating a New World Order or a New International Economic Order? They seated their own members at the top of the institutions of global trade, global banking and foreign policy.

For instance, the World Bank is one of the most critical mechanisms in the engine of globalization. Since the founding of the TC in 1973, there have been only seven World Bank presidents, all of whom were appointed by the President. Of these seven, six were pulled from the ranks of the TC!

- A.W. Clausen (1981–1986)

- Barber Robert McNamara (1968–1981)

- Conable (1986–1991)

- Lewis Preston (1991–1995)

- James Wolfenson (1995–2005)

- Paul Wolfowitz (2005–2007)

- Robert Zoellick (2007–present)

Another good evidence of domination is the position of U.S. Trade Representative which is critically involved in negotiating the many international trade treaties and agreements that have been necessary to create the New International Economic Order. Since 1977, there have been ten USTR's appointed by the President. Eight have been members of the TC!

- Robert S. Strauss (1977–1979)

- Reubin O'D. Askew (1979–1981)

- William E. Brock III (1981–1985)

- Clayton K. Yeutter (1985–1989)

- Carla A. Hills (1989–1993)

- Mickey Kantor (1993–1997)

- Charlene Barshefsky (1997–2001)

- Robert Zoellick (2001–2005)

- Rob Portman (2005–2006)

- Susan Schwab (2006–present)

This is not to say that Clayton Yeuter and Rob Portman were not friendly to Trilateral goals, because they clearly were.

The Secretary of State cabinet position has seen its share of Trilaterals as well: Henry Kissinger (Nixon, Ford), Cyrus Vance (Carter), Alexander Haig (Reagan), George Shultz (Reagan), Lawrence Eagleburger (G.H.W. Bush), Warren Christopher (Clinton) and Madeleine Albright (Clinton) There were some Acting Secretaries of State that are also noteworthy: Philip Habib (Carter), Michael Armacost (G.H.W. Bush),

Arnold Kantor (Clinton), Richard Cooper (Clinton).

Lastly, it should be noted that the Federal Reserve has likewise been dominated by Trilaterals: Arthur Burns (1970–1978), Paul Volker (1979–1987), Alan Greenspan (1987–2006). While the Federal Reserve is a privately-owned corporation, the President "chooses" the Chairman to a perpetual appointment. The current Fed Chairman, Ben Bernanke, is not a member of the TC, but he clearly is following the same globalist policies as his predecessors.

The point raised here is that Trilateral domination over the U.S. Executive Branch has not only continued and but has been strengthened from 1976 to the present. The pattern has been deliberate and persistent: Appoint members of the TC to critical positions of power so that they can carry out Trilateral policies.

The question is and has always been, do these policies originate in consensus meetings of the TC where two-thirds of the members are not U.S. citizens? The answer is all too obvious.

Trilateral-friendly defenders attempt to sweep criticism aside by suggesting that membership in the TC is incidental, and that it only demonstrates the otherwise high quality of appointees. Are we to believe that in a country of 300 million people only these 100 or so are qualified to hold such critical positions? Again, the answer is all too obvious.

Where Does the CFR Fit?

While virtually all TC members from North America have also been members of the CFR, the reverse is certainly not true. It is easy to over-criticize the CFR because most of its members seem to fill the balance of government positions not already filled by Trilaterals.

The power structure of the Council is seen in the makeup of its board of directors: No less than 44 percent (12 out of 27) are members of the Commission! If director participation reflected only the general membership of the CFR, then only 3-4 percent of the board would be Trilaterals.

Further, the president of the CFR is Richard N. Haass, a very prominent Trilateral member who also served as Director of Policy Planning for the U.S. Department of State from 2001–2003.

Trilateral influence can easily be seen in policy papers produced by the CFR in support of Trilateral goals.

For instance, the 2005 CFR task force report on the Future of North America was perhaps the major Trilateral policy statement on the intended creation of the North American Union. Vice-chair of the task force was Dr. Robert A. Pastor, who has emerged as the "Father of the North American Union" and has been directly involved in Trilateral operations since the 1970's. While the CFR claimed that the task force was "independent," careful inspection of those appointed reveal that three Trilaterals were carefully chosen to oversee the Trilateral position, one each from Mexico, Canada and the United States: Luis Rubio, Wendy K. Dobson and Carla A. Hills, respectively. Hills has been widely hailed as the principal architect of the North American Free Trade Agreement (NAFTA) that was negotiated under President George H.W. Bush in 1992.

The bottom line is that the CFR, thoroughly dominated by Trilaterals, serves the interests of the TC, not the other way around!

Trilateral Globalization in Europe

The content of this paper thus far suggests ties between the TC and the United States. This is not intended to mean that Trilaterals are not active in other countries as well.

Thus, since 1973 and in parallel with their U.S. Hegemony, the European members of the TC were busy creating the European Union. In fact, the EU's Constitution was authored by Commission member Valéry Giscard d'Estaing in 2002–2003, when he was President of the Convention on the Future of Europe.

The steps that led to the creation of the European Union are unsurprisingly similar to the steps being taken to create the North American Union today. As with the EU, lies, deceit and confusion are the principal tools used to keep an unsuspecting citizenry in the dark while they forge ahead without mandate, accountability or oversight.

Conclusion

It is clear that the Executive Branch of the U.S. was literally hijacked in 1976 by members of the TC, upon the election of President Jimmy Carter and Vice-President Walter Mondale. This near-absolute domination, especially in the areas of trade, banking, economics and foreign policy, has continued unchallenged and unabated to the present.

Windfall profits have accrued to interests associated with the TC, but the effect of their "New International Economic Order" on the U.S. has been nothing less than devastating.

The philosophical underpinnings of the TC are pro-Marxist and pro-socialist. They are solidly set against the concept of the nation-state and in particular, the Constitution of the United States. Thus, national sovereignty must be diminished and then abolished altogether in order to make way for the New World Order that will be governed by an unelected global elite with their self-created legal framework.

If you are having negative sentiment against Trilateral-style globalization, you are not alone. A 2007 Financial Times/Harris poll revealed that less than 20 percent of people in six industrialized countries (including the U.S.) believe that globalization is good for their country while over 50 percent are outright negative towards it. While citizens around the world are feeling the pain of globalization, few understand why it is happening and hence, they have no effective strategy to counter it.

The American public has never, ever conceived that such forces would align themselves so successfully against freedom and Liberty. Yet, the evidence is clear: Steerage of America has long since fallen into the hands of an actively hostile enemy that intends to remove all vestiges of the very things that made us the greatest nation in the history of mankind.

(Wood, Patrick. "The Trilateral Commission: Usurping Sovereignty," Third World Traveler. https://thirdworldtraveler.com/New_World_Order/Trilateral_UsurpSovereign.html)

"Subpage not available."

TRILATERAL COMMISSION INSIDERS USUALLY RUN FOR AND WIN

It started in 1952. Nearly every person elected as president of the United States since then—and nearly every opponent—has belonged to a secretive, globalism-oriented organization known as the Council on Foreign Relations.

Some presidents and their challengers have belonged to additional clubs of internationalists—the Bilderberg Group and the Trilateral Commission. Running mates, too, more often than not have had ties to the groups.

That the groups exert enormous influence on public policy is indisputable. What is disputed is whether such groups are, as adherents and members argue, just discussion forums for movers and shakers, or, as critics have long alleged, secret societies shaping a New World Order from behind the scenes. On that last point at least, no one could challenge the critics: All these groups operate in considerable secrecy, away from the scrutiny of the American public.

Regardless of how one characterizes them, the fact that virtually all presidents belong to the same secret clubs prompts the author of a new book to wonder if the 2008 election will also be a contest between globalist insiders. Judging from the list of frontrunners of each party, Daniel Estulin, author of "The True Story of the Bilderberg Group," may be on to something.

According to a variety of sources, the following presidential candidates are either members of one of the groups or have strong ties: Hillary Rodham Clinton, Rudy Giuliani, Mitt Romney, Barack Obama, John McCain, John Edwards, Fred Thompson, Joe Biden, Chris Dodd and Bill Richardson.

Mike Huckabee, though not a member, spoke to the CFR in September. Since then, his political star has risen to the point that he has become a top-tier candidate.

So often throughout recent history it has been the case.

Ever since Democrat Adlai Stevenson challenged Republican Dwight D. Eisenhower in 952 and 1956, the odds have significantly favored those with membership in the elite groups.

In 1964, President Lyndon B. Johnson was not a member. Neither was his opponent, Barry Goldwater. But Johnson had already staffed his administration with plenty of insiders.

In 1968, it was Nixon versus club member Hubert H. Humphrey.

In 1972, it was Nixon again against Democratic Party CFR member George McGovern.

In 1976, it was CFR Republican Gerald Ford losing to CFR Democrat Jimmy Carter.

In 1980, Ronald Reagan was not a member, but his running mate, George H.W. Bush, was. So were both of his opponents—Carter and independent John Anderson. Assuming office, however, Reagan quickly named 313 CFR members to his team.

In 1984, another CFR member, Walter Mondale, was nominated by the Democratic Party to challenge Reagan.

In 1988, CFR member Bush took on CFR member Michael Dukakis.

In 1960, both John F. Kennedy and Richard M. Nixon were members.

In 1992, Bush was challenged by an obscure governor from Arkansas,

Bill Clinton, who won the "trifecta" by being a member of the CFR, TC and Bilderberg Group.

In 1996, Clinton was challenged by CFR member Bob Dole.

In 2000, CFR member Al Gore ran against non-member George W. Bush, but his running mate, Dick Cheney, was.

In 2004, Bush was challenged by CFR member John Kerry.

"David Rockefeller, whose family financed the CFR, is a common denominator among these parallel groups," writes Estulin. "Not only is he the CFR chairman emeritus, but he also continues to provide financial and personal support to the TC, CFR and Bilderberg Group."

What is the agenda behind these groups, which Estulin says are comprised of "self-interested elitists protecting their wealth and the investments of multinational banks and corporations in the growing world economy at the expense of developing nations and Third World countries"?

"The policies they develop," he writes, "benefit them as well as move us towards a one-world government."

Those questioning Estulin's conclusion as mere speculation need only recall organizational financer David Rockefeller's own words as recorded in his "Memoirs."

"Some even believe we are part of a secret cabal working against the best interests of the United States, characterizing my family and me as 'internationalists' and conspiring with others around the world to build a more integrated global political and economic structure – one world, if you will," he wrote. "If that's the charge, I stand guilty, and I am proud of it."

With regard to insider roles in recent U.S. presidential races, two of the most interesting were 1976 and 1992.

"In the spring of 1972, a high-profile group of men gathered for dinner with W. Averell Harriman, the grand old man of the Democratic Party, a Bilderberger and a member of the CFR," writes Estulin. "Also present were Milton Katz, a CFR member and director of international studies at Harvard, Robert Bowie, who would later become deputy director of the CIA, George Franklin, David Rockefeller's coordinator for the TC, and Gerald Smith, U.S. ambassador-at-large for non-proliferation matters. The focus of their discussion was the not-too-distant 1976 presidential elections. Harriman suggested that if the Democrats wanted to recapture the White House, "we had better get off our high horses and look at some of those southern governors." Several names cropped up. Among them were Ruben Askew, governor of Florida, and Terry Sanford, former governor of North Carolina and, at the time, president of Duke University."

Katz reportedly informed David Rockefeller of the viability of Jimmy Carter, then governor of Georgia. According to the author, he could be sold politically to the American people. At a dinner in London, recorded by the London Times, Rockefeller got acquainted with Carter and became convinced he could become the next U.S. president. Carter was invited to join the TC and quickly accepted.

Later, U.S. News and World Report would have this to say about the Carter administration: "The Trilateralists have taken charge of foreign policy-making in the Carter administration, and already the immense power they wield is sparking some controversy. Active or former members of the TC now head every key agency involved in mapping U.S. strategy for dealing with the rest of the world."

In 1992, Estulin concludes Bill Clinton was similarly "anointed" for the presidency at the 1991 Bilderberg Conference in Baden-Baden. Following the meeting, Clinton immediately took a trip to Russia to meet with Soviet Interior Minister Vadim Balatin, then serving Mikhail Gorbachev. Later, when Boris Yeltsin won the presidential election, Bakatin became the new chief of the KGB.

The meeting went unnoticed in most of the press, with the exception of the Arkansas Democrat, whose headline told the story: "Clinton has powerful buddy in U.S.S.R— New head of KGB."

Estulin's book, first written in 2005 in Spain, has been translated into 24 languages, most recently this English edition. He has covered the Bilderberg Group as a journalist for more than 15 years.

(WND Staff, "Will Secret Clubs Pick Next Prez?" World Net Daily, November 1, 2007)

TRILATERAL COMMISSION MEMBERSHIP

North American Chairman: Thomas Foley

- Partner, Akin Gump Strauss Hauer & Feld, Washington DC

- Former US Ambassador to Japan

- Former Speaker of the US House of Representatives

- European Chairman: Peter Sutherland

- Chairman, BP p.l.c., London

- Chairman, Goldman Sachs International

- Special Representative of the United Nations Secretary-General for Migrations

- Former Director General, GATT/WTO, Geneva

- Former Member of the European Commission

- Former Attorney General of Ireland

- Pacific Asian Chairman: Yotaro Kobayashi

- Chief Corporate Advisor, Fuji Xerox Co., Ltd., Tokyo

- North American Deputy Chairman: Allanee Gotlieb

- Senior Adviser, Bennett Jones LLP, Toronto, ON

- Chairman, Sotheby's, Canada

- Former Canadian Ambassador to the United States

NORTH AMERICAN DEPUTY CHAIRMAN: LORENZO ZAMBRANO

- Chairman of the Board and Chief Executive Officer, CEMEX, Monterrey, NL, Mexico

EUROPEAN DEPUTY CHAIRMAN: HERVE DE CARMOY

- Chairman, Almatis, Frankfurt-am-Main

- Former Partner, Rhône Group, New York & Paris

- Honorary Chairman, Banque Industrielle et Mobilière Privée, Paris

- Former Chief Executive, Société Générale de Belgique

EUROPEAN DEPUTY CHAIRMAN: ANDRZEJ OLECHOWSKI

- Founder, Civic Platform

- Former Chairman, Bank Handlowy

- Former Minister of Foreign Affairs and of Finance, Warsaw

PACIFIC ASIAN DEPUTY CHAIRMAN: HAN SUNG-JOO

- President, Korea University, Seoul

- Former Korean Minister for Foreign Affairs

- Former Korean Ambassador to the United States

PACIFIC ASIAN DEPUTY CHAIRMAN: SHIJURO OGATA

- Former Deputy Governor, Japan Development Bank

- Former Deputy Governor for International Relations, Bank of Japan

NORTH AMERICAN VICE CHAIRMAN: JOSEPH S. NYE JR.

- Distinguished Service Professor at Harvard University, John F. Kennedy School of Government, Harvard University, Cambridge, MA

- Former Dean, John F. Kennedy School of Government

- Former US Assistant Secretary of Defense for International Security Affairs

NORTH AMERICAN DIRECTOR: MICHAEL J. O'NEIL

EUROPEAN DIRECTOR: PAUL REVAY

PACIFIC ASIA DIRECTOR: TADASHI YAMAMOTO

FORMER NORTH AMERICAN CHAIRMEN

- Paul A. Volcker (1991–2001), Honorary North American Chairman

- David Rockefeller (1977–1991), Founder and Honorary North American Chairman

- Gerard C. Smith (1973–1977)

FORMER EUROPEAN CHAIRMEN

- Otto Graf Lambsdorff (1992–2001), Honorary European Chairman

- Georges Berthoin (1976–1992), Honorary European Chairman

- Max Kohnstamm (1973–1976)

FORMER JAPANESE CHAIRMEN

- Kiichi Miyazawa, Acting Chairman (1993–1997)

- Akio Morita (1992–1993)

- Isamu Yamashita (1985–1992)

- Takeshi Watanabe (1973–1985)

EXECUTIVE COMMITTEE

- Erik Belfrage

  Senior Vice President, Skandinaviska Enskilda Banken

  Director, Investor AB, Stockholm

- C. Fred Bergsten

  Director, Peterson Institute for International Economics, Washington, DC

  Former US Assistant Secretary of the Treasury for International Affairs

- Georges Berthoin t

  International Honorary Chairman, European Movement

  Honorary Chairman, he Jean Monnet Association

  Honorary European Chairman, the Trilateral Commission

- Jorge Braga de Macedo

  President, Tropical Research Institute, Lisbon

  Professor of Economics, Nova University at Lisbon

  Chairman, Forum Portugal Global

Former Minister of Finance

- Zbigniew Brzezinski
- Counselor, Center for Strategic and International Studies, Washington, DC
- Robert Osgood

    Professor of American Foreign Affairs, Paul Nitze School of Advanced International Studies, Johns Hopkins University

    Former Assistant to the President for National Security Affairs

- François Bujon de l'Estang, Ambassadeur de France

    Chairman, Citigroup France, Paris

    Former Ambassador to the United States

- Richard Conroy

    Chairman, Conroy Diamonds & Gold, Dublin

    Member of Senate, Republic of Ireland

- Vladimir Dlouhy

    Senior Advisor, ABB

    International Advisor, Goldman Sachs

    Former Czechoslovak Minister of Economy

    Former Czech Minister of Industry & Trade, Prague

- Bill Emmott

    Former Editor, *The Economist*, London

- Nemesio Fernandez-Cuesta

Executive Director of Upstream, Repsol-YPF

Former Chairman, Prensa Española, Madrid

- Michael Fuchs

  Member of the German Bundestag

  Former President, National Federation of German Wholesale & Foreign Trade, Berlin

- Antonio Garrigues Walker

  Chairman, Garrigues Abogados y Asesores Tributarios, Madrid

- Toyoo Gyohten

  President, the Institute for International Monetary Affairs

  Senior Advisor, the Bank of Tokyo-Mitsubishi, UFJ, Ltd., Tokyo

- Stuart Harris

  Professor of International Relations, Research School of Pacific and Asian Studies, Australian National University

  Former Vice Minister of Foreign Affairs, Canberra

- Carla A. Hills

  Chairman and Chief Executive Officer, Hills & Company, Washington, DC

  Former US Trade Representative

  Former US Secretary of Housing and Urban Development

- Karen Elliott House

Writer, Princeton, New Jersey

Senior Fellow, Belfer Center for Science and International Affairs, John F. Kennedy School of Government, Harvard University, Cambridge, Massachusetts

Former Senior Vice President, Dow Jones & Company

Publisher, *The Wall Street Journal*

- Mugur Isărescu

  Governor, National Bank of Romania, Bucharest

  Former Prime Minister of Romania

- Baron Daniel Janssen

  Honorary Chairman, Solvay, Brussels

- Béla Kadar

  Member of the Hungarian Academy, Budapest

  Member of the Monetary Council of the National Bank

  President of the Hungarian Economic Association

  Former Ambassador of Hungary to the OECD, Paris

  Former Hungarian Minister of International Economic Relations and Member of Parliament

- Lord Kerr of Kinlochard

  Deputy Chairman and Senior Independent Non-Executive Director of Royal Dutch Shell

  Member of the House of Lords

  Director of Rio Tinto, the Scottish American Investment Trust, London

Former Secretary General, European Convention, Brussels

Former Permanent Undersecretary of State and Head of the Diplomatic Service, Foreign & Commonwealth Office, London

Former British Ambassador to the United States

- Sixten Korkman

  Managing Director, the Research Institute of the Finnish Economy (ETLA) and Finnish Business and Policy Forum (EVA), Helsinki

- Count Otto Lambsdorff

  Partner, Wessing Lawyers, Düsseldorf

  Chairman, Friedrich Naumann Foundation, Berlin

  Former Member of German Bundestag

  Honorary Chairman, Free Democratic Party

  Former Federal Minister of Economy

  Former President of the Liberal International

  Honorary European Chairman, the Trilateral Commission, Paris

- Lee Hong-Koo

  Chairman, Seoul Forum for International Affairs

  Former Prime Minister of Korea

  Former Korean Ambassador to the United Kingdom and the United States

- Marianne Lie

Director General, Norwegian Shipowners Association, Oslo

- Cees Maas

  Honorary Vice Chairman of the ING Group and former Chief Financial Officer, Amsterdam

  Former Treasurer of the Dutch Government

- Roy MacLaren

  Former Canadian High Commissioner to the United Kingdom

  Former Canadian Minister of International Trade, Toronto, Ontario

- Minoru Makihara

  Senior Corporate Advisor, Mitsubishi Corporation, Tokyo

- Sir Deryck C. Maughan

  Managing Director and Chairman, KKR Asia, Kohlberg Kravis Roberts & Co., New York, New York

  Former Vice Chairman, Citigroup

- Minoru Murofushi

  Counselor, ITOCHU Corporation, Tokyo

- Indra K. Nooyi

  Chairman of the Board and Chief Executive Officer, PepsiCo, Inc., Purchase, New York

- Yoshio Okawara

  President, Institute for International Policy Studies, Tokyo

Former Japanese Ambassador to the United States

- Susan Rice

Senior Fellow, Foreign Policy Studies and Global Economy and Development Programs, Brookings Institution, Washington, DC

Former Assistant Secretary of State for African Affairs

Former Special Assistant to the President and Senior Director for African Affairs, National Security Council

- Luis Rubio

President, Center of Research for Development (CIDAC), Mexico City, DF

- Silvio Scaglia

Chairman, Fastweb, Milan

Former Managing Director, Omnitel

- Guido Schmidt-Chiari

Chairman, Supervisory Board, Constantia Group

Former Chairman, Creditanstalt Bankverein, Vienna

- Carlo Secchi

Professor of European Economic Policy and former Rector, Bocconi University

Vice President, ISPI, Milan

Former Member of the Italian Senate and of the European Parliament

- Tøger Seidenfaden

Editor-in-Chief, *Politiken*, Copenhagen

- Petar Stoyanov

  Former President of the Republic of Bulgaria

  Member of the Bulgarian Parliament

  Chairman, Parliamentary Group of United Democratic Forces

  Chairman, Union of Democratic Forces, Sofia

- Harri Tiido

  Undersecretary for Political Affairs, Estonian Ministry of Foreign Affairs, Tallinn

  Former Ambassador of Estonia and Head of the Estonian Mission to NATO, Brussels

- George Vassiliou

  Former Head of the Negotiating Team for the Accession of Cyprus to the European Union

  Former President of the Republic of Cyprus

  Former Member of Parliament and Leader of United Democrats, Nicosia

- Paul Volcker

  Former Chairman, Wolfensohn & Co., Inc., New York

- Frederick H. Schultz

  Professor Emeritus, International Economic Policy, Princeton University

  Former Chairman, Board of Governors, US Federal Reserve System

Honorary North American Chairman and former North American Chairman, the Trilateral Commission

- Marko Voljč

  Chief Executive Officer, K & H Bank, Budapest

  Former General Manager of Central Europe Directorate, KBC Bank Insurance Holding, Brussels

  Former Chief Executive Officer, Nova Ljubljanska Banka, Ljubljana

- Panagis Vourloumis

  Chairman and Chief Executive Officer, Hellenic Tellecommunications Organization (OTE), Athens

- Jusuf Wanandi

  Vice Chairman, Board of Trustees, Centre for Strategic and International Studies, Jakarta

- Serge Weinberg

  Chairman of the Supervisory Board, Accor

  Chairman and Chief Executive Officer, Weinberg Capital Partners

  Former Chairman Management Board, Pinault-Printemps-Redoute

  Former President, Institute of International and Strategic Studies (IRIS), Paris

- Heinrich Weiss

  Chairman, SMS, Düsseldorf

  Former Chairman, Federation of German Industries, Berlin

NEW WORLD ORDER QUOTES

- General Douglas MacArthur: "I am concerned for the security of our great nation; not so much because of any threat from without, but because of the insidious forces working from within."

- US President Franklin D. Roosevelt in a letter written November 21, 1933, to Colonel E. Mandell House: "The real truth of the matter is, as you and I know, that a financial element in the large centers has owned the government of the U.S. since the days of Andrew Jackson."

- Bill Clinton, *USA Today* on March 11, 1993, page 2a: "We can't be so fixated on our desire to preserve the rights of ordinary Americans."

- Strobe Talbot, President Clinton's Deputy Secretary of State, *Time Magazine*, July 20, 1992: "In the next century, nations as we know it will be obsolete; all states will recognize a single, global authority. National sovereignty wasn't such a great idea after all."

- Woodrow Wilson, *The New Freedom* (1913): "Since I entered politics, I have chiefly had men's views confided to me privately. Some of the biggest men in the United States, in the Field of commerce and manufacture, are afraid of something. They know that there is a power somewhere so organized, so subtle, so watchful, so interlocked, so complete, so pervasive, that they better not speak above their breath when they speak in condemnation of it."

- Attorney General Janet Reno, Associated Press on December 10, 1993: "Gun registration is not enough. Waiting periods are only a step. Registration is only a step. The prohibition of private firearms is the goal."

- *American Mercury Magazine*, December 1957, p. 92: "The invisible Money Power is working to control and enslave mankind. It financed Communism, Fascism, Marxism, Zionism, Socialism. All of these are directed to making the United States a member of a World Government."

- H. G. Wells in his book *The New World Order*, 1940: "It is the system of nationalist individualism that has to go.... We are living in the end of the sovereign states....In the great struggle to evoke a Westernized World Socialism, contemporary governments may vanish....Countless people...will hate the New World Order....and will die protesting against it."

- *The Chicago Tribune*, 1951: "Those who absorbed the Elmer Davis [Rhodes scholar and head of OWI], Office of War Information training have pushed the British concept of policing the world with American soldiers and economic aid and have fought for a world federation under which the United States would surrender its sovereignty."

- Henry Kissinger, Bilderberger Conference in Evians, France, 1991: "Today, America would be outraged if U.N. troops entered Los Angeles to restore order. Tomorrow they will be grateful! This is especially true if they were told that there were an outside threat from beyond, whether real or promulgated, that threatened our very existence. It is then that all peoples of the world will plead to deliver them from this evil. The one thing every man fears is the unknown. When presented with this scenario, individual rights will be willingly relinquished for the guarantee of their well-being granted to them by the World Government."

- American Jewish Committee's official mag, *Commentary*, November 1958, p. 376: "The International government of the United Nations, stripped of it's legal trimming, then, is really the International Government of the United States and the Soviet Union acting in Unison."

- Benjamin Disraeli, first Prime Minister of England, *Coningsby, the New Generation*, 1844: "The world is governed by very different personages from what is imagined by those who are not behind the scenes."

- George W. Malone, US Senator (Nevada), speaking before Congress, 1957: "I believe that if the people of this nation fully understood what Congress has done to them over the last 49 years, they would move on Washington; they would not wait for an election....It adds up to a preconceived plan to destroy the economic and social independence of the United States!"

- Congressman Larry P. McDonald, 1976, killed in the Korean Airlines 747 that was shot down by the Soviets: "The drive of the Rockefellers and their allies is to create a one-world government combining super capitalism and Communism under the same tent, all under their control....Do I mean conspiracy? Yes I do. I am convinced there is such a plot, international in scope, generations old in planning, and incredibly evil in intent."

- General Colin Powell, April 21, 1993, receiving the UN-USA Global Leadership Award: "The United Nations will spearhead our efforts to manage the new conflicts [that afflict our world]....Yes the principles of the United Nations Charter are worth our lives, our fortunes, and our sacred honor."

- New York Mayor, John Hylan: "The real menace of our Republic is the invisible government which like a giant octopus sprawls its slimy legs over our cities, states and nation. At the head is a small group of banking houses... This little coterie...run our government for their own selfish ends. It operates under cover of a self-created screen...seizes...our executive officers...legislative bodies...schools...courts...newspapers and every agency created for the public protection."

- US Senator Barry Goldwater, his book *No Apologies*, 1964: "The Trilateral Commission is intended to be the vehicle for multinational consolidation of the commercial and banking interests by seizing control of the political government of the United States. The Trilateral Commission represents a skillful, coordinated effort to seize control and consolidate the four centers of power--Political, Monetary, Intellectual, and Ecclesiastical."

- British Prime Minister Benjamin Disraeli, 1876: "The governments of the present day have to deal not merely with other governments, with emperors, kings and ministers, but also with the secret societies which have everywhere their unscrupulous agents, and can at the last moment upset all the governments' plans."

- President Harry Truman: "For some time I have been disturbed by the way the CIA has been diverted from its original assignment. It has become an operational and at times a policy making arm of the government."

- Myron Fagan: "The idea was that those who direct the overall conspiracy could use the differences in those two so-called ideologies [Marxism/fascism/socialism v. democracy/capitalism] to enable them [the Illuminati] to divide larger and larger portions of the human race into opposing camps so that they could be armed and then brainwashed into fighting and destroying each other."

• Thomas Jefferson once famously remarked that it is better to have a newspaper without a government than a government without a newspaper.

ROUND TABLE GROUPS

The Round Table Groups stemmed from a secret society (Quigley's phrase) created by British magnate Cecil Rhodes to unite the world—beginning with the English-speaking dominions—under "enlightened" elitists like himself.

The post–World War I proposal for a League of Nations came from the Round Table Group's machinations.

The post–World War I of the Versailles Peace Conference was a covert network.

The post–world War I of the Versailles Peace Conference decided to establish a front organization to the existing Round Table Group in England and in each dominion.

ROYAL INSTITUTE OF INTERNATIONAL AFFAIRS

The post–World War I of the Versailles Peace Conference is called the Royal Institute of International Affairs.

Royal Institute of International Affairs was made up of existing Round Table Group.

Bilderberg Group Council on Foreign Relations and the Trilateral Commission

(New World Order)

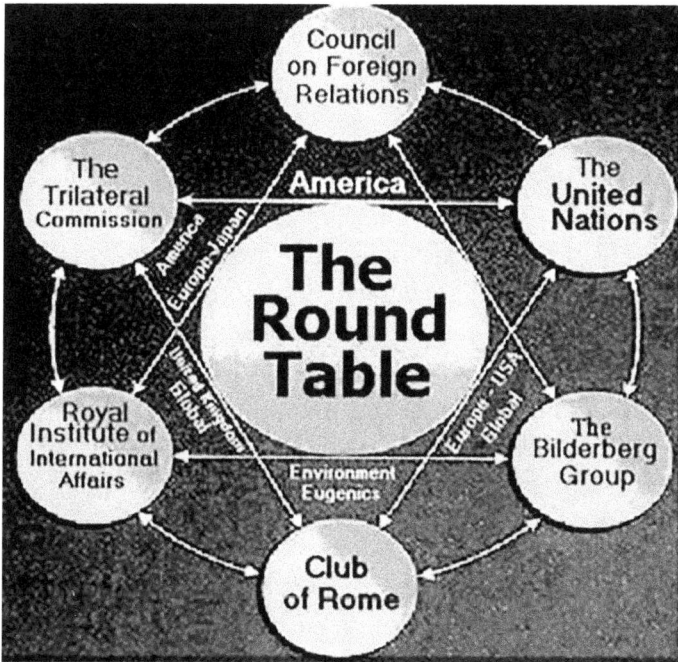

Figure A

ROUND TABLE NETWORK CLUB OF ROME (TREATY OF ROME)

PREAMBLE

His Majesty the King of the Belgians, the President of the Federal Republic of Germany, the President of the French Republic, the President of the Italian Republic, Her Royal Highness The Grand Duchess of Luxembourg, Her Majesty The Queen of the NetherlandsDetermined to lay the foundations of an ever closer union among the peoples of Europe,

Resolved to ensure the economic and social progress of their countries by common action to eliminate the barriers which divide Europe,

Affirming as the essential objective of their efforts the constant improvement of the living and working conditions of their peoples,

Recognising that the removal of existing obstacles calls for concerted action in order to guarantee steady expansion, balanced trade and fair competition,

Anxious to strengthen the unity of their economies and to ensure their harmonious development by reducing the differences existing between the various regions and the backwardness of the less favored regions,

Desiring to contribute, by means of a common commercial policy, to the progressive abolition of restrictions on international trade,

Intending to confirm the solidarity which binds Europe and the overseas countries and desiring to ensure the development of their prosperity, in accordance with the principles of the Charter of the United Nations,

Resolved by thus pooling their resources to preserve and strengthen peace and liberty, and calling upon the other peoples of Europe who share their ideal to join in their efforts,

Have decided to create a European Economic Community and to this end have designated as their Plenipotentiaries:

His Majesty The King of the Belgians: Mr. Paul-Henri Spaak, Minister for Foreign Affairs, Baron J. Ch. Snoy et d'Oppuers, Secretary-General of the Ministry of Economic Affairs, Head of the Belgian Delegation to the Intergovernmental Conference.

The President of the Federal Republic of Germany: Dr. Konrad Adenauer, Federal Chancellor, Professor Dr. Walter Hallstein, State Secretary of the Federal Foreign Office.

The President of the French Republic: Mr. Christian Pineau, Minister for Foreign Affairs,

Mr. Maurice Faure, Under-Secretary of State for Foreign Affairs.

The President of the Italian Republic: Mr. Antonio Segni, President of the Council of Ministers, Professor Gaetano Martino, Minister for Foreign Affairs.

Her Royal Highness The Grand Duchess of Luxembourg: Mr. Joseph Bech, President of the Government, Minister for Foreign Affairs, Mr. Lambert Schaus, Ambassador, Head of the Luxembourg Delegation to the Intergovernmental Conference.

Her Majesty The Queen of the Netherlands: Mr. Joseph Luns, Minister for Foreign Affairs, Mr. J. Linthorst Homan, Head of the Netherlands Delegation to the Intergovernmental Conference.

ROUND TABLE NETWORK

There exists a ruling elite connection between the Bilderberg Group and the two other secretive groups: the Council on Foreign Relations and the Trilateral Commission.

The Bilderberg Group, the Council on Foreign Relations, and the Trilateral Commission are secretive ruling elite groups that do not allow the mainstream media to cover in depth their meetings.

The Bilderberg Group's combined wealth exceeds the combined wealth of all United States citizens.

The Bilderberg Group, the Council on Foreign Relations, and the Trilateral Commission corporate tycoons keep track of world events and prominent politicians.

The Bilderberg Group, the Council on Foreign Relations, and the Trilateral Commission are shadow governments with a top priority to erase the sovereignty of all national governments and state government sovereignties within their borders to place them under global corporate control that will take over their economies under a New World Order.

The Bilderberg Group, the Council on Foreign Relations, and the Trilateral Commission have insource and outsource members where the insource members make up the hardcore nucleus of the group, and the outsource are innocently and remotely related to the group.

The Bilderberg Group, the Council on Foreign Relations, and the Trilateral Commission contains members are famous politicians and financiers of the world whose political affiliations range from liberal to conservative (George W. Bush, George Soros, Gerald Ford, George McGovern, and Jimmy Carter).

The Bilderberg Group, the Council on Foreign Relations, and the Trilateral Commission are private clubs whose parallel world remains unseen in the daily struggles of most of humanity, where there exists a cesspool of deception, lies, double talk, insinuation, blackmail, and bribery.

The Bilderberg Group, the Council on Foreign Relations, and the Trilateral Commission are a surreal world of double and triple agents, of changing loyalties, of professional psychotic assassins, brainwashed black ops agents, soldiers of fortune, and mercenaries whose primary sources of income are the dirtiest and most despicable government-run subversive missions the kind that can never be exposed.

The Bilderberg Group, the Council on Foreign Relations, and the Trilateral Commission have set about to loot the entire planet.

Almost all the presidential candidates of both parties have belonged to at least one of these following organizations: Bilderberg Group, Council on Foreign Relations, and Trilateral Commission.

The Bilderberg Group, the Council on Foreign Relations, and the Trilateral Commission members run the central banks of the world and are poised to control discount rates, money supply, interest rates, gold prices, and which countries receive or do not receive loans.

The Bilderberg Group, the Council on Foreign Relations, and the Trilateral Commission have invitation-only membership.

The Bilderberg Group, the Council on Foreign Relations, and the Trilateral Commission earliest members were handpicked from among none other than the Fabian Socialists who ultimately supported global government.

The Bilderberg Group baptized Bill Clinton in 1991, where he attended their conference in Baden-Baden and was anointed to the United States presidency.

The Bilderberg Group sent Bill Clinton to Moscow to get his KGB student-era, anti-Vietnam war files "buried" before he announced his candidacy for president, which happened some two and a half months later.

Clinton is a member of the three groups (Bilderberg Group, Council on Foreign Relations, and Trilateral Commission).

Hillary Clinton is a member of the Bilderberg Group.

Many of the US congressmen and senators are members of the Bilderberg Group, the Council on Foreign Relations, and the Trilateral Commission,

People who are in major policymaking positions are members of the Bilderberg Group, the Council on Foreign Relations, and the Trilateral Commission,

People who are in the field of foreign relations are members of the Bilderberg Group, the Council on Foreign Relations, and the Trilateral Commission.

People of the press are members of the Bilderberg Group, the Council on Foreign Relations, and the Trilateral Commission.

People who are leaders within the CIA, FBI, and IRS are members of the Bilderberg Group, the Council on Foreign Relations, and the Trilateral Commission.

People within governmental organizations in Washington are members of at least one of these organizations (of the Bilderberg Group, the Council on Foreign Relations, and the Trilateral Commission).

Since most prominent members of mainstream media are members of the Bilderberg Group, Council on Foreign Relations, and Trilateral Commission—whom Edith Kermit Roosevelt, granddaughter of Theodore Roosevelt, called "this legitimate Mafia"—Americans do not obtain their news from independent sources.

Jim Lehrer, *The News Hour*, who is the cornerstone of PBS's programming, is a Council on Foreign Relations member.

Dwayne Andreas, who was chairman of *The News Hour*, was a member of the Trilateral Commission. Paul Gigot, David Gergen, William Kristol, and William Safire, *News Hour* journalists, are members of one or more of the Bilderberg Group, the Council on Foreign Relations, and the Trilateral Commission groups.

Since the inception of these organizations, almost every American president belonged to either the Bilderberg Group, the Council on Foreign Relations, or the Trilateral Commission groups.

When we consider that the American presidents were members in either the Bilderberg Group, the Council on Foreign Relations, or the Trilateral Commission groups, the ruling elite are leading the American people into a new world government.

When the public is led to believe that its own best interests are being served while the Council on Foreign Relations policy is being carried out, the deception is complete.

If the "" become too independent a chapter in the book is complete like "The Watergate Con-Game."

Since Richard Nixon, a Council on Foreign Relations, an "anointed one" member, became insubordinate and was unwilling to submit to the shadow government, the Council on Foreign Relations carefully crafted Nixon's demise to demonstrate to subsequent chief executives the price they would pay for disregarding the agenda of those who anoint them.

David Rockefeller and other United States Trilateralists, Bilderbergers, and the Council on Foreign Relations members have dismantled the industrial might of the United States government.

When the cabal (Bilderberg Group, the Council on Foreign Relations, and the Trilateral Commission) gradually began collapsing the United States economy as far back as the 1980s, the current housing bubble explosion/credit crunch/mortgage meltdown is the result.

Bilderberg Group, the Council on Foreign Relations, and the Trilateral Commission created an American yard sale.

Bilderberg Group, the Council on Foreign Relations, and the Trilateral Commission have engineered an economic meltdown, driving hundreds of thousands and eventually millions of businesses and individuals into bankruptcy.

Bilderberg Group, the Council on Foreign Relations, and the Trilateral Commission are key players so that these big three ruling elite organizations can buy up the train wreck left behind for pennies on the dollar, which becomes a brilliant fast-track strategy toward owning the world.

Bilderberg Group, the Council on Foreign Relations, and the Trilateral Commission became successful in employing a strategy for planetary economic hegemony as the cacophony of their carefully engineered global economic cataclysm reverberates across America and around the world in the final months of 2007. Moreover, it was never about buyers who didn't read the fine print when taking out liar loans.

Bilderberg Group, the Council on Foreign Relations, and the Trilateral Commission, the shadow governments, anointed silver-tongued ruling elite politicians and central bankers ultimately to skillfully continue to steal governments from people and replace them with transnational corporations.

No one could have said it better than David Rockefeller, founder of the Trilateral Commission, a Bilderberg member, and board member of the Council on Foreign Relations (Chairman Emeritus) in his *Memoirs*: "Some even believe we are part of a secret cabal working against the best interests of the United States, characterizing my family and me as 'internationalists' and of conspiring with others around the world to build a more integrated global political and economic structure-one world, if you will. If that's the charge, I stand guilty, and I am proud of it."

Bilderbergers and the Council on Foreign Relations and Trilateral Commission reek of totalitarianism.

BILDERBERG GROUP (AMERICAN FREE PRESS)

- Sen. John Edwards's standout "performance" at the super-secret Bilderberg meeting in Italy last month may have been a key reason for his selection as John Kerry's vice presidential running mate, according to *The New York Times*.

- Bilderberg and the Silent Media: The Bilderberg blackout in the US press is evidence that the owners of America's media are in collusion with the New World Order conspiracy.

- US Sen. John Edwards at Bilderberg: Among the one hundred or so invitees to the annual Bilderberg conference under way Sunday in a northern Italy resort is potential US vice president John Edwards.

The U.S. group is directed by Henry Kissinger, David Rockefeller, Paul Arthur Allaire and Richard Charles Albert Holbrooke.

Since 1953, the Bilderberg group has convened government, business, academic and journalistic representatives from the U.S., Canada and Europe with the express purpose of exploring the future of the North

Atlantic community. The international steering committee includes Conrad Black, publisher of newspapers throughout Canada, the U.S. and the London Telegraph and Jerusalem Post, Vernon Eulion Jordan, Jr., George J. Mitchell, Kissinger and Rockefeller.

On the agenda for the November [4–5, 1999] meeting [at the Library of Congress] is a panel discussion of the U.S. presidential elections and an exploration of the national security requirements for the 21st century. Among those involved in the discussion of the latter subject will be former U.S. Senators. Gary Hart and Warren Bruce Rudman, former Speaker of the House Newt Gingrich, journalist Leslie H. Gelb and Secretary of Defense William Sebastian Cohen. John McCain, at the special invitation of Kissinger, will speak at breakfast Friday morning and Albert Gore, Jr. will make a Thursday night dinner address, according to the agenda obtained by WorldNetDaily.

Others making presentations include Rep. Bill Thomas of California, Sen. Christopher John Dodd of Connecticut, Evan Bayh of Indiana and former White House Chief of Staff Erskine Bowles.

The U.S. group is directed by Henry Kissinger, David Rockefeller, Paul Arthur Allaire and Richard Charles Albert Holbrooke.

Bilderberg Group (United Press International)

The Bilderberg group of the world's elite, currently meeting in northern Italy and celebrating its 50th anniversary, casts an extensive shadow on the net.

Bilderberg: Its Long and Secret History: The roots of Bilderberg go back centuries, when international moneychangers would secretly manipulate the economy to enrich themselves and enslave ordinary people.

Bilderberg Big-Wigs Set to Meet in Italy: Bilderbergers say they do not know where their secret meeting will be held this year, so, in the spirit of brotherhood, American Free Press will help them. Go to Stresa, Italy, and chick into the five-star Grand Hotel des Iles Borromees June 3 to June 6.

Bilderberg Trying to Plug Leaks in Security: Angry over being discovered year after year, Bilderberg is taking an unprecedented step to prevent leaks - don't let the luminaries know where their secret meeting will be held until it's almost time to catch a plane.

Bilderberg Group (London Guardian)

Guess who's at super-secret Bilderberg meeting today: The 50th anniversary conference of the elite Bilderberg group—which many believe conspires semi-annually to foster global government—is under way in Stresa, Italy.

Bilderberg Group (World Net Daily)

George W. Bush: Getting His Orders at Bilderberg? US President George W. Bush's trip to Italy coincides neatly and quite conveniently with the annual meeting of the notorious Bilderberg Group, the world's ruling cabal of politicians, mega-corporate honchos and other gofers of the New World Order.

The secretive Bilderberg society, a group some believe conspires semi-annually to foster global government, will hold a steering committee meeting in Washington next month.

The Nov. 4-5 conference, featuring invited guests such as Vice President Al Gore and presidential candidate John McCain, is scheduled for the Library of Congress in the nation's capital and is sponsored by the American Friends of Bilderberg. The U.S. group is directed by Henry Kissinger, David Rockefeller, Paul Allaire and Richard C. Holbrooke.

Since 1953, the Bilderberg group has convened government, business, academic and journalistic representatives from the U.S., Canada and Europe with the express purpose of exploring the future of the North Atlantic community. The international steering committee includes Conrad Black, publisher of newspapers throughout Canada, the U.S. and the London Telegraph and Jerusalem Post, Vernon Jordan, George Mitchell, Kissinger and Rockefeller.

On the agenda for the November meeting is a panel discussion of the U.S. presidential elections and an exploration of the national security requirements for the 21st century. Among those involved in the discussion of the latter subject will be former U.S. Senators. Gary Hart and Warren Rudman, former Speaker of the House Newt Gingrich, journalist Leslie Gelb and Secretary of Defense William Cohen.

McCain, at the special invitation of Kissinger, will speak at breakfast Friday morning and Gore will make a Thursday night dinner address, according to the agenda.

Others making presentations include Rep. Bill Thomas of California, Sen. Christopher Dodd of Connecticut, Evan Bayh of Indiana and former White House Chief of Staff Erskine Bowles.

The list of potential invitees to the Washington conference includes the following:

Gen. Charles G. Boyd, Bill Bradley, Dianne Feinstein, Martin S. Feldstein, Gen. John R. Glavin, David Gergen, Sen. Kay Bailey Hutchison, Peter Jennings, Gen. Colin Powell, Sharon Percy Rockefeller, Gen. Brent Scowcroft, George Soros, George Stephanopoulos, Paul A. Volcker.

The November meeting at the Library of Congress is being billed to emphasize a globalist agenda and promote the idea that the notion of national sovereignty is antiquated and regressive.

Bilderberg Group (Turkish Newsline)

Turkish State minister leaves for Italy: Turkish State Minister Ali Babacan left on Thursday for Italy to attend Bilderberg Conference 2004.

Members of Dutch Labour Party at 52nd Bilderberg Conference: On behalf of the Netherlands some top executives from the world of business will attend the meeting that is ringed by secrecy.

Netherlands Telegraph

Bilderberg Planning To Put the Squeeze on U.S. Taxpayers: The internationalist Bilderberg group has called for higher U.S. taxes in the past, but this year "American guilt" will be the theme behind the locked and guarded gates of the plush resort in Stresa, Italy, June 3-6.

The Norwegian contribution to this year's Bilderberg Meeting is university chancellor Arild Underdal and industry leaders Egil Myklebust and Svein Aaser. Bilderberg is a secret club at which the word's elite decide how best to arrange tomorrow's world.

ELITE'S POWER (BOOKS ON CLANDESTINE GROUPS)

C. Wright Mills's book *The Power Elite* is familiar to most sociology students.

At the pinnacle of the government, the military and the corporations, a small group of men made the decisions that reverberated "into each and every cranny" of American life.

Insofar as national events are decided, the power elite are those who decide them.

For the first time in history, the territories of the United States made up a self-conscious mass society.

If the economy had once been a multitude of locally or regionally rooted, (more or less) equal units of production, it now answered to the needs of a few hundred corporations.

If the government had once been a patchwork of states held together by Congress, it now answered to the initiatives of a strong executive.

If the military had once been a militia system resistant to the discipline of permanent training, it now consumed half the national budget, and seated its admirals and generals in the biggest office building in the world.

The "awesome means of power" enthroned upon these monopolies of production, administration and violence included the power to prevent issues and ideas from reaching Congress in the first place.

Most Americans still believed the ebb and flow of public opinion guided political affairs.

But now we must recognize this description as a set of images out of a fairy tale.

They are not adequate even as an approximate model of how the American system of power works.

The powers of ordinary men are circumscribed by the everyday worlds in which they live, yet even in these rounds of job, family and neighborhood they often seem driven by forces they can neither understand nor govern.

The small groups of men standing at the head of the three monopolies represented a new kind of elite, whose character and conduct mirrored the antidemocratic ethos of their institutions.

The corporations recruited from the business schools, and conceived executive training programs that demanded strict conformity.

The military selected generals and admirals from the service academics, and inculcated "the caste feeling" by segregating them from the associational life of the country.

Less and less did local apprenticeships serve as a passport to the government's executive chambers.

Of the appointees in the Eisenhower administration, a record number had never stood for election at any level.

Above the apparent balance of powers, an intricate set of overlapping cliques shared in decisions having at least national consequences.

The nation's three top policy positions, secretary of state, treasury and defense, were occupied by former corporate executives.

For the first time in American history, men in authority are talking about an 'emergency' without a foreseeable end.

Such men as these are crackpot realists: in the name of realism they have constructed a paranoid reality all their own.

Elite's Power (Powerful Clandestine Groups)

The elite's power has a chokehold on the mass media.

The elite's power conspires to consolidate economic and political power on a global scale.

The elitists want to create a Common Market for the purpose of gradually building it into a government of Europe.

Confusion exists about the real influence of the elite, which makes it easier for skeptics to dismiss them; however, uncovering hard facts, a consistent and more solid picture emerges.

The elite's abuse of power is almost too nightmarish to contemplate.

The elite operate under guise of totalitarianism

The elite, who speculate in general terms, are specific individuals whose specific policies, specific dates, and specific venues are presented in black-and-white and become more real and more frightening.

The elite put into perspective the ideas of war and state terrorisms contrary to human nature.

The elite are a small proportion of mankind that produced war, oppression, and slavery that created an economic necessity for their positive benefit of wealth and power over the years.

The elite are individuals who literally feed on broken human spirits and spilt human blood.

The elite must discontinue their inhuman and detached unaccountable power scheming through open forums to satisfy the public's right to know on what is being planned in closed meetings whose members are the most wealthy and powerful people in the world.

The elite's power holds democracy and ordinary people with contempt.

The elite's immense economic power quite rightly leads one to question motives and plans.

The elite encourages speculation of "conspiracy fact."

The elite's growth of power was brought into being through the creation of the groups like the Bilderbergers, the Skull and Bones, the Council on Foreign Relations, and the Trilateral Commission, who are known to work against benefit of mankind.

GLOBAL ELITE

At the meetings, there was an ultra-elite conclave of banking, political, media, and industrial elites committed to world government.

The Common Market became the European Union through a series of steps.

The European Union has begun sapping political and economic powers from once-sovereign European nations.

The media moguls on both sides of the Atlantic provides protection counterparts in the political elite.

Thomas Jefferson once famously remarked that it is better to have a newspaper without a government than a government without a newspaper.

The free press docs not hold government accountable to the public.

The media is itself part of the ruling establishment.

The globalist elite controls the media.

The globalist elite controlled twenty-five papers.

An editor was furnished for each paper to properly supervise and edit information on matters considered vital to the interests of the globalist elite.

Georgetown University historian Carroll Quigley became the spine of the global power elitist network.

Quigley played a key role in mentoring many individuals who went on to occupy critical positions.

A Quigley student was Bill Clinton.

Bill Clinton paid homage to Quigley in his acceptance speech at the 1992 Democratic convention.

The global power elitist network became known as the Round Table Group.

The global power elitist network frequently would cooperate with the Communists, Socialists, or any other groups.

The aim of the global power elitist network would be to place the world's financial control in private hands.

The intent of the global power elitist network is to dominate the political system of each country.

The goal of the global power elitist network is to control the economy of the whole wide world.

The Council on Foreign Relations Notes

The Council on Foreign Relations is the American branch of a society that originated in England and believes that national boundaries should be obliterated and a one-world rule established.

President Woodrow Wilson and chief advisor Edward Mandell House, a Marxist, founded the Council on Foreign Relations in 1921 in New York city.

Edward Mandell House maintains that Socialism is Karl Marx's dream.

The Council on Foreign Relations influences both Democratic and Republican parties in the creation of a socialistic government.

The Council on Foreign Relations established a United States–controlled Central Bank.

The Council on Foreign Relations passed the Federal Reserve Act.

The Council on Foreign Relations brought into power a private central bank to create United States money taking away power from the federal government.

The Council on Foreign Relations capitalized on the ratification of the Sixteenth Amendment (the graduated income tax) to the United States Constitution—a Karl Marx scheme.

The Council on Foreign Relations was formed by House in 1921.

The Council on Foreign Relations would destroy the freedom and independence of the United States.

The Council on Foreign Relations leads the country of the United States toward one world government.

The Council on Foreign Relations attracted men of power.

The Council on Foreign Relations attracted men of influence.

The Council on Foreign Relations was financed through the tax-free Rockefeller Foundation and the Carnegie Foundation in the late 1920s.

The Council on Foreign Relations was funded by the American taxpayers' attribute to the Sixteenth Amendment.

The Council on Foreign Relations gained domination over the state department at the invitation of President Roosevelt in 1940.

The Council on Foreign Relations members have maintained this domination thus far.

The Council on Foreign Relations came to be known as the Invisible Government.

The Council on Foreign Relations' forty members of the United States delegation organized the meeting of the United Nations at San Francisco in 1945.

The Council on Foreign Relations is the American branch of a society that originated in England.

The Council on Foreign Relations has an Internationalist viewpoint.

The Council on Foreign Relations, along with the Atlantic Union Movement of the US, believes national boundaries should be obliterated into a one-world rule established.

The Council on Foreign Relations does not allow changing presidents to change the existing government administrators.

The Council on Foreign Relations members who have been held in office during the election of both Republican and Democratic presidents have controlled the operation of the executive branch of the United States government from 1945 to the present day.

The Council on Foreign Relations disregards the executive branch's choices on who will advise either Republican or Democratic presidents, whom the people of the United States elected to office.

The Council on Foreign Relations members control the United States government's strategies.

The Council on Foreign Relations members are those who both Republican and Democratic presidents have placed in key presidential advisory positions under the pressure of elections support to their candidacies.

The Council on Foreign Relations member Henry Kissinger was a Nixon placement.

The Council on Foreign Relations member Zbigniew Brzezinski, who replaced Kissinger and who was also a David Rockefeller protégé, was a Jimmy Carter placement.

The Council on Foreign Relations, regardless of different administration changes, its members were at times carried over to the next administration while new CFR member were added to guide the latest elected president who the people elected to carry on suppos-edly a new administration's policy.

The Council on Foreign Relations' sixteen-year former member Rear Admiral Chester Ward warned the American people of the organization's intentions.

The Council on Foreign Relations' sixteen-year former member Rear Admiral Chester Ward said that the most powerful clique in these elitist groups have one objective in common—to bring about the surrender of the sovereignty of the national independence of the United States.

The Council on Foreign Relations members are a second clique of international members who comprises the Wall Street interna-tional bankers and their key agents.

The Council on Foreign Relations members are a second clique of international members who primarily want the world banking monopoly from whatever power ends up in the control of global government.

The Council on Foreign Relations members' ultimate aim is to create a one-world socialist system.

The Council on Foreign Relations, with its treasonous activities to the United States Constitution, puts an end to the United States of America, making the country a part of their global government scheme.

The Council on Foreign Relations membership included Thomas Dewey, the Republican candidate for president in 1944 and in 1948.

The Council on Foreign Relations membership included Republicans Eisenhower and Nixon, as were Democrats Stevenson, Kennedy, Humphrey, and McGovern in later years.

The Council on Foreign Relations annual reports listed a membership of 1,878 members.

The Council on Foreign Relations included eleven United States senators.

The Council on Foreign Relations members contained more United States House of Congressmen's names than United States senators' names.

The Council on Foreign Relations' names list contained 284 United States government officials.

The Council on Foreign Relations Chairman of the Board at one time was David Rockefeller.

The Council on Foreign Relations members are running NBC and CBS, *The New York Times*, *The Washington Post*, *The Des Moines Register*, and many other important newspapers.

The Council on Foreign Relations members include leaders of *Time*, *Newsweek*, *Fortune*, *Business Week*, and numerous other publications.

The Council on Foreign Relations organization's members also dominate the academic world, top corporations, the huge tax-exempt foundations, labor unions, the military, and just about every segment of American life.

The Council on Foreign Relations promotes the destruction of US sovereignty.

The Council on Foreign Relations membership dominates almost every aspect of American life.

The Council on Foreign Relations is not known to most Americans.

The Council on Foreign Relations has never been exposed to the American public, a fact made possible that over 170 journalists, correspondents, and communications executives are members of its organization.

The Council on Foreign Relations' condition of membership is not to mention its organization name in their written words.

The Council on Foreign Relations' condition of membership is not to disclose CFR meetings' minutes.

The Council on Foreign Relations leads the American people into believing that they pick the presidential candidates of the United States.

The Council on Foreign Relations' members make the choice of picking Presidential candidates of the United States.

The Council on Foreign Relations members have been choosing presidential candidates for decades.

The Council on Foreign Relations members are on the Board of Governors of the Federal Reserve.

The Council on Foreign Relations members absolutely control the money and interest rates of the United States without benefit of Congress.

The Council on Foreign Relations members run a privately owned organization, the Federal Reserve, which has absolutely nothing to do with the United States of America.

The Council on Foreign Relations is dedicated to a one-world government.

The Council on Foreign Relations is financed by a number of the largest tax-exempt foundations.

The Council on Foreign Relations wields such power and influence over the American people's lives in the areas of finance, business, labor, military, education, and mass communication/media.

The Council on Foreign Relations organization becomes more familiar to every American concerned with good government.

The Council on Foreign Relations organization becomes more familiar to every American in preserving and defending the US Constitution, which is a free-enterprise system.

The Council on Foreign Relations controls the nation's right-to-know machinery.

The Council on Foreign Relations controls the news media, which is usually so aggressive in exposures to inform people.

The Council on Foreign Relations keeps the news media conspicuously silent when it comes to the its members and their activities.

The Council on Foreign Relations is the establishment.

The Council on Foreign Relations influences in key decision-making positions at the highest levels of government to apply pressure from above.

The Council on Foreign Relations has the power to finance.

The Council on Foreign Relations uses individuals and groups to bring pressure from below to justify the high-level decisions for converting the United States from a sovereign Constitution Republic into a servile member of a one-world dictatorship.

The Council on Foreign Relations' main goal is to create a one-world government.

The Council on Foreign Relations' function results in destroying the freedom and independence of all nations, especially including the United States complements of David Rockefeller, who continues to be the Chairman of the Board.

The Council on Foreign Relations the common, everyday American citizen needs to be told that there is a controlled government running the United States.

The Council on Foreign Relations' real goal is to make the United States into a carbon copy of a Communist state.

The Council on Foreign Relations will merge all nations into a one-world system run by a powerful few.

The Council on Foreign Relations is the key that will not allow the people of the United States to obtain their freedom with true independence from the yoke of international finance.

The Council on Foreign Relations controls the money of a country and controls everything in that country.

The Council on Foreign Relations must be known to every citizen of the United States.

The Council on Foreign Relations members should not be voted or promoted to office.

The Council on Foreign Relations is known as a secretive global-oriented organization whose members included almost everyone elected to the office of the president of the United States and nearly every opponent since 1952.

The Council on Foreign Relations was the English's Royal Institute of International Affairs in New York.

The Council on Foreign Relations boasts a membership of only about four thousand.

The Council on Foreign Relations roster includes literally hundreds of powerful figures occupying key positions in the media, including writers, reporters, editors, publishers, news anchors who deliver the news, and executives who select news and how it is covered.

The Council on Foreign Relations elitist members pull the strings in the media.

The Council on Foreign Relations clique has, for decades, had a virtual stranglehold on the executive branch of the United States as well as much of the academe.

The Council on Foreign Relations member of the board David Rockefeller specifically identified *The New York Times* and *The Washington Post* as key media organs of the power elite.

The Council on Foreign Relations redoubt papers, *The New York Times* and *The Washington Post*, set the tone for most news coverage, defining issues, and setting the limits of "respectable" opinion.

The Council on Foreign Relations is the closest thing to a ruling establishment in the United States.

The Council on Foreign Relations members are the people who have managed our international affairs and our military-industrial complex for more than half a century.

The Council on Foreign Relations' 10 percent or more of the membership is comprised of journalists and other media figures.

The Council on Foreign Relations membership includes editorial page editor, deputy editorial page editor, executive editor, managing editor, foreign editor, national affairs editor, business and financial editor, and writers.

The Council on Foreign Relations membership includes owners, management, and editorial personnel for the other media giants such as *The New York Times*, *The Wall Street Journal*, *Los Angeles Times*, NBC, CBS, and ABC.

The Council on Foreign Relations media heavyweights do not merely analyze and interpret foreign policy for the United States; they help make it.

The Council on Foreign Relations news media power does not check against the abuse of power by our ruling elite, but it is instead a key part of a political cartel.

The Council on Foreign Relations establishment media act as the ruling elite's voice conditioning the public to accept, and even embrace, Insider designs that otherwise might not be politically attainable.

At the Majestic Hotel in Paris in 1919, the Round Table Groups of the United States and Britain emerged out from under a cloak of secrecy and officially became the (American) Council on Foreign Relations and the (British) Royal Institute for International Affairs.

The Council on Foreign Relations bylaws absolutely prohibit their members from discussing this elite organization.

The Council on Foreign Relations ruling members have decided that the US government should adopt a particular policy. Once this happens, their extensive research facilities are used to develop arguments to support the new policy, and the Council on Foreign Relations makes every effort to discredit any opposition.

The Council on Foreign Relations' lust to take away the United State's sovereignty and independence pervasively exists throughout most of its membership.

The Council on Foreign Relations had, during the last six administrations (before Mr. Reagan's second term), to have half of the Council members assume official government positions or to act as consultants at one time or another.

The Council on Foreign Relations controllers like David Rockefeller used the media to convince Reagan to make their puppet George Bush Reagan's vice presidential running mate.

The Council on Foreign Relations had twenty-eight members in the Reagan administration after his election.

THE BILDERBERG NOTES

The Bilderberg Group founder was Joseph Retinger (an American Freemason) and Prince Bernhard of the Netherlands in 1954.

The Bilderberg Group, whose founder Joseph Retinger, was concerned about the growth of anti-Americanism in Western Europe.

The Bilderberg group name was the name of the hotel in Oosterbeek, the Netherlands, where the group met for the first time.

The Bilderberg Group was formed during the Cold War period after the Second World War.

The Bilderberg Group, the NATO organization ,aimed at strengthening the bond of the western nations against the threat of communism.

The Bilderberg Group's declared purpose was to bind politically the United States of America with Europe against the United Socialistic Soviet Republic, diminishing the global communist threat to the monetary interests of the United States and Europe.

The Bilderberg Group's members meet regularly, presumably once a year at various locations around the world.

The Bilderberg Group's members are made up of some of the most influential people within the global arena.

The Bilderberg Group's members are all informed persons of authority and influence in their respective countries.

The Bilderberg Group's membership is heavily laden with the Council on Foreign Relations, the Pilgrims Society, the Trilateral Commission, and the famous Round Table members, which was founded in 1910 and who denies its existence.

The Bilderberg Group and the Round Table group prescribe for a more efficient form of global empire such that Anglo-American domination could be extended throughout the twentieth century.

The Bilderberg Group's membership includes dominant leaders in the business, media, and political world.

The Bilderberg Group attendees include central bankers, defense experts, mass media press barons, government ministers, prime ministers, royalty, international financiers, and political leaders from Europe and North America.

The Bilderberg Group is made up of a powerful group of politicians and businesspeople who want to create a One World Government where international and national sovereignties disappear.

The Bilderberg Group's invited members are a sinister ministered group of elitists who operate entirely through self-interest.

The Bilderberg Group meetings are held under strict secrecy as the invited members plan for the future global world or One World Government.

The Bilderberg Group organization maintains an extremely low profile.

The Bilderberg Group's written reports or studies rarely are published for the public under the official sponsorship of its organization.

The Bilderberg Group's participants have denied for many years the very existence of its dynasty.

The members of the Bilderberg press (*The New York Times*, *The Washington Post*, *Newsweek Magazine*, *The Financial Times* and *Time*

Magazine) are usually in attendance; therefore, under the code of silence, publicity is avoided to the outside world.

The Bilderberg Group's events will not be reported by the corporate media, even though the selected media people would have been aware of those events many weeks or even months ago.

The Bilderberg Group, literally speaking, wants to produce a dictatorial One World Empire with intermediaries eliminated, placing political power into the hands of a few chosen people.

The Bilderberg Group wants to produce a dictatorial One World Empire that suppresses unwarranted competition to maximize concentration of industries.

The Bilderberg Group wants to produce a dictatorial One World Empire that makes it possible through their iron-grip control of the World Bank, the International Monetary Fund, and the World Trade Organization to establish absolute control over prices, goods, and raw materials.

The Bilderberg Group wants to produce a dictatorial One World Empire that analyzes the present into primitive components and their interrelations.

The Bilderberg Group, literally speaking, wants to produce a dictatorial One World Empire that architects a strategy of selective manipulation, reconstruction, introduction, and abolition of components and interrelations.

The Bilderberg Group organization shares political power with the Rockefeller family of the United States and the Rothschild family of Europe.

The Bilderberg Group organization is scarcely known to the people of the world.

The Bilderberg Group encourages conspiracy theorists who maintain that the group had orchestrated the move to a common European currency.

The Bilderberg Group encourages conspiracy theorists who maintain that the group had Bill Clinton elected president of the United States after he agreed to sign onto NAFTA.

The Bilderberg Group was blamed for instigating the war within Yugoslavia, disposing the Serbs of Yugoslavia dictator Slobodan Milosevic.

The Bilderberg Group's term *nationalism* is an obscenity because it's equated with patriotism.

The Bilderberg Group's secrecy and its connections to power elites have provided fodder for many who believe that the group is part of a conspiracy.

The Bilderberg Group as a society are the puppet masters of a New World Order.

The Bilderberg Group has been pulling the strings of humankind since at least 1954.

The Bilderberg Group intends to dissolve the sovereignty of the United States and other countries into a supranational structure similar to the European Union.

The Bilderberg Group's long-term purpose is to build a One-World Empire.

The Bilderberg Group is not the end but the means to a future One World Government.

The Bilderberg Group will decide the fate of the world.

The Bilderberg Group deals with the Bank of England, Bank of Canada, Bank of Russia, National Bank of Ukraine, European Central Bank, Central Bank of Ireland, and the USSR's Gosbank.

The Bilderberg Group cannot be able to develop its plan for the world if it is subjected to publicity in the coming years.

The Bilderberg Group understands that the world is more sophisticated and is prepared to march toward a world government.

The Bilderberg Group prefers the supranational sovereignty of intellectual elites and world bankers to the national autodetermination practices of the centuries.

The Bilderberg Group meeting in Baden, Germany, included the then-governor Bill Clinton and Dan Quayle.

The Bilderberg Group contains members who are considered to be global elite.

The Bilderberg Group helps some secret groups of people who control world events and hide their agenda from public knowledge.

The Bilderberg Group's membership is made up of groups of people—politicians, heads of multinational companies, directors of world banking organizations, and royalty—who decide policies that determine the way ordinary people will live and/or die.

The Bilderberg Group finds it relatively easy to control the masses when everyday groups of people give away their power and freedom, fearing to step out from the comfort of their everyday comforts.

The Bilderberg Group knows if you control governments and the media, you control the world.

The Bilderberg Group knows that the people of the United States will not demand answers.

The Bilderberg Group knows that the people of the United States will not demand a government's action to problems like globalization and a New World Order government.

The Bilderberg Group backed Tony Blair of New Labour Party in the May 1997 UK general elections.

The Bilderberg Group's member is Mr. Andrew Knight, the chief executive of News International, the parent of *The Sun*, a British paper.

The Bilderberg Group invited Mr. Tony Blair as a guest of an the annual meeting in 1993, together with his colleague Kenneth Clarke, who are on opposite sides.

The Bilderberg Group's attendees also were once Margaret Thatcher and Denis Healey contrary to the thought of having lived in a democracy where your vote actually counted.

The Bilderberg Group's attendees were Tony Blair and Margaret Thatcher could account for why Margaret Thatcher was one of Tony Blair's first guests at Number Ten.

The Bilderberg Group treats the United States presidential candidates the same way.

The Bilderberg Group represents everyone since the Jimmy Carter candidacy in both parties, Democrat or Republican, at top secret meetings held annually in hidden locations.

The Bilderberg Group evolved directly from the "satanic-communist" Illuminati—Royal Institute of International Affairs relationship—and the Council on Foreign Relations with the help of Mr. Rittenhouse and his breed of religious isolationists at Liberty Lobby.

The Bilderberg Group owns the central banks, such as the Federal Reserve in the United States, and is therefore in a position to determine discount rates, money supply levels, the price of gold, and which countries should receive loans.

The Bilderberg Group decides who should be allowed to run for the offices of president, prime minister, chancellor, and other leading positions in governments around the world.

The Bilderberg Group believes that world history is not the result of coincidences, but rather precise planning.

The Bilderberg Group was formed more than half a century ago to become a powerful group to take the fate of this planet into hand and steer the world in the direction of a secret brand of internationalism.

The Bilderberg Group caused numerous crucial events in politics and economics through subtle manipulation.

The Bilderberg Group's goal is total global control.

The Bilderberg Group selected Bill Clinton to become United States president.

The Bilderberg Group has a proven history of acting in a king-maker capacity, yet they are unelected and unaccountable to anyone.

The Bilderberg Group's directives are driven towards undermining national sovereignty and establishing a world order that benefits their elite interests.

The Bilderberg Group groomed both Bill Clinton and Tony Blair before becoming president and prime minister.

The Bilderberg Group selected John Edwards as John Kerry's running mate in the 2004 presidential election.

The Bilderberg Group met secretly every year.

The Bilderberg Group did not allow the media in to interview any of the participants.

The Bilderberg Group has armed guards at all the doors of their meeting establishments.

The Bilderberg Group's member attendees would exit meetings hiding their faces, ashamed, so as not to be photographed or be interviewed, sneaking out to their limousines for the airport.

The Bilderberg Group attendees were one hundred of the world's most wealthy and powerful individuals, including Hillary Clinton, George H. W. Bush, David Rockefeller, Gov. George Pataki of New York, the president of the Federal Reserve Bank, Henry Kissinger, and Queen Beatrix of the Netherlands, whose family owns Royal Dutch Shell Oil, at a five-star hotel in Ottawa, Ontario, Canada.

The Bilderberg Group's participants are chosen very carefully with the help of secret world power centers through their careers.

The Bilderberg Group selects those participants who have reached key positions in their country's political scene who will begin to implant the Bilderberg decisions, plans, and programs.

The Bilderberg Group is elitist, undemocratic, and unaccountable.

The Bilderberg Group builds self-serving world government, pulling strings behind the scenes and planting their candidates in politics positions of power to serve the needs of the insider group members.

The Bilderberg Group criticizer, Prime Minister Margaret Thatcher of Britain, was ousted from power.

The Bilderberg Group's participants were President Bush's top White House aide and high officials of the state, defense, and treasury departments.

The Bilderberg Group Club has grown beyond its idealistic beginnings to become a shadow world government.

The Bilderberg Group uses telecommunications technology and new methods of behavior engineering to manipulate and convert individual conduct.

The Bilderberg Group attempts to place the United States into an electronic global police state in the next century.

The Bilderberg Group's United States participants emphatically break the Logan Act of the United States where it is absolutely illegal for elected officials to meet in private with influential business executives to debate and design public policy.

The Bilderberg Group meetings follow a traditional protocol founded in 1919, in the wake of the Paris Peace Conference held at Versailles, by the Royal Institute of International Affairs (RIIA) based at Chatham House in London.

The Bilderberg Group's ultimate goal is to transform earth into a prison planet, bringing about a single globalized marketplace under a One World Government using a United World Army policy force.

The Bilderberg Group organizes wars and elects and deposes political leaders.

The Bilderberg Group has helped to oil the wheels of global politics and globalization for the past half a century.

TRILATERAL COMMISSION NOTES

The Trilateral Commission was formed to redirect attention away from the Council on Foreign Relations.

The Trilateral Commission represents a union of the three non-communist industrial regions of North America, Europe, and Japan.

The Trilateral Commission opportunity existed to legalize its creation.

The Trilateral Commission was formed with the blessing of the Bilderberger Group and the Council on Foreign Relations.

The Trilateral Commission organized on July 23–24, 1972, at the 3,500-acre Rockefeller estate at Pocantico Hills, New York.

The Trilateral Commission founding chairman was David Rockefeller.

The Trilateral Commission was made of leaders in business, banking, government, and mass media in North America, Europe, and Japan.

The Trilateral Commission emerged from Rockefeller's reading of Zbigniew Brzezinski's book entitled *Between Two Ages*.

The Trilateral Commission is founded on the thoughts of Zbigniew Brzezinski, who idealized the theories of Karl Marx.

The Trilateral Commission consists of initializing a New World Order, which is to be an economic linkage between Japan, Europe, and the United States.

The Trilateral Commission require changes in the modern world it.

The Trilateral Commission would cause the American system to gradually accommodate itself to an emerging international context, with the United States government called upon to negotiate, to guarantee, and, to some extent, to protect the various arrangements that have been contrived even by private business.

The Trilateral Commission will band together the international upper class to protect their interests.

The Trilateral Commission brings to power political leaders of developed nations to ensure that the global financial interests of the Rockefellers and other ruling elites are protected from the masses.

The Trilateral Commission literature also states, exactly as Brzezinski's book had proposed, that the more advanced Communist states could become partners in the alliance, leading to world government.

The Trilateral Commission carries out Brzezinski's proposal, which chairman David Rockefeller put into practice.

The Trilateral Commission affects the affairs of the United States, which no longer acts in its original governmental interest by not winning wars and by constantly tying to international agreements, pacts, and conventions.

The Trilateral Commission forces the United States leaders to developed blatant preferences for Communist USSR, Communist Cuba, and Communist China while they continue to work for world government, which has always been the goal of Communism.

The Trilateral Commission activities are overseen and guided through the efforts of David Rockefeller, who ends up controlling it.

The Trilateral Commission expanded its dominant membership base to incorporate economically smaller but emerging countries within its regional structure in 2001.

The Trilateral Commission was accorded a handful of members in a Holy Globalism tinfoil festival, Mexico, as were Asia-Pacific countries such as Australia, Indonesia, Malaysia, New Zealand, the Philippines, Singapore, South Korea, and Thailand.

The Trilateral Commission objectives illustrate best great power of the elite.

The Trilateral Commission can make or break any president or candidate for president.

The Trilateral Commission made Jimmy Carter in his efforts to become president and broke Senator Barry Goldwater in his failed attempt.

The Trilateral Commission's center or bull's-eye is made up of the inner circle members who are the decision-makers and who are 100 percent informed in involving the ideas of the Global Union movement, which David Rockefeller is the only "obvious" member of this group.

The Trilateral Commission inner ring is a group that is made up of the officers and directors.

The Trilateral Commission is a Global Union movement.

The Trilateral Commission's center ring is made up of the leaders and implementers who are probably 80 percent informed by the members of the inner circle and who are moderately involved in the Global Union movement.

The Trilateral Commission's outer ring are members who are included for camouflage purposes only, and most of them belong to the Council on Foreign Relations.

The Trilateral Commission reproduced powerful commercial and political interests that were committed to private enterprises, economic freedoms, and stronger collective management of global problems.

The Trilateral Commission members are influential politicians and banking and business executives.

The Trilateral Commission members are in the media.

The Trilateral Commission members are intellectual leaders.

The Trilateral Commission members are trade union chiefs.

The TC became known to be the Shadow Government of the West.

The Trilateral Commission was created by leaders of the Council on Foreign Relations.

The Trilateral Commission is a tool to develop a global government throughout the world.

The Trilateral Commission reveals that David Rockefeller and other elites want a global government dictatorship.

The Trilateral Commission leads to the Council on Foreign Relations, which also plays a part in the movement toward a one world government along with the Bilderberg Group.

The Trilateral Commission's director became Zbigniew Brzezinski, who David Rockefeller appointed.

The Trilateral Commission's primary goal was to place a Trilateral-influenced president in the White House in 1976.

The Trilateral Commission's goal is to groom an appropriate candidate who would be willing to cooperate with its objectives.

The Trilateral Commission, through Rockefeller and Brzezinski, selected a handful of well-known liberal Democrats and a scattering of Republicans (liberal-internationalist) to serve as members.

The Trilateral Commission accepted Jimmy Carter, who was an obscure one-term Democratic governor, to join.

The Trilateral Commission had 284 of its members placed in Jimmy Carter's administration along with the Council on Foreign Relations members' assignments.

The Trilateral Commission placed Walter Mondale and Dr. Henry Kissinger in Jimmy Carter's administration.

The Trilateral Commission helped Jimmy Carter to win the nomination and the presidency.

The Trilateral Commission mobilized the money power of the Wall Street bankers, the intellectual influence of the academic community—subservient to the wealth of the great tax-free foundations—and the media controllers represented in the membership of the Council on Foreign Relations.

The Trilateral Commission overnight made Jimmy Carter a presidential candidate.

The Trilateral Commission power, the Rockefeller empire, and the Council on Foreign Relations media influence helped Jimmy Carter make his way to the presidency, establishing the first full-fledged Trilateral administration appointments of numerous Trilateralists to key policymaking positions to carry out the Trilateral agenda to the maximum.

The Trilateral Commission is founded using federal taxes that the people of the United States are forced to pay for totalitarian plans to create a New World Order.

The Trilateral Commission is international, and it is intended to be the vehicle for multinational consolidation of the commercial and banking interests by seizing control of the political government of the United States.

The Trilateral Commission represents a skillful coordinated effort to seize control and consolidate the four centers of power — political, monetary, intellectual, and ecclesiastical.

The Trilateral Commission created by David Rockefeller was a substitute for him to select members whose purposes he defines, which he funded.

The Trilateral Commission's members were accepted after going through David Rockefeller's screening method.

The Trilateral Commission lowers to the position of using coolie countries who have nothing but raw material and supply the manpower, which goes against principles of the people of the United States.

The Trilateral Commission allows international bankers and international industrialists to act together to control the United States, which is a super state, to enslave the world for their own satisfaction.

The Trilateral Commission takes away the wealth of the people and working capital of the United States that has either been locked in the vaults of certain banks and the great corporations or exported to foreign countries for the benefit of the foreign customers of these banks and corporations.

The Trilateral Commission padlocks the warehouses and coal yards and grain elevators that are full, and the great banks and corporations hold the keys.

The Trilateral Commission original members are still in positions of power through several presidential terms of office where they are able to implement policy.

The Trilateral Commission's goal is to get rid of the United States sovereignty as well as of its national independence and the United States under the rule of a one world government.

The Trilateral Commission's power under the President Carter administration has taken charge of foreign policymaking.

The Trilateral Commission's active or former members head every key agency involved in mapping United States strategy in dealing with the rest of the world.

The Trilateral Commission is seen to have a conspiracy at work under the Trilateral Commission concentration of power.

The Trilateral Commission develops a democratic dictatorship with the corporate elitists in control with the uninformed people's consent.

The Trilateral Commission has acquired a reputation for being the Shadow Government of the West.

The Trilateral Commission founder is David Rockefeller, who is the most conspicuous representative today of the ruling class containing a multinational fraternity of men who shape the global economy and manage the flow of its capital.

The Trilateral Commission has given a private citizen, David Rockefeller, the privileges of a head of state.

The Trilateral Commission made David Rockefeller the most powerful man in America.

The Trilateral Commission forces journalists to destroy truth.

The Trilateral Commission toasts an independent press for rich men behind the scenes.

The Trilateral Commission makes the most important foreign, economic, and domestic policy decisions of the United States government.

The Trilateral Commission sets goals and guidelines for the administration.

The Trilateral Commission allows the economic officials of the largest countries to think in terms of managing a single world economy.

The Trilateral Commission manages international economies among countries.

The Trilateral Commission forced President Carter to appoint Cyrus Vance, Michael Blumenthal, and Harold Brown, who were Trilateralist members.

The Trilateral Commission forced President Carter to appoint fourteen additional Trilateralist members to his administration.

The Trilateral Commission needs in the three regions of the world (Japan, Europe, and North America) to essentially introduce to all those nations the concept of a global New World Order.

The Trilateral Commission Carter Cabinet members were Trilateralists of David Rockefeller's new organization.

The Trilateral Commission emphasis on international economics during the oil crisis forced many developing nations to borrow excessively.

The Trilateral Commission caused private multinational banks, particularly Rockefeller's Chase Manhattan, to loan countries during the oil crisis.

The Trilateral Commission will manage and create a system that will rule the world.

The Trilateral Commission is a coterie of international conspirators with designs on covertly ruling the world.

The Trilateral Commission is to take over all key policymaking positions in the United States government.

The Trilateral Commission constitutes a conspiracy to seek and gain control of the United States government in order to create a New World Order government.

The Trilateral Commission wants a handful of people to run the government.

The Trilateral Commission doesn't believe that the people themselves can run their lives.

The Trilateral Commission wants an elitist government that makes decisions for people's lives.

The Trilateral Commission had at least ten members in Ronald Reagan's administration after his election.

The Trilateral Commission's elite class of individual members keep moving the United States toward accepting a totalitarian New World Order.

The Trilateral Commission was created by multinational companies in order to dominate American foreign policy.

The Trilateral Commission economic plans leaned toward the controlling of energy sources, food production, and the international monetary system.

The Trilateral Commission is orchestrating, meshing, and gearing to accomplish a the New World Order.

The Trilateral Commission has rejected the United States Constitution and the democratic political process.

The Trilateral Commission objective is to obtain the wealth of the world for their own use under the guise of "public service."

The Trilateral Commission objective is to obtain one-world socialist government to control.

The Trilateral Commission objective is primarily to gain control of the American presidency.

The Trilateral Commission has taken over the presidency of the United States and the key cabinet departments of the federal government.

The Trilateral Commission is a private organization dedicated to the subordination of the domestic interests of the United States to the international interests of the multinational banks and corporations.

The Trilateral Commission contains a new crop of economists, which will create a new international economic system.

The Trilateral Commission will ultimately create a new world economic system that will affect jobs in America and elsewhere.

The Trilateral Commission will ultimately create a new world economic system that will affect the prices consumers pay.

The Trilateral Commission will ultimately create a new world economic system that will affect freedom of individuals and nations.

The Trilateral Commission original members are in positions of power throughout the world and in the United States.

The Trilateral Commission members hold key positions in United States government and other member countries' governments.

The Trilateral Commission members implement strategies that are dictatorial commands, acquiring a reputation of it being a shadow government.

The Trilateral Commission membership is made up of over three hundred members who only are interested in promoting close international cooperation, especially among noncommunist industrial nations.

The Trilateral Commission members are top bankers, industrialists, businessmen, labor leaders, scholars, politicians, senators, and governors.

The Trilateral Commission's purpose is to engineer an enduring partnership among the ruling classes of North America, Western Europe, and Japan in order to safeguard the interests of Western capitalism in an explosive world.

The Trilateral Commission attitude is to trilateralize the people, governments, and economies of all nations, which must serve the needs of multinational banks and corporations.

The Trilateral Commission is a Rockefeller family operation through and through.

The Trilateral Commission's teamwork must be dedicated to the fashioning of a more just and equitable world order.

The Trilateral Commission changes the international system for a global one.

The Trilateral Commission approach is strictly economic, and total reliance is placed on materialism.

The Trilateral Commission emphasizes the necessity of eliminating artificial barriers to world commerce, tariff, export duties, and quota.

The Trilateral Commission proposes to substitute an international economy managed and controlled by international monetary groups.

The Trilateral Commission dominated the executive branch of the United States government, which provided all the necessary political leverage needed to skew United States and global economic policies to the Trilateralists' own benefit.

The Trilateral Commission has become an expert at using crises (and creating them in some instances) to manage countries toward the New World Order.

The Trilateral Commission dominates and transcends both political parties.

Resume (Mob Rule)

The Bill of Rights came into effect on December 15, 1791, which guaranteed a noncentralized federal government republic under the Tenth Amendment. The Tenth Amendment outlaws the use of referendums. However, in 1913, the Seventeenth Amendment was ratified, allowing the United States senator to be people elected in violation of the Tenth Amendment.

Comparing the flow charts "Federal Government Republic" and "Federalism," a federal government republic became a centralized nonfederal government republic under federalism.

Federalism, a product of the Seventeenth Amendment, forced the loss of state governments' and people's sovereignties, which open the door to secret organizations like the following:

- Council on Foreign Relations (CFR)

- Bilderberg Group

- Trilateral Commission (TC)

Very simply, the Trilateral Commission (TC) supports both sides of the aisle's candidates for president of the United States. The object of the TC is to control the election of the presidents of the United States, whereas the Council on Foreign Relations (CFR) controls the media, giving support to the same TC presidential candidates.

After the election, the CFR executes payback-time suggestions to the president elect. The mob rule CFR makes suggestions of CFR or TC members for key executive branch positions of the new presidential administration, which also will have CFR members of previous residential administrations, resulting in over a period of time accumulative mob rule CFR appointments.

Voting in a completely new administration does not guarantee a change in executive policies over the old replaced administration.

FEDERALISM: A PATH TO A NEW WORLD ORDER VIOLATES THE TENTH AMENDMENT AND THE BILL OF RIGHTS

United States Constitution Seventeenth Amendment Clause 1: The Senate of the United States shall be composed of two Senators from each State, elected by the people thereof, for six years; and each Senator shall have one vote.
United States Constitution Article I; Section 3
The Senate of the United States shall be composed of two Senators from each state, chosen by the legislature thereof, for six years; and each Senator shall have one vote.

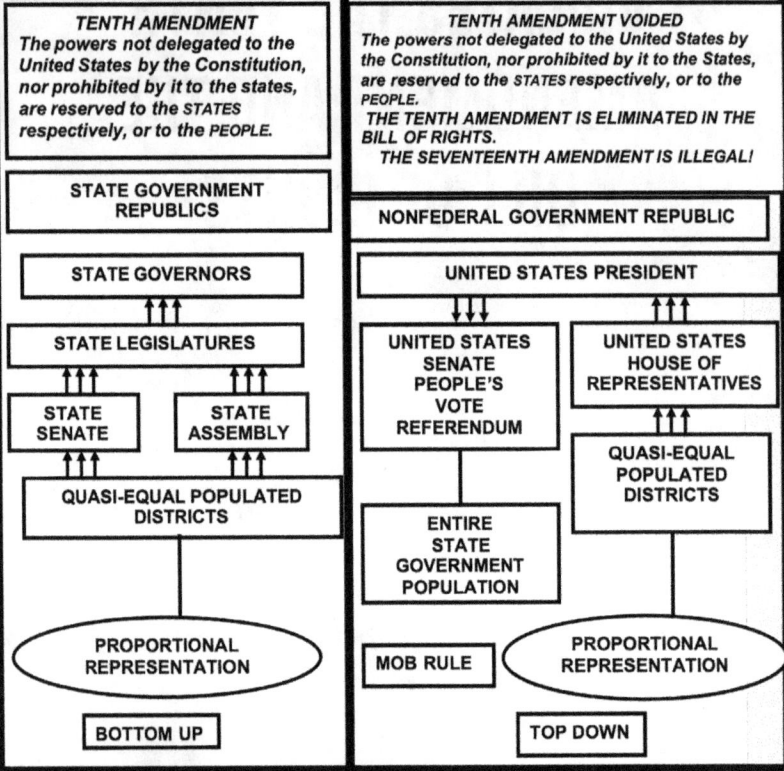

TENTH AMENDMENT	TENTH AMENDMENT VOIDED
The powers not delegated to the United States by the Constitution, nor prohibited by it to the states, are reserved to the STATES respectively, or to the PEOPLE.	*The powers not delegated to the United States by the Constitution, nor prohibited by it to the States, are reserved to the STATES respectively, or to the PEOPLE.* *THE TENTH AMENDMENT IS ELIMINATED IN THE BILL OF RIGHTS.* *THE SEVENTEENTH AMENDMENT IS ILLEGAL!*

STATE GOVERNMENT REPUBLICS	NONFEDERAL GOVERNMENT REPUBLIC
STATE GOVERNORS	**UNITED STATES PRESIDENT**
↑↑↑	↓↓↓ ↑↑↑
STATE LEGISLATURES	**UNITED STATES SENATE PEOPLE'S VOTE REFERENDUM** / **UNITED STATES HOUSE OF REPRESENTATIVES**
↑↑↑ ↑↑↑	↑↑↑
STATE SENATE / **STATE ASSEMBLY**	**QUASI-EQUAL POPULATED DISTRICTS**
↑↑↑ ↑↑↑	
QUASI-EQUAL POPULATED DISTRICTS	**ENTIRE STATE GOVERNMENT POPULATION**
PROPORTIONAL REPRESENTATION	**MOB RULE** / **PROPORTIONAL REPRESENTATION**
BOTTOM UP	**TOP DOWN**

FEDERALISM

THE RIGHT OF THE HUMAN BEING

By: Donald D. Marchi

It is the birthright of every human being to be **happy**. This is not a right granted by a creator, but a right inherited from the beginningless time of the Universe. It is the most important pursuit of all human beings. *Happiness*—it is the purpose behind and the first cause of all human action. All action ideally ends in happiness, right?

But no—we can't always be happy. Things happen. Dependent origination occurs. Some events are good, some bad, and we suffer based on desire. Thus, the struggle between the good and the bad begins, and finding happiness becomes more difficult. We call this **Life**—and the **pursuit of happiness**.

We all have different ideas of what happiness means. In the United States, our Founding Fathers created, through a form of government, the **American Dream**. It is the lynchpin of our pursuit of happiness. But this dream is not possible without a Constitution that creates the paths to follow.

The path to happiness is a responsibility shared by the people and their elected government—a government that must deeply understand the needs of all, rooted in the origins and experiences of the people. This is paramount. It is a duty bestowed upon all people and their governments throughout the Universe.

It is the responsibility of each human being to help build a government that creates and protects paths to happiness. A person should not, knowingly or unknowingly, place the burden of their own happiness on the back of another. We call this **personal responsibility**, a cornerstone of all successful governments.

Likewise, no government should place the burden of a person not under its care onto those who are. This fundamental truth drives the creation of constitutional governments wherever human beings exist.